University of Edinburgh

In Memory of the late

A. G. Carmichael

*the University Court have the honour
to present to*

Miss Carmichael

this copy of the

ROLL OF HONOUR
1914-1919

UNIVERSITY OF EDINBURGH
ROLL OF HONOUR
1914—1919

VOL.2

Record of War Service

HILL, ALBERT EDWARD.
Student of Arts, 1912-13. Inns of Court O.T.C., July 1915. 17th London Regiment (T.), 2nd Lieut. July 1916; Lieut. Jan. 1918; Acting Captain Sept. 1918.

HILL, DAVID McGOWAN.
Student of Law. King's Own Scottish Borderers, 2nd Lieut.

HILL, JAMES GILL.
M.B., Ch.B. 1912. R.A.M.C., Lieut. March 1915; Captain Sept. 1915; Major Dec. 1918; Lieut.-Col. Jan 1919. 2nd Northern Field Ambulance and 35th General Hospital, Calais. M.C. Dec. 1918.

HILL, JAMES LESLIE.
Morrison's Academy, Crieff. Student of Arts and Medicine, 1905-9 and 1912-17; M.A. 1909; M.B., Ch.B. 1917. O.T.C. Infantry, 1909-15, Cadet. R.A.M.C., Lieut. May 1917; Captain May 1918.

HILL, JAMES ROLAND.
M.B., Ch.B. 1907. R.A.M.C., Captain Sept. 1914; Acting Major March 1918. 30th Field Ambulance.

HILL, JOHN McADAM.
Royal School, Dungannon. M.B., Ch.B. 1907. Vol. Medical Staff Corps, 1902-7, Sergeant. R.A.M.C., Lieut. Dec. 1914; Captain Dec. 1915. 2nd Highland Light Infantry; 10th Duke of Cornwall's Light Infantry, and 5th Royal Irish Regiment. Order of St Sava (5th Class), July 1915.

HILL, KENNETH JAMES COWAN.
Edinburgh Academy. O.T.C. 1909-14, Cadet L/Corporal. Student of Science, 1914-15 and 1918-20; B.Sc. 1920. O.T.C. Engineers, Oct. 1914 to Dec. 1915, Cadet. R.E., 2nd Lieut. Dec. 1915; Lieut. July 1917.

HILL, RICHARD PERCY.
M.B., C.M. 1896. Australian Army Medical Corps, Captain.

HILL, ROBERT.
George Watson's College. Cadet Corps 1906-8. Student of Science, 1908-11 and 1919; B.Sc. 1919. O.T.C. Infantry, 1909-14, Cadet L/Corporal. 3rd Durham Light Infantry (S.R.), 2nd Lieut. Aug. 1914; Lieut. Feb. 1915; Captain March 1916. France. Wounded July 1915. Invalided out 1918.

HILL, WILLIAM GEOFFREY.
Malvern College. Student of Medicine, 1916 and 1919. University O.T.C. Infantry, 1916-17. 15th Sherwood Foresters, 2nd Lieut. Dec. 1917. Wounded at Voormezeele, Belgium, Sept. 1918. Invalided out Jan. 1919.

Record of War Service

HILL, WILLIAM HUGH.
: Blairlodge. M.B., C.M. 1896; M.D. 1902; D.P.H. 1906. R.A.M.C. (T.), Lieut. Oct. 1915; Captain April 1916. France Jan. 1916 to April 1919. Sanitary Officer, 55th Division, No. 4 Mobile (Hygiene) Laboratory, and Acting D.A.D.M.S. (San.) Second Army. Dispatches and Médaille des Epidémies 1918.

HILLCOAT, ROBERT GUY.
: Edinburgh Academy. M.A. 1909; LL.B 1911. O.T.C. Infantry, Sept. to Oct. 1914, Cadet. 23rd Royal Fusiliers, Lieut. Oct. 1914; Captain July 1915. 205th Division Employment Coy., Labour Corps. Attached R.A.O.C. H.Q., Third Army. France Nov. 1915. Dispatches Dec. 1918 and July 1919.

HILL SCOTT, CONRAD.
: Student of Law, 1914-15. O.T.C. Infantry, Feb. to Oct. 1915, Cadet. 3/9th Royal Scots (T.), 2nd Lieut. 1915; Lieut. 1917; Captain 1917. France. Invalided out.

HINWOOD, HARRY CLIVE.
: M.B., Ch.B. 1913. O.T.C. Artillery, Oct. 1908-14, Cadet B.S.M. R.F.A. (S.R.), 2nd Lieut. Aug. 1914. France Dec. 1914. Prisoner of War, March 1915. R.A.M.C., Lieut. July 1918.

HIRD, FREDERICK WAISTELL.
: George Watson's College; First XI. Cadet Corps to 1907, L/Corporal. M.B., Ch.B. 1914. O.T.C. Medical, Nov. 1910 to April 1914, Cadet. R.A.M.C., Lieut. Dec. 1914; Captain Aug. 1915. M.C. July 1918. Dispatches June 1917.

HISCOCK, ALFRED WALTER.
: Ancrum School. Student of Science, 1918. Lovat Scouts, Private Sept. 1914. Machine-Gun Corps, 2nd Lieut. May 1917. Gallipoli, Egypt, and France.

HISLOP, DAVID HALL.
: George Watson's College. M.A. 1903. Minister, U.F. Church of Scotland. Artists' Rifles, Private 1915. Argyll and Sutherland Highlanders, 2nd Lieut. 1916; Lieut. March 1918. France. Wounded 1917.

HISLOP, DAVID MURDOCH.
: M.A. 1911. O.T.C. Infantry, Feb. 1910 to April 1913, Cadet. 5th Highland Light Infantry (T.), Private; L/Corporal.

HISLOP, FRANCIS DANIEL.
: Boroughmuir School; First XI. Student of Arts, 1911-14 and 1918-19; M.A. 1915 (Hons. Hist.) 1919. 5th Royal Scots (T.), June 1909; 2nd Lieut. Oct. 1914; Lieut. May 1915; Temp. Captain April 1916; Acting Captain Jan. 1917. Machine-Gun Corps, Feb. 1918 to Jan. 1919. Gallipoli Sept. 1915; Egypt Jan. 1916; France March 1916 to June 1917.

Record of War Service

HISLOP, GORDON.
Leith Academy. M.A. (Hons. Engl.) 1909. Vans Dunlop Scholar. 5th Royal Scots (T.), Private Sept. 1914. 10th and 2nd Durham Light Infantry, 2nd Lieut. May 1917; Lieut. Nov. 1918.

HISLOP, LAWRENCE.
Glasgow High School. University O.T.C. Engineers, June to Dec. 1917, Cadet. Royal Air Force, 2nd Lieut. Dec. 1917; Lieut. July 1918.

HISLOP, STEPHEN LUNN.
Broughton School. Student of Medicine, 1918. R.E. and R.G.A., 2nd Lieut. March 1918.

HISLOP, THOMAS ALEXANDER.
Student of Arts, 1910-14; M.A. (Hons. Classics) 1914. Scots Greys, Trooper, Sept. 1914.

HISLOP, WILLIAM.
Ayr Academy. M.A. 1908. Schoolmaster. No. 4 Coy. Q.R.V.B., Royal Scots, 1903-6, Private. A.S.C. (M.T.), Private Dec. 1915.

HOBKIRK, ANDREW MOSS.
Boroughmuir School. Student of Science, 1916 and 1919. O.T.C. Artillery, April to Dec. 1917, Cadet; Officer Cadet Dec. 1917. R.G.A., 153rd Heavy Battery, 2nd Lieut. June 1918. Salonika.

HODGSON, ALBERT ERNEST.
Sir Wm. Turner's Grammar School, Coatham, Redcar, Yorks. M.B., Ch.B. 1903; M.D. 1911; D.P.H. (Camb.) 1906. R.A.M.C., Lieut. Jan. 1915; Captain Jan. 1916.

HODGSON, STEWART.
George Heriot's School. M.B., Ch.B. 1911. R.A.M.C., Lieut. June 1915; Captain June 1916. Wounded March and Oct. 1918. M.C. July 1918.

HODSDON, Sir JAMES WILLIAM BEEMAN.
Sherborne. Student of Medicine, 1877-80; M.R.C.P. (Edin.) 1883; F.R.C.S. (Edin.) 1883; M.D., M.S. (Ireland) 1881. Lecturer and Examiner in Clinical Surgery. R.A.M.C. (T.), Major July 1908. 2nd Scottish General Hospital. Dispatches March and Aug. 1919. K.B.E. 1920.

HOGARTH, BERTRAM WHEWELL.
M.R.C.P. (Eng.) 1890; L.R.C.P. (Lond.) 1890; M.B., B.S. (Lond.) 1891; B.Sc. (P.H.) (Edin.) 1894; M.D. (Lond.) 1894. 5th Royal Lancaster Regiment, Major. Transferred R.A.M.C., Major May 1915. 3rd West Lancashire Field Ambulance. France 1915.

HOGARTH, JAMES BURNET.
M.B., Ch.B. 1914; M.D. 1919; F.R.C.S. (Edin.) 1918. R.A.M.C. (T.), Lieut. Aug. 1916; Captain March 1917. London Mounted Brigade Field Ambulance, and 2/8th Lancashire Fusiliers. City of London Military Hospital. France. 1917.

Record of War Service

HOGARTH, RANDAL FAIR.
Berwick Grammar School. Student of Arts, 1918. A.S.C. (M.T.), Feb. 1917; L/Corporal July 1918 to Feb. 1919.

HOGG, GEORGE WILLIAM.
George Heriot's School. O.T.C. 1914-16. Student of Science, 1918. Royal Air Force, Cadet Aug. 1918.

HOGG, HENRY SCOTT ANDERSON.
M.B., Ch.B., 1905. R.A.M.C., Lieut. March 1917; Captain March 1918.

HOGG, ROBERT.
Moray House School. M.A. 1912. Schoolmaster. R.A.S.C. (M.T.), Private Nov. 1918.

HOILE, HENRY JOHN.
Dundee High School. M.A. (St Andrews); M.B., Ch.B. 1900. R.A.M.C., Lieut. June 1915; Captain Jan. 1918. Med. Exp. Force, July 1915 to June 1916. Egyptian Exp. Force, July 1917 to April 1919.

HOLE, GILBERT LINDSAY DOUGLAS.
Edinburgh Academy; First XV. and XI. Student of Law, 1901-6. Writer to the Signet, 1906. 10th King's Liverpool Regiment (Liverpool Scottish), Private May 1916; 2nd Lieut. Jan. 1917; Lieut. July 1918. France July 1917 to Feb. 1918. Ypres, Cambrai, Festubert, and La Bassée.

HOLE, RICHARD BRASSEY.
M.B., Ch.B. 1903. R.A.M.C., Major July 1915; Acting Lieut.-Col. Egypt and France. Dispatches.

HOLLAND, HENRY TRISTRAM.
Loretto. M.B., Ch.B. 1899; F.R.C.S. (Edin.) 1907. Beluchistan Indian Defence Force, Captain. Mention 1919. Kaisar-i-Hind Medal (2nd Class).

HOLMDEN, FRANK ALFRED AMPHLETT.
M.B., C.M. 1889. Colonial Office Forces, Surgeon-Captain 1893. Matabele War, 1893; South African Campaign, 1899-1902. R.A.M.C., Captain May 1915; Major Feb. 1916. Southern Command, 1915-19. Dispatches Feb. and April 1901. D.S.O. April 1901.

HOLMDEN, HARRY FOSTER.
Auckland College, New Zealand. M.B., Ch.B. (Hons.) 1911; M.D. 1913; F.R.C.S. (Edin.) 1913. O.T.C. Infantry, Feb. 1909 to April 1912, Cadet. R.A.M.C., Lieut. June 1915; Captain June 1916; Major Jan. 1918. 14th Casualty Clearing Station, two years. Dispatches (German East Africa), Sept. 1918.

HOLMES, FRANK.
Student of Medicine, 1911-14 and 1916-18. M.B., Ch.B. 1918. O.T.C. Infantry, Oct. 1912-14, Cadet; and Medical, Cadet Staff Sergeant May 1917; 2nd Lieut. Oct. 1917; 8th Seaforth Highlanders, 2nd Lieut. Sept. 1914; Lieut. Nov. 1914; Captain Oct. 1915. R.A.M.C., Lieut. Oct. 1918; Captain Oct. 1919. France, Black Sea.

Record of War Service

HOLMES, JOHN ROBERT.
M.B., C.M., 1886. R.A.M.C., Major. 4th London Field Ambulance.

HOLMES, NOEL ROWLAND HUTCHINSON.
Student of Medicine, 1913-15 and 1918-19. O.T.C. Artillery, Dec. 1914 to Feb. 1915, Cadet. R.F.A. (T.), 2nd Lieut. Feb. 1915; Lieut.; Acting Captain. Gallipoli Sept. 1915; Palestine. Dispatches April 1918.

HOLMES, NORMAN.
Municipal School, Barrow-in-Furness. University O.T.C. Artillery, Dec. 1916 to June 1917, Cadet; Officer Cadet, June 1918.

HOLMES, THOMAS DANIEL HILL.
Rugby. M.B., C.M. 1887; M.D. 1891. R.A.M.C., Lieut. Aug. 1916; Captain Aug. 1917; Major March 1918.

HOME, BRUCE F.
Royal High School; First XI. Student of Medicine, 1918. 9th Royal Scots, Private Aug. 1914; Sergeant July 1915. R.G.A., 2nd Lieut. Dec. 1915; Lieut. July 1917; Acting Captain July 1918. France.

HOME, GEORGE.
Wanganui College, New Zealand. M.B., C.M. 1892; M.D. 1895; D.P.H. (Lond.) 1897. N.Z. Medical Corps, Captain Aug. 1914; Major July 1915; Lieut.-Col. Oct. 1918. O.C. No. 2 N.Z. General Hospital. O.B.E. 1919; C.B.E. 1920.

HOME, WILLIAM.
M.A. 1904. 11th Argyll and Sutherland Highlanders. Gordon Highlanders, Captain Sept. 1914; Major.

HOME, WILLIAM EDWARD.
Rugby. B.Sc. 1882; M.B., C.M. 1885; M.D. 1895; M.R.C.P. (Edin.) 1901; D.P.H. (Edin.) 1907. No. 4 Coy. Q.E.R., 1879-85, Colour-Sergeant. Royal Navy, 1885; Fleet Surgeon 1901. Staff Surgeon, Royal Canadian Navy, Esquimalt Naval Hospital, July 1914. R.A.M.C., Major 1916. H.M. Hospital Ship *Glenart Castle*. Egypt, Italy, and China, 1919-20. O.B.E. 1919.

HOME-HAY, NINIAN EDWARD MILES.
M.B., Ch.B. 1914. O.T.C. Infantry, Oct. 1908 to May 1912, Cadet. R.A.M.C., Lieut., 69th Field Ambulance.

HOMER, PERCY C. H.
University O.T.C. Medical, May 1913 to Sept. 1914, Cadet. R.A.M.C., Private. H.Q. Staff, 3rd Cavalry Division, France.

HONEYFORD, JOHN.
M.B., Ch.B. 1910; M.D. 1912; F.R.C.S. (Edin.) 1914. R.A.M.C., Lieut. Nov. 1915. Resident Surgeon, Edinburgh War Hospital; Senior Assistant Surgeon, Bristol Military Orthopædic Centre; and Surgeon, Beaufort War Hospital.

Record of War Service

HONEYMAN, STANLEY.
Edinburgh Academy. M.B., Ch.B. 1913. O.T.C. Medical, Jan. 1909 to April 1913, Cadet Corporal. R.A.M.C., Lieut. Oct. 1914; Captain Oct. 1915.

HOOD, ALEXANDER.
George Watson's College. M.B., Ch.B. 1910. O.T.C. Artillery, Oct. 1908 to Dec. 1909, Cadet Sergeant. R.A.M.C. (Indian Contingent), Lieut. 1912; Captain March 1915; Temp. Major 1918. D.A.D.M.S. France 1914-16; India 1916-20.

HOOD, JOHN HAMILTON.
Campbell College, Belfast. M.B., Ch.B. 1913. O.T.C. Medical, 1910-12, Cadet. R.A.M.C., Lieut. Aug. 1914; Captain Aug. 1915; Acting Major Oct. 1918.

HOOD, LIONEL JOHN.
M.B., Ch.B. 1900. Resident, R.I.E. R.A.M.C., Lieut. Oct. 1915; Captain Sept. 1918. Egypt and France.

HOOD, WILLIAM NIMMO.
George Heriot's School. O.T.C. 1914-16. Student of Medicine, 1916-19. O.T.C. Medical, June to Sept. 1918, Cadet. Royal Navy, Surgeon Sub-Lieut., Nov. 1918.

HOPE, EDWARD WILLIAM.
M.B., C.M. 1878; B.Sc. and M.D. 1881; D.Sc. (P.H.) 1887; L.R.C.P. (Lond.) 1879. R.A.M.C. (T.), Major Jan. 1909. Sanitary Officer. O.B.E. 1918.

HOPE, HARRY REGINALD.
Botelar Grammar School, Warrington. O.T.C. 1915-17, Cadet Sergeant. University O.T.C. Artillery, 1917-18, Cadet Corporal; Officer Cadet March 1918. Tank Corps, 2nd Lieut. March 1919.

HOPE, JAMES.
Lasswade Academy. Student of Arts and Science, 1909-14; M.A. 1912; B.Sc. 1914. R.E., Signals, Corporal Aug. 1915; Sergeant; 2nd Lieut. Dec. 1917; Captain Jan. 1918. Australian Mounted Division. Gas Services, Egypt.

HOPE, JAMES.
Fettes College. O.T.C. 1912-14. University O.T.C. Infantry, 1916-17, Cadet. Royal Highlanders (Black Watch), Private Feb. 1917. France. Wounded. M.M.

HOPE, JAMES ARTHUR.
Morrison's Academy, Crieff. M.A. 1885; LL.B. 1889. Writer to the Signet, 1889. A.S.C. (T.), Lieut.-Col. 1908. Scottish Horse Brigade, T. and S. Column. Military Representative, 1916-18. V.D.

HOPE, JOHN CHARLES DAVID.
Edinburgh Academy. O.T.C. to 1916. Student of Science, 1918-19. O.T.C. Artillery, April to Aug. 1916, Cadet; Ambulance Driver. Croix Rouge Française Oct. 1916 to May 1918. Royal Air Force, Pupil Pilot, May 1918 to Feb. 1919. Croix de Guerre (French) April 1918.

Record of War Service

HOPE, JOHN PATON.
  Royal High School. Student of Medicine, 1913-15 and 1917-20; M.B., Ch.B., 1920. R.N.V.R., Surgeon-Probationer.

HOPE, LESLIE PARKINSON.
  Edinburgh Academy. O.T.C. 1908-9. Student of Arts and Divinity, 1910-14 and 1918-19; M.A. 1913. O.T.C. Artillery, 1911-14, Cadet Bombardier. Lothians and Border Horse, Private March 1914. Mobilised Aug. 1914. Highland Cyclist Battn., 2nd Lieut. June 1915. King's African Rifles, Lieut. Nov. 1917 to April 1919.

HOPE, THOMAS.
  George Watson's College. M.A. 1913. R.A.M.C. (T.), Private April 1915; Acting L/Corporal July 1915 to June 1917. 59th General Hospital, France, 1917-19.

HOPKIRK, DUDLEY STUART.
  Broughton School. Student of Arts, 1915-16 and 1919; M.A. 1919. 3rd Highland Light Infantry, Private May 1917; Corporal June 1918.

HORNE, JAMES WILLIAM.
  Daniel Stewart's College. B.Sc. 1892. 1st and 2nd London Scottish (T.), Sanitary Section, Private Aug. 1914; L/Corporal Feb. 1915. France Nov. 1914 to Aug. 1915. Ministry of Munitions, 1916-19.

HORNE, JOHN HOWARD.
  George Watson's College. M.B., Ch.B. 1907. No. 4 Coy. Q.R.V.B., Royal Scots, 1905-7, Private. Indian Medical Service, Lieut. Jan. 1909; Captain Jan. 1912. Egyptian Exp. Force, 1914-20.

HORNE, JOHN L. (See p. 749.)

HORNE, ROBERT JOHN MAULE.
  Daniel Stewart's College. M.A. (Hons. Classics) 1904; B.Sc. 1913; M.B., Ch.B. 1917; D.P.H. 1919. Assistant in Physiology, 1913-14. Forth R.G.A. (T.), 1894, Major April 1912. South African Campaign, 1900-2. Coast Defence, Aug. 1914 to Jan. 1919. Mention 1917 and 1918. T.D.

HORSBURGH, BENJAMIN.
  George Heriot's School. M.A. 1888. Ceylon Artillery Volunteers, Captain July 1900; Major.

HORSFORD, CYRIL.
  Bedford Modern School. M.B., Ch.B. 1898; M.D. 1902; F.R.C.S. (Eng.). R.A.M.C., Lieut. June 1917; Captain June 1918. Aural Specialist. Italy.

HORTON, WILFRED WINNAL.
  Shrewsbury. M.B., Ch.B. 1880; M.D. 1884. R.A.M.C. (T.), Lieut. Sept. 1915; Captain March 1916. R.M.O., 6th Gloucestershire Regiment. Invalided out Nov. 1917.

Record of War Service

HORWITZ, SAMUEL SALMON.
Student of Medicine, 1912-15. O.T.C. Medical, Nov. 1914 to April 1915, Cadet. 3rd Sherwood Foresters, 2nd Lieut. 1915; Lieut. Feb. 1916.

HOSKING, ARCHER.
Wanganui College, N.Z. M.B., C.M. 1896. Volunteers and Territorial Force for nineteen years. N.Z. Medical Corps, Major May 1917.

HOSSACK, JAMES.
Boroughmuir School; First XV. and XI. Student of Arts, 1914-16 and 1918-19; M.A. 1919. R.N.V.R., Signalman, June 1916. H.M.S. *Rule*, Mystery Ship, and North American Convoy Service.

HOSSACK, WILLIAM.
Boroughmuir School; First XV. and XI. Student of Arts, 1915-16 and 1918-20; M.A. 1920. R.N.V.R., Sept. 1916; Signalman, Jan. 1917. North American Convoy Service. Torpedoed May 1917.

HOTCHKIS, JAMES NAPIER.
Edinburgh Academy. Student of Law, 1881-5. Writer to the Signet, 1887. South African Campaign, 1900-1. Mobilised. Highland Cyclist Battn., Captain Aug. 1914. Transferred R.F.A., Jan. 1915, and Highland Light Infantry, July 1916. France July 1915 to Jan. 1916; Malta Nov. 1917-19.

HOTCHKISS, ALEXANDER DICK.
Falkirk High School. M.A. 1911. Schoolmaster. Canadian Engineers, 6th Field Coy., L/Corporal July 1918.

HOUGHTON, CECIL HOBART.
Corrig School, Kingstown. M.B., Ch.B. 1902. No. 4 Coy. Q.R.V.B., Royal Scots, 1897-1900, L/Corporal. R.A.M.C., Lieut. Aug. 1916. No. 1 Ambulance Train, France.

HOWARD, DOUGLAS WALTER.
Mile End House School, Portsmouth. University O.T.C. Infantry, March to Aug. 1914, Cadet. 9th Royal Scots, Corporal Aug. 1914. 2nd London Regiment (Royal Fusiliers), 2nd Lieut. Dec. 1916; Lieut. June 1918. Attached 2/7th Lancashire Fusiliers, Feb. 1917. Prisoner of War in Germany, March to Nov. 1918. M.C. June 1918.

HOWARD-JONES, JOHN.
M.B., C.M. 1890; B.Sc. (P.H.) 1892; D.Sc. (P.H.) 1893; M.D. 1899. R.A.M.C. (T.), April 1897; Major Nov. 1908. Mobilised Aug. 1914; Lieut.-Col. Feb. 1915 to Jan. 1919. 2/1st Welsh Field Ambulance; 321st East African Field Ambulance. S.M.O., 205th Brigade. T.D. 1917. Dispatches March 1919.

Record of War Service

HOWARTH, RICHARD.
  Falkirk High School. Student of Medicine, 1915-16 and 1918-19. O.T.C. Artillery, Sept. 1915 to Oct. 1916. Artists' Rifles, Private Oct. 1916. 5th Bedfordshire Regiment, 2nd Lieut. March 1917. Attached Royal Air Force, March to July 1918. India 1917; Egypt 1918.

HOWDEN, HERBERT.
  University Battery, E.C.A.V., 1900; 2nd Lieut. 1905; Lieut. 1906. O.T.C. Artillery, Captain 1909; Major and O.C. Aug. 1912 to Oct. 1914. R.F.A., Temp. Major Oct. 1914-20. France and The Rhine.

HOWDEN, ROBERT KENYON.
  Maritzburg College; First XI. M.B., C.M. 1896. South African Campaign, Natal Medical Corps, Captain 1900-1. South African Medical Corps, Captain 1916-19.

HOWIE, GEORGE WYLLIE.
  George Watson's College. Student of Arts, 1917. O.T.C. Infantry, Feb. to Aug. 1917, Cadet L/Corporal; Officer Cadet Aug. 1917. 9th Highland Light Infantry, 2nd Lieut. Nov. 1917; Lieut. May 1919. France 1918.

HOWIE, JAMES COLLINS.
  George Heriot's School. O.T.C. 1909-11, Cadet Colour-Sergeant. M.A. (Hons. Maths.); B.Sc. 1914. Schoolmaster. 9th and 3rd, attached 13th Royal Scots (T.), Private Nov. 1915; L/Corporal May 1916; 2nd Lieut. Nov. 1916. France. Wounded April 1917. Invalided out Jan. 1918.

HOWIE, PHADLALLAH ELIOS EL.
  Moray House School. M.B., C.M. 1887. Surgeon, Volunteer Forces, Gordon Highlanders, 1897-1906. R.A.M.C., Lieut. Aug. 1916. 43rd General Hospital, Salonika. Invalided out Sept. 1917.

HOY, CHARLES FERRIER.
  Broughton School. Student of Arts, 1909-15; M.A. 1915. Schoolmaster. R.G.A., Gunner June 1915; L/Corporal Aug. 1918. Sound Ranging Section, Field Survey Battn., R.E.

HOYLAND, HAMILTON.
  University O.T.C. Medical, Dec. 1907 to March 1908, Cadet. 4th Suffolk Regiment (T.), 2nd Lieut.; Lieut. June 1916.

HOYLAND, STANLEY WALL.
  Framlingham College; First XI. Cadet Corps 1900-4, Cadet Colour-Sergeant. M.B., Ch.B. 1916; L.R.C.P. & S. (Edin.). O.T.C. Medical, 1908-13, Cadet Sergeant. R.A.M.C. (S.R.), Lieut. 1913; Captain Dec. 1916. France Aug. 1914 and 1916. No. 12 Stationary Hospital; Egypt 1917; German and Portuguese East Africa 1917-18, attached 2nd W.I. Regiment, 4/4th King's African Rifles.

Record of War Service

HUCKETT, ALFRED EDWARD.
Blackheath, London; First XI. M.B., Ch.B. 1909. R.A.M.C., Lieut. Sept. 1915; Captain Sept. 1916. France June 1916 to March 1917 and Nov. 1917 to Dec. 1918. Invalided out Jan. 1919.

HUDSON, ALEXANDER ROBERT.
Oldenham; First XI. O.T.C. 1907-10. Student of Medicine, 1911-14. Scottish Horse, 2nd Lieut. Aug. 1914; Lieut. Oct. 1914; Captain June 1915. Transferred R.F.C., Oct. 1916. Reverted to Lieut., Royal Air Force. France. Wounded and taken Prisoner Aug. 1917.

HUDSON, ARTHUR AINSLIE.
Uppingham. M.B., C.M. 1892; M.D. 1896; F.R.C.S. (Edin.) 1896. South African Campaign, 1900-1. Cape Medical Staff Corps, Captain. R.A.M.C., Lieut. Oct. 1914; Captain June 1915. Eye Specialist.

HUGHES, JAMES.
George Watson's College. M.A. 1913. Schoolmaster. A.S.C., Private Jan. 1915; Corporal Feb. 1916; Sergeant May 1916; Staff Sergeant Sept. 1916. Suvla Bay Aug. to Dec. 1915; Egypt Jan. 1916; Khartoum April 1918 to Aug. 1919.

HUGHES, MERRITT YERKES.
Everett High School, U.S.A. B.A. and M.A. (Boston, U.S.A.); M.A. (Edin.) 1918. American Exp. Force, Intelligence Police, Private July 1918; Sergeant Oct. 1918.

HUGHES, SAMUEL.
L.S.A. (Lond.) 1884; M.R.C.S. (Eng.) and M.B., C.M. (Edin.) 1885. R.A.M.C. (T.), Lieut. 1908; Captain Oct. 1915. 3rd East Anglian Field Ambulance.

HUGHSON, A. J.
Student of Arts. 4th King's Own Scottish Borderers, Corporal. 9th Royal Scots, Lieut. July 1917. Croix de Guerre.

HUGO-BRUNT, HUGO. (See p. 749.)

HUIE, D. H.
Loretto. Student of Law. Chartered Accountant, 1889. 9th Royal Scots (T.), 2nd Lieut. Oct. 1900; Major Oct. 1909.

HUME, DAVID LIONEL LUMSDEN.
Kirkcaldy High School. O.T.C. 1907-10, Cadet Sergeant. Student of Arts and Divinity; M.A. 1913. R.A.M.C., Private Nov. 1915. R.H.A., Officer Cadet Nov. 1916. R.G.A., 2nd Lieut. Feb. 1917; Lieut. Aug. 1918; Acting Captain July 1918. France. Dispatches Nov. 1918.

HUME, JOHN.
Royal High School; First XV. and XI. B.Sc. 1914. A.I.C. O.T.C. Infantry, 1910-13, Cadet. 9th Royal Scots (T.), Private Sept. 1914; L/Corporal; Sergeant, R.E., 2nd Lieut. June 1916; Lieut. Dec. 1917; Acting Captain (Divisional Gas Officer), Aug. 1918. France. Croix de Guerre (Belgium), Jan. 1919.

Record of War Service

HUME, ROBERT MARSHALL.
George Heriot's School. O.T.C. 1909-10, Cadet Corporal. Student of Medicine, 1910-15; M.B., Ch.B. 1915. 9th Royal Scots (T.), Private 1911. Mobilised Aug. 1914. R.A.M.C., Lieut. Aug. 1915; Captain Aug. 1916. France 1915-16.

HUME, WALTER ALAN.
George Heriot's School. M.A. 1908. Schoolmaster. R.A.M.C., Private Dec. 1914. R.F.A. (T.), 2nd Lieut. March 1917; Lieut. Sept. 1918. France May 1915 to Oct. 1916; Palestine Jan. 1918 to March 1919.

HUME, WILLIAM WATSON.
George Watson's College. Student of Science. A.S.C. (M.T.), Private. Meerut Division, Indian Contingent. France 1914.

HUMPHRIS, FRANCIS HOWARD.
Highgate School. L.R.C.P. (Lond.) 1895; M.R.C.S. (Eng.) 1895; F.R.C.P. (Edin.) 1900; M.B., Ch.B. 1900. R.A.M.C. (T.), Captain Aug. 1914; Major Sept. 1914. 3rd London General Hospital. Egypt. Dispatches Sept. 1917.

HUNT, KEITH FLASHMAN.
Pretoria High School. Student of Science, 1912-13 and 1918-19. O.T.C. Engineers, Oct. 1913 to Sept. 1914, Cadet. Scottish Horse, Private Sept. 1914; Sergeant Nov. 1914; 2nd Lieut. July 1915. Seconded, R.F.C., Pilot Aug. 1916; Lieut. July 1917. Prisoner of War two years.

HUNTER, ALAN DAVID.
Clifton Bank, St Andrews; First XI. Student of Law, 1913-15. Solicitor, 1919. O.T.C. Artillery, Dec. 1914 to Feb. 1915, Cadet. R.F.A., 2nd Lieut. Feb. 1915; Lieut. Feb. 1917; Acting Major July 1917. Wounded April 1918. M.C.

HUNTER, ALEXANDER.
Royal High School. Student of Arts, 1910-15; M.A. 1913; Hons. Classics 1915. Schoolmaster. Royal Scots, Private Feb. 1916; L/Corporal. Military Police.

HUNTER, ANDREW.
George Heriot's School. M.A. 1895; B.Sc. 1899; M.B., Ch.B. 1901. Professor of Pathological Chemistry, University of Toronto. Canadian Army Medical Corps, Captain June 1916.

HUNTER, ANDREW EDWIN.
George Watson's College. M.B., Ch.B. 1901; M.D. 1905. R.A.M.C., Lieut. June 1916. Mesopotamia.

HUNTER, ARTHUR JOSEPH GORDON.
George Watson's College. M.B., Ch.B. 1910; M.D. 1913; F.R.C.S. (Edin.) 1914. R.A.M.C. (T.), Lieut. Oct. 1914; Captain April 1915. 3rd Lowland Field Ambulance. Gallipoli, Egypt, Palestine, and France. M.C. Dec. 1917.

Record of War Service

HUNTER, CHARLES LAMB.
: Royal High School. M.A. 1902. Minister, Church of Scotland. Chaplain (Captain), May 1916, R.F.A., 276th Brigade; 55th Division, R.A.

HUNTER, EVAN AUSTIN.
: Fettes College. B.A. (Oxford). Student of Law, 1909-11. Writer to the Signet, 1912. A.S.C. (Scottish Horse Mounted Brigade), 2nd Lieut. Sept. 1914; Lieut. and Captain Feb. 1915; Staff Captain (Q.M.G. 3), War Office, Dec. 1917 to March 1919. France March 1917. Invalided home. Dispatches. O.B.E. (Military) 1919.

HUNTER, FREDERICK ARTHUR.
: George Watson's College. O.T.C. 1908-12. University O.T.C. Artillery, Dec. 1914 to March 1915, Cadet. R.F.A., 2nd Lieut. May 1915. R.F.C., Pilot Observer, Feb. 1916. Commander Kite Balloon Section. France May 1915 to Sept. 1916. Egypt and Palestine Dec. 1917 to May 1919.

HUNTER, GEORGE ALEXANDER.
: George Watson's College. University O.T.C. Infantry, May 1916, Cadet; Officer Cadet Nov. 1916. 1/4th King's Own Scottish Borderers, 2nd Lieut. March 1917; Lieut. Egypt and Palestine.

HUNTER, GILBERT ROBERTSON.
: George Watson's College. O.T.C. 1914-17, Cadet Corporal. Student of Science, 1918-19. O.T.C. Artillery, May 1917 to Feb. 1918, Cadet Sergeant; Officer Cadet, Feb. 1918. R.F.A., 43rd Reserve Battery, 2nd Lieut. Aug. 1918. Gas Instructor.

HUNTER, JAMES KERR. (See p. 750.)

HUNTER, JAMES YOUNG.
: M.A. 1900. Schoolmaster. A.S.C. (M.T.), Private 1918-19. Attached 34th Battn., Machine-Gun Corps, France.

HUNTER, JOHN.
: George Watson's College. M.B., Ch.B. 1910. R.A.M.C., Lieut. June 1917; Captain June 1918.

HUNTER, JOHN.
: Boroughmuir School. M.A. 1913. Schoolmaster. 6th Royal Scots (T.), Private Nov. 1914; Sergeant. 6th Border Regiment, 2nd Lieut. April 1917; Lieut. Senussi Campaign, N.-W. Egypt, and France.

HUNTER, JOHN.
: Windsor Park School, Musselburgh. M.B., Ch.B. 1902; D.P.H. (Edin.) and (Glasg.). Vol. Medical Staff Corps, 1899-1902, Private. R.A.M.C., Lieut. June 1915. Invalided out June 1916. National Service, Medical Boards 1917-18.

HUNTER, JOHN HENRY GRAHAM.
: Student of Medicine, 1909-14. M.B., Ch.B. 1913. O.T.C. Artillery, Feb. 1909 to Oct. 1914, Cadet Sergeant. R.A.M.C., Lieut. Sept. 1914; Captain Sept. 1915.

Record of War Service

HUNTER, JOHN WILLIAM ALEXANDER.
Derby School. Student of Medicine, 1912-14 and 1918-19. O.T.C. Artillery, Oct. 1913-14, Cadet. R.F.A., 2nd Lieut. Aug. 1914; Lieut. Dec. 1915; Acting Captain March 1918.

HUNTER, NORMAN CRICHTON.
Clifton Bank, St Andrews. Student of Law, 1915-16 and 1919-20. O.T.C. Artillery, Nov. 1915 to Feb. 1916, Cadet; Officer Cadet Feb. 1916. R.F.A., 2nd Lieut. July 1916; Lieut. July 1917. M.C. Oct. 1918.

HUNTER, ROBERT LESLIE.
Daniel Stewart's College. Cadet Corps 1913-16, Sergeant. Student of Science, 1918. Inns of Court O.T.C., Private May 1915; Officer Cadet Nov. 1918.

HUNTER, THOMAS WRIGHT.
Oxenford House, Jersey. Student of Law, 1911-12. 15th Royal Scots, Private Sept. 1914; 2nd Lieut. March 1915; Captain March 1917 to Jan. 1919. France.

HUNTER, WILLIAM.
Ayr Academy. M.B., C.M. 1883; M.D. 1886; F.R.C.P. (Lond.) 1896. Demonstrator of Physiology, 1883-4. British Military Sanitary Mission, Serbia, 1915. President, Advisory Committee, Prevention of Disease, Gallipoli, Egypt, Salonika, Malta, and Palestine. Eastern Command, 1917-19. Order of St Sava, Serbia, June 1915. C.B. and Dispatches (Dardanelles) Jan. 1916.

HUNTER, WILLIAM ALAN.
M.A. 1912. Schoolmaster. 6th Royal Scots, College Coy., Corporal. 2nd Rhodesia Regiment, Nov. 1914; 2nd Lieut. Feb. 1917; Lieut. Aug. 1917; Captain April 1919. Military Labour Corps, East Africa. Dispatches Jan. and March 1919.

HUNTER, WILLIAM HARRY.
George Watson's College. M.B., C.M. 1895; F.R.C.S. (Edin.). Civil Surgeon, South African Campaign, 1900-2. South African Medical Corps, Captain May 1918. Central Africa (Nyasaland).

HUNTER, WILLIAM LANGWILL.
South Africa. Athletics. Student of Medicine, 1911-15 and 1918-19. Athletic Champion, 1912-14 and 1918-20. O.T.C. Artillery, 1914, Cadet. Lothians and Border Horse, Private Sept. 1914. R.N.V.R., Surgeon-Probationer, Jan. 1915 to Sept. 1918. H.M. Ships *Goshawk*, *Marne*, *Bluebell*, and *Gabriel*.

HURST, JOHN THOMAS.
Skipton Grammar School. M.B., C.M. 1900. R.A.M.C., Lieut. April 1915; Captain April 1916. 2nd Royal Warwickshire Regiment. Twice Mentioned in Dispatches (Somme). M.C. 1917.

Record of War Service

HURWORTH, JAMES ERNEST.
Kingswood, South Africa. First XV. and XI. Cadet Corps 1901-7, Lieut. Student of Medicine, 1910-14 and 1916-17; M.B., Ch.B. 1917. O.T.C. Artillery, Oct. 1912-14, Cadet. R.F.A. (S.R.), 2nd Lieut. Sept. 1914; Lieut. June 1915. South African Medical Corps, Captain April 1917. France 1914-16; Salonika 1916; German East Africa 1917-18. Dispatches May 1915 and Feb. 1918.

HUSBAND, ALBERT LEWIS.
M.B., C.M. 1895; M.D. 1903. R.A.M.C., Lieut. Aug. 1916; Captain Aug. 1917. Ophthalmologist to War Office, Cannock Chase Area.

HUSBAND, JAMES.
Edinburgh Academy. M.B., Ch.B. 1899; F.R.C.S. (Edin.). Indian Medical Service, Lieut. June 1901; Major Dec. 1912. Med. Exp. Force. Mesopotamia and East Africa. Dispatches (East Africa) Jan. 1918.

HUSBAND, JAMES WILLIAM.
Dundee High School. M.A. 1905; LL.B. 1908. 5th Royal Highlanders (Black Watch) (T.), 2nd Lieut.; Lieut. July 1917; Acting Captain April 1918.

HUSBAND, ROBERT BLYTH.
Daniel Stewart's College. Cadet Corps 1914-18, Cadet Corporal. Student of Arts, 1918-19. O.T.C. Artillery, Feb. to Oct. 1918, Cadet. R.F.A., Officer Cadet Oct. 1918.

HUSBAND, THOMAS GIBSON.
Knox Institute, Haddington. B.Sc. 1912. A.M.I.C.E. O.T.C. Engineers, 1909-11, Cadet. Canadian Engineers, Sapper Aug. 1914; L/Corporal Nov. 1915; Corporal May 1916; 2nd Lieut. July 1916; Lieut. Jan. 1918; Acting Captain Sept. 1918 to March 1919. France Feb. 1915 to March 1919. Dispatches Nov. 1917.

HUSKIE, CHARLES.
Fettes College. Student of Arts, 1913-14. 1st Battn. City of Edinburgh Vol. Regiment, Private Feb. 1917.

HUSSAIN, SYED A.
Student of Arts, 1913-15. Indian Field Ambulance.

HUTCHEON, ARCHIBALD.
B.L. 1906. 5th Gordon Highlanders (T.), 2nd Lieut.

HUTCHINSON, DONALD HENRY.
Repton. M.B., C.M. 1896; M.D. 1898. R.A.M.C., Lieut. 1916. Mesopotamia. Dispatches 1918.

HUTCHINSON, EDWARD DE WARRENNE.
M.B., C.M. 1879; M.D. 1882. Indian Medical Service, Major.

Record of War Service

HUTCHINSON, THOMAS EDGAR.
Miller Institution, Thurso. Student of Arts, 1918-19. 4th Argyll and Sutherland Highlanders, Private May 1918.

HUTCHINSON-LOW, RICHARD MARSDEN.
M.B., C.M. 1873; L.R.C.P. & S. (Edin.) 1873. Q.E.R., 1869-73. Yeomanry and R.E., Major (retired) 1898. Rejoined Army Medical Service, 1914. Royal Defence Corps, Central Reserve. Prisoner of War Detention Barracks, London. O.B.E.

HUTCHISON, ADAM FRASER.
Boroughmuir School. Student of Law, 1912-13. R.F.A., 2nd Lieut. Aug. 1914; Lieut. June 1916; Captain Jan. 1918. France. M.C. June 1918.

HUTCHISON, ALICE MARION.
M.B., Ch.B. 1899; M.D. 1905. Scottish Women's Hospital, Calais; Chief M.O. Oct. 1914 to April 1915. Malta 1915; Serbia 1915 to Feb. 1916; Macedonia Oct. 1916-17. R.A.M.C., Aldershot, 1917-20. Order of St Sava (3rd Class), (Serbian).

HUTCHISON, ALEXANDER ROBERT.
King's School, Bruton, Somerset. Student of Science, 1913-14. Lothians and Border Horse (T.), Private March 1912. Mobilised Aug. 1914. R.E., Sapper 1916. Gallipoli 1915; Senussi Campaign and Sinai Desert 1916; Palestine 1917-18.

HUTCHISON, SIR ROBERT.
Kirkcaldy High School, and Oliver's Mount, Scarborough; First XI. Student of Arts and Medicine, 1891-2. 4th Dragoon Guards, 2nd Lieut. Feb. 1900, Major; Brevet Lieut.-Col. 1915; Brevet Col. and Brigadier-General 1916; Major-General 1917. France Aug. 1914. War Office, 1916-19. Adjutant-General, Army of the Rhine, June 1919. C.B., D.S.O., K.C.M.G. Officer, Cross of the Order of the Crown of Belgium 1916; Croix de Guerre March 1918; Order of Leopold; Commander of the Crown of Italy; American Distinguished Service Medal. Five times Mentioned in Dispatches.

HUTCHISON, WILLIAM.
George Watson's College. M.B., Ch.B. 1900; D.P.H. (Camb.). R.A.M.C., Lieut. April 1915; Captain April 1916. France.

HUTTON, GORDON CAMPBELL.
Student of Medicine, 1913-14. 9th Royal Scots, Private. France, Officer Cadet. 2nd King's Own Scottish Borderers, 2nd Lieut. Dec. 1916; Lieut. 2/119th Rajputana Infantry, Indian Army.

HUTTON, JAMES.
George Watson's College. Student of Law, 1909-15. O.T.C. Artillery, Aug. 1914 to Feb. 1915, Cadet. R.F.A. (S.R.), 2nd Lieut. Feb. 1915; Lieut. Jan. 1917. Royal Air Force, Pilot July 1918; Captain Jan. 1919. Dispatches Jan. 1919.

Record of War Service

HUXTABLE, ROBERT BEVERIDGE.
The Hutchins School, Hobart. M.B., C.M. 1891. O.C. Thursday Island Defences, Aug. to Dec. 1914. Australian Army Medical Corps, Lieut.-Col. May 1915; Col. and A.D.M.S. Nov. 1916. 7th Australian Field Ambulance, May 1915. 1st Australian Division, Nov. 1916, Major (Hon. Lieut.-Col.). Commanding 2nd Infantry (Kennedy) Regiment, Commonwealth Military Forces. V.D. May 1917; D.S.O. June 1917; C.M.G. June 1918. Dispatches Dec. 1916, June and Dec. 1917, May and Dec. 1918.

HYSLOP, BALFOUR STUART.
George Watson's College. M.B., Ch.B. 1898. R.A.M.C., Lieut. Nov. 1916.

ILLINGWORTH, ANDREW EDWARD.
George Heriot's School. Student of Law, 1913-14. 9th Royal Scots, Private Aug. 1914. 8th Cameron Highlanders, 2nd Lieut. July 1915. Transferred Yorkshire Regiment, Dec. 1915; Lieut. Jan. 1917. India Jan. 1916.

ILLINGWORTH, CHARLES FREDERIC WILLIAM.
Heath School, Halifax. Student of Medicine, 1916-17 and 1918. O.T.C. Artillery, March to Sept. 1917, Cadet; Officer Cadet Sept. 1917. Royal Air Force, 2nd Lieut. Feb. 1918. France.

IMPEY, ROBERT LANCE.
Kingswood College, Grahamstown, S.A. First XV. and XI. Cadet Corps, 1905-8, Cadet Sergeant. Student of Medicine, 1911-15; M.B., Ch.B. 1915. O.T.C. Medical, 1913-15, O.C. R.A.M.C. (S.R.), Lieut. Aug. 1914; Captain June 1916; Major May 1918. 139th Field Ambulance, France, 1916-17. D.A.D.M.S., German East Africa, 1917-18; British East Africa and Uganda, 1918. Invalided out March 1919. M.C. (France) Sept. 1916. Dispatches (East Africa) Sept. 1917.

INCH, ALEXANDER STEVEN.
M.A. 1885. Minister, U.F. Church of Scotland. Chaplain, 9th Argyll and Sutherland Highlanders, Captain May 1909.

INCH, THOMAS DOUGLAS.
George Watson's College. M.B., Ch.B. 1913. Freeland Barbour Scholar. O.T.C. Medical, 1908-14, Cadet Q.M.S. R.A.M.C. (T.), Unattached List, Lieut., Acting Captain, and O.C. Medical Unit, Aug. 1914. R.A.M.C. (S.R.), Jan. 1915, Captain April 1915; Acting Major May 1918. France Jan. 1915; D.A.D.M.S., XVth Corps, Jan. 1917; Italy Oct. 1917. M.C. Jan. 1918; Croce di Guerra Nov. 1918; O.B.E. Jan. 1919. Twice Mentioned in Dispatches.

INCH, WILLIAM HAROLD.
George Watson's College. Student of Medicine, 1905-9. No. 4 Coy. Q.R.V.B., Royal Scots, 1905-7, Private. 8th Royal Scots (T.), 1907; Lieut. 1909; Captain Jan. 1915; Acting Major Dec. 1916; Staff Captain April 1919. France Nov. 1914-17 and 1918-20; Festubert, Givenchy, Beaumont Hamel, and Arras. The Rhine.

Record of War Service

INGLES, JOHN STEWART.
Dumfries Academy; First XI. Student of Arts, 1913-15 and 1918-20; M.A. 1920. O.T.C. Infantry, Oct. 1914 to July 1915, Cadet. Argyll and Sutherland Highlanders, 2nd Lieut. July 1915; Lieut. July 1917.

INGLIS, DAVID WILLIAM.
Daniel Stewart's College. M.A. 1897. Minister, U.F. Church of Scotland. Chaplain, 4th Class, Feb. 1916.

INGLIS, FRANCIS.
Daniel Stewart's College; First XI. B.Sc. 1911. Labour Corps, Private April 1917 (permanently lame since 1912). Clerk, attached Scottish Command H.Q.

INGLIS, GEORGE JOHN.
Edinburgh Academy. O.T.C. 1915-17. University O.T.C. Artillery, Jan. to Sept. 1918. R.F.A., Officer Cadet Sept. 1918; 2nd Lieut. May 1919.

INGLIS, GORDON STEWART.
Edinburgh Academy. B.Sc. 1913. O.T.C. Engineers, Feb. 1910 to June 1914, Cadet C.Q.M.S. R.E. (T.), Dundee Fortress Coy., Sapper Oct. 1914; 2nd Lieut. Nov. 1914; Lieut. March 1916; Acting Captain Nov. 1915; Adjutant July 1916 to Jan. 1918; Acting Major Sept. 1918. 1st Lowland Field Coy. France. Dispatches Jan. 1916. M.C. Jan. 1917.

INGLIS, JAMES McDONALD.
Prince of Wales College, Charlottetown, Canada. M.A. 1872. Minister, Church of Scotland. Chaplain 1885, 4th Royal Scots Fusiliers, and 4th Scottish General Hospital, Colonel 1915. V.D. T.D.

INGLIS, JAMES PRINGLE PARK.
M.B., Ch.B. 1905. R.A.M.C., Lieut. July 1916; Captain Sept. 1917. No. 11 General Hospital, Alexandria, Egypt.

INGLIS, JOHN.
Royal High School; First XV. B.Sc. 1895. O.T.C. Engineers, Feb. to March 1915, Cadet. 16th Royal Irish Rifles, Pioneer; 2nd Lieut. March 1915. R.E., 2nd Lieut. Nov. 1915; Captain Feb. 1916. Egypt and Palestine 1915-19.

INGLIS, JOHN ANDREW.
George Watson's College. Student of Arts and Divinity, 1908-15; M.A. 1912. O.T.C. Infantry, 1908-14, Cadet Corporal. 3rd, 1st, and 6th Royal Highlanders (Black Watch), 2nd Lieut. Dec. 1914; Lieut. Oct. 1915; Captain Oct. 1917. Attached 2nd Highland Light Infantry. France. Twice Wounded. Dispatches 1915.

INGLIS, JOSEPH ELLIS.
Edinburgh Academy and Sedbergh; First XV. and XI. Cadet Corps 1904-8, Cadet Sergeant. Student of Law, 1909-12. Writer to the Signet, 1913. O.T.C. Infantry, 1909-11, Cadet. R.G.A. (T.), 2nd Lieut. 1911; Lieut. 1912. Mobilised Aug. 1914; Captain June 1916; Acting Major Jan. 1917; Staff Captain. Heavy Artillery Nov. 1918. France. Dispatches May 1916. M.C. Jan. 1918.

Record of War Service

INGLIS, ROBERT CHARLES.
Berwick Grammar School and Kirkcaldy High School. B.Sc. 1906. A.M.I.C.E. O.T.C. Feb. to May 1915, Cadet. 14th Argyll and Sutherland Highlanders, Private June 1915. R.E. (Northumberland Division), 2nd Lieut. Dec. 1915; Lieut. May 1917.

INGLIS, ROBERT J. M.
Student of Science, 1902-3. A.M.I.C.E. R.E. (T.), Oct. 1905; Captain May 1911. University O.T.C. Engineers, 1910-19, Captain and O.C. Instructing Officer 1914-15.

INGLIS, W. G. S.
George Watson's College. Student of Medicine, 1913-14. R.F.A. (T.), 1st Lowland Brigade, Gunner.

INGS, GEORGE ARTHUR.
Student of Medicine; L.R.C.P. & S. (Edin.) and L.F.P.S. (Glasg.) 1890. Canadian Army Medical Corps, Major July 1915.

INKSTER, ROBERT GASKIN.
Royal High School. Student of Medicine, 1915-16 and 1917-19. R.F.A., Gunner Jan. 1916; Officer Cadet. France 1917. Invalided out May 1918.

INNES, ALBERT JAMES LANGLANDS.
Student of Medicine, 1912-14 and 1918-19. O.T.C. Medical, 1914-15, Cadet. R.A.M.C. (T.), 3rd Lowland Field Ambulance, Hon. Lieut.

INNES, JOHN.
Portobello School. Student of Arts and Science, 1914-15 and 1918-19. 16th Royal Scots, Private Dec. 1914. R.E., Corporal July 1915. R.F.A., Officer Cadet. R.G.A., 2nd Lieut. Nov. 1917. France 1915. Wounded at Loos, Sept. 1915.

INNES, LAURENCE WALROND.
George Watson's College. O.T.C. 1908-10. Student of Medicine, 1911-14 and 1917-19; M.B., Ch.B. 1918. O.T.C. Infantry, April 1911 to Sept. 1914, Cadet Sergeant. 7th Royal Scots (T.), 2nd Lieut; Captain Dec. 1916.

INNES, LESLIE WALROND.
Student of Science, 1911-14 and 1918-20; B.Sc. 1920. O.T.C. Infantry, April 1911 to June 1914, Cadet Sergeant. Forth R.G.A. (T.), 2nd Lieut.; Lieut. June 1916; Acting Major June 1917. Dispatches.

INNES, RICHARD HARTLEY ROSE.
Student of Medicine, 1912-14. O.T.C. Artillery, 1912-14, Cadet. South African Mounted Rifles, Field Artillery, Gunner Aug. 1914-15. R.N.V.R., Surgeon-Probationer, Oct. 1915 to Nov. 1919. German S.W. Africa 1914-15.

Record of War Service

INNES-SMITH, STUART WILLIAM.
Epsom College; First XV. O.T.C. 1914. Student of Medicine, 1915-16. O.T.C. Infantry, 1915, Cadet. Argyll and Sutherland Highlanders, Private Nov. 1915. M.M. Oct. 1918.

IRELAND, JOHN.
Royal High School. B.Sc. 1911. O.T.C. Engineers, 1910-11, Cadet Corporal. R.E., 81st Field Coy., 2nd Lieut. Oct. 1914; Lieut. July 1915. France. Wounded at Bazentin-le-Petit (Somme), July 1916. M.C. Aug. 1916.

IRELAND, RICHARD MORISON.
Edinburgh Institution; First XI. Student of Law, 1906-9. Writer to the Signet, 1910. 5th and 9th Royal Scots (T.), 2nd Lieut. Sept. 1914; Lieut. May 1915; Captain Oct. 1916. 1st Essex Regiment. Gallipoli Sept. to Dec. 1915; France Aug. 1916 to April 1919. Invalided home Dec. 1915. Wounded at Beaumont Hamel Nov. 1916.

IRELAND, WALTER EDWARD.
Edinburgh Collegiate School. M.A. 1874. Minister, U.F. Church of Scotland. 1st V.B., Argyll and Sutherland Highlanders, Private June 1916.

IRVINE, NORMAN MORRIS.
Forfar Academy. Student of Science, 1913-14 and 1918-19. 9th Royal Scots, 13th Argyll and Sutherland Highlanders, and Royal Air Force, Lieut.

IRVINE, QUENTIN.
Radley College. B.A. (Oxford). Student of Science, 1918-19. 16th Middlesex Regiment, Private Aug. 1914. 3rd Argyll and Sutherland Highlanders, 2nd Lieut. April 1915; Lieut. July 1917. France June to Nov. 1916.

IRVINE, RICHARD CHARLES.
M.B., Ch.B. 1902. R.A.M.C., Lieut; Captain Oct. 1915; Acting Major Jan. 1918. 15th Casualty Clearing Station. Indian Exp. Force, Lahore Division.

IRVINE FORTESCUE, JOHN FAITHFUL.
Aberdeen Grammar School. Student of Divinity, 1918. A.S.C., Lieut. June 1915.

IRVINE-JONES, CHARLES IRVINE.
Daniel Stewart's College. Student of Medicine, 1916-17 and 1918-19. O.T.C. Medical, March 1918 to Feb. 1919, Cadet. 40th and 39th Training Reserve Battn., Private July 1917. 4th Argyll and Sutherland Highlanders.

IRVING, ROBERT JAMES.
Solihull; First XI. B.Sc. 1891; M.B., Ch.B. 1902. R.A.M.C., Lieut. Jan. 1915; Captain 1915. 2nd Southern General Hospital.

ISAAC, GEORGE WASHINGTON.
"Bedfords," Clifton, Bristol. M.B., C.M. 1882. R.A.M.C. (V.), July 1918. 1st City of London R.A.S.C. (M.T.).

Record of War Service

ISRAEL, ELIE BENJAMIN.
Jeppe High School, Johannesburg. Student of Medicine, 1910-15; M.B., Ch.B. 1915. O.T.C. Medical, Nov. 1914 to June 1915, Cadet. R.A.M.C., Captain Oct. 1916.

IVORY, WILLIAM HOLMES.
Edinburgh Academy; First XI. Student of Law. Writer to the Signet, 1908. 8th and 5/6th Royal Scots (T.), 2nd Lieut. June 1915; Lieut. July 1917. France Sept. 1917 to Dec. 1918.

JACK, ARNOLD CHATER.
Merchiston Castle. O.T.C. 1912-16, Cadet L/Corporal. University O.T.C. Artillery, 1916-17, Cadet B.Q.M.S.; Officer Cadet Sept. 1917. R.F.A., 256th Brigade, 2nd Lieut. Feb. 1918 to Jan. 1919. France, 51st (Highland) Division.

JACK, DAVID.
Miller Institution, Thurso. Student of Arts, 1914-17 and 1918-20; M.A. (Hons. Maths.) 1920. Medically unfit 1915-16. R.G.A., Signaller July 1917.

JACK, DONALD GEORGE. (See p. 750.)

JACK, JAMES GORDON.
George Watson's College. Cadet Corps 1906-7. Student of Law, 1909-13. Writer to the Signet, 1914. O.T.C. Infantry, March 1909 to June 1912, Cadet. Forth R.G.A., Gunner Nov. 1915; Bombardier March 1916. 1st Highland Light Infantry, 2nd Lieut. Feb. 1917. 4th Labour Coy., France, June 1917 to Jan. 1918. Invalided out June 1918.

JACK, JOHN GRAY.
George Heriot's School. M.B., Ch.B. 1899. R.A.M.C., Lieut. July 1916.

JACK, JOHN ROBERT KAY.
Boroughmuir School. Student of Arts, 1913-15. 6th Royal Scots (T.), Private Nov. 1912. Ministry of Munitions, 1915-17. Royal Air Force, Air Mechanic May 1917. Labour Corps, 2nd Lieut. Feb. 1918. France. Invalided out April 1919.

JACK, ROBERT PATON.
Hamilton Academy. M.B., C.M. 1886; D.P.H., F.P.S. (Glasg.) 1889. 2/6th Scottish Rifles (T.), Major. Mobilised Sept. 1914; Lieut.-Col. June 1916. Transferred to R.A.M.C., Aug. 1917. France.

JACK, THOMAS.
M.A. 1906. Schoolmaster. 4th Royal Scots (T.), Private 1900; Colour-Sergeant; 10th Border Regiment, 2nd Lieut. Jan. 1915. Machine-Gun Corps, Lieut. Aug. 1916. Gallipoli, Egypt, and Palestine.

JACK, WILLIAM CALDERHEAD.
Ayr Academy; First XV. O.T.C. 1912-18, Cadet L/Corporal. Student of Medicine, 1918. O.T.C. Artillery, Jan. to Aug. 1918, Cadet Corporal. R.F.A., Officer Cadet Sept. 1918.

Record of War Service

JACKSON, EDWARD SIDDALL.
George Watson's College. O.T.C. 1905-10, Cadet Corporal. Student of Medicine, 1911-14 and 1918-19. O.T.C. Artillery, Jan. 1912 to Oct. 1914, Cadet. R.F.A., 14th Division, 2nd Lieut. Oct. 1914; Lieut.

JACKSON, FREDERICK STANLEY.
Collegiate School, St Anne's. Student of Medicine, 1902-4. A.S.C. (M.T.), 2nd Lieut. June 1917. France.

JACKSON, GEORGE ERSKINE.
Haileybury; First XV. B.A. (Oxford) 1895. Student of Law. Writer to the Signet, 1898. Fife and Forfar Yeomanry (Highland Mounted Brigade), Staff, Captain Aug. 1914; Major March 1918. Gallipoli Sept. to Dec. 1915. Palestine and Syria. D.A.A. and Q.M.G., Egypt, June 1916 to July 1919. Dispatches March 1917 and June 1919. M.C. June 1918. O.B.E. June 1919.

JACKSON, PETER McGREGOR.
Perth Academy. Student of Law, 1914-15. Chartered Accountant, 1919. 1/5th Border Regiment, Private June 1915, 2nd Lieut. Nov. 1917. 32nd Division.

JACKSON, ROBERT.
Lancaster School. M.B., C.M. 1885. No. 4 Coy. Q.E.R., 1881-6, Private. Army Medical Service, 1893. Mobilised Aug. 1914. R.A.M.C. (T.), Colonel March 1913, and A.D.M.S., West Lancashire Division; 55th Division. France 1915-17. T.D. Dispatches June 1917.

JACKSON, THOMAS.
Cheltenham. M.A. 1902. No. 4 Coy. Q.R.V.B., Royal Scots, 1897-1900. 3rd Highland Light Infantry, 1900. South African Campaign, 1900-1, Captain 1904; Temp. Major 1918; Brevet Major June 1919. Attached 2nd Royal Scots Fusiliers, France Oct. to Dec. 1914. Wounded Dec. 1914. Chief Instructor, O.C. Battn. Oxford. Dispatches March 1918 and June 1919.

JACKSON, THOMAS WILLIAM.
Northampton School; First XI. M.B., Ch.B. 1913. R.A.M.C., Lieut. Oct. 1915; Captain Oct. 1916. 2/1st East Anglian and 55th Field Ambulances. 8th East Surrey Regiment, and Military Hospital, Bury St Edmunds. M.C. April 1918.

JACKSON, WALTER DALGLEISH.
George Watson's College and Aberdeen Grammar School; First XV. Student of Medicine, 1918-20. 1/4th Gordon Highlanders, Private March 1914. Mobilised (under age) Aug. 1914. O.T.C. Artillery, June 1916 to Feb. 1917, Cadet Corporal; Officer Cadet Feb. 1917. R.F.A., 2nd Lieut. Sept. 1917; Acting Captain Aug. 1918; Lieut. March 1919. France. Dispatches Aug. 1918. Wounded at Arras June 1918 and Morlancourt Aug. 1918.

Record of War Service

JAFFRAY, WILLIAM STEVENSON.
   Daniel Stewart's College. Student of Arts and Divinity, 1884-91; D.D. 1920. Chaplain, 4th Class, 1891; 1st Class, 1910. Principal Presbyterian Chaplain, Aug. 1919. South African Campaign, 1900. France 1914-18; Salonika and Black Sea 1918-19. C.M.G. June 1915; Order of St Sava (2nd Class), Serbia, Nov. 1918; C.B.E. June 1918. Five times Mentioned in Dispatches.

JAGGER, FRANCIS FIELD CUNNINGHAM.
   Shrewsbury. M.B., Ch.B. 1900. R.A.M.C. (T.), Lieut. Aug. 1915; Captain Feb. 1916. M.O., 2/2nd Company of London Yeomanry; 2/5th King's Own Yorkshire Light Infantry. O.C. No. 3 Mobile X-Ray Unit.

JAMAL-UD-DIN.
   Student of Medicine, 1909-14; M.B., Ch.B. 1913. Indian Medical Service, Lieut. Aug. 1914; Acting Captain Sept. 1915; Captain Aug. 1917. Med. Exp. Force.

JAMES, ALASTAIR KER.
   Edinburgh Academy. O.T.C. 1913-14. Student of Medicine, 1914-15 and 1918-19. O.T.C. Infantry, Oct. 1914 to March 1915, Cadet L/Corporal. 7th attached 5/6th Royal Scots (T.), 2nd Lieut. March 1915; Lieut. Nov. 1915. France.

JAMES, BENJAMIN. (See p. 750.)

JAMES, JOSEPH FRAIN.
   M.B., Ch.B. 1905. Indian Medical Service, Captain March 1910.

JAMES, WALTER TIMOTHY.
   King Edward's School, Birmingham; First XV. M.B., Ch.B. 1899; M.D. 1917. No. 4 Coy. Q.R.V.B., Royal Scots, 1895-8, Private. Civil Surgeon, South African Field Force, 1901-2. R.A.M.C., Lieut. Jan. 1915; Captain Jan. 1916. 6th King's Own Scottish Borderers, 1915. Mesopotamia 1916.

JAMESON, GEORGE BERNARD.
   M.B., C.M. 1890; M.D. 1895. R.A.M.C. (T.), Lieut. 2nd East Lancashire Field Ambulance.

JAMESON, JAMES CONWAY.
   Edinburgh Academy; First XV. and XI. M.B., C.M. 1888; D.P.H. (Camb.) 1904. R.A.M.C., July 1891. Indian Frontier, 1897-8; South African Campaign, 1899-1902. Lieut.-Col. and O.C. No. 12 General Hospital, Aug. 1914; No. 11 Stationary Hospital, July 1917 to March 1919. Dispatches Jan. 1918.

JAMESON, JOHN GORDON.
   Edinburgh Academy. B.A., LL.B., and Advocate, 1903. M.P. Scottish Horse (T.), Captain Sept. 1914; Major Feb. 1916. 710th Labour Coy.

JAMESON, WILFRID.
   M.A. 1911. Schoolmaster. 7th Royal Scots (T.), Private.

JAMIE, GEORGE HOPE.
   George Watson's College; First XI. Student of Arts and Divinity, 1909-15; M.A. 1914. Minister, Church of Scotland. O.T.C. Artillery, Dec. 1914 to Sept. 1915, Cadet. Chaplain, 1st Royal Scots Fusiliers (Jhansi, India).

Record of War Service

JAMIE, WILLIAM DALLAS.
George Watson's College. M.A. 1910. 9th Royal Scots (T.), Private Nov. 1915. 7/8th King's Own Scottish Borderers, 2nd Lieut. May 1917; Lieut. Nov. 1918. France 1917-19. Croix de Guerre with Palm Nov. 1918.

JAMIESON, ALEXANDER BROWN.
M.B., Ch.B. 1910. R.A.M.C., Lieut.

JAMIESON, ANDREW STEWART.
Royal High School. Student of Law, 1898-9. Solicitor, 1899. R.N.V.R., 2nd R.N. Brigade, Clyde Division, Paymaster-Lieut.-Commander March 1913.

JAMIESON, ARCHIBALD MONCRIEFF.
M.A. 1890. Schoolmaster. 8th Royal Scots (T.), Sergeant 1883.

JAMIESON, ARCHIBALD WILLIAM.
Merchiston Castle. Student of Law, 1894-5. R.G.A., Nova Scotia, Captain.

JAMIESON, ARTHUR.
Anderson Institute, Lerwick. M.A. 1912. Schoolmaster. 16th Royal Scots, Private Dec. 1914; Corporal April 1915. R.E., Corporal July 1915; Sergeant Sept. 1915; C.S.M. Jan. 1916; 2nd Lieut. May 1917; Lieut. Nov. 1918. France Aug. 1915 to Jan. 1919. M.C. Oct. 1917; Bar to M.C. Oct. 1918.

JAMIESON, ERIC.
Rose's Academical Institution, Nairn. M.A. 1910; M.B., Ch.B. 1915. O.T.C. Artillery, 1911-15, Cadet B.S.M. R.A.M.C., Lieut. May 1915; Temp. Captain Dec. 1915; Captain (Regulars) Dec. 1918. 23rd Combined Field Ambulance and Acting D.A.D.M.S., Third Indian Army Corps, Mesopotamia; Persia. Dispatches July 1918.

JAMIESON, HAROLD.
Nairn Academy. Student of Arts and Medicine, 1912-15 and 1918-19; M.A. 1915. O.T.C. Artillery, Oct. 1914 to March 1915, Cadet. R.F.A., 2nd Lieut. April 1915; Lieut. Sept. 1917. France, Ypres.

JAMIESON, JAMES BRYCE.
M.A. 1900; B.D. Minister, Church of Scotland. Chaplain, King's Own Scottish Borderers.

JAMIESON, JAMES FORBES.
B.Sc. 1907. No. 4 Coy. Q.R.V.B., Royal Scots, 1904-7, Private. 27th Hyderabad Mounted Rifles (V.), (Indian Defence Force), Private 1912.

JAMIESON, JOHN.
Daniel Stewart's College. M.B., Ch.B. 1901; M.D. South African Campaign, 1901-2. R.A.M.C., Lieut. April to Oct. 1918. 100th Field Ambulance.

JAMIESON, JOHN ALEXANDER.
George Watson's College. M.B., Ch.B. 1907; M.D. 1911. No. 4 Coy. Q.R.V.B., Royal Scots, 1903-7, L/Corporal. R.A.M.C., Lieut. May 1917; Captain May 1918. Mesopotamia.

Record of War Service

JAMIESON, JOHN BOYD.
George Watson's College. Cadet Corps 1888. M.B., C.M. 1897; M.D. 1902; F.R.C.S. (Edin.) 1900. No. 4 Coy. Q.R.V.B., Royal Scots, 1891-1904, Lieut. (Surgeon). R.A.M.C. (T.), Lieut. 1908; Major 1909; Lieut.-Col. Sept. 1919. Lowland Division Train. Scottish Coast Defences; S.M.O. Forth Garrison, from April 1919.

JAMIESON, JOHN DUNCAN.
George Heriot's School. Student of Arts, 1912-16; M.A. 1916. Minister, Baptist Church. 9th and 3rd Royal Scots, Private March 1916; 2nd Lieut. Jan. 1917; Lieut. July 1918 to March 1919. Attached 4th West Surrey Regiment and 5th South Wales Borderers. India and Mesopotamia.

JAMIESON, ROBERT HILLHOUSE.
M.B., Ch.B. 1907; M.D. 1910; F.R.C.S. (Edin.) 1909. R.A.M.C., Lieut. July 1916. 33rd Stationary Hospital, Salonika.

JAMIESON, SYDNEY.
Horton College, Ross, Tasmania. B.A. (Sydney); M.R.C.S. (Eng.); L.R.C.P. (Lond.); M.B., C.M. 1888. Australian Army Medical Corps, May 1915, Lieut.-Col. 3rd Australian General Hospital.

JAMIESON, WALTER.
Leith Walk School. M.A. 1910. Schoolmaster. 5th Royal Scots (T.), Corporal Sept. 1914; Sergeant Dec. 1914; Lieut. April 1915. Egypt and France. Wounded July 1917.

JANAKIRIAMIAH, TANGUTURI.
M.B., Ch.B. 1915. Indian Field Ambulance.

JARDINE, JOHN.
George Heriot's School. M.B., Ch.B. 1904; M.D. 1909; D.P.H. (Edin.) 1905; F.R.C.S. (Edin.) 1908. R.A.M.C., Lieut. Dec. 1914; Captain Dec. 1915. O.B.E. Dispatches 1918.

JARDINE, MAURICE KIRKPATRICK.
Westminster School. O.T.C. 1906-10. Student of Medicine, 1911-16. O.T.C. Medical, Feb. 1916, Cadet. B.R.C.S. Nov. 1914. Hospital Ships *Glenart* and *Gloucester Castle*, April to Oct. 1915, Dardanelles. R.N.V.R., Surgeon Sub-Lieut., May 1916 to April 1919. H.M.T.B. Destroyers *Trident*, *Tancred*, and *Walker*.

JARDINE, WILLIAM.
George Watson's College. M.A., B.Sc. 1912. R.A.M.C., Private July 1915; Sergeant Feb. 1916. France 1916-19; Somme, Arras, Amiens, and Le Cateau.

JARDINE, WILLIAM CHRISTOPHER.
M.B., Ch.B. 1909. O.T.C. Infantry, Oct. 1908 to Jan. 1910, Cadet L/Corporal. R.A.M.C., Lieut.; Captain Oct. 1915.

Record of War Service

JARVIS, OSWALD DUKE.
  Forfar Academy. Student of Medicine, 1910-15; M.B., Ch.B. 1915. O.T.C. Medical, Nov. 1910 to May 1914, Cadet Sergeant. R.A.M.C., Lieut. (S.R.) Aug. 1914; Lieut. (Regulars) Aug. 1915; Temp. Captain Feb. 1916; Captain Feb. 1919. Mesopotamia. Dispatches Feb. 1919. O.B.E. June 1919.

JEFFCOAT, LESLIE FRASER EILOART.
  M.B., Ch.B. 1914. O.T.C. Infantry, Jan. 1909 to July 1912, Cadet. R.A.M.C., Lieut.; Captain May 1916.

JEFFREY, JOHN.
  Sedbergh. M.B., Ch.B. 1899; F.R.C.S. (Edin.) 1902. British Red Cross, France, 1915. R.A.M.C., Lieut. May 1917; Captain May 1918. Egypt.

JEFFREY, JOHN GEORGE ALEXANDER.
  George Heriot's School. O.T.C. 1910-14. Student of Science, 1918. 15th Highland Light Infantry, 2nd Lieut. Dec. 1915; Lieut July 1917 to Jan. 1919; Acting Captain Sept. 1917 to March 1918. M.C. April 1918.

JEFFREY, JOHN STEWART.
  George Watson's College. O.T.C. 1914-17. Student of Science, 1918-19. O.T.C. Artillery, April to Nov. 1918, Cadet. R.F.A., Officer Cadet Nov. 1918.

JENKINS, CHARLES CUNNINGHAM.
  Ayr Academy; First XV. and XI. Student of Arts, 1914-15 and 1919. 16th 18th, and 3rd Royal Scots, Private March 1916; Sergeant. 4th and 12th Highland Light Infantry.

JENKINS, GEORGE JOHN.
  M.B., C.M. 1895; F.R.C.S. (Eng.) 1902. R.A.M.C. (T.), Captain June 1915. London General Hospitals. Member of Advisory Committee to the War Office. O.B.E. (Military). Dispatches.

JENKINS, GEORGE McLAREN.
  Dunfermline High School. Student of Arts and Science, 1911-14; M.A. 1919. O.T.C. Infantry, Oct. 1912 to Oct. 1914, Cadet. 9th and 1st King's Own Scottish Borderers, 2nd Lieut. Oct. 1914; Lieut. July 1917. 51st and 2nd Machine-Gun Corps. Gallipoli, France, and The Rhine. Wounded 1916. M.C. Dec. 1918.

JENKINS, GERALD KERR.
  Daniel Stewart's College. Student of Arts, 1913-14. O.T.C. Artillery, Oct. 1913 to Aug. 1914, Cadet. R.F.A., 2nd Lieut. Aug. 1914; Major Jan. 1917. France May 1916. Italy. M.C. Jan. 1918.

JENKINS, WILLIAM JOHN.
  George Watson's College; First XV. Student of Science, 1911-14. O.T.C. Artillery, Nov. 1912 to Sept. 1914, Cadet. R.F.A., 2nd Lieut. Sept. 1914; Lieut. Oct. 1917. France 1915-16; Mesopotamia 1917-18; Palestine 1918.

Record of War Service

JENNINGS, NORMAN.
   Carlisle Grammar School. Student of Medicine, 1912-17; M.B., Ch.B. 1916. O.T.C. Medical, April 1913-14, Cadet. Royal Navy, Surgeon-Probationer, March 1915-16; Surgeon Jan. 1917. Yorkhill War Hospital; R.N. Hospital, Haslar; H.M. Ships *Waveney* 1915-16, and *Highflyer* 1917-19.

JENNINGS, WILLIAM ERNEST.
   M.B., C.M. 1887; M.D. 1903; D.P.H. (Ireland) 1903. Fellow, Syndic, and Examiner, Bombay University. Indian Medical Service, 1887; Lieut.-Col. 1907; Colonel 1916; Major-General 1919. Staff and Marine Surgeon, Bombay, and A.D.M.S., Poona Division. K.H.P. 1919. Knight of Grace, Order of St John of Jerusalem, 1914. Dispatches June and Aug. 1918.

JOBSON, COLIN LIVINGSTONE.
   Royal High School. M.A. 1912. Schoolmaster. 6th attached 4th Royal Scots (T.), Private Aug. 1914; Corporal.

JOBSON, ERIC WILLIAM CHARLES.
   Stratford High School, New Zealand. O.T.C. 1916-17. Student of Medicine, 1918. N.Z. Rifle Brigade, Private. N.Z. Medical Corps. France 1917-18.

JOCKEL, GEORGE ROBERT MARSHALL.
   Royal High School. Student of Law, 1904-6; Law Agent, 1907. Royal Scots, Private Nov. 1915. 5th and 21st Highland Light Infantry, 2nd Lieut. Aug. 1917 to Jan. 1919.

JOE, ALEXANDER.
   Brechin High School. Student of Medicine, 1912-15 and 1918-19. O.T.C. Infantry, Oct. 1914 to July 1915, Cadet. R.N.V.R., Surgeon-Probationer, July 1915 to April 1918. Taken Prisoner at Battle of Jutland May 1916, returned March 1918. D.S.C. (Jutland) May 1916.

JOHNS, WILLIAM WILTON.
   M.B., Ch.B. 1907; M.D. 1910; L.R.C.P. & S. (Edin.) and L.F.P.S. (Glasg.) 1906. Edinburgh and Border Hospital, Dunkirk, 1914. R.A.M.C., Lieut. Aug. 1916; Captain Aug. 1917. 43rd General Hospital, Salonika.

JOHNSON, CECIL WILLOUGHBY.
   Bishop Cotton School, Simla. Q.E.R., 1878-82, Private. R.A.M.C., Surgeon 1885; Lieut.-Col. 1905. Retired 1912. South African Campaign, 1899-1902; Egypt 1885-6; India 1897. Mobilised Sept. 1914-19.

JOHNSON, ERNEST HUGH. (See p. 750.)

JOHNSON, GEORGE MACNESS.
   Charterhouse. Student of Medicine, 1912-14. 9th Royal Scots, Private Nov. 1914. 4th Cameron Highlanders, 2nd Lieut. April 1915; Lieut. Aug. 1915. Royal Newfoundland Regiment from May 1916, Acting Captain 1916. Attached 79th Carnatic, 108th Infantry, and Wallajahbads. France, Mesopotamia, India, Oct. 1917, and Persia.

Record of War Service

JOHNSON, REGINALD NOEL.
Grey College, South Africa. First XV. and XI. Student of Medicine, 1912-15 and 1917-19. O.T.C. Infantry, Oct. 1914 to Jan. 1915, Cadet. R.A.M.C. (T.), Scottish Horse Brigade Field Ambulance, Private Dec. 1914; Corporal Feb. 1915; Sergeant April 1915 to Aug. 1917.

JOHNSON, WILLIAM PRIDEAUX SELBY.
Dukes School, Alnwick. M.B., Ch.B. 1908. R.A.M.C., Lieut. April 1917; Captain April 1918. France. Wounded at Passchendaele Sept. 1917.

JOHNSTON, CHARLES ARTHUR.
M.B., C.M., 1888. Indian Medical Service, Lieut.-Col. July 1911. C.B. D.S.O.

JOHNSTON, F. C.
Glenalmond. Student of Arts, 1902-4. 18th Royal Fusiliers (Public Schools and University Corps), Private.

JOHNSTON, GEORGE.
George Watson's College. Student. 6th Scottish Rifles, Sergeant.

JOHNSTON, GEORGE GILBERT H.
George Heriot's School; First XV. and XI. M.A. 1900. Schoolmaster. A.S.C., Lieut. Aug. 1915; Captain April 1917. France 1915.

JOHNSTON, HENRY HALCRO.
Dollar Institution and Edinburgh Collegiate School. M.B., C.M. 1880; M.D. 1893; B.Sc. (P.H.) 1893; D.Sc. 1894. Rugby International, 1877. R.A.M.C., 1881; Colonel (Retired) 1913. Rejoined Dec. 1914 to Oct. 1916, and June 1917 to April 1919. Malakand 1897-8. South African Campaign, 1899-1902. Gibraltar 1915. A.D.M.S, Western District, Scottish Command, 1916; Northern Command, 1917-19. C.B. (Military) 1902; C.B.E. (Military) June 1919.

JOHNSTON, HUGH BARR.
Student of Science. O.T.C. Engineers, 1912-15, Cadet. 13th Royal Scots, 2nd Lieut. 23rd Machine-Gun Corps, Lieut. Aug. 1916. Gallipoli Oct. 1915. France.

JOHNSTON, JAMES HALCRO.
George Watson's College. B.Sc. 1913. O.T.C. Engineers, Oct. 1910 to April 1914, Cadet. Simla Volunteers, 1914 to Jan. 1916. 2nd Q.V.O., Sappers and Miners (I.A.R.O.), Rawal Pindi, 2nd Lieut. Jan. 1916; Lieut. Jan. 1917. Mesopotamia Nov. 1916-20. Wounded Feb. 1917. Dispatches June 1919.

JOHNSTON, JAMES HUNTER.
M.B., C.M. 1892. R.A.M.C., Lieut.; Captain March 1916.

JOHNSTON, JAMES McLAUCHLAN.
Trinity Academy, Leith. Student of Medicine, 1919. O.T.C. Artillery, July 1917 to Feb. 1918, Cadet. R.G.A., Officer Cadet Feb. 1918.

Record of War Service

JOHNSTON, JAMES THOMAS.
Student of Medicine, 1913-18. M.B., Ch.B. 1918. O.T.C. Artillery, Oct. 1914 to April 1915, Cadet. R.N.V.R., Surgeon-Probationer.

JOHNSTON, JOHN.
Annan Academy. M.A. 1905. Schoolmaster. No. 4 Coy. Q.R.V.B., Royal Scots, 1902-6, L/Corporal. 3rd V.B. King's Own Scottish Borderers, 1898. 6th Royal Scots (T.), 2nd Lieut. Oct. 1909; Lieut. Aug. 1914; Captain Sept. 1915; Staff Captain March 1918; Staff Major Oct. 1918; Staff Lieut.-Col. July 1919. Attached 13th Leicestershire Regiment, Nov. 1916. France Dec. 1916. Dispatches Dec. 1917, Dec. 1918, and July 1919. O.B.E. June 1919.

JOHNSTON, JOHN DORRENS.
Student of Medicine, 1914-15 and 1917-18. O.T.C. Artillery, 1914-15, Medical, 1918-19, Cadet. 14th Argyll and Sutherland Highlanders, Private. France 1916-18.

JOHNSTON, JOHN MACPHERSON.
Dundee High School. M.B., Ch.B. 1903; M.R.C.S. (Eng.); L.R.C.P. and D.P.H. (Lond.). R.A.M.C., Lieut. Aug. 1914; Captain Aug. 1915. Sanitary Officer, Mudros and Egypt, 1915-17. Dispatches July 1917.

JOHNSTON, LEWIS INGLIS.
George Heriot's School. O.T.C. 1914-17, Cadet L/Corporal. Student of Medicine, 1918. R.G.A., Officer Cadet July 1917.

JOHNSTON, MATTHEW JAMES.
Royal School, Dungannon; First XI., Football. M.B., Ch.B. 1907; M.D. 1919. R.A.M.C., Lieut. Dec. 1914; Captain Dec. 1915 to Jan. 1919. 2nd Ambulance Flotilla. France Feb. 1915 to Jan. 1919. M.C. Nov. 1918.

JOHNSTON, ROBERT JOHN.
George Watson's College. M.B., C.M. 1892. R.A.M.C., Captain Aug. 1914; Military Hospital, Ayr.

JOHNSTON, THOMAS BAILLIE.
George Watson's College; First XI. M.B., Ch.B. 1906. Lecturer on Anatomy, 1907-14. R.A.M.C., Lieut. Feb. 1916; Captain March 1918. 22nd Field Ambulance. France 1917; Italy 1918. Dispatches May 1918.

JOHNSTON, WILLIAM DAVID STONEY.
Nelson College, New Zealand. Cadet Corps. N.Z. Territorials, Lieut. M.B., Ch.B. 1907; M.D. 1910. N.Z. Medical Corps, Captain Oct. 1917.

JOHNSTON, WILLIAM HENRY.
B.A. (New Zealand). M.B., Ch.B. 1911; M.D. 1915. O.T.C. Infantry, Jan. 1909 to June 1910, Cadet. R.A.M.C., Lieut.; Captain March 1918.

Record of War Service

JOHNSTONE, CECIL H. C.
Student of Law, 1907-8. R.F.A. (T.), 1st Lowland Brigade, Lieut.; Captain June 1916.

JOHNSTONE, CHARLES BRAND.
Rossall. M.B., C.M. 1897. L.R.C.P. & S. (Edin.) and L.F.P.S. (Glasg.) 1897. R.A.M.C., Lieut. Nov. 1914; Captain May 1915; Major Jan. 1917. 1st Midland Field Ambulance.

JOHNSTONE, DAVID ANDREW.
Lochmaben School. M.B., C.M. 1894. R.A.M.C., Lieut. Oct. to Dec. 1918.

JOHNSTONE, FREDERICK JOHN CARLYLE.
Edinburgh Academy. O.T.C. 1908-10. Student of Medicine, 1909-17. M.B., Ch.B. 1916. O.T.C. Artillery, Oct. 1910 to Oct. 1914, Cadet B.S.M. R.F.A. (S.R.), 2nd Lieut. Aug. 1914; Lieut. June 1915 to April 1916. R.A.M.C. (S.R.), Lieut. Nov. 1916; Captain Nov. 1917. Senior M.O., Turkana Expedition, 1918; Northern Frontier and British East Africa. Dispatches (East Africa) June 1919.

JOHNSTONE, JAMES LOCKHART.
Fettes College. O.T.C. 1913-16. University O.T.C. Artillery, 1917-18, Cadet; Officer Cadet Aug. 1918. R.G.A. (T.), 2nd Lieut. April 1919.

JOHNSTONE, JAMES MACKERSIE.
Lanark Grammar School. M.B., Ch.B. 1902. 8th Highland Light Infantry (T.), Lieut. April 1908; Captain June 1912. R.A.M.C. (T.), Captain July 1915.

JOHNSTONE, JOHN MILLER.
Selkirk High School. Student of Medicine, 1911-16. M.B., Ch.B. 1916. O.T.C., Medical, Oct. 1914 to March 1916, Cadet Corporal. R.A.M.C., Lieut. April 1916; Captain May 1917.

JOHNSTONE, ROBERT WILLIAM.
George Watson's College. M.A. 1900; M.B., Ch.B. 1903; M.D. 1906; M.R.C.P. and F.R.C.S. (Edin.) 1906. University Assistant. No. 4 Coy. Q.R.V.B., Royal Scots, 1899-1902, Private. Red Cross Royal Victoria Hospital, 1914-17. R.A.M.C., Lieut. April 1917. France April to Oct. 1917. Deputy Commissioner and Commissioner, Ministry of National Service, London, Oct. 1917 to May 1919. O.B.E. Jan. 1919. C.B.E. March 1920.

JOLLY, GEORGE ADAM.
George Watson's College. M.B., Ch.B. 1901. Indian Medical Service, Captain; Major March 1914. East Africa.

JOLLY, GORDON GRAY.
George Watson's College. M.B., Ch.B. 1907; D.P.H. (Edin.); D.T.M. (Lond.). University Battery, E.C.A.V., 1904-8, Sergeant. Indian Medical Service, 1908; Captain 1911; Local Major Dec. 1917; Temp. Major May 1918. East Africa 1914-19. D.A.D.M.S. Sanitation, 1917-19. Dispatches Aug. 1918. C.I.E. June 1919.

Record of War Service

JOLLY, WILLIAM ADAM.
M.B., Ch.B. 1906; D.Sc. 1910. Consultant, South African Medical Corps; Cape Peninsula Garrison Regiment, Private.

JONES, BENJAMIN.
M.B., C.M. 1886; M.D. 1890; D.P.H. (Lond.). R.A.M.C., Lieut. May 1915; Captain 1916.

JONES, DAVID HARRIS.
Dundee High School. M.A. 1908; M.B., Ch.B. 1915. Vans Dunlop Scholar, 1907. O.T.C. Medical, April 1908 to Nov. 1912, Cadet. R.A.M.C., Lieut. Aug. 1915; Captain Aug. 1916 to June 1919.

JONES, DAVID JOHN.
M.B., C.M. 1888. R.A.M.C., Captain Feb. 1916. H.M. Hospital Ship *Tagus*, Mediterranean, Feb. to Dec. 1915; H.M. Hospital Ship *Brighton*.

JONES, EDGAR VAUGHAN.
M.B., Ch.B. 1901. South African Medical Corps, Captain Nov. 1914 to May 1916. R.A.M.C., Temp. Hon. Lieut. May 1916; Captain 1916-18. Welsh Hospital, Netley.

JONES, EDWARD HUGHES.
M.B., C.M. 1890; M.D. 1909. R.A.M.C., Lieut.; Captain Sept. 1915.

JONES, ERNEST RANKIN GRIFFITHS.
George Watson's College. Student of Arts, 1911-15; M.A. 1915. 3rd and 5th King's Royal Rifle Corps, Rifleman June 1916; Officer Cadet Dec. 1916; 2nd Lieut. March 1917; Lieut. Sept. 1918 to Feb. 1919. Salonika July 1917.

JONES, FRANCIS ARTHUR.
Wrexham County School. Student of Medicine, 1918. R.G.A., 123rd Siege Battery, Gunner Jan. 1916.

JONES, FRANK.
St Bees School, Cumberland; First XV. and XI. Rifle Corps 1905-7. Student of Medicine, 1910-17; L.R.C.P. & S. (Edin.) and L.R.F.P. & S. (Glasg.) 1917. O.T.C. Infantry, May 1909 to May 1912, Cadet. R.A.M.C., Lieut. Aug. 1917; Captain 1918. German East Africa.

JONES, HENRY.
Broughton School. Student of Arts, 1914. O.T.C. Engineers, Nov. 1914 to Aug. 1915, Cadet. R.E., No. 2 Special Coy., Corporal Aug. 1915; Sergeant Oct. 1917. France Aug. 1915 to Feb. 1919.

JONES, IDWAL WYNNE.
Friars School, Bangor. M.B., Ch.B. 1912. O.T.C. Medical, April 1908 to Nov. 1912, Cadet. R.A.M.C., Lieut. Oct. 1915; Captain Oct. 1916. 131st Field Ambulance, France, 1915-16. Salonika 1916-17; Mesopotamia 1918-19. 152nd Casualty Clearing Field Ambulance (Indian Army). Afghan War, India, 1919.

Record of War Service

JONES, JOHN HASTIE.
  George Watson's College. M.B., Ch.B. 1909; D.P.H. No. 4 Coy. Q.R.V.B., Royal Scots, 1904-8, L/Corporal. R.A.M.C., Lieut. June 1917; Captain June 1918. 130th Brigade, R.F.A. 52nd General Hospital, Constantinople.

JONES, JOHN POLIN.
  Student of Science. R.G.A. (Hong Kong), Lieut.

JONES, LIONEL BAKER.
  Christ College, Brecon; First XV. and XI. Student of Medicine, 1914. O.T.C. Infantry, Oct. 1914 to May 1915, Cadet. Inns of Court O.T.C. May to Sept. 1915. 6th Welsh Regiment, 2nd Lieut. Sept. 1915. R.F.C. and Royal Air Force, Aug. 1916; Lieut. April 1917 to July 1919. M.C. April 1917.

JONES, WILLIAM.
  King's School, Chester. Student of Medicine, 1919. Royal Army Ordnance Corps May 1916.

JORDAN, JOHN GREGORY.
  M.B., C.M. 1883. Indian Medical Service, Lieut.-Col. Sept. 1906.

JOSEPH, EDWARD GORDON.
  Wanganui Collegiate School. First XV. Student of Medicine, 1915-19; M.B., Ch.B. 1918; M.R.C.S., L.R.C.P. Otago Mounted Rifles, Private Dec 1914. Gallipoli. Wounded.

JOSS, DOUGLAS MACKINTOSH.
  George Watson's College. M.A. 1903. Minister, U.F. Church of Scotland. V.A.D. 1914-16. Y.M.C.A., France. Chaplain, France, 22nd General Hospital, 1916-17. Attached 4th King's Own Scottish Borderers, Dunfermline, 1917-19.

JOUBERT, CHARLES PIETER MARAIS.
  Grey College. Student of Medicine, 1909-14; M.B., Ch.B. 1914. R.A.M.C., Lieut. April 1915. France and Dardanelles.

JOUBERT, JAN HENDRIK HOFMEYR.
  Victoria College, Stellenbosch. Volunteers, Lieut. M.B., Ch.B. 1905. South African Medical Corps, Captain Aug. 1914.

JOYNT, NORMAN LOCKHART.
  Cork Grammar School. M.B., Ch.B. 1912. M.Sc. (Londonderry). R.A.M.C. (S.R.), Lieut. Aug. 1914; Captain April 1915. M.C. July 1916.

JUDD, KENNETH ERIC.
  Grammar School, Karachi. O.T.C. 1905-10, Cadet L/Corporal. First XI. Student of Medicine, 1916 and 1919. Indian Defence Force, Private Aug. 1914-16; Officer Cadet Sept. 1917. Royal Air Force, 2nd Lieut. Nov. 1917; Lieut. April 1918 to Jan. 1919. France.

Record of War Service

JUNNER, JAMES.
Student of Law, 1877-9. Royal Defence Corps (T.), Major Nov. 1914. 4th Reserve Battn., Queen's Supernumerary, Major. No. 1 Railway Guards Coy., S.N.R.

KAPUR, KANHAYA LAL.
M.B., Ch.B. 1912; D.P.H. 1914. Indian Medical Service, Temp. Lieut. Dec. 1914; Temp. Captain Dec. 1915. Indian Field Ambulance. France 1915; Mesopotamia 1916-19.

KAVANAGH, HENRY EDWARD.
Sacred Heart College. Student of Medicine, 1913-15 and 1916-17. N.Z. Medical Corps, Private Oct. 1914.

KAY, ALFRED GOODWYN.
Ayr Academy. M.B., C.M. 1879; L.R.C.S. (Edin.) 1876. R.A.M.C., 1881; Lieut.-Col. 1901; Retired 1908. Brevet Colonel June 1917. Egyptian Expedition, 1882-3. Mention 1917.

KAY, DAVID MILLER.
Morrison's Academy, Crieff. M.A. and B.Sc. (St Andrews); B.D. 1893; D.D. 1907. Professor of Hebrew, St Andrews University. St Andrews University Garrison Artillery, 1883-1909, Lieut. Chaplain Dec. 1914; Major July 1916. France Jan. 1915; Gallipoli June 1915; Macedonia Feb. 1916; Black Sea Dec. 1918 to Aug. 1919. D.S.O. Four times Mentioned in Dispatches.

KAY, JOHN HUNTER.
Ayr Academy. M.B., Ch.B. 1903. R.A.M.C., Lieut. Dec. 1916; Captain Dec. 1917.

KAY, ROBERT.
George Watson's College. Student of Law, 1905-8. Chartered Accountant, 1909. R.G.A., Lieut. June 1916. Wounded.

KEAY, JAMES WILLIAM.
M.B., Ch.B. 1903; M.D. 1906; F.R.C.P. (Edin.) 1910; D.P.H. (Glasg.) 1909. R.A.M.C. (T.), Captain June 1910; Major Aug. 1914; Acting Lieut.-Col. 1916-17. 2/3rd Lowland and 315th London Field Ambulances. Royal Air Force.

KEDDIE, DAVID DAWSON.
Student of Arts, 1915-16. O.T.C. Infantry, Nov. 1915 to May 1916, Cadet. Private in the Army.

KEDDIE, ROBERT RAMSAY.
Student of Arts, 1905-7. O.T.C. Infantry, May to Oct. 1916, Cadet. 6th King's Own Scottish Borderers, 2nd Lieut. Oct. 1916. France.

KEENE, EDGAR HORATIO DOUGLAS.
Wesley and Ormond Colleges. M.A. (Melbourne) 1901. Student of Medicine, 1914 and 1918-19. Australian Army Medical Corps, Private. 1st Australian Sanitary Section, and 1st Australian Casualty Clearing Station, France.

Record of War Service

KEEP, ARTHUR CORRIE.
 Edinburgh Collegiate School; First XV. M.B., C.M. 1882; M.D. 1885; M.R.C.S. (Eng.) 1882. R.A.M.C., Captain Feb. 1915; Major Feb. 1919. France 1915-19. M.C. June 1916.

KEIGHLEY, JAMES PHILIP. (See p. 750.)

KEIR, IVAN COCHRANE.
 Bath College; First XV. and XI. M.B., Ch.B. 1903; M.D. 1906; D.P.H. (Oxford) 1909. R.A.M.C. (T.), Lieut. Sept. 1914; Captain Dec. 1914. 2/1st S.-W. Mounted Brigade Field Ambulance; No. 10 General Hospital, Rouen; No. 2 Rest Camp, and 2/2nd Wessex Field Ambulance.

KEITH, DAVID BARROGILL.
 M.A. 1911; LL.B. 1913. O.T.C. Infantry, June 1909 to July 1911, Cadet. 10th Scottish Rifles, Lieut.; Captain May 1916. M.C.

KEITH, WILLIAM SINCLAIR.
 George Heriot's School. Student of Arts, 1906-14; M.A. 1911. Schoolmaster. 4th and 6th Royal Scots, Private 1906-11. R.G.A., Gunner 1915-17; 2nd Lieut. 1917; Lieut. 1919. France 1917. Gassed Dec. 1917, March and June 1918.

KELLEY, ERNEST BRACEWELL.
 Student of Medicine, 1910-16; M.B., Ch.B. 1916. O.T.C. Medical, April 1909 to July 1913, Cadet. Royal Navy, Surgeon-Probationer; Surgeon April 1916.

KELLIE, EDWARD.
 Berwickshire High School, Duns. Student of Science, 1911-15 and 1919-20; B.Sc. 1920. R.E., Corporal July 1915. R.G.A. (S.R.), 2nd Lieut. Dec. 1917.

KELLY, WILLIAM.
 Aberdeen Grammar School, and Morrison's Academy, Crieff; First XV. O.T.C. 1916-17. University O.T.C. Infantry, 1917, Cadet; Officer Cadet Nov. 1917. Labour Corps, 2nd Lieut. Feb. 1918. 26th Royal Welsh Fusiliers, France, May 1918-19.

KELMAN, JOHN.
 Royal High School. M.A. 1884; D.D. 1907. Minister, U.F. Church of Scotland. Chaplain, 4th Class; University O.T.C., 1909-19. Y.M.C.A., France, Chaplain. O.B.E. 1918.

KELT, JAMES COOK.
 Daniel Stewart's College; Athletics. Student of Medicine, 1915-16. O.T.C. Infantry, May to June 1915, Cadet. 14th Argyll and Sutherland Highlanders, Private June 1915. 5th Loyal North Lancashire Regiment, 2nd Lieut. Jan. 1918; Lieut. July 1919. The Rhine.

KEMP, ALEXANDER JAMES OGILVIE.
 Daniel Stewart's College. Student of Law, 1913-14 and 1918-19; Law Agent, 1919. 4th Royal Scots (T.), Private 1908; 2nd Lieut. Oct. 1913; Lieut. Sept. 1914; Captain March 1916.

Record of War Service

KEMP, PETER.
Milne's Institution, Fochabers. M.A. (Aberdeen). Student of Divinity, 1914-15. 14th Argyll and Sutherland Highlanders, Private July 1915; L/Corporal. Gordon Highlanders, 2nd Lieut. April 1917; Lieut. Aug. 1918. Attached King's African Rifles, Nov. 1917 to June 1919.

KEMP, PHILIP ROWLAND.
Newport Grammar School, Isle of Wight. Student of Medicine, 1916-18. Royal Navy, H.M.S. *Woolston*, Surgeon Sub-Lieut., Oct. 1918. Baltic and Gulf of Riga.

KENDALL, JAMES.
Farnham Grammar School, Surrey. M.A., B.Sc. 1910; D.Sc. 1915. Professor of Chemistry, Columbia University, New York. O.T.C. Infantry, May 1909-11, Cadet. U.S. Naval Reserve Force, Lieut. Aug. 1917 to Jan. 1919. France and Italy.

KENNAWAY, CHARLES GRAY.
Perth Academy. Student of Arts and Law, 1910-14; M.A. 1913. 2/6th Royal Highlanders (Black Watch) (T.), 1909. Mobilised Aug. 1914. 1st Grenadier Guards, Lieut.; Captain March 1916; Staff Captain 1919. France. Wounded Oct. 1917. The Rhine.

KENNAWAY, CHARLES GRAY.
Aberdeen Grammar School. University O.T.C. Infantry, 1917-18, Cadet; Officer Cadet March 1918. Guards, Machine-Gun Corps, 2nd Lieut. Sept. 1918.

KENNEDY, ALEXANDER.
Knox Institute, Haddington. Student of Arts, 1909-11, 1914-15, and 1918-19; M.A. 1919. Y.M.C.A. Work, 1915-17. R.E. (Special Coy.), Sapper Feb. 1917. Educational Instructor, Feb. 1919. Gassed April 1918.

KENNEDY, ALEXANDER SCOTT.
Student of Law, 1912-14. O.T.C. Artillery, July to Sept. 1915, Cadet. R.F.A., 2nd Lieut. Sept. 1915.

KENNEDY, ANGUS JOHN AITCHISON.
Daniel Stewart's College; First XV. and XI. Student of Law, 1911-13. Chartered Accountant, 1914. 1st Lovat Scouts (T.), May 1912; Lieut. Aug. 1914; Captain Feb. 1916. M.C. June 1918.

KENNEDY, ARCHIBALD COWAN.
George Watson's College. O.T.C. 1908-11, Cadet L/Corporal. Student of Arts and Divinity, 1910-14 and 1918-19; M.A. 1914. O.T.C. Artillery, Oct. 1911-14, Cadet. R.F.A., 31st Brigade, 2nd Lieut. Aug. 1914; Lieut. June 1915; Captain and Adjutant, Nov. 1917; Adjutant and Liaison Officer, British Artillery, 1st Hellenic (Larissa) Division, Macedonia. France Jan. 1915; Neuve Chapelle. Wounded May 1915.

Record of War Service

KENNEDY, DAVID.
George Watson's College and Kirkcaldy High School; First XV. O.T.C. 1914-17. Student of Medicine, 1918. Royal Air Force, Lieut. 1917-19.

KENNEDY, DUNCAN.
B.L. 1904. Writer to the Signet, 1908. O.T.C. Artillery, July to Aug. 1915, Cadet. Royal Army Ordnance Corps, Lieut. Sept. 1915; Captain Oct. 1918. Salonika for three years. M.B.E. June 1919.

KENNEDY, GEORGE JAMES.
Royal High School. Student of Science, 1912-14. O.T.C. Engineers, Oct. 1912 to Aug. 1914, Cadet. 5th Royal Scots (T.), Private Aug. 1914; L/Corporal Dec. 1914. Gallipoli; Wounded May 1915. Discharged Sept. 1916.

KENNEDY, JAMES CRAWFORD.
M.B., Ch.B. 1900; M.D. (Gold Medal) 1907; D.T.M. and H. (Camb.). R.A.M.C., Nov. 1900; Lieut.-Col. March 1918. India and Mesopotamia. Dispatches (India) Aug. 1918.

KENNEDY, JAMES TURNER.
Keiss School, Caithness. M.A. 1907. Minister, U.F. Church of Scotland. R.A.M.C., Private April 1916. Chaplain, 4th Class, Sept. 1917. Dispatches May 1919.

KENNEDY, NORMAN DOUGALL.
George Watson's College. Student of Arts, 1913-16 and 1918-19; M.A. 1919. O.T.C. Infantry, Oct. 1913 to Jan. 1916, Cadet. 4th King's Own Scottish Borderers (T.), 2nd Lieut. Jan. 1916; Lieut. July 1917; Acting Captain Dec. 1918. Wounded April and Aug. 1917. M.C. June 1919.

KENNEDY, PETER.
Broughton School, Edinburgh. Student of Arts, 1907-14; M.A. 1911. Schoolmaster. R.A.M.C., Private Oct. 1915; L/Corporal Aug. 1917; Corporal Dec. 1917; Sergeant Jan. 1918 to Sept. 1919. Russia.

KENNEDY, THOMAS DYMOCK.
Perth Academy; First XV. and XI. M.A. (St Andrews). First XV. M.B., Ch.B. 1910. No. 4 Coy. Q.R.V.B., Royal Scots, Corporal. Singapore Mutiny, Feb. 1915. R.A.M.C., Lieut. May 1915; Captain May 1916. Med. and Egyptian Exp. Forces. Dispatches (Egypt) Dec. 1916.

KENNEDY, WALTER PHILLIPS.
George Heriot's School. O.T.C. 1914-16. Student of Science, 1916-17 and 1918-19. R.A.M.C., Private May 1917.

KENNEDY, WILLIAM NICOL WATSON.
George Watson's College; First XV. Cadet Corps 1905-6, Cadet Sergeant. M.B., Ch.B. 1912; M.D. 1920; D.P.H. (Edin.) 1914. University Battery, E.C.A.V. and O.T.C. Artillery, 1906-9, Cadet. R.A.M.C. (T.), Lieut. Feb. 1915; Captain Aug. 1915; Major Sept. 1918. D.A.D.M.S. (Sanitation). France 1915; Salonika 1916; North Russia 1918-19. O.B.E. (Military) June 1919.

Record of War Service

KENNEDY-FRASER, DAVID.
George Watson's College. M.A., B.Sc. 1909. Assistant Professor in Education, Cornell University, U.S.A., 1914-16. Lecturer in Education, 1919. R.G.A., Oct. 1916; 2nd Lieut. March 1917; Lieut. Sept. 1918. Intelligence Corps, France. Dispatches.

KENNETH, JOHN HENRY.
Glasgow University O.T.C., 1909. Student of Arts, 1911-13 and 1919. R.A.M.C., Private Dec. 1914; Corporal 1916-18. 23rd Casualty Clearing Station, France, 1915.

KENNISH, ALAN CHARLES EDWARD FORBES.
Epsom College; First XV. and XI. O.T.C. 1909-14, Officer Cadet. Student of Medicine, 1913-14. Oxford and Buckinghamshire Light Infantry (T.), 2nd Lieut. Aug. 1914; Lieut. France March 1915. O.C., 80th Trench Mortar Battery, Aug. 1915. Wounded Sept. 1916. Royal Air Force, July 1918.

KENT, JOHN ROBERT.
Kirkwall Burgh School. Student of Arts, 1913-15 and 1919; M.A. 1919. O.T.C. Artillery, 1914-15, Cadet Bombardier. R.F.A., 2nd Lieut. Aug. 1915; Lieut. July 1917; Acting Captain Aug. 1917 to Feb. 1919. M.C. Sept. 1918.

KENWOOD, HENRY RICHARD.
M.B., C.M. 1887; L.R.C.P. (Lond.) 1888; D.P.H., R.C.P.S. (Eng.) 1891. R.A.M.C., Hon. Lieut.-Col. Oct. 1914. Army Sanitary Committee. C.M.G. Twice Mentioned in Dispatches.

KENYON, RICHARD.
Daniel Stewart's College. M.B., C.M. 1893. R.A.M.C., Lieut. Nov. 1915. Malta and Egypt.

KEOGH, Sir ALFRED.
LL.D. 1909. Army Medical Service, Lieut.-General, 1913; Surgeon-General; Director-General. G.C.B. G.C.V.O. C.H. Grand Officer Legion of Honour; Grand Officer Order of the Crown (Belgium); Order of White Eagle (Serbia).

KER, ALLAN EBENEZER. *V.C.* (See p. 753.)

KER, CLAUD BUCHANAN.
Malvern College. Cadet Corps 1884-6, Cadet Officer. M.B., C.M. 1890; M.D. 1896; F.R.C.P. (Edin.) 1901. Lecturer on Fevers. R.A.M.C. (T.), 1895; Major April 1908. Prisoners of War Camp, Stobs, Nov. 1915.

KERMACK, STUART GRACE.
Fettes College. M.A. 1908; LL.B. 1910. Assistant Lecturer in Mercantile Law, 1913-14. O.T.C. Artillery, 1905-9, Cadet. R.F.A. (T.), 1st Lowland Brigade, 1911; Lieut. 1914; Captain June 1916. Egyptian Army, 1918-19.

KERR, ALEXANDER LIVINGSTONE.
Sydney Grammar School, New South Wales. M.B., C.M. 1888; M.D. 1890; M.R.C.S. (Eng.) 1889; F.R.C.S. (Edin.) 1890. Australian Army Medical Corps, Hon. Captain March 1916; Temp. Major Feb. 1917. P.M.O., April 1919.

Record of War Service

KERR, ALEXANDER MALCOLM.
 Broughton School, Edinburgh. Student of Medicine, 1914-15 and 1918-19. Non-Combatant Corps, Private April 1916.

KERR, CHARLES.
 Dundee High School. M.B., C.M. 1893. Clinical Medical Tutor, St Andrews. R.A.M.C., Lieut.; Captain Dec. 1912; Major Jan. 1916. 1st Scottish General Hospital; 21st General Hospital, Alexandria, 1915-16, and 27th General Hospital, Cairo, 1916-19. Dispatches Feb. 1916, July 1917, and March 1919. O.B.E. June 1919.

KERR, DONALD.
 Student. Australian Imperial Force.

KERR, DOUGLAS JAMES ACWORTH.
 St Paul's, London. O.T.C. 1908-12, Cadet Sergeant. Student of Medicine, 1912-14 and 1917-20; M.B., Ch.B. 1920. O.T.C. Artillery, Oct. 1912-14, Cadet Corporal. R.F.A., 2nd Lieut. Sept. 1914; Lieut. Sept. 1915; Captain; Adjutant. 49th Brigade, Oct. 1915. France.

KERR, FRANCIS FERGUSON.
 Manitoba University. First XV. M.B., C.M. 1898; M.D. 1903. 1st Battn., Lancashire Volunteer Regiment, Major 1915. Red Cross, Prestwich; Stanley House Hospital, Manchester.

KERR, FRANCIS KENNETH.
 Daniel Stewart's College; First XV. and XI. M.B., Ch.B. 1900. R.A.M.C., South African Campaign, 1900-1; Lieut. Nov. 1914; Captain Aug. 1916; Acting Major Sept. 1918; Acting Lieut.-Col. Sept. 1919. Royal Scots Fusiliers. Med. Exp. Force 1915. France 1916-17; Salonika 1918-19; Black Sea 1919-20. M.C. 1917.

KERR, HENRY BIRKMYRE.
 Bruntsfield School. George Heriot's School O.T.C., 2nd Lieut. M.A., B.Sc. 1909. Schoolmaster. 17th Royal Scots, Lieut.

KERR, HUGH ROBERT.
 George Heriot's School; First XV. O.T.C. 1909-14, Cadet Corporal. Student of Science, 1914-15. O.T.C. Infantry, Oct. 1914 to April 1915, Cadet Corporal. 24th Northumberland Fusiliers, 2nd Lieut. April 1915; Lieut. July 1917. Wounded April and Dec. 1917.

KERR, JAMES.
 George Watson's College. Student of Science, 1918. R.F.A., 1/1st Lowland Brigade, Gunner Sept. 1914. 11th Gordon Highlanders, 2nd Lieut. Sept. 1915. R.F.C., April 1916, Lieut. Oct. 1916; Captain Aug. 1917; Royal Air Force to Jan. 1919. A.F.C. June 1919.

Record of War Service

KERR, JAMES HENRY.
Grantown-on-Spey Grammar School. Student of Medicine, 1912-18; M.B., Ch.B. 1917. O.T.C. Artillery, Oct. 1913-15, Cadet. Royal Navy, Surgeon-Probationer, Dec. 1915; Surgeon Jan. 1918 to Aug. 1919.

KERR, JAMES ROBERTSON.
M.B., Ch.B. 1905. University R.A.M.C. (V.), 1900-5, Corporal. R.A.M.C., Lieut. July 1916 to Aug. 1917. South African Medical Corps, Captain April 1918 to Aug. 1919.

KERR, JOHN FRASER.
Falmouth Grammar School. Student of Medicine, 1912-16 and 1917-19 L.R.C.P. & S. (Edin.). Royal Navy, Surgeon-Probationer, Jan. 1916 to July 1917. H.M.T.B. Destroyers *Miranda* and *Skilful*.

KERR, LAWRENCE.
Dunbar Burgh School. Student of Arts, 1913-14. 4th, 6th, and 12th Royal Scots (T.), Private Nov. 1913; Officer Cadet Feb. 1917; 2nd Lieut. June 1917; Lieut. and Intelligence Officer, Dec. 1918. Gallipoli and Palestine May 1915 to Jan. 1917; France Oct. 1917; The Rhine Jan. 1919. Gassed at Ypres, April 1918.

KERR, PETER MURRAY.
Dumfries Academy. M.B., C.M. 1887. 1/5th King's Own Scottish Borderers (T.), 1891; Lieut.-Col. Gallipoli 1915. Mention. T.D.

KERR, ROBERT.
George Watson's College. Cadet Corps 1906-8. M.A. 1912. O.T.C. Infantry, Oct. 1908-13, Cadet Sergeant, and Unattached List, T.F., 2nd Lieut. May 1915; Lieut. Oct. 1916.

KERR, ROBERT BROWNE.
Spier's School, Beith; First XV. and XI. Student of Arts, 1911-15. M.A. (Hons. Classics) 1915. O.T.C. Infantry, March 1912 to May 1915, Cadet. Munitions, March to Nov. 1915. Royal Scots Greys, 2nd Dragoon Guards, Private Nov. 1915; Corporal (Instructor) 1916 to April 1919.

KERR, ROY RUSSELL.
George Watson's College. M.B., Ch.B. 1909. O.T.C. Medical, 1909-12, Cadet Corporal. Resident, R.I.E., 1910-11. R.A.M.C., Lieut. Sept. 1914. H.M. Hospital Ship *Asturias* and 1st Welsh Regiment. Royal Navy, Surgeon, Dec. 1915-19. R.N. Hospital, Haslar; H.M.S. *Amethyst*.

KERR, SAMUEL KERR GIFFORD.
Blairlodge. M.A. 1897; LL.B. 1901. Writer to the Signet, 1901. Q.R.V.B., Royal Scots, 1900-5, Private. 3rd V.B. Royal Scots, Private Dec. 1916.

KERR, STEPHEN H. C.
Royal High School; First XV. Student of Law, 1907-9. Chartered Accountant, 1909. Lothians and Border Horse (T.), Private March 1905; Sergeant. France and Balkans.

Record of War Service

KERR, WILLIAM.
Edinburgh Academy. O.T.C. 1914-16, Cadet L/Corporal. Student of Medicine. O.T.C. Artillery, Oct. 1916 to May 1917, Cadet Bombardier; Officer Cadet May 1917. R.F.A., 2nd Lieut. Oct. 1917. Wounded Sept. 1918.

KERR, WILLIAM SMITH.
M.B., C.M. 1890; F.R.C.S. (Edin.) 1903. R.A.M.C. (T.) 1903. Major Nov. 1915; Temp. Lieut.-Col. Jan. 1916 to Feb. 1917.

KERRIGAN, HERBERT WALLACE.
Magherafelt, Co. Derry. M.B., Ch.B. 1912; L.R.C.P. & S. (Edin.) and L.R.F.P.S. (Glasg.) 1908. R.A.M.C. (T.), Lieut. Sept. 1915; Captain March 1916. France.

KESTING, NORMAN GOTTFRIED.
Inverness Royal Academy, and Rutherford College, Newcastle-on-Tyne. M.A. 1906. Minister, Church of Scotland. 2nd Lovat Scouts (T.), Private.

KHAMBATTA, FREDOON POCHAJI.
New High School, Bombay. First XI. Student of Science, 1918. Bombay University Infantry, attached 116th Mahrattas, Private Oct. 1917; Acting Corporal Dec. 1917 to 1918.

KHAN, GHULAM HUSSAIN.
Student of Arts, 1913-15 and 1917-20. Indian Field Ambulance, Dec. 1914.

KHAN, MOHAMMAD JAN.
Student of Arts and Law, 1911-15; M.A. 1914; Barrister. Indian Field Ambulance, Dec. 1914.

KHAN, WORASAT HOSAIN.
Student of Arts, 1912-15. Indian Field Ambulance.

KHAW, IGNATIUS JAMES OO KEK.
M.B., Ch.B. 1913. Indian Medical Service, Lieut. Nov. 1914; Captain Nov. 1915 to Dec. 1919. Mesopotamia Feb. 1916; India Dec. 1918 to Nov. 1919.

KIDD, ALEXANDER EDWARD.
Dundee High School. M.B., C.M. 1894; D.P.H. (St Andrews) 1901. R.A.M.C. (T.), 1903; Major Aug. 1914; Temp. Lieut.-Col. Jan. 1916. 2/3rd Highland Field Ambulance and 33rd Stationary Hospital. Order of St Sava (3rd Class), Oct. 1917; Gold Cross of the Redeemer (Greece), Aug. 1918. O.B.E. June 1919. Dispatches Jan. 1916, July and Nov. 1917, and Jan. 1919.

KIDSTON, NOËL WALLACE.
M.B., Ch.B. 1906. R.A.M.C., Captain Nov. 1913; Acting Major March 1918.

KIERNANDER, WILLIAM DIXIE.
Dollar Academy; First XV. O.T.C. 1906-9. Student of Medicine, 1909-14 and 1919-20. 1/2nd Scottish Horse (T.), Private Aug. 1914. 7th Coy. Imperial Camel Corps, July 1916. Royal Air Force, Cadet April 1918; Flight Cadet Sept. 1918. Gallipoli Sept. 1915; Egypt and Palestine Dec. 1915 to March 1919. Wounded at Raja Jan. 1917.

Record of War Service

KILGOUR, DAVID.
University Library Assistant. R.N.V.R., Ordinary Seaman, June 1918.

KILGOUR, GILBERT INNES.
Burntisland School. M.A. (Hons. Engl.) 1907. Schoolmaster. Royal Scots, Private March 1917; 2nd Lieut. July 1918.

KILGOUR, JAMES.
George Watson's College. M.A. 1913. Schoolmaster. R.N.V.R., H.M. Transport *Princess Juliana*, Wireless Telegraphist.

KILGOUR, JAMES.
Servitor, University. 6th Royal Highlanders (Black Watch), Private Jan. 1915; L/Corporal.

KING, ARCHIBALD.
George Watson's College. M.A. (Hons. Maths.) 1904; B.Sc. (Special Distinction, Mathematics and Astronomy) 1904. R.G.A., Sept. 1916; 2nd Lieut. Nov. 1916; Lieut. May 1918. France 1918.

KING, ARTHUR.
Student of Medicine, 1914-15 and 1918-19. 14th Argyll and Sutherland Highlanders, Private May 1915; L/Corporal. King's Own Yorkshire Light Infantry, 2nd Lieut. Dec. 1917.

KING, DAVID BARTY.
Clifton Bank, St Andrews. M.A.; M.B., Ch.B. 1899; M.D. 1902; M.R.C.P. (Edin.) 1902. County of London War Hospital, Epsom, 1915. R.A.M.C., Major June 1917. O.B.E. Dec. 1919.

KING, GEORGE.
M.B., C.M. 1896. Indian Medical Service, Jan. 1899; Major (Retired). Hospital Ship to France, India, Egypt, Salonika, and Gallipoli.

KING, JOHN WILLIAM.
Tynecastle School. University O.T.C. Artillery, Feb. to Sept. 1918, Cadet; Officer Cadet Sept. 1918. R.F.A., 2nd Lieut. April 1919.

KING, ROBERT BUCHANAN.
Uppingham. B.A.; Student of Law, 1904-7. Advocate, 1906. 7th Argyll and Sutherland Highlanders (T.), 2nd Lieut. Oct. 1914. Wounded May 1915.

KING, STANLEY BRIGHT.
Silcoates School, Wakefield; First XI. and XV. Student of Arts, 1914-16. R.A.M.C. (T.), Private Nov. 1915; L/Corporal April 1916; Corporal Feb. 1918. 1st Welsh Field Ambulance. Egyptian Exp. Force, May 1917 to Aug. 1919.

KINGSCOTE, ERNEST.
Collége Communale, Boulogne. M.B., C.M. 1882; L.R.C.S. (Edin.). Wiltshire Yeomanry, Captain 1915-18. Intelligence Department, War Office. Censor.

Record of War Service

KINLOCH, C.
    Student. Scottish Horse (T.), Private. 13th Royal Highlanders (Black Watch), Lieut. July 1917.

KINMONT, PATRICK.
    Dundee High School. M.B., Ch.B. 1897; M.D. 1908; F.R.C.S. (Edin.) 1901. South African Campaign, 1900. R.A.M.C., Lieut. Nov. 1915. 21st Stationary Hospital, Salonika.

KINNEAR, JOHN WILSON.
    Arbroath High School. Student of Music, 1913-15 and 1916-18. R.F.A. (T.), 2/1st Forfar Battery, 2/2nd Highland Brigade, Gunner April 1915. 8th Cameron Highlanders, 2nd Lieut. Aug. 1915.

KINNEAR, WILLIAM.
    Dundee High School. M.B., C.M. 1888; M.D. 1901. Army Medical Service (T.), 1891. Mobilised Aug. 1914; Colonel 1914-15. A.D.M.S., Highland Division; A.D.M.S., 64th Division, May 1915. Invalided out Nov. 1917. K.H.P.

KINNES, JAMES RAMSAY.
    M.A. (Hons. Mod. Lang.) 1912. Schoolmaster. 14th Royal Scots (Interpreters' Corps), Hon. 2nd Lieut. Aug. 1914; 2nd Lieut. Jan. 1915; Lieut. Feb. 1917. General Staff, 1916. France. Gassed and Wounded. Prisoner of War in Germany, March 1918.

KIPPEN, JAMES WILLIAM.
    Perth Academy. Student of Medicine, 1889-94. 7th King's Own Scottish Borderers, Sergeant; Warrant Officer, Class I.

KIPPEN, JOHN SYME.
    Malvern College. O.T.C. 1913-16. Student of Law, 1917-18. O.T.C. Engineers, May 1917 to Feb. 1918, Cadet Corporal; Officer Cadet Feb. 1918. R.E. (Signal Service), 2nd Lieut. July 1918. Attached 312th Brigade, R.F.A.

KIRK, DAVID LEWIS
    George Watson's College. Student of Law, 1902-4. Solicitor before the Supreme Courts, 1910. Edinburgh Volunteers Unit, Sept. 1914. Inns of Court O.T.C., Feb. 1916. A.S.C., 2nd Lieut. Dec. 1916; Lieut. June 1918 to May 1919.

KIRK, EDWARD WILFRID.
    George Watson's College. M.B., Ch.B. 1908; F.R.C.S. (Edin.). R.A.M.C., Lieut. Aug. 1914; Captain Dec. 1916. France 1916-18. Bangour Military Hospital, 1918-19.

KIRK, JAMES.
    M.B., C.M. 1895; M.D. 1897. Colonial Forces, Straits Settlements, Major June 1906. Penang 1915-16. R.A.M.C., Captain, Ophthalmic Specialist, Malta and Curragh Commands, July 1916; Edinburgh 1917 to Feb. 1918.

Record of War Service

KIRK, JAMES BALFOUR.
George Watson's College. Student of Medicine, 1911-14 and 1915-17; M.B., Ch.B. 1917. O.T.C. Artillery, 1911-14, Medical, 1916-18, Cadet. 9th Royal Scots, Private Aug. 1914. R.F.A., 2nd Lieut. Dec. 1914 to March 1916; 2nd Lieut., Unattached List, T.F., Oct. 1916. R.A.M.C., Lieut. Aug. 1917; Captain Aug. 1918. France 1915-16. Attached Political Department, Med. Exp. Force, March 1918. Mesopotamia Aug. 1918-19.

KIRK, JOHN PAUL.
George Watson's College. Student of Law, 1914. 9th Royal Scots, Private March 1915. Seaforth Highlanders, 2nd Lieut. Dec. 1915; Lieut. June 1917. France; Arras 1917-18. Wounded. Dispatches (Buzancy) July 1918.

KIRK, ROBERT.
Dumfries Academy. Student of Law, 1912-14. O.T.C. Infantry, Aug. 1915, Cadet. 1st and 3rd King's Own Scottish Borderers, 2nd Lieut. Oct. 1915; Lieut. July 1917. France.

KIRK, ROBERT.
M.B., C.M. 1876; M.D. 1879; L.R.C.P. (Edin.) 1876; F.R.C.S. (Edin.) 1881. R.A.M.C. (T.), Lieut.-Col. July 1882. 10th Royal Scots (T.). V.D.

KIRKLAND, HUGH MACMILLAN.
Edinburgh Academy. Student of Science, 1916-18. O.T.C. Artillery, Oct. 1916 to Jan. 1918, Cadet; Officer Cadet Jan. 1918. R.E., 406th Field Coy., 2nd Lieut. April 1918. France Oct. 1918.

KIRKLAND-WHITTAKER, HARRY.
M.B., Ch.B. 1904; M.D. 1906; L.S.A. (Lond.) 1900; L.R.C.S. (Edin.) 1904. R.A.M.C., Lieut. 1915; Captain Dec. 1916.

KIRKNESS, FREDERICK JOHN.
Trinity Academy. M.B., Ch.B. 1913. O.T.C. Infantry, May 1909-12, Cadet Corporal. R.A.M.C., Lieut. Sept. 1915; Captain Sept. 1916. 18th King's Liverpool Regiment; 96th and 67th Field Ambulances; 38th Stationary and 53rd General Hospitals. D.G.T., G.H.Q, France.

KIRKNESS, JAMES MATHIESON.
M.B., Ch.B. 1903; M.D. 1906; F.R.C.S. (Edin.). R.A.M.C. (T.), Lieut. 1910; Captain Aug. 1914; Major Oct. 1918. 1st East Lancashire Brigade, R.F.A. Transferred Royal Air Force Medical Service, March 1918. Egypt, Gallipoli, and Palestine. Invalided home Oct. 1916.

KIRKPATRICK, ROGER.
Edinburgh Academy. M.B., C.M. 1881; M.D. 1894; M.R.C.S. (Eng.) 1881. Q.E.R., 1877-80, Private. Army Medical Service, 1882; Colonel 1912. C.M.G. Dispatches 1915. C.B. 1917.

Record of War Service

KIRKWOOD, IAN MUIR.
George Watson's College. Student of Medicine, 1917 and 1919. O.T.C. Artillery, Oct. 1916 to July 1917, Cadet; Officer Cadet July 1917. R.G.A., 2nd Lieut. Dec. 1917. France Jan. 1918 to Jan. 1919.

KIRKWOOD, JAMES.
George Watson's College. M.B., Ch.B. 1902; F.R.C.S. (Edin.) 1909. Indian Medical Service, 1903; Major July 1914. East Africa.

KIRKWOOD, WALTER CHARLES CAMPBELL.
Royal High School. M.B., C.M. 1893. No. 4 Coy. Q.R.V.B., Royal Scots, 1888-91, Private. R.A.M.C., Lieut. March 1915; Captain March 1916.

KIRKWOOD, WILLIAM DOUGLAS.
Kelso High School. Cadet Corps 1898-1902, Cadet Pipe-Major. M.B., Ch.B. 1910; M.D. 1913. O.T.C. Artillery, 1905 to Dec. 1910, Cadet. Wrest Park Hospital, Bedford, 1915. R.A.M.C., Lieut. 1916; Captain Nov. 1917.

KIRSOPP, EDGAR CRAIG BUCHANAN.
Linlithgow Academy. Student of Law, 1912-14 and 1918-19; B.L. 1919. O.T.C. Infantry, Feb. 1912 to Aug. 1914, Cadet L/Corporal. 10th Royal Scots (T.), Aug. 1914; Lieut.; Captain June 1916. General Staff, Jan. 1918. M.C. March 1918; Bar to M.C. Oct. 1918.

KIRTON, AUBREY CECIL.
Harrison College, Barbados. O.T.C. 1906-11, Cadet Sergeant. Student of Medicine, 1911-16; M.B., Ch.B. 1916. R.A.M.C., Surgeon-Lieut. Sept. 1917; Surgeon-Captain Sept. 1918. British West Indies Regiment.

KITCHEN, HUGH MELVILLE.
St Joseph's College, Náini Tál. O.T.C. 1906-12, Cadet Corporal. University O.T.C. Engineers, Sept. 1914 to Sept. 1915, Cadet. 13th Highland Light Infantry, 2nd Lieut. Sept. 1915. Machine-Gun Corps, March 1916, Lieut. Jan. 1917; Captain March 1918. France July 1916 to Feb. 1919. M.C. Sept. 1918; Bar to M.C. Nov. 1918.

KITCHIN, JAMES TYSON.
St Bees, Cumberland. M.B., C.M. 1887; M.D. 1892; D.P.H., R.C.P.S. (Ireland) 1900. Abram Peel War Hospital, Bradford, July to Dec. 1917. R.A.M.C., Captain Jan. 1918 to Feb. 1919. M.O., 52nd Stationary Hospital, France.

KITTOW, DIGORY EDWARD.
Student of Medicine, 1908-12. O.T.C. Artillery, Oct. 1914 to Nov. 1914, Cadet. R.F.A., 2nd Lieut. Nov. 1914; Lieut. Feb. 1916.

KLINGLER, FREDERICK.
Daniel Stewart's College. Student of Law, 1909-12. 9th Royal Scots (T.), Private.

Record of War Service

KNIGHT, DENIS ATHELSTONE.
Harrison College, Barbados. O.T.C. 1906-10, Cadet Corporal. Student of Medicine, 1912-18; M.B., Ch.B. 1918. O.T.C. Infantry, 1914, Cadet. R.N.V.R., Surgeon-Probationer, Dec. 1914. Royal Navy, Surgeon-Lieut. July 1918.

KNIGHT, JAMES St PIERRE.
Methodist College, St John's, Newfoundland. First XI. M.B., Ch.B. 1910. O.T.C. Artillery, 1906 to Feb. 1911, Cadet. R.A.M.C., Lieut. Oct. 1915; Captain Oct. 1916. Royal Newfoundland Regiment, Major Oct. 1918. D.A.D.M.S., Newfoundland Contingent, Dec. 1918. Dispatches (France) 1917. O.B.E. 1919.

KNIGHT, JOHN TAYLOR.
Broughton School, Edinburgh. Student of Science, 1912-15 and 1918-20; B.Sc. 1920. R.E. (Special Brigade), Sapper June 1915; Corporal July 1915; Officer Cadet March 1917. R.F.A., 2nd Lieut. Aug. 1917; Lieut. Feb. 1919. France. Wounded Sept. 1915 and March 1918. M.M. Sept. 1915.

KNIGHT, WILFRED EDWYNE.
Royal High School. M.B., Ch.B. 1902; L.R.C.P. & S. (Edin.) 1902; L.F.P.S. (Glasg.) 1902. Natal Medical Corps, 1906. South African Medical Corps, Captain 1910-19. German East African Campaign, 1917-18.

KNIGHT-COUTTS, CECIL.
Daniel Stewart's College. Student of Medicine, 1900-3. University Battery, E.C.A.V., Corporal. R.F.A., 2nd Lieut. April 1915; Lieut. Dec. 1915; Captain Jan. 1917. Twice Wounded. M.C.

KNOX, JOHN.
George Watson's College. O.T.C. 1915-16. Student of Medicine, 1916-17. O.T.C. Artillery, 1917, Cadet Bombardier; Officer Cadet July 1917. R.G.A., 493rd Siege Battery, 2nd Lieut. Dec. 1917. France; Somme, Cambrai, 1918.

KNOX, ROBERT.
M.B., C.M. 1892; M.D. 1897; M.R.C.S. (Eng.) and L.R.C.P. (Lond.) 1892. R.A.M.C. (T.), Captain Aug. 1914. 4th London General Hospital.

KNOX, ROBERT WELLAND.
Westminster. M.B., C.M. 1896; F.R.C.S. (Eng.) 1914. Indian Medical Service, July 1897, Major; Lieut.-Col. Jan. 1917; Acting Colonel and A.D.M.S. Nov. 1919. Egypt. D.S.O. Order of White Eagle (Serbia), 4th Class; Officer of Crown of Italy. Dispatches Feb. 1915, June 1916, March 1917 and 1918.

KNUTHSEN, LOUIS FRANCIS.
Edinburgh Academy; First XV. and XI. M.B., Ch.B. 1893; M.D. 1901. R.A.M.C., Nov. 1914, Hon. Major April 1917. O.C. No. 5 B.R.C. Hospital, Wimereux, France, 1914. Dispatches 1917. O.B.E. (Military) 1919. Associate, Order of St John of Jerusalem 1919; Médaille de Reconnaissance; Médaille d'honneur des Epidémies.

Record of War Service

KOCK, JULIUS GEORGE DE.
  M.B., Ch.B. 1907; M.D. 1909. 16th Royal Scots, Lieut.

KOEPPERN, JOHN HENRY.
  Student of Science, 1911-13. R.A.M.C., No. 2 Section, Field Coy., Private.

KOHLER, LEO JOHN.
  Blairgowrie High School. Student of Law, 1914-15. 14th Argyll and Sutherland Highlanders, Private May 1915. M.M. Sept. 1918.

KOZMA, PAULIN.
  Student of Science, 1913-15. Russian Army.

KRAMER, HERMANN.
  South African College. M.B., Ch.B. 1902; M.D. 1906; M.R.C.P. and F.R.C.S. (Edin.). South African Medical Corps, Captain Aug. 1917. Military Hospitals, Mailland, Potchefstroom, and Wynberg. Assistant Medical Inspector of Recruits, Cape Town.

KRIEL, PIETER EDOUARD.
  French Hoek School, South Africa. Student of Medicine, 1913-15 and 1917-19. O.T.C. Infantry, May 1915 to March 1916, Cadet. 9th Royal Scots (T.), Private Sept. 1914 to May 1915. 4th South African Infantry, Private Dec. 1915; L/Corporal Sept. 1916 to April 1917.

KROGH, ANDRÉ LEWIS.
  M.B., Ch.B. 1911; M.D. 1918. R.A.M.C., Lieut.; Captain May 1916.

KYLES, DAVID.
  Student of Arts, 1918. 2/1st Lothians and Border Horse, Private Nov. 1915. 2nd Gloucestershire Regiment. Salonika and Russia.

LABAT, GERRIT HENDRIK WILLEM DE.
  Worcester School, Cape Colony. M.B., Ch.B. 1897. South African Medical Corps, Captain Sept. 1917.

LACK, LEWIS ALBERT HODGKINSON.
  M.B., Ch.B. 1903. Indian Medical Service, Captain; Major Sept. 1917.

LAIDLAW, GEORGE PALMER.
  Hoddom School, Ecclefechan. M.A. 1905; B.Sc. 1909. Glasgow University O.T.C., 1913-14, Cadet. 2/6th attached 2nd Argyll and Sutherland Highlanders, 2nd Lieut. Oct. 1914; Lieut. June 1916.

LAIDLAW, WILLIAM.
  Broughton School, Edinburgh. Student of Arts, 1916-17. O.T.C. Infantry, Sept. 1916 to April 1917, Cadet. King's Own Scottish Borderers, Private April 1917. Tank Corps, 2nd Lieut. Nov. 1917. M.C. Nov. 1918.

Record of War Service

LAIDLER, PERCY WARD.
L.R.C.P. & S.; L.D.S. (Edin.) and L.R.F.P. & S. (Glasg.) 1914. University O.T.C. Infantry, Dec. 1908. South African Medical Corps, Captain May 1916. Invalided out March 1918.

LAING, ALEXANDER PATERSON.
George Watson's College. Student of Science, 1914-15 and 1918-20; B.Sc. 1920. O.T.C. Engineers, Sept. 1914 to Feb. 1915, Cadet. R.E. (T.), 1st Highland Field Coy., 2nd Lieut. Feb. 1915. France April 1915. Invalided home Feb. 1917. Employed Admiralty.

LAING, ALFRED MARTIN.
Robert Gordon's College, Aberdeen. M.A. (Aberdeen); LL.B. 1903; Advocate, 1904. 1st and 2nd Seaforth Highlanders, Lieut. Dec. 1914; Captain Aug. 1916. Attached 1st Essex Regiment, Gallipoli, May to Aug. 1915.

LAING, ARTHUR CECIL.
Student of Medicine, 1909-15; M.B., Ch.B. 1915. R.A.M.C., Lieut. Aug. 1915; Captain Aug. 1916. 1/2nd Highland Field Ambulance; 7th Argyll and Sutherland Highlanders. France. M.C. and Croix de Guerre (French) 1919.

LAING, DAVID.
George Watson's College; First XV. and XI. M.B., C.M. 1884; M.D. 1887. R.F.A. (T.), 1888; Lieut.-Col. Jan. 1912. O.C. 2/2nd Highland Brigade. Mention. T.D.

LAING, FRANCIS MILLAR.
Royal High School. University O.T.C. Infantry, 1917; Cadet Sergeant; Officer Cadet Oct. 1917. R.E., Signal Service, Sapper Feb. 1918 to Jan. 1919.

LAING, FREDERICK ROBERT.
M.B., Ch.B. 1908. R.A.M.C., 1909, Captain 1913; Acting Major Feb. 1918; Brevet Major June 1919. R.F.A., Indian Contingent. France 1915. British Military Hospital, Italy, 1917. D.A.D.M.S., 41st Division, March to Dec. 1918. 139th Field Ambulance, Jan. to May 1919. Croix de Guerre (Belgian) Jan. 1919.

LAING, GEORGE DAVISON.
Boston Grammar School. Athletics. M.B., Ch.B. 1899; M.D. 1906. Northumberland Yeomanry, Private 1900. South African Campaign, 1901-2. R.A.M.C., Captain Oct. 1915; Acting Major Sept. 1918. 36th Casualty Clearing Station. School of Instruction, Aug. 1918. Dispatches Dec. 1917 and Dec. 1918.

LAING, HENRY WILLIAM.
Perth Academy. M.B., C.M. 1875; M.D. 1879.; L.R.C.S. (Edin.) 1875. R.A.M.C., Captain Oct. 1914; Major Sept. 1916; Brevet Lieut.-Col. June 1917. 2/7th Royal Highlanders (Black Watch), (T.). 191st Infantry Brigade, Jan. 1918. 310th London Field Ambulance, Feb. 1919.

Record of War Service

LAING, HARRY GORDON MATHEWSON.
Royal High School. University O.T.C. Artillery, Dec. 1917 to Aug. 1918, Cadet. R.G.A., Officer Cadet Aug. 1918.

LAING, JOHN MACKINTOSH.
Fettes College. O.T.C. 1907-11. Student of Arts, 1911-14; M.A. 1914. O.T.C. Infantry, Sept. to Oct. 1914, Cadet. 9th Scottish Rifles, 2nd Lieut. Oct. 1914; Lieut. Sept. 1915; Captain Oct. 1918. M.C. Nov. 1918.

LAING, WILLIAM MACKIE.
M.A. (St Andrews) 1911. Student of Divinity, 1911-14. Minister, Church of Scotland. Chaplain, 4th Class, Sept. 1916.

LAIRD, DAVID ANDERSON.
George Watson's College. M.B., Ch.B. 1913. O.T.C. Infantry, 1909-10, Medical, 1910-12, Cadet. R.A.M.C., Lieut. Sept. 1914; Captain Sept. 1915. France Oct. 1914 to Sept. 1915, and April 1916 to Sept. 1917. Prisoner of War in Germany, Oct. 1915 to Jan. 1916. Mesopotamia Jan. 1918; India, N.-W. Frontier, and Punjab, May to Oct. 1919. Dispatches Jan. 1916.

LAKEY, JOHN.
Boroughmuir School. Student of Arts, 1914-17 and 1918-19. 2nd Scots Guards, Private Jan. 1917.

LALTOO, JACOB.
Student of Medicine, 1913-17. Indian Field Ambulance, 1914.

LAMB, ANDREW HENRY COWAN.
M.A. 1903; LL.B. and Writer to the Signet, 1907. Army Pay Department, Acting Paymaster, Aug. 1915; Captain and Temp. Paymaster to July 1919.

LAMB, GEORGE MILLAR.
George Watson's College, and Morrison's Academy, Crieff. Cadet Battn. (Highland), 1914-15, and O.T.C. 1915-16. Student of Medicine, 1918-19. O.T.C. Artillery, Jan. to Nov. 1918, Cadet Sergeant. R.F.A., Officer Cadet Nov. 1918.

LAMB, JAMES HENDERSON.
M.B., Ch.B. 1912. R.N.V.R., Surgeon. H.M.S. *Calgarian*.

LAMB, JOHN.
Glasgow High School. B.D. 1909. Minister, Church of Scotland. Chaplain, 4th Class, Jan. 1918.

LAMB, JOHN.
Portree School. Student of Arts, 1912-14. O.T.C. Infantry, Oct. 1913-14, Cadet. 15th Royal Scots, Private. 8th, 6th, and 3rd Cameron Highlanders, 2nd Lieut. Nov. 1914; Lieut. July 1917; Captain Aug. 1918. Overseas 1915-16. 1st Lovat Scouts, May to Aug. 1918. R.N.V.R., Lieut. Aug. 1918. H.M. Ships *Excellent* and *Riviera* (Black Sea), Aug. 1918 to May 1919.

Record of War Service

LAMBAH, VISHWA MITRA.
Edward's Mission College, Peshawar. First XI. Student of Medicine and Science, 1908-15. M.B., Ch.B. 1912; B.Sc. (P.H.) 1915. Indian Field Ambulance, Sept. 1914; Indian Medical Service, Nov. 1914; Indian Hospital, Brighton.

LAMBERT, CHARLES DAVID.
Merchiston Castle. Cadet Corps 1905-8. Student of Science, 1914-15. O.T.C. Artillery, 1914-15, Cadet. R.F.A., 2nd Lieut. Feb. 1915; Lieut. Jan. 1917.

LAMBERTON, JAMES.
George Watson's College. M.B., Ch.B. 1912. R.A.M.C. (T.), Lieut. 1914; Captain Sept. 1915. Eastern Brigade Field Ambulance; 1st Northumberland Fusiliers, France, two years.

LAMBIE, CHARLES GEORGE.
Stanley House, Bridge of Allan. Student of Medicine, 1909-14; M.B., Ch.B. 1914. Assistant to Professor of Materia Medica. R.A.M.C., Lieut. Nov. 1915; Captain Nov. 1916. 49th Brigade, R.F.A.; 39th and No. 11 Mobile Labour, France; 23rd Stationary Hospital, Mesopotamia; 6th Division, Labour, Poona, India. M.C. Sept. 1918.

L'AMIE, FREDERICK WILLIAM.
George Heriot's School. M.A., B.Sc. 1910. Schoolmaster. R.G.A., Gunner; Bombardier.

LAMOND, ALEXANDER M.
Perth Academy. Student of Law, 1915-16 and 1918-19. 8th Royal Highlanders (Black Watch), Private Nov. 1915.

LAMOND, JOHN LOGAN.
Royal High School. Student of Medicine, 1910-17; M.B., Ch.B. 1916. O.T.C. Medical, June 1910 to March 1915, Cadet Q.M.S. Royal Navy, H.M.S. *Orotava*, Surgeon-Lieut. Nov. 1916.

LAMONT, DONALD.
Raining's School, Inverness. M.A. 1899. Examiner in Celtic. Minister, Church of Scotland. Chaplain, 1914, Highland Mounted Brigade; Scottish Horse (T.). Gallipoli and Egypt.

LAMONT, DONALD COLIN.
Inverness Royal Academy. Student of Medicine, 1913-18; M.B., Ch.B. 1918. O.T.C. Medical, Feb. 1916 to July 1918, Cadet. R.A.M.C. (S.R.), Lieut. Aug. 1918; Captain Sept. 1919. 3rd British General Hospital, Basra, Mesopotamia.

LAMONT, HENRY MACLAURIN.
Edinburgh Academy. Student of Arts and Divinity, 1888-96; M.A. 1891; B.D. 1896. Minister, Church of Scotland. Officiating Clergyman, 2/10th Royal Scots, Summer 1916 and 1917. 2nd King's Own Scottish Borderers (Volunteers), Private 1917.

Record of War Service

LAMONT, JOHN CHARLES.
  Liverpool College. M.B., C.M. (Hons.) 1885; M.R.C.S. (Eng.) 1885. Demonstrator of Anatomy, 1886-7. Indian Medical Service, Surgeon-Captain, 1887; Lieut.-Col. 1907. Retired 1908. Chin-Lushai Expedition, 1889-90; Manipur Expedition, 1891. Re-employed. India 1915-19. C.I.E. 1919.

LAMONT, JOSEPH.
  M.A. 1914. O.T.C. Artillery, Oct. 1909 to Nov. 1912, Cadet. Army Veterinary Corps, Corporal Jan. 1914; Q.M.S. R.A.S.C., 2nd Lieut. Feb. 1919.

LAMONT, JOSEPH LAURIE.
  Treherne and Manitoba College, Winnipeg. First XV. B.A. (Manitoba) 1911; Student of Medicine, 1913-17; M.B., Ch.B. 1917. O.T.C. Medical, March 1915-17, Cadet Sergeant. Royal Navy, Surgeon-Lieut., July 1917 to Feb. 1919. H.M. Ships *Oakly* and *Cupar*. Attached 8th, 3rd, and 7th North Sea Fast Minesweeping Flotillas.

LAMPORT, HENRY CHRISTOPHER.
  Rondebosch College, Cape Town. M.B., C.M. 1888. R.A.M.C. (T.), 1889; Major 1902; Lieut.-Col. Sept. 1918. 2nd West Lancaster Brigade, R.F.A.; 1/7th Devon Regiment. Queensferry, Alexandra Palace, and Aylesbury Military Hospitals.

LANDALE, WELLWOOD MAXWELL.
  Fettes College; First XV. and XI. Student of Arts and Divinity, 1889-92; M.A. 1892. Minister, Church of Scotland. Chaplain to the Forces, 4th Class, Nov. 1917-19.

LANDSBOROUGH, WILLIAM.
  M.B., Ch.B. 1902. R.A.M.C., Lieut. Oct. 1915; Captain Oct. 1916. Dispatches June 1919.

LANE, CECIL ALEXANDER.
  M.B., Ch.B. 1884; L.R.C.P. (Edin.) 1882. R.A.M.C., Lieut.-Col. Aug. 1915; Colonel, A.M.S., Jan. 1917. Burma, 1887. A.D.M.S., Abbotabad and Sialkot Brigades; 2nd (Rawal Pindi) Division. India, 1914-17.

LANG, ANDREW.
  Kilmarnock Academy. Student of Arts, 1913-14. O.T.C. Infantry, Feb. to Sept. 1914, Cadet. 15th Royal Scots, Private Sept. 1914; 2nd Lieut. Aug. 1917; Acting Captain Oct. 1918 to Nov. 1919.

LANG, ERIC CHRISTISON.
  George Watson's College. M.B., Ch.B. 1910. O.T.C. Artillery, Oct. 1908 to Nov. 1911, Cadet. R.A.M.C., 1912; Captain March 1915; Temp. Lieut.-Col. April 1918. 1st Leicestershire Regiment. Field Ambulance, France, 1914; India. D.S.O. (Rue du Bois) March 1915. Dispatches.

LANG, FERDINAND WILSON. (See p. 750.)

LANGLANDS, CAIRNS KER.
  George Watson's College; First XV. O.T.C. 1914-18, Cadet Lieut. Student of Science, 1918. Royal Air Force, Cadet May 1918; Flight Cadet Sept. 1918.

Record of War Service

LANGLANDS, CHARLES BABINGTON.
George Watson's College, and Larchfield School, Helensburgh; First XV. Student of Science, 1919. O.T.C. Artillery, Feb. to Oct. 1917, Cadet Bombardier; Officer Cadet Oct. 1917. R.F.A., 2nd Lieut. March 1918. France July 1918-19.

LANGLANDS, DAVID NASMYTH.
Royal High School. Student of Law, 1913-15. 2/1st Lothians and Border Horse, Private April 1915.

LANGLANDS, JOHN BRYCE.
George Watson's College; First XV. O.T.C. 1914-15, Cadet Corporal. Student of Medicine, 1918. Highland Light Infantry, 2nd Lieut. July 1915; Lieut. July 1917. France 1916-18.

LANGWILL, ARCHIBALD.
Royal High School. M.B., Ch.B. 1911. R.A.M.C., Lieut. Dec. 1914; Captain Dec. 1915. 1st Rifle Brigade, France, 1915. Isolation Hospital, Amara, Mesopotamia, 1916-19.

LANGWILL HAMILTON GRAHAM.
Royal High School. M.B., C.M. 1889; M.D. 1898; F.R.C.P. (Edin.). R.A.M.C. (T.), Captain July 1908. 2nd Scottish General Hospital.

LANGWILL, JAMES.
Royal High School; First XV. M.B., Ch.B. 1908; M.D. 1912. Assistant to Professor of Clinical Surgery, 1912-14. No. 4 Coy. Q.R.V.B., Royal Scots, Private. R.A.M.C., Lieut. Oct. 1916; Captain Oct. 1917. 21st Stationary Hospital, and 83rd Field Ambulance, Salonika (Struma Front).

LANGWILL, LYNDESAY GRAHAM.
Royal High School. Student of Commerce, 1919. O.T.C. Infantry, March to Sept. 1916, Cadet; Officer Cadet Sept. 1916. 2/1st Fife and Forfar Yeomanry attached 14th Royal Highlanders (Black Watch), 2nd Lieut. Dec. 1916; Lieut. June 1918; Signalling Officer. France.

LARGE, DAVID TORQUIL MACLEOD.
M.B., Ch.B. 1910. R.A.M.C., Captain March 1915. M.C.

LARKINS, FRANCIS EDMOND.
St John's College, Winnipeg. M.B., Ch.B. 1904; M.D. 1908; D.P.H. (Edin.) 1906. R.A.M.C., May 1917.

LATIF, SHAIKH ABDUL.
B.A., B.Sc. 1912. A.M.I.C.E. Lieut. July 1916. Assistant Engineer, Railway in Waziristan Field, 1917, and Field Service, N.-E. Railway, India.

LATIMER, SYDNEY JAMIESON MUIR.
Merchiston Castle. O.T.C. 1915-16. University O.T.C. Artillery, June 1917 to May 1918, Cadet; Officer Cadet May 1918. R.F.A., 2nd Lieut. April 1919.

Record of War Service

LAUCHLAN, ROBERT.
 Royal High School. Student of Medicine, 1919. O.T.C. Artillery, Sept. 1914 to Oct. 1915, Cadet. R.F.A., 2nd Lieut. Oct. 1915; Lieut. Oct. 1917.

LAUDDIE, ABDURRAHMAN KHAN.
 M.B., Ch.B. 1901. Indian Medical Service, Major Sept. 1914.

LAUDER, THOMAS CAMPION.
 M.B., Ch.B. 1897; L., L.M., R.C.P. & S. (Ireland) 1894; B.Sc. (P.H.) 1920. R.A.M.C., Lieut.-Col. March 1915.

LAUGHTON, NORMAN BLAKE.
 Student of Medicine, 1910-15; M.B., Ch.B. 1915. O.T.C. Medical, Nov. 1914-15, Cadet. R.A.M.C., Lieut. Aug. 1915; Captain Aug. 1916. Gallipoli Oct. to Dec. 1915; Egypt Jan. 1916 to Dec. 1917; Palestine Dec. 1917 to Nov. 1918; Arabia and Egypt 1919.

LAURIE, ALAN RUPERT.
 Derby School; First XI. O.T.C. 1904-10, Cadet Sergeant. Student of Medicine, 1910-15; M.B., Ch.B. 1915. O.T.C. Medical, Nov. 1914 to Aug. 1915, Cadet, R.A.M.C., Lieut. Aug. 1915; Captain Feb. 1916. Dispatches Jan. 1919.

LAURIE, ALBERT ERNEST.
 Bonnington Academy. Student of Arts, 1885. Canon, Episcopal Church of Scotland. Chaplain, 4th Class, 1914; Senior Chaplain (Major) 1918. Dispatches 1915. M.C. 1916; Bar to M.C. 1917.

LAW, CHARLES DONALDSON.
 Student of Medicine. L.R.C.P. & S. (Edin.) and L.F.P.S. (Glasg.) 1898. R.A.M.C., Captain April 1915. 51st General Hospital.

LAW, JOHN SPENCE.
 Forfar Academy. M.B., C.M. 1883. R.A.M.C., Major April 1915. Norfolk War Hospital.

LAWL, JAG MOHAN.
 M.B., Ch.B. 1907. Indian Medical Service, Lieut.

LAWRENCE, GEORGE ALLISON.
 George Watson's College. M.A. 1909. Schoolmaster. 10th Seaforth Highlanders, Private Dec. 1914; Sergeant Instructor Sept. 1915. Household Brigade, Officer Cadet June 1918.

LAWRENCE, GEORGE CLARKE.
 George Watson's College. M.A. 1913. Cameron Highlanders, Private March 1916. Highland Light Infantry. Royal Scots, 2nd Lieut. June 1917. France 1916; Egypt 1917-19.

LAWRENCE, IRVINE.
 Servitor, University. 16th Royal Scots, Private May 1915. Malta.

Record of War Service

LAWRENCE, LEONARD ARTHUR.
Church of England Grammar School, Geelong, Victoria, and Melbourne University. Student of Medicine, 1914. O.T.C. Medical, 1914-15, Cadet. Attached 1st Australian Auxiliary Hospital, Harefield Park, July to Oct. 1915. 4th and 9th Royal Dublin Fusiliers, 2nd Lieut. Jan. 1916; Lieut. Dec. 1916; Acting Captain and Adjutant June 1917. The Black Sea. Dispatches Dec. 1917.

LAWRIE, JAMES McLELLAN.
Falkirk High School. University O.T.C. Artillery, July 1917 to March 1918, Cadet; Officer Cadet March 1918. R.G.A., 2nd Lieut. Sept. 1918.

LAWRIE, JAMES RUSSELL.
Bathgate Academy. Student of Arts, 1911-14 and 1918-19; M.A. 1919. Schoolmaster. 3rd and 5th Highland Light Infantry, Private Feb. 1916; Sergeant. Attached N.C.O. School of Musketry.

LAWRIE, JOHN HOLLIS DRUMMOND.
Daniel Stewart's College. Cadet Corps 1912-14. Student of Medicine, 1919. Royal Scots, Private March 1915. 4th and 17th Scottish Rifles, 2nd Lieut. May 1915; Lieut. April 1917; Captain Sept. 1917 to Oct. 1918. France. Wounded at the Somme Sept. 1916.

LAWRIE, MAURICE BERTRAM.
Normal College and South African College. M.B., Ch.B. 1912; F.R.C.S. (Edin.) 1919. R.A.M.C. South African Medical Corps, Captain Dec. 1914. Dispatches Dec. 1916. M.C. July 1917; Bar to M.C. Oct. 1917.

LAWRIE, THOMAS.
St Boswells School. M.A. 1886. Minister, U.F. Church of Scotland. 1st Kincardineshire Volunteer Regiment, Private June 1917; Lieut. Sept. 1917.

LAWRIE, WILLIAM DUNCAN.
George Watson's College. M.B., C.M. 1892; M.D. and F.R.C.S. (Edin.) 1900, R.A.M.C., Lieut. May 1915; Captain May 1916.

LAWSON, ALEXANDER.
Student of Arts, 1910-13; M.A. 1919. Schoolmaster. 6th Royal Highlanders (Black Watch), Private Nov. 1915. Attached 51st Division, Dec. 1916 to April 1918. Prisoner of War April to Nov. 1918.

LAWSON, ANDREW HAROLD BALVAIRD.
George Watson's College. O.T.C. 1914-16. Student of Arts, 1919. O.T.C. Artillery, 1917-18, Cadet; Officer Cadet. R.F.A., 2nd Lieut. Feb. 1919.

LAWSON, CHARLES BUNBURY.
Dover College. M.B., C.M. 1889. R.A.M.C., 1892; Lieut.-Col. Aug. 1914; Brevet Colonel Feb. 1915. South Africa, 1899-1900. Dispatches Jan. 1915.

Record of War Service

LAWSON, FREDERICK.
George Heriot's School. O.T.C. 1914-16. University O.T.C. Engineers, 1917-18, Cadet Corporal; Officer Cadet Sept. 1918. Royal Scots, 2nd Lieut. April 1919.

LAWSON, JAMES.
Merchiston Castle; First XI. Cadet Corps 1902-8. B.Sc. (St Andrews). Student of Medicine, 1908-15; M.B., Ch.B. 1915; M.D. 1920. B.R.C.S. (Dresser), 1914. Attached Meerut Casualty Clearing Hospital. R.A.M.C. (S.R.), Lieut. April 1915; Captain Nov. 1915. 60th Field Ambulance, 1915-16; Machine-Gun Corps, 1917. Royal Air Force, 1918-19. France 1914; North Russia 1918-19. Dispatches Dec. 1916.

LAWSON, JAMES SEGGIE WATERSTONE.
Royal High School. Student of Arts, 1914-15. O.T.C. Infantry, Feb. 1915 to March 1916, Cadet L/Corporal; Officer Cadet March 1916. 3rd and 10th Argyll and Sutherland Highlanders, 2nd Lieut. Aug. 1916; Lieut. Feb. 1918.

LAWSON, JOSEPH ILLINGWORTH.
Merchiston Castle. M.B., Ch.B. 1913. R.A.M.C. (S.R.), Lieut. Sept. 1914; Captain April 1915. 7th Field Ambulance, The Rhine. Dispatches June 1918. M.C. Aug. 1918.

LAWSON, ROBERT.
Lanark Grammar School. Student of Medicine, 1910-15 and 1919. M.B., Ch.B. 1915; M.D. 1919. R.A.M.C., Lieut. July 1915; Captain Jan. 1916. 3rd Lowland Field Ambulance. Wounded July 1916. M.C. July 1918.

LAWSON, ROBERT SHARP.
Morrison's Academy, Crieff. M.A. 1906; M.B., Ch.B. 1910; F.R.C.S. (Eng.) 1916. Anatomy Staff, 1912-14. O.T.C. Medical, 1906-9, Cadet. Royal Navy, Surgeon-Lieut., Jan. 1915 to June 1919. H.M.S. *Zealandia*; H.M. Hospital Ships *Plassey* and *St Margaret of Scotland*; Royal Naval Hospital, Chatham.

LAWSON, THOMAS EBENEZER.
Student of Medicine, 1909-14. L.R.C.P. & S. (Edin.) and L.R.F.P.S. (Glasg.) 1914. O.T.C. Infantry, 1910, Medical, 1911-13, Cadet. R.A.M.C., Lieut. Sept. 1914; Captain Sept. 1915 to April 1919. 46th Field Ambulance.

LAWSON, WILLIAM DALRYMPLE.
George Watson's College. Student of Law, 1906-11. Chartered Accountant, 1911. 9th Royal Scots (T.), Private Aug. 1914. Argyll and Sutherland Highlanders, 2nd Lieut. Feb. 1915. Machine-Gun Corps, Lieut. Sept. 1916; Acting Major Feb. 1918. France 1915-18. Wounded July 1916 and April 1918.

LAWSON, WILLIAM THOMSON.
George Watson's College. Student of Medicine, 1910-14. R.A.M.C., Scottish Horse, Sept. 1914. 3/7th Durham Light Infantry, 2nd Lieut. Aug. 1915; Lieut. June 1917. France. Wounded at Somme Oct. 1916.

Record of War Service

LAWTON, ROBERT.
Peebles Burgh and County School. M.A. 1904. Schoolmaster. R.G.A., Gunner July 1917.

LAY, ARTHUR CROALL HYDE.
Edinburgh Academy. O.T.C. Student of Arts and Commerce, 1918. O.T.C. Infantry, 1918, Officer Cadet. King's Own Scottish Borderers, 2nd Lieut.

LEACH, ABRAHAM.
Giggleswick. M.B., Ch.B. 1902. R.A.M.C, Lieut. Feb. 1915; Captain Feb. 1916. Mesopotamia and India.

LEADBETTER, JAMES GREENSHIELDS GREENSHIELDS. (See p. 750.)

LEAKEY, ALEXANDER BAZETT.
M.B., Ch.B. 1902. R.A.M.C., Lieut. Feb. 1906; Captain Jan. 1915. France.

LEARMONT, JOHN.
Dumfries Academy. Student of Arts and Medicine, 1910-15 and 1917-19; M.A. 1913; M.B., Ch.B. 1919. O.T.C. Infantry, Nov. 1910-13, and Artillery, Oct. 1914-15, Cadet. R.N.V.R., Surgeon-Probationer, Oct. 1915 to Sept. 1917.

LEARMONTH, WILLIAM WADDELL.
Linlithgow Burgh School. Student of Law, 1895-7 and 1917-19. Solicitor Jan. 1899. 1st Volunteer Battn., Royal Scots, Private March 1917 to Aug. 1918.

LEARY, GERALD FERDINAND VICTOR.
M.B., Ch.B. 1907. R.A.M.C. (S.R.), Lieut. June 1912; Captain Aug. 1915; Acting Major April 1918. 25th Casualty Clearing Station. Dardanelles, Serbia, and Salonika, Dispatches Nov. 1917.

LEARY, THOMAS GARNET STIRLING.
Bangor College, Ireland. M.B., Ch.B. 1900; M.D. and F.R.C.P. (Edin.) 1904. University Battery, E.C.A.V., 1895-8, Bombardier. Australian Army Medical Corps, Captain April 1915; Major Nov. 1919. 1st, 3rd, and 5th Australian General Hospitals. Gallipoli. Invalided from Gallipoli.

LEASK, JAMES BRUCE.
Student of Arts, 1911-15; M.A. 1919. O.T.C. Infantry, Oct. 1911-14, Cadet. 10th Argyll and Sutherland Highlanders, 2nd Lieut. Nov. 1914; Lieut. Sept. 1915; Acting Captain Jan. to Nov. 1916; Staff Lieut. June to Nov. 1917; Staff Captain Nov. 1917; Captain May 1918. Egypt. Dispatches (E.E.F.) June 1918 and June 1919. Order of Nile (4th Class), March 1919. O.B.E. (Military) June 1919.

LEBURN, WILLIAM GILMOUR.
Dollar Academy and Merchiston Castle. O.T.C. 1914-17. University O.T.C. Artillery, 1917-18, Cadet Bombardier; Officer Cadet June to Nov. 1918.

Record of War Service

LECHLER, ARTHUR NORMAN.
St Lawrence College, Kent; First XI. Cadet Corps 1906-8. Student of Science Engineering, 1912-14 and 1918-19. 9th Royal Scots (T.), Private Sept. 1914. Manchester Regiment, 2nd Lieut. March 1915. R.F.C., Lieut. March 1918. Egypt. Wounded. Prisoner of War April 1917 to Sept. 1918. Mentioned in Dispatches March 1916.

LECHLER, JOHN HOWARD.
M.B., Ch.B. 1907. R.A.M.C., Lieut. 1916; Captain April 1917.

LECKIE, ARTHUR JAMES BRUCE.
M.B., Ch.B. 1908; M.D. 1912. R.A.M.C., Lieut.; Captain Feb. 1918.

LECKIE, JOSEPH PRIMROSE.
Cupar School, Fife. Student of Medicine, 1913-14 and 1917-19. O.T.C. Artillery, Oct. 1913-14, Cadet. R.F.A., 2nd Lieut. Sept. 1914; Lieut. Feb. 1917.

LECKIE, ROBERT WESTLANDS.
George Watson's College. M.A. 1910. Probationer, U.F. Church of Scotland. O.T.C. Artillery, Aug. to Sept. 1914, Cadet. R.F.A., 2nd Lieut. Sept. 1914; Lieut. July 1917; Acting Captain Sept. 1917; Temp. Captain June 1919. 11th Division, Ammunition Column, Egypt and Salonika, 1916. France 1917-18. Wounded at Cambrai Dec. 1917.

LECKIE, WILLIAM GORDON.
George Watson's College. Student of Science, 1919. O.T.C. Artillery, Jan. to Nov. 1915, Cadet Bombardier; Officer Cadet Dec. 1915. R.G.A., 2nd Lieut. July 1916; Lieut. Jan. 1918. France. Dispatches April 1918.

LEDGER, ARCHIBALD GEORGE KIRKWOOD.
Christ's Hospital. M.B., Ch.B. 1906; M.D. 1909. R.A.M.C., Lieut. May 1915; Captain May 1916.

LEDIARD, HENRY AMBROSE.
Cheltenham College. Student of Medicine, 1866. Cumberland and Border Regiment (V.), Private May 1916; 2nd Lieut. Oct. 1916. Surgeon, Chadwick and Engelthwaite Military Auxiliary Hospitals.

LEE, ALAISTER FRASER.
George Watson's College. M.B., Ch.B. 1907; M.D. 1909. No. 4 Coy. Q.R.V.B., Royal Scots, 1902-6, Private. R.A.M.C. (T.), Highland Mounted Brigade Field Ambulance, 1912-14. Lovat Scouts, 1914; Captain April 1915. Dardanelles, Egypt, Salonika, and France. M.C. Dec. 1916.

LEE, DAVID CHISHOLM.
George Watson's College. M.B., Ch.B. 1912. N.Z. Medical Corps, Captain Oct. 1915. Gallipoli, Egypt, and France; Somme, Messines, Passchendaele 1917.

LEE, JAMES.
M.B., C.M. 1896; M.D. 1902. R.A.M.C., Lieut.

Record of War Service

LEE, JAMES ARTHUR.
Student of Science, 1910-11. Durham R.G.A., Anti-aircraft, Lieut. 1916.

LEEBODY, HENRY ALFRED.
Academical Institution, Londonderry; First XV. M.B., C.M. 1895. Volunteer Medical Staff Corps, 1894-5, Private. Army Medical Service (T.), 1906; Brevet Major June 1917; Brevet Lieut.-Col. Jan. 1919; Acting Colonel June 1919. A.D.M.S., Scottish Command.

LEEBODY, JOHN GALWAY.
Merchiston Castle. O.T.C. 1914-18, Cadet Sergeant. Student of Medicine, 1918. Royal Air Force, Cadet May 1918.

LEEMING, JOHN HERKLOTS.
Aldenham Grammar School. Student of Medicine, 1887-90; M.D. (Toronto) 1886; L.R.C.P. (Lond.) 1886. Canadian Army Medical Corps, Captain and Brigade Sanitary Officer, Nov. 1914; Major Dec. 1917. 4th Field Ambulance. France.

LEES, DAVID.
Ayr Academy. M.A. 1903; M.B., Ch.B. 1907; F.R.C.S. (Edin.) 1918. No. 4 Coy. Q.R.V.B., Royal Scots, 1900-7, Colour-Sergeant. R.A.M.C., Lieut. Dec. 1915; Captain Dec. 1916. 2nd Irish Guards; 1st Welsh Guards; No. 4 Field Ambulance; No. 34 Casualty Clearing Station, and No. 9 Stationary Hospital. Wounded 1916 and 1917. D.S.O. July 1917. Dispatches Jan. 1918.

LEES, HARRY RANKINE.
Edinburgh Academy. Student of Science, 1906-7. 2/7th Argyll and Sutherland Highlanders Oct. 1914; Captain Feb. 1916; Major March 1918. M.G. Officer, 193rd Infantry Brigade, Beirout, Syria. Dispatches Aug. 1917.

LEES, WALTER ARTHUR CLARK.
Fettes College; First XV. and XI. Student of Arts, 1901-2. 9th, 14th, and 15th Argyll and Sutherland Highlanders, Private Oct. 1914; Sergeant July 1915. Invalided out Jan. 1916. Ministry of National Service.

LEESON, JOHN RUDD.
M.B., C.M. 1876; M.D. 1882; M.R.C.S. (Eng.) 1875. R.A.M.C. (V.), Captain June 1917. 2nd V.B. Middlesex Regiment. St John's Ambulance.

LEGGAT, GEORGE LEGGAT.
Dundee High School; M.B., Ch.B. 1911; D.P.H., R.C.P.S. (Edin.) 1913. R.A.M.C., Lieut. Dec. 1914; Captain Dec. 1915; Lieut.-Col. June 1919. Med. Exp. Force. Dispatches and O.B.E. (Military) June 1919.

LEGGATE, ARCHIBALD RENWICK.
M.B., Ch.B. 1908. R.A.M.C., Lieut.; Captain March 1918. No. 3 Native Labour General Hospital, France.

Record of War Service

LEGGATE, ROBERT.
Stonehouse School, Lanarkshire. M.A. 1908. Schoolmaster. 15th Highland Light Infantry, Private June 1918. France 1918-19.

LEGGE, SYDNEY BUXTON.
Edinburgh Academy. M.B., Ch.B. 1906; M.D. 1910. R.A.M.C., Lieut. Nov. 1915.

LEGROS, RENÉ PIERRE.
Lycée of Rennes, France. M.A. (Hons. Mod. Lang.) 1912. Assistant Lecturer in French, London University. French Army, Aug. 1914. Staff Interpreter (10th Region), 1914-15. 13th Hussar Regiment (Liaison Officer), attached 136th Infantry Regiment, 1916. Aviation, Observer and Instructor of Aerial Gunnery, 1917-19.

LE HARIVEL, PHILIPPE CHARLES GUILLAUME.
Daniel Stewart's College. M.A. (Hons. Mod. Lang.) 1911. Schoolmaster. A.S.C., Private Nov. 1915 to Feb. 1919. France July 1916.

LEIGHTON, GERALD ROWLEY.
Nelson College, New Zealand. M.B., C.M. 1895; M.D. 1901; L.R.C.P. & S. (Edin.) and L.F.P.S. (Glasg.) 1895. A.S.C., Captain April 1915; Major April 1917; Lieut.-Colonel to June 1920. Technical Adviser, Ministry of Food and National Salvage Council; Inspector of Food Contracts for W.O. and Admiralty. Dispatches 1917. O.B.E.

LEIGHTON, PATRICK ALEXANDER.
M.B., Ch.B. 1898; M.D. 1903. R.A.M.C., Lieut. Dec. 1916; Captain Dec. 1917; Major Oct. 1918 to May 1919. France.

LEITCH, ALFRED.
M.B., Ch.B. 1906. Mile End Military Hospital, London, March to Dec. 1916. R.A.M.C., Lieut. Dec. 1916; Captain Dec. 1917. France Jan. 1917.

LEITH, JAMES MACKENZIE.
B.L. 1877. R.G.A. 1880, Hon. Lieut.-Col. holding Staff Appointment.

LEITH, WILLIAM.
Student of Law. Solicitor 1895. 1/3rd Forth R.G.A., Gunner.

LEJEUNE, FRANCIS ARNOLD.
Sedbergh. Cadet Corps 1902-6, Corporal. University O.T.C. Artillery, Feb. to July 1916, Cadet Sergeant; Officer Cadet July 1916. R.G.A. (S.R.), 2nd Lieut. Oct. 1916; Lieut. April 1918. France.

LEMON, JOHN WORKMAN.
Student 1892. French Red Cross, 1915. Officer Cadet. A.S.C. (M.T.), 2nd Lieut. Nov. 1916. Labour Corps, June 1917.

LEMPRIERE, PHILIP CHARLES.
George Watson's College. O.T.C. 1909-11. M.A. 1911. Minister, Episcopal Church of Scotland. Chaplain, 4th Class, July 1917 to Sept. 1918. Attached R.F.A., 255th Brigade. France; third Ypres, Cambrai, Lys, Marne, and Arras.

Record of War Service

LENNOX, DAVID
Dumfries Academy. Student of Medicine, 1909-15; M.B., Ch.B. 1917. O.T.C. Artillery, Oct. 1910 to Sept. 1914, Cadet. R.F.A., 2nd Lieut. Sept. 1914; Lieut. Aug. 1915. R.A.M.C., Lieut. May 1917; Captain May 1918.

LENNOX, JOHN.
George Watson's College. M.A. 1888. Minister, U.F. Church of Scotland. Chaplain (Hon. Captain), South African Native Labour Corps, Oct. 1916. France. Sub-Director of Education, Boulogne, Oct. 1918 to Feb. 1919. Dispatches Jan. 1918 and June 1919. O.B.E. June 1919.

LESLIE, ARCHIBALD STEWART.
B.A. (Oxford) 1895. Student of Arts, 1889-90. Writer to the Signet, 1898. Q.R.V.B., Royal Scots, Private 1896-1902. Scottish Horse (T.), Lieut. 1903. Mobilised Aug. 1914; Captain; Major; Lieut.-Col. June 1916. D.A.D. Forestry, April 1917. C.M.G. Jan. 1918. Dispatches. T.D. 1918.

LESLIE, JAMES.
Fettes College. B.Sc. 1905. R.E. (T.), City of Edinburgh Fortress, 2nd Lieut. 1908; Lieut. 1909; Captain June 1916. Mention Feb. 1917.

LESLIE, JOHN GORDON.
M.B., C.M. 1893. R.A.M.C., Lieut. 1915; Captain Aug. 1918. M.O., H.M. Hospital Ship *Braemar Castle*. Med. Exp. Force.

LESLIE, LEONARD.
George Watson's College; First XV. M.B., Ch.B. 1909; M.D. 1911. O.T.C. Medical, 1906-8, Cadet. R.A.M.C., Lieut. Oct. 1916; Captain Oct. 1917; Acting Major June 1918. Egypt. Dispatches April 1918.

LESLIE, ROBERT MILLER.
Arbroath High School. Student of Arts, Science, and Law, 1911-14 and 1918-20; M.A. 1919. O.T.C. Infantry, Dec. 1911 to Sept. 1914, Cadet. 5th Royal Highlanders (Black Watch) (T.), 2nd Lieut. Sept. 1914; Temp. Lieut. March 1915; Lieut. June 1916. Dispatches Dec. 1917.

LESLIE, THOMAS LESLIE.
B.Sc. 1910. O.T.C. Infantry, Oct. 1908, Cadet Sergeant. 35th Scinde Horse, Lieut.; Captain Sept. 1915. Indian Exp. Force.

LESSELLS, JAMES.
Dunfermline High School. Student of Arts, 1918. 8th Cameron Highlanders, Private June 1916. Machine-Gun Corps Sept. 1916 to Feb. 1919. France, 8th Division, 1916-18; Somme, Ypres, Passchendaele. Prisoner of War March to Nov. 1918.

LESSELS, JOHN.
Student of Law, 1911-14. 4th Royal Scots (T.), Sergeant; 2nd Lieut. Sept. 1917. Tank Corps, 2nd Lieut. April 1918.

Record of War Service

LESTER, JOHN BROWN.
 M.B., C.M. 1890; M.D. 1913; F.R.C.P. (Edin.) 1918. R.A.M.C., Lieut. 1916; Captain 1917; Major 1919. Egyptian Exp. Force.

LETHEM, GORDON JAMES.
 Mill Hill School; First XV. M.A. 1908; LL.B. (Distinction) 1909. Barrister-at-Law. Rugby "blue." Liaison Officer, Allied Forces in Cameroons, Maiduguji Column, 1914.

LETHEM, WILLIAM ASHLEY.
 Mill Hill School; First XV. M.B., Ch.B. 1913; M.D. 1920. O.T.C. Artillery, 1908-12, Cadet Sergeant. R.A.M.C. (S.R.), Lieut. 1913; Captain April 1915. Hon. Artillery Coy., and 1st Argyll and Sutherland Highlanders. France 1914; Gallipoli, Serbia, Salonika, and Constantinople. Dispatches 1917. M.C. June 1918.

LEVACK, JOHN SUTHERLAND.
 M.B., Ch.B. 1908. R.A.M.C., Lieut.; Captain July 1914.

LEVEY, SYDNEY.
 Jeppe High School, Johannesburg. Cadet Corps 1910-14, L/Corporal. Student of Medicine, 1914-20; M.B., Ch.B. 1920. Anatomy Staff, 1917. Royal Navy, H.M.S. *Aubretia*, Surgeon-Probationer.

LEVIN, JOSEPH JOHN.
 M.B., Ch.B. 1910. O.T.C. Artillery, Nov. 1908 to Feb. 1911, Cadet. South African Medical Corps, Captain. 5th Mounted Brigade, Northern Force. German South-West Africa, Kanbeb, 1915.

LEVY, LOUIS.
 Student of Medicine, 1912-14; M.B., Ch.B. 1914. O.T.C. Infantry, Jan. 1909 to July 1913, Cadet Sergeant. R.A.M.C., Lieut.

LEWARS, JOHN MITCHELL.
 George Watson's College. O.T.C. 1914-16, Cadet Corporal. Student of Arts, 1919. O.T.C. Artillery, 1916-17, Cadet Corporal; Officer Cadet April 1917. R.G.A. (T.), North Scottish, 2nd Lieut. June 1917; Lieut. Dec. 1918.

LEWIS, ARTHUR JAMES.
 George Watson's College; First XV. and XI. M.B., Ch.B. 1904; M.D. 1906. No. 4 Coy. Q.R.V.B., Royal Scots, 1899-1903, Corporal. R.A.M.C., Lieut. May 1915; Captain May 1916. France 1916-19.

LEWIS, CYRIL.
 Bedford School. M.B., C.M. 1891; M.D. 1897. Volunteer Medical Staff Corps, 1887-91, Staff Sergeant. R.A.M.C., Major Dec. 1908. 3rd Western General Hospital.

Record of War Service

LEWIS, LIONEL ARTHUR.
M.B., Ch.B. 1910. R.A.M.C. (S.R.), Lieut. Sept. 1914; Captain April 1915. France Nov. 1914.

LIDDELL, DAVID.
Student of Arts, 1913-15. R.E., Corporal.

LIDDELL, JOHN KENNETH CRAWFORD.
George Watson's College, and Perth Academy. Student of Medicine, 1912-15 and 1918-19. O.T.C. Infantry, 1914-15, Medical, 1918-19, Cadet. R.N.V.R., Surgeon-Probationer, 1915-18.

LIDDELL, MABEL ISABEL.
Seymour Lodge, Dundee. Student of Arts, 1914-17; M.A. 1917. Q.M.A.A.C., Oct. 1918 to July 1919. American Expeditionary Forces in France.

LIDDELL, ROBERT VICTOR.
Eltham College, London. First XV. and XI. O.T.C. 1916-18, Cadet Sergeant. Student of Medicine, 1918. 2nd Artists' Rifles (2/28th London Regiment) Oct. 1918.

LIDDELL, RONALD MORTON.
Weymouth College. M.B., Ch.B. 1907; L.R.C.P. & S. (Edin.) and L.F.P.S. (Glasg.) 1907. R.A.M.C., Lieut. Feb. 1917; Captain Feb. 1918.

LIDDELL, WILLIAM.
M.A., B.Sc. 1912. 3rd Scots Guards, Private.

LIDDLE, WILLIAM JOHN.
George Watson's College. O.T.C. 1914-16. Student of Medicine, 1918. R.E. (Wireless), Sapper 1916-19.

LIGGINS, JAMES BULL.
Student of Medicine, 1913-14 and 1915-18; M.B., Ch.B. 1918. R.A.M.C., Private 1914; L/Corporal. Attached 3rd Northumberland Fusiliers. N.Z. Medical Corps, Lieut. 1918.

LIGHTBODY, WILLIAM ARTHUR.
Merchiston Castle. O.T.C. 1912-14. University O.T.C. Artillery, 1916-17, Cadet; Officer Cadet Feb. 1917. R.G.A. (Forth), 2nd Lieut. May 1917 to July 1918. Indian Mounted Artillery, July 1918, Lieut. Nov. 1918-19.

LILICO, GORDON.
St Bees School, Cumberland; First XV. O.T.C. 1906-9. Student of Medicine, 1909-15; M.B., Ch.B. 1915. O.T.C. Infantry, 1910-13, Medical, 1914, Cadet. R.N.V.R., Surgeon-Probationer, Dec. 1914. Royal Navy, Surgeon, Oct. 1915. H.M. Ships *Oropesa, Conqueror, Vernon, Doris, Fox,* and *Prince George,* 1914-19.

LILICO, WILLIAM.
George Heriot's School. M.B., Ch.B. 1902; M.D. 1910. R.A.M.C., Lieut. June 1917; Captain June 1918. India 1917-18.

Record of War Service

LILLEY, PHILIP WILLIAM.
Arbroath High School. M.A. (Hons. Classics) 1905. Minister, U.F. Church of Scotland. Y.M.C.A. Work in France, 1915 and 1917. Chaplain, 4th Class, June 1918. 1/4th Gordon Highlanders, The Rhine.

LILLIE, JOHN ADAM.
Aberdeen Grammar School; First XV. and XI. M.A. (Aberdeen); LL.B. 1910. Advocate, 1912. Lothians and Border Horse, Private. Mobilised Aug. 1914. Discharged. Military Recruiting Staff, Lieut. May 1917. Ministry of National Service

LILLIE, WILLIAM.
Miller Institution, Thurso, and Aberdeen University. University O.T.C. Infantry, July to Aug. 1917, Cadet. R.G.A., Gunner Oct. 1917.

LIM, ROBERT KHO SENG.
George Watson's College. O.T.C. 1911-13. Student of Medicine, 1913-19; M.B., Ch.B. 1919. Lecturer in Physiology. Indian Field Ambulance, Oct. 1914.

LINDORES, ALFRED GEORGE.
George Heriot's School. University O.T.C. Artillery, 1917-18, Cadet. R.F.A., Gunner April 1918; Signaller Aug. 1918 to Jan. 1919.

LINDSAY, CREIGHTON HUTCHINSON.
Rainey School, Magherafelt. M.B., Ch.B. 1901; M.D. 1906; D.P.H. (Camb.) 1907. University Battery. E.C.A.V., 1897-1900, Gunner. R.A.M.C., Lieut. 1907; Major Aug. 1914; Acting Lieut.-Col. Aug. 1915; Acting Colonel Aug. 1917. 87th Field Ambulance, Gallipoli, April 1915; Egypt Jan. 1916; France March 1916. A.D.M.S., France and Germany, 1917-19. C.M.G. 1915; D.S.O. 1918. Seven times Mentioned in Dispatches.

LINDSAY, GEORGE.
Auchengray School. M.A. 1911. Athletics. Schoolmaster. 8th Royal Scots (T.), Private Nov. 1905; Sergeant; 2nd Lieut. Jan. 1915; Lieut. Jan. 1916. France 1914.

LINDSAY, JAMES.
M.B., Ch.B. 1906. West African Medical Staff, Captain. Prisoner of War to 1916. Cameroons.

LINDSAY, ROBERT STRATHERN.
Clifton College. O.T.C. 1908-12, Cadet Captain. Student of Law, 1912-14 and 1919-20. 9th Royal Scots (T.), 2nd Lieut. 1913; Lieut. Nov. 1914; Captain June 1916. Acting Brigade Major, 184th and 183rd Infantry Brigades, July 1918 to Feb. 1919. France Feb. 1915 to March 1919. M.C. Jan. 1917.

LINDSAY, THOMAS.
Daniel Stewart's College. M.B., Ch.B. 1911. O.T.C. Infantry, Oct. 1908 to May 1910, Cadet Colour-Sergeant. R.A.M.C. (S.R.), Lieut. May 1910; Captain Nov. 1913; Major May 1918. No. 2 General Hospital and No. 14 Field Ambulance, France. Wounded Sept. 1918.

Record of War Service

LINDSAY, W. C. S.
Daniel Stewart's College. University O.T.C. Infantry, March 1909 to May 1910, Cadet. 9th Royal Scots, 2nd Lieut. May 1910; Acting Captain May 1915; Captain June 1916; Acting Major April 1918. France Feb. 1915 to July 1919. Wounded. Dispatches Feb. 1918 and March 1919. M.C.

LINDSAY, WALKER STEWART.
M.B., Ch.B. 1912. O.T.C. Medical Nov. 1909 to April 1912, Cadet. R.A.M.C., Lieut.; Captain Jan. 1916. France. O.B.E.

DE LINGEN-KILBURN, JOHN ROBERT.
Student of Arts and Divinity, 1912-15; M.A. 1912; B.D. 1917. Minister, Church of Scotland. O.T.C. Infantry, 1914, Cadet. 12th Middlesex Regiment, 2nd Lieut. Nov. 1914 to April 1915. Intelligence Officer, North Russia.

LINKIE, THOMAS MUIR.
Royal High School. Student of Arts, 1911-16; M.A. (Hons. Engl.) 1916. O.T.C. Infantry, Oct. 1914 to Jan. 1916, Cadet. 8th Cameron Highlanders, Private July 1916. 1/7th and 3rd Gordon Highlanders, 2nd Lieut. Aug. 1918. France 1917 and Oct. 1918. Attached 10th Scottish Rifles.

LINKLATER, GEORGE JAMES IRVINE.
George Watson's College. M.B., Ch.B. 1912. Surgeon, Troopship, Aug. to Dec. 1914. R.A.M.C. (T.), Lieut. March 1915; Captain Sept. 1915. 3rd Lowland Field Ambulance. Palestine. Wounded at Gaza April 1917. Dispatches Oct. 1918 and March 1919. O.B.E. (Military) June 1919.

LINTON, ALEXANDER.
George Watson's College. M.A. (Hons. Mod. Lang.) 1913. O.T.C. Artillery, Oct. 1909 to Nov. 1912, Cadet. 13th and 3rd Royal Scots, 2nd Lieut. Jan. 1915; Lieut. Aug. 1916; Staff Captain April 1918. France, Hill 70; The Rhine. Intelligence Corps, 1917-18. Censor, 1918-19. Dispatches. M.C. Sept. 1915.

LINTON, FREDERICK THOMAS CHURCHILL.
George Watson's College. M.A. 1900; M.B., Ch.B. 1903; D.P.H. (Camb.) 1908. R.A.M.C. (T.), Captain April 1915-19. Attached H.Q. Staff, Chatham, Nov. 1916 to April 1919.

LIPETZ, HARRY.
George Heriot's School. Student of Science, 1913-16 and 1918-20; B.Sc. 1920. R.E. (Special Coy.), Sapper April 1916.

LIPETZ, SAM.
George Heriot's School. O.T.C. 1914-15. Student of Medicine, 1915 and 1918. R.F.A., Driver (Signaller) Aug. 1916; 2nd Lieut. Nov. 1917 to June 1918.

LISHMAN, WILLIAM.
Queen Elizabeth's Grammar School, Hexham. Student of Arts, 1912-15; M.A. 1915. Durham University O.T.C. Sept. to Dec. 1915. Y.M.C.A., Feb. to April 1916. R.G.A., 44th Anti-Aircraft Coy., Gunner May 1917.

Record of War Service

LISTER, THOMAS.
Royal High School. M.A. 1911. Chartered Accountant, 1915. R.G.A. (T.), 2nd Lieut. Nov. 1915; Lieut. June 1916.

LISTON, REGINALD PROSPER St LEGER.
Ampleforth College. O.T.C. 1912-16, Cadet Corporal. Student of Medicine, 1916-19. O.T.C. Artillery, Feb. 1917-18, Cadet. R.F.A., Officer Cadet March 1918.

LISTON, WALTER LYLE.
Trinity Academy, Leith. Student of Arts, 1912-14. 4th Royal Scots (T.), Private June 1914; 2nd Lieut. May 1917; Lieut. Nov. 1918.

LITHGOW, EDWIN MALCOLM.
M.B., Ch.B. 1898; F.R.C.S. (Edin.). 10th Royal Highlanders (Black Watch), Captain Sept. 1914. R.A.M.C., Captain July 1917. France and Salonika.

LITHGOW, JOHN DAVIS.
M.B., C.M. 1898; F.R.C.S. Assistant Surgeon, Ear and Throat Department, R.I.E. R.A.M.C., Lieut. Oct. 1914; Captain Oct. 1915-18. Royal Air Force, 1918. France 1914. 1/1st S.M. Field Ambulance, Ypres, 1917.

LITSTER, RICHARD JAMES.
George Watson's College. O.T.C. 1915-17. University O.T.C. Infantry, April 1917, Cadet L/Corporal; Officer Cadet. 8th Seaforth Highlanders, 2nd Lieut. March 1918. France 1918.

LITT, JOHN PERCY.
Shrewsbury. M.B., Ch.B. 1910; M.D. 1913; D.P.H. (Liverpool). R.A.M.C. (S.R.), Lieut. Sept. 1914; Captain April 1915. Captain (Reg.) Jan. 1917; Acting Major Sept. to Dec. 1918 and Feb. 1919. Med. Exp. Force, May to Sept. 1915. Salonika Nov. 1915-19. 82nd General Hospital, Constantinople. Dispatches July 1917. Greek Order of Redeemer (Chevalier), Oct. 1918.

LITTLE, JOHN.
Wallace Hall, Dumfries. Student of Law, 1892-5. Solicitor, 1897. 13th Reserve Brigade, Oct. 1914, Staff Sergeant. Instructor of Musketry. Lieut. 1915; Captain Aug. 1915. Secretary, Perth T.F. Association, Aug. 1916.

LITTLE, JOHN ELWES.
Kelso High School. Student of Medicine, 1915-16. R.A.M.C., Oct. 1914, Sergeant. Dispenser, H.M. Hospital Ships *Herefordshire* and *Devonlea*, and Mayo Hospital, Lahore, India.

LITTLE, PAUL MacDONALD.
St Mary's Hall, Cardiff. Student of Medicine, 1910-15; M.B., Ch.B. 1915. R.A.M.C., Lieut. Aug. 1915; Captain Aug. 1916. 6th Leicestershire Regiment, France. M.C. 1916; Bar to M.C. 1918.

Record of War Service

LIVESAY, ARTHUR WILLIAM BLIGH.
Isle of Wight College. M.B., C.M. 1892; F.R.C.S. (Edin.). Royal Navy, Nov. 1895; Surgeon-Commander, Nov. 1911. R.N. Hospitals, The Cape, 1914-16; Granton 1918, and Invergordon 1919.

LIVINGSTON, GEORGE ROBERT.
Edinburgh Academy. M.B., C.M. 1895; M.D. 1904; L.M. (Dublin); F.R.C.S. (Edin.) 1916. No. 4 Coy. Q.R.V.B., Royal Scots, Colour-Sergeant. R.A.M.C. (V.) and (T.), 1900; Major 1913. Mobilised Aug. 1914 to May 1919. 1/5th King's Own Scottish Borderers. Casualty Clearing Station, 52nd (Lowland) Division, Dardanelles. H.M. Hospital Ship *Herefordshire*. 21st General Hospital, Alexandria.

LIVINGSTONE, ARCHIBALD McDONALD.
Student of Arts and Science, 1909-14; B.Sc. 1912. O.T.C. Artillery, Aug. to Sept. 1914, Cadet. R.F.A., 2nd Lieut. Sept. 1914; Lieut.; Acting Major May 1918. Wounded 1917. M.C. June 1917.

LIVINGSTONE, ARTHUR PRINGLE.
George Watson's College. University O.T.C. Artillery, Oct. to Nov. 1914, Cadet. R.F.A., 2nd Lieut. Nov. 1914; Acting Lieut. Sept. 1916; Lieut. Feb. 1917; Acting Captain March 1917. R.F.C., Aug. 1917; Adjutant, 48th, 16th, and 80th Squadrons, April 1918. France 1915-19; Egypt 1919-20. Wounded 1916.

LIVINGSTONE, JOHN.
Perth Academy. M.B., C.M. 1891. Assistant to Professor of Clinical Medicine, 1891-2. Westmorland and Cumberland Yeomanry, Surgeon-Lieut. 1902; Surgeon-Captain. R.A.M.C. (T.), Major Aug. 1914. France 1915. 3rd Welsh Field Ambulance, Army Medical Department, War Office. T.D. 1919.

LIVINGSTONE, THOMAS HILLHOUSE.
Uppingham. M.B., Ch.B. 1899; M.D. and F.R.C.S. (Edin.) 1903. R.A.M.C. (T.), Lieut. May 1908; Captain 1909. Mobilised Aug. 1914 to April 1919. Northumbrian Division, T. and S. Column. Ear, Nose, and Throat Specialist, 1st Northern General Hospital.

LIVINGSTONE-LEARMONTH, BASIL LOCKHART.
M.B., C.M. 1896. R.A.M.C., Lieut. July 1915; Captain July 1916. H.M. Hospital Ship *Aquitania*.

LLEWELLYN, RICHARD BEVAN.
Llandovery School. M.B., Ch.B. 1913. R.A.M.C., Lieut. Nov. 1914; Captain Nov. 1915.

LLOYD JOHN STANLEY.
MB., Ch.B. 1912. O.T.C. Medical, Jan. 1909 to May 1912, Cadet. R.A.M.C., Lieut. Sept. 1914; Captain Sept. 1915; Acting Major. France. Dispatches.

Record of War Service

LLOYD, NIGEL FITZROY.
    MB., Ch.B. 1908. Royal Navy, Surgeon Oct. 1914.

LLOYD, RAYMOND LIONEL.
    M.B., Ch.B. 1913. South African Medical Corps, Captain Nov. 1915. M.C. 1916.

LLOYD, THOMAS JONES.
    Pencader School. Student of Medicine, 1910-15. M.B., Ch.B. 1915. O.T.C. Medical, 1914-15, Cadet. R.A.M.C., Lieut. Dec. 1915; Captain Dec. 1916.

LLOYD-EVANS, VAUGHAN.
    Warwick School; First XV. M.B., Ch.B. 1907; F.R.C.S. (Edin.) 1912. R.A.M.C., Lieut. July 1916; Captain July 1917. Salonika.

LOCHRANE, CHARLES DAMIEN.
    Stonyhurst College. M.B., Ch.B. 1904; M.D. 1908; F.R.C.S. (Edin.) 1906. R.A.M.C., Lieut. May 1918. Egginton War Hospital.

LOCHRANE, NEALE LEO.
    Stonyhurst College. Cadet Corps 1902-4. M.B., Ch.B. 1912; M.D. 1914. R.A.M.C., Lieut. Sept. 1914; Captain April 1915. France and Salonika. Dispatches Oct. 1917.

LOCKERBIE, JAMES BLACKLAY.
    George Heriot's School. M.B., Ch.B. 1904; F.R.C.S. (Edin.) 1908. R.A.M.C. (T.), Captain May 1915.

LOCKHART, JAMES BALFOUR.
    Cambuslang School. Student of Arts and Science, 1912-14 and 1919-20; M.A. (Hons. Maths.), B.Sc. 1920. R.A.M.C., Private Sept. 1914; Acting Sergeant March 1917. Officer Cadet Sept. 1918 to Jan. 1919. 1/2nd Lowland Field Ambulance, 1914-17. Gas School, Egypt, 1917-18.

LOCKHART, PETER.
    Grange School, Grangemouth. M.A. 1913. R.F.A., 31st Battery, Gunner Oct. 1914; 2nd Lieut. March 1918. France.

LOCKHART, ROBERT.
    Kirkcaldy High School; First XV. and XI. O.T.C. Cadet Corporal. Student of Medicine, 1918-19. 12th Royal Scots, 2nd Lieut. Dec. 1915; Lieut. July 1917. France. M.C. Sept. 1916.

LOCKHART, THOMAS THOMSON RANKIN.
    M.A. 1913; B.Sc. 1918. R.E., Sapper June 1915; Corporal July 1915; Sergeant March 1916; 2nd Lieut. April 1916; Lieut. Oct. 1917; Captain July 1918. France 1915. Italy. Wounded Nov. 1916. Dispatches Jan. 1917. M.C. Oct. 1917. "Encomium" Comando Supremo, Italian Army, Dec. 1918.

LODGE, WILFRID JOHN.
    B.A. (Oxford). Student of Arts, 1909-10. 15th Royal Scots, Lieut.; Major Aug. 1916. France.

Record of War Service

LOGAN, GEORGE.
George Watson's College; First XV. O.T.C. 1909-11. Student of Science, 1912-13. Lothians and Border Horse, Private Feb. 1914. R.G.A., 2nd Lieut. Nov. 1914; Lieut. June 1916; Captain Sept. 1916. France and Italy 1916-18. Dispatches Feb. 1918. Order of the Crown of Italy, April 1918.

LOGAN, INNES.
George Watson's College and Kelso High School; First XV. and XI. Cadet Corps 1900-2. M.A. 1907. University Battery, E.C.A.V., 1903-8, Sergeant. Minister, U.F. Church of Scotland. Chaplain, 4th Class, Sept. 1914. R.F.A., 1914. France 1915-19. 2nd Royal Scots, 1915-16; 1st Scots Guards, 1917-19. Hon. C.F. 1919. Dispatches June 1916.

LOGAN, JOHN ROBERT.
M.B., C.M. 1880. R.A.M.C. (T.), Captain July 1908. 1st Western General Hospital, Liverpool.

LOGAN, VICTOR DONALD ORR.
Liverpool College. M.B., Ch.B. 1909. University Battery, E.C.A.V., 1904-8, Gunner. R.A.M.C., Lieut. Oct. 1914; Captain Oct. 1915. 17th General Hospital. France and Med. Exp. Force.

LOGAN, WILLIAM ROBERTSON.
Kelso High School and George Watson's College. M.B., Ch.B. 1909; M.D. 1913; F.R.C.P. 1919. Clinical Pathologist, R.I.E. University Battery, E.C.A.V., 1904-8, Gunner. RA.M.C., Lieut. June 1915; Captain June 1916. Bacteriologist in Lemnos, Port Said, and Salonika.

LOGIE, HENRY CREELMAN.
M.A. 1904. Schoolmaster. R.G.A., 51st Siege Battery, Gunner Feb. 1916. France.

LOGIE, JOHN MOFFAT.
Arbroath School. M.B., Ch.B. 1910. R.A.M.C., Lieut. April 1915.

LORD, JOHN ROBERT.
Owens College, Manchester. M.B., C.M. 1896. University Battery, E.C.A.V. R.A.M.C., Lieut.-Col. May 1915. Horton War Hospital. C.B.E. (Military) 1919. Mention.

LORIMER, ALEXANDER PATRICK GORDON.
Edinburgh Academy; First XV. M.B., Ch.B. 1905. University Battery, E.C.A.V., 1900-3, Gunner. Indian Medical Service, 1906, Captain; Major Sept. 1918. War Hospitals, India, 1914-16. Mesopotamia July 1916-18; 122nd Indian Field Ambulance; 2/7th Gurkhas. Palestine 1918-19; Waziristan Aug. to Oct. 1919. Dispatches (Mesopotamia) 1918.

Record of War Service

LORIMER, DUNCAN.
George Watson's College. M.B., Ch.B. 1902; B.Sc. 1903; F.R.C.S. (Edin.) 1907. R.N.V.R. 1912; Surgeon 1914. H.M. Ships *Bacchante* 1914, and *Malaya* 1915-17. R.N. Hospital, Granton, 1917-19.

LORIMER, JAMES.
M.B., Ch.B. 1908. R.N.V.R., H.M.S. *London*, Surgeon.

LORNIE, ALBERT CHRISTIAN.
George Watson's College. Student of Medicine, 1914 and 1918-20. O.T.C. Infantry, Oct. 1914 to March 1916, Cadet; and Medical, Oct. 1916 to March 1917, Cadet Sergeant. R.N.V.R., H.M.S. *Peregrine*, Surgeon-Probationer, March 1917.

LORNIE, FRANKLIN ROSS TAYLOR.
George Watson's College. Student of Arts and Divinity, 1911-14 and 1916-17; M.A. 1914. Minister, Church of Scotland. O.T.C. Infantry, 1912-14, Cadet. 6th Royal Scots (T.), 2nd Lieut. June 1914; Lieut. March 1915. Egypt and France. Invalided out Aug. 1917.

LORNIE, JAMES.
Perth Academy. M.A. (Hons. Maths. and Nat. Phil.); B.Sc. 1898. Singapore Volunteer Corps (Veterans' Coy.), Private Nov. 1914. Intelligence Department.

LORNIE, PETER.
Perth Academy. M.B., Ch.B. 1906; M.D. 1912. R.A.M.C., Lieut. Nov. 1915; Captain Nov. 1916. O.B.E. June 1919.

LORRAINE, JOSEPH CURRIE.
M.B., Ch.B. 1908; F.R.C.S. (Edin.) R.A.M.C., Lieut. March 1915; Captain March 1916.

LORRAINE, NORMAN STANLEY REES.
Royal High School. Student of Medicine, 1910-15. M.B., Ch.B. 1915. O.T.C. Medical, 1910-14, Cadet Sergeant. R.A.M.C. (S.R.), Lieut. Aug. 1914; Captain Jan. 1916. Military Hospital, Catterick. France 1915-16; Italy and Egypt 1917-18.

LOTHIAN, DOUGLAS BEGBIE McC.
George Watson's College. O.T.C. 1909-12. Student of Medicine, 1914-15 and 1917-19. 9th Royal Scots (T.), Private April 1915. Machine-Gun Corps. France June to Nov. 1916. Invalided out July 1917.

LOUDEN, JOHN GRAHAM.
Dunfermline High School. Student of Medicine, 1910-15; M.B., Ch.B. 1915. R.A.M.C., Lieut. Sept. 1918. 43rd Field Ambulance.

LOUDON, ANDREW WALKER BUIST.
M.B., Ch.B. 1902; M.D. 1906. R.A.M.C. (S.R.), Captain Nov. 1913; Acting Lieut.-Col. March 1918.

Record of War Service

LOUDON, JOHN ALEXANDER.
: Ayr Academy. University O.T.C. Infantry, Aug. to Dec. 1916, Cadet. 9th and 1st Seaforth Highlanders, Pioneer, Dec. 1916; 2nd Lieut. April 1917; Lieut. Oct. 1918. France.

LOUW, ADRIAN HOFMEYR.
: Victoria College, Cape Province. M.B., Ch.B. 1911. Tennis "Blue." South African Medical Corps, Captain Aug. 1914; Major 1917. Twice Mentioned in Dispatches.

LOUW, EGBERT WARWICK.
: Student of Medicine, 1910-15; M.B., Ch.B. 1914. R.A.M.C., Lieut.

LOUW, HENDRIK JACOBUS.
: Student of Medicine, 1912-14 and 1917-19. O.T.C. Artillery, Oct. 1914 to March 1915, Cadet. R.F.A., 2nd Lieut. March 1915.

LOVE, WILLIAM.
: George Watson's College; First XV. O.T.C. 1912-15. Student of Medicine, 1915-16. O.T.C. Artillery, May 1915 to March 1916, Cadet; Officer Cadet March 1916. 3/3rd Scottish Horse, 2nd Lieut. July 1916; Lieut. Jan. 1918. Attached 1st Herts. Yeomanry. Mesopotamia and Persia.

LOVELOCK, CHARLES WILLIAM. (See p. 750.)

LOW, CHARLES MacRITCHIE.
: Daniel Stewart's College. B.Sc. 1911. A.M.I.C.E. Canadian Engineers, Sapper Jan. 1915; Corporal Nov. 1915; Sergeant Feb. 1916; C.S.M. Sept. 1917; Lieut. April 1918. Wounded June 1915.

LOW, DAVID.
: Perth Academy. Student of Medicine, 1918. R.E. (Special Brigade), Sapper May 1916; Officer Cadet Nov. 1918 to Jan. 1919.

LOW, DAVID HALYBURTON.
: George Watson's College. M.A. 1906. Lecturer in English, University of Belgrade. General List, Field Censor's Staff, 2nd Lieut. Sept. 1916; Lieut. 1917.

LOW, GEORGE CARMICHAEL.
: Madras College, St Andrews. M.A. (St Andrews); M.B., C.M. 1897; M.D. 1910; M.R.C.P. (Lond.) 1918. Indian Medical Service, Captain June 1917; Major June 1918.

LOW, HERBERT BRUCE.
: Uppingham. Cadet Corps 1898-1902, Cadet Sergeant. M.B., Ch.B. 1907; M.D. 1911. No. 4 Coy. Q.R.V.B., Royal Scots, March 1902-8, Lieut. 7th Durham Light Infantry (Combatant), 1914-15. Transferred to R.A.M.C. (T.), Captain April 1915; Acting Major Jan. 1918. 2nd Northumbrian Field Ambulance. France April 1915 to Dec. 1918. Dispatches Jan. 1916, June 1918, and Jan. 1919. M.C. Jan. 1917; Bar to M.C. Nov. 1918.

Record of War Service

LOW, JAMES.
Student of Science, 1913-15. 16th Royal Scots, Private.

LOW, JAMES LAWSON.
M.A. 1908. Schoolmaster. 5th Gordon Highlanders (T.), 1898; Lieut. 1913; Acting Captain Jan. 1915; Captain Oct. 1915; Acting Major Jan. 1916. Wounded June 1915. Dispatches Jan. 1916, June 1918, Jan. and March 1919. O.B.E. June 1919.

LOW, JAMES WOTHERSPOON.
George Watson's College. O.T.C. 1906-9. Student of Science, 1910-14; B.Sc. 1914 Demonstrator, Zoology Department, 1914. 4th Royal Scots (T.), 2nd Lieut. 1911 Mobilised Aug. 1914; Captain Sept. 1914. R.T.O., March 1918 to May 1919.

LOW, JOHN BRUCE.
M.B., Ch.B. 1913. O.T.C. Artillery, March 1909 to Dec. 1911, Cadet. R.A.M.C. Lieut.; Captain Dec. 1915.

LOW, JOHN INCH.
Blairgowrie High School. M.A. (Hons. Engl.) 1901. Schoolmaster. 3rd Royal Scots, Private Aug. 1917; Officer Cadet May 1918. A.S.C. (H.T. & S.), 2nd Lieut. July 1918 to June 1919. Mesopotamia 1918-19.

LOW, WALTER JOHN.
Harrow; First XI. O.T.C. 1912-16, Cadet L/Corporal. University O.T.C. Infantry, May to Sept. 1917, Cadet; Officer Cadet Sept. 1917. 1st Scots Guards, 2nd Lieut. Jan. 1918. France Aug. to Nov. 1918; The Rhine 1919.

LOWE, ARTHUR HAMILTON.
Lincoln Grammar School. M.B., C.M. 1893; D.P.H. (Ireland) 1911. R.A.M.C., Captain May 1915. Sanitary Officer, Poperinghe. 2nd Brigade, R.F.C.

LOWNIE, JOHN DONALDSON.
George Watson's College. Student of Law, 1899-1904. Writer to the Signet, 1908. 3/6th Royal Scots (T.), 2nd Lieut. July 1915; Lieut. Feb. 1917. Attached Machine-Gun Corps, Oct. 1916. France. Wounded at Messines June 1917.

LOWSON, JOHN HUGH.
George Watson's College, and Edinburgh Academy. Student of Law, 1907-11. Writer to the Signet, 1912. 12th Royal Scots, 2nd Lieut. Aug. 1914; Lieut. Dec. 1914. R.F.C., Flying Officer (Observer), Aug. 1916. France. Wounded and taken Prisoner Sept. 1916 to Dec. 1918.

LUCAS, FREDERICK RICHARD.
George Watson's College. Student of Medicine, 1903-10; L.R.C.P. & S. (Edin.) and L.R.F.P.S. (Glasg.) 1913. 9th Royal Scots (T.), University Coy., 1902; Captain Oct. 1909; Major July 1916. Attached R.A.M.C., 1917. France 1915. Dispatches Feb. 1917.

LUCRAFT, HARRY STEPHENSON.
Student of Medicine, 1912-15 and 1918-19; M.B., Ch.B. 1919. R.N.V.R., Surgeon-Probationer. H.M. Ships *Onslaught* and *Hildebrand*.

Record of War Service

LUCY, REGINALD HORACE.
: Malvern College; First XI. M.B., C.M. 1885; F.R.C.S. (Eng.) 1888. R.A.M.C. (T.), Major Sept. 1908. 4th Southern General Hospital, Aug. 1914 to June 1916. Invalided June 1916. Hill House Auxiliary Hospital, Guildford, 1917-18.

LUGTON, ALEXANDER DRYSDALE.
: Boroughmuir School; First XV. Student of Arts, 1914-15 and 1918-20. 16th Royal Scots, Private Nov. 1914; L/Corporal Aug. 1918. Transferred 34th Battn. Machine-Gun Corps.

LUKE, FRANCIS RICHARD.
: Fettes College. M.B., Ch.B. 1911. University Battery, E.C.A.V., and O.T.C. Artillery, 1906-9, Cadet. South African Medical Corps, Captain April 1917 to Sept. 1918.

LUKE, JOHN ANNANDALE.
: Edinburgh Academy. Student of Medicine, 1913-15. 15th Royal Scots, Private Oct. 1914. Cameron Highlanders, 2nd Lieut. April 1915; Lieut. June 1916; Acting Captain Feb. 1919. France.

LUMLEY, ALLAN A.
: Royal High School and Tonbridge School. O.T.C. 1913-17, Cadet Corporal. University O.T.C. Artillery, Dec. 1917 to July 1918, Cadet Corporal. R.G.A., Officer Cadet Aug. 1918; Temp. 2nd Lieut. April 1919.

LUMSDEN, GEORGE JAMES SANDERSON.
: Royal High School. Student of Law, 1912-14. O.T.C. Infantry, Sept. to Nov. 1914, Cadet Corporal. 10th Gordon Highlanders, 2nd Lieut. Nov. 1914. 7th Cameron Highlanders, Lieut. March 1916; Captain and Adjutant April 1917; Brigade Major Oct. 1918. 44th Infantry Brigade, France; Irish Reserve Brigade. Wounded at Loos Sept. 1915. Dispatches June and Dec. 1917. M.C. Dec. 1917.

LUMSDEN, JAMES.
: M.A. 1904. Diplômé, Dijon University. Schoolmaster. R.A.M.C., Private May 1915; Staff Sergeant Nov. 1915. 92nd Field Ambulance attached 97th Infantry Brigade, 37th Division, France, Nov. 1915 to Feb. 1919.

LUMSDEN, JAMES MICHAEL.
: Birley Street School, Manchester; First XI. Student of Divinity. O.T.C. Infantry, 1914-15, Cadet. 1st and 2nd Seaforth Highlanders, 2nd Lieut. April 1915; Lieut. April 1916; Acting Captain and Adjutant May 1918.

LUMSDEN, JOHN.
: M.A. 1908. Diplômé, Dijon University. Schoolmaster. 1/7th Royal Highlanders (Black Watch), Private Oct. 1916. France, 51st (Highland) Division. Intelligence Staff, Second and First Armies. Croix de Guerre avec Palme, Aug. 1917.

Record of War Service

LUMSDEN, JOHN LOWSON.
Royal High School. Student of Arts, 1878-80. Fife Light Horse, 1888. 2/1st Fife and Forfar Yeomanry (T.), Major 1906; Retired 1912; Rejoined Sept. 1914. South African Campaign, 1900. T.D.

LUMSDEN, THOMAS ARNOT.
George Heriot's School. Student of Science, 1912-15, 1916-17 and 1918-19; B.Sc. 1917; M.A. (Hons. Maths.) 1919. R.E. (Special Brigade), Corporal July 1915 to April 1917. Munitions, April 1917 to Dec. 1918.

LUNAN, JAMES DOUGLAS.
Daniel Stewart's College. Student of Science, 1912-14. O.T.C. Artillery, 1913-14, Cadet. R.F.A., 2nd Lieut. Sept. 1914; Lieut. Nov. 1915; Captain Aug. 1917.

LUNDIE, ALEXANDER.
M.B., Ch.B. 1903. R.A.M.C., Lieut.; Captain Aug. 1915.

LUNN, JAMES GEORGE.
Morrison's Academy, Crieff. M.A. 1908. Minister, U.F. Church of Scotland. Chaplain, 4th Class, June 1917. 2/4th Royal Scots Fusiliers. 12th Brigade, R.G.A., Hon. Chaplain, 4th Class.

LUPTON, ALFRED CRICHTON.
M.B., C.M. 1895. Surgeon-Lieut. Coldstream Guards, 1898; Captain 1901; Major 1905. 1st Life Guards, Surgeon-Captain. South African Campaign, 1899-1901.

LUSK, SAMUEL FINLAY.
Ballymoney, County Antrim. M.B., C.M. 1895. R.A.M.C., Lieut. Aug. 1916; Captain Aug. 1917.

LUSK, THOMAS GIBSON.
Larne Grammar School, County Antrim. M.B., C.M. 1894. University Battery, E.C.A.V., 1889-92, Sergeant. R.A.M.C., Captain Sept. 1915 to May 1919. 4th Sherwood Foresters and 3rd Northumberland Fusiliers. Tyne Garrison, 1919.

LYALL, GEORGE.
George Heriot's School. Student of Arts and Divinity, 1913-16; M.A 1916. R.A.M.C., Private April 1916. H.M. Hospital Ship *Mandilla* and 75th Field Ambulance.

LYALL, WILLIAM LESLIE.
George Watson's College. M.B., C.M., 1896; F.R.C.P. (Edin.); D.P.H. (Edin.) 1915. R.A.M.C., Captain Aug. 1914; Major Jan. 1918. France; Somme, Ancre, and Arras.

LYELL, ARTHUR LINDSAY.
Haileybury. O.T.C. 1913-17, Cadet L/Corporal. University O.T.C. Artillery, Sept. 1917 to April 1918, Cadet Corporal; Officer Cadet April 1918. R.F.A., 2nd Lieut. Aug. 1918. France. Wounded Oct. 1918.

Record of War Service

LYELL, DAVID.
B.Sc. South African Campaign, 1900-2. R.E. Rejoined Captain Sept. 1914; Major and Lieut.-Col. Aug. 1916; Colonel Nov. 1916. Chief Rly. Const. Engineer, Dpty. Director of Rlys., France. Dispatches Dec. 1915, June and Dec. 1917, June and Dec. 1918, and June 1919. D.S.O. Order of Leopold, and Croix de Guerre (Belgium) June 1917. C.M.G. June 1918. C.B.E. June 1919. Commander of the Portuguese Order Avis, March 1919. Legion of Honour (Officer), June 1919.

LYELL, THOMAS.
Student of Law, 1904-6. 5th Royal Highlanders (Black Watch) (T.), Captain Jan. 1916. M.C.

LYLE, FREDERICK WILLIAM.
M.B., C.M. 1889; M.D. 1895. R.A.M.C., Lieut; Captain May 1918.

LYLE, SAMUEL.
M.B., Ch.B. 1901. R.A.M.C., Lieut. Dec. 1914; Captain Dec. 1915. 25th Casualty Clearing Station till Jan. 1917. Gallipoli, Serbia, and Macedonia. Grantham Military Hospital, 1917-18. National Service, Deputy Commissioner of Medical Services, Jan. 1918; Commissioner, East Central Region, July 1918. C.B.E. Jan. 1919.

LYNDEN-BELL, EDWARD HORACE LYNDEN.
Philbirds, Maidenhead; First XI. M.B., C.M. 1882. R.A.M.C., Aug. 1883, Colonel 1912. Burmah Campaign, 1885-9. France 1914. Dispatches Oct. 1914. C.B. 1915. Knight of Grace of St John of Jerusalem.

LYON, DAVID MURRAY.
George Watson's College. M.B., Ch.B. 1910; M.D. 1920; F.R.C.P. (Edin.); D.P.H. Lecturer in Pathology. O.T.C. Infantry, 1905-11, Cadet Colour-Sergeant. R.A.M.C. (S.R.), Lieut. 1912; Captain April 1915; Acting Major Jan. 1918. Divisional Officer, No. 6 General Hospital, France. Dispatches Feb. 1915.

LYON, MALCOLM MURRAY.
Nottingham High School; First XI. O.T.C. 1912-13, Cadet Corporal. Student of Medicine, 1914-16. O.T.C. Infantry, April to Dec. 1915, Cadet. Highland Light Infantry (S.R.), 2nd Lieut. Dec. 1915; Lieut. June 1917. France. Wounded and taken Prisoner at Beaumont Hamel (Somme) Nov. 1916.

LYONS, WILLIAM CAMPBELL.
Foyle College, Londonderry. M.B., Ch.B. 1910; D.P.H. 1913. R.A.M.C. (T.), Lieut. Feb. 1916; Captain Aug. 1916.

MACADIE, GEORGE ALEXANDER.
Miller Institution, Thurso. Student of Medicine, 1914 and 1918-19. 5th Seaforth Highlanders, Private Feb. 1912. France 1915-18.

McADOO, ROBERT.
M.B., Ch.B. 1913. R.A.M.C. (T.), Lieut.; Captain April 1915. 1st Scottish Horse.

Record of War Service

McAFEE, CHARLES S. V.
Student of Arts, 1908-11. R.F.A., Bombardier.

McAFEE, DUNCAN JOHN.
Merchiston Castle. Cadet Corps 1899-1903. M.B., Ch.B. 1910. L.M. (Rotunda). R.A.M.C., Lieut. Sept. 1915; Captain Sept. 1916. 105th Field Ambulance. 35th Battn. Machine-Gun Corps. M.C. Feb. 1918.

McAINSH, DUNCAN TAYLOR.
Royal High School. Student of Arts and Medicine, 1909-14; M.A. 1920. O.T.C. Infantry, Oct. 1909 to Aug. 1914, Cadet Corporal. R.A.M.C. (T.), Scottish. Horse Field Ambulance, Private Sept. 1914. 13th Argyll and Sutherland Highlanders, 2nd Lieut. Aug. 1915; Lieut. July 1917; Acting Captain June 1919. France. M.C. Sept. 1918.

MACALISTER, CHARLES JOHN.
M.B., C.M. 1884; M.D. 1895; F.R.C.P. (Lond.) 1909. 6th V.B., King's Liverpool Regiment, 1888. Liverpool Scottish (T.), 1890, Major. Physician in charge of Administrative Centre and War Hospitals, Liverpool, 1914-19.

MACALISTER, JAMES McLAGAN.
Daniel Stewart's College. M.A. 1904. Minister, Presbyterian Church of Canada. Canadian Army Medical Corps, No. 1 Canadian General Hospital, Private March 1916-19. No. 9 Canadian Field Ambulance, France.

M'ALISTER, WILLIAM MALCOLM.
M.A. 1910. M.B., Ch.B. 1918. R.N.V.R., Surgeon-Probationer.

M'ALLAN, JAMES.
Aberdeen Grammar School. M.A. (Aberdeen) 1911. Student of Science, 1916-17. M.R.C.V.S. (Royal Dick College) 1918. Scottish Horse (T.), Farrier Q.M.S. Aug. 1914. Gordon Highlanders, 2nd Lieut. Aug. 1916. Royal Army Veterinary Corps, Lieut. July 1918. Russia. Order of St Stanislaus (3rd Class) with Swords, March 1919.

McALLEY, ROBERT IAN.
Brechin High School. Student of Medicine, 1918. 2nd Scots Guards, Private March 1917; Corporal. France. Wounded and Discharged Nov. 1918.

MACALLISTER-HEWLINGS, WILLIAM FREDERICK.
Wyggeston Grammar School. M.B., C.M. 1893. University Battery, E.C.A.V., 1890-3, Gunner. R.A.M.C. (T.), 1890; Major Oct. 1914. 4th Leicestershire Regiment, France. D.A.D.M.S., 50th Division, Aug. 1918. Dispatches Jan. 1918.

M'ALLUM, STUART GERALD.
Royal High School; First XV. M.B., C.M. 1889; M.D. 1893; D.P.H. 1910. South African Campaign, 1900-1. R.A.M.C. (S.R.), Major May 1913; Acting Lieut.-Col. May 1917. 2nd Cavalry and 140th Field Ambulances, and 40th Stationary Hospital, 1914-19. France 1914. D.S.O. and Dispatches Jan. 1919.

Record of War Service

McALPINE, CHARLES BOYD.
: Royal High School; First XV. Student of Arts, 1912-15 and 1918-19; M.A. (Hons. Hist.) 1919. O.T.C. Infantry, Oct. 1913 to July 1915, Cadet Sergeant. 2nd Cameron Highlanders, 2nd Lieut. Aug. 1915; Lieut. April 1917; Acting Staff, Captain Nov. 1918 to Jan. 1919.

M'ALPINE, DAVID BROWN.
: Student of Arts, 1909-14; M.A. 1913. O.T.C. Infantry, Jan. 1910 to Sept 1914, Cadet L/Corporal. 9th Royal Scots (T.), Private.

M'ALPINE, EDWARD GEORGE.
: Royal High School. Student of Arts, 1908-14; M.A. 1912. O.T.C. Infantry, May 1910 to Sept. 1914, Cadet Sergeant. 6th Bangalore, Coorg, and Mysore Battn., Indian Defence Force, 2nd Lieut. Nov. 1914; Lieut. July 1916.

MACALPINE, RODERIC ALEXANDER MURDO.
: George Watson's College; First XV. O.T.C. 1915-17, Cadet L/Corporal. Student of Science, 1918-19. O.T.C. Infantry, Oct. 1917 to Sept. 1918, Cadet Sergeant-Major; Officer Cadet. Cameron Highlanders, 2nd Lieut. Dec. 1918.

MACANDREW, J. M.
: Student. Seaforth Highlanders, Captain; Hon. Major. Recruiting Officer.

McARTHUR, DANIEL EDWARD.
: Galashiels Academy. Student of Science, 1916-17 and 1918-19. O.T.C. Artillery, Oct. 1916 to July 1917; Cadet Sergeant; Officer Cadet July 1917. R.G.A. (T.), 20th (Forth) Fire Command, 2nd Lieut. March 1918 to June 1919.

MacARTHUR, DONALD HECTOR COLIN.
: Wakefield Grammar School. M.B., Ch.B. 1905; M.D. 1913. R.A.M.C. 1908; Captain Feb. 1912; Temp. Major 1918. Field Ambulance, Indian Exp. Force. Mesopotamia. Dispatches. O.B.E.

MACARTHUR, DONALD RODERICK.
: Nicolson Institute, Stornoway. Student of Science, 1918 R.F.A., Sept. 1914; 2nd Lieut. Oct. 1914. R.G.A. May 1915; Lieut. Aug. 1916; Acting Captain March 1917. France. Wounded at the Somme Aug. 1916, and at Ypres July 1917.

McARTHUR, WILLIAM NEIL.
: Dunfermline High School. Student of Medicine, 1918. 1/5th Argyll and Sutherland Highlanders, Nov. 1915; Corporal; Officer Cadet.

MACASKIE, WILFRID VICTOR.
: M.B., Ch.B. 1910. R.A.M.C., Lieut. Oct. 1914; Captain Oct. 1915; Major Jan. 1918. Dardanelles, Salonika, and Egypt. M.C. and Dispatches June 1918.

MACASKILL, DONALD.
: Student of Arts, 1912-14. 10th Argyll and Sutherland Highlanders, L/Corporal.

Record of War Service

MACAULAY, DONALD.
Rainings School, Inverness. M.A. 1887; M.B., C.M. (Hons.) 1892. No. 4 Coy. Q.R.V.B., Royal Scots. South African Campaign, Civil Surgeon, 1900-2. South African Medical Corps (S.R.O.), U.D.F., Major Sept. 1914; Lieut.-Col. Nov. 1914. R.A.M.C., Lieut.-Col. Aug. 1915. S.A.M.C., Jan. 1918. German S.-W. and E. Africa and Eastern Mediterranean, 1914-18. O.B.E. (Military) Feb. 1919.

MACAULAY, DOUGLAS IAN OTTO.
Charterhouse. Student of Medicine, 1913-15 and 1917-20; M.B., Ch.B. 1920. O.T.C. Medical, Oct. 1914 to July 1915, Cadet. R.N.V.R., Surgeon-Probationer, Aug. 1915 to Nov. 1917. H.M.S. *Redpole*.

MACAULAY, GEORGE JAMES RONALDSON.
Edinburgh Academy. O.T.C. 1914-16. Student of Arts, 1916-17 and 1918-19. O.T.C. Artillery, Oct. 1916 to June 1917, Cadet; Officer Cadet June 1917. R.F.A., 2nd Lieut. Nov. 1917. Prisoner of War in Germany March 1918.

MACBEAN, DONALD.
Tarbert School, Loch Fyne. Student of Divinity, 1914-16 and 1918-19. R.A.M.C., Private April 1916; L/Corporal.

MACBEAN, DUNCAN.
George Watson's College. Student of Arts and Science, 1908-10. O.T.C. Infantry, Oct. 1909 to July 1913, Cadet. 6th Cameron Highlanders, 2nd Lieut. April 1915; Lieut. July 1917. 2/4th King's African Rifles.

MACBEATH, ANDREW GILBERT WAUCHOPE.
Royal High School. Student of Arts, 1917 and 1919. O.T.C. Infantry, Dec. 1917 to July 1918, Cadet; Officer Cadet July 1918. Highland Light Infantry, 2nd Lieut. May 1919.

MACBETH, JOHN STEWART.
George Watson's College; First XV. Cadet Corps 1905-7, Cadet Corporal. Student of Arts and Medicine, 1908-14 and 1917-19; M.A. (Hons. Classics) 1912. O.T.C. Artillery, March 1909 to Feb. 1912, Cadet. Scottish Horse, Private Aug. 1914; L/Corporal; 2nd Lieut. March 1915; Lieut. Dec. 1916. Machine-Gun Corps, Salonika, Aug. 1916 to Jan. 1918.

McCAA, JAMES IRELAND.
Edinburgh Academy. Student of Medicine, 1914-15 and 1918-19. O.T.C. Infantry, Oct. 1914 to June 1915, Cadet L/Corporal. 5th Royal Scots Fusiliers (T.), 2nd Lieut. March 1915; Lieut. Sept. 1915; Captain July 1916.

MACCABE, JOSEPH. (See p. 750.)

McCAIG, JOSEPH.
George Watson's College. M.B., Ch.B. 1913. R.A.M.C., Lieut. Oct. 1918.

McCALL, GEORGE GRACIE.
George Heriot's School. O.T.C. 1909-14, Cadet Corporal. Student of Science, 1914-15 and 1918-19. R.E., July 1915-17. R.G.A., 2nd Lieut. 1917.

Record of War Service

McCALL, ROBERT.
Ayr Academy; First XI. M.A., B.Sc. 1912. A.I.C. O.T.C. Infantry, 1910-11 and 1914-15, Cadet. R.E., Corporal July 1915. Woolwich Arsenal, 1917-19.

McCALLUM, JAMES RUSSELL.
Daniel Stewart's College. Student of Science, 1911-14 and 1919; B.Sc. 1920. O.T.C. Artillery, Oct. 1913-14, Cadet. R.F.A. (S.R.), 93rd Brigade, 2nd Lieut. Aug. 1914; Lieut. June 1915; Acting Captain Sept. 1916; Captain Nov. 1917; Acting Major April 1917. France Nov. 1914 to Feb. 1919. Dispatches Jan. 1918. M.C. Nov. 1917; Bar to M.C. March 1918.

M'CALLUM, PETER.
Student of Medicine, 1910-14; M.B., Ch.B. 1914. O.T.C. Medical, 1914-15, Cadet Sergeant. R.A.M.C. (S.R.), Lieut. April 1915; Captain Oct. 1915. M.C.

M'CALLUM, RODERICK.
M.A. (Hons. Maths.) and B.Sc. (Distinction, Nat. Phil.) 1914. R.A.M.C., Private Feb. 1915. 55th Field Ambulance. France July 1915.

M'CALLUM, WILLIAM TOPP.
Daniel Stewart's College. University O.T.C. Artillery, Feb. to July 1916, Cadet; Officer Cadet July 1916. R.F.A. (S.R.), 2nd Lieut. Oct. 1916; Lieut. April 1918. Egypt and Salonika Nov. 1916 to June 1918; India.

MacCARTHY, ALEXANDER BREMNER.
Epsom College. M.B., Ch.B. 1897. R.A.M.C., Lieut. Jan. 1917. France (Somme) April 1917 to Jan. 1918.

McCARTNEY, JAMES ELVINS.
Warwick School; First XV. O.T.C. 1906-10, Cadet Sergeant. Student of Medicine, 1910-15; M.B., Ch.B. 1915. Assistant to Professor of Pathology. O.T.C. Infantry, June 1911 to Aug. 1914, Cadet Corporal. 5th Worcestershire Regiment, 2nd Lieut. Aug. 1914; Lieut. March 1915. R.A.M.C., Lieut. Sept. 1915; Captain Sept. 1916.

McCLEAN, JOHN GERALD.
Royal Academical Institution, Belfast. University O.T.C. Infantry, May to Aug. 1915, Cadet. 9th Royal Scots, Private Aug. 1915; Corporal. France. Wounded April 1917. Prisoner of War April 1918.

McCLELLAN, ALEXANDER GEORGE.
Taunton School. Student of Medicine, 1911-16 and 1918-19. O.T.C. Artillery, 1912-16, Cadet. R.F.A. (S.R.), Officer Cadet March 1916; 2nd Lieut. Dec. 1916.

McCLURE, ALEXANDER ROBERT.
Castle-Douglas School. Student of Medicine, 1918. Hon. Artillery Company, Dec. 1914. R.E., 36th Divisional Signal Company, Lieut. July 1917. France 1915.

Record of War Service

McCLURE, IAN HYSLOP.
Dumfries Academy; First XI. Student of Medicine, 1915-16 and 1918-19. O.T.C. Artillery, Feb. to Aug. 1916, Cadet. R.N.A.S. and Royal Air Force, Nov. 1916, Lieut. Invalided out.

McCLYMONT, ALEXANDER WATSON.
George Watson's College; First XV. Student of Arts and Divinity; M.A. (Hons. Phil.) 1901. Minister, U.F. Church of Scotland. Chaplain, 4th Class, Nov. 1917. 50th, 58th, 18th, and 61st Casualty Clearing Stations. Liege Sub-Area and No. 9 B.R.C. Hospital. France 1915-16 and 1917-19; Lys April 1917.

McCLYMONT, JAMES ALEXANDER.
Ayr Academy. M.A. 1867; B.D. 1870; D.D. 1894. Minister, Church of Scotland. Chaplain, 1884; 1st Class, 1909; Hon. Chaplain, July 1914. Mobilised Sept. 1914. Hon. C.F. Nov. 1917; Principal Chaplain, July 1918. 2nd Scottish General Hospital and Forth Garrison. V.D. Dispatches Dec. 1917.

McCLYMONT, JAMES DOUGLAS.
Dalbeattie School. M.A. 1909. Schoolmaster. R.G.A., Gunner July 1916. Attached 227th and 22nd Siege Batteries.

McCONAGHEY, JOHN CUNNINGHAM.
United Services College, Westward Ho! First XV. and XI. M.B., Ch.B. 1898; M.D. 1905. R.A.M.C., Lieut. Dec. 1914-15. Civil Medical Practitioner, Central Military Hospital, Aylesbury, June 1916 to Oct. 1918.

McCONAGHY, CHRISTOPHER BIRDWOOD.
United Services College, Westward Ho! M.B., Ch.B. 1900. No. 4 Coy. Q.R.V.B., Royal Scots, 1895-8, Private. Indian Medical Service, June 1901; Major Dec. 1912. Mesopotamia Aug. 1916 to May 1918.

McCONCHIE, JAMES FLEMING.
Royal Academical Institution, Belfast. Student of Medicine, 1912-14 and 1917-20; M.B., Ch.B. 1920. Anatomy Staff, 1919. R.A.M.C., 62nd Field Ambulance, Private Sept. 1914; L/Corporal 1915. 5th King's Own Scottish Borderers (T.), 2nd Lieut. July 1916-17.

McCONNELL, ALBERT EDWARD PEEL.
M.B., Ch.B. 1913. O.T.C. Medical, June 1910 to April 1914, Cadet. R.A.M.C. (T.), Lieut.; Captain April 1915; Acting Major March 1918. 2nd South Midland Field Ambulance. M.C.

McCONNELL, ALFRED JOSEPH.
Ballymena Academy. M.B., Ch.B. 1909. R.A.M.C., Lieut. May 1917; Captain May to Dec. 1918. Salonika.

Record of War Service

McCONNELL, GEORGE.
  Foyle College, Londonderry; First XV. and XI. M.B., Ch.B. 1906; L.M. (Dublin). Rugby "Blue" and Irish International. R.A.M.C. (T.) attached Royal Serbian Army, Lieut. Nov. 1914; Captain May 1915. Divisional Medical Officer, 64th General and 33rd Stationary Hospitals.

McCOOL, PATRICK.
  St George's College, Weybridge; First XI. M.B., Ch.B. 1911. O.T.C. Medical, 1908-12, Cadet Sergeant. 23rd London General Hospital, 1915-17. R.A.M.C., Lieut. Sept. 1917; Captain March 1918; Major Sept. 1918. Military Hospital, Hemel Hempstead.

MACCORMAC, HENRY.
  M.B., Ch.B. 1903; M.D. 1916; F.R.C.P. (Lond.) 1909. French Red Cross, Jan. 1915. R.A.M.C., Lieut. and Captain June 1915; Major Dec. 1916; Acting Lieut.-Col.; Dermatologist. France Jan. 1915-19. Dispatches Nov. 1918 and 1919. C.B.E. (Military) 1919. Médaille d'Honneur de l'Assistance publique.

McCORMACK, TERENCE JOSEPH.
  Blackrock College, County Dublin. Athletics. University O.T.C. Infantry, March to July 1917, Cadet L/Corporal. Fife Volunteer Force, Aug. 1916. 9th King's Own Yorkshire Light Infantry, 2nd Lieut. Dec. 1917; Lieut. June 1918. France Aug. 1918. Wounded Nov. 1918.

MACCORMICK, SIR ALEXANDER.
  M.B., Ch.B. 1880; M.D. 1885; F.R.C.S. (Eng.) 1900. No. 4 Coy. Q.E.R. to 1881, Private. South African Campaign. Australian Army Medical Corps, Colonel; 3rd Australian General Hospital, Consulting Surgeon.

McCOWAN, PETER KNIGHT.
  Perth Academy. M.B., Ch.B. 1912. O.T.C. Artillery, July 1909 to Feb. 1912, Cadet. R.A.M.C., Lieut. July 1916; Captain July 1917; Major Sept. 1918. 10th Royal Highlanders (Black Watch), Secunderabad, C.F.A.; 15th Casualty Clearing Hospital, Asia Minor.

McCRACKEN, ALLAN SOMERVILLE.
  George Watson's College. Student of Medicine, 1914-16 and 1917-19. O.T.C. Artillery, Oct. 1914 to May 1916. 10th Seaforth Highlanders, Private 1916; 2nd Lieut. 1917. France 1917-18; Somme, Arras, Cambrai.

McCRACKEN, ANGUS MURRAY.
  Oundle School. O.T.C. 1909-12, Cadet Sergeant. Student of Science, 1913-14. O.T.C. Artillery, Oct. 1913 to Aug. 1914, Cadet. R.F.A. (S.R.), 2nd Lieut. Aug. 1914; 2nd Lieut. (Regulars) May 1915; Acting Captain Sept. 1916; Lieut. July 1917; Acting Major June 1918-19; Adjutant. 147th Brigade, Oct. 1915 to Aug. 1916. M.C. and Dispatches (Gallipoli) Nov. 1915.

Record of War Service

McCRACKEN, KENNETH MILNE.
Epsom College. O.T.C. 1908-12, Cadet L/Corporal. Student of Medicine, 1912-14 and 1918-19. O.T.C. Artillery, Feb. 1913 to Oct. 1914, Cadet. Scottish Horse, Private Aug. 1914. R.F.A. (S.R.), 2nd Lieut. Sept. 1914; Lieut. June 1915; Acting Captain Nov. 1916; Captain Nov. 1917. Attached Royal Air Force, Jan. 1918. Wounded and Gassed July 1917.

McCREADIE, HAROLD WILLIAM LEWIS.
Daniel Stewart's College. Student of Science, 1918-19. O.T.C. Engineers, Dec. 1913 to Oct. 1914, Cadet. R.E. (T.), City of Dundee (Fortress), Sapper Oct. 1914. R.A.S.C. (M.T.), 2nd Lieut. Jan. 1917; Lieut. July 1918. France Sept. 1915.

M'CRINDLE, JAMES DOIG.
M.B., C.M. 1896; D.P.H. (Camb.) 1901. R.A.M.C. (T.), Sanitary Section, Captain Jan. 1909.

McCRIRRICK, NORMAN.
Student of Arts, 1909-10. Royal Air Force, Lieut.-Instructor.

MACCULLIE, ALLAN NICOLSON.
Stromness School. Student of Arts, 1912-15; M.A. 1915. 2nd and 3rd Scots Guards, Private Nov. 1915; L/Corporal Oct. 1916; Corporal June 1918; L/Sergeant Oct. 1918. France Feb. 1917. Gassed at Ypres Aug. 1917.

MacCULLOCH, ANDREW FRANCIS.
George Heriot's School. M.A., B.Sc. 1914. A.I.C. Research Scholar, Bacteriology. O.T.C. Infantry, 1910-13, Cadet. R.F.A. (T.), 1st Lowland Brigade, 2nd Lieut. July 1915; Lieut. Aug. 1916; Captain Aug. 1918. Mesopotamia. Invalided out. Indian Army Reserve, Aug. 1918.

McCULLOCH, HUGH.
Leith Academy. Student of Science, 1911-14. 6th and 11th Royal Scots, Private Aug. 1914; L/Corporal Nov. 1914. 5th Connaught Rangers, 2nd Lieut. Jan. 1915; Lieut. July 1917 to April 1919.

McCULLOCH, JOHN LEITCH. (See p. 750.)

MacCULLOCH, MELLIS.
Falkirk High School. Student of Medicine, 1919. 2/7th Argyll and Sutherland Highlanders, Private April 1915. R.E. (Special Coy.), L/Corporal.

M'CUNE, LANCELOT GORDON.
M.B., Ch.B. 1907. R.A.M.C., Lieut.; Captain May 1916; Acting Major Jan. 1918.

M'CUNE, WILLIAM SIMPSON.
M.B., Ch.B. 1907. R.A.M.C. (V.). South African Campaign, 1899-1901. R.A.M.C. (T.), Lieut. Jan. 1914; Captain April 1915. R.G.A. Invalided out Feb. 1919.

McCUTCHEON, JOHN.
M.B., Ch.B. 1906. Royal Navy, Surgeon.

Record of War Service

McDAVID, JAMES WALLACE.
: M.A., B.Sc. 1908; D.Sc. 1915; M.Sc. (Vict.). O.T.C. Artillery, Nov. 1908-10, Cadet. R.F.A. (S.R.), Lieut. Oct. 1910; Captain Aug. 1916. France. Nobel's Explosive Works.

MACDIARMID, EUAN.
: Edinburgh Academy; First XV. O.T.C. 1914-17, Cadet Pipe-Major. Student of Arts, 1918-19. O.T.C. Artillery, 1918, Cadet Bombardier. R.F.A., Officer Cadet Oct. 1918.

McDIARMID, PATRICK JAMES.
: Perth Academy. Student of Medicine, 1914-15 and 1918-19. O.T.C. Artillery, Oct. 1914 to May 1915, Cadet. 14th Argyll and Sutherland Highlanders, Private May 1915. Transferred 7th Royal Highlanders (Black Watch), June 1916.

MACDIARMID, PETER.
: M.B., Ch.B. 1905; M.D. 1911. R.A.M.C., Hon. Captain Jan. 1915; Hon. Lieut.-Col. Oct. 1917. Alder Hey Military Surgical Hospital, Liverpool. O.B.E. June 1919.

MACDONALD, A. A.
: Student of Arts. 5th Seaforth Highlanders (T.), L/Corporal.

MACDONALD, ADAM DAVIDSON.
: Dundee High School. Student of Arts and Science, 1913-15. Neil Arnott Scholar. M.A. 1919. O.T.C. Infantry, 1915-16, Cadet. 12th Scottish Rifles, 2nd Lieut. Jan. 1916. R.N.A.S., July 1916; R.N.V.R., Lieut. Oct. 1917. Royal Air Force, Captain April 1918. Dispatches.

MACDONALD, ALASTAIR HUGH.
: Forres Academy. Student of Law, 1912-14. 6th Seaforth Highlanders, Dec. 1914; Lieut. June 1916; Acting Captain and Adjutant April 1918; Temp. Captain, 1919; Staff Captain "A," First Army. France. M.C. and two Bars.

MACDONALD, ALEXANDER RAMSAY.
: Arbroath High School. Student of Science, 1914 and 1919. O.T.C. Artillery, Aug. to Oct. 1915, Cadet. R.F.A., 156th Brigade, and R.H.A., 2nd Lieut. Oct. 1915; Lieut. July 1917. France. Wounded Dec. 1917.

MACDONALD, ANDREW EDWARD.
: Benedict's Abbey, Fort Augustus. Student of Law, 1899-1901. 4th Cameron Highlanders, Captain; Major June 1916; General Staff, Dec. 1917.

MACDONALD, ANGUS.
: Dunfermline High School. Student of Medicine, 1915-16 and 1919. R.N.V.R., H.M. T.B.D. *Nicator*, Surgeon-Probationer, April 1917.

MACDONALD, ANGUS.
: Greenock Academy. Student of Science, 1911-14. O.T.C. Artillery, Oct. 1908 to Nov. 1913, Cadet B.S.M. R.F.A. (S.R.), 2nd Lieut. Aug. 1914; Lieut June 1915; Captain Nov. 1917. France. Wounded June 1915.

Record of War Service

MACDONALD, ANGUS GRAHAM.
Keith School. M.B., C.M. 1890; M.D. 1911; D.P.H. (Manchester) 1909, and D.T.M. (Liverpool) 1910. No. 4 Coy. Q.R.V.B., Royal Scots, 1886-90, Private. R.A.M.C., Lieut. Oct. 1916; Captain March 1917; Major Jan. 1919. Assistant to Consultant in Malaria, War Office. O.B.E. June 1919.

MACDONALD, ANGUS HUGH.
Bell Baxter Academy, Cupar Fife. Student of Law. Solicitor, 1907. R.G.A. (T.), April 1910; Temp. Captain May 1915; Captain May 1917. Argyll Mountain Battery and 4th Highland (Mountain) Brigade. Gallipoli, Egypt, and Salonika. Dispatches June 1915. M.C. Oct. 1915.

McDONALD, CHARLES.
Student of Medicine, 1911-17. M.B., Ch.B. 1916. Royal Navy, Surgeon-Probationer, Dec. 1914; Surgeon Oct. 1916. H.M.S. *Eaglet*.

McDONALD, DAVID THOMPSON.
George Watson's College. Student of Medicine, 1914-15 and 1918-19. Anatomy Staff, 1919. O.T.C. Artillery, Nov. 1914 to Aug. 1915, Cadet. 7th Northumberland Fusiliers (T.), 2nd Lieut. Sept. 1915; Lieut. July 1917.

MacDONALD, DONALD.
Taunton School; First XV. and XI. M.A. 1910; B.Sc. 1915. O.T.C. Infantry, 1908-16, Cadet. Somerset Light Infantry, 2nd Lieut.; Temp. Captain 1916-17. Attached Staff, 20th Division, 1918.

MACDONALD, DONALD.
Royal High School. Student of Arts, 1916. O.T.C. Artillery, 1916, Cadet Sergeant; Officer Cadet July 1916. R.F.A., 2nd Lieut. Oct. 1916; Lieut. April 1918. 20th Heavy Battery, R.G.A. Egypt Dec. 1916; Salonika Feb. 1917 to Jan. 1919.

MACDONALD, DONALD ROBERTSON. (See p. 751.)

MACDONALD, DOUGLAS OVENSTONE.
Student of Medicine, 1911-15 and 1916-18. M.B., Ch.B. 1918. O.T.C. Artillery, Oct. 1912-14, Cadet. R.F.A., 2nd Lieut. Sept. 1914. R.A.M.C. (S.R.), Lieut. June 1918. Mesopotamia, France, Germany.

MACDONALD, DUNCAN DAVID FARQUHARSON.
Sharp's Institute, Perth. Student of Arts and Divinity, 1879; M.A. 1885. Minister, Church of Scotland. 2nd V.B. King's Own Scottish Borderers, Private Feb. 1917. Recruiting Officer. Chaplain, March 1918.

MACDONALD, ERIC.
Greenock Academy. Student of Science, 1910-14. O.T.C. Artillery, 1908-12, Cadet B.S.M. R.F.A., 2nd Lieut. Aug. 1915; Lieut. July 1917. M.C.

MACDONALD, GEORGE.
Fettes College; First XV. and XI. M.A. 1907; M.B., Ch.B. 1911. R.A.M.C., Lieut. Feb. 1916; Captain Feb. 1917.

Record of War Service

MacDONALD, GEORGE.
Royal High School. B.Sc. 1910. A.M.I.C.E. O.T.C. Engineers, Jan. 1910 to Dec. 1913, Cadet Corporal. A.S.C. (M.T.), Sept. 1914. R.E., 2nd Lieut. Feb. 1915; Lieut. Sept. 1915; Acting Adjutant Sept 1915 to Oct. 1917.

MACDONALD, GEORGE ALEXANDER.
George Watson's and Daniel Stewart's Colleges. M.B., Ch.B. 1914. O.T.C. Medical, 1910-14, Cadet Corporal. R.A.M.C. (S.R.), Lieut. Feb. 1914. Mobilised Jan. 1915; Captain July 1915.

MACDONALD, GEORGE S.
Kelso High School; First XV. University O.T.C. Artillery, 1917-18, Cadet. Royal Air Force, Flight Cadet, Feb. 1918.

McDONALD, HECTOR ARCHIBALD.
Linlithgow Academy. Student of Science, 1917-20. O.T.C. Artillery, Dec. 1917 to June 1918, Cadet; Officer Cadet June 1918. R.G.A., 2nd Lieut. April 1919.

MACDONALD, HECTOR JOHN.
Royal High School. Student of Medicine, 1916 and 1918. O.T.C. Artillery, 1916-17, Cadet Sergeant. R.F.A. (S.R.), 176th Brigade, 2nd Lieut. May 1917.

MACDONALD, IAN FARQUHARSON.
George Watson's College. Cadet Corps 1906-8, Corporal. Student of Arts and Medicine, 1910-13. O.T.C. Artillery, 1912-14, Cadet. R.F.A., 2nd Lieut. Sept. 1914; Lieut. July 1915. 178th, 179th, and 6th "B" Reserve Brigades. France. M.C. Feb. 1918.

MACDONALD, IAN GEORGE.
George Watson's College. Student of Science, 1918. 1/2nd Lovat Scouts, Sept. 1914; 2nd Lieut. Nov. 1917. Attached 5th Seaforth Highlanders.

MACDONALD, JACK.
George Watson's College. M.B., Ch.B. South African Medical Corps, Captain.

MACDONALD, JAMES.
Sharpe Educational Institution, Perth. M.A. 1901; LL.B. 1902. Advocate, 1902. General List, Lieut. Dec. 1916. War Office. Labour Department, Ministry of Munitions, Dec. 1917-18.

MACDONALD, JAMES ALEXANDER.
Student of Arts and Medicine, 1907-14; M.A. 1910. O.T.C. Artillery, 1908-13, Cadet B.S.M. R.F.A., Lieut. Jan. 1917; Acting Major Aug. 1917. France and Italy. D.S.O.; Croix de Guerre; Ordre du Mérite.

McDONALD, JAMES HALDANE.
M.B., C.M. 1894. Indian Medical Service, Lieut.-Col. July 1914.

Record of War Service

MACDONALD, JAMES HAROLD.
George Watson's College. M.A. 1899; LL.B. 1901. Writer to the Signet, 1904. 5th V.B. Royal Scots, 2nd Lieut. Dec. 1896. 7th and 9th Royal Scots (T.), Captain and Adjutant; Major June 1916. France April 1917. Wounded and invalided home May 1917. Tay Defences, 1918-19. T.D. May 1919.

MACDONALD, JAMES RONALD.
Madras College, St Andrews. M.A. 1880. Minister, Church of Scotland. 3rd V.B. King's Own Scottish Borderers, Private April 1918; Corporal July 1918-19.

MACDONALD, JOHN.
Student of Arts, 1913-14. 3/1st Lovat Scouts, Private March 1915; 2nd Lieut. Aug. 1916; Lieut. Feb. 1918. India and Mesopotamia 1917-18.

MACDONALD, JOHN.
M.B., Ch.B. 1908; L.R.C.P. & S. (Edin.) and L.F.P.S. (Glasg.) 1908. Australian Army Medical Corps, Captain; Major April 1917. 2nd Light Horse Regiment. Dardanelles 1915.

MACDONALD, JOHN ALEXANDER.
Inverness Royal Academy. Student of Arts, 1913-15. O.T.C. Artillery, Oct. 1914 to Sept. 1915, Cadet. R.F.A., 2nd Lieut. Oct. 1915; Lieut. July 1916. 3rd Highland (Howitzer) and 8th Brigades.

McDONALD, JOHN ROUGH.
George Watson's College. O.T.C. 1914-15, Cadet L/Corporal. Student of Medicine, 1915-16 and 1918-19. Anatomy Staff, 1919. O.T.C. Infantry, 1915-17, Cadet; Officer Cadet. 11th Border Regiment, 2nd Lieut. April 1917. France 1917-18; Nieuport, Ypres. Wounded Nov. 1917. M.C. Feb. 1918.

MacDONALD, JOHN VALENTINE.
George Watson's College. M.B., Ch.B. 1908. Indian Medical Service, Captain 1913; Brevet Major 1919. 29th Punjabis; 176th Indian Field Artillery. British East Africa and South Persia. Dispatches. M.C.

MACDONALD, NORMAN DORAN.
Student of Law, 1884-8. Advocate, 1888. 9th Royal Scots (T.), Captain. France. Prisoner of War in Germany (Gütersloh) June 1915.

MACDONALD, NORMAN JAMES.
Dollar Academy. O.T.C. 1906-11. Student of Law, 1918. Royal Canadian Dragoons, Sergeant Aug. 1914. Royal Scots, 2nd Lieut. Nov. 1916. M.C. March 1917.

MACDONALD, PATRICK THOMSON TULLOCH.
Aberdeen Grammar School. M.A. (Aberdeen) 1903; M.B., Ch.B. 1914. R.A.M.C., Lieut. Sept. 1915; Captain Sept. 1916 to April 1919. France Feb. 1917 to April 1919.

Record of War Service

MacDONALD, PETER HAY.
M.B., Ch.B. 1899. Cert. T.M. (Lond.). R.A.M.C., Lieut. Jan. 1915; Captain Jan. 1916; Major March 1918 to April 1919. 11th Sherwood Foresters, France. Glencorse Depôt, Royal Scots. Dundee War Hospital. Wounded at first Battle of the Somme.

MacDONALD, RANALD.
Daniel Stewart's College; First XV. M.B., Ch.B. 1908; M.D. 1913. Volunteer Medical Staff Corps, 1903-7, Sergeant. R.A.M.C., Lieut. July 1915; Captain July 1916; Major and D.A.D.M.S., Oct. 1918. Mudros July 1915; Alexandria and Port Said. O.B.E. and Dispatches June 1919.

MACDONALD, ROBERT ARTHUR SCRYMGEOUR.
Broughton School, Edinburgh. Student of Science, 1915-17 and 1918-20. O.T.C. Infantry, Oct. 1915 to March 1917, Cadet; Officer Cadet March 1917. King's Own Scottish Borderers and Machine-Gun Corps, 2nd Lieut. Sept. 1917.

MACDONALD, ROBERT SIMPSON.
Harris Academy, Dundee. Student of Arts, 1915-16. O.T.C. Infantry, Oct. 1915 to July 1916, Cadet. Royal Highlanders (Black Watch), Private July 1916. Machine-Gun Corps, France. Wounded July 1917.

MACDONALD, RONALD ANNANDALE.
Edinburgh Academy. O.T.C. 1914-17, Cadet Corporal. Student of Medicine, 1919. O.T.C. Artillery, May to Dec. 1917, Cadet Corporal; Officer Cadet Dec. 1917. R.F.A., 2nd Lieut. Aug. 1918.

MACDONALD, RONALD ROSS MUNRO.
Royal Academy, Tain. Student of Law, 1910-12. 4th Seaforth Highlanders, Lieut.; Captain June 1917. 2nd Garrison Battn., Northumberland Fusiliers.

McDONALD, SAMUEL.
Robert Gordon's College, Aberdeen. Student of Law, 1918. 5th Gordon Highlanders, 2nd Lieut. 1907; Major Dec. 1914; Lieut.-Col. May 1918. France. Wounded. Four times Mentioned in Dispatches. D.S.O. Jan. 1916; two Bars to D.S.O. Jan. 1918; C.M.G. July 1919.

McDONALD, STUART.
Dumfries Academy. M.A. (Durham); M.B., C.M. 1896; M.D. 1907; F.R.C.P. (Edin.) 1904. Examiner in Pathology, 1904-8; Professor of Pathology, Durham University. Durham University O.T.C. Infantry, 2nd Lieut. 1912; Captain 1914. R.A.M.C. (T.), March 1915. Pathologist, 1st Northern General Hospital. Inspector, Bacteriological Laboratories, Northern Command.

MACDONALD, STUART A.
George Watson's College. University O.T.C. Artillery, 1917, Cadet; Officer Cadet Aug. 1917. R.G.A. (S.R.), 2nd Lieut. Dec. 1917 to June 1919.

Record of War Service

MACDONALD, WILLIAM.
  Inverness High School. M.B., Ch.B. 1909; M.D. 1913. R.A.M.C., Lieut. April 1915; Captain April 1916 to Dec. 1918. France.

MACDONALD, WILLIAM ALEXANDER.
  Royal High School. Rugby International. Student of Law. Solicitor. 6th Gordon Highlanders (V.) and (T.), Major June 1913. France Nov. 1914-18. T.D. Médaille de la Reconnaissance Française (3rd Class).

MACDONALD, WILLIAM KELMAN.
  George Watson's College. M.B., Ch.B. 1907; M.D. 1910. R.A.M.C., Lieut. June 1915; Captain June 1916.

MACDONALD, WILLIAM KING HAMILTON.
  M.A. 1899. Minister, Presbyterian Church of England. 4th V.B. Northumberland Fusiliers, Private Nov. 1917; 2nd Lieut. Aug. 1918.

MACDONALD, WILLIAM MARSHALL.
  Otago High School, New Zealand. First XV. B.Sc. (New Zealand); M.B., Ch.B. 1895; M.D. 1911; M.R.C.P. (Lond.) 1918. Médecin-Major Assimilé, French A.M.S., Assistant Neurologist, June 1915. N.Z. Medical Corps, April 1917; Major and Temp. Lieut.-Col. N.Z. Exp. Force April 1918. C.B.E. (Military) Dec. 1918.

MACDONALD, WILLIAM SUTHERLAND.
  George Watson's College. Student of Medicine, 1914-15 and 1918-19. O.T.C. Artillery, 1914-15, Cadet. 14th Argyll and Sutherland Highlanders, Private May 1915; 2nd Lieut. Border Regiment. France 1916-17 and 1918. Gassed. M.C. May 1918.

McDOUGAL, ARTHUR ROBERT.
  Edinburgh Academy. Student of Science, 1897-8. Lothians and Border Horse, 1902; Sergeant Aug. 1914. Fife and Forfar Yeomanry (T.), Lieut. Nov. 1914; Acting Captain Dec. 1916; Captain April 1918. 14th (Fife and Forfar Yeomanry). Royal Highlanders (Black Watch). Gallipoli, Egypt, Palestine, and France.

McDOUGAL, JOHN WALTER.
  Kelso High School. Student of Law, 1911-14. King's Own Scottish Borderers, 2nd Lieut. Oct. 1914; Captain Aug. 1916. Dispatches April 1917.

MacDOUGALL, ALEXANDER JAMES.
  Clifton College. M.B., C.M. 1894. R.A.M.C. July 1896; Major 1908; Lieut.-Col. March 1915; Temp. Colonel Dec. 1917. France. Dispatches Feb. 1915 and Dec. 1918. C.M.G.

McDOUGALL, DUNCAN.
  George Watson's College. M.A. 1909. Minister, Free Church of Scotland. Chaplain to Royal Naval Brigade, interned in Holland, June 1915 to Dec. 1916.

MacDOUGALL, G. A.
  Student of Science, 1892-3. 9th Canadian Field Artillery, Major. France 1915.

Record of War Service

McDOUGALL, JAMES CURRIE.
: M.A. 1914; B.Sc. 1916. O.T.C. Infantry, 1915-16, Cadet; Officer Cadet April 1916. 4th Argyll and Sutherland Highlanders, 2nd Lieut. Aug. 1916; Lieut. Feb. 1918. 7th North Staffordshire Regiment. 1st Duke of Wellington's Regiment. India, Baku, Mesopotamia, Dec. 1916.

McDOUGALL, JOHN GORDON.
: M.B., Ch.B. 1900. R.A.M.C., Lieut.

MacDOUGALL, ROBERT STEWART.
: M.A. (Hons. Nat. Sc.) 1889; D.Sc. 1898. Lecturer in Agricultural Entomology. O.T.C. Infantry, June 1916-18, Lieut. Lecturer to Troops at Home and in France, 1917-18.

McDOUGALL, WILLIAM STEWART.
: Chanonry School, Aberdeen. M.B., C.M. 1889. R.A.M.C., Lieut. Aug. 1916.

McDOWALL, DAVID.
: George Watson's College. University O.T.C. Artillery, 1916, Cadet; Officer Cadet Sept. 1916. North Scottish R.G.A. (T.), 2nd Lieut. Dec. 1916; Lieut. June 1918. 17th Siege Battery, R.G.A., France. Wounded.

McDOWALL, IRVINE.
: Harrison College, Barbados. Student of Medicine, 1910-15; M.B., Ch.B. 1915. British West Indies Regiment, Surgeon-Lieut. Nov. 1917; Surgeon-Captain Nov. 1918. 57th General Hospital, Marseilles.

McDOWALL, ROBERT JOHN STEWART.
: George Watson's College. O.T.C. 1907-9, Cadet L/Corporal. Student of Medicine, 1910-15; M.B., Ch.B. 1915. O.T.C. Medical, Dec. 1914-15, Cadet. R.A.M.C. (T.), Lieut. Nov. 1915; Captain May 1916; Major May 1919. 91st Sanitary Section, Egypt. D.A.D.M.S., G.H.Q., Egyptian Exp. Force.

McDOWALL, WILLIAM ANDSON. (See p. 751.)

MacDUFF, PETER
: M.A. 1883. Schoolmaster. 1/7th Royal Highlanders (Black Watch) (T.), 1884; Major Aug. 1915; Lieut.-Col. 1916. Area Commandant, Third Army Staff, July 1917-19. T.D. 1908.

McEACHRAN, DAVID.
: Broughton School, Edinburgh; First XV. Student of Medicine, 1912-17; M.B., Ch.B. 1917. O.T.C. Medical, Aug. 1914 to July 1915, Cadet. Royal Navy, Surgeon-Probationer, July 1915. H.M.S. *Linnet*. R.A.M.C., Lieut. Aug. 1917; Captain Aug. 1918.

MacECHERN, CHARLES.
: Inverness High School. Student of Arts, 1885-7. First XI. Association. United States Army, Nevada Regiment, 1898; Corporal; Quartermaster. Spanish American War and Great War.

Record of War Service

MacECHERN, DUGALD.
Inverness High School. M.A. 1887; B.D. 1890. First XI. Association. Minister, Church of Scotland. 5th Seaforth Highlanders, Private and 2nd Lieut. Jan. 1915; Lieut. Aug. 1915.

MacEDWARD, LACHLAN.
Kingussie School. Student of Arts, 1912-15; M.A. 1915. 14th Argyll and Sutherland Highlanders, Private May 1915; Lewis Gun, L/Corporal Jan. 1917; Corporal April 1917. Wounded July 1917.

M'EWAN, GEORGE CLAZY.
Edinburgh Academy. O.T.C. 1909-10. Student of Medicine, 1910-14 and 1915-17; M.B., Ch.B. 1916. O.T.C. Artillery, Oct. 1910 to Aug. 1914, Cadet Corporal. R.F.A. (S.R.), 2nd Lieut. Aug. 1914; Lieut. June 1915. R.A.M.C. (S.R.), Lieut. Jan. 1917; Captain Jan. 1918. France. Wounded May 1915.

McEWAN, JOHN GORDON.
George Watson's College. O.T.C. 1910-12. Student of Science, 1913-14. 15th Royal Scots, Private Sept. 1914. R.F.C., 2nd Lieut. May 1915; Lieut. June 1916. Wounded and Prisoner of War in Germany, Jan. 1916 to Nov. 1918.

McEWAN, PETER.
Perth Academy. M.A. 1901; M.B., Ch.B. 1905; F.R.C.S. (Edin.) 1907. Assistant in Surgery, 1906-7. R.A.M.C. (T.), Lieut. April 1915; Captain Oct. 1915. 2/1st West Riding Casualty Clearing Station, France. Croix de Guerre (French) May 1918.

McEWEN, BRUCE.
Fettes College. M.A. 1897; D. Phil.; B.D. 1900. Gunning Lecturer. Minister, Church of Scotland. 8th Royal Scots (T.) Oct. 1905, Captain Jan. 1911; Major May 1915. Machine-Gun Corps, April 1917 to Feb. 1918. France Nov. 1914 to June 1916. Dispatches Dec. 1917.

McEWEN, EWYN ALASTAIR.
Edinburgh Academy. Student of Law, 1909-10. Lothians and Border Horse, Private Sept. 1914. 3/9th, 3rd, and 2nd Argyll and Sutherland Highlanders (S.R.), 2nd Lieut. Feb. 1915; Lieut. Oct. 1915; Captain Aug. 1916; Acting Major Feb. 1919. 1st Cameron Highlanders, May to Aug. 1915. France 1915-19; The Rhine 1919. Wounded at Cambrai Aug. 1915. M.C. Oct. 1917; Bar to M.C. Oct. 1918.

MacEWEN, JOHN DUGALD.
George Watson's College. M.A. 1905; M.B., Ch.B. 1910; F.R.C.S. (Edin.) 1913. Anatomy Staff, 1913-14. R.A.M.C., Lieut. March 1915; Captain March 1916; Acting Major 1918. Turkey 1915. 40th Stationary Hospital, France.

Record of War Service

McEWEN, THOMAS.
George Watson's College. Student of Medicine; L.R.C.P. & S. (Edin.), L.R.F.P.S. (Glasg.) 1910. O.T.C. Medical, 1908-9, Cadet Q.M.S. R.A.M.C. (S.R.), Lieut. May 1914; Captain April 1915; Acting Major Jan. 1918. Egypt and France. Wounded. M.C.

McEWEN, WALTER DOUGLAS.
Ewart High School, Newton-Stewart. Student of Science, 1918. Royal Scots, Private Aug. 1914. Machine-Gun Corps, March 1916 to Dec. 1918.

MacEWEN, WILLIAM GEORGE.
George Watson's College; First XV. M.A. (Hons. Maths.), B.Sc. 1913. Neil Arnott and Gray Scholar. O.T.C. Artillery, Oct. 1910 to July 1914, Cadet Q.M.S. R.F.A. (S.R.), 2nd Lieut. June 1914; Lieut. April 1915; Temp. Captain Sept. 1915; Captain July 1917. Attached R.H.A. Royal Arsenal, July 1917. France. Wounded at Loos Sept. 1915. Mention Aug. 1918.

MacFARLANE, BRYCE McINTYRE.
George Watson's College. Student of Medicine, 1918. Seaforth Highlanders, Private Aug. 1915, L/Corporal Nov. 1915; Corporal Jan. 1916; Acting Sergeant Jan. 1917. Royal Highlanders (Black Watch), 2nd Lieut. June 1917; Lieut. Dec. 1918.

MACFARLANE, DAVID WILSON.
Boroughmuir School. Student of Science, 1918. 1/4th King's Own Scottish Borderers, Private Jan. 1918. Wounded Sept. 1918.

MACFARLANE, DUGALD.
Royal High School. Student of Arts and Divinity, 1889-95. Minister, Church of Scotland. Chaplain, 1/5th Seaforth Highlanders; Captain Dec. 1914. 51st Division, France.

McFARLANE, FRITIOF NORMAN.
Whitgift Grammar School, Croydon. O.T.C. 1909-12. Student of Medicine, 1914-15 and 1918-19. O.T.C. Artillery, Oct. 1914 to May 1915, Cadet. R.F.A., 44th Battery, 2nd Lieut. May 1915; Lieut. July 1917. Mesopotamia and Persia June 1916 to Feb. 1919.

MACFARLANE, JAMES.
Student of Law, 1900-2. 2nd Rhodesian Regiment, L/Corporal. British East Africa.

MACFARLANE, PETER REID CHALMERS.
George Heriot's School. Student of Science, 1912-15 and 1918-19; B.Sc. 1919. 8th Seaforth Highlanders, Private April 1915; L/Corporal; Sergeant Aug. 1916. Royal Air Force, Officer Cadet Aug. 1918. France.

Record of War Service

McFARLANE, WILFRID.
: George Watson's College. M.B., Ch.B. 1902; L.R.C.P. & S. (Edin.), and L.F.P.S. (Glasg.) 1902. R.A.M.C., Lieut. Dec. 1914; Captain Dec. 1915. M.C. Dec. 1916, and Bar to M.C. Nov. 1917.

McFEE, WILLIAM GEORGE.
: M.B., C.M. 1885. R.A.M.C. (T.), Captain.

MACFIE, JOHN DANIEL ALEXANDER.
: Montrose Academy and Dunfermline High School. Student of Arts, 1913-14. O.T.C. Artillery, Aug. to Sept. 1914, Cadet. 11th and 9th Royal Highlanders (Black Watch), 2nd Lieut. Sept. 1914. R.F.C., May 1916. Wounded and taken Prisoner Aug. 1916. Repatriated Sept. 1917. Invalided out Sept. 1918.

MACFIE, ROBERT ANDREW SCOTT.
: Oundle School. M.A. (Camb.). Cambridge University Rifle Volunteers, 1887-9. B.Sc. 1891. Liverpool Scottish, 1900-7. 1/10th Liverpool (Scottish) Regiment, Aug. 1914; Colour-Sergeant Sept. 1914; C.Q.M.S. Feb. 1915; R.Q.M.S. Aug. 1917. France Nov. 1914 to Sept. 1916, and Feb. 1917 to April 1919. Dispatches July 1919. M.M. Oct. 1916.

MACFIE, RONALD BUTE.
: George Watson's College. M.B., Ch.B. 1910; F.R.C.S. (Edin.) 1912. O.T.C. Artillery, Oct. 1906 to Dec. 1909. R.A.M.C., Captain Dec. 1914; Major Jan. 1918. 36th Casualty Clearing Station. Dispatches Feb. 1919. O.B.E. June 1919.

MACFIE, THOMAS HATELY.
: George Watson's College. M.B., C.M. 1895. R.A.M.C., Lieut. Jan. 1916-18. M.O., Men's V.A.D., Sussex 47. Egyptian Exp. Force.

MACFIGGANS, ROBERT.
: Falkirk High School. Student of Arts, 1916-17 and 1918-19. R.G.A., Gunner July 1917.

McGARRITY, JOHN.
: George Watson's College. Student of Medicine, 1910-16; M.B., Ch.B. 1915. O.T.C. Medical, Nov. 1914 to May 1916, Cadet. Resident, R.I.E., Oct. 1915 to March 1916. R.A.M.C., Lieut. May 1916; Captain May 1917. India, Palestine, and Egypt, June 1916-19. Hospital Ship, Mediterranean, 1918-19.

MACGARROL, ROBERT.
: Inverness Royal Academy. Student of Medicine, 1912-16 and 1918-19. O.T.C. Infantry, Oct. 1914 to Nov. 1915, and Medical, Dec. 1915-16, Cadet. R.N.V.R., Surgeon-Probationer, June 1916 to Oct. 1918. H.M.S. *Ruby*.

McGEACHY, JAMES ANDREWS.
: Daniel Stewart's College. Cadet Corps 1913-16; Cadet Corporal. Student of Science, 1916-17. O.T.C. Artillery, 1917, Cadet; Officer Cadet Aug. 1917. R.E., 63rd Field Coy., 2nd Lieut. Nov. 1917; Lieut. May to Aug. 1919.

Record of War Service

McGEORGE, JAMES.
Merchiston Castle. Student of Law, 1909-11. Law Agent, 1913. 5th King's Own Scottish Borderers (T.), Lieut.; Captain June 1916.

MacGIBBON, JAMES.
George Watson's College. M.A. 1884; B.D. 1887. Minister, Church of Scotland. Chaplain, April 1915-16. Chaplain (T.), 2nd Class, 1917. France, Festubert, 1915. Dispatches and M.C. June 1916. Order of St Sava (Class V.), May 1919.

MacGIBBON, THOMAS ARTHUR.
Invercargill High School, New Zealand. M.B., Ch.B. 1905; M.D. 1918; F.R.C.S. (Edin.) 1911; B.A., B.Sc. N.Z. Medical Corps, Captain 1908; Lieut.-Col. 1916. A.D.M.S., Canterbury Military District, 1916-18.

MacGILCHRIST, ARCHIBALD CURRIE.
M.B., Ch.B. 1898; M.D. 1909; M.R.C.P. (Lond.) 1908. Indian Medical Service, Major July 1911.

McGILCHRIST, JOHN.
M.A. 1901. Student of Medicine, 1911-16 and 1918-19. 3rd Seaforth Highlanders, Private.

McGILL, HENRY MONCRIEFF.
Durham. O.T.C. 1914-15, Cadet L/Corporal. Student of Medicine, 1918. Argyll and Sutherland Highlanders, Corporal March 1916. Highland Light Infantry, 2nd Lieut. Nov. 1916; Lieut. May 1918.

McGILL, NEIL.
Aitkenhead School. Student of Arts, 1910-13. Chaplain (Captain) May 1916 to July 1917. France. 9th Highland Light Infantry. Somme. Boulogne Base Hospital.

MacGILLIVRAY, ALEXANDER GORDON.
Edinburgh Academy. Student of Medicine, 1912-15 and 1918-20; M.B., Ch.B. 1920. Dresser, 2nd Scottish General Hospital, Craigleith, Sept. 1914 to July 1915. 2/7th Lancashire Fusiliers, 2nd Lieut. July 1915; Lieut. Dec. 1916.

McGILLIVRAY, DONALD.
Jarrow School. Student of Arts, 1915-16 and 1918-19. 2nd Scottish Rifles, Private March 1916; Corporal July 1917; Officer Cadet July 1918. 3rd Royal Highlanders (Black Watch), 2nd Lieut. Jan. 1919. France.

MacGILLIVRAY, FRANCIS PATRICK.
Edinburgh Academy. O.T.C. 1911-12. Student of Medicine, 1913-14. O.T.C. Infantry, 1913-14, Cadet. Machine-Gun Corps, Sept. 1914, 2nd Lieut. Feb. 1915; Lieut. July 1916. Transferred 7th Royal Scots. Dispatches Dec. 1917.

McGLASHAN, DUNCAN ALEXANDER.
Edinburgh Academy. O.T.C. 1910-12. Student of Science, 1914-15. R.E., Dispatch Rider, and L/Corporal Jan. 1915; 2nd Lieut. May 1916; Lieut. Nov. 1917.

Record of War Service

McGLASHAN, JEFFREY BLACKSTOCK.
George Watson's College. M.A. 1910; LL.B. 1913. Writer to the Signet, 1919. 9th Royal Scots, Private Sept. 1914. 3rd and 6th Argyll and Sutherland Highlanders, 2nd Lieut. Jan. 1915; Lieut. June 1916. France, 51st Division, and Italy Jan. 1917 to Nov. 1918. Gassed near Maing, Valenciennes, Oct. 1918.

McGLASHAN, KEITH BUCHANAN.
George Watson's College. M.B., Ch.B. 1910; M.D. 1912; F.R.C.S. (Edin.); D.P.H. 1913. Anatomy Staff, 1912-13. O.T.C. Medical, 1908-10, Cadet Corporal. R.A.M.C. (S.R.), Captain Aug. 1914. M.O., 6th Lancers. France 1914-15; Mons, Marne, Neuve Chapelle; Mesopotamia. Wounded May 1915. Dispatches twice.

McGOWAN, JOHN POOL.
M.A. 1900; M.B., Ch.B. (Hons.) 1904; M.D. (Gold Medal) 1908; D.T.M. & H. 1906; B.Sc. 1907; M.R.C.P. (Edin.) 1913. R.A.M.C., Lieut. May 1917; Captain May 1918 to April 1919. Pathologist. France.

MACGOWN, JOHN CECIL.
Bedford Grammar School; First XV. O.T.C. 1911-14. Student of Medicine, 1913-14 and 1918-19. R.A.M.C. (T.), Scottish Horse Field Ambulance, Private Sept. 1914. 2/1st Scottish Horse, 2nd Lieut. July 1915; Lieut. July 1917. R.F.C., Oct. 1916 to Feb. 1919. Prisoner of War July 1917 to Dec. 1918.

MACGREGOR, ALASTAIR DUNCAN ATHOLL.
M.A. 1905; B.A. (Oxford). Nigerian Land Contingent, West Africa.

McGREGOR, ALEXANDER.
George Watson's College. M.A. 1896. Indian Defence Force, Private Sept. 1914; Corporal 1917.

McGREGOR, ALEXANDER LEE.
Student of Medicine, 1916-18. German West Africa, 1914-15, Burgher in Potchefstroom Commando. R.N.V.R., Surgeon-Probationer, April 1918.

McGREGOR, ANDREW MURRAY.
S.A. College, Cape Town. First XV. Cadet Corps 1892, Captain. M.A. (Cape) 1896; B.D. 1899. Minister, Dutch Reformed Church. Chaplain to 1st Mounted Brigade (Captain) Nov. 1914. South African Exp. Force, German South-West Africa, 1914-15.

MACGREGOR, ARCHIBALD GORDON.
Edinburgh Academy. O.T.C. 1910-12. Student of Science, 1912-15. O.T.C. Engineers, Oct. 1913 to Feb. 1915, Cadet L/Corporal. R.E. (T.), Signal Service, 2nd Lieut. Feb. 1915; Temp. Lieut. Oct. 1915; Lieut. June 1916. 27th (Lowland) Infantry Brigade, 9th Division, France, and The Rhine, April 1917 to Jan. 1919. M.C. Sept. 1918; Croix de Guerre (Belgium) Jan. 1919.

Record of War Service

MACGREGOR, AUGUSTUS WALLACE.
: Edinburgh Academy. M.A. 1887; LL.B. 1892. Writer to the Signet, 1892. 12th Provisional Battn. King's Own Scottish Borderers, 2nd Lieut. Nov. 1915; Lieut. July 1917. 314th and 315th Coys. Royal Defence Corps, 1916-17; 4th Reserve Battn. King's Own Scottish Borderers, 1917-19.

MACGREGOR, CHARLES THOMPSON.
: East Calder School. M.A. 1895. Schoolmaster. 5th Royal Scots (T.), Private Dec. 1914; Sergeant April 1915.

MACGREGOR, DAVID HUTCHISON.
: George Watson's College. M.A. (Hons. Phil.) 1898. Professor of Economics, Leeds University. R.E., West Riding Division (Signal Coy.), 2nd Lieut. Aug. 1915; Lieut. July 1917; Captain Oct. 1918. General Staff, G.H.Q., Oct. 1918 to Feb. 1919. France 1915-17; Italy 1918-19. Dispatches May 1918. M.C. Aug. 1917.

MacGREGOR, DAVID ROBERTSON.
: B.Sc. (St Andrews); M.B., Ch.B. 1902. R.A.M.C., Lieut. Oct. 1915; Captain 1916-17. 29th General Hospital, Salonika.

MACGREGOR, DONALD GRANT.
: Merchiston Castle and Rossall. Student of Science, 1913-14. 2nd Rhodesian Regiment, Private 1914; Corporal to March 1919. Africa.

McGREGOR, DUNCAN.
: Leith Academy. M.A. 1905. Schoolmaster. 6th V.B. Royal Scots (College Coy.), 1902-5. R.E., Corporal July 1915; Sergeant Aug. 1917. Croix de Guerre (Belgium) Dec. 1917.

MACGREGOR, DUNCAN CAMPBELL.
: George Watson's College. Cadet Corps 1905-6. M.A. 1911. Assistant, Greek, 1913-15. 9th Royal Scots, Private Aug. 1914. 8th Cameron Highlanders, 2nd Lieut. Jan. 1915; Lieut. June 1916. Intelligence Corps.

MACGREGOR, DUNCAN GREGOR.
: University O.T.C. Infantry, Sept. to Nov. 1914, Cadet. 13th Royal Scots, 2nd Lieut.

McGREGOR, ERIC.
: Pontypridd School. Student of Science, 1911-13. A.M.I.C.E. R.E. (T.), Field Coy., Sapper April 1915; L/Corporal June 1915; 2nd Lieut. Oct. 1915; Lieut. June 1916; Acting Captain June 1918. France March 1916. Dispatches June 1917 and Jan. 1918. M.C. June 1918.

McGREGOR, GEORGE.
: George Watson's College. M.A. 1909. Schoolmaster. 9th, 3/7th, attached 13th and 2nd Royal Scots, Private May 1915; 2nd Lieut. Aug. 1915; Lieut. Aug. 1916. France, Arras.

Record of War Service

MACGREGOR, GEORGE BARBOUR.
 George Watson's College. M.B., Ch.B. 1906. R.A.M.C., Lieut. Feb. 1915; Captain Feb. 1916; Acting Major Dec. 1918. 22nd Manchester Regiment; Prisoners of War Hospital, Oswestry. France; Somme 1916, Passchendaele 1917, La Bassée 1918. Wounded 1916; Gassed 1918. Dispatches Oct. 1917. M.C.

MACGREGOR, IAN GREGOR. (See p. 751.)

McGREGOR, JAMES ALLISTER.
 Pontypridd School; First XV. and XI. M.A. 1911. Rugby "Blue." 8th Argyll and Sutherland Highlanders (T.), 2nd Lieut. June 1915; Lieut. July 1917. France 1916-18. M.C. Jan. 1918.

MACGREGOR, JAMES COCHRAN STEVENSON.
 Merchiston Castle, and Bootham School, York. Student of Arts, 1914-15. O.T.C. Infantry, Jan. to March 1915, Cadet. B.R.C.S. July 1915. Officer Cadet Feb. 1916. R.G.A., 2nd Lieut. June 1916; Lieut. Dec. 1917 to Jan. 1919. Intelligence Corps, Nov. 1918.

MACGREGOR, JAMES MAXWELL.
 Kirkcaldy High School; First XV. Student of Arts, 1913-15. Royal Navy, Telegraphist, March 1916; Warrant Telegraphist, 1917-19. H.M. Ships *Beluga, Killingholme, Haldon*, and *Bilbrough*. Mediterranean and Ægean Sea, Nov. 1917 to Aug. 1919. Torpedoed April 1916, and Mined Aug. 1917.

MACGREGOR, JOHN.
 M.A. 1903; LL.B. 1906. Advocate, 1907. 4th Royal Scots Fusiliers, Lieut. June 1916.

McGREGOR, JOHN ROBERTSON.
 M.B., Ch.B. 1903. South African Medical Corps, Lieut.

McGREGOR, JOHN ROY.
 Pontypridd School; First XI. Cadet Corps 1900-3, Corporal. M.B., Ch.B. 1911; D.P.H. (Sheffield). No. 4 Coy. Q.R.V.B., Royal Scots, 1903-8, L/Corporal. R.A.M.C., Lieut. Aug. 1917; Captain Aug. 1918. German East Africa. Prisoner of War July and Aug. 1918.

MACGREGOR, ROBERT BARR.
 Dunbar School. Student of Medicine, 1913-18; M.B., Ch.B. 1918. O.T.C. Infantry, 1914-15, Medical, 1915-18, Cadet Staff Sergeant. R.A.M.C., Lieut. Sept. 1918; Captain Sept. 1919. General Base Hospital, Marseilles. H.M.A.T. *Valdivia, Egypt*, and *Dongola*.

MACGREGOR, ROBERT FORRESTER DOUGLAS.
 George Watson's College and Merchiston Castle. M.B., Ch.B. 1908. Indian Medical Service, Lieut. 1910; Captain 1913; Brevet Major Jan. 1919. 128th Indian Field Ambulance, France. 7th (Meerut) Division, Egyptian Exp. Force, 1919. Mesopotamia 1916-17; Palestine and Syria, 1918. Dispatches Oct. and Dec. 1916, and March 1918. M.C. Dec. 1916.

Record of War Service

McGREGOR, RONALD MALCOLM.
: George Heriot's School. O.T.C. 1913-16, Cadet Sergeant. Student of Science, 1916-17 and 1919-20. O.T.C. Infantry, 1916-17, Cadet. 53rd Training Reserve Battalion, Private March 1917. R.F.C., 2nd Lieut. Oct. 1917. France.

McGREGOR, WILLIAM McPHERSON.
: George Watson's College. Student of Science, 1912-15; B.Sc. 1915. A.S.C. (M.T.), Private Sept. 1916. Transferred to Ministry of Munitions, Dec. 1918.

McGUIRE, THOMAS. (See p. 751.)

McHARDY, ARCHIBALD.
: George Heriot's School; First XV. and XI. M.A. 1911. Licentiate, Church of Scotland. O.T.C. Infantry, June 1910-14, Cadet. R.A.M.C., Private Sept. 1914; Sergeant Jan. 1915; Staff Sergeant Sept. 1916 to May 1917. 54th Field Ambulance. Chaplain, 4th Class, Highland Light Infantry, June 1917 to Aug. 1919. France. M.C. June 1919.

McHARDY, HORATIUS R.
: Dundee High School; First XI. Student of Science, 1917. O.T.C. Artillery, Aug. 1917 to March 1918, Cadet; Officer Cadet March 1918. R.G.A., 2nd Lieut. Oct. 1918.

McHARDY, IAN.
: Pulteney Town Academy. First XI. M.A. 1912. O.T.C. Artillery, 1909-13, Cadet. Artillery Reserve of Officers, 2nd Lieut. Aug. 1914. 3rd King's Own Scottish Borderers, Aug. 1914; Lieut. April 1915; Acting Captain Feb. 1916 to May 1918 and Feb. to Dec. 1919. Dispatches Feb. 1917 and Aug. 1919.

MacHARDY, WILLIAM.
: Student of Law, 1892-3. Solicitor, 1897. 4th Scottish Horse (T.), Sergeant.

McHATTIE, THOMAS JOHN TYNDALE.
: M.B., Ch.B. 1897; M.D. 1909. University Volunteer Medical Staff Corps, 1893-7, L/Corporal. R.A.M.C. (T.), Captain Sept. 1914; Major Jan. 1918. 3rd London Field Ambulance and No. 25 Stationary Hospital, Rouen.

McHUTCHON, EDWIN GRAY.
: Ayr Academy. M.A. 1912. O.T.C. Infantry, 1910-13, Cadet. 5th Royal Scots Fusiliers (T.), 2nd Lieut. Sept. 1914. R.E., 65th Division, Signalling Coy., Lieut. June 1916; Acting Captain May 1918-19. No. 2 Wireless Signalling Squadron, Med. Exp. Force. Twice Mentioned in Dispatches (Mesopotamia). O.B.E. June 1919.

McILWAINE, ALFRED LINDSAY.
: Grammar School, Melbourne. Student of Medicine, 1910-14 and 1916-19; M.B., Ch.B. (Hons.) 1918. 19th Northumberland Fusiliers, Private Aug. 1914; 2nd Lieut. Feb. 1915; Lieut. March 1915; Captain and Adjutant May 1915 to Sept. 1916. Pioneer Battalion, 35th Division.

Record of War Service

McINNES, AENEAS EDE.
Bower Parish School, Caithness. M.A. 1884. Minister, Church of Scotland. 1st Battn. Border Volunteers, Private March 1917; L/Corporal June 1917.

McINNES, IAN WHITTON.
George Watson's College. O.T.C. 1914-17, Cadet L/Corporal. Student of Arts, 1918-19. O.T.C. Infantry, Sept. 1917 to Aug. 1918, Cadet Sergeant; Officer Cadet Aug. 1918. 4th Royal Highlanders (Black Watch), 2nd Lieut.

MacINNES, JOHN.
Portree School. Student of Arts, 1913-14 and 1918-20; M.A. 1920. M'Kinnon Bursar. 4th Cameron Highlanders (T.), Private Aug. 1914; 2nd Lieut. Oct. 1915; Lieut. July 1917 to March 1919.

McINTOSH, ALEXANDER MORRISON.
George Watson's College. M.B., Ch.B. 1898; F.R.C.S. (Edin.) 1903. Tutor, Clinical Surgery. R.A.M.C. 1895, Lieut.-Col. Nov. 1915; Acting Colonel Nov. 1915 to April 1919. A.D.M.S., 52nd, 65th, and 67th Lowland Divisions. Gallipoli and Egypt. Three times Mentioned in Dispatches. T.D. 1918. C.M.G. June 1919.

McINTOSH, ALEXANDER PHILP.
Boroughmuir School. Student of Arts, 1912-15 and 1918-19; M.A. 1919. 16th Royal Scots, Private Nov. 1914; R.E. (Special Brigade), Sergeant. M.M. Dec. 1917.

McINTOSH, ARTHUR EDWIN.
Royal High School; First XV. and XI. Student of Science, 1918. 1/1st Lothians and Border Horse, Private Oct. 1914. 7th Dragoon Guards, 2nd Lieut. May 1917; Lieut. Nov. 1918.

McINTOSH, GEORGE WISHART.
Kirkcaldy High School. M.B., C.M. 1896; B.Sc. (P.H.) 1902. 7th Royal Highlanders (Black Watch) 1903; Captain Feb. 1913. Transferred to R.A.M.C. (T.), Major Oct. 1915. Dispatches March 1919.

McINTOSH, GILBERT EDWARDS.
Harris Academy, Dundee; First XI. University O.T.C. Artillery, 1917-18, Cadet; Officer Cadet April 1918. R.F.A., 2nd Lieut. Dec. 1918.

McINTOSH, HUGH P. F.
Student of Arts, 1913-15. R.A.M.C., Private. 9th Argyll and Sutherland Highlanders, Lieut. July 1916. Twice Wounded. M.C.

McINTOSH, JAMES EDWARD.
Royal Grammar School, Newcastle. Student of Arts, 1911-14; M.A. 1914. Licentiate, U.F. Church of Scotland, July 1919. R.A.M.C., Private Nov. 1915 to Dec. 1918. 13th Field Ambulance. Wounded Nov. 1917.

McINTOSH, JAMES WILSON.
George Watson's College. M.B., Ch.B. 1897; B.Sc. (P.H.) 1899; F.R.C.S. (Edin.) 1910. R.A.M.C. (T.), Captain Sept. 1914; Temp. Major Dec. 1914 to June 1919.

Record of War Service

McINTOSH, JOHN.
Webster's Seminary, Kirriemuir. Student of Arts and Science, 1913-15 and 1918-20; M.A. 1920. O.T.C. Infantry, 1914, Cadet. 16th Royal Scots, Private Dec. 1914. R.E., Corporal July 1915; Sergeant March 1916; C.Q.M.S. June 1918; Officer Cadet Nov. 1918. Royal Scots, 2nd Lieut. April 1919.

McINTOSH, JOHN GEORGE HUNTER.
Edinburgh Academy; First XV. and XI. B.A. (Camb.) 1899. Student of Law, 1899-1903. Writer to the Signet, 1903. South African Campaign, 1900-1. Scottish Horse (T.), Lieut. Sept. 1914; Captain Dec. 1915. Lovat Scouts. Gallipoli, Egypt, Salonika, and France Aug. 1915 to Nov. 1918.

McINTOSH, JOHN NEWTON.
Bury St Edmunds School. M.B., Ch.B. 1913. R.A.M.C. (S.R.), Lieut. Sept. 1914; Captain April 1915-19. France Sept. 1914; India 1915, 23rd Combined Field Ambulance; Mesopotamia 1916; France, Egypt, and Palestine, 1917.

McINTOSH, ROBERT.
Dundee High School; First XI. Student of Science, 1912-14. O.T.C. Engineers, Oct. 1913-15, Cadet. R.E., 2nd Lieut. Nov. 1915; Lieut. July 1917. Palestine and France.

McINTOSH, ROBERT.
M.A., B.Sc. 1906. Schoolmaster. R.A.M.C., Private Sept. 1916; Acting L/Corporal 1917; Corporal July 1918; Acting Sergeant Oct. 1918.

McINTOSH, ROBIN S.
Student of Arts. 6th Royal Scots (T.), Lieut. Aug. 1914; Captain Sept. 1914; Major Jan. 1917. 2/5th South Staffordshire Regiment.

McINTOSH, THOMAS PEARSON.
Burntisland School. B.Sc. 1912. 15th Royal Scots, Private Sept. 1914. 12th Scottish Rifles, 2nd Lieut. March 1915; Lieut. July 1917. 5th Royal Inniskilling Fusiliers.

McINTOSH, THOMAS STEVEN.
Dollar Academy. M.A. 1902; M.B., Ch.B. 1906; M.D. 1911; M.R.C.P. (Edin.); D.P.H. (Lond.). R.A.M.C., Lieut. April 1915; Captain April 1916. Sanitary Officer, Aldershot Command, and Boulogne.

MACINTYRE, ALEXANDER.
Oban High School. Student of Arts, 1912-15. O.T.C. Infantry, May to Aug. 1915, Cadet. King's African Rifles, 2nd Lieut. Aug. 1915; Lieut. July 1917. France and East Africa. Wounded in France April 1917.

MACINTYRE, ALEXANDER.
George Watson's College. Student of Medicine, 1913-14 and 1919-20. O.T.C. Artillery, Aug. 1915 to March 1916, Cadet; Officer Cadet March 1916. 17th Bengal Cavalry, 2nd Lieut. Oct. 1916; Lieut. Oct. 1917. India and Egypt.

Record of War Service

McINTYRE, ALEXANDER GRAY.
George Watson's College and Dollar Academy. M.B., C.M. 1893; M.D. 1898. R.A.M.C., Lieut. May 1917; Captain May 1918.

MACINTYRE, DAVID LOWE, V.C. (See p. 755.)

McINTYRE, HUGH DAVID.
Madras Academy, Cupar. Student of Arts, 1877. 5th Argyll and Sutherland Highlanders, Jan. 1880. Sudan 1885; Upper Burma 1886-9; Tirah 1897-8; China 1900-1. Brigadier-General Dec. 1914; Hon. Brigadier-General April 1917. 100th Infantry and 12th Reserve Brigades. Staff, France, 1917-18.

MACINTYRE, HUGH ROSS.
George Watson's College. M.B., Ch.B. 1904; M.D. 1908. R.A.M.C., Lieut. Dec. 1914; Captain Dec. 1915; Major Jan. 1918 to April 1919. 9th Clearing Hospital. France; Somme 1916, Messines 1917. Italy, Piave, 1918. Dispatches Jan. 1917 and June 1919. M.C. June 1917; Bar to M.C. Oct. 1917; D.S.O. Nov. 1918.

McINTYRE, JAMES CHARLES FAIRLIE.
Grove Academy, Broughty Ferry. Student of Science, 1918. 10th (Lovat Scouts) Cameron Highlanders, Private Sept. 1914.

McINTYRE, ROBERT BROWN.
George Heriot's School; First XI. O.T.C. 1916-17. University O.T.C. Infantry, 1917-18, Cadet; Officer Cadet Feb. 1918. 4th Gordon Highlanders, 2nd Lieut. July 1918; Lieut. Jan. 1920. Attached 2nd Lincolnshire Regiment. France Sept. 1918; The Rhine Feb. to Sept. 1919; India Nov. 1919.

McINTYRE, ROBERT EDMOND.
Daniel Stewart's College. M.A. 1913. Licentiate, U.F. Church of Scotland. R.A.M.C., Private Aug. 1914; Corporal. 40th Field Ambulance. R.G.A., 360th Siege Battery, Lieut.; Captain; Acting Major Jan. 1917. Gallipoli 1915.

McINTYRE, ROBERT GORDON.
Dingwall Academy. Student of Medicine, 1915-16 and 1917-19. Anatomy Staff, 1919. R.N.V.R., Surgeon Sub-Lieut., March 1918.

McINTYRE, WILLIAM B. R. W.
Dollar Academy. Student of Arts, 1913-14. Argyll and Sutherland Highlanders, Private Sept. 1914. Wounded.

McINTYRE, WILLIAM KEVERALL.
Hutchins School, Hobart, Tasmania, and Sydney University. Student of Medicine, 1911-15; M.B., Ch.B. 1915. O.T.C. Medical, Aug. 1914 to July 1915, Cadet Sergeant-Major. South African Campaign, 1900-1. R.A.M.C., Lieut. July 1915; Captain July 1916; Major Jan. 1918 to April 1919. 80th Field Ambulance. Macedonia 1916. Dispatches Dec. 1917. M.C. Jan. 1918; Greek M.C. (2nd Class) 1919.

Record of War Service

McISAAC, JAMES WATSON.
M.A. 1911; LL.B. 1913. Writer to the Signet, 1915. Gordon Highlanders, Private Oct. 1916. Highland Light Infantry, 2nd Lieut. April 1917; Lieut. Oct. 1918. Salonika.

MacIVER, DONALD PATRICK.
Royal High School; First XV. Student of Medicine, 1913-14 and 1918-19. O.T.C. Infantry, Oct. 1913 to Sept. 1914, Cadet. R.A.M.C., Scottish Horse Field Ambulance, Private Sept. 1914. Argyll and Sutherland Highlanders, 2nd Lieut. May 1915. 1st Garrison Battn. Gordon Highlanders, India, March 1917 to July 1918; Lieut. July 1917; Hon. Lieut. Sept. 1918. Wounded. M.C. May 1916.

McIVER, EVANDER.
Student of Medicine, 1912-15. O.T.C. Infantry, Feb. 1913, Cadet. R.A.M.C. (T.), Scottish Horse Brigade Field Ambulance, Private.

MACIVER, ISAAC HUNTER.
Nicolson Institute, Stornoway, and Aberdeen University. Student of Medicine, 1918. 4th Gordon Highlanders, April 1912, 2nd Lieut. Aug. 1915; Lieut. Sept. 1915; Acting Captain March 1918. 4th Seaforth Highlanders. France 1915. Mention Aug. 1919.

McIVER, JOHN CHRISTIAN.
George Watson's College. Student of Arts, 1911-14 and 1918-19; M.A. (Hons. Classics) 1919. Argyll and Sutherland Highlanders, Private Sept. 1914; 2nd Lieut. May 1915; Lieut. July 1917; Acting Captain Sept. 1918. France 1914-15, Neuve Chapelle; Egypt 1916; Salonika 1916-18. Wounded 1915. Dispatches (Salonika) Oct. 1917.

MacIVER KENNETH IAN.
Royal High School; First XV. and XI. M.A. 1907. Minister, U.F. Church of Scotland. Y.M.C.A. Work, Egypt, 1915; France 1916. Chaplain, 4th Class, 10th Scottish Rifles, April 1918.

MacIVER, LEWIS JAMES.
Royal High School; First XV. Student of Arts, 1912-14; M.A. 1919. O.T.C. Infantry, 1913-14, Cadet. 12th Argyll and Sutherland Highlanders, 2nd Lieut. Sept. 1914; Lieut. Jan. 1915; Captain July 1915. France 1916-17; Salonika 1918-19.

MacIVER, S. L.
University O.T.C. Artillery, Dec. 1914 to May 1915, Cadet. R.F.A., 2nd Lieut. May 1915; Lieut. July 1917; Acting Captain Dec. 1917. M.C.

McIVOR, ARNOTT.
Assistant, Chemistry Department. 5th Royal Scots (T.), Private.

McKAIL, JAMES.
M.A. (Glasg.). M.B., Ch.B. 1909. R.A.M.C., Lieut. Sept. 1915. 3rd London General Hospital.

Record of War Service

MACKAY, ADAM.
M.A., 1900; B.D. 1903. Minister, Church of Scotland. Scottish Churches Huts, 1916-17. Chaplain, 4th Class, June 1918.

MACKAY, ALEXANDER MORRISON.
Manchester Grammar School. M.B., Ch.B. 1912. O.T.C. Medical, April 1908 to Aug. 1912, Cadet Sergeant. R.A.M.C. (T.), Lieut. Aug. 1914; Captain Aug. 1915; Acting Major Jan. 1918. 1st Field Ambulance, East Lancashire Division. Dispatches June 1919.

MACKAY, ARTHUR GEORGE.
George Watson's College. Student of Medicine, 1912-14 and 1918-20. 13th Royal Scots, Private Jan. 1915. France July 1915. Prisoner of War in Germany, May 1916 to Nov. 1918.

MACKAY, DAVID NORMAN.
George Watson's College. Student of Law, 1898-1900. Solicitor, 1900. No. 4 Coy. Q.R.V.B., Royal Scots, 1900-4. R.N.V.R., Lieut. Aug. 1916. H.M. Ships *Thalia* and *Lavatera*.

MACKAY, DONALD.
Miller Institution, Thurso. M.A. 1904. Schoolmaster. R.F.A., 180th Brigade, Gunner Jan. 1915; Bombardier Feb. 1915; 2nd Lieut. Aug. 1915; Lieut. Sept. 1916; Adjutant Oct. 1916; Captain; Acting Major Feb. 1918. Wounded April 1918. Dispatches Jan. 1917. M.C. Oct. 1917; Bar to M.C. June 1918.

MACKAY, DONALD.
Tain Royal Academy. Student of Arts, 1916-17 and 1918-19. 2/5th Gordon Highlanders, Private July 1917. 10th Seaforth Highlanders and R.A.M.C.

MACKAY, DONALD WILLIAM.
George Watson's College. M.A. (Hons. Men. Phil.) 1914. O.T.C. Artillery, Oct. 1909 to Feb. 1913, Cadet Bombardier. R.G.A., 2nd Lieut. Aug. 1914; Lieut. June 1915; Captain Nov. 1917; Acting Major Oct. 1917. O.C. 287th Siege Battery. France March 1916-19; The Rhine March to Nov. 1919.

MACKAY, ERIC BRYCE.
Glasgow Academy; First XV. and XI. O.T.C. 1914-17, Cadet L/Corporal. University O.T.C. Artillery, Oct. 1917 to Feb. 1918, Cadet. R.G.A., Officer Cadet March 1918; 2nd Lieut. Sept. 1918 to Jan. 1919.

MACKAY, GEORGE.
George Watson's College. O.T.C. 1912-14. Student of Science, 1914. O.T.C. Engineers, Dec. 1914 to July 1915, Cadet. 14th Royal Scots, 2nd Lieut. July 1915; Lieut. Nov. 1916; Captain Dec. 1918. Machine-Gun Corps. France; Somme 1916, Arras 1917. Dispatches July 1918. M.C. June 1919.

MACKAY, GEORGE MUNRO.
M.A. 1902; M.B., Ch.B. 1909. South African Medical Corps, Captain Jan. 1916. 9th South African Infantry.

Record of War Service

MACKAY, GEORGE REGINALD EDWARD GRAY.
> Merchiston Castle; First XV. and XI. Cadet Corps 1899-1903, Sergeant. M.B., Ch.B. 1909. R.A.M.C. (T.), Lieut. Nov. 1914; Captain May 1915; Acting Major Jan. 1918. 1/2nd Highland Field Artillery Brigade. France and Italy. M.C. and Bar; Italian Bronze Medal Jan. 1919.

MACKAY, GEORGE STIBBARD.
> George Watson's College. Student of Medicine, 1913-14 and 1917-19. Anatomy Staff, 1919. Scottish Horse (T.) Field Ambulance, Private Sept. 1914. Royal Highlanders (Black Watch), 2nd Lieut. June 1915; Lieut. July 1917 to May 1918. Salonika. M.C. Feb. 1918.

MACKAY, GEORGE WILLIAM JOHN.
> Kingussie School. Student of Medicine, 1916-17 and 1918-19. Hockey "Blue." O.T.C. Medical, April 1918-19, Cadet Royal Navy, Signal Unit, Sept. 1917; Signaller Sub-Instructor, March 1918.

MACKAY, HENRY.
> Tain Royal Academy. Student of Arts and Medicine, 1912-15 and 1918-20; M.A. 1915; M.B., Ch.B. 1920. O.T.C. Infantry, 1915-16, Cadet. R.N.V.R., Surgeon-Probationer, March 1918. H.M.S. *Polyanthus*.

MACKAY, HENRY JOHN.
> M.B., C.M. 1884; M.D. 1894. Army Medical Service (V.), Surgeon-Lieut. 1891; Major. R.A.M.C. (T.), Lieut.-Col. 1908; Colonel and A.D.M.S., 1912-17. Wessex Division, 1917-18, Bedford District.

MACKAY, IAN CAMPBELL.
> Student of Medicine, 1910-15; M.B., Ch.B. 1915. O.T.C. Infantry, May 1910, and Medical, Nov. 1912 to Sept. 1914, Cadet. R.A.M.C. (S.R.), Lieut. Sept. 1914; Captain Sept. 1915.

MACKAY, JAMES FORBES.
> M.B., Ch.B. 1907; M.D. 1911; D.P.H. (Edin.) 1909. R.A.M.C., Captain April 1918. Red Cross Hospital, Netley.

MACKAY, JAMES REAY SUTHERLAND.
> Merchiston Castle; First XI. Cadet Corps 1897-1905, Cadet Sergeant. Student of Medicine, 1905-14 and 1915-16; M.B., Ch.B. 1916. O.T.C. Artillery, May 1910 to Nov. 1912, Cadet. 13th Argyll and Sutherland Highlanders, 2nd Lieut. Sept. 1914; Lieut. Dec. 1914. R.A.M.C., Jan. 1917; Captain Jan. 1918. Palestine.

MacKAY, JAMES STRACHAN.
> M.A. 1907. Diplômé Université de Rennes (France). No. 4 Coy. Q.R.V.B., Royal Scots, 1899-1902, Private. Tank Corps, Private April 1917; L/Corporal Oct. 1917; Corporal Oct. 1918.

Record of War Service

McKAY, JOHN BROWN.
M.A. 1907; B.Sc. 1912. 4th King's Own Scottish Borderers (T.), 2nd Lieut. Oct. 1914; Lieut. May 1915; Captain June 1915. Ministry of Munitions, 1917-18, and Board of Agriculture, 1918. Invalided out Feb. 1919.

MACKAY, JOHN CHIENE.
Edinburgh Academy. O.T.C. 1910-12, Cadet L/Corporal. Student of Medicine, 1911-14. O.T.C. Artillery, 1913-15, Cadet. R.F.A. (T.), 2nd Lieut. Nov. 1914; Lieut. June 1916; Acting Captain May to Nov. 1918. 1/3rd Highland (Howitzer) Brigade. Wounded July 1918. M.C. June 1917; Bar to M.C. Sept. 1918.

MACKAY, JOHN MACLACHLAN.
Robert Gordon's College, Aberdeen. LL.B. 1903. Barrister-at-Law. Athletics. President, Celtic Society. 10th Seaforth Highlanders, Lieut.; Captain Jan. 1916. India Feb. to April 1916; Mesopotamia 1916; India 1917-19; N.-W. Frontier, Exp. Force, 1919.

MACKAY, MAGNUS ROSS.
Portree. M.B., Ch.B. 1912. O.T.C. Medical, 1907-10, Captain. R.A.M.C., Lieut. Oct. 1914; Captain Oct. 1915. France, Balkans, and Transcaucasia. M.C. Jan. 1917.

MACKAY, NORMAN DOUGLAS.
B.Sc. 1903; M.B., Ch.B. 1904; D.P.H. 1912; M.D. 1913. R.A.M.C., Lieut. March 1915. 20th General Hospital and 1st London Scottish.

MACKAY, PATRICK ROBSON.
Student of Arts, 1873-4. D.D. (St Andrews). Minister, U.F. Church of Scotland. Chaplain, 4th Class, 1908; 1st Class Nov. 1917; Principal Chaplain July 1918. Scottish Command. Mention 1917. C.B.E. 1919.

MACKAY, RALPH WILLIAM.
Student of Law, 1907-8. 5th Seaforth Highlanders, Lieut. July 1917. Attached 3rd King's African Rifles, Oct. 1917.

MACKAY, ROBERT MITCHELL.
Student of Medicine, 1909-14 and 1915-16; M.B., Ch.B. 1914; M.D. 1916. R.A.M.C., Lieut.

MACKAY, WILLIAM.
Edinburgh Academy; First XI. Student of Arts, 1904-5, and Law, 1908-9. Law Agent, 1912. 1st V.B. Cameron Highlanders, 1906-8. 4th Cameron Highlanders (T.), 2nd Lieut. 1913; Lieut. Sept. 1914; Temp. Captain Sept. 1915; Captain June 1916. France 1914-15, 7th Division. Wounded at Neuve Chapelle 1915.

MACKAY, WILLIAM.
Fort William High School. Student of Medicine, 1916-17 and 1918-19. O.T.C. Artillery, June to Aug. 1917, Cadet. Royal Air Force, 2nd Lieut. Aug. 1917. 139th and 34th Squadrons. Indian Exp. Force.

Record of War Service

MACKAY, WILLIAM BERTIE.
Edinburgh Institution. M.B., C.M. (Hons.) 1884; M.D. 1896; M.R.C.S. (Eng.) 1885. R.A.M.C. (T.), 1889; Major 1903; Lieut.-Col. June 1916. No. 4 General Hospital, France, 1915. T.D. 1909. Dispatches 1915 (twice) and 1916. C.M.G. 1916. Hon. Associate, Order of St John of Jerusalem.

MACKAY, WILLIAM MURRAY.
Durham School. M.B., Ch.B. 1899. No. 4 Coy. Q.R.V.B., Royal Scots, and Volunteer Medical Staff Corps, 1894-9, Private. Surgeon, South African Field Force, 1900-1. R.A.M.C. (T.), 2nd and 6th Durham Light Infantry; Surgeon-Lieut. March 1902; Major March 1914 to Dec. 1918. France. Wounded at Ypres.

MACKEAN, HUGH.
Edinburgh Institution. M.A. 1893. Minister, Episcopalian Church of Scotland. Chaplain, 4th Class, Aug. 1914. Forth Garrison. Mention 1918.

McKEAND, WILLIAM IAN.
Edinburgh Academy. O.T.C. 1908-9. Student of Law, 1912-14. O.T.C. Infantry, 1914-15, Cadet. 7th Border Regiment, 2nd Lieut. Jan. 1915; Lieut. Nov. 1916; Captain June 1917. 2nd Lancashire Infantry Brigade, France; The Rhine. M.C.

McKEE, GEORGE.
Dumfries Academy. M.A. 1914. Schoolmaster. 6th and 15th Royal Scots, Private Jan. 1915; L/Corporal Feb. 1915; Corporal Oct. 1915. Tank Corps. Egypt Sept. 1915 to May 1916. France May 1916 to Feb. 1919.

McKELVEY, DANIEL.
Omagh Academy, Co. Tyrone. M.B., Ch.B. 1913; M.D. 1919. R.A.M.C., Lieut. Nov. 1914; Temp. Captain Nov. 1915; Acting Major May 1918 to April 1919; Captain May 1918. France 1914-19. Wounded Oct. 1918. M.C. July 1917; first Bar to M.C. Sept. 1918, second Bar Oct. 1918. Dispatches and Croix de Guerre avec Palme, Sept. 1918.

McKELVIE, DAVID BLYTH.
Buckhaven School. M.A. 1910. Schoolmaster. 1st Royal Scots, Private Dec. 1914; 2nd Lieut. May 1916; Lieut. Nov. 1917. Egypt; Salonika May 1916. Wounded Sept. 1916. Invalided out Sept. 1918.

McKELVIE, JOHN DOUGLAS.
Norwich Grammar School. M.B., Ch.B. 1905; M.D. 1909. No. 4 Coy. Q.R.V.B., Royal Scots, 1901-5, Private. R.A.M.C., Lieut. Feb. 1918; Captain Feb. 1919. Attached Armoured Car Unit. Mesopotamia and Persia.

MACKELVIE, THOMAS.
Royal High School. Student of Law, 1888-90. Argyll and Bute Artillery Volunteers, 2nd Lieut. 1897. 4th Highland Mountain Brigade. R.G.A. (T.), Captain 1908; Major July 1914. Gallipoli 1915. Wounded. Dispatches and C.M.G. Nov. 1915.

Record of War Service

MACKENNA, DAVID LOCKHART.
Dumfries Academy; First XI. M.B., Ch.B. 1908. R.A.M.C., Lieut. March 1916; Captain March 1917-18.

MACKENNA, ROBERT WILLIAM.
Dumfries Academy, and Royal High School, Edinburgh. M.A. 1896; M.B., Ch.B. 1898; M.D. 1908. President, S.R.C. R.A.M.C. (T.), Captain Nov. 1914; Major Sept. 1918. 1st West General Hospital, Liverpool. 57th General Hospital, France, 1917-18.

MACKENZIE, ALBERT ALEXANDER.
Madras College, St Andrews; First XV. and XI. M.A. (St Andrews); LL.B. 1906. Solicitor, 1911. R.F.A., 2nd Lieut. Oct. 1914; Lieut. June 1916. Gallipoli, Egypt, and France.

MACKENZIE, ALEXANDER.
Kingussie High School. Student of Arts and Divinity, 1907-14; M.A. 1911. O.T.C. Artillery, Feb. to Aug. 1916, Cadet. R.G.A. (S.R.), 2nd Lieut. June 1917; Lieut. Dec. 1918. Anti-Aircraft Royal Artillery. France.

MACKENZIE, ALEXANDER.
George Watson's College. Student of Arts, 1915. R.F.A., 155th Army Brigade, Gunner Nov. 1916; 2nd Lieut. July 1918. France; Cambrai and Maubeuge.

MACKENZIE, ALEXANDER.
Wick High School. Student of Arts, 1912-14. 1st Seaforth Highlanders, Private Sept. 1915; L/Corporal.

MACKENZIE, ALEXANDER DONALD.
Merchiston Castle. Cadet Corps 1904-7. B.Sc. 1911. O.T.C. Engineers, 1909-11, Cadet. R.E. (T.), City of Edinburgh (Fortress), 2nd Lieut. June 1912; Lieut. Dec. 1914; Temp. Captain April 1915; Captain June 1916; Acting Major Nov. 1918. 1st (Tank) Bridging Battn., R.E. O.B.E. June 1919.

MACKENZIE, ALFRED JAMES.
George Heriot's School. M.A. 1913. O.T.C. Infantry, Dec. 1909 to Dec. 1912, Cadet. Scottish Horse (T.), Private; 2nd Lieut. May 1918.

MACKENZIE, ALISTER THOMAS.
Tain Royal Academy. M.A. 1904; M.B., Ch.B. 1907; M.D. (Gold Medal) 1909. D.P.H. (Camb.) 1906. R.A.M.C., Lieut. July 1917; Acting Major Jan. 1918-19. Egyptian Exp. Force. Dispatches March 1919.

MCKENZIE, ARCHIBALD.
Hilton College, Natal. College Guards, 1872-7, Captain and O.C. M.B., C.M. (Hons.) 1883; M.D. 1890; M.R.C.S. (Eng.) 1883. M.O., Durban Light Infantry, 1884. Natal and South African Medical Corps, Major; Lieut.-Col. April 1916. South African Campaign, 1899-1902. No. 3 Base Hospital, Durban, 1914-19.

Record of War Service

McKENZIE, ARCHIBALD DUNCAN.
   Durban High School; First XI. Cadet Corps, 1896-1903, R.S.M. M.B., Ch.B. 1909. University Battery, E.C.A.V., 1904-8, Lieut. South African Medical Corps, Captain Aug. 1914; Major Jan. 1916-19. German South-West and German East Africa. Dispatches (East Africa) 1917.

MacKENZIE, DAVID.
   Fettes College; First XV. LL.B. 1907. 6th Royal Highlanders (Black Watch), (T.), 2nd Lieut. Oct. 1914; Lieut. Feb. 1915; Captain June 1916. Attached 4th Hampshire Regiment, Mesopotamia, 1917-18.

McKENZIE, DAVID KINNELL.
   George Watson's College. Student of Arts and Science, 1913-15 and 1919. O.T.C. Infantry, Oct. 1914 to March 1915, Cadet. 12th Argyll and Sutherland Highlanders, 2nd Lieut. March 1915; Lieut. Sept. 1916. France 1918.

MACKENZIE, DONALD.
   Fortrose Academy. Student of Medicine, 1916-19. O.T.C. Medical, 1918-19, Cadet. R.N.V.R., Western Mediterranean Sloop Flotilla, Surgeon Sub-Lieut. Oct. 1918.

MACKENZIE, DONALD FINLAYSON.
   M.A. 1882. Minister, U.F. Church of Scotland. Chaplain, 4th Class, May 1912. 4th Seaforth Highlanders.

MACKENZIE, DONALD FRANCIS.
   Dover College, Kent; First XV. and XI. M.B., Ch.B. 1905; D.T.M. (Liverpool). R.A.M.C., 1907; Captain 1910; Major Jan. 1919; Acting Lieut.-Col. 59th Field Ambulance, Aug. 1916 to May 1919. France, Indian Corps, Sept. 1914. D.S.O. Jan. 1917. Dispatches Jan. and June 1917 and March 1919.

MACKENZIE, DONALD FRANCIS.
   Sciennes School. Student of Arts and Divinity, 1907-10 and 1914; M.A. 1911. O.T.C. Artillery, Dec. 1914 to July 1915, Cadet Corporal. R.F.A. (T.), 2nd Lieut. July 1915; Lieut. June 1916; Acting Captain and Adjutant July 1918 to May 1919. Headquarters, 42nd D.A.C., France.

MACKENZIE, DONALD ROSS.
   Daniel Stewart's College; First XV. and XI. Student of Law, 1912-14. O.T.C. Artillery, Nov. 1912 to Aug. 1914, Cadet. R.F.A. (S.R.), 2nd Lieut. Aug. 1914; Captain Nov. 1917. France Jan. 1915; Macedonia Oct. 1915. Dispatches Nov. 1917. M.C. Jan. 1918.

MACKENZIE, EBENEZER VICTOR GLADSTONE.
   Daniel Stewart's College. Student of Law, 1902-4. 7th and 10th Seaforth Highlanders, 2nd Lieut.; Lieut. March 1917.

MacKENZIE, EDWARD BRIGGS DRAKE.
   Glenalmond. O.T.C. 1915-16. Student of Science, 1916-17. O.T.C. Artillery, Nov. 1916 to Aug. 1917, Cadet Bombardier. R.F.A., Officer Cadet Aug. 1917; 2nd Lieut. Jan. 1918; Lieut. July 1919. France March 1918 to Feb. 1920.

Record of War Service

MACKENZIE, ERIC FRANCIS WALLACE.
 Wellington College, New Zealand. First XV. M.B., Ch.B. 1914. Rugby "Blue."
 R.A.M.C., Lieut. Oct. 1914; Captain Oct. 1915; Major and D.A.D.G. A.M.S., War
 Office, June 1918. France; Neuve Chapelle, Festubert, Givenchy, Aubers Ridge,
 and Loos. Wounded at Somme Sept. 1916. Dispatches Jan. 1916 and June 1918.
 M.C. Sept. 1915. O.B.E. June 1919.

MACKENZIE, ERIC LOFTS.
 Kimberley High School and George Watson's College. Cadet Corps 1903-8,
 Cadet C.S.M. M.B., Ch.B. 1914. O.T.C. Artillery, 1909-14, Cadet Corporal.
 R.A.M.C., Lieut. Aug. 1914; Captain Aug. 1915; Acting Major May 1918.
 France, 1st Division (four years). Dispatches Feb. 1916. M.C. Jan. 1917.

MACKENZIE, FRANCIS BURNETT.
 Boroughmuir School. Student of Arts, Science, and Medicine, 1905-14 and
 1918-20; M.A. 1909. 4th Royal Scots (T.), 2nd Lieut. Feb. 1912; Lieut. and
 Captain June 1915; Major Dec. 1916. Machine-Gun Corps, Divisional Officer
 1917. Gallipoli 1915. Dispatches 1915 and 1917. D.S.O. 1918. M.C. 1915.

MACKENZIE, GEORGE.
 Assistant, Chemistry Department. Royal Highlanders (Black Watch), Sergeant
 1914-19.

MACKENZIE, GEORGE.
 Bell Baxter School, Cupar-Fife. Student of Law, 1914-15. R.G.A., 137th, 219th,
 and 184th Siege Batteries, 2nd Lieut. March 1916. Wounded April 1917.

MACKENZIE, GEORGE EDWARD.
 Lycée de Douai. M.A. 1910; B.D. (Aberdeen). Minister, Church of Scotland.
 9th Highland Light Infantry (Glasgow Highlanders), Jan. 1915. 4th Seaforth
 Highlanders, 2nd Lieut.; Captain June 1915. R.F.A., 153rd Brigade, Lieut.
 Aug. 1916. France. Wounded. Invalided out Jan. 1919.

MACKENZIE, GEORGE OMOND.
 George Watson's College. Student of Arts, 1918. 2/1st Lothians and Border
 Horse, Private Jan. 1915 to Dec. 1916. Librarian, Scottish Command.

MACKENZIE, HARRY MALCOLM.
 Royal High School; First XV. and XI. M.B., Ch.B. 1899; D.P.H. (Camb.) 1903.
 University Battery, E.C.A.V., 1894-9, Sergeant. Indian Medical Service, Lieut.
 1900; Major 1911; Lieut.-Col. July 1919. Egypt 1914-15. H.M.S. *Hardinge*,
 July 1915 to March 1916. India.

MACKENZIE, HECTOR BRUCE.
 Waitaki High School, New Zealand. Athletics. Cadet Corps 1903-10. Student
 of Medicine, 1912-15 and 1917-18; M.B., Ch.B. 1918. N.Z. Medical Corps,
 2nd Lieut. Aug. 1915; Lieut. July 1916.

Record of War Service

MACKENZIE, HECTOR WILLIAM GAVIN.
George Watson's College. M.A. 1876; M.A. and M.D. (Camb.); M.R.C.S. (Eng.); F.R.C.P. (Lond.). R.A.M.C., Captain Dec. 1908. 2nd London Hospital.

MACKENZIE, HENRY DEEDES NUTT.
M.B., C.M. 1893; M.D. 1897. R.A.M.C., Captain, attached R.F.A., 95th Brigade, France.

MACKENZIE, IAN A.
Student of Arts and Law, 1910-14. O.T.C. Infantry, Oct. 1909 to April 1912, Cadet. 72nd Seaforth Highlanders, Lieut. Canadian Exp. Force.

MACKENZIE, JAMES MOIR.
Fettes College; First XV. Student of Law, 1909-13. Writer to the Signet, 1911. First XV. R.N.V.R., Temp. Sub-Lieut. Oct. 1914; Temp. Lieut. Jan. 1915; Adjutant, 4th Battn. Royal Naval Division, 1915; Sub-Lieut. March 1916; Lieut. March 1917. H.M. Ships *Loyal* 1916, *Tempest* 1917, and *Shakespeare* 1918-19.

McKENZIE, JOHN.
Royal High School. M.B., Ch.B. 1901; D.P.H. (Edin.). R.A.M.C., Lieut. April 1915; Captain April 1916. France. Wounded at Somme Aug. 1916.

MACKENZIE, JOHN EDWIN.
Larchfield, Helensburgh, and Royal High School. B.Sc. 1889; D.Sc. 1901; Ph.D. (Strasburg). Lecturer in Chemistry. Highland Artillery Volunteers, 1890. Bombay Light Horse, 1906-7. O.T.C. Artillery, 2nd Lieut. 1909; Lieut. 1909; Captain 1912; Major and O.C. Oct. 1914. Acting Adjutant, Edinburgh Contingents O.T.C. 1914-19. O.C. School of Instruction, Artillery and Infantry Officers, 1915-16. France Feb. 1916. Mention March 1918.

McKENZIE, JOHN FRASER.
Boroughmuir School. Student of Arts, 1915. R.F.A., 22nd Brigade, 7th Division, Gunner May 1916.

MACKENZIE, JOHN KENNEDY.
M.A. 1913; Student of Divinity. Licentiate, Church of Scotland. 8th Cameron Highlanders, 2nd Lieut. Draft Conducting Officer, Machine-Gun Depôt, France.

MACKENZIE, JOHN TOLME.
Student of Medicine; L.R.C.P. & S. (Edin.) and L.R.F.P.S. (Glasg.) 1911. R.A.M.C., Lieut. Aug. 1915; Captain Aug. 1916. 13th Northumberland Fusiliers. France Sept. 1915 to Aug. 1917. M.C.

MACKENZIE, JOHN WILLIAM.
Royal Academy, Inverness; First XI. M.B., Ch.B. 1898; M.D. 1903. R.A.M.C. (T.), 1905; Major June 1917; Acting Lieut.-Col. Aug. 1917 to June 1919. Highland Mounted Brigade Field Ambulance, 1911-17. Suvla. Egyptian Exp. Force. 44th Stationary Hospital, Kantara, 1917-19. Dispatches Dec. 1916 and Jan. 1919. O.B.E. (Military) Jan. 1919.

Record of War Service

MACKENZIE, KENNETH.
Otago High School, New Zealand. Cadet Corps 1900-2, Cadet Sergeant. M.B., Ch.B. 1908; M.D., F.R.C.S. (Eng.). Anatomy Staff, 1910-11. 9th Royal Scots 1904-6, Private. N.Z. Medical Corps, Captain June 1917.

MACKENZIE, KENNETH WILLIAM.
Grammar School, Aberdeen; First XV. and XI. M.B., Ch.B. 1905. Scottish Hockey International. Indian Medical Service, 1905-12. Captain (Retired). R.A.M.C., Lieut. Oct. 1914; Captain Feb. 1915; Major; Acting Lieut.-Col. Feb. 1918. France. No. 11 Hospital, Boulogne. 52nd Light Infantry, March 1916. D.A.D.M.S., 2nd Division, Nov. 1916. No. 6 Field Ambulance, 1918-19. M.C. Aug. 1916; Bar to M.C. Nov. 1916; D.S.O. July 1918. Twice Mentioned in Dispatches.

MACKENZIE, LIONEL DO AMARAL.
Tain Royal Academy. M.A. 1911; LL.B. 1913. Advocate. O.T.C. Infantry, Feb. 1909 to July 1910, Cadet. 7th Royal Scots, June 1909. 2nd Gordon Highlanders, Lieut. April 1915; Captain June 1917; Brevet Major Jan. 1918; Staff Captain March 1917; Brigade Major June 1917 to May 1919; Adjutant July 1919. France 1914-18. Dispatches Jan. and June 1918, and Jan. 1919. M.C. Dec. 1916; D.S.O. Jan. 1919.

MACKENZIE, MALCOLM DRUMMOND.
Stellenbosch High School. 3rd Western Province Rifles, 1913-15, Corporal. South African Mounted Rifles, Field Artillery, Gunner Feb. to Sept. 1915. O.T.C. Artillery, 1915-16, Cadet. R.F.A. (S.R.), 2nd Lieut. Jan. 1916; Lieut. July 1917. German S.-W. Africa 1915. France May 1916 to Nov. 1917. Wounded at Passchendaele Dec. 1917. M.C. June 1917.

MACKENZIE, MAURICE GORDON.
George Heriot's School. O.T.C. 1909-13, Cadet Colour-Sergeant. Student of Law, 1915-17; B.L. 1920. R.G.A., 1/1st Kent (T.), Heavy Battery, Signaller May 1917; Wireless Operator. 1/1st Lowland (City of Edinburgh) R.G.A.

MACKENZIE, PERCIVAL.
Royal Academy, Inverness. M.A. 1907. Minister, Church of Scotland. Royal Artillery, Dec. 1915. Royal Army Ordnance Corps, Lieut. Inspector of Ordnance Machinery.

MACKENZIE, ROBERT.
Tain Royal Academy. M.A. 1894. Schoolmaster. 1st V.B. Sutherland Highlanders, Private 1888-1900. 1st V.B. Royal Highlanders, Private Jan. 1915; C.S.M.

MACKENZIE, ROBERT NINIAN.
Inverness College. M.B., Ch.B. 1917. O.T.C. Artillery, Jan. 1912 to Oct. 1915, Cadet. R.A.M.C., Lieut. Nov. 1917; Captain Nov. 1918.

Record of War Service

MACKENZIE, RONALD PIERSON.
Edinburgh Academy; First XI. M.B., C.M. 1889; D.P.H. (Camb.). Civil Surgeon, South African Campaign, 1900-1. South African Medical Corps, Lieut.-Col. Sept. 1914. German East and West Africa and South Africa. C.M.G.

MACKENZIE, R. W. K.
M.B., Ch.B. R.A.M.C., Captain. M.C.

MACKENZIE, THOMAS.
M.A. 1918; B.Sc. Technical Chemist. Royal Navy Experimental Section, Mechanic.

MACKENZIE, THOMAS.
Larchfield, Helensburgh. M.B., C.M. 1886; M.D. 1891; M.A. (Glasg.). 7th (I.O.M.) V.B., Liverpool Regiment, 1895; Captain; Major Feb. 1915. R.A.M.C., Major Oct. 1915; Lieut.-Col. (Local, Malta) Aug. 1916. O.C. Prisoners of War Camp, 1914-15. Cotonera Military Hospital, Malta; 30th Coy. R.A.M.C., 1915-19. V.D. Mention March 1918.

MACKENZIE, THOMAS ARCHIBALD.
Royal High School. M.B., Ch.B. 1903. R.A.M.C., Lieut. Feb. 1916 to April 1917 attached 131st Indian Cavalry Field Ambulance. U.S.A. Medical Corps, Captain July 1917; Major Feb. 1919.

MACKENZIE, WILLIAM.
Fortrose and Dingwall Academies. M.B., Ch.B. 1913; D.P.H., D.T.M. O.T.C. Infantry, Oct. 1909 to April 1913, Cadet L/Corporal. R.A.M.C., Lieut. Aug. 1914; Captain Oct. 1915. 9th South Staffordshire Regiment. Dispatches July 1916, Jan. 1918, and Jan. 1919. D.S.O. July 1918.

MACKENZIE, WILLIAM.
Golspie School. Student of Science, 1918. 51st Graduate Battn. Gordon Highlanders, Private May 1918.

McKERCHAR, JOHN.
Dumfries Academy. M.B., Ch.B. 1912. O.T.C. Artillery, March 1909 to Feb. 1912, Cadet. R.A.M.C. (S.R.), Lieut. Sept. 1914; Captain April 1915. 1/4th Somerset Light Infantry.

McKERRON, ROBERT GORDON.
Kelso High School. M.A. (Hons. Classics) 1893. Graves Registration Units, Lieut. Dec. 1916. France 1916-17.

McKERROW, ALEXANDER ROBERT CAMPBELL.
Portmadoc School. Student of Medicine, 1911-14 and 1917-18; M.B., Ch.B. 1918. Rugby "Blue." O.T.C. Artillery, Jan. 1912 to Sept. 1914, Cadet Bombardier, R.F.A., 2nd Lieut. Sept. 1914. R.A.M.C., Lieut. May 1918. Gallipoli 1915.

Record of War Service

McKERROW, JAMES CLARK.
 St Bees School, Cumberland. M.B., Ch.B. 1912. O.T.C. Infantry, Dec. 1908 to April 1912, Cadet Sergeant. Vol. Gen. R. of O. 1912. R.A.M.C., Lieut. 1915; Captain 1916. 2nd South Lancashire Regiment. Wounded Oct. 1914.

McKERROW, MUNGO.
 Robert Gordon's College, Aberdeen. Student of Medicine, 1910-14 and 1916-17; M.B., Ch.B. 1917. O.T.C. Infantry, Feb. 1909 to Jan. 1914, Cadet L/Corporal. 11th (Lonsdale) Border Regiment, L/Corporal Oct. 1914; 2nd Lieut. Nov. 1914; Lieut. Sept. 1915 to April 1917. Royal Navy, Surgeon-Lieut. May 1917. France Nov. 1915 to July 1916. H.M.S. *Armadale Castle*, Aug. 1917 to Jan. 1919. M.C. June 1916.

MACKESSACK, ROBERT JOHN.
 Elgin Academy. M.A. (Aberdeen); M.B., Ch.B. 1904; M.D. 1909. R.A.M.C., Lieut. Aug. 1916; Captain Aug. 1917.

MACKIE, ARTHUR WELLWOOD.
 Dumfries Academy. Student of Medicine, 1911-15 and 1917-20. O.T.C. Medical, May 1912 to March 1915, Cadet. R.N.V.R., Surgeon-Probationer, March 1916. Invalided out March 1917.

MACKIE, DAVID TAYLOR.
 Daniel Stewart's College. Student of Medicine, 1919. 1/10th Royal Scots, Private Aug. 1914. 2/5th Scottish Rifles, March 1915; L/Corporal April 1915; Royal Military College, Jan. 1916. 2nd Royal Scots, 2nd Lieut. Aug. 1916; Lieut. Feb. 1918. France. Wounded. Invalided out Jan. 1919.

MACKIE, DONALD McDONALD.
 Viewpark; First XV. and XI. University O.T.C. Engineers, 1914-15, Cadet. R.E. (T.), Lowland Division, 2nd Lieut. July 1915; Lieut. June 1916. Egyptian Exp. Force, Dec. 1915 to May 1919.

MACKIE, GEORGE.
 M.B., Ch.B. 1899. R.A.M.C. (T.), Acting Lieut.-Col. Aug. 1916; Major Feb. 1918. D.S.O.

McKIE, HENRY ERSKINE.
 Morrison's Academy, Crieff; First XV. and XI. O.T.C. 1913-15. Student of Science, 1919. R.F.A. (41st Division, Artillery), 2nd Lieut. Oct. 1915; Lieut. July 1917. M.C. Jan. 1918.

MACKIE, JAMES FRASER.
 Student of Medicine, 1913-15 and 1917-20. O.T.C. Infantry, 1914, Cadet. 6/7th Royal Scots Fusiliers, 2nd Lieut. Dec. 1914 to Sept. 1917. Wounded Aug. 1916.

Record of War Service

MACKIE, JOHN.
: Leith Academy. M.A. (Hons. Maths.) 1911; B.Sc. Assistant in Natural Philosophy. O.T.C. Infantry, Sept. 1914 to March 1915, Cadet Sergeant. 8th Royal Scots (T.), 2nd Lieut. March 1915; Lieut. April 1917. France July 1916-18. British Military Mission, U.S.A., July to Oct. 1918. France Dec. 1918 to Jan. 1919. Gas Officer, 1917-19.

McKILLOP, ALEXANDER CAMERON.
: M.B., Ch.B. 1909. O.T.C. Medical, Oct. 1908 to June 1909, Cadet Staff Sergeant. N.Z. Medical Corps, Major.

MACKILLOP, JAMES.
: Servitor. 1st Cameron Highlanders, 1885-1901. Soudan, 1885-6; South Africa, 1900-1. 3rd attached 7th and 8th Cameron Highlanders, Private Oct. 1914; Corporal Nov. 1915; Sergeant March 1917 to Aug. 1918. 40th Training Reserve Battn.

McKINLAY, ROBERT.
: Campbell College, Belfast; First XV. Student of Medicine, 1910-15; M.B., Ch.B. 1915. O.T.C. Medical, Oct. 1910 to May 1914, Cadet L/Corporal. R.A.M.C. (S.R.), Lieut. Aug. 1914; mobilised April 1915; Captain Oct. 1915; Acting Major Jan. 1918; Major (Regulars) 1919. D.A.D.M.S., Black Sea, March 1919. Dispatches (Salonika) Jan. 1919.

MACKINLAY, WILLIAM HARRISON.
: M.B., C.M. 1892. R.A.M.C., Lieut.

McKINNA, HENRY DRUMMOND.
: Huddersfield Municipal College. Student of Medicine, 1915-16 and 1918-19. O.T.C. Artillery, Oct. 1915 to July 1916, Cadet. 3rd and 8th Cameron Highlanders, July 1916. 3rd Argyll and Sutherland Highlanders, 2nd Lieut. March 1917; Lieut. Nov. 1918. M.C. Nov. 1917.

McKINNEY, EBENEZER ARCHIBALD MORRISON.
: George Heriot's School. Student of Medicine, 1918-20. Royal Scots, Private Sept. 1914. Wounded and Gassed.

McKINNEY, JAMES WILFRED.
: Royal School, Dungannon. M.B., Ch.B. 1912. R.A.M.C., Lieut. Feb. 1915; Captain Feb. 1916; Major Jan. 1918. 6th Field Ambulance. The Rhine. Dispatches July 1917.

MACKINNON, ERIC.
: George Watson's College; First XV. Student of Science, 1911-13 and 1918-19; B.Sc. 1919. O.T.C. Engineers, 1912-14, Cadet. 9th Royal Scots (T.), Private Sept. 1914; L/Corporal. 13th and 10th Argyll and Sutherland Highlanders, 2nd Lieut. Nov. 1915; Lieut. July 1917. France 1915 and 1916-17; second Ypres and Somme. Wounded at Arras May 1917.

Record of War Service

MACKINNON, JOHN.
    M.B., C.M. 1894. R.A.M.C., Captain Sept. 1916. East Africa.

MACKINNON, MALCOLM.
    Student of Medicine. East African Medical Service, Captain.

MACKINNON, PATRICK.
    George Watson's College; First XV. and XI. B.Sc. 1912. O.T.C. Engineers, 1909-12, Cadet. Canadian Engineers, 2nd Field Coy., Sapper Aug. 1914. R.E., 2nd Lieut. Aug. 1915; Lieut. Oct. 1916; Captain 1919. France 1915 17; second Ypres, Festubert, Somme, Messines; Egypt and Asia Minor 1917-19. Wounded Feb. and Oct. 1916 and June 1917. Twice Mentioned in Dispatches. M.C. Aug. 1917.

MACKINNON, PATRICK.
    George Heriot's School. O.T.C. 1913-16. Student of Arts, 1916 and 1918-19. O.T.C. Artillery, 1916-17, Cadet; Officer Cadet June 1917. R.F.A. (S.R.), 2nd Lieut. Dec. 1917. Wounded Aug. 1918. Invalided out March 1919.

MACKINNON, WILLIAM DONALD.
    George Heriot's School. O.T.C. 1909-11. Student of Medicine, 1911-17; M.B., Ch.B. 1917. O.T.C. Medical, Nov. 1915 to July 1917, Cadet. R.A.M.C. (S.R.), Lieut. Oct. 1917; Captain Oct. 1918. Invalided out March 1919.

MACKINTOSH, ALLAN HENRY GRANT.
    Royal Academy, Inverness. M.B., Ch.B. 1909. M.O. (Civilian), 3/3rd West Riding Brigade, R.F.A., 1914-16. R.A.M.C., Lieut. May 1917. Invalided out April 1918.

MACKINTOSH, CHARLES.
    Edinburgh Academy; First XV. and XI. B.A. (Oxford); LL.B. 1914. O.T.C. Infantry, Sept. 1914, Cadet. 4th Royal Scots (T.), Lieut. Sept. 1914; Captain July 1917; Staff Captain, 229th Infantry Brigade. Gallipoli, Palestine, and France. Dispatches June 1918. M.C. June 1919.

MACKINTOSH, HUGH CAMERON. (See p. 751.)

MACKINTOSH, IAN.
    George Watson's College. O.T.C. 1914-15. Student of Arts, 1918. 1st Cameron Highlanders, 2nd Lieut. Aug. 1915; Captain June 1918. France. M.C. Dec. 1918.

MACKINTOSH, JAMES.
    Banff and Fordyce Academies. Student of Arts, 1913-14. 5th Cameron Highlanders, Private Sept. 1914; L/Corporal; 2nd Lieut. Oct. 1916; Lieut. April 1918.

MACKINTOSH, JOHN.
    Nairn Academy. B.D. 1870. Minister, Church of Scotland. Chaplain, 2nd Battn. V.S.R., 1895; Chaplain, 3rd Class, 1905; 2nd Class 1910. 2nd Scottish General Hospital for seven months.

Record of War Service

MACKINTOSH, J. KYLE.
Student. Highland Mounted Brigade (T.), Major.

MACKINTOSH, WILLIAM DRUMMOND.
George Watson's College. Student of Science, 1910-15; B.Sc. 1914. O.T.C. Engineers, Jan. 1912 to Oct. 1914, C.Q.M.S. R.E. (S.R.), 81st Field Coy., 2nd Lieut. Oct. 1914; Lieut. Oct. 1915; Captain Nov. 1917; Acting Major Sept. 1917. France; Loos, Somme, Ancre, third Ypres. Wounded April 1918. Dispatches Aug. 1919. M.C. 1916; Bar to M.C. June 1918.

MACKINTOSH, WILLIAM JOHN.
Royal Academy, Inverness. Student of Medicine, 1918. 7th Cameron Highlanders, Oct. 1916; L/Corporal Jan. 1918. France. Wounded and Prisoner of War March 1918.

MacLACHLAINN, ALASTAIR MACKINTOSH.
Cheltenham. O.T.C. 1906-11, Cadet Colour-Sergeant. Student of Medicine, 1912-14 and 1917-19. O.T.C. Artillery, 1912-14, Medical, 1918-19, Cadet. 1/1st Scottish Horse Brigade Field Ambulance, Private Sept. 1914; L/Corporal Nov. 1915. Imperial Camel Corps Field Ambulance. France, Med. Exp. Force, and Palestine.

MACLACHLAN, ALASTAIR DUNLOP BANKS.
George Watson's College. O.T.C. to 1912, Cadet L/Corporal. Student of Arts, 1913-14. 16th Royal Scots, Private Jan. 1915; 2nd Lieut.; Lieut. Machine-Gun Corps. 8th Rajputs; 1/150th Indian Infantry, Staff Captain and R.T.O., Indian Army. France, Salonika, and India. Wounded at the Somme. M.C. July 1916.

MACLACHLAN, ALEXANDER KENNETH.
M.B., Ch.B. 1909. R.A.M.C. (T.), Lieut. Jan. 1913; Captain April 1915; Acting Major March 1919. Egypt.

McLACHLAN, ANGUS ELRICK WILLIAM.
George Heriot's School; First XV. O.T.C. 1913-17, Cadet Sergeant. Student of Medicine, 1918. 3rd and 2nd Royal Scots, May 1917; 2nd Lieut. Aug. 1917; Lieut. Feb. 1919.

MACLACHLAN, CHARLES FELLOWES.
George Watson's College. Student of Medicine, 1909-15; M.B., Ch.B. 1915. O.T.C. Infantry, 1908-12, Cadet. R.A.M.C., Lieut. 1915; Captain Jan. 1917. France 1916-18; Somme, Ancre, Cambrai; Salonika 1918; S. Russia. M.C.

MACLACHLAN, CHARLES FELLOWES MONCRIEFFE.
Crieff Academy. Student of Arts and Law, 1900-6 and 1910-12. Writer to the Signet, 1907. 16th Royal Scots, Private Nov. 1914. 11th and 9th Gordon Highlanders, 2nd Lieut. March 1915; Lieut. July 1916; Captain Dec. 1917; Adjutant Aug. 1916 to March 1918. 1/1st Highland Cyclist Battn., Acting Adjutant April 1918. France Oct. 1915 to March 1918. Dispatches May 1917.

Record of War Service

McLACHLAN, DONALD GORDON STEWART.
George Heriot's School. O.T.C. 1913-16, Cadet L/Corporal Student of Medicine, 1918. Royal Scots, Aug. 1916; 2nd Lieut. Jan. 1917; Lieut. July 1918. Attached 8th Welsh Regiment. India and Mesopotamia.

MACLACHLAN, ROBERT CLEPHANE.
M.B., Ch.B. 1900. R.A.M.C., Captain Nov. 1915.

MACLAGAN, DAVID WHITESIDE.
Edinburgh Academy. M.B., Ch.B. 1898. R.A.M.C., Lieut. Nov. 1915; Captain Nov. 1916 to Feb. 1919. M.O., 3rd South Staffordshire Regiment, and H.M.S. *Britannic*. Embarkation Staff, Southampton. Dispatches 1918.

MACLAGAN, DOUGLAS CRAIG.
Royal High School. Student of Law, 1899-1901. 5th Royal Scots (T.), Captain Aug. 1914; Major Jan. 1915; Temp. Lieut.-Col. April to June 1916. Gallipoli. D.S.O. Oct. 1915.

MACLAGAN, JOHN.
George Watson's College. M.A. 1903. Minister, Church of Scotland. R.F.A., 157th Brigade, 2nd Lieut. March 1915; Lieut. Dec. 1915. France.

MACLAGAN, JAMES PHILIP DALRYMPLE.
Haileybury. Student of Medicine, 1911-14. R.F.A. (T.), 1st Lowland Brigade, Gunner Sept. 1914. 2/7th Royal Scots, 2nd Lieut. March 1915; Lieut. Nov. 1915. R.F.C. and Royal Air Force, Pilot Oct. 1916 to Aug. 1919. France.

MACLAGAN, PHILIP WHITESIDE.
Berwick Grammar School. M.B., Ch.B. 1910; M.D. 1917. R.A.M.C., Lieut. Aug. 1914; Captain Aug. 1915. Isolation Hospital, Aldershot, 1914-18. France Jan. 1918. Dispatches Sept. 1917. M.C. Oct. 1918.

MacLAGAN, WILLIAM FERGUSON.
George Watson's College. M.A. 1901; LL.B. 1903. Law Agent. R.H.A. and R.G.A., Gunner April 1917; 2nd Lieut. May 1918. Wounded Oct. 1918.

MacLANACHAN, WILLIAM.
Student of Medicine, 1914-15 and 1917-18. O.T.C. Infantry, Jan. to July 1915, Cadet. Royal Air Force, 2nd Lieut.

McLAREN, ALISTAIR JAMES.
Dingwall Academy. Student of Arts, 1915-16 and 1918-19. O.T.C. Artillery, 1916, Cadet. R.F.A., Gunner Sept. 1916. France. M.M. (Zonnebeke) Jan. 1918.

McLAREN, DONALD JAMES.
Bedford Grammar School. M.B., Ch.B. 1910. Associate, South Australian School of Mines. 2/4th Somerset Light Infantry (T.), Feb. 1913; Captain and Adjutant Oct. 1914. R.A.M.C., Captain Feb. 1916. Third Afghan War.

Record of War Service

McLAREN, HAMISH DUNCAN.
Fordyce Academy, Banff; First XI. Student of Science, 1915-16. O.T.C. Engineers, Oct. 1915 to June 1916, Cadet. R.N.V.R., Signaller Dec. 1916. R.N.A.S., Probationer Flight Officer, Nov. 1917. Royal Air Force, Pilot Feb. 1918; Captain Sept. 1918. France. D.F.C. and Croix de Guerre with Palm (French) Oct. 1918; Bar to D.F.C. Nov. 1918.

McLAREN, JAMES BOSWELL PATERSON.
Linlithgow Academy. Student of Medicine, 1909-16; M.B., Ch.B. 1916. O.T.C. Medical, 1915-16, Cadet. R.A.M.C., Lieut. May 1916; Captain May 1917. 20th Nottingham and Derbyshire Regiment; 59th Labour Group; 10/11th Highland Light Infantry; 16th Field Ambulance; No. 2 Labour Group. France. Dispatches Jan. 1919.

McLAREN, JAMES CORRIGALL.
Invergordon Academy. Student of Arts, 1917-19. 4th Seaforth Highlanders, Private April 1918.

MacLAREN, MURRAY.
Grammar School, St John, New Brunswick. B.A.; M.B., C.M. 1884; M.D. 1888; M.R.C.S. (Eng.) 1885; LL.D. Canadian Army Medical Corps, May 1889; Lieut.-Col.; Colonel April 1915. O.C. No. 1 Canadian General Hospital; D.D.M.S., Canadians; Canadian Hospital, Buxton. England and France Sept. 1914-19. C.M.G. and Dispatches Jan. 1916.

McLAREN, PATRICK DUNCAN.
M.A. 1912; M.B., Ch.B. 1916. O.T.C. Medical, Nov. 1915 to Jan. 1917, Cadet. R.A.M.C., Lieut. Jan. 1917; Captain Feb. 1918. Mesopotamia.

McLAREN, RORY ERIC.
M.B., Ch.B. 1907; M.D. 1910; D.P.H. (Edin.) 1908. R.A.M.C., Lieut.

McLAREN, THOMAS.
Edinburgh Academy; First XV. Student of Medicine, 1915. 4th Highland Light Infantry, 2nd Lieut. Nov. 1915; Lieut. July 1917; Acting Captain May 1918. France.

McLAREN, THOMAS DICK.
Edinburgh Institution. Student of Arts and Medicine, 1890-9; M.B., Ch.B. 1899. R.A.M.C., Lieut. Oct. 1915; Captain Oct. 1916 to July 1918.

McLAREN, WILLIAM SMAIL.
Alloa School. M.B., Ch.B. 1911; D.P.H. (Edin.) 1913. R.A.M.C., Lieut. July 1916; Captain July 1917 to March 1919. 9th Gloucestershire Regiment, France.

McLAUGHLIN, JAMES NEIL.
Clongower Wood College, Ireland. M.B., Ch.B. 1906; M.D. 1910. R.A.M.C. (V.), 1902-8, Sergeant. R.A.M.C. (S.R.O.), Lieut. 1908; Captain 1912; Brevet Major 1917. No. 8 Stationary Hospital, Boulogne. Invalided out 1918. Dispatches 1915.

Record of War Service

MacLAURIN, CHARLES.
Sydney Grammar School. M.B., C.M. 1895. Australian Army Medical Corps, Lieut.-Col. Aug. 1915. No. 3 London General Hospital and No. 2 Australian Casualty Clearing Station.

MACLEAN, ALEXANDER.
George Watson's College; First XV. M.B., C.M. 1889. Royal Navy, Aug. 1889; Surgeon-Captain June 1919. D.S.O. May 1916.

MacLEAN, ALEXANDER FRASER.
Morrison's Academy, Crieff. M.A. 1905; B.Sc. 1908. 16th Royal Scots, Private Nov. 1914; Sergeant 1915; 2nd Lieut. 1915; Captain 1916. 15th Divisional Gas Officer; Area Gas Officer, No. 3 District.

MACLEAN, ALEXANDER MILLER.
Royal High School. M.A. 1884; B.D. 1887; D.D. 1919 Minister, Church of Scotland. Army Chaplain, 4th Class, 1897. Mobilised Dec. 1914; 2nd Class, Sept. 1917. France. C.M.G. and Dispatches Jan. 1916. T.D. 1917.

McLEAN, ANGUS.
Dunbar Burgh School. Student of Science, 1911-14; B.Sc. 1914; C.D.A. (Edin.). Lothians and Border Horse (T.), Private Nov. 1912. Mobilised Aug. 1914; Sergeant. R.F.A., 1st Lowland Brigade, 2nd Lieut. Nov. 1915; Lieut. July 1917. France, 61st Divisional R.A., May 1916. Wounded June 1917; Gassed Sept. 1917.

MacLEAN, CHARLES ALLAN.
Tobermory School. M.A. 1914; B.Sc. 1920. 6th and 4th Royal Scots, Private 1910; L/Corporal. 11th Argyll and Sutherland Highlanders, 2nd Lieut. Jan. 1915; Captain Feb. 1917. Dispatches 1917. M.C. and Croix de Guerre 1918; M.B.E. 1919.

MACLEAN, DONALD McDONALD.
Fettes College; First XV. M.A. 1901. Minister, U.F. Church of Scotland. Scottish Red Cross Mobile Unit, Rouen (Driver) 1916-17. Chaplain, 4th Class, May 1917. Salonika. Dispatches Jan. 1919.

MacLEAN, EVAN VICTOR.
Student of Law, 1908. Law Agent. Indian Army Volunteers, 2nd Lieut. June 1915; Lieut. June 1916. R.F.A. and R.F.C., France and Egypt, 1915-19.

MACLEAN, EWEN JOHN.
M.B., Ch.B. 1889; M.D. 1891; M.R.C.P. (Lond.) 1896. R.A.M.C. (T.), 1909; Major; Brevet Lieut.-Col. June 1919; Lieut.-Col. 3rd Western General Hospital; Officers' Hospital, Eaton Hall, Chester.

MacLEAN, HECTOR.
George Watson's College. Student of Law, 1914-16. Chartered Accountant, 1919. R.F.A., Gunner Aug. 1916; Bombardier Jan. 1917; 2nd Lieut. Jan. 1918. France 1915-19.

Record of War Service

MacLEAN, HENRY JOHN.
Timaru High School, New Zealand. M.B., Ch.B. 1900; F.R.C.S. (Edin.) 1909. N.Z. Medical Corps, Captain 1901; Major 1914; Lieut.-Col. March 1917; Colonel 1919. C.B.E. and Dispatches 1918.

McLEAN, IAN.
Otago Boys' High School, New Zealand. Student of Medicine, 1918. N.Z.F.A., Gunner, 1915-18. Egypt and France. Wounded at Messines 1917.

McLEAN, JAMES YOUNGER.
Edinburgh Academy. University O.T.C. Artillery, 1909-12 and 1914, Cadet. R.F.A., 4th Northumbrian Brigade, 2nd Lieut. Oct. 1914; Lieut. July 1915. R.F.C., June 1916; Captain Sept. 1916. O.C. 22nd Balloon Coy., France, and Salonika. Dispatches (France) July 1915 and (Salonika) Nov. 1917. M.C. Jan. 1918.

McLEAN, JOHN.
Tain Royal Academy; First XV. and XI. Student of Law, 1897-8 and 1918-19. Law Agent, 1897. 1st Ross Volunteers, Private 1883-5. No. 5 Coy. Q.E.R., 1885-91; 2nd V.B. Royal Scots, Edinburgh, 1917-18.

MACLEAN, JOSEPH.
Easdale School. Student of Arts, 1914-16. Schoolmaster. R.G.A., Gunner June 1916. Italy and France.

McLEAN, KENNETH.
B.Sc. 1913. O.T.C. Artillery, Feb. 1900 to Nov. 1912, Cadet. 4th Gurkha Rifles (I.A.R.O.), Lieut.

MACLEAN, KENNETH ALEXANDER.
M.B., Ch.B. 1910; D.P.H. (Edin.). No. 4 Coy. Q.R.V.B., Royal Scots, 1906-8. O.T.C. Infantry, Dec. 1908-10, Cadet Corporal. R.A.M.C., Lieut. Aug. 1914; Captain Aug. 1915. 35th Field Ambulance; 21st General Hospital, Alexandria. Palestine (Ismailia).

MACLEAN, MURDO.
Inverness Royal Academy. M.A. 1899; M.B., Ch.B. 1906. R.A.M.C., Lieut. May 1915. 2nd Northern General Hospital, Leeds.

MacLEAN, NEIL ADAM.
George Watson's College. M.A. 1908; LL.B. 1911; and Advocate. President. S.R.C. 3rd Royal Scots, Private Nov. 1916; L/Corporal July 1917; 2nd Lieut. Oct. 1918.

MacLEAN, RICHARD.
B.Sc. (Distinction) 1910. O.T.C. Engineers, 1908-11, Cadet. Bombay, Baroda and Central India Railway Volunteers, 2nd Lieut. to Jan. 1915. R.E. (Railway Troops), 2nd Lieut. Aug. 1915; Lieut. Feb. 1916; Captain Jan. 1917; Acting Major June 1918 to Feb. 1919. 260th Coy. R.E. France Oct. 1915 to May 1918. Dispatches Nov. 1918.

Record of War Service

McLEAN, ROBERT.
Edinburgh Academy; First XV. and XI. B.Sc. 1904. University Battery, E.C.A.V., 1902-4; Gunner. R.E., Captain Sept. 1915. Aden and Mesopotamia; France.

MACLEAN, ROBERT ALLAN.
Kent Road School, Glasgow. Student of Science, 1918. 1st and 2nd King's Own Royal Lancaster Regiment, 2nd Lieut. Jan. 1918.

MACLEAN, RODERICK.
Student of Law, 1899-1902. Chartered Accountant, 1902. 4th Cameron Highlanders (T.), Captain Aug. 1914; Major Jan. 1916.

McLEAN, WILLIAM FARQUHAR.
Fordyce Academy, Banffshire. M.B., Ch.B. 1912; M.D. 1920. O.T.C. Medical, 1909-11, Cadet Corporal. R.A.M.C. (S.R.), Lieut. 1911; Captain April 1915; Acting Major Jan. 1918; Acting Lieut.-Col. July 1918. France 1914 and 1916-19. Mediterranean 1915. Dispatches Jan. 1915. M.C. June 1918.

McLELLAN, ARCHIBALD.
Edinburgh Academy. O.T.C. 1914-16. University O.T.C. Artillery, 1917-18, Cadet Sergeant. R.G.A., Officer Cadet Sept. 1918.

McLEMAN, JOHN.
Kirkcaldy High School. O.T.C. 1908-9. Student of Medicine, 1910-14 and 1917-20; M.B. 1920. O.T.C. Infantry, 1909-12, Cadet. R.A.M.C. (T.), Scottish Horse Brigade Field Ambulance, Private Sept. 1914. 7th Durham Light Infantry, Lieut. July 1917.

MACLENNAN, ALISTAIR. (See p. 751.)

MACLENNAN, ANDREW.
George Watson's College. M.B., C.M. 1884. R.A.M.C. (T.), Captain Aug. 1915. Royal Air Force Medical Service, Oct. 1918 to Feb. 1919.

MACLENNAN, IAN.
Student of Medicine, 1914-15. O.T.C. Infantry, 1914-15, Cadet. 11th Royal Highlanders (Black Watch), Lieut. July 1917. Prisoner of War March 1918.

McLENNAN, JOHN.
Student. 8th Royal Scots (T.), Lieut.

MACLENNAN, RODERICK DIARMID.
Oban High School, and Gore High School, Southland, New Zealand; First XI. Cadet Corps till 1914. Student of Arts and Divinity, 1916-17. O.T.C. Artillery, 1916-17, Cadet; Officer Cadet June 1917. R.G.A., 2nd Lieut. Nov. 1917. France. Wounded Sept. 1918.

MACLENNAN, WILLIAM DONALD ROSS.
Boroughmuir School. Student of Arts and Science, 1910-14; M.A. (Hons. Maths.); B.Sc. 1914. Schoolmaster. R.F.A., Gunner 1915; 2nd Lieut. Aug. 1916; Lieut. Feb. 1917. R.G.A., France, Oct. 1916 to Nov. 1918.

Record of War Service

MacLEOD, ALEXANDER GORDON.
Manchester Grammar School. M.B., Ch.B. 1909. R.A.M.C., Lieut. March 1915; Captain March 1916; Acting Major March to June 1919.

MACLEOD, BANNATYNE.
Clare College, Cambridge. Student of Arts, 1876-7. 2/4th Seaforth Highlanders (T.), Major Nov. 1914.

MacLEOD, CHARLES GORDON.
M.A.; M.B., C.M. 1889; M.D. 1911. Australian Army Medical Corps (Reserve), Hon. Major Nov. 1909. Ophthalmic Surgeon, Garrison Hospital, Sydney, 1914-15, and No. 4 Australian General Hospital, Randwick, 1915-18.

MacLEOD, IAN RONALDS.
George Watson's College. Student of Medicine, 1899-1909 and 1910-11; L.R.C.P. & S. (Edin.) and L.R.F.P.S. (Glasg.) 1910. 7th Cameron Highlanders, Lieut. 1914. R.A.M.C., Captain July 1916.

MacLEOD, JAMES STRACHAN.
George Watson's College. Student of Law, 1894-6. Solicitor before the Supreme Courts. South Africa, 1899-1902. Royal Highlanders (Black Watch). 8th Durham Light Infantry, Major; Lieut.-Col. July 1918. Attached 8th Lancashire Fusiliers. France 1914. Wounded Oct. 1915, and Gassed 1918. D.S.O. and twice Mentioned in Dispatches.

MACLEOD, JOHN ANDREW.
Golspie School. M.B., Ch.B. 1906; D.P.H. (Edin.) 1913. R.A.M.C., Lieut. Aug. 1914; Captain Aug. 1915. Wounded July 1916. Invalided out June 1919. Dispatches Jan. 1916.

MACLEOD, MALCOLM.
M.A. 1906. Minister, U.F. Church of Scotland. Y.M.C.A., Rouen, Jan. to Sept. 1915. Chaplain, 4th Class, 1/4th Gordon Highlanders, June 1916.

MacLEOD, MURDO.
Nicolson Institute, Stornoway. Student of Arts, 1914-16; M.A. 1920. R.F.A., 148th Brigade, Gunner April 1916; Bombardier June 1916; Corporal 1917; Sergeant Instructor (Education) 1918.

MACLEOD, NEIL.
George Watson's College. Student of Medicine, 1912-15 and 1916-18; M.B., Ch.B. 1918. O.T.C. Artillery, Oct. 1913 to Aug. 1914, Cadet. 9th Royal Scots, Private Aug. 1914. Royal Navy, Surgeon-Probationer, Jan. 1915; Surgeon June 1918 to April 1919. H.M. Ships *Sandfly*, *Nicator*, *Africa*, *Prince Rupert*, and *Princess Royal*. Dispatches (Jutland).

MACLEOD, NORMAN.
Dingwall Academy. Student of Medicine, 1918. 1st Royal Highlanders (Black Watch), Private Jan. 1917. Wounded.

Record of War Service

MACLEOD, ROBERT ALEXANDER MACKENZIE.
 M.B., C.M. 1900; M.D. 1906; D.P.H. (Edin.) 1911. R.A.M.C., Lieut. May 1915; Captain May 1916 to April 1919.

McLEOD, TORQUIL WILLIAM.
 Royal Academy, Tain; First XI. University O.T.C. Artillery, 1916, Cadet; Officer Cadet Dec. 1916. R.G.A., 123rd Siege Battery, 2nd Lieut. March 1917 to July 1918. Wounded Aug. 1917. Invalided out July 1918.

MACLEOD, WILLIAM BERNERA.
 M.B., C.M. 1891. Royal Navy, Fleet Surgeon, Nov. 1910. H.M.S. *Impregnable*, Devonport.

McLINTOCK, JAMES MAITLAND.
 George Heriot's School; First XV. Student of Science and Medicine, 1914-15. R.E. (Special Brigade), Corporal July 1915-17. Royal Air Force, Lieut. 1917-18. France 1915-17.

MACLUCKIE, REGINALD WILLIAM.
 B.Sc. 1900. 3rd Argyll and Sutherland Highlanders, 2nd Lieut.

MACLURE, EDWIN BAIN.
 M.A. 1912. 15th Royal Scots, Private Sept. 1914. 9th Royal Scots Fusiliers, 2nd Lieut. June 1915. Machine-Gun Corps, Jan. 1916; Lieut. June 1917.

McMASTER, ARCHIBALD COTTERELL.
 Prince Albert College, Auckland, New Zealand. M.B., Ch.B. 1905; F.R.C.S. (Edin.) 1908. N.Z. Medical Corps, Lieut. 1911. R.A.M.C. (T.), Lieut. Aug. 1914; Captain Dec. 1915 to March 1919. 3rd Lowland Field Ambulance, 1914-15; Edinburgh and Perth War Hospitals, 1915-18. Italy 1918.

MACMEEKEN, JOHN WEST.
 Lanark Grammar School. M.A. 1909; B.Sc. 1911. O.T.C. Infantry, March 1909 to Jan. 1910, Cadet. Princess Patricia's Canadian Light Infantry, Private. France, Somme. Invalided out April 1918.

McMENAMIN, FRANCIS DE SALES.
 St Columb's, Londonderry. M.B., Ch.B. 1912. R.A.M.C., Lieut. Dec. 1914; Captain Dec. 1915; Major Jan. 1919. Gallipoli, Salonika, and France M.C. May 1918.

McMENEMY, JOHN JOSEPH.
 St Joseph's College, Dumfries. Student of Arts, 1916-17 and 1918-19; M.A. 1920. O.T.C. Artillery, 1918, Cadet. 4th Seaforth Highlanders (S.R.), Private Sept. 1918.

MACMICHAEL, DAVID COLVILLE.
 Royal High School; Athletics. M.A. 1886; B.D. 1891. Minister, Church of Scotland. Colombo Town Guard and Artillery, 1914-17. Hon. Chaplain, Ceylon Defence Force (Captain) Oct. 1917.

Record of War Service

McMICHAEL, GEORGE VERT THOMSON.
George Watson's College. M.B., Ch.B. 1911; D.P.H. (Edin.) 1912. R.A.M.C., Lieut. June 1915; Captain June 1916; Acting Major Jan. to July 1918; Captain July 1918 to Jan. 1919. France Sept. 1915 to Jan. 1919.

McMILLAN, ARTHUR ROBERT GOW.
Fettes College. M.A. 1905. Advocate, 1910. 9th Royal Scots (T.), 2nd Lieut. Oct. 1915; Lieut. July 1917.

MACMILLAN, CHARLES CLARKE.
M.B., C.M. 1897. Royal Navy, Staff Surgeon; Fleet Surgeon May 1914. R.N. Hospital, Malta. D.S.O. Nov. 1900.

MACMILLAN, COLIN HUGH.
B.Sc. 1910. O.T.C. Infantry, 1909-10, and Engineers, 1910-13, Cadet Sergeant. R.E., Fourth Army H.Q., Signal Coy., Lieut. Sept. 1914; Captain Sept. 1915.

MACMILLAN, HUGH AGNEW.
George Watson's College; First XV. Cadet Corps 1905-8. M.B., Ch.B. 1913. O.T.C. Artillery, Oct. 1910 to June 1914, Cadet. R.A.M.C., Lieut. Oct. 1914; Captain April 1915; Acting Major April 1918; Acting Lieut.-Col. June 1918. 1st Northumbrian Midland Field Hospital, and 2/4th Leicestershire Regiment. France. Wounded Sept. 1917. Dispatches Jan. 1919. M.C. Sept. 1917.

McMILLAN, JAMES ARTHUR.
Ewart High School, Newton Stewart. Student of Law, 1904-6. 7th Scottish Rifles, 2nd Lieut. June 1912; Lieut. June 1915; Captain April 1916. 52nd Division. Gallipoli, Egypt, and Palestine. Wounded at Gallipoli June 1915, and Palestine Nov. 1917.

McMILLAN, JAMES ATHOLE.
George Watson's College; First XI. Student of Science, 1912-14 and 1918-19; B.Sc. 1919. R.A.M.C. (T.), 3rd Lowland Field Ambulance, Private Nov. 1914. R.F.A., 2nd Lieut. Nov. 1915; Lieut. July 1917. France. Wounded Oct. 1918.

McMILLAN, JOHN JAMES.
M.B., Ch.B. 1903; M.D. 1909. R.A.M.C., Lieut. Oct. 1915; Captain April 1918.

MACMILLAN, JOHN McCALLUM ANDERSON.
M.A. 1896; M.B., Ch.B. 1900; L.R.C.P. (Lond.) 1901; F.R.C.S. (Eng.) 1908. Indian Medical Service, Lieut. 1903; Captain 1906; Major Feb. 1918; Acting Lieut.-Col. Feb. 1917 to June 1919. Egyptian Exp. Force, 1914-19. Dispatches Jan. 1920.

MACMILLAN, JOHN MELROSE.
Edinburgh Institution. M.A. 1895; B.A.; LL.B. (Camb.) 1899. Solicitor. 4th Duke of Cornwall's Light Infantry, Lieut. Nov. 1914. Royal Defence Corps, March 1916 to Jan. 1919; Captain July 1917.

Record of War Service

MACMILLAN, ROBERT JAMES ALAN.
 George Watson's College; First XV. M.B., Ch.B. 1909; D.T.M. & H. (Liverpool) 1913. E.C.A.V., 2nd Lieut. 1905. Forth R.G.A. (T.), Captain 1908. Uganda Medical Service, 1913-16; Major Dec. 1915. R.G.A. (T.), Major Jan. 1917. German East Africa, 1914-16; France and The Rhine, 1916-19. Dispatches May 1918 and July 1919. D.S.O. April 1919.

MACMILLAN, SAMUEL RONALD.
 Bathgate Academy. Student of Medicine, 1918. Royal Navy, Telegraphist Dec. 1917.

McMORLAND, JOHN BRUCE.
 Clifton Bank, St Andrews, and Edinburgh Academy. M.B., Ch.B. 1906. R.A.M.C., Lieut. May 1916; Captain April 1918.

McMULLAN, GEORGE.
 Blairlodge; First XV. M.B., Ch.B. 1906; M.D. 1913; F.R.C.S. (Edin.) 1919. R.A.M.C., Lieut. April 1915; Captain April 1916; Acting Major Dec. 1918.

McMURTRIE, ALEXANDER CHURCH BRODIE.
 M.B., Ch.B. 1906; M.D. 1910; D.P.H. (Edin.) 1907; F.R.C.S. (Edin.) 1909. R.A.M.C., Lieut.; Captain May 1916. M.C.

MacNAB, ROBERT ALLAN.
 Kingussie School. Student of Medicine, 1912-14 and 1918-19. 4th Cameron Highlanders (T.), Private Jan. 1911; Sergeant July 1915. R.E., 2nd Battn. (Special Brigade), Lieut. April 1916. France Feb. 1915 to Jan. 1918.

MACNAB, WILLIAM JOHNSTON.
 George Watson's College. M.B., Ch.B. 1906. R.A.M.C., Lieut. June 1915-16; Captain Nov. 1917 to Jan. 1919.

MACNAB, WILLIAM URQUHART.
 Kingussie School. M.A. 1912. Royal Naval Reserve (T.), Deck Hand, Oct. 1916.

McNAIR, ANDREW.
 Kilmarnock Academy. Student of Arts and Medicine, 1901-8. 8th Cameron Highlanders, Private Nov. 1914. 4th Royal Scots Fusiliers, 2nd Lieut. March 1915; Lieut. July 1917 to June 1919. Wounded Nov. 1917.

MACNAIR, DAVID.
 Bede Collegiate School, Sunderland. M.B., Ch.B. 1908; M.D. 1912. R.A.M.C. (T.), Lieut. Dec. 1909; Captain June 1913. 25th Field Ambulance. Prisoner of War.

McNAIR, HERBERT.
 Preston Grammar School; First XI. Student of Medicine, 1916 and 1918-19. O.T.C. Artillery, 1916-17, Cadet Bombardier; Officer Cadet July 1917. R.F.A. (S.R.), 2nd Lieut. Dec. 1917. France May to Oct. 1918. M.C. April 1919.

Record of War Service

MACNAIR, ROBERT.
George Watson's College; First XV. Student of Medicine, 1912-18; M.B., Ch.B. 1919. O.T.C. Medical, 1916, Cadet. R.N.V.R., Surgeon-Probationer, March 1916.

MACNAIR, ROBERT ALASTAIR CUNNINGHAM.
Royal High School; First XV. Student of Medicine, 1916-17 and 1918-19. 6th East Kent Regiment (The Buffs), Acting Corporal; Officer Cadet.

MACNAUGHTON, ARNOLD INGRAM.
Merchiston Castle; First XV. and XI. O.T.C. 1908-17, Cadet Officer. University O.T.C. Artillery, 1917-18, Cadet, Acting Bombardier; Officer Cadet Jan. 1918. R.G.A., 2nd Lieut. July 1918.

MACNAUGHTON, DUNCAN.
Edinburgh Academy. M.A. 1914; LL.B. 1920. 9th Royal Scots (T.), Piper Aug. 1914. 3rd Gordon Highlanders, 2nd Lieut. Jan. 1915; Lieut. 1916 to Jan. 1917. France, attached 1st Gordon Highlanders, March 1915. Wounded Aug. 1915.

MACNAUGHTON, FRANCIS GEORGE.
Merchiston Castle. O.T.C. 1905-9. M.B., Ch.B. 1914; M.D. 1920. O.T.C. Infantry, 1909-13, Cadet Colour-Sergeant. R.A.M.C. (S.R.), Lieut. April 1914; Captain April 1915. Wounded July 1917.

McNAUGHTON, STEWART.
Middlesbrough High School. M.B., Ch.B. 1905; M.D. 1915; D.P.H. (Camb.). 1908; D.T.M. and H. 1909. R.A.M.C., Lieut. Feb. 1916; Captain Feb. 1917.

McNAUGHTON, WILLIAM.
Morrison's Academy, Crieff; First XV. and XI. M.B., Ch.B. 1910. Forth R.G.A., 1905-12, Lieut. R.A.M.C., Lieut. Jan. 1912; Captain March 1915; Brevet Major June 1917. India, Mesopotamia, and Afghanistan. Dispatches June 1917, April 1918, Feb. and May 1919. O.B.E. May 1919.

MacNEIL, CELIA MARY COLQUHOUN.
M.B., Ch.B. 1913. R.A.M.C. (Auxiliary Section), Sept. 1915. Leith War Hospital, 1915-17. 14th General Hospital, France (Sisters and Q.M.A.A.C. Section), Equiv. Major, 1917-19.

McNEIL, CHARLES.
M.A. 1901. M.B., Ch.B. (Hons.) 1905. M.D. 1908; F.R.C.P. (Edin.) 1913. Assistant Physician, R.I.E. Scottish Branch B.R.C.S., attached No. 11 Stationary Hospital, Rouen, Nov. 1914. R.A.M.C., Temp. Captain Feb. 1916; Temp. Major May 1917. Dispatches Jan. 1918.

McNEIL, DAVID BELL.
M.A. 1908. Schoolmaster. Forth R.G.A. (T.), Gunner May 1916; Bombardier Aug. 1916; 2nd Lieut. Nov. 1917. France. Dispatches Nov. 1918.

Record of War Service

McNEIL, ROBERT PATRICK.
George Watson's College. M.B., Ch.B. 1902. South African Medical Service, Captain Oct. 1914. M.O., 1st Natal Carbineers in German South-West Africa, and 1st Cape Corps in German East Africa, May 1916. M.C. Jan. 1917.

McNEILL, DAVID.
Royal High School. M.A. 1910. Schoolmaster. R.G.A., 151st Siege Battery, Gunner Dec. 1915; 2nd Lieut. May 1917; Lieut. Nov. 1918; 99th Brigade, Oct. 1918. Education Officer. 19th Corps Heavy Artillery, France.

McNEILL, FERGUSON.
Boroughmuir School. Student of Arts, 1911-15 and 1916-17; M.A. 1917. O.T.C. Infantry, June to Aug. 1915, Cadet. 6th Royal Scots (T.), 2nd Lieut. Aug. 1915; Lieut. July 1917. Wounded. Invalided out July 1917.

McNEILL, GEORGE.
M.B., Ch.B. 1902; F.R.C.S. (Edin.). R.A.M.C., Captain May 1916; Acting Major March 1918. France 1916.

McNEILL, N. A.
Student of Science, 1908-14. Scots Guards, Captain; Major April 1918.

MACNEILL, ROBERT ARCHIBALD.
Dollar Academy. M.B., Ch.B. 1899. R.A.M.C., Lieut. Dec. 1915. Rejoined March 1917; Captain Sept. 1917. Dispatches May 1918.

MacNISH, DAVID.
Dumfries Academy. M.A. 1882; M.B., C.M. 1887. Auxiliary Hospital, Neuilly sur Seine, Jan. to Oct. 1915. R.A.M.C., Lieut. Oct. 1915; Captain May 1916.

MACONOCHIE, ERIC REGINALD DELME.
Blairlodge; First XV. Cadet Corps 1899-1903, Corporal. M.B., Ch.B. 1908; F.R.C.S. (Edin.) 1911. Lothians and Border Horse, Private 1903-6. R.A.M.C., Lieut. April 1915; Captain April 1917; Major Jan. 1918. France, Egypt, Palestine, and Salonika.

McOUAT, JOHN THOMSON.
Glenalmond; First XV. O.T.C. 1913-17, Cadet Sergeant. Student of Medicine, 1918. Argyll and Sutherland Highlanders, Private Nov. 1917. 5th Battn. G.M.G.C., 2nd Lieut. Sept. to Dec. 1918.

MacOWAN, DAVID.
Stirling High School. M.A., B.Sc. 1910. Lothians and Border Horse, Private Nov. 1915.

MACPHAIL, HECTOR DUNCAN.
George Watson's College. M.A. 1904; M.B., Ch.B. 1908; M.D. 1911. R.A.M.C., Major May 1915. Northumberland War Hospital. O.B.E.

Record of War Service

MACPHAIL, IAIN ROSS.
 Epsom College. Student of Medicine, 1911-18. R.A.M.C., Scottish Horse Field Ambulance, Private Aug. 1914 to May 1915. R.N.V.R., Surgeon Sub-Lieut. H.M.S. *Millbrook*.

MACPHAIL, JOHN MURDO.
 George Watson's College. M.B., Ch.B. 1906. M.D. 1913. R.A.M.C., Lieut. April 1915; Captain April 1916.

MACPHAIL, WILLIAM MALCOLM.
 George Watson's College. O.T.C. 1909-13, Cadet Pipe-Major. Student of Medicine, 1913-15 and 1917-19. M.B., Ch.B. 1919. O.T.C. Infantry, Oct. 1913 to Sept. 1915, Cadet Pipe-Major. R.N.V.R., Surgeon-Probationer, Sept. 1915. 1st and 13th Destroyer Flotillas.

MACPHERSON, ALEXANDER.
 Royal High School. Student of Medicine, 1913-15. R.N.V.R., Surgeon-Probationer, Aug. 1915. H.M. Ships *Rother*, *Nigella*, *Petard*, and *Verbena*.

MACPHERSON, ALEXANDER.
 George Heriot's School. M.A. 1911; B.Sc. 1912. Lothians and Border Horse (T.), Private May 1914. Scottish Horse, 2nd Lieut. Sept. 1916. Transferred to R.F.A., Oct. 1917. Attached University O.T.C. Artillery, Aug. 1918.

MACPHERSON, ALEXANDER.
 George Watson's College. M.A. 1911. 16th Royal Scots, Private. 3rd King's Own Scottish Borderers, 2nd Lieut May 1917; Lieut.

MACPHERSON, ANGUS GORDON ROBERTS.
 Student of Science, 1918. Royal Air Force, Armament School, Uxbridge, Flight Cadet.

MACPHERSON, CHARLES JAMES.
 Kingussie School; First XI. M.A. (Hons. Classics) 1902; Ph.D. (Berlin). Intelligence Corps, 2nd Lieut. Sept. 1914; Lieut. Oct. 1915; Captain June 1918. General Staff (Operations), France, Sept. 1914 to Aug. 1919. Poland. Wounded Aug. 1917. Dispatches July 1916 and Jan. 1917. M.C. July 1918.

MACPHERSON, DONALD JAMES ROBERTSON.
 Morrison's Academy, Crieff; First XV. Student of Science, 1914-15 and 1918-19. O.T.C. Artillery, Oct. 1914 to March 1915, Cadet Bombardier. R.F.A. (S.R.), 2nd Lieut. April 1915; Lieut. Sept. 1916; Acting Captain and Adjutant, Dec. 1916 to Feb. 1917. France Nov. 1915 to Dec. 1917; Italy Dec. 1917 to Jan. 1919. Dispatches June 1918,

MACPHERSON, GEORGE WILLIAM KINNAIRD.
 Dingwall Academy. M.A. 1912; B.D. 1915. Licentiate, Church of Scotland. O.T.C. Infantry, Jan. 1910 to July 1913, Cadet. 8th and 4th Seaforth Highlanders, Lieut. Feb. 1915; Captain June 1916. France.

Record of War Service

MACPHERSON, HUGH ROSS.
    Wick High School. Student of Science, 1914-15 and 1918-19; M.A. 1920. O.T.C. Artillery, Oct. 1914 to March 1915, Cadet. R.F.A., 2nd Lieut. March 1915; Lieut. Feb. 1917. Wounded in Mesopotamia April 1916.

MACPHERSON, IAN GRAHAM.
    Rossall; First XV. and XI. O.T.C. 1914-18, Cadet Sergeant. Student of Medicine, 1918. R.F.A., 212th Battery, Officer Cadet Sept. 1918.

MACPHERSON, JAMES EWAN.
    Leith Academy. Student of Arts, 1910-12. 9th and 12th Royal Scots (T.), 1910; Major Jan. 1917. 90th Punjabis. France. North-West Frontier, India. Wounded at Arras. Twice Mentioned in Dispatches.

MACPHERSON, JAMES MURRAY.
    George Watson's College. Student of Medicine, 1912-18; M.B., Ch.B. 1918. O.T.C. Infantry, 1914-15, Cadet. R.N.V.R., H.M.S. *Itchen*, Surgeon-Probationer, July 1915. R.A.M.C., Lieut. Sept. 1918. 39th Field Ambulance, Mesopotamia.

MACPHERSON, JOHN.
    Inverness Academy. M.B., C.M. 1882; M.D. 1896; F.R.C.P. (Edin.) 1891. R.A.M.C., Hon. and Temp. Lieut.-Col. April 1917. C.B. June 1917.

MACPHERSON, JOHN DUNCAN GRAHAM.
    Craigmount; First XV. and XI. M.B., C.M. 1896. First XV. and XI. R.A.M.C., Lieut. Jan. 1898; Captain Jan. 1901; Lieut.-Col. March 1915. 38th Casualty Clearing Station (Somme and Ancre), and 6th Conv. Depôt, Etaples, Feb. 1916 to June 1918. King George's War Hospital, India, July 1918.

MACPHERSON, JOHN LUMSDEN.
    Madras College, St Andrews. M.A. (St Andrews); B.L. 1888. 6th and 7th Royal Highlanders (Black Watch) (T.), 2nd Lieut. 1890; Hon. Major 1905. O.C. Depôt 1914; Major and O.C. 2/7th and 3/7th Battns. 1915-16; Lieut.-Col. 1917. 3/7th Gordon Highlanders, Acting Lieut.-Col. 1916. Mention Feb. 1917. T.D.

MACPHERSON, JOHN MALCOLM.
    Boroughmuir School. M.A. (Hons. Engl.) 1913. 4th King's Own Scottish Borderers (T.), Private Aug. 1914; Sergeant Sept. 1914; C.Q.M.S. May 1915; 2nd Lieut. June 1916; Lieut. Dec. 1917.

MACPHERSON, JOHN STUART.
    George Watson's College; First XV. O.T.C. 1912-17, Cadet Officer. Student of Arts, 1918. Officer Cadet Sept. 1917. 2nd Argyll and Sutherland Highlanders, 2nd Lieut. Jan. 1918. France.

Record of War Service

MACPHERSON, MALCOLM MUNRO.
: Elgin Academy. 6th Seaforth Highlanders (T.), 1909-12, L/Corporal. Student of Arts and Divinity, 1911-15; M.A. 1919. O.T.C. Infantry, 1912-14, Cadet L/Corporal. 6th Seaforth Highlanders, 2nd Lieut. Oct. 1914; Lieut. Jan. 1915; Acting Captain Jan. 1916; Captain March 1918. Transferred Labour Corps, Feb. 1917-19. Wounded April 1916. Dispatches March 1919. O.B.E. June 1919.

MACPHERSON, STANLEY NORFOLK.
: Ayr Academy. University O.T.C. Infantry, 1917, Cadet. 1st Gordon Highlanders, Private Aug. 1917; L/Corporal Sept. 1917; Corporal Oct. 1918; Sergeant Jan. 1919. France; The Rhine. M.M. and Dispatches Oct. 1918

MACPHERSON, THE HON. THOMAS STEWART.
: George Watson's College. M.A. (Hons. Classics) 1897. No. 4 Coy. Q.R.V.B., Royal Scots, 1895-7, Private. Chota Nagpur Light Horse, Indian Defence Force, Trooper April 1917.

MACPHERSON, WILLIAM EWEN.
: George Heriot's School. University O.T.C. Infantry, 1917, Cadet; Officer Cadet Aug. 1918. Royal Air Force, 2nd Lieut. Nov. 1918; Lieut. April 1919. D.F.C. Nov. 1919.

MACPHERSON, SIR WILLIAM GRANT.
: Fettes College. M.A. (Hons. Classics) 1879; M.B., C.M. 1882; LL.D. 1919. Army Medical Service, 1882; Surgeon-General July 1914. D.D.G.A.M.S., War Office, Oct. 1914. D.M.S., First Army, Nov. 1915, and Macedonian Exp. Force to April 1916. D.D.G.M.S., G.H.Q., France, to June 1918; Major-General 1918. H.Q., Southern Command. C.M.G. 3rd Class, Sacred Treasure (Japan). Japanese Red Cross Decoration. K.H.P. 1912-18. C.B. Feb. 1915. Commander, Legion of Honour 1916; Commander, Crown of Italy 1917. K.C.M.G. Jan. 1918. Nine times Mentioned in Dispatches.

MACQUEEN, JOHN.
: The College, Inverness. M.B., Ch.B. 1914. O.T.C. Artillery, 1912-13, Cadet. Lovat Scouts, Private Aug. 1914. R.F.A., 2nd Lieut. Sept. 1914; Lieut. April 1915. Transferred R.A.M.C., Captain June 1915. France Jan. 1915; second Ypres. Attached Royal Highlanders, Baghdad, Mesopotamia, April 1916. Egypt (Alexandria) July 1917; Palestine Jan. 1918. Dispatches (Mesopotamia) Aug. 1917.

MACQUEEN, JOSEPH GORDON.
: M.B., Ch.B. 1911. R.A.M.C., Lieut. Dec. 1914; Captain Nov. 1917. No. 3 General Hospital, France, 1915.

MACQUEEN, RONALD CHESNEY.
: Eastbourne College. Cadet Corps 1901-4. M.B., Ch.B. 1909; F.R.C.S. (Eng.) 1913. Princess Club Hospital, Bermondsey, 1914-15. R.A.M.C., Lieut. Sept. 1915; Captain Sept. 1916; Acting Major March 1919. Military Hospital, Rugeley.

Record of War Service

MacRAE, ALEXANDER MURRAY.
Dornoch Academy. Student of Medicine, 1912-14 and 1917-20; M.B., Ch.B. 1919. O.T.C. Infantry, Oct. 1914 to July 1915, Cadet L/Corporal. R.N.V.R., Surgeon-Probationer, June 1915 to Sept. 1917. H.M. Ships *Cameleon* 1915, *Ossary* 1915-16, *Spitfire* 1916-17, and *Narcissus* 1917.

MACRAE, ANDREW THOMAS WATTERS.
George Watson's College. Student of Medicine, 1913-15. O.T.C. Infantry, Oct. 1914 to March 1915, Cadet L/Corporal. 10th Seaforth Highlanders, Lieut. April 1916; Acting Captain Oct. 1917. France 1916-18. Wounded 1916.

MACRAE, ANGUS.
George Watson's College. Student of Arts and Medicine, 1912-14 and 1919; M.A. 1919. O.T.C. Infantry, Nov. 1913 to April 1915, Cadet L/Corporal. 4th Seaforth Highlanders, 2nd Lieut. April 1915; Lieut. June 1916. Wounded and taken Prisoner March 1918.

McRAE, DAVID MILLER.
Materia Medica Laboratory. R.F.A. (T.), 1st Lowland Brigade, Driver 1913. France. 51st Highland Division, Oct. 1915 to Feb. 1917; and 96th Brigade, Sept. 1917 to May 1919.

MACRAE, DONALD ALASTAIR.
Tain Royal Academy, and Aberdeen University. Student of Medicine, 1911-14. O.T.C. Medical, Sept. 1912 to Aug. 1914, Cadet. R.A.M.C. (T.), Private. Scottish Horse Brigade Field Ambulance.

MACRAE, DONALD CAMERON.
The College, Inverness. Student of Medicine, 1914-15 and 1918-19. O.T.C. Infantry, 1914-15, Cadet. 14th Argyll and Sutherland Highlanders, Private May 1915. 1/6th Royal Highlanders (Black Watch), to March 1919. M.M. Oct. 1918.

MACRAE, DUNCAN FREDERICK.
M.B., Ch.B. 1910. R.A.M.C. (T.), Lieut. Sept. 1914; Captain April 1915. 280th Brigade, R.F.A., Feb. 1915. No. 6 Stationary Hospital, France, Oct. 1916 to Nov. 1918.

McRAE, DUNCAN JAMES.
M.B., Ch.B. 1907; M.D. 1920. R.A.M.C., Lieut.; Captain Aug. 1915. France.

MACRAE, GEORGE GORDON.
George Watson's College. O.T.C. 1915. Student of Medicine, 1917 and 1919. O.T.C. Infantry, Oct. 1917 to June 1918, Cadet; Officer Cadet July 1918. 3rd Gordon Highlanders, 2nd Lieut. March 1919.

MACRAE, HUGH.
The College, Inverness. Student of Law, 1899-1901. Chartered Accountant, 1903. R.F.A., Lieut. University Battery, E.C.A.V., 1898-1904, B.S.M.; Lieut. 1904-8. R.F.A., Lieut. Dec. 1914. France 1915-16; The Somme. Wounded 1915 and 1916. Controller of Demob. Statistics.

Record of War Service

MACRAE, IAN MACPHERSON.
　　M.B., Ch.B. 1903. Indian Medical Service, Major March 1916. Egyptian Exp. Force.

MACRAE, JOHN LEWIS.
　　Blairlodge. M.B., C.M. 1891. Indian Medical Service, 1892; Lieut.-Col. 1912. Banu 1897-8; China 1900. Stationary Hospital, Mardan, N.W.F.P., India.

MACRAE, KENNETH DUNCAN CAMERON.
　　M.B., Ch.B. 1901. R.A.M.C., Lieut.; Captain Feb. 1916.

MACRAE, KENNETH WILLIAM DUNCAN.
　　Boteler Grammar School, Warrington. M.B., Ch.B. 1905. R.A.M.C., Lieut. Sept. 1916; Captain Sept. 1917. Mesopotamia and France.

McRITCHIE, ROBERT.
　　Edinburgh Academy. University O.T.C. Artillery, 1918, Cadet Bombardier. R.G.A., Officer Cadet Oct. 1918.

McROBBIE, WILLIAM ALEXANDER.
　　Aberdeen Grammar School. University O.T.C. Artillery, 1916, Cadet. 4/2nd Highland Field Coy., R.E. (T.), 2nd Lieut. Feb. 1917; Lieut. Aug. 1918. 148th Army Troops Coy. France.

MACTAGGART, JACK AULD.
　　Glasgow Academy; First XI. O.T.C. 1912-14, Cadet Sergeant. University O.T.C. Artillery, 1916-17, Cadet Corporal. Clyde R.G.A. (T.), Officer Cadet April 1917; 2nd Lieut. Sept. 1917 to March 1919. 443rd Siege Battery, France, June to Oct. 1918. Wounded Oct. 1918.

McTURK, JOHN NORMAN.
　　M.B., Ch.B. 1906; M.D. 1909. R.A.M.C., Lieut. July 1916. 41st General Hospital, Salonika, 1916. Rejoined Nov. 1918. Order of St Sava (5th Class).

McVEAN, NORMAN NEIL GEORGE COWAN.
　　George Watson's College. M.B., Ch.B. 1905. Indian Medical Service, 1906, Captain. France 1914; Egypt, Syria, and Aden, 1915. Invalided out Jan. 1917.

MacVEAN, PATRICK WILLIAM.
　　M.B., C.M. 1893. Royal Navy, Surgeon; Staff-Surgeon (Retired).

McVEY, JAMES.
　　Bo'ness Academy. Student of Arts, 1918. 52nd Graduating Battn. Highland Light Infantry, Private May 1918.

McVICKER, DANIEL.
　　Coleraine Institution, and Queen's College, Belfast. M.B., Ch.B. 1913; F.R.C.S. (Edin.) 1920. O.T.C. Artillery, 1910-13, Cadet. R.A.M.C., Lieut. Oct. 1914; Captain Oct. 1915. 2nd Coldstream Guards, 1917. France Jan. to Aug. 1915, and June 1916 to Aug. 1917. Italy June 1918 to Aug. 1919. Wounded Aug. 1917. Dispatches Jan. 1916. M.C. Sept. 1917.

Record of War Service

McVICKER, JOSEPH WALLACE.
: Coleraine Institution; First XV. Student of Medicine, 1916. O.T.C. Medical, Oct. 1916 to June 1917, Cadet. Royal Air Force, 3rd Air Mechanic, Sept. 1917.

McVIE, HERBERT JAMES.
: Holy Cross Academy. Student of Arts, 1914-15. O.T.C. Infantry, April to Sept. 1915, Cadet. 16th Royal Scots, 2nd Lieut. Sept. 1915; Lieut. July 1917. France. Wounded April 1917. Invalided out March 1919.

McVITTIE, JOHN COULTHARD.
: Annan Academy. Student of Medicine, 1918. 4th Reserve Battn., Border Regiment, Private June 1918; Corporal Dec. 1918.

McWALTER, THOMAS.
: Student of Arts, 1908-14. 4th Royal Scots (T.), Private; L/Corporal.

MacWATT, The Hon. ROBERT CHARLES.
: Royal High School. M.B., C.M. 1886; B.Sc. (P.H.) 1897; F.R.C.S. (Eng.) 1911. Fellow of the Punjab University. Indian Medical Service, 1887; Lieut.-Col.; Colonel Jan. 1918. A.D.M.S., N.-W. Frontier of India. Inspector General, Civil Hospitals, Punjab. Chief Malaria and Plague M.O., Punjab. Kaisar-i-Hind Medal (1st Class) 1908. C.I.E. Jan. 1916.

MACWHIRTER, ALASTAIR STEWART.
: George Heriot's School. Student of Science, 1919. O.T.C. Artillery, Aug. 1917 to March 1918, Cadet. 9th Royal Scots, Private Nov. 1914 to July 1915 (under age); Officer Cadet March 1918. R.F.A., 2nd Lieut. Aug. 1918.

McWILLIAM, WILLIAM NICHOLSON.
: Academical Institution, Dublin, and King's College, London. Student of Science, 1914-15. O.T.C. Infantry, Oct. 1914 to Feb. 1915, Cadet. Highland Cyclist Battn., Royal Highlanders (Black Watch), 2nd Lieut. Feb. 1915; Lieut. Jan. 1916; Captain March 1917.

MABBOTT, JOHN DAVID.
: Berwickshire High School, Duns. Student of Arts, 1915-17 and 1918-19. M.A. 1919. O.T.C. Artillery, Nov. 1916 to Aug. 1917, Cadet Sergeant; Officer Cadet, Aug. 1917. Forth R.G.A. (T.), 2nd Lieut. Jan. to Dec. 1918.

MADDOCK, EDWARD CECIL GORDON.
: Rossall. M.B., Ch.B. 1898; M.D. 1911; D.T.M. (Liverpool) 1905; D.P.H. (Camb.) 1906; F.R.C.S. (Edin.) 1911. Volunteer Medical Staff Corps, 1894-8, Private. Indian Medical Service, 1899; Major Jan. 1911; Lieut.-Col. Jan. 1919. Y. Indian General Hospital, Dec. 1914 to March 1915. H.M. Hospital Ship *Takalo*, 1916-17. D.A.D.M.S., Bombay, 1917-18. 160th I.C. Field Ambulance, 1918-19. Egyptian Exp. Force. Dispatches June 1919.

Record of War Service

MADDOX, RALPH HENRY.
Haileybury. M.B., C.M. and M.R.C.S. (Eng.) 1887; D.T.M. (Liverpool) 1907. Indian Medical Service, 1892; Lieut.-Col. 1912. Waziristan, 1894-5; Suakim, 1896; Tirah, 1897. Mesopotamia, June 1916 to Nov. 1918. Kaisar-i-Hind Medal (2nd Class), 1902. Dispatches June 1917, April 1918, and March 1919. C.I.E. June 1919.

MADGE, JOHN BRISTO CULLEY.
George Watson's College. Student of Medicine, 1912-14. O.T.C. Artillery, Oct. 1912 to Sept. 1914, Cadet. R.F.A., 2nd Lieut. Sept. 1914; Lieut. March 1915. Royal Air Force. France. Wounded and taken Prisoner Sept. 1917.

MAGRATH, CHARLES WILLIAM STANFORD.
Rossall. M.B., C.M. 1880; M.D. 1892. R.A.M.C., 1881; Lieut.-Col. 1901; Retired 1911. Re-employed Oct. 1914. Egyptian War, 1882-4; Burmese War, 1886-7. Dispatches Feb. 1917 and March 1919.

MAILER, JOHN.
Boroughmuir School. Student of Arts, 1917-19. 53rd T.R. (Y.S.), Highland Light Infantry, Private Oct. 1918.

MAILER, ROBERT.
Stirling High School. M.B., Ch.B. 1917. O.T.C. Infantry, 1914, Medical, 1915-17, Cadet. R.A.M.C. (S.R.), Lieut. Aug. 1917; Captain Aug. 1918.

MAIN, GEORGE ANDERSON.
George Watson's College; First XV. and XI. O.T.C. 1914-17, Cadet Sergeant. Student of Science, 1918-19. O.T.C. Artillery, Aug. 1917 to March 1918, Cadet Corporal; Officer Cadet March 1918. R.E., 2nd Lieut. June 1918.

MAIN, NORMAN STEWART.
Linlithgow Academy. M.A. and LL.B. 1906. Law Agent, 1908. 10th and 2nd Royal Scots, 2nd Lieut. Sept. 1914; Captain June 1916.

MAIN, ROBERT MAXWELL.
Circus Place School, Edinburgh. Student of Arts, 1876-7, and Law, 1880-2. 7th Royal Scots, Lieut.-Col. and Hon. Colonel; Retired 1908. Intelligence Officer (Lieut.-Col.), Aug. 1914 to Jan. 1919. Haddington and Berwick. V.D. 1904.

MAIR, ROBERT CUMMING THOMSON.
Keith Grammar School. M.A. (Hons. Aberdeen); LL.B. 1905. Solicitor. 6th Seaforth Highlanders (T.), 2nd Lieut. 1912; Lieut. Aug. 1914; Captain 1915; Quartermaster Dec. 1917. M.C. June 1917.

MAIR, WILLIAM.
Dollar Academy and George Watson's College. M.A. 1896; B.Sc. 1899; M.B., Ch.B. 1901; M.D. 1908. R.A.M.C., Lieut. June 1917; Captain June 1918 to April 1919.

Record of War Service

MAITLAND, ALEXANDER.
Harrow. B.A. (Oxford); LL.B. and Advocate, 1903. R.G.A. (T.), 2nd Lieut. Sept. 1914; Lieut. April 1915; Captain April 1916. France.

MAITLAND, PETER BROWN.
Campbeltown School. Student of Medicine, 1912-15. O.T.C. Infantry, Jan. 1911 to Feb. 1914, Cadet L/Corporal. R.A.M.C. (T.), 3rd Lowland Field Ambulance, Private Oct. 1914; Corporal Dec. 1914. Attached R.E. 1916, and A.S.C., France. Wounded at Combles, Sept. 1916.

MALCOLM, DAVID.
Perth Academy. M.A. 1904. Schoolmaster. R.F.A., Gunner April 1918.

MALCOLM, EDWARD ELLICE.
Edinburgh Academy; First XV. and XI. Student of Arts and Law, 1894-1900; M.A. 1897. Writer to the Signet, 1901. Commandant, Lochaber District Guides. Ministry of National Service. 1st V.B., Cameron Highlanders, Private May 1917; Lieut. June 1917; Captain Oct. 1918.

MALCOLM, JOHN WRIGHT.
Walsall Grammar School. O.T.C. 1906-10, Cadet Sergeant. Student of Medicine, 1910-15. M.B., Ch.B. 1915. O.T.C. Medical, May 1911 to Sept. 1914, Cadet Sergeant. R.A.M.C. (S.R.), Lieut. Aug. 1914; Captain Feb. 1916; Major Dec. 1918. Attached 8th Royal Highlanders (Black Watch). The Rhine. M.C. Nov. 1916; Bar to M.C. April 1918.

MALCOLM-SMITH, GEORGE LOUIS.
Edinburgh Academy. O.T.C. 1909-12. Student of Medicine, 1912-17; M.B., Ch.B. 1917. O.T.C. Medical, 1914-17, Cadet Staff-Sergeant. R.A.M.C. (S.R.), Lieut. Aug. 1917; Captain Aug. 1918. East African Exp. Force. Dispatches 1919.

MALHOTRA, RAM CHANDR.
M.B., Ch.B. 1911. Indian Medical Service, Lieut. May 1915. Attached 25th Punjabis.

MALIK, ABDUL RASHID.
Gordon Mission College, Rawal Pindi. Student of Science and Arts, 1917-19. Military Police, Sub-Inspector, Mesopotamia, Feb. 1915 to Jan. 1917.

MALINS, HERBERT.
Malvern College; First XI. B.A. (Oxford). M.B., C.M. 1898; F.R.C.S. (Edin.). South African Campaign, 1900-1. R.A.M.C., Lieut. Sept. 1915. Invalided out March 1916.

MALLACE, ALEXANDER CROSS.
George Heriot's School. M.A. 1904; M.B., Ch.B. 1908. R.A.M.C. (T.), Lieut. April 1913. Mobilised Aug. 1914; Captain April 1915; Major Jan. 1918. 1/2nd Highland Field Ambulance. 51st (Highland) Division. France. M.C. April 1918. Dispatches May 1918.

Record of War Service

MALLINSON, JOHN.
George Heriot's School. Student of Science, 1912-15 and 1918-20. O.T.C. Infantry, May to Aug. 1915, Cadet. 10th Scottish Rifles, 2nd Lieut. Sept. 1915; Lieut. July 1917 to Sept. 1918. France. Wounded June 1916 and April 1917.

MALLOCH, DUNCAN.
George Watson's College. Student of Medicine, 1910-15; M.B., Ch.B. 1915. O.T.C. Medical, 1914-15, Cadet. R.A.M.C., Lieut. Aug. 1915; Captain Aug. 1916. 97th Field Ambulance, 150th Brigade, R.F.A.; 12th Casualty Clearing Station and No. 3 Mobile Laboratory. France, 1915-18; Somme 1916; Arras and Cambrai 1917; Maubeuge 1918. Dispatches Dec. 1918. M.C. June 1919.

MALLOCH, JOHN.
Stirling High School. M.B., Ch.B. 1909. R.A.M.C., Lieut. Sept. 1915. 17th Motor Ambulance Convoy. Salonika.

MALONE, DESMOND SCOTT.
George Heriot's School. Student of Medicine, 1918. The Cameronians (Scottish Rifles), Private Dec. 1915; Corporal July 1917 to Feb. 1919.

MALONE, JOSEPH ARCHIBALD EDWARD.
Royal High School; First XV. and XI. Student of Arts and Medicine, 1878-9 and 1881-3. Q.E.R., 1881-3, Private. Bechuanaland, 1884-5. South African Campaign, 1899-1901. Westminster Dragoons, Lieut. Sept. 1914; Adjutant Oct. 1914; Captain Nov. 1914.

MALONEY, WILLIAM JOSEPH.
George Heriot's School. M.B., Ch.B. 1905; M.D. 1907; F.R.C.S. 1912. R.A.M.C., Lieut. 4th Worcestershire Regiment. Wounded at Dardanelles 1915.

MALSEED, ALFRED.
Academical Institution, Londonderry. M.B., Ch.B. 1904. Volunteer Medical Staff Corps, Nov. 1900-4, L/Corporal. R.A.M.C., Lieut. Oct. 1915; Captain Nov. 1916. King's Own Yorkshire Light Infantry and 5th Liverpool Regiment. France 1916-18. M.C.

MANFORD, GILBERT CUMMING.
Edinburgh Institution. Student of Law, 1909-14 Writer to the Signet, 1914. 14th Highland Light Infantry, 2nd Lieut. Nov. 1914; Lieut. April 1916; Captain and Adjutant June 1916 to May 1919. Attached Staff, France, and Scottish Command H.Q. France June 1916-18. M.C. June 1918.

MANIFOLD, COURTNAY CLARKE.
Clifton College. M.B., C.M. 1886. Indian Medical Service, 1887; Colonel; Major-General Dec. 1917. China (Peking), and Tirah. D.D.M.S. of Anzac. France 1916-17. Dispatches 1916 and 1917. C.B. 1914; C.M.G. 1917. K.H.P. Croix de Guerre.

Record of War Service

MANIFOLD, JOHN ALEXANDER.
    George Watson's College. M.B., Ch.B. 1907. R.A.M.C., Captain July 1912; Acting Lieut.-Col. Jan. 1917; Brevet Major. D.S.O.; M.C. Twice Mentioned in Dispatches.

MANION, ROBERT JAMES.
    Student of Medicine, 1901-6. M.D., C.M. (Toronto) 1904; L.R.C.P. & S. (Edin.), and L.F.P.S. (Glasg.) 1906. Canadian Army Medical Corps, Captain Jan. 1916. France. M.C. (Battle of Arras).

MANN, ALAN COWAN.
    George Watson's College; First XI. M.B., Ch.B. 1913. O.T.C. Artillery, Oct. 1909 to April 1914, Cadet. R.A.M.C., Lieut.; Captain. France. M.C. June 1918; Bar to M.C. Sept. 1918. Twice Mentioned in Dispatches.

MANN, CHARLES.
    Daniel Stewart's College; First XV. Student of Science, 1918. R.E. (T.), City of Edinburgh (Fortress), Jan. 1915; L/Corporal June 1915; Corporal July 1915; Officer Cadet Dec. 1916. 1/10th and 17th Royal Scots, 2nd Lieut. March 1917; Lieut. Aug. 1918.

MANN, DAVID.
    Collegiate School, Broughty Ferry. M.B., Ch.B. 1906; F.R.C.S. (Edin.) 1908. R.A.M.C., Lieut. Nov. 1915; Captain Nov. 1916. France.

MANN, FRED.
    Arbroath High School. Student of Arts, 1910-14; M.A. (Hons. Classics) 1914. O.T.C. Infantry, Nov. 1910 to Oct. 1913, Cadet. R.A.M.C. (T.), 3rd Lowland Field Ambulance, Private Oct. 1915. Egypt. 75th Field Ambulance, France.

MANN, JAMES CAMERON.
    Leith Academy. Student of Science, 1917-19. O.T.C. Artillery, 1917-18, Cadet Bombardier; Officer Cadet May 1918. R.G.A., 2nd Lieut. Feb. 1919.

MANN, JAMES STEWART.
    Nottingham High School; First XI. Student of Medicine, 1913-18; M.B., Ch.B. 1918. O.T.C. Medical, April 1915-18, Cadet Corporal. R.A.M.C., Lieut. May 1918; Captain May 1919. Salonika, July 1918 to June 1919.

MANN, NORMAN FLEETWOOD.
    High School, Durban, Natal. First XI. Cadet Corps 1896-1905; Cadet Sergeant-Major. M.B., Ch.B. 1910. University Battery, E.C.A.V., 1905-10, Sergeant, R.A.M.C., Captain Oct. 1914 to Nov. 1917. Free State Rebellion, and German S.-W. Africa.

Record of War Service

MANNING, EDYR RODESTON.
: Sydney Church of England Grammar School. Student of Medicine, 1913-14. Lothians and Border Horse, Private Aug. 1914. 14th Reserve Regiment of Cavalry, 2nd Lieut. Sept. 1914; Lieut. Feb. 1915. R.F.C., Feb. 1916; Pilot June 1916; Captain and Flight Commander Feb. 1917; Squadron Commander Sept. 1917; Major Jan. 1918. France, attached 15th Hussars, March 1915, and R.F.C. June 1916 and April 1917. Wounded at second Ypres Aug. 1915, and first Somme Aug. 1916. M.C. June 1917.

MANSFIELD, EDWARD.
: Bowen House, Brisbane. Student of Medicine, 1909-14; M.B., Ch.B. 1914. O.T.C. Medical, Jan. 1910 to April 1913, Cadet. R.A.M.C., Lieut.

MANSFIELD, GERALD STEWART.
: Clifton College. M.B., C.M. 1890. R.A.M.C. Oct. 1892; Major (Retired) 1912; Rejoined April 1915; Lieut.-Col. Dec. 1917; D.A.D.M.S., Central Force, and H.Q., Eastern Command; A.D.M.S. Dispatches 1915.

MANSON, JOHN.
: Student of Arts, 1912-14. 4th Royal Scots (T.), Private July 1913. Seaforth Highlanders, 2nd Lieut. April 1918.

MANUEL, JAMES.
: Student of Medicine, 1911-16; M.B., Ch.B. 1916. O.T.C. Medical, Nov. 1914 to April 1916, Cadet Corporal. R.A.M.C., Lieut. May 1916; Captain May 1917. Dispatches Nov. 1917. M.C. Dec. 1917; Bar to M.C. March 1918.

MANUEL, TERTIUS PETER.
: Edinburgh Institution. Student of Law, 1898-1903. Writer to the Signet, 1903. O.T.C. Infantry, 1915, Cadet. 3/6th Royal Scots (T.), 2nd Lieut. July 1915; Lieut. Feb. 1917. Machine-Gun Corps. Overseas March to Aug. 1917.

MANWARING-WHITE, RICHARD.
: Pocklington School, Yorks; First XI. M.B., Ch.B. 1903; M.D. 1906; F.R.C.S. 1914. R.A.M.C., Lieut. June 1918. Military Hospital, Alder Hey, Liverpool.

MARBURG, CHARLES LOUIS HERMANN.
: Merchiston Castle, and Pembroke College, Cambridge. Rugby "Blue." O.T.C. 1903-9, Cadet Sergeant. Student of Law, 1912-13. Rugby "Blue." 9th Royal Scots (T.), Lieut. Aug. 1914; Captain June 1916. Wounded at Gaza Nov. 1917.

MARGETTS, HORACE PALMER.
: Student of Medicine, 1908-11; L.R.C.P. & S. (Edin.) and L.R.F.P.S. (Glasg.) 1915. Royal Navy, Surgeon Feb. 1915. O.B.E.

MARJORIBANKS, JAMES LESLIE.
: Royal High School. M.B., C.M. 1896; M.D. 1904; D.P.H. (Edin.) 1904. Indian Medical Service, 1897; Major; Lieut.-Col. Jan. 1917. Transport Ship *Assaye*.

Record of War Service

MARKSMAN, LEO BASIL CLYDE.
George Watson's College; First XV. and XI. Cadet Corps 1904-6, Colour-Sergeant. M.B., Ch.B. 1911. Secretary, University Union. R.A.M.C. (S.R.), Lieut. Nov. 1914; Captain May 1915 to Nov. 1919. India.

MARR, ALEXANDER MURRAY.
George Heriot's School; First XV. O.T.C. 1910-13, Cadet Corporal. Student of Medicine, 1913-14 and 1918-19. O.T.C. Artillery, 1914-15, Cadet. 13th, 3rd, and 5/6th Royal Scots, 2nd Lieut. April 1915; Lieut. July 1917; Acting Captain and Adjutant Dec. 1917. Egypt Nov. 1915; France March 1916 to May 1918.

MARR, THOMAS GRAHAM.
Falkirk High School. Student of Law, 1914-16. R.A.S.C., Private.

MARSHALL, ARCHIBALD COOK.
Dunfermline High School. Student of Arts and Law, 1908-11 and 1917-18; M.A. 1918. 4th and 6th Royal Scots (T.), Private March 1910; Sergeant Dec. 1914; 2nd Lieut. Feb. 1915; Lieut. April 1916. 14th Army Cyclist Corps. France and Salonika.

MARSHALL, CHARLES EDWARD.
M.B., Ch.B. 1903; L.R.C.P. & S. (Edin.). Australian Army Medical Corps, Major April 1917. 1st Australian Casualty Clearing Station. 27th Battn. Australian Imperial Forces, Gallipoli, and 14th Australian Field Artillery.

MARSHALL, DANIEL GROVE.
Brightwell's Academy, Shrewsbury. M.B., C.M. 1885. Lecturer on Tropical Diseases. Indian Medical Service, 1888; Major (Retired); Temp. Lieut.-Col. Oct. 1918. Burmah 1891-2; N.W.F. 1892 and 1897; China (Peking) 1900. Consultant in Malaria, Scottish Command.

MARSHALL, DAVID.
George Watson's College. M.A. 1905; B.L. (Distinction) 1909. Solicitor, 1909. Fife and Forfar Yeomanry, Sergeant Aug. 1914; 2nd Lieut. May 1915; Lieut. Oct. 1916; Captain July 1917. Machine-Gun Corps (Cavalry). Suvla, Egypt, and Palestine. M.C. Nov. 1917.

MARSHALL, FREDERICK.
Royal High School. Student of Law, 1890-2. Chartered Accountant, 1893. A.S.C., Lieut. July 1915; Captain May 1917.

MARSHALL, GEORGE GUTHRIE.
George Watson's College; First XV. M.B., Ch.B. 1912. Resident, R.I.E., 1913-14. R.A.M.C., Lieut. Sept. 1914; Captain April 1915; Acting Major May 1917. R.M.O., 10th Gloucestershire Regiment; 9th Sherwood Foresters, and 35th Field Ambulance, France. Dispatches.

Record of War Service

MARSHALL, GEORGE LESLIE.
M.A. 1909. 48th Canadian Highlanders, Lieut. Oct. 1915. Canadian Machine-Gun Corps, April 1918.

MARSHALL, HENRY RISSIK.
Marlborough. B.A. (Oxford) 1912. Student of Law, 1913-14. Lanarkshire Yeomanry (T.), 2nd Lieut. Oct. 1912; Lieut. April 1915. 6th Highland Light Infantry, Acting Captain Oct. 1915; Captain 1917 to April 1919. Gallipoli Oct. 1915; Egypt and Sinai 1917, and Palestine to Jan. 1919.

MARSHALL, JAMES RISSIK.
Marlborough. B.A. (Oxford). Student of Law, 1909-12; LL.B. 1912; Advocate, 1912. Lothians and Border Horse (T.) June 1913, Lieut.; Captain July 1917.

MARSHALL, JOHN FORSYTH.
Stirling High School. Student of Arts, 1911-15; M.A. 1915. Oxford University O.T.C. Infantry, Oct. 1914 to March 1915. 13th, 10th, and 11th Highland Light Infantry, 2nd Lieut. March 1915; Lieut. April 1917; Captain Sept. 1917; Adjutant Oct. 1916 to Feb. 1919. France Dec. 1915 to Feb. 1919. Dispatches Jan. 1918. M.C. June 1918.

MARSHALL, LEGH RICHMOND HERBERT PETER.
Radley College. M.B., Ch.B. 1907; M.D. 1909. Red Cross Hospitals, Peebles, 1915. R.A.M.C., Lieut. Feb. 1916; Captain Feb. 1917. East Africa 1916-19, Dispatches 1917 and 1918. O.B.E. Jan. 1919.

MARSHALL, ROBERT IAN.
Edinburgh Academy; First XV. and XI. O.T.C. 1914-17, Cadet Corporal, Student of Commerce, 1919-20. O.T.C. Artillery, 1917-18, Cadet B.S.M.; Officer Cadet March 1918. R.F.A., 190th Brigade, 2nd Lieut. Aug. 1918.

MARSHALL, ROBERT WADDELL. (See p. 751.)

MARSHALL, WILLIAM EDWARD.
Perth Academy. M.B., C.M. 1902; D.P.H. (St Andrews) 1906. R.A.M.C., Lieut. Aug. 1908; Captain Feb. 1912; Brevet Major June 1918. 2nd Leinster Regiment. Hospital Ship *Clan MacGillivray*; 33rd Field Ambulance; 9th West Yorkshire Regiment and Hejaz Operations (Arabia). M.C. Sept. 1916; Order of the Nile (4th Class), Sept. 1917. Dispatches 1917 and 1919.

MARTIN, BERNARD DAVIS.
George Watson's College. O.T.C. 1912-15, Cadet L/Corporal. Student of Science, 1918. 4th North Staffordshire Regiment (S.R.), 2nd Lieut. April 1915; Lieut. July 1917. Wounded. Inavlided out Jan. 1919.

MARTIN, CHARLES de CATERET.
M.B., Ch.B. 1913. O.T.C. Artillery, Nov. 1908 to Feb. 1911, Cadet. Indian Medical Service, Lieut.; Captain Aug. 1917.

Record of War Service

MARTIN, CLAUDE BUIST.
    M.B., C.M. 1890. Army Medical Service, 1892; Colonel Aug. 1918. Chitral, 1895. South Africa, 1899-1902. A.D.M.S., General H.Q., Salonika Dec. 1917. Army of Black Sea, Constantinople. Dispatches Nov. 1917 and Jan. 1919. C.M.G. Jan. 1919; Order of St Sava 1917.

MARTIN, DAVID.
    Royal High School. Student of Law, 1911-12. Machine-Gun Corps, 2nd Lieut. April 1915; Lieut. Nov. 1916; 32nd Machine-Gun Corps and 15th Highland Light Infantry, France; 256th Machine-Gun Corps, Mesopotamia.

MARTIN, DAVID HENRY.
    Robert Gordon's College, Aberdeen. Student of Law, 1902-4. 5th Gordon Highlanders, Captain Nov. 1915; Major. 2/6th and 28th Durham Light Infantry, April 1918.

MARTIN, DONALD.
    M.A. 1895. Minister, U.F. Church of Scotland. Chaplain, 4th Class, 7th Cameron Highlanders, June 1916; Hon. Chaplain Dec. 1918.

MARTIN, DOUGLAS.
    Daniel Stewart's College. M.B., Ch.B. 1913. D.T.M. & H.; D.P.H. (Edin.). R.A.M.C., Lieut. July 1917; Captain July 1918. 66th General Hospital, Salonika, 1917-18. 2nd H.A.C., Italy, March to Nov. 1918.

MARTIN, ERNEST WILLIAM.
    Royal Grammar School, Sheffield; First XV. and XI. M.B., Ch.B. 1899. City of London Military Hospital, 1915. R.A.M.C., Lieut. Jan. 1916; Captain Jan. 1917. 20th Casualty Clearing Station and 28th Ambulance Train. Medical Research, Fort Pitt, Chatham.

MARTIN, FRANK ASHCROFT.
    George Watson's College. O.T.C. 1914-17, Cadet Sergeant. Student of Science, 1918. Officer Cadet March 1917. Royal Air Force, 2nd Lieut. May 1917; Lieut. and Captain April 1918. Wounded Oct. 1917.

MARTIN, GEORGE EWART.
    M.A. 1910; M.B., Ch.B. 1913. R.A.M.C. (T.), Lieut. Dec. 1914; Captain June 1915; Major June 1919. 3rd North General Hospital; 3rd and 21st Casualty Clearing Stations. The Rhine. Dispatches July 1919.

MARTIN, GEORGE MITCHELL.
    Daniel Stewart's College. Student of Arts and Science, 1910-15; M.A. (Hons. Maths.) and B.Sc. 1915. O.T.C. Artillery, Feb. to July 1915, Cadet. R.F.A., 2nd Lieut. July 1915; Lieut. June 1917. France. Wounded Nov. 1917.

MARTIN, HAROLD OLIVER.
    University School, Southport. Student of Medicine, 1913. L.R.C.P. & S. (Edin.), Royal Navy, Surgeon-Lieut., June 1915.

Record of War Service

MARTIN, HENRY COOKE.
　Royal Academical Institution, Belfast. M.B., Ch.B. 1903. R.A.M.C., Lieut. July 1917; Captain July 1918. 72nd Field Ambulance and 12th Royal Fusiliers. France.

MARTIN, HENRY RANALD.
　Inverness College. Student of Medicine, 1919-20. O.T.C. Infantry, Jan. 1917 to March 1918, Cadet L/Corporal; Officer Cadet March 1918. 1st Cameron Highlanders, 2nd Lieut. Oct. 1918. India.

MARTIN, JAMES FITZGERALD.
　Bath College. M.B., Ch.B. 1899; D.P.H. (Lond.), 1911. R.A.M.C., Lieut. Dec. 1899; Lieut.-Col. Dec. 1917. South Africa, 1899-1902; D.A.D.M.S., 1915-18; D.A.D.G., War Office, Sept. 1918. France Aug. 1914 to Aug. 1918. Dispatches Jan. and May 1915, Nov. 1916, Nov. 1917, and May 1918. C.M.G. June 1915; Knight of Grace, St John of Jerusalem, 1918; C.B.E. June 1919.

MARTIN, JOHN JAMES BLACK.
　Student of Arts, 1913-15. O.T.C. Artillery, Oct. 1914 to May 1915, Cadet. R.F.A. (S.R.), 2nd Lieut. May 1915.

MARTIN, JAMES SACKVILLE.
　M.B., C.M. 1895; M.D. 1900; M.R.C.S. (Eng.) and L.R.C.P. (Lond.) 1897. R.A.M.C., Lieut. Dec. 1914; Captain Dec. 1915.

MARTIN, JOHN ROBSON.
　George Watson's College. O.T.C. 1906-11, Cadet L/Corporal. Student of Arts and Divinity, 1911-15; M.A. 1915. O.T.C. Infantry, 1912-14, Cadet. R.A.M.C., Private Nov. 1915. 8th attached 6th Seaforth Highlanders, 2nd Lieut. May 1917; Lieut. Nov. 1918 to July 1919. France 1916-18; third Arras and third Marne. Wounded July 1918.

MARTIN, JOHN SIMSON STUART.
　M.B., Ch.B. 1911. Indian Medical Service, Lieut.; Captain Jan. 1915. 127th Indian Field Ambulance.

MARTIN, JOSEPH.
　Whithorn School. Student of Medicine, 1915-16 and 1917-19. O.T.C. Medical, May 1918 to Feb. 1919, Cadet. R.E., No. 2 Special Coy., Pioneer July 1916.

MARTIN, MARTIN McCALL.
　George Watson's College. Student of Law, 1915-16. 9th Royal Scots (T.), Private. 13th Rifle Brigade, 2nd Lieut. Oct. 1917. France 1916-17 and 1918-19. Twice Wounded.

MARTIN, OLAUS McLEOD.
　M.A. 1911. 21st Cavalry, Indian Army, 2nd Lieut. Lahore.

MARTIN, PETER.
　Broughton School, Edinburgh; First XV. Student of Science, 1912-14. R.A.M.C. (T.), 1911, Corporal. 1/4th King's Own Scottish Borderers and 1/4th Royal Scots. Gallipoli. Chemist, T.N.T. Factory, Edinburgh, 1916-17.

Record of War Service

MARTIN, ROBERT HENRY.
 M.B., Ch.B. 1902. Volunteer Medical Staff Corps, 1897-1902, Cadet Corporal. South Africa, 1900-1. R.A.M.C., Lieut. March 1918; Captain March 1919.

MARTIN, SAMUEL EDGAR.
 Newry School. M.B., Ch.B. 1905. Barrister-at-Law. Volunteer Medical Staff Corps, 1900-5, Cadet Sergeant. R.A.M.C., Lieut. May 1915; Captain March 1918. Major July 1918.

MARTIN, THOMAS MUIRHEAD.
 George Watson's College. M.B., C.M. 1892; M.D. 1901; L.R.C.P. & S. (Edin.) and L.F.P.S. (Glasg.) 1892. R.A.M.C., Major July 1917. Ministry of Pensions, Special Medical Board.

MARTIN, WILLIAM BRUCE.
 George Watson's College. O.T.C. 1911-12. Student of Science, 1913-14. 4th Royal Scots (T.), Private Aug. 1914. 13th Northumberland Fusiliers, 2nd Lieut. Jan. 1915. Machine-Gun Corps, Nov. 1915; Lieut. Aug. 1916; Acting Captain Oct. 1918. 30th Battn., Machine-Gun Corps, Boulogne. France 1916-17 and 1918; The Rhine 1918-19; Egyptian Exp. Force 1919. Wounded June 1917.

MARTIN, WILLIAM LEWIS.
 George Watson's College. M.A. (Hons. Nat. Sc.) 1890; B.Sc. 1893; M.B., C.M. 1895; D.P.H. (Edin.) 1911. Dipl. Psych. (Edin.) 1912; M.R.C.P. (Edin.) 1919. R.A.M.C. (V.), 1895, Captain. R.A.M.C. (T.), Major Aug. 1914. Attached 6th Royal Scots (T.). D.C.M.S., Ministry of National Service and Ministry of Pensions. O.B.E. (Military) June 1918. T.D.

MARTINDALE, WALTER OLSEN.
 Edinburgh Institution. University O.T.C. Artillery, 1917-18, Cadet Bombardier. R.G.A., Officer Cadet March 1918.

MARTINE, THEODORE CHARLES.
 Edinburgh Academy. O.T.C. 1914-18, Cadet Sergeant. Student of Science, 1918. Foot Guards, Officer Cadet July 1918. Scots Guards, 2nd Lieut. March 1919.

MARTINE, WILLIAM ROBERT.
 Fettes College. O.T.C. 1913-16, Cadet L/Corporal. Student of Medicine, 1919. O.T.C. Infantry, Aug. 1916 to Jan. 1917, Cadet L/Corporal; Officer Cadet Jan. 1917. Highland Light Infantry, 2nd Lieut. April 1917; Lieut. Oct. 1918. North Russia Oct. 1918-19. M.B.E. Feb. 1920.

MARTYN-CLARK, WALTER IRELAND.
 Edinburgh Academy, and Wygeston School, Leicester; First XI. M.B., Ch.B. 1906. West African Medical Staff, 1911; Captain Oct. 1915 to March 1919. Attached 3rd and 1st Nigerian Regiments. South Nigeria, 1914-15; Cameroons. 1915-16; German East Africa, 1917-18, and Nigeria 1919.

Record of War Service

MARWICK, JAMES ELRICK.
George Watson's College. Student of Science, 1910-11. Lothians and Border Horse (T.), Private 1914; Corporal 1915; Sergeant Sept. 1915. Army Remount Service, Staff-Sergeant Oct. 1915; 2nd Lieut. April 1918. France and Salonika. Wounded Sept. 1918.

MARWICK, ROBERT ELRICK.
Royal High School. M.B., Ch.B. 1906. R.A.M.C., Lieut. July 1916. Field Ambulance and Corps Artillery. President, Medical Recruiting Board. France.

MARWICK, WILLIAM.
Kirkwall Burgh School. Student of Medicine, 1910-14 and 1918-19. O.T.C. Infantry, Oct. 1911-15, Cadet. 5th Cameron Highlanders, Corporal April 1916. M.M. June 1918. France July 1916 to Nov. 1918. Wounded at Butte de Warlencourt Oct. 1916.

MASON, CHARLES ARTHUR.
Rossall. Cadet Corps 1905-6. M.B., Ch.B. 1912. O.T.C. Artillery, Jan. 1909 to April 1913, Cadet. R.A.M.C., Lieut. Oct. 1914; Captain April 1915. France. Invalided home Oct. 1916. Garrison Duty, India, May 1917.

MASON, JOHN.
North Merchiston School. M.A. 1907. Schoolmaster. 10th Royal Scots (T.), 1908; Captain 1912.

MASON, JOHN BLACK.
Edinburgh Academy. M.B., Ch.B. 1902. R.A.M.C., Lieut. April 1915; Captain April 1916. 5th Northamptonshire Regiment. 64th Brigade, R.F.A.; 37th Field Ambulance and No. 2 Motor Ambulance Convoy. France. Croix de Guerre (Belgian) 1918.

MASON, JOHN WHARTON.
Clifton College; First XV. and XI. O.T.C. 1906-9, Cadet L/Corporal. Student of Medicine, 1912-14 and 1918-19. R.F.A., Aug. 1914, Captain. Dispatches Jan. 1916. M.C. Sept. 1916.

MASON, PHILIP WOODGATE.
Wellington College, New Zealand. First XV. M.B., Ch.B. 1903. Volunteer Medical Staff Corps, 1898-1903, Sergeant. R.A.M.C., Lieut. Oct. 1914; Captain April 1915. 1st S.W. Mounted Brigade Field Ambulance. Salonika, Dec. 1916 to March 1919.

MASON, VICTOR HAROLD.
Hymers College. Cadet Corps 1903-8, Cadet Sergeant. M.B., Ch.B. 1914. R.A.M.C., Lieut. April 1915; Captain April 1916; Major Feb. 1918. M.C.

Record of War Service

MASON-MACFARLANE, DAVID JAMES.
Edinburgh Institution. M.B., Ch.B. 1885; M.D. 1888; L.R.C.P. & S. (Edin.) and L.F.P.S. (Glasg.) 1885. Resident, R.I.E., 1885. 1st and 4th Seaforth Highlanders, 1889; Lieut.-Col. 1913; Brevet Colonel July 1918; Colonel Aug. 1918 to March 1919. France, Meerut Division, Nov. 1914. Wounded at Neuve Chapelle March 1915. T.D. 1910. Dispatches 1915 and 1916. C.M.G. June 1915; C.B.E. 1919.

MASON-MACFARLANE, FRANK NOEL.
Student of Medicine, 1914-15. O.T.C. Infantry, Oct. 1914, Cadet. R.F.A., 2nd Lieut.; Captain July 1915; Brigade Major May 1918. M.C. and Bar.

MASSIE, VICTOR GEORGE.
George Watson's College. Student of Medicine, 1915-16 and 1917-19. R.N.V.R., Surgeon Sub-Lieut. April 1918.

MASSON, JAMES.
George Watson's College. M.A. 1894; B.Sc. 1897; M.B., Ch.B. (Hons.) 1899; F.R.C.S. (Edin.) 1910. Indian Medical Service, Lieut. 1901; Captain 1904; Major 1912; Lieut.-Col. April 1918. Indian Frontier, Palestine, and Syria.

MASTERS, ARTHUR MURRAY.
M.B., Ch.B. 1910; M.D. 1914. R.A.M.C., Lieut. Jan. 1916; Captain Jan. 1917. India.

MATHER, ALEXANDER WILLIAM.
George Watson's College. Cadet Corps 1904-6. M.B., Ch.B. 1912; M.D. 1916. O.T.C. Artillery, 1909-11, Cadet. R.A.M.C., Lieut. Jan. 1916; Captain Jan. 1917 to April 1919. France; Somme 1916, Arras 1917, Passchendaele 1917.

MATHESON, ALISTER RODERICK.
Edinburgh Academy. Student of Medicine, 1912-17; M.B., Ch.B. 1917. O.T.C. Medical, Nov. 1915 to Feb. 1916, Cadet. Royal Navy, Surgeon-Probationer, Feb. 1916; Surgeon July 1917 to June 1919.

MATHESON, CHARLES.
Gordon College, Aberdeen. M.A. (Aberdeen) 1903. Student of Arts, 1909-10. Artists' Rifles O.T.C. April 1915; Sergeant 1915; C.Q.M.S. 1917. Instructor in Map Reading.

MATHESON, FARQUHAR WILLIAM.
George Watson's College. M.B., C.M. 1883. R.A.M.C., Lieut.; Captain June 1916.

MATHESON, JOHN.
Miller Institution, Thurso. Student of Arts, 1913-14 and 1919-20. 4th Royal Scots (T.), Private Aug. 1914; Corporal March 1916; Sergeant April 1916. Gallipoli 1915; Egypt 1916; Palestine 1917; and France 1918.

Record of War Service

MATHESON, JOHN CARSTAIRS.
   Falkirk High School. M.A. 1899. Schoolmaster. 9th Seaforth Highlanders, Private Dec. 1915; L/Corporal Jan. 1917; Corporal May 1918. France Sept. 1916 to Feb. 1919.

MATHEWSON, GEORGE DOUGLAS.
   George Watson's College. M.B., Ch.B. and B.Sc. 1905; F.R.C.P. (Edin.) 1912. Assistant to Professor of Medicine. R.A.M.C., Captain July 1916; Acting Major Feb. 1918. Dispatches 1919.

MATHEWSON, JOHN.
   George Watson's College. M.A. 1902; M.B., Ch.B. 1906; M.D. 1910. R.A.M.C. Lieut. Dec. 1917; Captain Dec. 1918 to April 1919. 74th General Hospital, France.

MATHEWSON, WILLIAM RICHARD.
   Dunfermline High School. Student of Science and Medicine, 1912-17; B.Sc. 1915; M.B., Ch.B. 1917. O.T.C. Medical, Feb. 1916 to April 1917, Cadet L/Corporal. R.A.M.C., Lieut. May 1917; Captain June 1918. Mesopotamia.

MATHIE, WILLIAM.
   Glasgow High School. University O.T.C. Artillery, 1916, Cadet; Officer Cadet, Aug. 1916. R.G.A. (T.), 2nd Lieut. Nov. 1916; Lieut. May 1918.

MATHIESON, ALEXANDER.
   M.B., Ch.B. 1905. R.A.M.C., Lieut. June 1915; Captain June 1916; Acting Major Dec. 1918. Salonika June 1916 to Feb. 1919. Transcaucasia March to Sept. 1919.

MATHISON, ARCHIBALD DOUGLAS E.
   Student of Law, 1900-4. Writer to the Signet, 1905. 2/5th Royal Scots (T.), 2nd Lieut. Sept. 1914; Lieut. 1916; Captain 1917. France for two years.

MATLEY, CHARLES STUART.
   George Watson's College. Student of Law, 1912-14 and 1918-19; B.L. 1919. O.T.C. Infantry, 1912-14, Cadet. 9th, 15th, and 17th Royal Scots, 2nd Lieut. Aug. 1914; Temp. Lieut. Oct. 1914; Temp. Captain March 1916; Lieut. and Captain Aug. 1917 to Jan. 1919; Acting Major Aug. 1917 to March 1918. France.

MATTHEW, ANDREW.
   George Watson's College. Student of Science, 1918. 9th Royal Scots (T.), Private Nov. 1914. France.

MATTHEW, CHARLES GEEKIE.
   Edinburgh Academy. M.B., C.M. 1885. Royal Navy, Surgeon 1889; Staff Surgeon 1901; Fleet Surgeon 1905; Retired 1909; Recalled Aug. 1914; Surgeon-Captain 1918.

Record of War Service

MATTHEW, EDWIN.
  M.A. (Aberdeen) 1889; M.B., C.M. (Hons.) 1897; M.D. 1908. R.A.M.C., Captain 1908. 2nd Scottish General Hospital; Edinburgh War Hospital, Bangour.

MATTHEW, FREDERICK CRICHTON.
  Royal High School. M.A. 1897; M.B., Ch.B. 1900; M.D. 1903; F.R.C.S. Volunteer Medical Staff Corps, 1895-1900; Staff-Sergeant. R.A.M.C., Lieut. July 1915; Captain July 1916. Dardanelles and Salonika.

MATTHEWS, ALEXANDER.
  Ewart High School, Newton Stewart. Student of Law, 1914-15. O.T.C. Artillery, Nov. 1915 to July 1916, Cadet. 140th Siege Battery, R.G.A., 2nd Lieut. Aug. 1916; Acting Captain Sept. 1917 to April 1919. Dispatches Dec. 1918.

MATTHEWS, REGINALD JOHN.
  Newport School, Monmouthshire. Student of Medicine, 1918. Bristol University O.T.C., Feb. to April 1917, Cadet. R.F.C., April 1917; 2nd Lieut. Aug. 1917. Devonshire Regiment, Jan. 1918, Captain May 1918. 23rd Light Trench Mortar Battery. France May to Sept. 1918.

MAUGHAN, JOHN ST. AUBYN.
  Student of Medicine, 1901-3; L.R.C.P. & S. (Edin.) L.R.F.P.S. (Glasg.) 1903. Volunteer Medical Staff Corps, 1900-3. R.A.M.C., Lieut. 1904; Captain 1908; Major July 1915. D.S.O. and Dispatches Jan. 1917.

MAUNSELL, EDWARD CHARLES CECIL.
  M.B., Ch.B. 1901; M.D., D.T.M. and H. 1910. Indian Medical Service, Major Jan. 1914. 94th Russell's Infantry.

MAX, DAVID JOHN.
  M.B., Ch.B. 1914. Royal Navy, Surgeon-Lieut. March 1916 to June 1919.

MAXTON, GEORGE SCRIMGEOUR.
  Perth Academy. M.A. 1913. Schoolmaster. Army Ordnance Corps, Private 1915; L/Corporal. London Scottish, Sergeant.

MAXWELL, AYMER D.
  Trent College, Derbyshire. Student of Medicine, 1910-14 and 1918-19. 7th and 9th Royal Scots (T.), 2nd Lieut. Sept. 1912; Lieut. Sept. 1914; Captain Sept. 1915. M.C. Dec. 1917.

MAXWELL, JAMES.
  Bathgate Academy. Student of Arts, 1910-12. R.A.M.C., Private Feb. 1916; Acting L/Corporal Aug. 1917. 9th Gloucestershire Regiment, Acting Corporal May 1918; Officer Cadet Nov. 1918; 2nd Lieut. Sept. 1919. Vardar Front. Attached Serbian Army. Serbian Cross of Charity.

MAXWELL, JAMES.
  George Watson's College. M.B., Ch.B. 1912; M.D. 1915. R.A.M.C., Lieut. May 1915; Captain Dec. 1917; Acting Major May 1918. H.M. Hospital Ship *Aquitania*, 1914; Stoke-on-Trent War Hospital.

Record of War Service

MAXWELL, JAMES REID.
Arbroath and Dundee High Schools. M.A. 1898. Schoolmaster. R.A.M.C. (T.), 1/3rd Lowland Field Ambulance, Private Sept. 1914. 8th Cameron Highlanders, 2nd Lieut. Aug. 1915; Lieut. July 1917. Dispatches March 1919.

MAXWELL, JOHN.
Ayr Academy. O.T.C. 1912-17, Cadet Corporal. Student of Law, 1919-20. O.T.C. Infantry, May to Nov. 1917, Cadet; Officer Cadet Nov. 1917. 3rd Seaforth Highlanders, 2nd Lieut. March 1918. France. Wounded Oct. 1918.

MAXWELL, JOHN HUGH.
Repton. Student of Science, 1914-15. O.T.C. Infantry, Nov. 1914 to Aug. 1915, Cadet L/Corporal. 3rd King's Own Scottish Borderers, 2nd Lieut. Aug. 1915; Lieut. July 1917. Wounded Oct. 1918. M.C. Oct. 1918.

MAXWELL, JOHN MILLAR.
Portobello School. M.A. (Hon. Maths. and Nat. Phil.) 1913. Schoolmaster. R.F.A., Gunner Oct. 1915; Bombardier May 1916. R.E., Corporal Oct. 1918.

MAXWELL, RAYMOND.
M.B., C.M. 1892; M.D. 1899. Hon. Surgeon, R.I.E. South African Medical Corps Reserve, Captain April 1915; Temp. Major and Temp. Lieut.-Col. Feb. 1917. No. 2 General Hospital, Sept. 1917; S.M.O., Kimberley, and No. 5 General Hospital, Sept. 1918 to Jan. 1919. O.B.E. July 1919.

MAXWELL, VICTOR WILLIAM.
Kirkcaldy High School. O.T.C. 1909-15, Cadet Sergeant. Student of Arts and Medicine, 1915-16 and 1918-19. O.T.C. Infantry, March to Sept. 1916, Cadet L/Corporal; Officer Cadet. 7th Royal Highlanders (Black Watch), 2nd Lieut. Dec. 1916; Lieut. June 1918.

MAXWELL, WILLIAM MAURICE.
Repton. O.T.C. 1912-14. Student of Science, 1914-15. O.T.C. Infantry, 1914-15, Cadet Corporal. 6th Scottish Rifles (T.), 2nd Lieut. May 1915; Lieut. July 1916. Machine-Gun Corps. France Jan. 1916 to Oct. 1917, and June to Nov. 1918.

MAXWELL, WILLIAM WALKER.
George Watson's College. M.B., Ch.B. 1898; M.D. 1903; M.R.C.S. (Eng.) 1900. R.A.M.C., Lieut. May 1915; Captain Nov. 1915. No. 3 Australian, and Nos. 4, 25, and 54 Casualty Clearing Stations. Royal Air Force, and Second Army Trench Mortars, France.

MAYA-DAS, FRANCIS XAVIER.
M.B., Ch.B. 1918. Indian Field Ambulance, Dresser. Dispenser, Indian Convalescent Home, New Milton, Hants, 1914-16, and Dresser, Indian Base Hospital, Suez, 1916.

MAYBERRY, ROBERT JOHN.
M.B., Ch.B. 1902. R.A.M.C., Lieut. Dec. 1915; Captain Dec. 1916. Egypt for two years.

Record of War Service

MAYBIN, JOHN ALEXANDER.
  Ayr Academy. M.A. (Hons. Classics) 1912. R.F.A., Gunner March 1917; 2nd Lieut. July 1918.

MAYBIN, WILLIAM.
  Ayr Academy; First XV. and XI. Student of Arts, 1903-4. 15th Canadian Battn., Private Aug. 1914; Corporal and C.S.M. 1915; Lieut. 1916; Captain Dec. 1917; Major 1918. Dispatches 1915. M.M. 1916; M.C. 1918.

MAYNARD, EDWARD FORSTER.
  University School, Hastings. M.B., C.M. 1889; M.D. 1892; M.R.C.P. (Lond.) 1891. R.A.M.C. (T.), Major 1908; Lieut.-Col. 1911. Dispatches Feb. 1917. 2nd Eastern General Hospital, Brighton.

MAYNE, WILLIAM JOHN FITZGERALD.
  Kelvin House, Belfast. M.B., Ch.B. 1908; D.P.H. (Belfast) 1914. Athletics. Volunteer Medical Staff Corps 1902-5, L/Corporal, and No. 4 Q.R.V.B., Royal Scots, 1905-8. R.A.M.C. (T.), Lieut. Dec. 1914; Captain Sept. 1916; Brevet Major June 1918 to April 1919. 10th Irish Division Train, Suvla Bay, 1915; Sanitary Officer, 16th Army Corps, Salonika, 1916-18; Mobile Laboratories, 1918-19. Constantinople 1919. Dispatches Nov. 1917.

MEADOWS, GEORGE STEPHEN.
  M.B., C.M. 1890. 2/4th Duke of Cornwall's Light Infantry, Sept. 1894; Major Dec. 1914; Acting Lieut.-Col. May 1918. India Nov. 1914 to Jan. 1916, and Aug. 1917 to Nov. 1919. Aden and Egyptian Exp. Forces, 1916-17.

MEADOWS, ROBERT THORNTON.
  M.B., C.M. 1885; M.D. 1892; D.P.H. (Eng.) 1895. 2nd V.B. Duke of Cornwall's Light Infantry. A.M.S. (R. of O.), Surgeon-Major. R.A.M.C., Major Aug. 1915. Hospital Ships *Oxfordshire, Guildford Castle,* and *Dongola.* D.S.O. 1917.

MEARES, NEVILLE CHARLES SIMS.
  Oakfield School, Newport, Mon. University O.T.C. Artillery, 1916-17, Cadet Bombardier; Officer Cadet May 1917. R.G.A. (S.R.), 2nd Lieut. Sept. 1917; Lieut. March 1919. 128th Siege Battery, France, Nov. 1917 to Jan. 1919.

MEARNS, ALEXANDER.
  Montrose Academy. M.B., Ch.B. 1912. O.T.C. Infantry, 1909-13, Cadet Corporal. R.A.M.C., Lieut. Dec. 1914; Captain Dec. 1915; Major Jan. 1918. Dispatches Jan. 1919.

MEEKE, HUGH CRAIG.
  Royal Academical Institution, Belfast. Student of Arts and Divinity; M.A. 1897. Chaplain, 4th Class, 1905; 3rd Class, Jan. 1915; 2nd Class, June 1915. France 1914-15. Senior Chaplain, 15th Division and East African Exp. Force, 1915-17; Assistant Principal Chaplain, Egyptian Exp. Force, 1917-19. Dispatches 1914, 1915, 1917, and 1918. D.S.O. 1918.

Record of War Service

MEIKLE, ALEXANDER JAMIESON.
George Watson's College. M.B., C.M. 1892; M.D. 1894; L.R.C.P. & S. (Edin.) and L.F.P.S. (Glasg.) 1892. Australian Army Medical Corps, Lieut.-Col. 4th Field Ambulance. Dispatches.

MEINÉ, FELIX ADOLPH.
Dale College, Kingwilliamstown, and Rhodes University, Grahamstown. First XV. Student of Medicine, 1912-14 and 1918-19. O.T.C. Artillery, Feb. 1913 to Aug. 1914, Cadet. R.G.A., 2nd Lieut. Aug. 1914; Lieut. June 1915; Captain May 1917. 66th Siege Battery, and 6th Heavy Artillery Group, France.

MEKIE, DAVID.
Daniel Stewart's College. M.A. 1894. Schoolmaster. R.A.M.C. (T.), Private July 1915; Corporal Oct. 1915; Sergeant June 1916; Sergeant-Major Oct. 1917. 2nd Scottish General Hospital.

MELDRUM, JAMES WILLIAM.
Daniel Stewart's College. M.A. 1902. Schoolmaster. 15th London Regiment (Civil Service Rifles), Private Jan. 1916; Corporal to Jan. 1919.

MELDRUM, ROY.
Robert Gordon's College, Aberdeen. University O.T.C. Artillery, 1917-18, Cadet. Royal Tank Corps, Officer Cadet Feb. 1918.

MELL, FELIX OSWALD NEWTON.
M.B., C.M. 1894. Indian Medical Service, Major; Lieut.-Col. Jan. 1916. C.I.E.

MELLES, JOSEPH WILLIAM.
Sykes' School, Woodford Green, Essex. M.A. 1878. 1st Argyllshire Volunteer Regiment, Lieut. April 1917. Head Coast Watcher, Admiralty.

MELLO, PHILIP DE.
Student of Arts, Science, and Medicine, 1913-17; L.R.C.P. & S. (Edin.) and L.F.P.S. (Glasg.) 1905. Indian Medical Service, Lieut.

MELLOR, EDWARD STANLEY.
Rossall. Cadet Corps 1906-9. Student of Medicine, 1909-15; M.B., Ch.B. 1914. Royal Navy, Surgeon-Lieut. Dec. 1914. H.M. Ships *Wildfire* 1914-15, *Amaryllis* 1916-18, and *Mackay* 1919. Royal Marine Barracks, Chatham, 1918-19.

MELLOR, JOSEPH CROSLAND.
Kirkcaldy High School. O.T.C. 1907-12, Cadet Sergeant. Student of Science, 1912-15 and 1918-19; B.Sc. 1919. O.T.C. Artillery, Oct. 1914 to June 1915, Cadet. R.F.A. (T.), 2nd Lieut. June 1915; Lieut. June 1916; Acting Captain June 1918. 21st and 321st Brigades. India 1918.

MELVILLE, CHARLES HENDERSON.
Uppingham. M.B., C.M. 1885; D.P.H. (Lond.) 1901. No. 4 Coy., Q.E.R., 1882-5, Private. R.A.M.C., 1886; Brevet Colonel 1912. Army Medical Service, Colonel March 1915 to Aug. 1919. Hazara Expedition, 1888. Egypt 1915 and 1916. C.M.G. Jan. 1918. Twice Mentioned in Dispatches.

Record of War Service

MELVILLE, CHARLES WILLIAM FRANCIS.
M.B., Ch.B. 1898. Indian Medical Service, Major July 1917; Temp. Lieut.-Col. Oct. 1917.

MELVILLE, DAVID.
George Watson's College; First XV. and XI. M.B., C.M. 1892; M.D. 1898; D.P.H. (Edin.) 1904. South African Campaign, 1900-2. East African Medical Service, Lieut. Aug. 1915; Captain Dec. 1915; Major July 1917. Transferred South African Medical Corps. Invalided out Dec. 1917. Died November 1919.

MELVILLE, FREDERICK ROBERT.
George Heriot's School. B.Sc. 1911. A.M.I.C.E. O.T.C. Engineers, 1910-12, Cadet. Bombay Volunteer Rifles (Scots Coy.), Aug. 1916.

MELVILLE, GEORGE.
Harris Academy, Dundee. Student of Science, 1919. O.T.C. Engineers, 1914-15, Cadet. R.E., Sapper April 1915; 2nd Lieut. Sept. 1915; Lieut. July 1917.

MELVILLE, GEORGE.
East Linton School. M.B., C.M 1891; D.P.H. (Edin.) 1901. Army Medical Reserve, 6th V.B., Royal Scots, Surgeon-Lieut. 1896; Surgeon-Major April 1908. South African Campaign. R.A.M.C. (T.), attached 8th Royal Scots, Captain 1908. Mobilised Aug. 1914 to Feb. 1917.

MELVILLE, HENRY BRUCE.
M.B., C.M. 1885. Indian Medical Service, Lieut.-Col. April 1917.

MELVILLE, KENMURE DUNCAN.
George Watson's College and Blairlodge. Cadet Corps 1890-3. M.B., Ch.B. 1900; M.D. 1904. Q.R.V.B., Royal Scots, 1896-9, Private. R.A.M.C., Lieut. July 1916; Captain July 1917. 42nd and 49th General Hospitals, Salonika; 62nd General Hospital, Italy. Dispatches June 1919. Italian "Souvenir" Medal July 1919.

MELVIN, MORAY.
Fraserburgh Academy. Student of Medicine, 1913-18; M.B., Ch.B. 1918. Demonstrator in Anatomy. O.T.C. Medical, May 1916 to July 1918, Cadet Sergeant. R.A.M.C., Lieut. Oct. 1918; Captain Oct. 1919. Russia (Murmansk).

MELVIN, WILLIAM GEORGE.
Aberdeen Grammar School. Student of Science, 1904-5. M.I.C.E. F.S.I. 1st King George's Own Sappers and Miners, 2nd Lieut. Aug. 1916; Lieut. 1917; Captain 1918-19. Nos. 1 and 7 Engineer Field Park. Mohmand Blockade, N.-W. Frontier, 1916-17. South Persian Field Force, 1918-19.

MENZIES, DANIEL.
Morrison's Academy, Crieff. Student of Law, 1911-13 and 1918-19. Law Agent, 1914. 1/6th and 5th Royal Highlanders (Black Watch), Private July 1914; 2nd Lieut. Sept. 1916; Lieut. March 1918. Machine-Gun Corps. France. Wounded March 1918. M.C.

Record of War Service

MENZIES, DOUGLAS H.
    George Watson's College. Student of Law, 1898-1900 and 1903-4. Law Agent. 1st Lovat Scouts and 10th Cameron Highlanders, Private Sept. 1914. Gallipoli, Egypt, Salonika, and France.

MENZIES, EDWARD GORDON DEWAR.
    George Watson's College. M.B., Ch.B. 1899. R.A.M.C., Lieut. Sept. 1916-17.

MENZIES, HENRY GREY.
    Glen Urquhart School. M.A. 1911. Schoolmaster. Canadian Infantry, 2nd Lieut. Oct. 1915. R.G.A., 266th Siege Battery, 2nd Lieut. Sept. 1917; Lieut. March to April 1919. France.

MENZIES, JAMES ACWORTH.
    Dunfermline High School. M.B., C.M. 1890; M.D. 1894. R.A.M.C. (T.), Lieut. May 1915; Captain Nov. 1915 to Sept. 1918. 1st Northern General Hospital.

MENZIES, JACK McKENZIE.
    Aylwin College, Arnside. Student of Science, 1909-12. O.T.C. Artillery, Feb. 1910-13, Cadet. R.F.A., 2nd Lieut. Aug. 1914; Lieut. Jan. 1916; Captain April 1917; Major May 1917 to June 1919. Dispatches Jan. 1916, Jan. 1918, and June 1919. M.C. June 1918. D.S.O. June 1919.

MENZIES, JAMES ROBERTSON.
    Edinburgh Institution. M.B., Ch.B. 1913; L.R.C.P. & S. (Edin.); L.R.F.P.S. (Glasg.) 1913; M.D. 1920. O.T.C. Infantry, 1909-14; Lieut. 1909. R.A.M.C. (T.), Captain April 1915; Major July 1918; Acting Lieut.-Col. Jan. 1919. 3rd Lowland Field Ambulance, France.

MENZIES, JOHN STEWART.
    Forfar Academy. M.A. 1908. Schoolmaster. 4th Royal Scots (T.), Private Dec. 1915. Palestine and France. Wounded three times.

MENZIES, NEIL GRAHAM.
    Daniel Stewart's College; First XV. and XI. University O.T.C. Infantry, 1917. 7th Argyll and Sutherland Highlanders, Private Aug. 1917. France. Wounded at the Marne July 1918.

MENZIES, PATRICK DROUGHT NORTH.
    Fettes College. Student of Law, 1900-4. Writer to the Signet and Law Agent, 1906. O.T.C. Infantry, 1916, Cadet; Officer Cadet March 1916. 2/1st Fife and Forfar Yeomanry, 2nd Lieut. Nov. 1916; Lieut. May 1918. France.

MENZIES, ROBERT.
    George Watson's College, and Morrison's Academy, Crieff; First XV. and XI. Student of Law, 1911-14. Chartered Accountant, 1914. 9th Royal Scots (T.), Private 1909; 2nd Lieut. Oct. 1914; Lieut. April 1915; Temp. Captain Aug. 1917; Temp. Major Feb. 1918; Captain and Brevet Major June 1919. France Feb. 1915 to March 1916, and attached Staff, France, July 1916 to Aug. 1919. Wounded Jan. 1916. Dispatches June 1917, June 1918, and June 1919. O.B.E. June 1918.

Record of War Service

MENZIES, THOMAS.
M.A. 1890. Schoolmaster. 1st Battn. Kincardineshire Volunteer Regiment, 2nd Lieut. Dec. 1916; Lieut. May 1917; Captain and O.C. Jan. 1918.

MENZIES, WILLIAM MENZIES.
M.B., Ch.B. 1909. R.A.M.C., Captain May 1918. Twice Mentioned in Dispatches.

MERCER, EBENEZER BEATTIE.
Edinburgh Institution. Student of Medicine, 1918. R.F.C., Corporal; 2nd Lieut. Feb. 1917.

MERCER, WALTER.
George Watson's College. M.B., Ch.B. 1912. O.T.C. Medical, 1910-12. R.A.M.C., Lieut. Oct. 1915; Captain Oct. 1916. Edinburgh War Hospital. Mediterranean, France, and Italy.

MERCER, WILFRID BERNARD.
Brewood Grammar School. B.Sc. 1910. Warwickshire Yeomanry, 2nd Lieut. Dec. 1915; Lieut. July 1917. Machine-Gun Corps, July 1917. M.C. Feb. 1919.

MEREDITH-CLEMENTS, EVA.
M.B., Ch.B. 1908; M.D. 1911; D.P.H. R.A.M.C., May 1917.

MERRILES, ALEXANDER JOHNSON.
North Berwick High School. M.A. 1905; B.Sc. 17th and 4th Royal Scots, Jan. 1916; 2nd Lieut. Nov. 1916; Lieut. May 1918. France Jan. 1917-18.

MERWE, CAREL JOHANNES VAN DER.
M.B., Ch.B. 1907. South African Medical Corps, Captain.

MESSENGER, EDWIN SINCLAIR.
Carlisle Grammar School. Student of Medicine, 1917 and 1919. O.T.C. Artillery, July 1917 to Feb. 1918, Cadet Bombardier; Officer Cadet Feb. 1918. R.F.A., 2nd Lieut. Aug. 1918.

METCALFE, CLAUDE.
Student of Medicine, 1885-90. Nyasaland Volunteer Reserve, Private; attached King's African Rifles. Nyasaland 1899-1908, and 1914-17.

METHERELL, FREDERICK.
George Heriot's School. O.T.C. 1910-14, Cadet Sergeant. Student of Science, 1918. 9th Royal Scots, Private Oct. 1914. 1st Argyll and Sutherland Highlanders, 2nd Lieut. Dec. 1916; Lieut. July 1917. India and Mesopotamia.

METTAM, ALBERT EDWARD.
B.Sc. 1895. Royal Veterinary College, Dublin. O.T.C., Major and O.C. Died November 1917.

MEYER, REINHARD CARL JOHANNES.
M.B., Ch.B. 1908; M.D. and F.R.C.S. (Edin.) 1914. Royal Navy, Surgeon Aug. 1914. St Helena.

Record of War Service

MEYER, WILLIAM CHARLES BERNHARD.
Kimberley High School; First XV. and XI. Cadet Corps 1902-3, Cadet Sergeant-Major. B.A. (Cape); M.B., Ch.B. 1911; F.R.C.S. (Edin.) 1914. President, Royal Medical Society. O.T.C. Medical, April 1910-12, Cadet. R.A.M.C., Lieut. Aug. 1914; Captain March 1915; Acting Major Jan. 1918 to Dec. 1919. 17th Casualty Clearing Station, France. The Rhine. Dispatches 1916 and Jan. 1919.

MEYNELL, EDMOND LANGLEY.
Merchiston Castle. M.B., Ch.B. 1902; B.Sc. 1904. Volunteer Medical Staff Corps 1897 to 1903, Sergeant. R.A.M.C. (T.), Lieut. Oct. 1914; Captain April 1915. 24th Field Ambulance. France Nov. 1914.

MICHIE, ANGUS.
Charterhouse. Student of Medicine, 1911-14 and 1917-18. Royal Fusiliers, Public Schools Battn., Private Sept. 1914. 7th Sherwood Foresters, 2nd Lieut. May 1915; Lieut. Aug. 1916.

MIDDLETON, ARTHUR GILBERT MICHELSEN.
Student of Medicine, 1899-1904; L.R.C.P. & S. (Edin.) and L.F.P.S. (Glasg.) 1905. Volunteer Medical Staff Corps, 1898-1902, Private. R.A.M.C., Lieut. Nov. 1914; Captain Nov. 1915; Major Nov. 1918-19. France. Wounded April 1917, and at Monchy June 1917. M.C. May 1917.

MIDDLETON, EDWARD LOGGIE.
M.B., Ch.B. 1909; M.D. 1919; D.P.H. (Edin.) 1912. R.A.M.C., Lieut. Dec. 1914; Captain Dec. 1915. Invalided out Feb. 1916.

MIDDLETON, GEORGE GLENDINNING.
Dollar Academy. M.B., Ch.B. 1907; D.P.H. (Edin.) 1910. No. 4 Coy. Q.R.V.B., Royal Scots, 1903-6, Private. R.A.M.C. (T.), Lieut. April 1913. Mobilised Aug. 1914; Captain April 1915; Acting Major Jan. 1918. Highland Field Brigade.

MIDDLETON, IAN CAMERON.
Stirling High School; First XV. Student of Medicine, 1916-17 and 1918-19. O.T.C. Medical, 1918-19, Cadet. 6th Cameron Highlanders, Private March 1917.

MILES, ALEXANDER.
George Watson's College. M.B., C.M. 1888; M.D. 1891; F.R.C.S. (Edin.) 1890. Senior Lecturer on Clinical Surgery. R.A.M.C. (T.), Captain 1908. Edinburgh and Border Hospital, Dunkirk, 1914-15. Edinburgh War Hospital, Bangour.

MILL, DOUGLAS ROBERT.
George Watson's College. Student of Science, 1911-15 and 1918-20; B.Sc. 1920. O.T.C. Infantry, 1911-15, Cadet Corporal. 16th Royal Scots, Private. Transferred R.E., Corporal Aug. 1915; Tank Corps 1916. France 1915-19.

MILL, GEORGE SCOTT.
George Watson's College. O.T.C. 1905-10. M.A. (Hons. Maths.); B.Sc. 1914. 3/5th Gurkha Rifles (I.A.R.O.), Lieut. May 1917; Acting Captain and Adjutant March 1918-19. N.-W. Frontier, India.

Record of War Service

MILL, GEORGE SYMERS.
 M.B., C.M. 1889; M.D. 1897. Volunteer Medical Staff Corps, 1886-9, Corporal. R.A.M.C. (T.) 1903; Major 1915. France 1915-19. King's Own Yorkshire Light Infantry (T.), 1915. No. 6 Hospital, Rouen; No. 2 Ambulance Train. War Hospital, Dewsbury.

MILL, JAMES.
 Dundee High School. Student of Arts, 1913-15 and 1919. Royal Air Force, 2nd Air Mechanic, Sept. 1917. Attached R.G.A.

MILL, JAMES DAVIDSON.
 Daniel Stewart's College. Student of Arts and Medicine, 1911-14 and 1918-19; M.A. 1914. O.T.C. Medical, 1912-14, Cadet Corporal. R.A.M.C. (T.). Scottish Horse Field Ambulance, Sergeant Sept. 1914. 13th Royal Highlanders (Black Watch), 2nd Lieut. July 1915; Lieut. Oct. 1917. King's Own Scottish Borderers. Instructor, Machine-Gun School, Lembet, Salonika, to Jan. 1918.

MILL, THOMAS.
 Otago High School. M.B., Ch.B. 1901; F.R.C.S. (Edin.) 1904. R.A.M.C., Major May 1915. N.Z. Medical Corps, Major Dec. 1915; Lieut.-Col. July 1916; Colonel Jan. to Nov. 1919. Bristol, Walton-on-Thames, and N.Z. Hospitals. C.M.G. Jan. 1918; C.B.E. June 1919. Mention March 1917 and Feb. 1918.

MILL, WILLIAM.
 Royal High School. M.A. (Hons. Engl.) 1911. Schoolmaster. O.T.C. Infantry, July to Sept. 1915, Cadet L/Corporal. 8th, 3rd, and 7th Cameron Highlanders, 2nd Lieut. Sept. 1915; Lieut. July 1917. Attached 13th West Riding Regiment. Brigade Signalling Officer. Cromarty, April 1917. Education Officer, 37th Division, Sept. 1918. Attached A.P.M., Lille, Dec. 1918 to June 1919.

MILL, W. A.
 M.B., C.M. R.A.M.C., Lieut. Dispatches.

MILLAR, ALEXANDER FLEMING WILKIE.
 Royal High School. M.B., Ch.B. 1909. No. 4 Coy. Q.R.V.B., Royal Scots, 1902-5, Private. R.A.M.C., Lieut. Jan. 1915. 43rd Field Ambulance. Invalided out July 1917.

MILLAR, BERTRAM ST CLAIR.
 Student of Medicine, 1912-14. Scottish Horse (T.), Private.

MILLAR, CHARLES.
 George Heriot's School; First XV. and XI. O.T.C. 1914-16, Cadet Corporal. Student of Science, 1918-20. O.T.C. Artillery, Aug. 1916 to Feb. 1917, Cadet. R.F.A., Officer Cadet Feb. 1917; 2nd Lieut. July 1917; Lieut. Jan. 1919. Anti-Aircraft Battery. Syria, Palestine, and Egypt, Dec. 1917 to Jan. 1919.

Record of War Service

MILLAR, GEORGE.
George Watson's College; First XV. M.B., Ch.B. 1914; F.R.C.S. (Edin.). O.T.C. Infantry, 1909-14, Cadet Corporal. R.A.M.C., Lieut. Oct. 1914; Captain Oct. 1915. 11th Highland Light Infantry. 2nd Scottish General Hospital. France. Wounded Sept. 1915. Dispatches Dec. 1915. M.C. (Battle of Loos) Jan. 1916.

MILLAR, JOHN.
Edinburgh Normal College. Junior Clerk of Senatus. 5th attached 12th Royal Scots, Sergeant 1914; 2nd Lieut. Aug. 1917; Lieut. Feb. 1919. France. Twice Wounded. Prisoner of War in Germany April to Nov. 1918. T.F. Long Service Medal, 1913.

MILLAR, JOHN SYDNEY LAWRENCE.
Edinburgh Academy. Student of Law, 1904-6. Writer to the Signet, 1906. 2nd Lovat Scouts (T.), Lieut. Aug. 1914; Captain June 1917 to May 1919. Attached R.E. (Signals), Khaiga Column, Egypt. Australian Mounted Division and 12th Cavalry Brigade. Gallipoli Sept. 1915; Egypt and Palestine 1915 to Sept. 1918.

MILLAR, ROBERT HOYER.
Student of Arts, 1874-5. Q.E.R. 1874-5, Private. 2nd (Angus) V.B. and 5th (T.) Royal Highlanders (Black Watch), Lieut. 1876; Captain and Hon. Major 1891 to 1906; Temp. Lieut.-Col. 1914-16. South African Campaign, 1900. Recruiting Officer, Sept. 1914 to May 1915. France 1915 and 1916. V.D.

MILLAR, ROBERT MARTIN.
Daniel Stewart's College. Student of Medicine, 1915-16 and 1919. 9th Royal Scots, Private March 1916; L/Corporal May 1917. R.G.A. (T.), 2nd Lieut. Jan. 1918.

MILLAR, THOMAS LOWE.
Arbroath High School. M.A. 1909. Schoolmaster. 7th King's Own Scottish Borderers, May 1915; Captain and Adjutant Aug. 1916. 15th Division Reception Camp. France.

MILLAR, THOMAS McWALTER.
George Heriot's and Broughton Schools. Student of Arts and Medicine, 1913-15 and 1918-19. O.T.C. Infantry, 1914, Cadet. 16th Royal Scots, Private Nov. 1914; 2nd Lieut. March 1915; Lieut. July 1917. France. Wounded April and July 1916.

MILLAR, WILLIAM GILBERT. (See p. 751.)

MILLAR CRAIG, DAVID.
Daniel Stewart's College. Student of Arts and Music, 1896-7. 5th Royal Scots (T.), Private 1900; 2nd Lieut. March 1915; Lieut. Sept. 1915; Acting Captain Dec. 1916; Staff Lieut. Aug. 1915 to July 1916. O.C. "Balloon Propaganda" for France 1918.

Record of War Service

MILLARD, PHILIP.
St John's School, Leatherhead. M.B., Ch.B. 1898; M.D. 1903. Civil Surgeon, attached R.A.M.C., South African Campaign, 1901-3. South African Medical Corps, Captain June 1916-19. East Africa and Nyasaland.

MILLER, ALEXANDER.
Cowdenbeath School. Student of Arts, 1911-15; MA. 1915. Schoolmaster. R.F.A., Nov. 1915; 2nd Lieut. Sept. 1918.

MILLER, ALEXANDER CAMERON.
Fort William Grammar School. M.B., C.M. 1883; M.D. 1888. R.A.M.C. (T.), 1892; Major 1908; Lieut.-Col. Sept. 1918 to March 1919. Battn. M.O., 1914-16. President, Recruiting Medical Board, 1916-17. Senior M.O., Dunfermline, 1917-19. T.D.

MILLER, ALEXANDER GRANT SCHAW.
Fettes College. B.A. (Camb.) 1913. Cambridge University O.T.C 1909-11. Student of Law, 1913 and 1919. 1st Fife and Forfar Yeomanry (T.), Cadet Sept. 1914; 2nd Lieut. Oct. 1914; Lieut. June 1916; Acting Captain and Adjutant Sept. 1916; Captain Jan. 1918 to March 1919. Attached 2/1st Highland Mounted Brigade. Mention Aug. 1919.

MILLER, ALFRED TENNANT.
Cheltenham College and Edinburgh Academy. M.A. 1888. 2/9th Highland Light Infantry (T.), 2nd Lieut. 1889; Major 1910; Lieut.-Col. 1915. France and Second Army of the Rhine. T.D. 1913.

MILLER, ANDREW CAIRNIE.
Perth Academy. Student of Law, 1914-15. O.T.C. Artillery, Nov. 1915 to March 1916, Cadet; Officer Cadet March 1916. R.F.A., 2nd Lieut.; Lieut. Jan. 1918; Acting Captain and Adjutant Aug. 1917 to Jan. 1918 and Jan. to May 1919. Trench Mortar Battery, 1916; 39th and 168th Brigades, Aug. 1917 to May 1919.

MILLER, CLAUDE WILLIAM HANDASYDE.
Edinburgh Academy. Student of Law, 1912-14. 9th Royal Scots (T.), Private Aug. 1914. 14th Argyll and Sutherland Highlanders, 2nd Lieut. Dec. 1914; Captain Sept. 1915; Major May 1918.

MILLER, DOUGLAS ALEXANDER.
Student of Medicine, 1912-14 and 1917-19; M.B., Ch.B. (Hons.) 1919. Athletics. O.T.C. Medical, 1913-14, Cadet. 3rd Cameron Highlanders, Private Aug. 1914. Scottish Horse Field Ambulance. 1st, 3rd, and 10th Royal Highlanders (Black Watch), 2nd Lieut. July 1915; Lieut. Aug. 1917. France and Salonika.

MILLER, GEORGE EDWARD.
Ayr Academy. O.T.C. 1911-14, Cadet Sergeant. Student of Science, 1914-15 and 1918-19. O.T.C. Infantry, Oct. 1914, and Engineers, Jan. to April 1915, Cadet. R.E., 2/1st Lowland Division, Dispatch Rider, April 1915; Special Coy. Corporal Aug. 1915. R.F.A., 2nd Lieut. Sept. 1918 to April 1919. France.

Record of War Service

MILLER, GEORGE WATERSON.
　　Dundee High School. B.Sc. 1895; M.B., Ch.B. 1898. No. 4 Coy. Q.R.V.B., Royal Scots, 1895-8, Corporal. R.A.M.C. (T.), Major Aug. 1914; Acting Lieut.-Col. Feb. 1918. 1st and 1/2nd Highland Field Ambulances, 1908 to March 1919. France, 51st Division. Dispatches May and Dec. 1917. D.S.O. Dec. 1917. T.D. May 1918. Croix de Guerre (French) Jan. 1919.

MILLER, GREGOR MACKENZIE.
　　Daniel Stewart's College; First XV. M.B., Ch.B. 1910. R.A.M.C., Lieut.; Captain Oct. 1916; Acting Major July 1918. 15th Sherwood Foresters. France Jan. 1916. M.C. July 1916.

MILLER, HUGH.
　　George Watson's College. O.T.C. 1915-17. Student of Medicine, 1918-19. O.T.C. Artillery, July 1917 to Feb. 1918, Cadet Bombardier; Officer Cadet Feb. 1918. R.G.A. (T.), 2nd Lieut. Aug. 1918.

MILLER, HUGH CRICHTON.
　　Fettes College. M.A. 1898; M.B., Ch.B. 1900; M.D. 1902; M.D. (Pavia) 1902. President, University Union. University Battery, E.C.A.V., 1894-1901, B.S.M. R.A.M.C., Lieut. Nov. 1915; Major Dec. 1916. No. 21 General Hospital, Alexandria. Neurologist, 4th London General Hospital.

MILLER, HUGH MORISON.
　　Edinburgh Academy and Loretto. M.A. 1909. Lecturer in English, Aberdeen University. 14th Royal Scots, 2nd Lieut. Feb. 1915; Lieut. Sept. 1915; Captain April 1916. Intelligence Corps, G.H.Q., France. Dispatches Nov. 1918.

MILLER, JAMES.
　　Edinburgh Academy. B.Sc. 1896; M.B., Ch.B. 1899; M.D. (Gold Medal) 1904. Lecturer, Pathology. R.A.M.C. (T.), Captain Dec. 1914; 2nd Scottish General Hospital.

MILLER, JAMES.
　　Kirkwall School. Student of Arts and Science, 1906-10 and 1913-14; M.A. 1909. O.T.C. Artillery, Oct. 1915 to Jan. 1916, Cadet. R.F.A., 180th Brigade, 2nd Lieut. Jan. 1916; Lieut. July 1917; Acting Captain and Adjutant Aug. 1917 to July 1919. Dispatches April 1918. M.C. June 1919.

MILLER, JAMES GRAHAM.
　　George Watson's College. M.B., C.M. 1887. 1st V.B. Northumberland Fusiliers, 2nd Lieut. Sept. 1917. R.A.M.C. (V.), Captain 1918.

MILLER, JAMES INNES.
　　Fettes College. O.T.C. 1909-11. Student of Arts, 1911-15; M.A. (Hons. Classics and Hist.) 1915. O.T.C. Artillery, 1912-15, Cadet Sergeant. R.F.A. (S.R.), 2nd Lieut. June 1915; Lieut. Dec. 1916; Captain July 1919. 59th Brigade, Gallipoli; 527th Howitzer Battery, Meerut Division, Mesopotamia.

Record of War Service

MILLER, JAMES MACBRIDE.
George Watson's College. Student of Arts, 1914-15. O.T.C. Artillery, 1914-15, Cadet. Forth R.G.A. (T.), 2nd Lieut. Feb. 1915; Lieut. June 1916; Acting Captain July 1916 to June 1918. France and The Rhine. M.C. Feb. 1919.

MILLER, JOHN.
George Watson's College. University O.T.C. Artillery, Jan. to Oct. 1918, Cadet. R.F.A., Officer Cadet Oct. 1918.

MILLER, JOHN GORDON.
Merchiston Castle. Cadet Corps to 1907. B.Sc. 1911. O.T.C. Artillery, Feb. 1908 to June 1914, Cadet Sergeant. R.F.A., 2nd Lieut. Aug. 1914; Lieut. March 1915; Captain July 1915. France.

MILLER, JOHN MORRISON.
Fettes College. O.T.C. 1914-16. University O.T.C. Artillery, 1916-17, Cadet; Officer Cadet May 1917. R.G.A., 2nd Lieut. Dec. 1917; Lieut. June to July 1919.

MILLER, JOHN TWEEDIE.
George Heriot's School. M.A. 1902. Schoolmaster. No. 95 Special Service Volunteer Coy., Private Jan. 1917; Sergeant Aug. 1917; C.S.M. Jan. 1918. 2nd V.B. Royal Scots, 2nd Lieut. Nov 1918.

MILLER, PETER WATERS.
Castletown School. Student of Arts and Divinity, 1909-15; M.A. 1913; B.D. 1915. Minister, Free Church of Scotland. Chaplain, 4th Class, Aug. 1918. 23rd Casualty Clearing Station. Lowland Division, France, and The Rhine.

MILLER, ROBERT WATSON HAMILTON.
Edinburgh Academy. O.T.C. 1909-10. Student of Medicine, 1910-16; M.B., Ch.B. 1916. O.T.C. Artillery, Oct. 1910-14, Cadet Corporal. R.F.A., 2nd Lieut. Oct. 1914-15. R.A.M.C. (S.R.), Lieut. Sept. 1916; Captain June 1917. 37th Indian General Hospital, Karachi, Jan. 1919.

MILLER, ROBERT WEBSTER.
Student of Medicine, 1908-14; M.B., Ch.B. 1914. R.A.M.C., Lieut. May 1916; Captain May 1917. Attached 2/9th and 2/2nd Gurkha Rifles. Marri Field Force, Baluchistan, 1918; Waziristan Field Force, 1919.

MILLER, SIDNEY CRAMOND.
George Watson's College. M.A. 1908. Canadian Infantry, Lieut.

MILLER, WILLIAM ARCHIBALD.
George Watson's College. M.B., Ch.B. 1910. R.A.M.C., Lieut. 1912; Captain May 1915; Acting Major Jan. 1917. D.S.O.; M.C.; Bar to M.C. Three times Mentioned in Dispatches.

MILLER, WILLIAM ARMOUR.
George Watson's College. Student of Law. Chartered Accountant, 1913. 29th Canadian Light Horse, Private. Saskatchewan Regiment, Lieut. Nov. 1916. M.M. Sept. 1916.

Record of War Service

MILLER, WILLIAM JOHN.
George Heriot's School; First XV. O.T.C. 1915-17, Cadet Sergeant. Student of Science, 1918-19. O.T.C. Artillery, Sept. 1917 to April 1918, Cadet Bombardier. R.G.A., Officer Cadet May 1918; 2nd Lieut. March 1919.

MILLIGAN, JOHN MONCREIFF.
George Heriot's School. Student of Law, 1896-8. 6th Royal Scots (T.), Captain; Major Oct. 1916. Attached 1/7th Royal Highlanders (Black Watch).

MILLIGAN, OSWALD BELL.
Edinburgh Academy. M.A. 1899; B.D. 1902. Minister, Church of Scotland Chaplain, 8th Royal Highlanders (Black Watch), Sept. 1914. Dispatches and M.C. 1916.

MILLN, GEORGE HERBERT STEPHEN.
M.B., Ch.B. 1903. Royal Navy, H.M.S. *Indus*, Surgeon-Lieut-Commander.

MILLN, JAMES DUFF SCOTT.
M.B., Ch.B. 1897. Royal Navy, Staff Surgeon; Fleet Surgeon Nov. 1913.

MILLS, BERNARD LANGLEY.
Marlborough. M.B., C.M. 1882; M.D. 1885; M.R.C.S. (Eng.) 1882; F.R.C.S. (Edin.) 1886; D.P.H. (Edin.) 1908. R.A.M.C., Jan. 1896. Indian Frontier and South African Campaign, Lieut.-Col. Jan. 1906. Rejoined Aug. 1914. Staff Officer, Army Bearer Corps, Western Command, India.

MILLS, EVERARD ARNOLD.
Student of Medicine, 1911-16; M.B., Ch.B. 1916. O.T.C. Medical, Nov. 1915 to July 1916, Cadet. R.A.M.C. (S.R.), Captain Feb. 1917; Acting Major March 1918. 7th Royal Sussex Regiment, 1918.

MILLS, HORACE MACAULAY.
Trent College, Derbyshire. M.B., Ch.B. 1910. R.A.M.C., Lieut. Dec. 1915. 12th Rifle Battn., and 2/3rd Field Ambulance.

MILLS, JAMES DICK WATSON.
Daniel Stewart's College. Student of Arts and Science, 1913-15 and 1919-20; B.Sc. 1920. O.T.C. Infantry, 1914, Cadet. 16th Royal Scots, Private Dec. 1914. R.E., Corporal July 1915. 3rd Northumberland Fusiliers, 2nd Lieut. Nov. 1917. Attached Durham Light Infantry. France.

MILLS, JOHN J.
Student of Arts, 1908-14. 9th Royal Scots (T.), Private; L/Corporal. 5th Royal Highlanders (Black Watch) (T.), 2nd Lieut.

MILLS, LAURENCE HITCHEN BARFOOT.
King Edward VI. Grammar School, Norwich. M.B., Ch.B. 1898. Auxiliary Hospitals (V.A.D.), Norwich, 1914-18. Ministry of National Service, Nov. 1917. R.A.M.C. (V.), Norfolk, Captain 1918.

Record of War Service

MILN, DAVID LESLIE.
King's School, Chester; First XI. O.T.C. 1913-15. University O.T.C. Artillery, 1917-18, Cadet Bombardier; Officer Cadet March 1918. R.G.A., 2nd Lieut. Feb. 1919.

MILNE, ALFRED ERNEST.
Student of Law, 1906-8. Writer to the Signet, 1911. 2/4th and 10th Royal Scots (T.), Private July 1916. Russia Sept. 1918. Wounded Oct. 1918.

MILNE, CHARLES IRVINE.
Montrose Academy, and George Watson's College. M.B., Ch.B. 1907. R.A.M.C., Lieut. May 1917; Captain May 1918 to Nov. 1919. North-West Frontier, India; North-West Frontier Force (Afghanistan), Aug. 1917 to Sept. 1919.

MILNE, COLIN.
Colston School, Bristol. Student of Medicine, 1911-16; M.B., Ch.B. 1916. O.T.C. Medical, Sept. 1914 to July 1916, Cadet. R.A.M.C. (S.R.), Lieut. Aug. 1916; Captain Feb. 1917. Aligharbi, Mesopotamia, April 1917 to Dec. 1918.

MILNE, DAVID.
Daniel Stewart's College; First XV. and XI. Student of Arts, 1913-15 and 1918-19. O.T.C. Infantry, Oct. 1914 to March 1915, Cadet. 9th Royal Scots (T.), Private March 1915; Corporal. France April 1915 to Oct. 1918. Wounded.

MILNE, EWAN THOMAS MITCHELL.
George Watson's College. O.T.C. 1909-10. Student of Arts and Science, 1911-14. 46th Punjabis, 2nd Lieut. 1914; Lieut. Dec. 1915; Captain Dec. 1918; Acting Major 1918-19. North-West Frontier, 1914-15; Mesopotamia 1915-16. 9th Bhopals, 1915-19. H.Q., Lucknow Division. Mention 1915.

MILNE, FRANK GARDYNE.
M.B., Ch.B. 1914. R.A.M.C., Lieut. Feb. 1915; Captain Feb. 1916; Acting Major Nov. 1918 to April 1919. Egypt and Palestine, July 1915 to April 1919.

MILNE, GEORGE WARDLAW.
Larchfield, Helensburgh, and Edinburgh Collegiate School; First XV. Student of Medicine, 1896-8; M.B., C.M. 1901; M.D. (Glasg.) 1911. South African Campaign, 1899-1902. R.A.M.C., Lieut. Oct. 1914; Captain Oct. 1915; Acting Major Nov. 1916; Acting Lieut.-Col. Dec. 1918. 1st Cameron Highlanders; Hospital Ship *St Denis*; Ambulance Trains "Warilsia" and "Valdinira," France, Oct. 1914. Dispatches April 1915 and Feb. 1919. O.B.E. April 1919.

MILNE, JAMES.
Forfar Academy. Student of Medicine, 1911-16; M.B., Ch.B. 1916. O.T.C. Medical, Jan. to July 1916, Cadet. R.A.M.C. (S.R.), Lieut. Aug. 1916; Captain Feb. 1917. 7th Middlesex Regiment. 280th Brigade, R.F.A. 2/2nd and 2/3rd London Field Ambulance.

Record of War Service

MILNE, JOHN.
Dunfermline High School. M.A. 1910. 2nd Lovat Scouts, Private Oct. 1914; Sergeant Nov. 1914; 2nd Lieut. May 1917; Lieut. Nov. 1918. Cameron Highlanders and Royal Highlanders (Black Watch). Wounded. Invalided out April 1919.

MILNE, JOHN BROWNLEE.
M.B., Ch.B. 1900. R.A.M.C., Captain. France.

MILNE, THOMAS.
Dunfermline High School; First XI. Student of Arts, 1912-15 and 1916-17; M.A. 1917. Maule Bursar. O.T.C. Infantry, Oct. 1913 to Sept. 1914, Cadet. 6th and 5th Cameron Highlanders, Private Sept. 1914; 2nd Lieut. Feb. 1915; Lieut. July 1917. King's African Rifles, Nov. 1917 to Feb. 1919. France Oct. 1915; East Africa Nov. 1917 to Feb. 1919. Wounded in France July 1916.

MILNE, THOMAS.
Largo School. Student of Arts, 1913-14. O.T.C. Infantry, 1914-15, Cadet. 10th Seaforth Highlanders, 2nd Lieut. Jan. 1915; Lieut. May 1916. German East Africa, attached 6th King's African Rifles, Dar-es-Salaam, Nov. 1917. M.C. May 1916.

MILNE, WILLIAM ROBERTSON.
Cruden Bay School. Student of Arts, 1918-19. 1st Gordon Highlanders, Private Sept. 1915.

MILNE, WILLIAM STUART.
M.B., Ch.B. 1902. R.A.M.C., Lieut., Netley Hospital.

MILNE-HOME, CHARLES ALEXANDER.
Haileybury. O.T.C. 1907-9. B.A.; LL.B. (Camb.) 1912. Student of Law, 1912-14. 6th King's Own Scottish Borderers, 2nd Lieut. Aug. 1914; Lieut. July 1917. Attached 16th Highland Light Infantry. The Rhine.

MINET, GASTON HENRI JOSEPH.
Student of Arts, 1916. Belgian Army, 4th Regiment d'Artillerie, Private June 1917; Brigadier (Corporal) May 1918; Maréchal des logis (Sergeant) Aug. 1918.

MIRYLEES, OSWALD MOIR.
M.B., Ch.B. 1905. R.A.M.C., Captain July 1918.

MITCHELHILL, JAMES.
George Watson's College. University O.T.C. Artillery, 1915-16, Cadet Bombardier; Officer Cadet June 1916. R.F.A., 2nd Lieut. Aug. 1916; Lieut. Feb. 1918; Captain Aug. to Nov. 1918. France. M.C. Jan. 1919.

MITCHELL, ALEXANDER.
George Heriot's School. M.A. 1902 (Hons. Engl. 1904; Hist. 1906). Lecturer in English. Edinburgh Volunteer Regiment. 3rd King's Own Scottish Borderers, Private July 1917. 16th Royal Scots. Twice Wounded.

Record of War Service

MITCHELL, ALEXANDER PHILP.
  Royal High School. M.B., Ch.B. 1907; M.D. 1909; Ch.M. 1913; F.R.C.S. (Edin.) 1912. R.A.M.C., Lieut. July 1918; Captain July 1919. Edinburgh War Hospital, Bangour.

MITCHELL, ANDREW ALEXANDER.
  Boroughmuir School. Student of Arts, 1913-14 and 1918-19; M.A. 1920. Royal Scots (T.), Private Feb. 1914.

MITCHELL, ARCHIBALD BROWNING.
  Daniel Stewart's College. M.B., Ch.B. 1911. O.T.C. Infantry, Dec. 1908 to Sept. 1914, Cadet Corporal. R.A.M.C., Lieut. Aug. 1914; Captain April 1915; Major Jan. 1918. Field Ambulances, Suvla Bay, July 1916; Macedonia, Serbia, and Palestine. M.C.

MITCHELL, CRAWFORD.
  Boroughmuir School. Student of Arts, 1918. 4th Royal Scots, Private June 1916.

MITCHELL, FREDERICK RITCHIE.
  Royal High School; First XV. and XI. Student of Medicine, 1918-19. O.T.C. Infantry, May to Nov. 1917, Cadet; Officer Cadet Nov. 1917. 7th Seaforth Highlanders, 2nd Lieut. April 1918.

MITCHELL, JAMES EBENEZER.
  Bearsden School. University O.T.C. Artillery, 1917, Cadet; Officer Cadet June 1917. R.G.A. (S.R.), 2nd Lieut. Nov. 1917; Lieut. May 1919.

MITCHELL, JAMES GALBRAITH.
  M.A. 1904; LL.B. 1907. 2nd and 18th Liverpool Regiment, Private; L/Corporal. Wounded July 1916.

MITCHELL, JOHN.
  Boroughmuir School. Student of Arts, 1912-14 and 1918-19; M.A. 1919. 9th Royal Scots, Private Aug. 1914. R.F.C., 1st Air Mechanic, March 1916. 1st Balloon Wing. France.

MITCHELL, JOHN STEVENSON.
  M.B., Ch.B. 1905; F.R.C.S. (Edin.) 1909. R.A.M.C., Lieut. Oct. 1915; Captain Jan. 1918. No. 20 Stationary Hospital, Salonika.

MITCHELL, LACHLAN MARTIN VICTOR.
  Inverness Royal Academy. M.B., Ch.B. 1909. O.T.C. Infantry to Sept. 1908, Cadet. R.A.M.C. (T.), Lieut. Jan. 1912; Captain April 1915; Temp. Major Sept. 1915; Acting Major Jan. 1918. Highland Mounted Brigade Field Ambulance. Gallipoli; Palestine. Dispatches June 1916 and Jan. 1919. O.B.E. (Military) Jan. 1917.

MITCHELL, THOMAS.
  M.A. 1907. Schoolmaster. 2/1st Scottish Horse, Corporal.

Record of War Service

MITCHELL, THOMAS SMITH.
Student of Medicine, 1901-6. Motor Machine-Gun Section, 2nd Lieut. Aug. 1915.

MITCHELL, WILLIAM ADAMSON McBAIN.
Montrose Academy. Student of Law, 1915-16. R.A.M.C., Private Aug. 1917; Corporal Feb. 1919.

MITCHELL, WILLIAM FRASER.
Dundee High School. Cadet Corps Jan. to June 1918. Student of Arts, 1918. 4th Seaforth Highlanders, Private July 1918.

MITCHELL, WILLIAM GEMMELL.
Royal High School. Student of Arts and Divinity, 1912-15 and 1918-19; M.A. 1915. R.A.M.C. (T.), Private July 1915; Corporal Sept. 1915. 3rd Lowland Field Ambulance. Order of St Sava, 5th Class (Serbia), April 1919.

MITCHELL, WILLIAM GORDON.
M.A. 1880; M.B., C.M. 1885; M.D. 1892. No. 4 Coy. Q.R.V.B., Royal Scots, Private. R.A.M.C. (T.), Captain; Major Sept. 1916. 2/9th Argyll and Sutherland Highlanders, 1916. Attached Royal Air Force.

MITCHELL, WILLIAM LOW.
Dundee High School; First XV. and XI. M.A. (St Andrews); LL.B. 1909. Advocate, 1910. 5th Royal Highlanders (Black Watch) (T.), Lieut. 1905; Captain 1912. Signal Service, Jan. 1916. Commandant, Signals Schools, France, Nov. 1916 to Nov. 1918. France 1914-18.

MITCHELL, WILLIAM McGREGOR.
Student of Science and Medicine, 1912-14 and 1918-19; B.Sc., Veterinary, 1919. M.R.C.V.S. Assistant in Comparative Anatomy. Royal Veterinary College O.T.C., Lieut. 1912. R.A.V.C., Lieut. Sept. 1914; Captain Sept. 1915. France, attached Guards Division. Dispatches June 1915. M.C. June 1917.

MITCHELL, WILLIAM McKUTCHEON.
George Heriot's School. Student of Arts and Law, 1910-15 and 1919; M.A. (Hons. Econ. Sc.) 1915. 9th Royal Scots (T.), July 1915; 2nd Lieut. Nov. 1915; Lieut. April 1917; Acting Captain Feb. 1918. Attached Machine-Gun Corps. France. M.C. July 1917.

MITCHELL, WILLIAM SMITH.
Janitor and Bedellus. 2nd Royal Highlanders (Black Watch), 1887 to July 1909. South African Campaign, 1900-2. Rejoined as Colour-Sergeant Dec. 1914; Q.M.S. July 1915 to March 1918. Depôt, Perth.

MITCHELL-THOMSON, Sir WILLIAM, Bart.
LL.B. 1902. M.P. R.N.V.R., Hon. Lieut. K.B.E. June 1918.

MITRA, SAMARENDRA LAL.
M.B., Ch.B. 1913; B.Sc.; D.P.H., D.T.M. and H. Indian Medical Service, Temp. Lieut. May 1915; Temp. Captain May 1916. Indian Station Hospital, Lahore District.

Record of War Service

MITRA, SARAT CHANDRA.
: M.A. 1912; M.B., Ch.B. 1913. L.M. (Rotunda) 1915; L.M.R.C.P. (Ireland) 1914, Indian Medical Service, Lieut. May 1915; Captain May 1916. 16th Rajputs.

MITTON, JAMES BERTRAM.
: M.B., Ch.B. 1913. O.T.C. Artillery, 1908-11, Cadet. R.A.M.C. (S.R.), Lieut. Nov. 1914; Captain Nov. 1915. 33rd Field Ambulance. Suvla Bay. Wounded at Gallipoli. 4th London Field Ambulance, France, Sept. 1916. M.C.

MOFFAT, ALAN St JOHN.
: Repton. O.T.C. 1915-18, Cadet L/Corporal. Student of Medicine, 1918. King's Own Yorkshire Light Infantry, Aug. 1918; 2nd Lieut. March 1919.

MOFFAT, ALFRED GRIEVE.
: George Watson's College. Student of Science, 1918. 1st Gordon Highlanders, May 1916; 2nd Lieut. March 1917; Lieut. Oct. 1918. Wounded March 1918.

MOFFAT, FRANCIS JOHN CAMPBELL.
: George Watson's College; First XV. and XI. Student of Medicine, 1913-14. O.T.C. Artillery, Aug. to Sept. 1914, Cadet. 10th Gordon Highlanders, 2nd Lieut. Sept. 1914; Captain Dec. 1914; Acting Major July 1918. France. Three times Wounded. Dispatches Nov. 1917. D.S.O. Oct. 1917.

MOFFAT, ROBERT UNWIN.
: St Andrew's College, Grahamstown, Cape Colony. M.B., C.M. 1890; M.D. 1907. Africa, 1893. Uganda Mutiny, 1898. R.A.M.C., Lieut. Nov. 1914; Captain May 1915. 4th West Kent Regiment. C.M.G. 1898.

MOFFATT, ALEXANDER McRITCHIE.
: Merchiston Castle. O.T.C. 1907-9. Student of Science, 1910. O.T.C. Artillery, 1910-12, Cadet Trumpeter. 7th Argyll and Sutherland Highlanders, Lieut. Oct. 1914; Captain Feb. 1916; Major Oct. 1918. Royal Air Force, Flight Lieut. Egypt. Legion d'Honneur (Croix de Chevalier) May 1917. Dispatches May 1918.

MOIR, ALEXANDER HENRY MORHAM.
: George Watson's College; First XV. Student of Science, 1913-14 and 1918-19. 9th Royal Scots (T.), Private Aug. 1914; Lieut. July 1917; Acting Captain. France. M.C. Dec. 1918.

MOIR, GORDON.
: George Watson's College. O.T.C. 1916-18. Student of Medicine, 1917-18. O.T.C. Medical, April to Sept. 1918, Cadet. R.E., Signal Service, Sept. 1918.

MOIR, HENRY MAITLAND.
: George Watson's College. M.B., Ch.B. 1913. O.T.C. Infantry, Oct. 1909 to Dec. 1913, Cadet Corporal. R.A.M.C., Lieut. Nov. 1914; Captain Nov. 1915 to March 1919. France Feb. 1915.

Record of War Service

MOIR, JOHN.
M.D. R.A.M.C. (T.), Lieut.-Col.

MOIR, JOHN.
George Watson's College. Student of Science, 1912-13. R.F.A. (T.), 1st Lowland Brigade, Gunner Sept. 1914. 7th Argyll and Sutherland Highlanders, 2nd Lieut. Oct. 1915; Lieut. June 1917. Invalided home.

MOIR-PORTEOUS, DAVID JOHN.
George Watson's College. M.A. 1887; B.D. 1890. Minister, Church of Scotland. Chaplain 1907; 4th Class, 1908; 3rd Class, Dec. 1917. Stirling, 1915; Dundee, 1916. Birmingham Military Hospital, April 1918 to Aug. 1919.

MOLESWORTH, ERIC MACKINNON.
Fettes College. O.T.C. 1908-9. Student of Medicine, 1909-14; M.B., Ch.B. 1914. Royal Navy, Surgeon, Aug. 1914. H.M.S. *Hussar*. Mediterranean.

MÖLLER, CAREL THEODORUS.
M.B., Ch.B. 1905; L.R.C.P. & S. (Edin.) and L.F.P.S. (Glasg.) 1904. R.A.M.C., Major.

MOLONY, JOHN BARRÉ DE WINTON.
Glenalmond. Cadet Corps 1902-3. M.B., Ch.B. 1908; F.R.C.S. (Edin.). Indian Medical Service, Lieut. Dec. 1914; Captain Dec. 1915. Mesopotamia. Dispatches March 1918 and June 1919. O.B.E. (Military) May 1919.

MOLYNEAUX, JOHN JOSEPH.
Student of Medicine, 1910-15; M.B., Ch.B. 1914. O.T.C. Medical, Nov. 1914, Cadet. R.A.M.C. (S.R.), Lieut. Jan. 1915; Captain July 1915.

MONCREIFF, RICHARD HENRY FITZHERBERT.
Fettes College. Student of Law, 1903-5. Chartered Accountant, 1906. 9th Royal Scots (T.), March 1901; Captain March 1908; Major June 1916. France. War Office Staff, 1917-19. Twice Wounded. T.D. and Mention March 1919.

MONCUR, DAVID.
Broughton School, Edinburgh. M.A. 1908. Schoolmaster. Royal Scots, Jan. 1915; Sergeant Jan. 1916. Prisoner of War March 1917.

MONFRIES, CHARLES BABINGTON SMITH.
M.A. 1904. Schoolmaster. 17th Royal Scots, Captain March 1916; Temp. Major Sept. 1916. C.B.E.; O.B.E.

MONNINGTON, RICHARD CALDECOTT.
M.B., Ch.B. 1902. R.A.M.C., Lieut.; Captain Dec. 1915.

MONRO, DAVID CARMICHAEL.
Wellington College, New Zealand. M.B., Ch.B. 1911. R.A.M.C., Lieut. Aug. 1914; Captain Aug. 1915. 3rd Rifle Brigade; 44th Casualty Clearing Station, France. War and Station Hospital, Poona. Dispatches Jan. 1916.

Record of War Service

MONROE, JAMES.
M.B., Ch.B. 1898. R.A.M.C., Lieut.; Captain April 1917. Egypt May 1916.

MONSARRAT, KEITH WALDEGRAVE.
King William's College, Isle of Man. M.B., Ch.B. 1894; F.R.C.S. (Edin.) 1897. Lecturer, Operative Surgery, Liverpool University. R.A.M.C. (T.), 1898; Captain Dec. 1911; Brevet Major Jan. 1918. 1st Western General Hospital, Aug. 1914; 37th General Hospital, Salonika, June 1916. Dispatches June and Nov. 1917. Order of St Sava (Serbia) July 1917.

MONTEATH, HARRY HENDERSON.
Edinburgh Academy. B.A. (Oxford); LL.B. 1911. Writer to the Signet, 1911. A.S.C. (T.), 2nd Lieut. Dec. 1914; Lieut. May 1916; Acting Captain Oct. 1917 to Sept. 1919. Scottish Horse Brigade, Mesopotamia, March 1917 to Sept. 1919. Dispatches Jan. 1920.

MONTGOMERY, WALTER THOMAS HAROLD.
Student of Medicine. 2nd Royal Fusiliers (Sportsman's Battn.), 2nd Lieut.; Captain.

MOODIE, ANDREW MORRIS.
Dunfermline High School. M.A. 1911. Licentiate, U.F. Church of Scotland. 3rd London Scottish (T.), Private Jan. 1915. 7th Royal Highlanders (Black Watch), Acting Captain April 1917; Lieut. July 1917. France. Prisoner of War March to Dec. 1918. M.C. (Cambrai) Nov. 1917.

MOODY-STUART, KENNETH ANDREW.
M.B., Ch.B. 1904. University Battery, E.C.A.V., 1898-1908. O.T.C. Artillery, 1908-11, Captain 1909. R.F.A. (T.), 1st Lowland Brigade, Captain Sept. 1914; Acting Major June 1915; Major March 1918. France, 102nd Brigade. Italy, 31st Battery. Dispatches (Italy) Jan. 1919.

MOOLMAN, JUAN CHRISTIAN.
Student of Medicine, 1913-14. O.T.C. Artillery, Nov. 1913 to Aug. 1914, Cadet. R.H.A. (T.), Inverness-shire, 2nd Lieut.; Lieut. Dec. 1916. France.

MOON, CHRISTOPHER ROBERT CECIL.
Derby School; First XI. Cadet Corps 1902-6, 2nd Lieut. Student of Medicine, 1911-14 and 1915-16; L.R.C.P. (Edin.) 1918. Hockey International. O.T.C. Artillery, Sept. to Nov. 1914, Cadet. R.F.A., 2nd Lieut. Nov. 1914. Member of Recruiting and Pensions Medical Board.

MOONIE, WILLIAM BEATON.
Daniel Stewart's College; First XV. Mus. Bac. 1909. 3rd and 2/4th Cameron Highlanders, Private March 1916; L/Corporal. Attached Labour Corps.

MOORE, ARTHUR EISDELL.
Auckland Grammar School, New Zealand. First XV. M.B., Ch.B. 1911; M.D. 1913; F.R.C.S. (Eng.) 1919. R.A.M.C., Lieut. Nov. 1914; Captain Nov. 1915. France 1915; Mesopotamia 1916.

Record of War Service

MOORE, HAMILTON STEPHEN.
Kilmarnock Academy. Student of Medicine, 1910-16; M.B., Ch.B. 1916. R.A.M.C., Lieut. 1916; Captain 1917; Wounded Nov. 1917; Wounded and Prisoner of War May 1918. M.C. April 1918; Bar to M.C. May 1918.

MOORHOUSE, JAMES ERNEST.
Almondbury Grammar School. M.B., C.M. 1892; M.D. 1895. R.A.M.C. (H.H.R.), Captain Aug. 1914. Military Hospital, Stirling.

MORE, HUGH JAMES.
M.A. 1901; M.B., Ch.B. 1906; M.D. 1910. R.A.M.C., Lieut. Aug. 1914; Captain Aug. 1915. France 1914; Dardanelles, East Africa, Palestine, and Egypt.

MORE, JAMES ANTONY.
Madras College, St Andrews. Student of Science, 1913-14; B.Sc. 1920. R.G.A., 26th Heavy Battery, Gunner Aug. 1914; 2nd Lieut. Sept. 1915; Lieut. June 1916.

MORE, JOHN WILLIAM.
M.A. 1900; B.A. (Oxford). Sheriff-Substitute. General List, Lieut. Aug. 1916. Assistant Recruiting Officer and Military Representative, 1916-18. Appeal, National Service Representative.

MORE, JOHN WILSON.
Stirling High School. Student of Law, 1912-14. Solicitor, 1914. Lovat Scouts, Private June 1915 to Feb. 1919.

MORE, LANCELOT PAXTON.
M.B., C.M. 1891. R.A.M.C., 1892; Major July 1904; Lieut.-Col. Feb. 1915; Brevet Colonel Jan. 1917; Colonel and A.D.M.S., June 1918. H.Q., India, Oct. 1915 to Sept. 1918.

MORE, PAXTON St CLAIR.
St George's. M.B., C.M. 1891. Indian Medical Service, Jan. 1893; Lieut.-Col. Jan. 1913. O.C. Frontier War Hospital, Rawal Pindi. O.B.E. Aug. 1919.

MORGAN, BENJAMIN BRANFORD.
King Edward VI. School, Norwich. M.B., Ch.B. 1910; M.D. 1913. O.T.C. Artillery, Oct. 1908 to Jan. 1910, Cadet. R.A.M.C. (T.), 1st South Midland, Lieut. 1912; Captain April 1915. Dispatches June 1917.

MORGAN, EDWARD MERVYN LEWIS.
Wesley College, Melbourne. Student of Medicine, 1915. L.R.C.P. & S. (Edin.); L.R.F.P.S. (Glasg.) 1916. O.T.C. Medical, Sept. 1914, Cadet. R.A.M.C. (T.), Scottish Horse Brigade Field Ambulance, Private Sept. 1914. R.A.M.C. (S.R.), Lieut. Nov. 1916; Captain Nov. 1917. 33rd British General Hospital, Basra, March to Dec. 1917. Kharaq, Persia, Dec. 1917 to June 1919.

Record of War Service

MORGAN, HUGH TAYLOR.
M.B., C.M.; M.D. R.A.M.C. (T.), Captain. Rejoined Aug. 1914 to May 1919. 5th Southern General Hospital; 29th Stationary Hospital, Salonika, June 1916 to June 1918; 29th Stationary and Detention Hospitals, Cremona, Italy, 1918-19.

MORGAN, JAMES CUMMING.
Miller Institution, Thurso. M.A. 1901. Schoolmaster. Normal College, Capetown, Cadet Corps, Lieut. 1904-6. 9th Cameron Highlanders, Private July 1916; Corporal July 1918.

MORGAN, RODERICK.
M.A. 1907. Minister, U.F. Church of Scotland. Canadian Army Medical Corps, Private May 1916 to July 1919.

MORGAN, WILLIAM D.
George Watson's College; First XV. and XI. O.T.C. 1906-9, Cadet Sergeant. Student of Arts, 1909. O.T.C. Infantry, Oct. 1909 to Sept. 1911, Cadet. R.F.A., 2nd Lieut. Dec. 1912; Lieut. 1915; Captain Dec. 1916. D.S.O.; M.C.; Croix de Guerre (Belgian). Five times Mentioned in Dispatches.

MORIARTY, GERALD IRVING.
George Watson's College; First XI. MB., Ch.B. 1904. R.A.M.C., Lieut. April 1915; Captain April 1916. Hospital Ship, Mediterranean, 1915-16. Mesopotamia, Field Ambulance, 1916-17. Artillery Brigade, Egypt; Palestine, 1917-19.

MORISON, DAVID MURRAY.
George Watson's College; First XV. and XI. Student of Medicine, 1913-14 and 1916-19. 6th Royal Scots, Private Aug. 1914; 2nd Lieut. Dec. 1914; Lieut. July 1916. Border Regiment and Machine-Gun Corps. Wounded July 1916. Invalided out Sept. 1917.

MORISON, DUNCAN METCALFE.
Leys School. Cadet Corps 1903-6, Cadet L/Corporal. M.B., Ch.B. 1910. University Battery, E.C.A.V., 1905-7, Gunner. R.A.M.C., Lieut. Feb. 1915; Captain Feb. 1916; Acting Major Jan. 1918. 38th Field Ambulance, France. Dispatches May 1918. M.C. Sept. 1918.

MORISON, RUTHERFORD.
M.B., Ch.B. 1875; M.D. 1884; LL.D.; F.R.C.S. (Edin.) 1884; (Eng.) 1890; D.C.L. (Durham). Professor of Surgery, Durham University. R.N.V.R., Staff-Surgeon 1910; Surgeon, Northumberland War Hospital.

MORPETH, ROBERT SPOTTISWOODE.
George Watson's College. Student of Medicine, 1918-19. O.T.C. Infantry, June to Sept. 1915, Cadet. Cameron Highlanders, 2nd Lieut. Sept. 1915; Lieut. April 1917. France. Gassed Feb. 1917. Prisoner of War April 1918.

Record of War Service

MORRIS, GEORGE.
>George Watson's College. O.T.C. 1907-10. Student of Medicine, 1911-16; M.B., Ch.B. 1916. O.T.C. Medical, Nov. 1914 to April 1916, Cadet Sergeant-Major. R.A.M.C. (S.R.), Lieut. April 1916; Captain Oct. 1916. France. 29th Battn., Machine-Gun Corps. The Rhine. M.C. Dec. 1917.

MORRIS, JAMES ARTHUR.
>George Heriot's School; First XV. M.B., Ch.B. 1907; D.P.H. (St Andrews) 1913. No. 4 Coy. Q.R.V.B., Royal Scots, 1905-7, Private. R.A.M.C. (T.), Lieut. July 1912; Captain April 1915; Acting Major March 1918. *River Clyde*, Gallipoli, April 1915, and 89th Field Ambulance. 20th and 24th General Hospitals, France. Dispatches Sept. 1918.

MORRIS, JOHN CAMERON.
>George Watson's College. Student of Medicine, 1911-14 and 1916-18; M.B., Ch.B. 1918. R.A.M.C. (T.), Scottish Horse Brigade Field Ambulance, Private Sept. 1914. 5th Royal Scots Fusiliers, 2nd Lieut. July 1915. Egypt 1915 to Nov. 1916. R.A.M.C., Lieut. May 1918; Captain. Attached 98th Brigade, R.F.A. The Black Sea.

MORRIS, JOHN MUDIE.
>Forfar Academy. M.A., 1889; M.B., C.M. 1893; D.P.H. (Camb.). 2nd Royal Highlanders, Black Watch. 1st Glamorgan V.A., Lieut. R.A.M.C., Captain April 1916; Major April 1919. 3rd Western General Hospital; Military Hospital, Bath.

MORRISON, ALBERT JOHN McCLURE CHESNEY.
>M.B., Ch.B. 1913. R.A.M.C., Lieut. Oct. 1914; Captain Oct. 1915. No. 1 Stationary Hospital, Rouen. Wounded at Gallipoli June 1915, and France 1917.

MORRISON, ALEXANDER.
>Edinburgh Institution. Student of Law. Chartered Accountant, 1894. R.A.M.C., Lieut. and Quartermaster, Aug. 1914; Captain Aug. 1917.

MORRISON, CECIL JOHN RHODES.
>George Watson's College. O.T.C. 1914-17, Cadet L/Corporal. Student of Medicine, 1918-20. O.T.C. Artillery, Aug. 1917 to April 1918, Cadet Sergeant; Officer Cadet April 1918. R.F.A., 2nd Lieut. Feb. 1919.

MORRISON, DANIEL ANTON.
>M.A. 1900. Chaplain, 3rd Class (Major), Jan. 1915. R.A.M.C., France, 1914.

MORRISON, DAVID LYALL.
>George Watson's College. M.B., Ch.B. 1905; M.D. 1908. R.A.M.C., Lieut. Jan. 1917; Captain Jan. 1918. R.F.A., France and Italy. M.C. 1918.

MORRISON, DONALD JOHN.
>George Watson's College. Student of Medicine, 1911-15 and 1918-20; M.B., Ch.B. 1920. R.A.M.C. (T.), Scottish Horse Field Ambulance, Aug. 1914. R.N.V.R., Surgeon-Probationer, Aug. 1915 to Oct. 1918.

Record of War Service

MORRISON, JOHN.
George Watson's College, and School for Sons of Missionaries, Blackheath. M.B., Ch.B. 1907. Royal Navy, Surgeon-Lieut. Dec. 1914.

MORRISON, JOHN.
Galashiels Academy. Student of Science, 1913-15 and 1918-19. 16th Royal Scots, Private Dec. 1914. R.E. (Special Brigade), Corporal July 1915. France Aug. 1915 to June 1916. Gassed at Arras June 1916. M.M. June 1916.

MORRISON, JOHN TERTIUS.
George Watson's and Fettes Colleges. M.B., Ch.B. 1911; L.R.C.P. (Lond.) 1913; F.R.C.S. (Eng.) 1913. Ettles Scholar, 1911. Demonstrator of Anatomy, Liverpool University. R.A.M.C., Lieut. Oct. 1914; Captain Oct. 1915; Major Jan. 1919. France 1915-19. Surgical Observation (Research) Hut, 1916-18. Dispatches 1918. O.B.E. 1919.

MORRISON, KENNETH STEELE.
Fettes and George Watson's Colleges. O.T.C. 1908-9. Student of Arts, 1910-11. Chartered Accountant, 1919. O.T.C. Artillery, 1910-14, Cadet Bombardier. R.F.A. (S.R.), 2nd Lieut. Aug. 1914; Lieut. July 1915; Acting Captain Aug. 1916; Captain Nov. 1917. Royal Air Force. Gallipoli; France. Wounded and Prisoner of War Nov. 1917 to Aug. 1918. Invalided out Dec. 1918.

MORRISON, MALCOLM.
Royal Academy, Inverness. Student of Medicine, 1907-16; M.B., Ch.B. 1916. President, Celtic Society. O.T.C. Medical, 1908-14, Cadet Sergeant. R.A.M.C. (S.R.), Captain Feb. 1918. No. 8 Indian General Hospital, Mesopotamia.

MORRISON, NEIL.
George Watson's College. Student of Law, 1911-12. 9th Royal Scots (T.), Piper Sergeant. 8th Cameron Highlanders, 2nd Lieut. Dec. 1914; Captain Feb. 1916.

MORRISON, ROBERT VICTOR.
Foyle College, Londonderry. M.B., Ch.B. 1911; M.D. 1912. O.T.C., Medical, April 1909-11, Cadet. Indian Medical Service, Lieut. Jan. 1912, Captain Jan. 1915. 5th Light Infantry, Singapore, March 1914. Cameroons, West Africa, July 1915. Wounded Oct. 1915.

MORRISON, THOMAS STEPHEN.
Aberlour School. Student of Law, 1914-16. 2nd (H.S.) Garrison, Royal Scots, Private Oct. 1916.

MORRISON, WILLIAM.
Stirling High School. Student of Arts, 1915-16 and 1918-19; M.A. 1920. O.T.C. Artillery, 1915-16, Cadet Sergeant; Officer Cadet Aug. 1916. R.F.A., 2nd Lieut. Oct. 1916; Lieut. April 1918. France, Feb. to Nov. 1917, and April to Aug. 1918. Italy, Nov. 1917 to April 1918. M.C. Nov. 1918.

Record of War Service

MORRISON, WILLIAM ALEXANDER.
George Heriot's School; First XV. O.T.C. 1910-13, Pipe Major. Student of Science, 1913-14. R.F.A. (T.), 1st London Brigade, Gunner 1914. R.E. (Special Brigade), Corporal 1915. Canadian Railway Troops, Lieut. Jan. 1917; Captain and Adjutant, April 1918 to May 1919. France Oct. 1915.

MORRISON, WILLIAM GRAHAM.
Edinburgh Institution; First XV. and XI. Cadet Corps 1916. Student of Science, 1916-17 and 1919. O.T.C. Infantry, 1916-17, Cadet C.S.M.; Officer Cadet Oct. 1917. R.E., 2nd Lieut. Jan. 1918. 87th Field Coy., France, April 1918 to Feb. 1919.

MORRISON, WILLIAM KENNETH.
George Watson's College. M.B., Ch.B. 1913. Resident, R.I.E., 1913-14. O.T.C. Medical, March 1909-12, Cadet. R.A.M.C. (Regulars), Lieut. 1913; Captain March 1915. France 1914; Mesopotamia and Persia. Dispatches Aug. and Nov. 1917. D.S.O. Aug. 1917.

MORRISON, WILLIAM SHEPHERD.
George Watson's College. O.T.C. 1906-12, Cadet Sergeant. Student of Arts and Law, 1912-14; M.A. 1920. O.T.C. Artillery, 1912-14, Cadet. R.F.A. (S.R.), 2nd Lieut. Aug. 1914; Lieut. June 1915; Acting Captain Sept. 1916; Captain Nov. 1917 to Aug. 1919. France. Scottish Command Gas School, 1918-19. Wounded at Neuve Chapelle March 1915. Dispatches March and June 1915, Jan. 1916, and March 1919. M.C. March 1915.

MORTIMER, CYRUS MAXWELL.
Royal High School. Student of Arts and Divinity, 1919 O.T.C. Artillery, July to Nov. 1915, Cadet. R.F.A., Lowland Brigade, 2nd Lieut. Nov. 1915; Lieut. July 1917. Royal Air Force. A.F.C.

MORTIMER, JOHN ALEXANDER.
George Watson's College. M.B., Ch.B. 1909; M.D. 1911; M.R.C.P. (Edin.) 1911. R.A.M.C., Lieut. May 1915; Captain May 1916. 24th General Hospital, France.

MORTON, CHARLES JAMES.
M.B., C.M. 1886; M.D. 1890; L.R.C.P. & S. (Edin.) and L.F.P.S. (Glasg.) 1886. R.A.M.C., Lieut.; Captain Nov. 1915.

MORTON, EDWARD JOHN.
Daniel Stewart's College. M.B., Ch.B. 1902; F.R.C.S. (Edin.) 1906. R.A.M.C., Lieut. May 1915; Captain May 1916. 6th Duke of Cornwall's Light Infantry, France, and 40th D.A.C.

MORTON, EDWIN.
Wolverhampton Grammar School. M.A. (Oxford); M.B., C.M. 1885; M.D. 1888; D.P.H., R.C.P.S. (Ireland) 1912. R.A.M.C. (T.), Captain Nov. 1915. 3rd Southern General Base Hospital, Oxford.

Record of War Service

MORTON, HEW LESLEY MONTGOMERIE.
  Daniel Stewart's College. Student of Arts and Science, 1915. O.T.C. Artillery, Sept. 1915 to May 1916, Cadet; Officer Cadet May 1916. R.G.A., 2nd Lieut. Aug. 1916; Lieut. Feb. 1918.

MORTON, HUGH MURRAY.
  Grosvenor College, Carlisle; First XV. and XI. M.B., C.M. 1896. R.A.M.C. 1889; Major 1911; Lieut.-Col. March 1915; Temp. Colonel Oct. 1915 to March 1919. South African Campaign, 1899-1902. 35th Field Ambulance, Gallipoli, July 1915; A.D.M.S., 13th Division, Gallipoli, Egypt, and Mesopotamia, Oct. 1915 to March 1919; 32nd British General Hospital, Amara, Mesopotamia, March and April 1919. Dispatches Jan. 1919. D.S.O. Aug. 1917; C.B.E. June 1919.

MORTON, JAMES WILLIAM KINNIBURGH.
  Edinburgh Institution; First XV. and XI. Cadet Corps 1912-16, Cadet; 2nd Lieut. Student of Science, 1916-17 and 1919. O.T.C. Infantry, Oct. 1916 to April 1917, Cadet; Officer Cadet April 1917. Machine-Gun Corps (Infantry), 2nd Lieut. Oct. 1917. France. Wounded Aug. 1918.

MORTON, RALPH.
  Dumfries Academy; First XI. Cadet Corps 1917, Cadet Corporal. Student of Medicine, 1918. 4th Highland Light Infantry (Signal Section), Private July 1917.

MORTON, TERENCE CHARLES St CLESSIE.
  Student of Medicine, 1910-15; M.B., Ch.B. 1915. O.T.C. Medical, Sept. to Nov. 1914, Cadet L/Corporal. Royal Navy, Surgeon-Probationer, Dec. 1914; Surgeon July 1915. H.M. Ships *Carribean* and *Temeraire*, 1915-17. R.N.A.S., 1917-18. Royal Air Force Medical Service, Captain Nov. 1918-19. The Rhine.

MORTON, WILLIAM CUTHBERT.
  Queen's Royal College, Trinidad, B.W.I. M.A. 1896; M.B., Ch.B. 1903; M.D. 1910. University Battery, E.C.A.V. 2nd Northern General Hospital, March 1917. Re-education Department, Aug. 1917. R.A.M.C., Lieut. Oct. 1919. 2nd Northern General Hospital (Orthopædic). C.B.E. (Civil) Feb. 1919.

MOSES, OWEN St JOHN.
  M.B., C.M. 1896; M.D. 1900; B.Sc. (P.H.) 1900. Indian Medical Service, Major Dec. 1912.

MOSS, JOHN GREGORY OWEN.
  St Joseph's College, Darjeeling. M.B., Ch.B. 1912; M.D. 1917. O.T.C. Medical, 1908-11, Cadet. Indian Medical Service, Lieut. Jan. 1914; Captain Sept. 1915. 129th Baluchis and 107th Pioneers, 1914; 47th Sikhs, March 1915. France 1914. Hospital Ship *Letitia*, April to Dec. 1915. No. 1 Indian General Hospital and No. 2 Ambulance Train, Karachi, 1916-17. Waziristan, July 1917.

Record of War Service

MOTHERWELL, GAVIN BLACK.
Airdrie Academy and Glasgow High School. Student of Law, 1898-9. R.E. (T.), 52nd Lowland Division, 1888; Lieut.-Col. Sept. 1914. Gallipoli, Egypt, and Cyprus. Invalided from Gallipoli. Dispatches (Gallipoli) Dec. 1915.

MOTHERWELL, GAVIN BLACK LONDON.
Airdrie Academy and Glasgow High School. Student of Arts and Law, 1893-8, Writer to the Signet, 1900. 4th Royal Scots Fusiliers (T.), Lieut. Oct. 1914; Captain 1917. Appeal Military Representative. O.B.E. (Military) June 1919.

MOUAT, THOMAS BERNARD.
M.B., Ch.B. 1904; M.D. 1912; F.R.C.S. (Eng.) 1911. R.A.M.C., Captain Sept. 1914; Temp. Major May to Nov. 1917. 3rd Northern General Hospital. France. 59th General Hospital.

MOWAT, ALEXANDER.
Miller Institution, Thurso. O.T.C. Student of Arts, 1913-14. 4th Royal Scots (T.), Private 1914.

MOWAT, ARTHUR.
Pulteneytown Academy, Wick. Student of Arts, 1911-15; M.A. 1915. 5th Seaforth Highlanders, Private Nov. 1915; Sergeant June 1916; 2nd Lieut. March 1917; Lieut. Sept. 1918.

MOWAT, GEORGE.
Miller Institution, Thurso. Student of Arts, 1913-16 and 1918-19; M.A. 1916. R.F.A., Gunner Feb. 1916; Officer Cadet; 2nd Lieut. April 1919.

MOWAT, GEORGE THOMSON.
M.B., Ch.B. 1914. O.T.C. Infantry, 1909-13, Cadet. R.A.M.C., Lieut. Dec. 1914; Captain Dec. 1915. Italian Bronze Medal Jan. 1918.

MOWAT, HAROLD.
Tonbridge. M.B., Ch.B. 1905; M.D. 1907. R.A.M.C., Captain Nov. 1914. Royal Navy, Surgeon-Lieut. Dec. 1916 to Jan. 1919. Egypt 1915; France 1916; Dardanelles and North Sea, 1917-19.

MOWAT, JAMES COBBAN ROSS. (See p. 751.)

MOWAT, JAMES LAWSON.
Aberdeen Grammar School. University O.T.C. Artillery, 1917, Cadet; Officer Cadet Sept. 1917. R.G.A. (S.R.), 2nd Lieut. Feb. 1918. France March 1918 to July 1919. Croix de Guerre with Palm (French) Aug. 1918.

MOWAT, WILLIAM ALEXANDER.
Elliot Place School, Blackheath. M.A. 1898; B.D. 1902. Minister, Church of Scotland. Chaplain, 4th Class, June 1915.

MOYES, ANDREW HAIN.
George Heriot's School. University O.T.C. Infantry, Feb. to Sept. 1918, Cadet; Officer Cadet Sept. 1918. Royal Scots Fusiliers, 2nd Lieut. March 1919.

Record of War Service

MOYES, JOHN MURRAY.
    Fettes College; First XV. M.B., Ch.B. 1909. Dipl. Psych. Med. (Leeds) 1912. No. 4 Coy., Q.R.V.B., Royal Scots, 1906-8, and O.T.C. Infantry, Oct. 1908-9, Cadet Sergeant. R.A.M.C., Lieut. Sept. 1914; Captain Sept. 1915; Major Oct. 1918 to Feb. 1919. 5th London Regiment, May 1915. 12th Royal Scots Fusiliers, Oct. 1917 to Aug. 1918. 8th, 12th, 229th, and 94th Field Ambulances. France. Wounded May 1917. Dispatches Nov. 1917.

MOYES, ROBERT ESMOND.
    M.B., Ch.B. 1905; M.D. 1910. R.A.M.C., Lieut. Oct. 1917; Captain Oct. 1918. Mesopotamia and Palestine.

MUIR, CHARLES AUGUSTUS CARLOW.
    George Heriot's School. Student of Arts, 1912-14. 9th Royal Scots (T.), Private Oct. 1914. 1st King's Own Scottish Borderers, 2nd Lieut. Feb. 1915; Lieut. July 1917; Captain Sept. 1917. France Jan. 1915; Dardanelles Aug. 1915.

MUIR, JOHN.
    M.A. 1908. 1st Canadian Contingent, Sergeant.

MUIR, JOHN REID.
    George Watson's College. M.B., C.M. 1894. No. 4 Coy., Q.R.V.B., Royal Scots, 1890-5. Royal Navy, Staff Surgeon 1908; Fleet Surgeon Feb. 1916. Dispatches (Jutland) May 1916. Croix de Guerre (French).

MUIR, ROBERT.
    Hawick Academy. M.A. 1884; M.B., C.M. 1888; M.D. 1890; F.R.C.P. (Edin.) 1895; D.Sc. (Hon.); F.R.S. Professor, Pathology, Glasgow University. R.A.M.C. (T.), Lieut.-Col. 1908. 3rd Scottish General Hospital.

MUIR, ROYDEN McINTOSH.
    Wellington College. Cadet Corps. Student of Medicine, 1909-14. M.B., Ch.B. 1914. O.T.C. Infantry, 1909-12, Cadet. R.A.M.C., Lieut.

MUIRHEAD, A. BUCHAN.
    Student of Arts and Science. A.S.C., Special Service Clerk, 1915-19. Gallipoli, Egypt, and Salonika.

MUIRHEAD, ALEXANDER JAMES.
    Darlington Grammar School; First XI. Student of Medicine, 1912-17; M.B., Ch.B. 1917. O.T.C. Medical, Nov. 1914, Cadet. R.N.V.R., Surgeon-Probationer. H.M.S. *Midge*. Royal Navy, Surgeon May 1917. H.M. Ships *Superb, Valkyrie, Vürd, Pembroke, Victory, President*, and *Wildfire*.

MUIRHEAD, JAMES.
    Leith Academy. Student of Science, 1918-19. O.T.C. Artillery, Nov. 1916 to Jan. 1918, Cadet Sergeant; Officer Cadet Jan. 1918. R.F.A., 186th Brigade, 2nd Lieut. Aug. 1918. France. Wounded and gassed Oct. 1918.

Record of War Service

MUIRSMITH, ERIC WILLIAM.
Merchiston Castle. O.T.C. 1906-12, Cadet L/Corporal. Student of Law, 1914. Chartered Accountant, 1919. 8th Durham Light Infantry, 2nd Lieut. Nov. 1915; Lieut. March 1917; Captain Aug. 1918.

MUKAND, SAMUEL NEWMAN.
Muir Central College, Allahabad. First XI. M.B., Ch.B. 1910; D.P.H. (Edin.). Indian Medical Service, Lieut. Aug. 1917; Captain Aug. 1918. Bacteriologist, Carhwal Brigade, 7th Division (Meerut).

MULLER, CHARLES HEROLD.
South African College. M.B., Ch.B. 1903. South African Medical Corps, Captain 1914-15; Lieut.-Col. 1916-17. O.C. 4th Mounted Brigade Field Ambulance, East Africa. D.S.O. 1917.

MUNBY, WILLIAM MAXWELL.
M.B., Ch.B. 1904; Ch.M. 1909; F.R.C.S. (Eng.) 1909. R.A.M.C. (T.), Captain May 1915.

MUNCASTER, WILLIAM HENRY.
M.A. 1879; B.D. Minister, Congregational Church. Chaplain June 1916. Staff Captain, Sarcee Camp, Alberta; Garrison, Calgary. 89th Overseas Battn. Shorncliffe Camp; Military Hospitals, Orpington, Kent, and Wokingham, Berks.

MUNRO, ALEXANDER ROSE.
Student of Science, 1899-1900. 4th Seaforth Highlanders (T.), 2nd Lieut. 1903; Captain Oct. 1909; Major Feb. 1916; Staff Captain, 191st Infantry Brigade (21st Seaforth and Cameron Highlanders), May 1915. Assistant Records, Perth, Sept. 1916-19. Dispatches Feb. 1917. T.D. March 1919.

MUNRO, ANGUS.
M.A. 1913. O.T.C. Infantry, Oct. 1910 to April 1911, Cadet. 239th Canadian Regiment, Lieut. Dec. 1916.

MUNRO, DAVID.
M.A. (St Andrews) 1897. M.B., Ch.B. 1901; F.R.C.S. (Edin.) 1911. Indian Medical Service, Lieut. 1902; Major July 1913. Lieut.-Col. and P.M.O., Royal Air Force, India. H.M. Hospital Ship *Glenart Castle*, Nov. 1914. 10th Indian General Hospital, France and Mesopotamia, Aug. 1915. Officers' Hospital, Beit Naame, June 1916. D.A.D.M.S. Mesopotamia Sept. 1917; Palestine May to Dec. 1918. C.I.E. Aug. 1917. Twice Mentioned in Dispatches.

MUNRO, DAVID.
Surgical Department. R.A.M.C. (T.), Private 1908; Sergeant Aug. 1914; Staff-Sergeant Oct. 1915. 2nd Scottish General Hospital, Edinburgh, and 58th General Hospital, France.

Record of War Service

MUNRO, DONALD GEORGE MACLEOD.
Inverness Royal Academy. M.B., C.M. 1892; M.D. 1902; M.R.C.P. (Edin.) 1898. R.A.M.C., Lieut. June 1915; Captain Jan. 1916. 12th Berkshire Regiment, Med. Exp. Force. H.M. Hospital Ship *Mauritania*. France. Invalided home April 1918.

MUNRO, EDMUND BRODIE.
George Watson's College. M.B., Ch.B. 1905. Indian Medical Service, Lieut. 1907; Captain 1910; Major Aug. 1918. 89th Punjabis, and No. 12 Indian General Hospital, Mesopotamia. O.B.E. (Military) June 1919.

MUNRO, HORACE FREDERICK MONCRIEFF.
Daniel Stewart's College and Royal High School; First XI. M.A. 1906. No. 4 Coy., Q.R.V.B., Royal Scots, 1902-8; O.T.C. Infantry, 1908-9, Cadet. A.S.C. (S.R.), 2nd Lieut. 1909-11. A.S.C., Lieut. Nov. 1914; Captain Jan. 1915.

MUNRO, HUGH.
George Heriot's School. O.T.C. 1909-10, Cadet Sergeant. B.Sc. 1913. Nyasaland Volunteer Rifles, Nov. 1914. 6th Cameron Highlanders, April 1918 to March 1919. Wounded Sept. 1918.

MUNRO, HUGH LENNOX.
Brigg Grammar School. M.B., Ch.B. 1903; M.D. 1907. President, S.R.C. R.A.M.C. (T.), Lieut. Feb. 1911; Captain Aug. 1914. Dispatches Sept. 1917.

MUNRO, JAMES.
Daniel Stewart's College. M.A. (Hons. Engl.) 1905. Lecturer in Colonial History. Gordon Highlanders, Private April to Dec. 1916. Ministry of Munitions and Labour, 1916-19.

MUNRO, JAMES LORIMER.
George Watson's College. M.A. 1892. Minister, U.F. Church of Scotland. Scottish Churches Huts, Calais, 1916-17; France and Germany, 1918-19. Chaplain, 1st V.B. Royal Scots, Aug. 1917.

MUNRO, JAMES RAMSAY.
Moulton Grammar School, Lincolnshire. M.B., Ch.B. 1899; M.D. 1903. R.A.M.C., Lieut. June 1917; Captain June 1918.

MUNRO, RONALD MACKENZIE.
Dingwall Academy. M.A. 1905. Schoolmaster. 7th Royal Highlanders (Black Watch) (T.), 2nd Lieut. 1909; Lieut. July 1913; Temp. Captain July 1915; Captain June 1916.

MUNRO, STEWART GRAHAM.
University O.T.C. Artillery, Feb. 1910-13, Cadet. R.F.A., 2nd Lieut. Aug. 1914; Lieut. Sept. 1914; Captain; Major 1917. France 1915-19. M.C. and Bar to M.C.; Croix de Guerre avec Palme.

Record of War Service

MURCH, ANGUS HOPE.
Bancrofts School, Woodford, Essex. M.B., Ch.B. 1913. R.A.M.C., Lieut. Sept. 1915; Captain Sept. 1916.

MURDOCH, BARCLAY BROWN.
George Watson's College; First XV. M.A.; B.Sc. 1909. A.I.C. O.T.C. Artillery, 1908-13, Cadet. R.F.A., 2nd Lieut. Dec. 1914; Lieut. Dec. 1915; Acting Captain Sept. 1916. Wireless Officer, attached R.E., Aug. 1917 to Oct. 1918. France. Wounded 1916. Dispatches Jan. 1917.

MURDOCH, HUGH BRYDEN.
George Heriot's School. M.A., B.Sc. 1906. Schoolmaster. 5th Royal Scots (T.), Private. Wounded at the Dardanelles.

MURDOCH, HUGH COWAN.
Ayr Academy. Student of Science, 1899-1902. No. 4 Coy. Q.R.V.B., Royal Scots, 1898-1902, L/Corporal. 2nd V.B. (5th) and 4th Garrison Battns. Royal Scots Fusiliers (T.), 1903; 2nd Lieut.; Lieut.; Captain; Major 1917.

MURDOCH, JAMES ALEXANDER DOUGLAS.
Ayr Academy; First XV. M.A. 1902; B.L. (Glasg.). Law Agent, 1905. No. 4 Coy. Q.R.V.B., Royal Scots, 1899-1902, Private. Ayrshire Yeomanry (T.), 1906; Captain Sept. 1914. Egypt and Palestine. Wounded near Jerusalem Dec. 1917.

MURDOCH, JOHN DUNCAN.
Dundee High School. Student of Law, 1897-1900. Law Agent, 1903. R.E. Vol. and (T.), 2nd Lieut. 1896; Captain 1904; Major June 1916. France. M.C. and Dispatches Jan. 1916.

MURDOCH, JOHN PRYDE.
George Watson's College. M.A. 1895; B.D. 1903. Minister, U.F. Church of Scotland. Chaplain, 1918-19, 11th Corps, Fifth Army, France.

MURDOCH, THOMAS FLEMING.
George Watson's College. M.A. 1913. O.T.C. Infantry, June 1909 to July 1914, Cadet Sergeant Drummer. 3rd Royal Highlanders (Black Watch) (S.R.), 2nd Lieut. July 1914; Lieut. Jan. 1915; Captain Oct. 1915; Major Oct. 1917. Attached 2nd Liverpool Regiment. France Sept. 1914; The Black Sea. Wounded Oct. 1914 and May 1915. Dispatches June 1918.

MURDOCH, WILLIAM.
Warriston School, Moffat; First XV. and XI. M.B., Ch.B. 1914. R.A.M.C. (S.R.), Lieut. April 1915; Captain Nov. 1915; Acting Major March 1918. Wounded Aug. 1919. M.C. Jan. 1918; Bar to M.C. Sept. 1918.

MURISET, OLIVIER ARMAND JAMES NEEDHAM.
George Watson's College. M.B., Ch.B. 1910. R.A.M.C., Lieut. Sept. 1915; Captain Sept. 1916. France 1915-17 and 1918; Italy 1917-18.

Record of War Service

MURISON, CECIL CHARLES.
Student of Medicine. L.R.C.P. & S. (Edin.); L.F.P.S. (Glasg.) 1898; D.P.H. (Edin.) 1909; F.R.C.S. (Edin.) 1910. Indian Medical Service, Major July 1911.

MURISON, GILBERT-DE-HUSSEY.
University O.T.C. Medical, Oct. 1913 to Aug. 1914, Cadet. 11th and 3rd attached 2nd Royal Scots, 2nd Lieut. Aug. 1914; Lieut.; Captain July 1916.

MURISON, TAYLOR DAVID.
Student of Medicine, 1904-6; L.R.C.P. & S. (Edin.) and L.F.P.S. (Glasg.) 1907. Indian Medical Service, Captain Aug. 1911.

MURPHIE, WILLIAM.
Ayr Academy. Student of Arts, 1914-16. 11th Royal Scots, Private March 1916; 2nd Lieut. Jan. 1917; Lieut. July 1918 to March 1919.

MURPHY, SAMUEL WOOD.
George Heriot's School. Student of Law, 1901-3. Chartered Accountant, 1904. R.A.S.C., 2nd Lieut. May 1917; Lieut. Nov. 1918.

MURPHY, THOMAS CARLYLE.
Lanark Grammar School. M.A. 1912; B.D. 1920. Minister, Congregational Church. R.A.M.C., 3/3rd Highland Field Ambulance, Private Aug. 1915. Chaplain, 4th Class, Dec. 1916; Senior Chaplain, France and Italy, Sept. 1918.

MURRAY, ALEXANDER FREDERICK.
Ayr Academy. O.T.C. 1911-17, Cadet C.S.M. University O.T.C. Infantry, June 1917 to Feb. 1918, Cadet; Officer Cadet Feb. 1918. 1st Royal Scots Fusiliers, 2nd Lieut. July 1918. M.C. Nov. 1918.

MURRAY, ALEXANDER MACPHERSON.
Nicolson Institute, Stornoway. University O.T.C. Engineers, 1917-18, Cadet; Officer Cadet March 1918. R.E., Signal Service, 2nd Lieut. Aug. 1918.

MURRAY, ANDREW.
Student of Arts, 1910-13. 15th Royal Scots, Private.

MURRAY, ANDREW ROWAND.
Dumfries Academy. Student of Medicine, 1914-15 and 1916-19; M.B., Ch.B. 1920. O.T.C. Infantry, 1914-15, Medical, 1916-19, Cadet Sergeant. R.A.M.C., Private Aug. 1915.

MURRAY, ANGUS DONALD.
Golspie School. Student of Arts and Science, 1918. R.A.M.C., Private Aug. 1915. 58th and 106th Field Ambulances. France. M.C. (Passchendaele) Dec. 1917.

MURRAY, ARCHIBALD COLIN.
Student of Medicine, 1894-8 and 1912-14; M.B., Ch.B. 1914. R.A.M.C., Lieut. Aug. 1916; Captain Aug. 1917. France Nov. 1916 to April 1919; The Rhine April to Oct. 1919; North Russia Dec. 1919.

Record of War Service

MURRAY, CHARLES DAVID.
    Edinburgh Academy. M.A. 1885; LL.B. 1889; LL.D. 1919. Advocate, 1889. K.C.; M.P. Lieut.-Col., General Staff, War Office, 1915-17. British Recruiting Commission to U.S.A., 1917. C.M.G. 1918.

MURRAY, CHARLES GRAHAM.
    Harrison College, Barbados. M.B., C.M. 1893; M.D. 1905. R.A.M.C. (T.), Feb. 1909; Lieut.; Captain Oct. 1911; Major Sept. 1914.

MURRAY, CHARLES LEONARD LANTRÉ.
    Stellenbosch High School. Student of Medicine, 1918. South African Medical Corps, Private Feb. 1917; Corporal Dec. 1917.

MURRAY, CHRISTOFFEL CORNELIUS.
    M.B., Ch.B. 1910. South African Medical Corps, Captain. German East Africa.

MURRAY, DAVID KEITH.
    George Watson's College. Student of Arts and Law, 1881-7; B.L. and Law Agent, 1887. Artillery Volunteers, Colonel, Retired 1908. Caithness and Sutherland Volunteer Corps, Lieut.-Col. and County Commandant June 1917. V.D. 1907. Mention Sept. 1919.

MURRAY, DONALD NORMAN WATSON.
    Auckland Grammar School, New Zealand. M.B., Ch.B. 1902; M.D. 1904. Volunteer Medical Staff Corps, 1898-1901, Corporal. South African Campaign, 1900. N.Z. Medical Corps, Captain 1908; Major Aug. 1914; Lieut.-Col. Nov. 1915; Colonel Dec. 1918. N.Z. Exp. Force Aug. 1914. N.Z. Mounted Field Ambulance, 1915-18. A.D.M.S. The Rhine 1919. Dispatches Jan. and Dec. 1917 and Jan. 1919. D.S.O. Jan. 1917; C.M.G. Jan. 1919.

MURRAY, GEORGE BOYD.
    Royal High School; First XV. Student of Medicine, 1915-16. O.T.C. Infantry, Oct. 1915 to April 1916, Cadet. R.E., No. 3 Special Coy., Sapper April 1916; Corporal April 1917. France May 1916 to Feb. 1919. D.C.M. June 1919.

MURRAY, GEORGE STEWART.
    Daniel Stewart's College. M.B., Ch.B. 1901; M.D. 1905. R.A.M.C., Lieut. Oct. 1915; Captain Oct. 1916; Acting Major to May 1919. 30th General Hospital, France.

MURRAY, GRACE.
    M.A. 1911. Schoolmistress. Q.M.A.A.C. April 1918. France.

MURRAY, HENRY GARBOIS.
    Hampton School; First XV. and XI. Student of Arts, 1918. Royal Irish Rifles, 2nd Lieut. Nov. 1914; Lieut. July 1917; Acting Captain. France; Somme and Messines, 1915-17. Invalided out Jan. 1919.

MURRAY, JAMES ALEXANDER.
    M.A. 1910. Schoolmaster. R.F.A., 2nd Lieut.

Record of War Service

MURRAY, JAMES ELLIOT.
Sedbergh; First XV. and XI. M.B., Ch.B. 1906; M.D. 1908; L.M. (Dublin). R.A.M.C., Lieut. Nov. 1916. Machine-Gun Corps and Tank Corps, France.

MURRAY, JAMES MACKINNON.
George Watson's College. M.A. 1904. Licentiate, U.F. Church. Chaplain, 4th Class, Gordon Highlanders, Jan. 1917. 5th Cameron Highlanders, The Rhine. Croix de Guerre with Silver Star July 1918.

MURRAY, JAMES POTTER.
Ayr Academy. Student of Arts, 1912-16; M.A. 1916. Schoolmaster. 81st Coy., Machine-Gun Corps, Private April 1916.

MURRAY, JOHN GORDON.
Bathgate Academy. University O.T.C. Artillery, 1916-17, Cadet Bombardier. No. 1 V.A.D., Linlithgow. Royal Air Force, Officer Cadet Feb. 1917; Lieut. April 1918. Attached 3rd Grenadier Guards. Acting Flight Lieut. The Rhine.

MURRAY, JOHN KENNEDY.
Fettes College. O.T.C. 1910-12. Student of Medicine, 1913-16 and 1918-19. O.T.C. Infantry, Oct. 1914 to March 1916, Cadet. R.N.V.R., Surgeon-Probationer, May 1916 to March 1918.

MURRAY, JOHN McNAIR.
Christ's College Grammar School, New Zealand. First XV. Cadet Corps 1900-4, Hon. Lieut. M.B., Ch.B. 1911. Clinical Tutor, Medical, 1916. R.A.M.C., Lieut. July 1916; Captain Aug. 1917 to Jan. 1919; Acting Major Feb. 1918. Salonika and Palestine.

MURRAY, JOHN OLIVER.
Dumfries Academy. O.T.C. 1910. Student of Medicine, 1912-15 and 1917-19; M.B., Ch.B. 1919. President, S.R.C. O.T.C. Artillery, 1914-15, Cadet. R.F.A. (S.R.), 2nd Lieut. June 1915 to Feb. 1917. France. Dispatches July 1916.

MURRAY, KENNETH.
M.B., Ch.B. South African Medical Corps, Captain.

MURRAY, KENNETH.
Winchester. O.T.C. 1908-10. B.A. (Oxford). Student of Law, 1913-14 and 1918-19. Writer to the Signet, 1919. 2nd Lovat Scouts, 2nd Lieut. 1911; Lieut.; Captain June 1916. Gallipoli Sept. to Dec. 1915; Egypt Jan. to Aug. 1916; Salonika Sept. 1916 to Jan. 1917. Wounded at Salonika. Invalided out Oct. 1918.

MURRAY, PETER.
Perth Academy; First XV. and XI. Student of Science, 1914 and 1918-19; B.Sc. 1920. O.T.C. Engineers, 1914-15, Cadet. R.E., 2nd Field Coy., Lowland Division, 2nd Lieut Nov. 1915; Lieut. July 1917. France. Wounded April 1918. Dispatches April 1918.

Record of War Service

MURRAY, ROBERT B.
Bathgate Academy. Student of Arts, 1912-13. 15th Royal Scots, Private Sept. 1914; Corporal Nov. 1914; L/Sergeant Jan. 1915. R.E. (Special Coy.), Corporal July 1915; Sergeant May 1916. Royal Air Force, Officer Cadet Nov. 1917; 2nd Lieut. March 1918; Pilot. France. Prisoner of War Oct. 1918.

MURRAY, RONALD RODERICK.
George Watson's College. M.B., Ch.B. 1905; M.D. 1919; F.R.C.S. (Edin.) 1909. Northern Rhodesia Defence Force, Aug. 1914; Volunteers, Surgeon-Captain April 1915; Medical Corps, Captain Oct. 1917. Base Hospital, Abercorn, and Casualty Clearing Station, Fife, Northern Rhodesia, 1914-16. R.M.O., Northey's Force, June 1916; Field and Base Hospitals, German East Africa, April to Nov. 1917. Dispatches March 1917 and Sept. 1918. Invalided out Dec. 1917.

MURRAY, WILLIAM.
George Watson's College. O.T.C. 1906-10, Cadet Sergeant. Student of Law, 1913-14. 4th Royal Scots (T.), Private March 1913; Sergeant Sept. 1916; Colour-Sergeant Jan. 1919. Gallipoli June 1915; Egypt Jan. 1916; France April 1918 to April 1919.

MURRAY, WILLIAM.
Royal High School. M.B., C.M. 1891; M.D. 1895. R.F.A. (T.), 2nd Northumbrian Brigade, 2nd Lieut. 1903; Major July 1914. Mobilised Aug. 1914; Lieut.-Col. Oct. 1919. Attached R.A.M.C. July 1917 to Jan. 1919. Central Hospital, Hull, March 1918 to Jan. 1919.

MURRAY, WILLIAM.
Merchiston Castle. M.B., Ch.B. 1901; D.P.H. (Lond.). R.A.M.C., Lieut. Oct. 1917; Captain Oct. 1918. 29th Division, R.E., Dec. 1917 to March 1919.

MURRAY, WILLIAM.
George Watson's College. M.A. 1906. R.E., Signals, Sapper, Sept. 1914.

MURRAY-LYON, DAVID MURRAY.
Daniel Stewart's College. Student of Medicine, 1907-9. O.T.C. Artillery, 1907-8, Infantry, 1908-11, Cadet L/Corporal. 2nd, 15th, and 51st Highland Light Infantry, 2nd Lieut. 1911; Lieut. March 1914; Acting Captain March 1915; Captain Oct. 1915; Acting Major Dec. 1916; Acting Lieut.-Col. Nov. 1917; Temp. Lieut.-Col. June 1918; Brevet Major Jan. 1919; Temp. Major April 1919. 1st Liverpool Regiment and 5th Royal Scots Fusiliers. Wounded March 1915. France and The Rhine. Dispatches Jan. 1916, Dec. 1917, May and Dec. 1918. M.C. Feb. 1916; D.S.O. Feb. 1918.

MURRAY-LYON, OVINGTON.
Daniel Stewart's College. Student of Medicine, 1911-14. O.T.C. Artillery, 1910-14, Cadet. R.F.A., 2nd Lieut. Oct. 1914; Lieut. Oct. 1916; Captain Sept. 1918. France and the Black Sea, 1915-19. Wounded. M.C. March 1918.

Record of War Service

MURSELL, HENRY TEMPLE.
Mill Hill School, Middlesex. M.B., C.M. 1889; F.R.C.S. (Edin.) 1893; M.R.C.S. (Eng.); L.R.C.P. (Lond.). South African Campaign, 1900; South African Medical Corps, Lieut. 1907; Lieut.-Col. 1912; Colonel Jan. 1917. Surgeon, Cape, 1914-15. No. 1 General Hospital, Wynburg, 1916. A.D.M.S. Hon. Surgeon, Johannesburg Hospital. Dispatches. O.B.E. (Military) 1918.

MURTY, PYDAH VENKATA RAMANA.
Student of Medicine, 1909-14; M.B., Ch.B. 1914. Indian Medical Service, Lieut. March 1917; Captain March 1918.

MUSTARD, ALEXANDER LOW.
George Watson's College. M.A. 1909; LL.B. 1912. Writer to the Signet, 1912. 6th and 15th Royal Scots (T.), 2nd Lieut. 1910; Lieut. June 1914; Captain Sept. 1916. 6th Provisional Battn. (T.); 34th Division, Reinforcement Depôt; Command Depôts, 1918-19. France Feb. 1917. Wounded April 1918.

MYERS, BERNARD.
Wellington College, New Zealand. Cadet Corps 1883-5. M.B., C.M. 1898; M.D. 1900; M.R.C.S. (Lond.) 1898; M.R.C.P. (Lond.) 1912. N.Z. Medical Corps, Hon. Captain Feb. 1915. R.A.M.C., Major Aug. 1915. N.Z. Medical Corps, Lieut.-Col. Dec. 1915. N.Z. Military Hospital, Walton-on-Thames, 1915. A.D.M.S., 1916, and D.M.S., N.Z. Exp. Force, 1919. C.M.G. Aug. 1917. Dispatches Jan. and Aug. 1917.

MYLES, JOHN FREER.
Merchiston Castle; First XV. and XI. Cadet Corps 1902-8, Sergeant. B.A. (Oxford); LL.B. 1915. 8th Seaforth Highlanders, 2nd Lieut. Sept. 1914; Lieut. Nov. 1914; Captain July 1915. France. Wounded March 1916 and July 1917.

MYLES, WILLIAM HARRIS.
Dunbar School. M.A. 1911. Lecturer in Realistic Economics and Official Adviser in Commerce. O.T.C. Artillery, May to Aug. 1915, Cadet. R.G.A., 2nd Lieut. Aug. 1915; Lieut. July 1917; Acting Captain May 1917; Temp. Major March 1919. 223rd Siege Battery, France and The Rhine.

NAIDU, BANGALORE PASUPULATI BALAKRISHNA.
Madras Christian College, India. M.B., Ch.B. 1913; D.P.H. 1915; D.T.M. and M. Hy. (Liverpool). H.M. Transport ss. *Lysian*, 1915. Indian Medical Service, Temp. Lieut. Feb. 1916; Temp. Captain Feb. 1917. Bacteriologist, 83rd Combination Station Hospital, Mesopotamia. Dispatches Oct. 1918.

NAIRN, DAVID ROBERTSON.
Kirkcaldy High School. Student of Arts and Science, 1912-14 and 1918-19; M.A. 1919. Schoolmaster. Officer Cadet. Machine-Gun Corps (Motor), 2nd Lieut. Jan. 1915; Lieut. Nov. 1915.

Record of War Service

NAIRN, MATTHEW.
Assistant, Forensic Medicine Department. R.A.M.C., 1905; Acting Q.M.S. 1914; Warrant Officer II.; R.Q.M.S. 1917. No. 2 Motor Ambulance Convoy, France, Aug. 1914. Meritorious Service Medal.

NAISMITH, JAMES BERTRAM.
George Watson's College. M.A. (Hons. Engl.) 1910. University Battery, E.C.A.V., 1904-8, Gunner. R.G.A., 2nd Lieut. Nov. 1914; Lieut. Feb. 1917; Captain April 1918; Acting Major March 1918 to Jan. 1919. Dispatches Dec. 1918.

NAISMITH, JOHN OLIVER.
George Watson's College. M.A. 1906. Minister, U.F. Church of Scotland. University Battery, E.C.A.V., O.T.C. Artillery, 1903-10, Cadet B.Q.M.S. R.F.A. (S.R.), 2nd Lieut. 1910; Lieut. Jan. 1915; Acting Captain Aug. 1915; Captain Aug. 1916; Acting Major Sept. 1916. France 1914-18. Royal Military Academy, Woolwich, 1918-20. Dispatches June 1915, Jan. and July 1917. D.S.O. July 1917.

NALWA, IQBAL SINGH.
Student of Medicine, 1912-17; M.B., Ch.B. 1917. Indian Medical Service, Lieut. May 1918; Captain May 1919. M.O., 1st Yemen Infantry, Aden.

NANDKEOLYAR, RAM KISHERE LAL.
M.A. 1915. Barrister-at-Law. Indian Field Ambulance, Indian Vol. Aids Contingent 1914.

NAOROJI, SAROS ARDESHIR DADABHAI.
Student of Medicine, 1910-16 and 1920. Indian Field Ambulance, 1914.

NAPIER, ARCHIBALD DAVID MUTTER.
Edinburgh Academy. M.A. 1890. Writer to the Signet, 1893. 17th and 21st (2nd Tyneside Scottish) Northumberland Fusiliers, Captain Nov. 1914; Major July 1916. France Jan. 1916; Somme July 1916; Vimy Ridge and Arras. Invalided home April 1917. Dispatches April 1917.

NASH, JAMES THOMAS CHARLES.
M.B., C.M. 1886; M.D. 1899; D.P.H. (Camb.) 1899. Lecturer in Bacteriology, London University, 1900-1. R.A.M.C. (T.), Captain Jan. 1909. War Pensions.

NASH, JOHN BRADY.
St Patrick's College, Melbourne. Cadet Corps 1876. M.B., C.M. 1882; M.D. 1888. New South Wales Military Forces, Major 1885. Australian Army Medical Corps, Lieut.-Colonel. Egypt and Anzac.

NASMYTH, THOMAS GOODALL.
M.B., C.M. 1876; M.D. 1889; D.Sc. (P.H.) 1887; D.P.H. (Camb.) 1886; F.R.C.S. (Edin.) 1910; F.R.C.P. (Edin.) 1913. 1st V.B. (City of Edinburgh) Royal Scots, Private 1916-17. M.O., H.M. Factory, Gretna, May 1917 to Aug. 1918.

Record of War Service

NASON, WILLIAM SAMUEL.
: M.B., C.M. 1886. R.A.M.C., Lieut. April 1915; Captain April 1916. 77th Field Ambulance; 25th D.A.C.; 74th General Hospital, France, and M.O. 5th Worcestershire Regiment.

NEIL, JOHN CAMPBELL.
: Student of Medicine, 1909-14. M.B., Ch.B. 1914. R.A.M.C. Lieut.; Captain Feb. 1916. 70th Field Ambulance and 72nd General Hospital, France.

NEIL, NORMAN.
: Edinburgh Academy. O.T.C. 1914-16. Student of Science, 1916-17. O.T.C. Artillery, Nov. 1916 to Aug. 1917, Cadet Bombardier; Officer Cadet Aug. 1917. R.F.A., 2nd Lieut. Jan. 1918.

NEILL, ALEXANDER SUTHERLAND.
: M.A. 1912. Editor of *The Student*. Schoolmaster. Royal Scots Fusiliers, Private March 1917. R.G.A., 2nd Lieut. March 1918.

NEILL, JAMES HOOD.
: Royal High School. Student of Medicine, 1912-17; M.B., Ch.B. 1917. O.T.C. Medical, 1915-17, Cadet. R.A.M.C. (S.R.), Lieut. May 1917; Captain May 1918.

NEILL, NEIL SUTHERLAND.
: Forfar Academy. M.B., Ch.B. 1908. R.A.M.C., Lieut. Sept. 1916; Captain Sept. 1917.

NELSON, HENRY GRATTAN GUINNESS.
: M.B., Ch.B. 1910; M.D. 1913. R.A.M.C., Lieut. Feb. 1918; Captain March 1919. 47th General Hospital, France.

NELSON, WALLACE.
: George Heriot's School; First XV. O.T.C. 1915-18, Cadet Sergeant. Student of Medicine, 1918-19. Royal Air Force, Flight Cadet May 1918.

NEVE, ERNEST FREDERIC.
: Brighton Grammar School. M.B., C.M. 1882; M.D. (Gold Medal) 1885; M.R.C.S. (Eng.) 1882; F.R.C.S. (Edin.) 1886. Indian Defence Force, 1st and 3rd Punjab Rifles, Surgeon-Lieut., 1912; Surgeon-Captain, May 1916; Captain April 1917. India. Kaisar-i-Hind, 1st Class, 1918.

NEWCOMBE, HAROLD BERNARD. (See p. 751.)

NEWLANDS, WILLIAM.
: Bathgate Academy. Student of Arts, 1915-16. Army, Private Oct. 1916.

NEWMAN, RICHARD ERNEST UPTON.
: Clifton College. M.B., Ch.B. 1905. R.A.M.C., Major Jan. 1918; Acting Lieut.-Col. June 1917 to March 1919. M.C. June 1917. O.B.E. June 1919. Dispatches June 1915 and June 1919.

NEWTON, CHARLES HERDMAN.
: Loretto. M.B., Ch.B. 1915. O.T.C. Artillery, Nov. 1912 to June 1914, Cadet. R.A.M.C., Temp. Lieut. April 1915; Temp. Captain April 1916 to July 1919.

Record of War Service

NEWTON, CHARLES TREWEEKE HAND.
M.B., Ch.B. 1908; M.D. 1911; F.R.C.S. (Edin.) 1912. N.Z. Medical Corps, Aug. 1914; Major; Lieut.-Col. March 1916. D.S.O. Dispatches 1916 and 1917.

NEWTON, DUNCAN GRAY.
Edinburgh Academy; First XV. and XI. M.B., C.M. 1893; F.R.C.S. (Edin.) 1905. Lecturer on Vaccination, Sheffield University. Volunteer Medical Corps, Surgeon-Lieut., 1896; Captain 1900. R.A.M.C. (T.), Major Jan. 1914. M.O., 1/4th York and Lancaster Regiment, Aug. 1914. Military General Hospital, Rouen, Sept. 1915 to Oct. 1916; Military Hospital, Prees Heath, Salop, 1916-19. T.D.

NEWTON, JAMES WHITTET.
Dundee High School. B.Sc. (Agriculture) 1911; Forestry 1912. C.D.A. President S.R.C. Demonstrator in Zoology, 1912. O.T.C. Infantry, 1909-12, Cadet. Hon. Local Temp. Commandant, British East Africa, Oct. 1914. R.F.A., 2nd Lieut. Nov. 1915; Lieut. June 1916. Attached Nigerian Regiment.

NEWTON, JOHN McKENZIE.
Dundee High School. B.Sc. (Pure Science) 1899; (Engineering) 1900. M.I.M.E. 2nd V.B. Leicestershire Regiment, Private Feb. 1915; 2nd Lieut. July 1917.

NEWTON, ROBERT HENRY HERDMAN.
Loretto. M.B., Ch.B. 1913. Clinical Tutor in Medicine, R.I.E., 1919. Royal Navy, H.M.S. *King George V.*, Temp. Surgeon-Lieut., March 1915.

NICHOL, CHARLES EDWARD P. S.
Edinburgh Collegiate School. M.B., C.M. 1881. Army Medical Service, Captain 1882; Colonel 1912; Major-General 1916. Burma, 1885-7; South African Campaign, 1899-1902. D.D.M.S., Fifth Army Corps, and D.M.S., Fifth Army, France, April 1915 to Nov. 1916. D.S.O. 1902; C.M.G. and Dispatches 1916.

NICHOL, HARVEY.
George Watson's College. Student of Arts and Medicine, 1911-15 and 1918-19; M.A. 1914. O.T.C. Artillery, Oct. 1914 to April 1916, Cadet. R.N.V.R., Surgeon Sub-Lieut., Aug. 1916.

NICHOL, JOHN MacRAE SANDILANDS.
George Watson's College. Student of Medicine, 1912-14 and 1915-17; M.B., Ch.B. 1917. Anatomy Staff, 1919. O.T.C. Artillery, Dec. 1914 to March 1915, Cadet. R.N.V.R., Surgeon-Probationer, March 1915; Surgeon-Lieut., June 1917. H.M. Ships *Panther* and *Inflexible*.

NICHOL, ROBERT.
Minto School. M.A. 1901. Schoolmaster. R.G.A. (T.), 4th Highland Mountain Brigade, Gunner July 1915; 2nd Lieut. Sept. 1915; Lieut. June 1916.

NICHOLSON, BENJAMIN HUGH.
Edinburgh Academy. M.B., C.M. 1884. R.A.M.C. (T.), Captain May 1908. 1st Eastern General Hospital. Medical Referee, Pensions.

Record of War Service

NICHOLSON, DUNBAR.
Royal High School. M.A. 1900; LL.B. 1903. Law Agent, 1904. No. 4 Coy. Q.R.V.B., Royal Scots, Private 1896-1902. 8th Royal Scots (T.), 2nd Lieut. Feb. 1913; Lieut. Aug. 1914; Temp. Captain Sept. 1914; Captain July 1916. O.C. Administrative Centre and No. 149 T.F. Depôt, 1915-19.

NICHOLSON, GEORGE.
Student of Medicine, 1911-14 and 1916-19; M.B., Ch.B. 1918; M.D. 1920. O.T.C. Artillery, 1912-14, Cadet. R.F.A., 2nd Lieut. Aug. 1914; Lieut. Royal Navy, Surgeon 1918; H.M. Monitor 27, River Dwina, Russia. France 1915.

NICHOLSON, HARRY HENDERSON.
Broughton School, Edinburgh. Student of Arts, 1917 and 1919. O.T.C. Infantry March 1917-18, Cadet; Officer Cadet, 24th Tank Corps, March 1918.

NICHOLSON, JOHN GIBB.
Royal High School. M.A. 1904; M.B., Ch.B. 1908. Royal Navy, Temp. Surgeon March 1915. H.M. Ships *Albemarle*, *Phaeton*, and *Suva*.

NICHOLSON, NORMAN.
Royal High School. M.A. 1900. Minister, U.F. Church of Scotland. 4th V.B. King's Own Scottish Borderers, Private April 1915; 2nd Lieut. Sept. 1916. Y.M.C.A. (First Army, France) Feb. 1917

NICOL, GEORGE.
Clackmannan School. Student of Arts, 1888-93. Minister, Presbyterian Church of England. Chaplain, Guards Brigade, Captain Oct. 1915. Attached No. 5 Casualty Clearing Station. Dispatches 1917. O.B.E. (Military) June 1919. Hon. Chaplain Jan. 1919.

NICOL, JAMES LAUDER.
M.A. 1912. O.T.C. Infantry, May 1909 to Jan. 1912, Cadet. 8th Royal Scots (T.), 2nd Lieut.; Lieut. June 1916; Captain Jan. 1918. France. Wounded May 1915.

NICOL, THOMAS PATON.
University O.T.C. Infantry, May to Oct. 1916, Cadet Corporal; Officer Cadet. 1st, 4th, and 11th Scottish Rifles, 2nd Lieut. March 1917; Lieut. Sept. 1919. France; Egypt.

NICOLL, JAMES THOMSON BELL.
George Watson's College; First XV. O.T.C. 1914-17, Cadet L/Corporal. Student of Medicine, 1917 and 1919. O.T.C. Medical, March to Sept. 1918, Cadet. 2/28th London Regiment, Private Sept. 1918. Invalided out.

NICOLL, JOHN McDONALD.
M.B., C.M. 1892. R.A.M.C. (T.), Aug. 1914; Major April 1915; Lieut.-Col. 3/2nd Northumbrian Field Ambulance. France.

Record of War Service

NICOLL, WILLIAM ANDREW.
Broughton School, Edinburgh. Student of Arts, 1911-14; M.A. 1919. R.A.M.C. (T.), Private Jan. 1911; Corporal Aug. 1914. 6th Royal Scots, Corporal July 1915. R.N.V.R., Sub-Lieut. Nov. 1916. Royal Naval Division.

NICOLL, WILLIAM STEELE.
Harris Academy, Dundee. Student of Medicine, 1911-15. O.T.C. Artillery, Oct. 1913-15, Cadet. R.F.A. (S.R.), 2nd Lieut. April 1915.

NICOLSON, SIR ARTHUR JOHN FREDERICK WILLIAM, BART.
Merchiston Castle; First XV. Cadet Corps 1897-1901, L/Corporal. M.A. 1905; LL.B. Advocate, 1909. R.N.V.R., Lieut. Jan. 1915. H.M. Ships *Brilliant* and *Caroline*, Grand Fleet.

NICOLSON, HAROLD STANLEY.
Merchiston Castle. Student of Law, 1911-15. R.N.V.R., Lieut. Jan. 1915; H.M.S. *Resolution*.

NICOLSON, LEONARD THOMAS GREY.
Fettes College. O.T.C. 1911-14. Student of Arts, 1918-19. R.F.A., Gunner, attached Trench Mortar Battery. France 1915. Twice Wounded. Invalided out.

NICOLSON, LIONEL RUTHERFORD.
Merchiston Castle; First XV. Cadet Corps 1902-7, Sergeant. Student of Law, 1907-10 and 1914. Writer to the Signet, 1914. R.N.V.R., Lieut. Jan. 1915. H.M. Ships *Brilliant* and *Implacable*, Northern Patrol.

NICOLSON, MAGNUS ROBERT.
Broughton School, Edinburgh. Student of Arts, 1916-17 and 1918-19; M.A. 1920. R.F.A., Gunner June 1917.

NIELD-FAULKNER, SAMUEL AMERY.
Student of Medicine, 1917; L.R.C.P. & S. (Edin.), and L.R.F.P.S. (Glasg.). R.A.M.C., Lieut. July 1918; Captain July 1919. Royal Air Force Medical Service, Flight Lieut. Aug. to Dec. 1919. France; St Omer, Guines, and Arras.

NIGHTINGALE, JOHN.
Skipton Grammar School. M.B., C.M. 1888; M.D. 1903; D.P.H. (Eng.). No. 4 Coy. Q.E.R., 1884-7, Private. R.A.M.C. (T.), Major 1910; Acting Lieut.-Col. April 1916. France. Dispatches Nov. 1917 and April 1918. T.D.

NIGHTINGALE, PERCY ATHELSTAN.
M.B., C.M. 1890; M.D. 1898. R.A.M.C., Lieut.

NIMMO, CHARLES STUART.
George Watson's College; First XV. and XI. Student of Medicine, 1913-14 and 1916-20. Rugby International. 14th Royal Scots, Private Aug. 1914. 9th Seaforth Highlanders, 2nd Lieut. Nov. 1914; Lieut. Dec. 1916. Instructor in Topography to Royal Air Force Cadets.

Record of War Service

NIMMO, OSWALD PILLANS.
Student of Medicine, 1913-14. R.G.A. (T.), 2nd Lieut; Lieut. June 1916; Acting Captain Oct. 1916; Major. France.

NIMMO, ROBERT.
Perth Academy. Student of Law, 1915-17. Law Agent, July 1917. O.T.C. Infantry, 1917, Cadet. 15th Royal Scots, Private Sept. 1914 to April 1915; Officer Cadet Nov. 1917. 2/1st Scottish Horse, 2nd Lieut. Feb. 1918; Acting Captain Nov. 1918. Acting Staff Captain, 8th Cyclist Brigade, 1919.

NIMMO, WILLIAM AINSLIE.
Perth Academy; First XI. Student of Science, 1915-17. O.T.C. Infantry, 1915-17, Cadet L/Corporal; Officer Cadet June 1917. 9th Labour Coy., 2nd Lieut. Aug. 1917; Lieut. Feb. 1919. France.

NISBET, BRYCE RAMSAY.
George Watson's College. Student of Medicine, 1916-17. 79th T.R.B., Private April 1917. Machine-Gun Corps. Interpreter, Sixth Corps H.Q., The Rhine.

NISBET, F. C.
Student. R.E., 2nd Lieut.

NISBET, WALTER BLAKE.
Brisbane Grammar School, Queensland. M.B., C.M. 1885. Australian Army Medical Corps, Major April 1900; South African Campaign, 1900-1. Attached 4th Queensland South African Contingent. R.A.M.C., Major.

NISBET, WILLIAM JOHN.
M.B., Ch.B. 1909. R.A.M.C., Lieut. 1914; Captain Oct. 1915. Gallipoli and France.

NIVEN, EVAN.
Student of Medicine. Australian Army Medical Corps, Captain. Med. Exp. Force.

NIVEN, JAMES PARKER.
George Watson's College, and King's College, Aberdeen. 5th Gordon Highlanders, Private 1881-4. 5th Royal Scots, Private 1899; 2nd Lieut. 1904; Captain 1911. Adjutant, 2/5th and 6th Royal Scots, Oct. 1914. France July to Aug. 1916; Adjutant, Edinburgh Vol. Regiment, 1917. H.Q. Staff, Special Reserve Brigade, July 1917 to April 1919. Wounded July 1915. T.D. 1919. Dispatches.

NIXON, HORACE CLULOW.
Sedbergh. M.B., Ch.B. 1900; M.D. 1904. Royal Navy, Surgeon Dec. 1914.

NOAD, JOHN ELLIOTT MONCRIEFF.
Osborne and Dartmouth. Student of Science, 1911-14. A.M.I.C.E. O.T.C. Engineers, Oct. 1913 to Aug. 1914, Cadet. R.N.V.R. attached R.N. Brigade. Temp. Sub-Lieut. Sept. 1914. Antwerp. Interned in Holland.

Record of War Service

NOAKES, ALFRED WILLIAM HAMMOND.
King's College, London. Student of Law, 1913-16; B.L. 1916. R.G.A., 304th Siege Battery, Gunner July 1917. Egypt and Palestine Nov. 1917 to Feb. 1919.

NOBBS, ATHELSTANE.
Royal High School. M.B., C.M. 1892; M.D. 1901. Volunteer Medical Staff Corps, 1887-8, Private. R.A.M.C., Temp. Lieut., Hospital Ship and to Troops (Mediterranean), Nov. 1914 to Oct. 1915. Dardanelles Oct. 1915.

NOBBS, ERIC ARTHUR.
Edinburgh Academy. B.Sc. 1899; Ph.D. (Giessen); F.H.A.S. No. 4 Coy. Q.R.V.B., Royal Scots, 1896-9, Private. South African Campaign, 1899-1900, 1st Royal Scots (V.), Private. South African Forces, Staff Captain. Wounded July 1915. Dispatches 1915.

NOBBS, PERCY ERSKINE.
Edinburgh Collegiate School. M.A. 1896. F.R.I.B.A.; A.R.C.A. No. 4 Coy. Q.R.V.B., Royal Scots, 1897-1901, Private. 5th Northumberland Fusiliers, Lieut. March 1915; Captain April 1915; Major May 1917. Acting Director, Canadian Army Gymnastic Staff (Ottawa), 1916. O.C. Transatlantic Conductory Staff, 1917. Camouflage Park, R.E., France, 1918.

NOBLE, ALEXANDER BERTRAM.
Edinburgh Institution. M.A. 1897. Writer to the Signet, 1901. City of Edinburgh Vol. Regiment. Royal Scots, Private Oct. 1916.

NOBLE, DONALD.
Student of Law. 4th Cameron Highlanders (T.), 2nd Lieut. June 1915; Lieut. July 1915.

NOBLE, JAMES.
Trinity Academy, Leith. M.A. (Hons. Mod. Lang.) 1914. 1/4th Royal Scots (T.), Private July 1915.

NOBLE, ROBERT ORMISTON.
Jedburgh Grammar School. Student of Arts, 1916-17. O.T.C. Infantry, Nov. 1916 to Jan. 1918, Cadet Sergeant; Officer Cadet Jan. 1918. 3rd and 7th Seaforth Highlanders, 2nd Lieut. June 1918. France 1918.

NOBLE, THOMAS PATERSON.
M.B., Ch.B. 1911; M.D. 1913. R.A.M.C., Lieut.; Captain March 1916. Surgical Specialist, No. 2 Stationary Hospital, France.

NOLAN, ROBERT HOWARD.
Foyle College, Londonderry. M.B., Ch.B. 1905. Volunteer Medical Staff Corps, 1900-5, Private. R.A.M.C. (S.R.), Lieut.; Captain Nov. 1914 to Jan. 1916. Cameroons.

Record of War Service

NORFOR, ROBERT CHRISTOPHER.
Edinburgh Academy. O.T.C. 1914-15. University O.T.C. Artillery, 1916, Cadet. 10th (Works Battn.) Royal Scots Fusiliers, Private Jan. 1917; Sergeant Sept. 1917 to March 1918. Mention March 1919.

NORFOR, WILLIAM.
Dollar Academy and George Watson's College. Student of Law, 1884-5. Chartered Accountant, 1886. No. 4 Coy. Q.R.V.B., 2nd Lieut. 1882. 5th Royal Scots, Captain Oct. 1914. O.C. Prisoners of War Camps for three years.

NORMAN, GEORGE PERCY.
M.B., Ch.B. 1905; M.D. 1909. No. 4 Coy. Q.R.V.B., Royal Scots, 1900-4, Private. R.A.M.C., Lieut. April 1917.

NORMAN, HUBERT JAMES.
M.B., Ch.B. 1905. R.A.M.C., Lieut. March 1916; Captain April 1916.

NORMAN, JOSEPH MESSENGER.
Student of Medicine, 1911-16; M.B., Ch.B. 1917. O.T.C. Artillery, Oct. 1912 to April 1914, Cadet. 4th Border Regiment, 2nd Lieut. 1914. R.A.M.C. (S.R.), Lieut. May 1917; Captain May 1918. Burmah and North-West Frontier, India.

NORMAN, LOUIS SEPTIMUS FRANCIS DE ROHAN.
M.B., C.M. 1893; L.R.C.P. & S. (Edin.) and L.F.P.S. (Glasg.) 1887. R.E. (T.), 2nd Lieut. 1890; Major 1905. Resigned 1913. Mobilised R.E. 1914-17. Attached Durham R.G.A. (T.), and 32nd Battn. Middlesex Regiment. T.D.

NORMAND, CHARLES WILLIAM BLYTH.
Royal High School; First XV. M.A. (Hons. Maths.) and B.Sc. 1911; D.Sc. 1920. Simla Volunteer Rifles, Private Aug. 1914; 2nd Lieut. April 1915. I.A.R.O., 2nd Lieut. Feb. 1916; Lieut. Feb. 1917. Attached 105th Mahratta Rifles, 1916. Meteorologist, Mesopotamia, 1916-19. Dispatches 1917.

NORMAND, WILFRID GUILD.
Fettes College. B.A. (Oxford); LL.B. 1910. Advocate, 1910. R.E., Electric Light Coy., 2nd Lieut. June 1915; Lieut. Nov. 1916.

NORONHA, FREDERICK HONORATE.
St Joseph's College, Bangalore. M.B., Ch.B. 1910; D.P.H. (Camb.). Indian Medical Service, Temp. Lieut. July 1915; Temp. Captain 1916.

NORTHCOTE, AUGUSTUS BEAUCHAMP.
Denstone College, Staffs. M.B., C.M. 1888; M.D. 1892. R.A.M.C., Lieut. May 1915; Captain June 1916. 3rd Lancashire Fusiliers. H.M. Hospital Ship *Britannic*. Egypt.

NORTON, RICHARD.
George Heriot's School. Student of Medicine, 1918-19. Royal Air Force, 2nd Air Mechanic Aug. 1916.

Record of War Service

NOURSE, REGINALD H.
> Student of Medicine, 1903-10. R.A.M.C. (T.), Private 1914; L/Corporal 1915. 3rd London Field Ambulance.

NOWELL, ALGERNON JAMES PHILBRICK.
> M.B., Ch.B. 1906. R.A.M.C., Lieut. Sept. 1916; Captain Sept. 1917.

NUTT, WILLIAM HARWOOD.
> Sheffield Academy. M.B., Ch.B. 1903; M.D. 1905. South African Campaign, 1900-1. R.A.M.C. (T.), Captain 1909. Mobilised Aug. 1914-19. Radiologist, 3rd Northern General Hospital.

OAG, JAMES.
> George Watson's College. M.A. 1905; M.B., Ch.B. 1909. R.A.M.C., Lieut. Jan. 1916; Captain Jan. 1917. France.

OAG, WILLIAM DURHAM.
> Miller Institution, Thurso. University O.T.C. Infantry, July to Oct. 1917, and Medical, Oct. 1917 to July 1918, Cadet. 1/5th and 1/6th Seaforth Highlanders, Private Aug. 1914 to Oct. 1916 and Aug. 1918-19. France.

OBERLANDER, CHARLES FREDERICK ALFRED.
> B.A. (Cape) 1898; M.B., Ch.B. 1904. South African Medical Corps, Captain Feb. 1916; Major Feb. 1919. No 1 General Hospital, Wynberg, Cape.

O'BRIEN, ARTHUR JOHN RUSHTON.
> M.B., Ch.B. 1905; D.P.H. and B.Hy. (Durham). R.A.M.C. (V.), 1901-5, Private. R.A.M.C., Captain Oct. 1915 to July 1919. West Africa. Wounded July 1917. Dispatches (three times). M.C. Sept. 1916; Bar to M.C. July 1917.

O'BRIEN, CHARLES RICHARD.
> M.B., Ch.B. 1905. Indian Medical Service, Captain March 1909.

O'DEA, E. M.
> M.B., C.M. West African Medical Staff.

OGILVIE, ALEXANDER.
> Robert Gordon's College, Aberdeen. B.Sc. 1891. R.E. (T.), City of Edinburgh Fortress, 1888, Major and O.C. 1912; Temp. Lieut.-Col. July 1915; Brevet Lieut.-Col. June 1918; Lieut.-Col. May 1919. T.D. April 1911. Mentions Feb. 1917 and June 1918. O.B.E. June 1919.

OGILVIE, ALEXANDER.
> M.A. (Aberdeen). Student of Law, 1902-5. Writer to the Signet, 1905. R.F.A., Gunner May 1915; 2nd Lieut. July 1915; Lieut. June 1916. France.

OGILVIE, ALEXANDER THOMSON.
> Daniel Stewart's College. University O.T.C. Infantry, Oct. 1916 to May 1917, Cadet; Officer Cadet May 1917. Gordon Highlanders, 2nd Lieut. Aug. 1917; Lieut. Feb. 1919. France and The Rhine.

Record of War Service

OGILVIE, GEORGE.
George Heriot's School. Student of Medicine, 1915-16 and 1918-19. O.T.C. Medical, 1918, Cadet. R.G.A., Gunner May 1916. France 1917-18.

OGILVIE, GEORGE HAMILTON.
Repton. Cadet Corps 1902-5. B.Sc. 1911; Diploma in Forestry (Oxford). I.A.R.O., 1/10th, 2/10th, and 2/3rd Gurkha Rifles, 2nd Lieut. Jan. 1915; Acting Captain Dec. 1917; Captain Jan. 1919. India, Gallipoli, Mesopotamia, and Palestine. Wounded in Palestine Sept. 1918, and invalided home Nov. 1918. Dispatches Sept. 1918. M.C. June 1919.

OGILVIE, JAMES.
Student of Science, 1911-15. B.Sc. 1915. R.E., Corporal.

OGILVIE, JOHN.
Repton. M.A. 1900. North Scottish R.G.A. (T.), 2nd Lieut. May 1915; Lieut. May 1916; Acting Captain Oct. 1916 to Jan. 1919.

OGILVIE, PHILIP GORDON.
Repton. Student of Arts, 1907-8. I.A.R.O., 21st and 33rd Punjabis, 2nd Lieut. Feb. 1915. Ordnance Depôt, Bombay, Captain March 1917. Dispatches July 1919.

OGILVIE, WALTER HOLLAND.
Bedford Grammar School. M.B., C.M. 1891; B.Sc. (P.H.) 1893; D.Sc. (P.H.) 1898. No. 4 Coy. Q.R.V.B., Royal Scots, 1886-91, Sergeant. Indian Medical Service, 1893, Lieut.-Col. Jan. 1913; Temp. Colonel Sept. 1916; Brevet Colonel June 1919. Sudan 1896; China 1900; Thibet 1904. Dispatches Aug. 1917, Jan. and June 1919. C.M.G. Aug. 1917. Order of the Nile (3rd Class) March 1919.

OGILVIE, WILLIAM MACKAY.
George Watson's College. M.A. 1911; B.Sc. 1913. 9th Royal Scots (T.), Private Dec. 1914.

OGILVY, STEWART GRANT.
M.B., C.M. 1895; M.D. 1911. 1/10th Royal Scots (Cyclists Battn.) (T.), Major Nov. 1914. R.A.M.C., Major July 1917.

O'HALLORAN, HENRY.
St Mungo's Academy, Glasgow. Student of Arts, 1913-14. 4th Royal Scots, Private Aug. 1914; Staff Sergeant Nov. 1915. 6th Royal Irish Rifles, 2nd Lieut. May 1916; Acting Staff Captain Aug. 1917; Adjutant Oct. 1917. 1/124th Baluchistan Infantry, Indian Army, May 1918. Egypt Jan. 1916. Wounded at Gallipoli June 1915 and Salonika Sept. 1916. Dispatches 1917.

O'HANLON, LEONARD THOMAS.
Student of Law, 1912-13. Chartered Accountant, 1915. 3/4th King's Own Scottish Borderers (T.), 2nd Lieut. Dec. 1915; Lieut. July 1917. France. Wounded at St Julien near Ypres Sept. 1917, and at Gouzeaucourt Sept. 1918. Prisoner of War Sept. to Nov. 1918.

Record of War Service

OLDHAM, JOHN N.
George Heriot's School. O.T.C. 1917-18. Student of Science, 1919. O.T.C. Infantry, March to Oct. 1918, Cadet Sergeant; Officer Cadet Oct. 1918. Argyll and Sutherland Highlanders, 2nd Lieut. Dec. 1918.

OLDMEADOW, LLOYD JOHN HOLLIS.
Church Grammar School, Launceston, Tasmania. M.B., C.M. 1892; M.D. 1902; F.R.C.S. (Edin.) 1898. R.A.M.C., Lieut. Nov. 1915; Captain 1916.

OLIPHANT, ARTHUR HILTON.
George Watson's College and Edinburgh Academy. O.T.C. 1914-16. Student of Science, 1916-17. O.T.C. Infantry, 1917, Cadet. 55th T.R.B., Private Oct. 1917; Acting Sergeant April 1918. Attached 4th Highland Light Infantry; 9th Scottish Rifles. France.

OLIVER, ARCHIBALD.
George Watson's College. M.B., Ch.B. 1904; M.D. 1908; D.P.H. (Edin.) 1908. R.A.M.C. (T.), Lieut. Nov. 1914; Captain May 1915; Acting Major May 1918. D.A.D.M.S. (Sanitary), Salonika. Dispatches Oct. 1917. Chevalier of Order of Redeemer of Greece. Médaille des Épidémies en vermeil.

OLIVER, ARTHUR RUSKIN.
George Watson's College; First XV. and XI. O.T.C. 1914-17, Cadet L/Corporal. Student of Medicine, 1918-20. O.T.C. Artillery, Dec. 1917 to June 1918, Cadet Bombardier; Officer Cadet June 1918. R.F.A., 2nd Lieut.

OLIVER, CHARLES.
Broughton School, Edinburgh. Student of Arts, 1918-19. Royal Scots, Private Sept. 1916; L/Corporal.

OLIVER, JOHN ALEXANDER.
Ayr Academy; First XV. O.T.C. 1913-16. University O.T.C. Infantry, May to Dec. 1917, Cadet; Officer Cadet Dec. 1917. Royal Air Force, 2nd Lieut.

OLIVER, JOHN GILBERT.
George Watson's College; First XI. O.T.C. 1914-15. Student of Medicine, 1918-19. O.T.C. Artillery, May to Dec. 1916, Cadet; Officer Cadet Jan. 1917. R.F.A., 2nd Lieut. May 1917. Thrice Wounded.

OLIVER, JOHN WALTER.
George Heriot's School. O.T.C. 1909-12, Cadet Corporal. Student of Arts, 1912-14. 5th and 8th Royal Scots (T.), Private Sept. 1914; 2nd Lieut. Oct. 1917; Lieut. May 1919. Wounded Aug. 1915 and July 1918. Gallipoli; France.

OLIVER, MATTHEW JAMES.
Glenalmond; First XV. Cadet Corps 1879-81. M.B., C.M. 1886; D.P.H. (Edin.) 1890. 1st V.B. King's Own Scottish Borderers, Lieut. Coast Defences, 1918.

OLIVER, WILLIAM GEORGE BEAUCHAMP.
Edinburgh Academy. Student of Arts, 1913-17; M.A. 1916; (Hons. Mental Phil.) 1920. O.T.C. Infantry, 1914-15, Cadet. Royal Scots, Private Oct. 1916; Officer Cadet July 1917. Highland Light Infantry, 2nd Lieut. Sept. 1917.

Record of War Service

ORBELL, RONALD GRAEME SCOTT.
  Christ's College, Christchurch, New Zealand. M.B., Ch.B. 1904; M.D. 1908; L.M. (Dublin) 1905. N.Z. Medical Corps, Captain July 1915. Gallipoli. Dispatches Nov. and Dec. 1916. M.C. Aug. 1916.

ORCHARD, ALBERT JOHN.
  Christchurch High School, New Zealand. M.B., C.M. 1896. N.Z. Medical Corps, Captain Aug. 1916. France. Dispatches 1917. Mention 1919.

ORCHARD, JAMES EDWARD RUSSELL.
  M.B., Ch.B. 1910. R.A.M.C., Lieut. Nov. 1915; Captain Nov. 1916. France, India, and Mesopotamia.

ORD, ARTHUR FREDERICK TROTTER. (See p. 751.)

ORE, FREDERIC ALBERT.
  Congregational School, Caterham, Surrey. Student of Arts, 1914-16. R.A.M.C. (T.), Private Nov. 1915; Acting Corporal Feb. 1919. 1st Welsh Field Ambulance and 3rd Water Tank Coy., France.

ORME, LOGAN.
  Student of Arts, 1913-14. O.T.C. Infantry, May 1913 to Oct. 1914, Cadet. 3rd Argyll and Sutherland Highlanders, 2nd Lieut.

ORMISTON, GEORGE.
  Alloa Academy; First XI. Student of Medicine, 1916 and 1919. R.G.A., Gunner April 1917; Officer Cadet Oct. 1917; 2nd Lieut. March 1918. 50th, 11th, 299th, and 256th Siege Batteries. France and The Rhine.

ORMISTON, THOMAS MACLAY.
  Student of Medicine, 1915. Pharmacist. R.A.M.C., Private Nov. 1915; Corporal Feb. 1916; Sergeant March 1916; Lieut. May 1917; Captain May 1918.

ORMROD, GARFIELD.
  Shrewsbury. M.B., Ch.B. 1904. R.A.M.C., 1904; Captain 1909; Major Oct. 1915; Brevet Lieut.-Col. Jan. 1917; Acting Lieut.-Col. Aug. 1918. France, Salonika, and Russia. Dispatches 1917.

ORR, ALEXANDER MURDOCH.
  Bathgate Academy. Student of Arts, 1914-15. R.N.V.R., Ordinary Signalman, April 1916; Signalman Sept. 1916; Sub-Lieut. Nov. 1917; Lieut. Nov. 1918. Mine-sweeping, Sept. 1916. Sound Ranging, Feb. to Sept. 1919.

ORR, ANDREW CLARK.
  West Kilbride School. Student of Arts, 1914; M.A. 1915. Licentiate, Free Church of Scotland. Munitions, June 1915 to Jan. 1917. 4th Royal Scots Fusiliers, Private July 1917; Corporal Oct. 1917.

ORR, ARCHIBALD.
  Pumpherston School. Student of Science, 1914. O.T.C. Engineers, Nov. 1915 to Oct. 1916, Cadet; Officer Cadet Oct. 1916. King's Own Yorkshire Light Infantry, 2nd Lieut. Jan. 1917. R.E., 2nd Lieut. Nov. 1917; Lieut. May 1919. France March to Aug. 1917 and Jan. to April 1918. Wounded April 1918.

Record of War Service

ORR, JAMES.
George Watson's College. M.B., Ch.B. 1899. R.A.M.C., Lieut. June 1917; Captain June 1918.

ORR, JAMES.
Kirkcaldy High School. Student of Law, 1911-13. Chartered Accountant, 1914. 9th Royal Scots (T.), Private 1911. 11th and 13th Argyll and Sutherland Highlanders, 2nd Lieut. July 1915; Lieut. July 1917.

ORR, JAMES SYMINGTON.
Student of Medicine, 1917. O.T.C. Infantry, March to Oct. 1917, Cadet; Officer Cadet Oct. 1917. 1st Cameron Highlanders, 2nd Lieut. March 1918 to June 1919. France and The Rhine April 1918 to June 1919.

ORR, MATTHEW YOUNG.
Berwick Grammar School. Student of Arts and Science, 1902-6. 2/7th Royal Scots (T.), Private Aug. 1914; Sergeant 1915; 2nd Lieut. Oct. 1915; Lieut. July 1916; Captain Aug. 1917; Commandant, N.C.O.'s School of Instruction, Oct. 1916. 15th Scottish Rifles, Adjutant Feb. 1917 to April 1919. Dispatches Aug. 1918.

ORR, RYRIE.
Kirkcaldy School. M.A. 1885. J.P. 1st Special Service Vol. Battn., Private Nov. 1916; Corporal Jan. 1917; Sergeant Nov. 1917; 2nd Lieut. March 1918.

ORR, RYRIE J. ERSKINE.
George Watson's College. O.T.C. 1912-15. University O.T.C. Artillery, Sept. 1915 to May 1916, Cadet Corporal; Officer Cadet May 1916. R.G.A., 2nd Lieut. Aug. 1916; Lieut. Feb. 1918; Staff Captain and R.T.O. Dec. 1918. 253rd Siege Battery, France. Wounded at Messines.

ORWIN, JAMES STEWART.
M.B., Ch.B. 1905. Royal Navy, Surgeon; Staff-Surgeon.

OSBORNE, DENIS CALLENDER.
Foyle College, Londonderry; First XV. Student of Medicine, 1915-16 and 1919-20. O.T.C. Infantry, 1915, Cadet. Argyll and Sutherland Highlanders, Private Oct. 1915; Sergeant April 1916. 3rd Royal Inniskilling Fusiliers, 2nd Lieut. April 1917; Lieut. Oct. 1918. France. Wounded Aug. 1917.

OSLER, THOMAS HENRY.
Riversdale School, Cape. First XV. M.B., Ch.B. 1902. South African Medical Corps, Captain Nov. 1914. 24th Mounted Brigade Field Ambulance.

OSWALD, ANDREW BAIRD.
Glasgow High School. Glasgow University O.T.C., 1916, Cadet. University O.T.C. Artillery, 1917, Cadet Sergeant; Officer Cadet Aug. 1917. R.F.A., 2nd Lieut. Jan. 1918; Lieut. June 1919. 26th Army Brigade, France.

Record of War Service

OSWALD, DAVID JAMES TOSH.
Pocklington School; First XV. and XI. Student of Medicine, 1913-15 and 1918-20; M.B., Ch.B. 1920. O.T.C. Infantry, Oct. 1914-15, Cadet. R.N.V.R., H.M. Ships *Tigress* and *Nomad*, Surgeon Sub.-Lieut. Taken Prisoner at Battle of Jutland May 1916.

OSWALD, JOHN.
B.Sc. 1907. A.M.I.C.E. University Battery, E.C.A.V., 1904-8, Sergeant; Officer Cadet Feb. 1916. R.E., 2nd Lieut. July 1916; Lieut. Jan. 1918; Acting Captain Nov. 1917 to March 1919. Egypt and Palestine Sept. 1916 to Feb. 1918. Dispatches June 1918 and March 1919.

OSWALD, ROBERT.
George Watson's College. M.A. 1886; B.D. 1892. Minister, Church of Scotland. Chaplain, Highland Division (T.), Captain, 1899; Major 1909; Lieut.-Col., Lowland Mounted Brigade.

OSWALD-SMITH, HARRY.
George Watson's College. M.B., Ch.B. 1900. F.R.I.Ph. Rugby International (eleven "Caps"). R.A.M.C., Lieut. June 1915; Captain June 1916. France 1916-18. Invalided out June 1918.

OUTRAM, J. D.
Student of Law, 1891. Advocate, 1891. 3rd Highland Light Infantry, Captain and Hon. Major; Major May 1917. 1st Garrison Battn. Scottish Rifles.

OVENS, ROBERT BLACKSTOCK.
Edinburgh Academy. O.T.C. 1910. Student of Science, 1918-20. 8th Royal Scots, Private 1913; 2nd Lieut. Dec. 1914; Lieut. June 1916; Acting Captain April 1918 to Jan. 1919. France Nov. 1914 to Aug. 1918. M.C. Nov. 1916.

OWEN, ALLAN CAMERON.
Queen's College, New Zealand. M.B., Ch.B. 1902. Volunteer Medical Staff Corps, 1898-1902, Private. South African Campaign, 1900-1. N.Z. Medical Corps, Captain Sept. 1917.

OWEN, GEORGE ELMSLIE.
George Watson's College. O.T.C. 1915-17. Student of Science, 1918-19. O.T.C. Artillery, 1917-18, Cadet Corporal. R.G.A., Officer Cadet June 1918; 2nd Lieut. April 1919.

OWEN-MORRIS, WILLIAM GEORGE FREDERICK.
Birkenhead School; First XV. Student of Medicine, 1911-14 and 1916-18; M.B., Ch.B. 1917. Lothians and Border Horse, 1904; Corporal Aug. 1914. Welsh Horse (T.), 2nd Lieut. Jan. 1915; Lieut. R.A.M.C. (S.R.), Lieut. Jan. 1918; Captain Jan. 1919. 2nd Leinster Regiment. France. M.C. Oct. 1918.

OWEN-PRITCHARD, WILLIAM.
Student of Medicine; L.R.C.P. & S. (Edin.) and L.F.P.S. (Glasg.) 1901. East African Medical Staff, Captain Aug. 1914.

Record of War Service

OWLER, ALEXANDER WEBSTER.
George Heriot's School. M.A. 1914. Schoolmaster. 3rd Royal Scots Fusiliers, Private Feb. 1916. 19th Royal Scots. R.A.M.C. R.E., Meteorological Section, Sapper.

PACE, JOHN FRANCIS.
Stonyhurst College. M.B., Ch.B. 1911. O.T.C. Infantry, June 1909-11, Cadet. Civil Surgeon Aug. 1914. Royal Navy, Surgeon-Lieut. March 1915. H.M. Hospital Ships *Egmont*, *Victory*, *Otway*, *Hercules*, and *Crescent*.

PAGE, GEORGE FOSTER BRAITHWAITE.
Magdalen College School, Oxford. M.B., Ch.B. (Hons.) 1912. Royal Navy, H.M.S. *Centaur*, Surgeon April 1913; Acting Surgeon-Lieut.-Commander Aug. 1918; Surgeon-Lieut.-Commander April 1919. China 1914; East India 1915. R.N.A.S., France, 1916-17.

PAGE, RANDOLPH.
George Watson's College. Student of Science, 1917-18. O.T.C. Infantry, 1917-18, Cadet. Royal Air Force, Officer Cadet Feb. 1918; 2nd Lieut. France.

PAGET, ALFRED JAMES MEYRICK.
M.B., C.M. 1895; M.D. 1897. East Africa, 1900-4. S.M.O., Troops, British Somaliland, 1908-16. R.A.M.C., Lieut. April 1916.

PAISLEY, WILLIAM WALKER.
Glasgow Academy. O.T.C. 1915-17. University O.T.C. Engineers, Sept. 1917 to Feb. 1918, Cadet. R.N.V.R., Midshipman, Feb. 1918.

PALLETT, WILLIAM HORNER.
Blairlodge; First XV. and XI. Cadet Corps 1902-4, Sergeant. Student of Medicine, 1904-14; M.B., Ch.B. 1914. Q.R.V.B., Royal Scots, 1904-6, Private. R.A.M.C., Lieut. April 1917; Captain April 1918. Mesopotamia, East Africa, India.

PANDIT, JAI CHAND.
B.Sc. 1915. Indian Field Ambulance, 1914. Munitions, 1915. Assistant Port Engineer, Mesopotamia, 1917.

PANIKKAR KAVALAM, PADMANABHA.
Trivandrum School, India. M.B., Ch.B. 1913. D.T.M. & H. Indian Medical Service, Lieut. Jan. 1916; Captain Jan. 1917.

PANTON, HENRY FORBES.
Glenalmond. Cadet Corps 1899-1902. M.B., Ch.B. 1910. No. 4 Coy. Q.R.V.B., Royal Scots, 1906-8, Private. R.A.M.C., Lieut. 1912; Captain March 1915; Brevet Major June 1917. 29th Division, Med. Exp. Force. D.S.O.; M.C.

PANTON, J. BARRIE.
George Watson's College. Cadet Corps. Student of Medicine, 1906-12. O.T.C. Artillery, Oct. 1908 to Jan. 1913, Cadet Sergeant. N.Z. 2nd Brigade Field Artillery, Corporal, Aug. 1914. R.F.A., 2nd Lieut. Aug. 1915; Lieut. July 1917. Egypt, Dardanelles, N.Z. Contingent, and France, Guards Division.

Record of War Service

PARHAM, WILLIAM MASKELYNE.
 Merchant Taylors' School, London. M.B., C.M. 1889; M.D. 1902. Civil Surgeon, South Africa, 1900-2. R.A.M.C., Captain Sept. 1915; Major Dec. 1915. 47th Casualty Clearing Station, France. Invalided home 1917.

PARIS, GODFREY ANTHONY.
 Student of Medicine, 1911-17; M.B., Ch.B. 1916. O.T.C. Medical, Nov. 1914, Cadet. R.N.V.R., Surgeon-Probationer.

PARIS, JOHN.
 George Heriot's School. M.A. 1913. O.T.C. Infantry, Oct. 1910 to May 1914, Cadet. 5th Royal Highlanders (Black Watch) (T.), Private April 1916; L/Corporal May 1916; Sergeant Aug. 1916. 5th Border Regiment (T.), 2nd Lieut. Feb. 1917; Lieut. Aug. 1918.

PARISH, HENRY JAMES.
 Perth Academy. Student of Medicine, 1913-18; M.B., Ch.B. (Hons.) 1918. O.T.C. Medical, Feb. 1916 to July 1918, Cadet. R.A.M.C., Lieut. Sept. 1918; Captain Sept. 1919. 18th Stationary Hospital, Tiflis, the Black Sea.

PARK, GEORGE WILLIAMSON.
 Royal High School; First XV. and XI. M.B., C.M. 1893; B.Sc. (P.H.) 1896. Chief Censor, Penang, 1914. Penang Volunteers, Sergeant 1916-17. Bowhill Auxiliary R.C. Hospital, Selkirk, 1918.

PARK, ROBERT.
 Royal High School. M.B., Ch.B. 1911; M.D. 1914. R.A.M.C., Lieut. May 1915; Captain May 1916. France 1915-17. Wounded at Somme 1916. Torpedoed 1917.

PARK, THOMAS GLOVER.
 Student of Medicine, 1902-6. R.N.V.R., Sub-Lieut.

PARKER, HARRY GORDON.
 Durham School. M.B., Ch.B. 1912. Royal Navy, Temp. Surgeon Sept. 1914. R.A.M.C., Temp. Lieut. Aug. 1915; Captain Aug. 1916. France and The Rhine (three years). Field Ambulance. 51st Manchester Regiment.

PARKER, HERBERT GEORGE.
 Student of Medicine. F.R.C.S. (Edin.) 1897. R.A.M.C. (T.), 1901; Lieut.-Col. Nov. 1912. Egypt and Gallipoli. 1st Field Ambulance, Lancashire Division. Nell Lane Military Hospital, Manchester.

PARKER, JAMES SMITH.
 Student of Arts and Science, 1910-15; M.A. (Hons. Maths.) 1915; B.Sc. Schoolmaster. R.E. (Special Brigade), 4th Battn., Corporal July 1915. Munitions, 1916-19.

PARKER, ROBERT OVEREND.
 Dundee High School; Athletics. Student of Science, 1917-19. O.T.C. Engineers, March to Oct. 1918, Cadet. R.E., Officer Cadet Nov. 1918.

Record of War Service

PARKER, WYNDHAM.
King's School, Chester; First XI. M.B., Ch.B. 1913. O.T.C. Medical, Jan. 1908 to April 1914, Cadet Corporal. R.A.M.C., Lieut. June 1915; Captain June 1916. M.C. Nov. 1916. Italy. Dispatches Jan. 1919.

PARKES, WILLIAM HENRY.
M.B., C.M. 1892; M.D. 1919; F.R.C.S. (Honorary) 1919; M.R.C.P. (Lond.) 1919. N.Z. Medical Corps, 1897; Colonel March 1916. N.Z. General Hospital, Egypt, 1915. D.D.M.S., Jan. 1916; and D.M.S., N.Z. Exp. Force, 1917. C.M.G. Jan. 1916; C.B.E. Jan. 1918. Knight of Grace of St John 1918.

PARR, ALFRED ERNEST.
Ph.D. (Leipzig); M.S. in Agriculture (U.S.A.); B.Sc. 1904. Indian Army, United Provinces Horse (Northern Regiment), Sergeant 1914. 11th Lancers, 2nd Lieut. Aug. 1915; Lieut. 1916; Captain 1918. Indian Frontier 1916; Egypt and Palestine 1916-19. Twice Wounded. Dispatches 1917.

PARR, CLIFFORD HEATLEY.
B.Sc. 1913. 15th and 9th Royal Scots, Private Oct. 1914. 9th Royal Scots Fusiliers, 2nd Lieut. July 1915. 5th Reserve Cavalry Regiment, March 1916. 11th Hussars, Lieut. Nov. 1916 to March 1919. France.

PARR, THOMAS PARR.
Lymm Grammar School, Cheshire; First XI. Student of Medicine, 1913-17; M.B., Ch.B. 1916. St Andrews University O.T.C. 1910-14. R.A.M.C. (S.R.), Lieut. Aug. 1914; Lieut. Mobilised Jan. 1917; Captain July 1917; Lieut. (Regulars); Temp. Captain July 1919.

PARRY, EDGAR ROWE.
M.B., C.M. 1891. Indian Medical Service, 1893; Lieut.-Col. Jan. 1913. Chitral, 1895; Somaliland, 1903-4. 135th Indian Field Ambulance, Egypt, and 20th Indian General Hospital, Mesopotamia.

PARRY, EVAN ITHEL.
Student of Medicine; L.R.C.P. & S. (Edin.); L.R.F.P.S. (Glasg.) 1914. Rugby "Blue." Royal Navy, Temp. Surgeon Oct. 1914. H.M. Ships *Himalaya* and *Dreadnought*.

PARRY, FRANCIS MARDON.
M.B., Ch.B. 1898; D.P.H. (Camb.). South African Campaign, 1900-2. R.A.M.C., Lieut. 1900; Major 1912; Lieut.-Col. Dec. 1917.

PARSONS, JOHN ARTHUR.
Burnley Grammar School. M.B., C.M. 1895; M.D. 1899. R.A.M.C. (T.), Lieut. Sept. 1914; Captain April 1915. Royal Air Force Medical Service, Captain March 1918. Leicester Yeomanry. R.M.O., 14th Royal Welsh Fusiliers.

PARSONS, LAURANCE DUDLEY.
M.B., Ch.B. 1898. Ceylon Defence Force, Colombo Town Guard, 1917-19.

Record of War Service

PASQUAL, JAMES A.
Stonyhurst College, Blackburn. Student of Medicine, 1916-17 and 1918-19. O.T.C. Medical, May to Nov. 1917, Cadet. R.N.V.R., Surgeon Sub-Lieut.

PATERSON, ALEXANDER.
M.B., C.M. 1885. R.A.M.C., Lieut., attached 3rd Royal Highlanders (Black Watch). Palestine.

PATERSON, ALEXANDER GORDON.
Royal High School. M.A. 1879; M.B., C.M. 1884; M.D. 1886. Royal Berkshire Regiment, Vol. Battn., Surgeon-Captain. R.A.M.C., Hon. Temp. Major Nov. 1914. Hon. Associate, Order of St John of Jerusalem. Dispatches 1919.

PATERSON, ALEXANDER STEPHEN.
George Watson's College. M.B., Ch.B. 1906. Royal Navy, Surgeon May 1910; Surgeon-Lieut.-Commander May 1918. H.M. Ships *Egmont*, *Hussar*, *Columbella*, and *Theseus*. Mediterranean and Black Sea.

PATERSON, ARTHUR KEPPIE.
Edinburgh Academy. B.Sc. 1911. O.T.C. Infantry, May 1909 to Jan. 1910, Cadet, and Engineers, Feb. 1910 to Dec. 1915, Lieut. Transferred R.E., 65th Lowland Division, Captain March 1916. Invalided out Feb. 1918.

PATERSON, ARTHUR McMASTER.
Daniel Stewart's College. Student of Medicine, 1911-16. M.B., Ch.B. 1916. O.T.C. Medical, Oct. 1912-16. R.A.M.C. (S.R.), attached O.T.C., Lieut. Sept. 1914; Acting Captain March 1916; Captain Jan. 1917. France.

PATERSON, ARTHUR SPENCER.
Fettes College. O.T.C. 1914-18, Cadet L/Corporal. Student of Arts, 1918-19. Officer Cadet Aug. 1918. R.F.A., 2nd Lieut. April 1919.

PATERSON, ARTHUR THOMAS.
M.B., Ch.B. 1907; M.D. 1909; F.R.C.S. (Edin.) 1911. R.A.M.C., Lieut.; Captain. N.Z. Medical Corps, June 1918. 3rd N.Z. Hospital.

PATERSON, BASIL STANLEY McCHEYNE.
George Watson's College. O.T.C. 1913-15. Student of Arts, 1915-16. O.T.C. Artillery, Dec. 1915 to March 1916, Cadet; Officer Cadet March 1916. R.F.A., 2nd Lieut. July 1916; Lieut. Jan. 1918-19. France 1916-18 Somme; Le Cateau. Twice Wounded.

PATERSON, CHARLES EDWARD.
Edinburgh Institution. M.B., C.M. 1884; M.D. 1890. No. 4 Coy. Q.E.R., 1882-5, Corporal. 1st V.B.R. Berkshire Regiment, Lieut. 1st and 4th Hampshire Regiment, Cadet Battn., Captain 1910; Major 1911; Lieut.-Col. Nov. 1916; Colonel May 1918. V.A.D. B.R.C.S. 1912-15.

Record of War Service

PATERSON, DAVID.
Student of Law, 1895-7. Law Agent, 1902. R.F.A. (T.), 323rd Brigade, Captain May 1908; Temp. Major Oct. 1914; Major June 1916; Temp. Lieut.-Col. Dec. 1915. D.S.O. June 1919.

PATERSON, DONALD HUGH.
Winnipeg School. B.A. (Manitoba); Student of Medicine, 1912-16; M.B., Ch.B. 1916. Anatomy Staff, 1915-16. O.T.C. Medical, 1914-16, Cadet L/Corporal. R.A.M.C., Lieut. April 1916. Canadian A.M.C., Captain Dec. 1917. 1st Dorsetshires; 12th Suffolks; 135th and 91st Field Ambulances, France, 1916-17. Duchess of Connaught's and Petrograd Officers' Hospital, London, 1918-19.

PATERSON, DONALD ROSE.
M.B., C.M. 1883; M.D. 1887. R.A.M.C., Major 1908. 3rd Western General Hospital.

PATERSON, DOUGLAS GORDON.
George Heriot's School; First XV. and XI. O.T.C. 1913-17, Cadet Sergeant. Student of Medicine, 1918-19. Royal Air Force, 3rd Air Mechanic, June 1917; 2nd Lieut. Dec. 1917.

PATERSON, FRANK SALMON.
Edinburgh Academy; First XI. O.T.C. 1915-17. Student of Medicine, 1918-19. O.T.C. Artillery, July 1917 to Feb. 1918, Cadet; Officer Cadet Feb. 1918. R.G.A., 2nd Lieut. Aug. 1918.

PATERSON, GEORGE WILLIAM SIMLA.
George Watson's College. M.B., C.M. 1894. R.A.M.C., 1911; Captain Aug. 1914; Major and D.A.D.M.S., Scottish Command, 1919. Mention Aug. 1918.

PATERSON, HECTOR MACDONALD.
Dundee High School. University O.T.C. Artillery, Sept. 1917 to June 1918, Cadet. R.F.A., Officer Cadet June 1918.

PATERSON, HECTOR McLEOD.
Aberdeen Grammar School. Student of Arts, 1911-14. 12th and 13th Argyll and Sutherland Highlanders, Private Sept. 1914; 2nd Lieut. May 1915. North Staffordshire Regiment, Lieut. July 1917. France April 1916 to Nov. 1917. Invalided home Nov. 1917.

PATERSON, HUGH.
M.B., Ch.B. 1909; M.D. 1913. R.A.M.C. (T.), Lieut. 1905; Captain Aug. 1914; Acting Major Jan. 1918; Acting Lieut.-Col. 3rd Cameron Highlanders.

PATERSON, IAN.
Blairlodge. M.B., C.M. 1885. R.A.M.C. 1887, Major 1899. Relief of Chitral. South African Campaign, 1899-1902.

Record of War Service

PATERSON, JAMES.
George Watson's College. M.A. 1892. Minister, U.F. Church of Scotland. Hon. Chaplain 1916. France.

PATERSON, JAMES HENRY.
M.B., C.M. 1902; D.P.H. (Camb.) 1911. R.A.M.C., Lieut. Sept. 1914; Captain. Malta, France, and Egypt. Invalided out April 1918.

PATERSON, JAMES LEE HAMILTON.
Rutherford College, Newcastle-on-Tyne. M.B., Ch.B. 1906. R.A.M.C., Lieut. Feb. 1917; Captain Feb. 1918. Macedonia. Dispatches 1919.

PATERSON, JAMES RALSTON KENNEDY.
George Heriot's School. Student of Medicine, 1918-19. O.T.C. Infantry, Aug. to Oct. 1915, Cadet. Argyll and Sutherland Highlanders, 2nd Lieut. Oct. 1915; Lieut. July 1917. R.E. M.C. April 1918.

PATERSON, JOHN.
Ayr Academy. O.T.C. 1911-14. University O.T.C. Artillery, 1916-17, Cadet Bombardier; Officer Cadet May 1917. 122nd Brigade, R.F.A., 2nd Lieut. Nov. 1917; Lieut. May 1919. France. Gassed at Armentières, April 1918.

PATERSON, JOHN.
Ayr Grammar School. M.A. 1902. Schoolmaster. 3/1st Ayrshire Yeomanry, Private Nov. 1915. Attached 12th Highland Light Infantry. France Dec. 1916 to May 1917. Wounded at Arras April 1917.

PATERSON, JOHN CLYDE.
Fettes College. O.T.C. 1908-10. Student of Science, 1910-12. O.T.C. Engineers, 1910-12, Cadet. R.E., 2nd Lieut. Dec. 1914; Lieut. and Captain March 1916. Dispatches May 1917.

PATERSON, JOHN ROBERT.
Edinburgh Academy. O.T.C. 1914-16. Student of Medicine, 1919. O.T.C. Artillery, June 1916 to Jan. 1917, Cadet; Officer Cadet Jan. 1917. R.G.A., 2nd Lieut. April 1917; Lieut. Oct. 1918.

PATERSON, RANDOLPH ELLIOT.
St Ann's, Redhill, Surrey. M.B., Ch.B. 1911. N.Z. Medical Corps, Captain 1918. Government Hospital, Apia, Samoa.

PATERSON, THOMAS.
George Heriot's School. M.A. (Hons. Engl.) 1899. Schoolmaster. R.G.A., Gunner May 1916; Bombardier Dec. 1916; 2nd Lieut. Jan. 1918; Temp. Captain Jan. 1919. The Rhine.

PATERSON, VICTOR A. Y.
Perth Academy. Cadet Corps 1914-15, Acting Sergeant. Student of Arts, 1915-16 and 1918-19. O.T.C. Artillery, Nov. 1915 to May 1916, Cadet Corporal. R.F.A., Officer Cadet Sept. 1916; 2nd Lieut. Oct. 1916; Lieut. April 1918. France, Italy, and The Rhine. Wounded May 1917.

Record of War Service

PATERSON, WILLIAM.
Chefoo, N. China. University O.T.C. Infantry, Feb. to July 1918, Cadet. Chinese Labour Corps, 2nd Lieut. July 1918. France.

PATERSON BROWN, KEITH.
Merchiston Castle. Student of Medicine, 1911-16; M.B., Ch.B. 1916. O.T.C. Medical 1915-16, Cadet. R.A.M.C. (S.R.), Lieut. March 1916; Captain Sept. 1916. 40th British Field Ambulance. Mesopotamia, Caucasus. Dispatches April 1917.

PATLEY, HUBERT.
St John's College, Johannesburg. First XI. Student of Medicine, 1912-17; M.B., Ch.B. 1917. O.T.C. Medical, Feb. 1913 to March 1917, Cadet Staff-Sergeant. R.A.M.C., Lieut. May 1917; Captain May 1918.

PATON, ALEXANDER KELLY ROBERTSON.
Daniel Stewart's College. M.A. 1902. Minister, Presbyterian Church of England. A.S.C. (Northumbrian Division), Private Nov. 1914; Sergeant Feb. 1915; 2nd Lieut. June 1915; Temp. Lieut. Oct. 1916; Lieut. July 1917.

PATON, DAVID.
M.A. 1901. Schoolmaster. 9th Royal Scots (T.), Private June 1917; L/Corporal Sept. 1917.

PATON, DAVID DUNCAN.
M.A. 1900; M.B., Ch.B. 1903. R.A.M.C., Lieut. (Resigned). Australian Army Medical Corps, Hon. Major. Ophthalmic Surgeon, No. 8 General Hospital.

PATON, EBENEZER GRIEVE.
George Watson's College. O.T.C. 1915-17. University O.T.C. Artillery, 1917, Cadet; Officer Cadet Jan. 1918. Tank Corps, 2nd Lieut. Aug. 1918.

PATON, IAN ALEXANDER MORRIS.
George Watson's College. Student of Medicine, 1914-15 and 1918-19. Anatomy Staff, 1919. O.T.C. Artillery, Oct. 1914 to March 1916, Cadet; Officer Cadet March 1916. R.F.A., 95th Brigade, 2nd Lieut. July 1916; Lieut. Jan. 1918. France 1916-18. Wounded March 1918. Invalided out March 1919.

PATON, LEONARD CECIL.
George Watson's College; First XI. Student of Arts, 1910-14; M.A. (Hons. Classics) 1914. Oxford University O.T.C. Infantry, Oct. 1913 to July 1914, Cadet. 10th Scottish Rifles, 2nd Lieut. Nov. 1914; Lieut. Sept. 1915; Captain May 1918. Intelligence 1917-18. France. Three times Wounded, Sept. 1915. Invalided out March 1919. Dispatches Nov. 1915 and Jan. 1916. M.C. (Loos) Sept. 1915.

PATON, MONTGOMERY PATERSON.
M.A. (Hons.) and B.Sc., Distinction (St Andrews); M.B., Ch.B. 1911. R.A.M.C., Lieut. Aug. 1914; Captain Aug. 1915; Major Feb. 1918. 97th Brigade, R.F.A.; 10th King's Own Yorkshire Light Infantry; 64th Field Ambulance, and D.A.D.M.S. 21st Division. Dispatches. M.C. 1918; D.S.O. Jan. 1919.

Record of War Service

PATON, PETER FORSYTH.
    Allan Glen's School, Glasgow. University O.T.C. Infantry, Feb. to March 1917, Cadet. Royal Air Force, Officer Cadet; 2nd Lieut. May 1917; Lieut. March 1918. France and Italy.

PATON, WILLIAM BROWN.
    Lasswade School. M.A. 1912. Schoolmaster. R.E. (Special Brigade), Corporal July 1916.

PATON, WILLIAM CALDER.
    Glasgow Academy; First XV. and XI. M.A. 1906; M.B., Ch.B. 1910. Indian Medical Service, Lieut. 1912; Captain July 1915; Acting Major Sept. 1918; Brevet Major June 1919. 112th Indian Field Ambulance, Lahore Division, and 128th Combined Field Ambulance, Bozanti, Asia Minor. France Nov. 1914 to Sept. 1915; Mesopotamia Sept. 1915 to May 1918; Egypt and Palestine May 1918 to Feb. 1920. M.C. and Dispatches Jan. 1916.

PATRICK, JOHN CAIRNS.
    George Watson's College. Student of Arts and Commerce, 1919. O.T.C. Infantry, April 1912 to Sept. 1914, Cadet. 11th Royal Scots, 2nd Lieut. Sept. 1914; Lieut. Jan. 1915; Captain July 1916. France 1915-18; Loos and Somme. Wounded Aug. 1918.

PATRICK, RUSSEL.
    Edinburgh Academy. O.T.C. 1909-10. Student of Law, 1912-14. O.T.C. Artillery, Oct. 1912-14, Cadet. R.F.A. (S.R.), 2nd Lieut. Aug. 1914; Lieut. June 1915. R.H.A., Lieut. Feb. 1917; Captain Nov. 1917.

PATTEN, JOHN ALEXANDER.
    M.A. 1907. Minister of Congregational Church. Chaplain, 4th Class, June 1915; 3rd Class, May 1917. France Nov. 1915. Dispatches May 1917. M.C. March 1918.

PATTERSON, JAMES WATERS THORNTON.
    Wheelwright Grammar School, Dewsbury; First XI. Student of Medicine, 1915-16 and 1918-20. O.T.C. Artillery, 1917, Cadet Corporal; Medical 1918-19, Cadet. R.F.A., Officer Cadet Dec. 1917 to April 1918.

PATTERSON, NORMAN JOSEPH.
    Royal High School; First XV. and XI. Student of Medicine, 1912-13 and 1916-18; L.R.C.P. & S. (Edin.) 1919. Cricket "Blue." O.T.C. Artillery, Oct. 1913-14, Cadet. R.F.A., 23rd Brigade, 2nd Lieut. Oct. 1914. France. Wounded at Hooge Aug. 1915. Invalided out 1916. Dispatches Jan. 1916.

PATTERSON, WILLIAM GILCHRIST.
    George Heriot's School; First XV. O.T.C. 1914-18, Cadet Corporal. Student of Medicine, 1918-19. 53rd (Y.S.) Highland Light Infantry, Private July 1918.

Record of War Service

PATTERSON, WILLIAM JOHN.
M.B., Ch.B. 1904. R.A.M.C., Lieut.

PATTERSON, WILLIAM TYRRELL.
Student of Medicine, 1910-15; M.B. Ch.B. 1915. R.A.M.C., Lieut.; Captain Nov. 1916. 19th Motor Ambulance Convoy. East Africa.

PATTON, CLARE REGINALD.
M.B., Ch.B. 1912. O.T.C. Infantry, May 1909 to Feb. 1913, Cadet Sergeant. R.A.M.C., Lieut. Cameroons Exp. Force (Gold Coast), West Africa.

PATTON, WALTER SCOTT.
M.B., Ch.B. 1901. Indian Medical Service, Major Jan. 1914.

PATTULLO, HENRY ALEXANDER.
University O.T.C. Infantry, June 1916 to Feb. 1917, Cadet; Officer Cadet Feb. 1917. 3rd and 13th Royal Scots, 2nd Lieut. June 1917; Lieut. March 1919. France Aug. 1917-18. Jat Light Infantry, Indian Army, Sept. 1918. Mesopotamia March 1919. 1/8th Rajputs, Kurdistan. M.C. (Arras) March 1918.

PAUL, CUTHBERT BALFOUR.
M.B., Ch.B. 1900. R.A.M.C. (T.), Lieut.

PAUL, DAVID HUTCHEON.
Park Hurst School, Buxton. M.B., Ch.B. 1905; M.D. 1909. R.A.M.C., Lieut. Dec. 1914; Captain Dec. 1915 to Feb. 1919. Military Hospital, Oswestry.

PAUL, GEORGE GRAHAM.
Clifton Bank, St Andrews; First XI. M.A. (St Andrews). LL.B. 1909. Advocate, 1910. Nigerian Land Contingent, Private Sept. 1914; Sergeant Dec. 1915.

PAUL, HECTOR GILBERT.
Waid Academy, Anstruther; First XI. Student of Science, 1918-19. O.T.C. Engineers, April to Nov. 1918, Cadet L/Corporal; Officer Cadet Nov. 1918.

PAUL, KENNETH WARREN.
Montrose Academy. Student of Science, 1912-14. C.D.A. R.G.A., Gunner Aug. 1915.

PAUL, ROBERT LYALL.
Portobello School. Student of Law, 1916-17. O.T.C. Infantry, 1917-18, Cadet; Officer Cadet Feb. 1918. 5th Highland Light Infantry, 2nd Lieut. July 1918 to May 1919. Attached 18th Scottish Rifles, France, Sept. 1918.

PAUL, WILLIAM FORDYCE.
Bathgate Academy. M.A. 1914. Schoolmaster. Royal Scots, Private 1916; Corporal.

PAULIN, NEIL GODFREY.
Edinburgh Academy; First XI. B.A. (Oxford) 1909. Student of Law, 1910-14. R.F.A. (T.), 2nd Lieut. July 1911; Lieut. Aug. 1914; Captain June 1916. 86th Army F.A. Brigade, France, 1915-19. Wounded at third Ypres June 1917.

Record of War Service

PAWAN, JOSEPH LENNOX.
St Mary's College, Trinidad, B.W.I. M.B., Ch.B. 1912. Trinidad B.W.I. Light Infantry, Surgeon-Lieut. 1915.

PAWLETT, FRANCIS.
Oakham School. Student of Medicine, 1897-1900. Volunteer Medical Staff Corps, 1898-1900, L/Corporal. South African Campaign, 1900-2. 5th Battn. Canadian Infantry, Major Aug. 1914; Lieut.-Col. Aug. 1916. Attached Irish Guards and 2nd West Riding Regiment. France. Dispatches Jan. and March 1919. D.S.O. Sept. 1918.

PAYN, JOHN REDWOOD.
Pietermaritzburg College, Natal. Cadet Corps 1903-10, Cadet Corporal. Student of Medicine, 1911-14 and 1916-19; M.B., Ch.B. 1919. O.T.C. Artillery, Oct. 1911 to June 1913, Cadet. Forth R.G.A. (T.), 2nd Lieut. 1913; Captain June 1916.

PEACH, BENJAMIN NEEVE.
George Watson's College. B.Sc. 1910. O.T.C. Artillery, 1908-11, Cadet Bombardier. R.F.A., 2nd Lieut. Nov. 1914; Lieut. Dec. 1915; Captain Oct. 1917; Acting Major Dec. 1917; Major Oct. 1918. Salonika Sept. 1915.

PEAKE, ERNEST CROMWELL.
Blackheath School. M.B., Ch.B. 1898; M.D. 1915. Anglo-Belgian Red Cross, 1915. R.A.M.C., Lieut. Jan. 1915. Brook War Hospital, Woolwich, 1915-16.

PEARCE, CHARLES ROSS.
M.B., C.M. 1892. Indian Medical Service, Lieut.-Col. Jan. 1914.

PEARCE, JOHN LINDESAY.
M.B., Ch.B. 1905. R.A.M.C., Lieut. June 1915; Captain June 1916 to Jan. 1919. M.C. April 1917.

PEARSON, FRANK ROBERT TAYLOR.
M.A. 1892. Schoolmaster. Royal Air Force, June 1917; Acting Captain, Education Technical Group, to Feb. 1919.

PEARSON, JOHN HENRY HERBERT.
George Watson's College. M.B., Ch.B. 1908; M.D. 1913. R.A.M.C., Temp. Lieut. Dec. 1914; Temp. Captain Dec. 1915. France, Gallipoli, and Italy. Order of Leopold and Croix de Guerre (Belgian) 1917.

PECK, HERBERT.
Hutton Hall, Dumfries. M.B., C.M. 1896; M.D. 1899; L.R.C.P. & S. (Edin.) 1886; D.P.H. (Camb.) 1890. R.A.M.C. (T.), Captain and Sanitary Officer, 1909. 42nd Reserve Park, A.S.C. Medical Recruiting Board.

PEEBLES, ALEXANDER SPALDING MACKIE.
M.B., Ch.B. 1899; M.D. 1903. Indian Medical Service, Captain; Major March 1916.

Record of War Service

PEEBLES, JOHN GEORGE.
M.B., Ch.B. 1901. Royal Navy, Staff Surgeon; Fleet Surgeon Feb. 1918.

PEEBLES, THOMAS.
George Heriot's School; First XV. and XI. M.B., Ch.B. 1903. No. 4 Coy. Q.R.V.B., Royal Scots, 1898-1902, Private. R.A.M.C., Lieut. July 1916-17. 42nd General Hospital, Med. Exp. Force.

PEEK, JOHN HAROLD.
Maitland School, N.S.W. M.B., Ch.B. 1908; M.D. 1910; D.P.H. (Camb.) 1914. South African Campaign, 1899-1902. Australian Army Medical Corps, Hon. Captain 1911. R.A.M.C., Temp. Captain Sept. 1914; Temp. Major Jan. 1919. D.A.D.M.S. (Sanitation), Aldershot. Sanitary Officer, Italy. Dispatches Aug. 1917. Cavaliere della Corona d'Italia March 1918.

PEFFERS, ANDREW.
Forfar Academy. M.A. (St Andrews). First XI. St Andrews University O.T.C. 1910-13, Cadet Sergeant. Student of Medicine, 1913-14. 3rd Highland Light Infantry, 2nd Lieut. Aug. 1914; Lieut. Feb. 1915; Captain Dec. 1918. France March to Dec. 1915; Mesopotamia Jan. 1916 to Aug. 1919. Dispatches Aug. 1917. Legion of Honour (Chevalier) June 1919.

PEILL, ERNEST JOHN.
M.B., Ch.B. 1899; F.R.C.S. (Edin.) 1901. R.A.M.C., Lieut. Jan. 1917; Captain Jan. 1918; Major Sept. 1918. No. 3 Native Labour General Hospital, France. Dispatches July 1919.

PEIRSON, DUNCAN JAMES.
M.B., C.M. (Cape); M.B., C.M. (Edin.) 1898. South African Campaign, 1899-1902. South African Medical Corps, Captain Dec. 1915; Major Jan. 1916. 4th Field Ambulance.

PENBERTHY, CLIFFORD PEARCE.
Student of Medicine, 1911-16; M.B., Ch.B. 1916. O.T.C. Medical, 1916. South African Field Ambulance, Dresser. France. R.A.M.C., Captain Feb. 1917.

PENDRICH, WILLIAM JOHN.
Student of Law, 1910-12. 14th Argyll and Sutherland Highlanders, Private July 1915; Corporal July 1916.

PENFOLD, ERNEST ALFRED.
Portsmouth Grammar School. M.B., C.M. 1889. Royal Navy, Surgeon 1891; Staff Surgeon 1899; Fleet Surgeon 1907; (Surgeon-Commander 1918). Dispatches Sept. 1916. D.S.O. Jan. 1917; Order of St Stanislaus, 2nd Class (with Swords) June 1917.

PENMAN, ALEXANDER.
M.A. 1910. Schoolmaster. R.G.A., Gunner April 1917. Palestine and Macedonia.

Record of War Service

PENMAN, JOHN.
Dunfermline High School. M.A. (Hons. Classics) 1915. R.F.A., 34th Reserve Battery, Gunner April 1917; 2nd Lieut. May 1918. R.G.A., 71st Heavy Battery.

PENNEL, ALEXANDER NORVAL.
Student of Science, 1912-15. R.N.V.R., 2nd Lieut. Sept. 1915; Lieut. June 1917. Royal Air Force, Captain Aug. 1918. Malta.

PENTLAND-SMITH, ARCHIBALD LUMSDAINE.
Madras College, St Andrews. M.A., B.Sc. (St Andrews); M.B., C.M. 1895. R.A.M.C., Lieut. Jan. 1916; Edinburgh Castle and North Queensferry Hospitals. V.A.D. Hospital, Elie. H.M. Hospital Ship *Asturias*.

PEPPER, CHARLES EDWARD.
M.B., Ch.B. 1901. R.A.M.C., Lieut. Dec. 1914; Captain Nov. 1917. 1/8th Royal Warwick Regiment.

PERCIVAL, EDGAR.
Darlington Grammar School; First XI. M.B., Ch.B. 1913. O.T.C. Medical, Jan. 1909 to July 1913, Cadet Sergeant. R.A.M.C., Lieut. July 1913; Captain March 1915; Acting Lieut.-Col. June 1918. France and The Rhine. Dispatches Jan. 1915 and 1917. D.S.O. Sept. 1916; M.C. Nov. 1917.

PEREGRINE-JONES, D. J.
Old College School. Student of Science, 1918-20. R.E., Sapper Sept. 1914; Sergeant 1916; Officer Cadet 1916-17. Royal Welsh Fusiliers, 2nd Lieut. March 1917; Lieut. 1918. France.

PESEL, HOWARD GEORGE.
Loretto. M.B., Ch.B. 1901; M.D. 1903. R.A.M.C., Lieut. Jan. 1915; Captain Jan. 1916; Acting Major. France. No. 6 General Hospital, and 36th, 9th, and 41st Divisions. Italy and The Rhine. M.C.

PETER, JOHN.
Bo'ness Academy. M.A. 1912. Schoolmaster. 11th Battn. Scottish Rifles, Private July 1915. Salonika.

PETERKIN, GEORGE.
M.B., C.M. 1892; M.D. 1900; D.P.H. (Edin.) 1897. R.A.M.C., Captain and Sanitary Officer, 1909.

PETERKIN, WILLIAM BRUCE.
Loretto. O.T.C. 1913-14. University O.T.C. Infantry, May 1916 to Jan. 1918, Cadet Sergeant; Officer Cadet Feb. 1918. 10th and 3rd Royal Scots, 2nd Lieut. Aug. 1918 to Jan. 1919. Royal Air Force.

PETERSEN, GORDON.
Glenalmond; First XV. and XI. O.T.C. 1915-17, Cadet L/Corporal. Student of Science, 1918-19. O.T.C. Artillery, Dec. 1917 to Aug. 1918, Cadet Bombardier. R.F.A., Officer Cadet Aug. 1918.

Record of War Service

PETERSON, WILLIAM MURRAY.
    Glenalmond; First XV. O.T.C. 1912-16. University O.T.C. Artillery, Aug. 1916 to April 1917, Cadet. R.F.A., Officer Cadet April 1917; 2nd Lieut. Oct. 1917.

PETRIE, ALFRED ALEXANDER WEBSTER.
    Portsmouth Grammar School. Cadet Corps 1899-1902, Cadet Corporal. M.B., Ch.B. 1908; M.D. 1913; F.R.C.S. (Edin.) 1910; M.D. (Lond.) 1913. No. 4 Coy. Q.R.V.B., Royal Scots, 1902-8, L/Corporal. R.A.M.C., Lieut. June 1915; Captain June 1916. 3rd Stationary Hospital, France, and The Rhine.

PETTIGREW, FRANK W.
    Dunbar School. Technical Assistant, Surgery Department. Lothians and Border Horse, Private 1908. Transferred R.A.M.C., 1912; Corporal May 1914; Sergeant Aug. 1915; Acting Staff-Sergeant May 1917. 2nd Scottish General Hospital. Egyptian Exp. Force, Oct. 1915. Invalided out Sept. 1918.

PHEASE, RONALD NORMAN.
    Turriff School. Student of Medicine, 1910-15; M.B., Ch.B. 1915. O.T.C. Infantry, May 1910 to July 1913, Cadet. R.A.M.C., Lieut. July 1916; Captain July 1917. Transferred to Regulars, April 1919. Indian and Mesopotamian Exp. Forces.

PHILIP, CHARLES LYALL.
    George Watson's College. M.A. 1903. Red Cross Driver, 1916. I.A.R.O., 2nd Lieut. Aug. 1918. Supply and Transport and 8th (Indian) Cavalry.

PHILIP, COLIN CAMERON.
    Fettes College. O.T.C. 1909. M.B., Ch.B. 1914. O.T.C. Medical, Oct. 1909 to Jan. 1913, Cadet L/Corporal. R.A.M.C., Lieut. Jan. 1915; Captain July 1915. Lowland Field Ambulance, Egypt.

PHILIP, GEORGE HAROLD.
    Merchiston Castle; O.T.C. 1915-16. University O.T.C. Artillery, Aug. 1916 to March 1917, Cadet Bombardier; Officer Cadet March 1917. R.F.A., 2nd Lieut. Aug. 1917; Lieut. France. Gassed March 1918. Prisoner of War.

PHILIP, GEORGE MORRISON.
    Fettes College. Student of Science, 1911-14 and 1918; B.Sc. 1918. O.T.C. Engineers, 1911-14, Cadet. 15th Northumberland Fusiliers, 2nd Lieut. Nov. 1914; Lieut. Dec. 1915. Attached Royal Air Force, April to Nov. 1918. France. Wounded June 1916 and Oct. 1917. Dispatches March and Sept. 1916 and Dec. 1917. M.C. Jan. 1916; Bar to M.C. June 1916; D.S.O. June 1917.

PHILIP, JAMES RANDALL.
    Dundee High School. Student of Arts, 1917-19. O.T.C. Engineers, Jan. to Aug. 1918, Cadet; Officer Cadet Oct. 1918. R.G.A., 2nd Lieut. May 1919.

PHILIP, NORMAN McLEOD. (See p. 752.)

PHILLIPS, HENRY WHITBY.
    Atherstone Grammar School. M.B., C.M. 1881; M.D. 1886; M.R.C.S. (Eng.) 1881. Surgeon, Croydon District National Reserve. Surrey R.A.M.C. (V.), Captain Oct. 1917; Major Dec. 1918.

Record of War Service

PHILLIPS, HUGH RICHARD.
   Cheltenham. M.B., Ch.B. 1898; M.D. 1902. Royal Navy, Surgeon Aug. 1914-15. Hospital Ship *Soudan*. R.A.M.C., Captain Sept. 1918. King George's and other Hospitals, London.

PHILLIPS, JOHN.
   Southgate House School, Sunderland. M.B., C.M. 1888; L.R.C.P. & S. (Edin.); L.F.P.S. (Glasg.) 1887. R.A.M.C. (T.), Major 1908. 5th Southern General Hospital.

PHILLIPS, JOSEPH EVELYN.
   The Lodge School, Barbados. First XI. O.T.C. 1905-10, Cadet Sergeant. Student of Medicine, 1911-16. M.B., Ch.B. 1916. O.T.C. Infantry, Oct. to Dec. 1914, Cadet. R.N.V.R., Surgeon-Probationer, Dec. 1914-15. Royal Navy, Temp. Surgeon Oct. 1916. R.N. Hospital, Plymouth.

PHILLIPS, WILFRID WESTWOOD.
   Student of Medicine, 1910-15. M.B., Ch.B. 1914. O.T.C. Medical, 1914, Cadet. R.A.M.C., Lieut. Nov. 1914; Captain May 1915.

PHILP, HORACE ROBERT ANDREW.
   Royal High School. M.B., Ch.B. 1907. East African Medical Service. District Surgeon, Nyeri, 1915-16 and 1917-20. Kenya Province, Feb. 1916 to March 1917.

PICKERING, BERNARD.
   Leamington School. M.B., Ch.B. 1904. M.R.C.S. (Eng.) and L.R.C.P. (Lond.) 1905. R.A.M.C., Lieut. May 1915; Captain May 1916; Acting Major Jan. 1919.

PICKLES, FREDERICK.
   Bradford Technical College. M.A. 1893. Headmaster. St George's (Bristol) Cadet Corps, Captain. Bristol University Volunteer Battn., Private Oct. 1917.

PIERCE, HOWEL BULKLEY.
   Dinglewood School, Colwyn Bay; Athletics. Student of Medicine, 1913-15 and 1917-19. O.T.C. Infantry, 1914-15, Cadet. 12th and 2nd Royal Welsh Fusiliers, 2nd Lieut. July 1915; Lieut. Aug. 1917. Dispatches March 1918.

PIERCY, GEORGE BOWMAKER.
   Heaton Park Road School, Newcastle. Student of Arts and Divinity, 1903-9, Minister. R.A.M.C., 3rd Lowland Field Ambulance, Private Nov. 1914; Corporal Dec. 1914; Sergeant Jan. 1915. 4th Royal Scots (T.), 2nd Lieut. Oct. 1915; Lieut. July 1917. Egypt and Palestine. Invalided out Jan. 1918.

PINION, STANLEY.
   Methodist College, Belfast; First XV. M.B., Ch.B. 1910. R.A.M.C., Lieut. Oct. 1914; Captain Oct. 1915.

PIRIE, ALEXANDER HOWARD.
   Dundee High School. B.Sc. 1896; M.B., Ch.B. 1897. X-Ray Demonstrator. McGill University. Royal Scots, 1892-4. Royal Highlanders (Black Watch). M.O. London Scottish. Canadian Army Medical Corps, Lieut. 1901; Captain 1906; Major Jan. 1918. 3rd Canadian General Hospital (McGill), France 1914.

Record of War Service

PIRIE, JAMES HUNTER HARVEY.
    Robert Gordon's College, Aberdeen. B.Sc. 1899; M.B., Ch.B. 1902; M.D. 1907; F.R.C.P. (Edin.) 1910. R.A.M.C. (T.), Lieut. 1907; Captain 1909; Major March 1918. East African Medical Staff, Captain 1914. British and German East Africa, Aug. 1914-16.

PITCAIRN, ANDREW.
    Leven School. Student of Science, 1914. O.T.C. Artillery, Oct. 1914 to April 1915, Cadet. R.F.A., 2nd Lieut. April 1915; Lieut. June 1917. Mesopotamia. Dispatches Oct. 1917.

PITHIE, GRAHAM PRESTON.
    Dundee High School. Student of Medicine, 1917 and 1919. O.T.C. Artillery, Sept. 1917 to June 1918, Cadet. Royal Artillery, Officer Cadet June 1918.

PITT, JOHN.
    Royal High School. Student of Law, 1914-15. R.A.M.C., Private June 1915; Acting Sergeant 1916. No. 4 Ambulance Train, France.

PLAYFAIR, JOHN MAXWELL.
    Fettes College. O.T.C. 1916-17, Cadet L/Corporal. University O.T.C. Artillery, 1917, Cadet Bombardier; Officer Cadet Aug. 1917. R.F.A. (S.R.), 2nd Lieut. Feb. 1918; Lieut. Aug. 1919. 17th Division, Trench Mortar Brigade, France July 1918.

POAD, KENNETH.
    Leighton Park School, Reading; First XI. Student of Science, 1917-18. O.T.C. Infantry, 1917-18, Cadet. Inns of Court O.T.C., Private Oct. 1918.

POCKLEY, FRANCIS ANTILL.
    M.B., C.M. 1884; M.D. 1911. Australian Army Medical Corps, Major 1915.

POLE, DAVID GRAHAM.
    George Heriot's School. Student of Law, 1897-9. Solicitor before the Supreme Courts, 1901. No. 4 Coy. Q.R.V.B., Royal Scots, 1899, Private; S.S.C. Coy., 2nd Lieut. 1901; Captain (Retired) 1912. 12th Northumberland Fusiliers, Captain Aug. 1914; Major Feb. 1915; Lieut.-Col. Sept. 1915. France, Loos. Invalided home Dec. 1915.

POLE, LAURENCE WILLIAM.
    George Heriot's School. M.B., Ch.B. 1901; D.P.H. (Edin.) 1906. No. 4 Coy. Q.R.V.B., Royal Scots, 1897-1900, Private. R.A.M.C., Lieut. Nov. 1914; Captain Nov. 1915 to March 1919. R.M.O., R.E., 19th Division and Ninth Corps. H.Q. (School of Instruction). France.

POLLOCK, ALEXANDER JOHN.
    Student of Medicine, 1911-17; M.B., Ch.B. 1917; D.P.H. 1920. O.T.C. Medical, 1914-17, Cadet. Royal Navy, Surgeon-Lieut. Nov. 1917. Port Edgar Base.

POLLOCK, ALEXANDER NORMAN.
    M.B., Ch.B. 1913. Royal Navy, Temp. Surgeon Jan. 1915.

Record of War Service

POLLOCK, GEORGE.
M.B., Ch.B. 1906; M.D. 1914. R.A.M.C., Lieut. May 1915; Captain May 1916 to Nov. 1917.

POLLOCK, JOHN DONALD.
M.B., C.M. 1892; M.D. 1896. R.N.V.R., Hon. Surgeon 1915. H.M.S. *Gunner*. O.B.E. 1919.

POLLOCK, WALTER.
George Watson's College. University O.T.C. Infantry, 1909-11, Cadet. 9th, 11th, and 17th Royal Scots, Private March 1916. 34th Battn. Machine-Gun Corps, 2nd Lieut. June 1917; Lieut. Dec. 1918. France 1916-18, Somme.

POOLE, FREDERICK WILLIAM.
Edinburgh Institution. Student of Medicine, 1912-17; M.B., Ch.B. 1917. O.T.C., Medical, May 1912 to July 1917, Cadet Q.M.S. Royal Navy, Temp. Surgeon-Lieut. July 1917. Heligoland Battle, Nov. 1917. Mined off Heligoland, June 1918.

POOLE, LEOPOLD THOMAS.
Edinburgh Institution. M.B., Ch.B. 1910. O.T.C. Medical, 1908-10, Cadet Corporal. R.A.M.C., Lieut. 1912; Captain March 1915; Acting Lieut.-Col. Jan. 1918. Dispatches 1916, 1917, and 1918. M.C. Jan. 1917; D.S.O. April 1917.

POPE, JUSTIN JOHN.
Daniel Stewart's College. M.A., B.Sc. 1913. 14th Royal Scots, 2nd Lieut.; Lieut. 3rd Connaught Rangers, Captain July 1917. Salonika and Serbian Retreat. Invalided home June 1916. Boulogne 1917. M.C.

PORRITT, ERNEST EDWARD.
Wanganui School, New Zealand. M.B., C.M. 1896; M.D. 1903; F.R.C.S. (Edin.) 1898. Volunteer Medical Staff Corps, 1892-6, Private. N.Z. Medical Corps, Surgeon-Lieut. 1899; Lieut.-Col. Dec. 1915. Samoa 1916. Hospital Ship *Maheno*, 1917-19.

PORTEOUS, ALEXANDER JAMES DOW.
Knox Institute, Haddington. Cadet Corps 1908-14, Cadet Sergeant. Student of Arts, 1914-16. 2/8th Royal Scots (T.), Private Sept. 1916; L/Corporal March 1917; Officer Cadet Jan. 1918; 3rd attached 11th Royal Scots Fusiliers, 2nd Lieut. June 1918 to Feb. 1919.

PORTEOUS, EDWARD JOHN.
M.B., Ch.B. 1902. R.A.M.C., Captain Sept. 1914 to Oct. 1916. Cameroons Exp. Force. Croix de Guerre.

PORTEOUS, HAROLD BURNET.
M.B., Ch.B. 1906. R.A.M.C. (T.), Captain. 2nd S.W. Mounted Brigade Field Ambulance.

Record of War Service

PORTEOUS, HERBERT BRENTON.
King James I. Grammar School, Bishop Auckland. Student of Medicine, 1918-19. Argyll and Sutherland Highlanders, Private Oct. 1916; Piper Feb. 1917; L/Corporal Nov. 1917.

PORTEOUS, NORMAN.
Student of Science, 1907-8. A.M.I.C.E. R.E., Sapper Sept. 1914; 2nd Lieut. Nov. 1914; Lieut. July 1915; Acting Captain Aug. 1916; Captain Sept. 1917; Acting Major March 1919; Lieut.-Col. April to Dec. 1919. France. Dispatches June 1916, Jan. and March 1919. M.C. Jan. 1917; D.S.O. June 1919.

PORTEOUS, NORMAN WALKER.
Knox Institute, Haddington. Student of Arts, 1916-17. 56th T.R.B., Private April 1917; Officer Cadet Oct. 1917. 3rd attached 13th Royal Scots, 2nd Lieut. March 1918-19.

PORTEOUS, WILLIAM JAMES.
M.B., Ch.B. 1907; M.D. 1918. N.Z. Medical Corps, Captain Feb. 1917.

PORTER, ALLAN.
George Watson's College; First XI. M.B., Ch.B. 1910; M.D. 1914. R.A.M.C. Lieut. 1916; Captain Nov. 1917.

PORTER, HERDMAN.
Foyle College, Londonderry. M.B., Ch.B. 1902. R.A.M.C., Lieut. 1915. R.A.M.C. (V.), Major 9th Field Ambulance, Kent. Invalided out 1916.

PORTER, SIR JAMES.
LL.D. 1912; M.A., M.B., C.M. 1877; M.D. (Aberdeen). Royal Navy, Surgeon Vice-Admiral. Special Service, Aug. 1914 to Sept. 1917. C.B. 1902; K.C.B. 1910; K.C.M.G. (Dardanelles) 1916.

POSTLETHWAITE, WILLIAM BARRY.
Repton. O.T.C. 1908-10. Student of Medicine, 1910-15; M.B., Ch.B. 1915. O.T.C. Infantry, 1910-11, and Medical, 1911-14, Cadet. R.A.M.C. (S.R.), Lieut. Oct. 1914; Captain Oct. 1915; Acting Major, Jan. 1918 to May 1919. M.C. Sept. 1917; Bar to M.C. Sept. 1918.

POTTER, HARRY RADFORD.
Epworth College; First XI. Student of Medicine, 1916-17 and 1918-19. O.T.C. Infantry, May 1916-17, and Medical, April 1918 to Feb. 1919, Cadet. Hon. Artillery Coy., Private Aug. 1917. France.

POTTER, WILLIAM MISKIN.
Merchiston Castle. Cadet Corps 1902-8, Cadet Corporal. B.A. (Camb.) 1912. Student of Law, 1913-14. O.T.C. Infantry, Oct. to Nov. 1914, Cadet Sergeant. 10th and 8th Seaforth Highlanders, 2nd Lieut. Nov. 1914; Lieut. July 1917; Captain April 1918. France. Wounded and Gassed Oct. 1917.

Record of War Service

POTTINGER, DAVID.
    M.B., Ch.B. 1913. O.T.C. Infantry, May 1909 to Jan. 1911, Cadet. Lothians and Border Horse, Private 1911-14. R.A.M.C., Lieut. Oct. 1914; Captain Oct. 1915; Acting Major Jan. 1918. 33rd Casualty Clearing Hospital, Ludd, Egyptian Exp. Force. M.C. Aug. 1916.

POTTINGER, JOHN ALEXANDER.
    Kirkwall Burgh School. M.B., Ch.B. 1903; F.R.C.S. (Edin.) 1909. No. 4 Coy. Q.R.V.B., Royal Scots, 1899-1902, Private. N.Z. Medical Corps, Captain 1915. N.Z. Hospital Ship *Marama*, 1915-16. Egypt, Salonika, Malta, and France.

POTTS, ARTHUR EDWARD.
    George Heriot's School; First XV. B.Sc. 1912; M.Sc. (Cornell, U.S.). O.T.C. Artillery, 1910-12, Cadet. Princess Patricia's Canadian Light Infantry (McGill Coy.,) Private June 1915; Lieut. Jan. 1917. France. Wounded at Courcelettes and Arras.

POTTS, EDMUND THURLOW.
    M.B., Ch.B. 1901; M.D. 1903. R.A.M.C., Captain; Major Oct. 1915; Temp. Lieut.-Col. Nov. 1917. 4th Royal Scots Fusiliers, and No. 7 Field Ambulance. France; Mons, Aug. 1914, Le Cateau, Marne, and Aisne. Dispatches. C.M.G.; D.S.O. Feb. 1915.

POWER, MICHAEL PATRICK.
    Student of Science, 1906-7. L.R.C.P. & S. (Edin.), L.R.F.P.S. (Glasg.) 1913. R.A.M.C., Captain Dec. 1915. 5th Divisional Train, France. M.C.

POWER, REGINALD.
    Student of Medicine, 1909-14; M.B., Ch.B. 1914. R.A.M.C., Lieut.

POWRIE, ROBERT WALKER RENNIE.
    Perth Academy. Student of Science, 1915 and 1919. O.T.C. Engineers, 1915-16, Cadet. Royal Naval Air Service, 2nd Class Air Mechanic, March 1916; 1st Class, Sept. 1917; Leading Mechanic, April 1918; Petty Officer, June 1918.

PRASAD, BINDESHWARI.
    M.B., Ch.B. 1911. Indian Medical Service (Indian Contingent), Lieut. Dec. 1914.

PRASAD, KANTA.
    M.B., C.M. 1888; M.D. 1913. Indian Medical Service, Lieut.-Col. Jan. 1915. Lower Burma. Kaisar-i-Hind Gold Medal, June 1917.

PRENTICE, CHARLES WHITECROSS.
    George Watson's College. Student of Arts, 1915-16 and 1919. O.T.C. Artillery, March to Sept. 1916, Cadet; Officer Cadet Sept. 1916. Forth R.G.A. (T.), 2nd Lieut. Dec. 1916; Lieut. June 1918.

PRENTICE, WILLIAM BAIRD.
    Loretto. O.T.C. 1914-17. University O.T.C. Artillery, Aug. 1917 to March 1918, Cadet; Officer Cadet March 1918. R.G.A., 2nd Lieut. Oct. 1918.

Record of War Service

PRESTON, JAMES.
Boroughmuir School. Student of Arts, 1918-19. Royal Navy, H.M.S. *Royal Oak*, July 1917; A.B. Seaman Nov. 1917. Attached Wireless Staff as Decoder.

PRESTON, CLASSON O'DRISCOLL. (See p. 752.)

PRICE, ALEXANDER WILLIAM GORDON.
Mussoorie School, India. First XV. and XI. Cadet Corps, Sergeant. M.B., C.M. 1883. Q.E.R. 1879-83, Private. R.A.M.C. (H.H.R.), Captain Aug. 1914-19.

PRICE, ALFRED REES.
M.B., Ch.B. 1908. Royal Navy, Surgeon April 1912.

PRICE, ARTHUR CLEMENT.
M.B., Ch.B. 1911; D.T.M. & H. (Camb.). R.A.M.C., Lieut. June 1916; Captain June 1917. No. 3 Native Labour General Hospital; 73rd Field Ambulance; and 7th Northamptonshire Regiment.

PRICE, ARTHUR ERNEST.
Beauvale School, Nottinghamshire. Student of Science, 1918-19. R.H.A. and R.F.A. Aug. 1914; Lieut. March 1918; Acting Captain. France 1914.

PRICE, EDMUND GEORGE CHAMBERS.
George Watson's College. Cadet Corps 1905-8. M.B., Ch.B. 1913. O.T.C. Artillery, Feb. 1909 to June 1912, Cadet. R.A.M.C., Lieut. Oct. 1914; Captain Oct. 1915; Acting Major June 1918. France 1915-18. Dispatches.

PRICE, FREDERICK NOEL RITCHIE. (See p. 752.)

PRICE, LLOYD TURTON.
M.B., Ch.B. 1901. R.F.A. (T.), 2nd Highland Brigade, Surgeon-Lieut.

PRICE, RAYMOND HERBERT.
M.B., C.M. 1893; F.R.C.S. (Edin.) 1907. Indian Medical Service, Major; Lieut.-Col. July 1916.

PRIESTMAN, GEOFFREY.
Bradford Grammar School. Student of Medicine, 1918-19. R.A.M.C., Private Sept. 1914; Corporal Jan. 1915; Acting Sergeant 1917. 58th Casualty Clearing Station and 18th Field Ambulance.

PRIMROSE, ALEXANDER.
Pictou Academy, Nova Scotia. M.B., C.M. 1886; M.R.C.S. (Eng.) 1888. Canadian Army Medical Corps, Lieut.-Col. March 1915; Colonel 1917. 4th Canadian General Hospital, Salonika. Consulting Surgeon, Canadian Forces in England, 1917-18. Dispatches 1918. C.B. June 1918.

PRIMROSE, ALEXANDER FERGUSSON.
Fettes College. Student of Arts and Law, 1908-12 and 1917. 9th Royal Scots (V.), 1907. R.E., City of Edinburgh (Fortress), 2nd Lieut. 1909; Lieut. 1912; Captain Dec. 1914. O.B.E.

PRING-MILL, RICHARD.
Student of Medicine, 1911-13. O.T.C. Artillery, Oct. 1911 to June 1913, Cadet. R.F.A. (S.R.), 2nd Lieut. Jan. 1915, (Regulars) Feb. 1916; Lieut. Aug. 1917.

Record of War Service

PRINGLE, GEORGE LORAINE KERR.
Edinburgh Academy; First XV. M.B., C.M. 1893; M.D. 1897. R.A.M.C. (T.), Lieut. Oct. 1914; Captain May 1915; Acting Major Jan. 1918. 29th Casualty Clearing Station; 5th West Yorkshire Regiment (T.). France. M.C. June 1918.

PRINGLE, GEORGE TAYLOR.
Peebles High School. M.A. 1912; M.A. (Oxford). Inns of Court O.T.C., Dec. 1915, Private. R.G.A., 2nd Lieut. Oct. 1916. France Dec. 1916 to Sept. 1917. Invalided out July 1918. Ministry of Munitions and Labour, 1918-19.

PRINGLE, JOHN MILLIE.
Royal High School. M.B., Ch.B. (Hons.) 1914. R.A.M.C. (T.), Lieut. March 1916; Captain Sept. 1916; Major Dec. 1918. M.C. Nov. 1918.

PRINGLE, ROBERT NORMAN.
St Andrew's College, Grahamstown, South Africa. First XV. Cadet Corps, Sergeant-Major. M.B., Ch.B. 1899. No. 4 Coy. Q.R.V.B., Royal Scots, 1895-9, Corporal. South African Campaign, 1899-1902. South African Medical Corps, Captain Aug. 1914; Major Feb. 1915; Lieut.-Col. Sept. 1916. 21st Mounted Brigade and 1st South African Field Ambulances. Wounded in German S.-W. Africa. D.S.O. 1917; M.C. Aug. 1918.

PRINGLE-PATTISON, ANDREW ERNEST SETH.
George Watson's College. Cadet Corps 1905-7. M.B., Ch.B. 1913. O.T.C. Infantry, 1908-13, Cadet Sergeant. R.A.M.C., Temp. Lieut. Aug. 1914; Temp. Captain Aug. 1915; Captain (Reg.) Feb. 1918. France 1914. Wounded Oct. 1917.

PRINGLE-PATTISON, NORMAN SETH.
George Watson's College. M.A. 1908; LL.B. 1909. 9th and 7th Royal Scots (T.), 2nd Lieut. Sept. 1914; Lieut.; Captain June 1916. Gallipoli Aug. 1915. Invalided home Nov. 1915. France May 1917; Ypres, Cambrai, and St Quentin. Wounded March 1918.

PRIOR, NORMAN HENRY.
Auckland Grammar School, New Zealand. M.B., Ch.B. 1907. N.Z. Medical Corps, Captain Oct. 1915 to March 1919. M.C. Dec. 1916.

PRITCHARD, SYDNEY CLIFFORD.
M.B., Ch.B. 1899; M.D. 1903. R.A.M.C., Lieut. Sept. 1916; Captain Sept. 1917.

PROSSER, DAVID GRIFFITHS.
Edinburgh Academy. O.T.C. 1909-14, Cadet Officer. Student of Arts, 1914-15 and 1918-20; M.A. 1920. O.T.C. Infantry, Oct. 1914 to April 1915, Cadet Corporal. 11th Argyll and Sutherland Highlanders, 2nd Lieut. April 1915; Lieut. July 1917 to Jan. 1919. M.C. Aug. 1917.

PROUDFOOT, FRANK GREGOIRE.
Madras College, St Andrews. M.B., C.M. 1894; M.D. 1900. R.A.M.C. (T.), 1908; Major Aug. 1914. Queen's Own Oxfordshire Hussars (T.). Military Hospital, Brighton, and Ambulance Train, France. Wounded at second Ypres April 1915.

Record of War Service

PROUDFOOT, ROBERT.
Daniel Stewart's College; First XV. M.B., C.M. 1892; M.D. 1913; D.P.H. (Vict.) 1913. R.A.M.C. (T.), May 1911; Captain Nov. 1914; Acting Major May 1918. D.A.D.M.S., 53rd Division, Dec. 1915 to June 1918. Serbian Order of White Eagle, with Swords (4th Class), and Dispatches Sept. 1916.

PROUDFOOT, THOMAS CHARLES INNES.
Clifton Bank, St Andrews. University O.T.C. Artillery, Sept. 1916 to Aug. 1917, Cadet B.S.M. R.F.A. (S.R.), Officer Cadet Aug. 1917; 2nd Lieut. March 1918; Lieut. Aug. 1919. France May 1918. The Rhine Nov. 1918 to July 1919.

PROUT, WILLIAM THOMAS.
M.B., C.M. 1884. R.A.M.C., Major; Lieut.-Col. April 1916. Egypt, Suez Canal. Dispatches (Egypt) 1916; (Home) 1917. C.M.G.; O.B.E. 1919.

PROWSE, SAMUEL WILLIS.
M.B., C.M. 1893; M.D. 1896; F.R.C.S. (Edin.) 1898. Canadian Army Medical Corps, Lieut.-Col. 1916. No. 4 Canadian Casualty Clearing Station.

PRYDE, JAMES.
Royal High School. M.A. 1898; B.Sc. 1908. I.A.R.O. Aug. 1918; Captain Oct. 1918 to Jan. 1919. Recruiting Officer for Travancore.

PRYDE, ROBERT BEVERIDGE.
Lasswade School. Student of Arts, 1912-15 and 1919; M.A. 1919. Schoolmaster. 8th Royal Scots (T.), Private Feb. 1915; Corporal April 1915; Sergeant July 1916. France 1915.

PRYTHERCH, JOHN ROWLANDS.
Friars School, Bangor. M.B., Ch.B. 1900; M.R.C.S. (Eng.), L.R.C.P. (Lond.) 1900; D.P.H. (Ireland) 1910. R.A.M.C., Lieut. Aug. 1917; Captain Aug. 1918. Sanitary Officer, Egyptian Exp. Force, Alexandria.

PUCKLE, BRUCE HALE.
Uppingham. O.T.C. 1907-10, Cadet Corporal. Student of Science, 1913-14. O.T.C. Engineers, May to Sept. 1914, Cadet. 9th Welsh Regiment, 2nd Lieut. Sept. 1914; Lieut. Nov. 1914; Acting Major April 1916; Captain June 1918; Acting Lieut.-Col. Sept. 1918 to March 1919. Machine-Gun Corps. France and The Rhine (three years). D.S.O. and Dispatches (Somme) Jan. 1917.

PULLON, EDWIN DOUGLAS.
Leys School, Cambridge. Cadet Corps 1906-7, L/Corporal. B.Sc. 1910; M.B., Ch.B. 1912; M.D. 1920. South African Medical Corps, Dec. 1914; Captain; Major May 1918. German South-West Africa; Med. Exp. Force; Hospital Ship. German East Africa and Union of South Africa.

PURCHAS, ARTHUR CHALLINOR.
Auckland College and Grammar School, New Zealand. M.B., C.M. 1884; M.R.C.S. (Eng.) 1884. N.Z. Medical Corps, Major Aug. 1914 to March 1919.

Record of War Service

PURCHAS, FREDERICK MAURICE.
    M.B., C.M. 1896. Australian Army Medical Corps, Lieut. Aug. 1915. 3rd Australian Field Ambulance. Egypt; France March 1916, Ypres and Somme.

PURDOM, JAMES MATHERS.
    Broughton School, Edinburgh. Student of Law, 1913-14. 1/4th Royal Scots, Private 1910; Corporal Aug. 1914; C.Q.M.S. July 1916. Attached Egyptian Labour Corps, 2nd Lieut. May 1917; Lieut. Nov. 1918. France and Egypt.

PURDY, WILFRID JOHN.
    Student of Medicine, 1910-15; M.B., Ch.B. 1915. R.A.M.C., Lieut. March 1917; Captain March 1918. France. 10th Stationary Hospital, 13th and 36th Field Ambulances, 1917. 63rd Brigade, R.F.A., 1917. Burial Unit, France, 1919.

PURVES, JAMES EWART.
    Student of Medicine, 1912-17; M.B., Ch.B. 1917. O.T.C. Infantry, Dec. 1914 to Feb. 1915, Cadet. R.N.V.R., Surgeon-Probationer, Feb. 1915. Royal Navy, Surgeon-Lieut. Dec. 1917. H.M.S. *Gloucester*.

PURVES, KENNETH MACLENNAN.
    George Heriot's School. Student of Medicine, 1914-16 and 1917-19; M.B., Ch.B. 1920. O.T.C. Infantry, March 1915 to April 1916, Cadet. R.N.V.R., Surgeon-Probationer, April 1916-18 and July to Oct. 1918.

PURVES, ROBERT BLACK.
    Epsom College. M.B., Ch.B. 1895; F.R.C.S. (Edin.) 1899. Tutor, Clinical Surgery, 1899-1903. Lincolnshire Yeomanry, Surgeon Captain 1907. R.A.M.C. (T.), Major Aug. 1915; Acting Lieut.-Col. Feb. 1919. No. 2 Prisoners of War Hospital, Heliopolis, Cairo. Dispatches Nov. 1915. D.S.O. Sept. 1918.

PURVES, WILLIAM.
    Student of Arts, 1916-17. O.T.C. Infantry, March to Dec. 1917, Cadet Corporal; Officer Cadet Jan. 1918. 5th King's Own Scottish Borderers, 2nd Lieut. June 1918. France. Invalided home Nov. 1918.

PURVES, WILLIAM THOMPSON.
    M.A., 1894. A.M.I.M.E. R.N.V.R., Temp. Lieut. Nov. 1914.

PURVIS, GEORGE BURNETT.
    Kingswood College, Grahamstown, Cape Colony. Cadet Corps 1902-7. Student of Science, 1916. South African Forces, Heavy Artillery, Gunner 1914-15. German South-West Africa. R.F.C., Cadet. Royal Air Force, Flight Cadet.

PYMAN, BERTRAM.
    Malvern College. Student of Medicine, 1912-14. R.A.M.C. (T.), Scottish Horse Brigade Field Ambulance, Private Sept. 1914. Transferred A.S.C. (M.T.), Aug. 1915. Gallipoli, Egypt, and Palestine.

Record of War Service

PYOTT, ERNEST GEORGE.
George Watson's College; First XV. and XI. Student of Medicine, 1911-17; M.B., Ch.B. 1917. 9th and 12th Royal Scots, 2nd Lieut. Sept. 1914. South African Medical Corps, Captain April 1918. France; Loos and Ypres 1915, Cambrai and Le Cateau 1918.

QUIGLEY, JOHN.
Holy Cross Academy, Edinburgh. Student of Arts, 1914-15. Royal Scots, Private April 1917; L/Sergeant May 1917.

RABAGLIATI, ANDREA FRANCIS HONYMAN.
Bradford Grammar School. M.B., Ch.B. 1902; M.D. 1911; F.R.C.S. (Edin.) 1911. R.A.M.C., Lieut. 1914; Captain Nov. 1916. East Africa. Dispatches Sept. 1917.

RABAGLIATI, DUNCAN SILVESTRO.
Bradford Grammar School. B.Sc. 1902; M.R.C.V.S. 1904. Royal Army Vet. Corps, Captain Feb. 1916; Acting Major Aug. 1916. Egypt. O.C. No. 1 Camel Hospital, Feb. 1916 to July 1919. Dispatches Oct. 1916. O.B.E. (Military) 1919.

RABAGLIATI, HERMAN VICTOR.
M.A. 1906. President, S.R.C. Barrister, Lincoln's Inn. R.F.C. and Royal Air Force, 2nd Lieut. April 1916; Lieut. Nov. 1917; Captain May 1918. France Nov. 1916; Recording Officer, May 1917; Adjutant, XIII. Wing, May 1918 to Jan. 1919.

RADCLIFFE, FRANK.
M.B., Ch.B. 1912. R.A.M.C., Lieut. May 1915. O.B.E. Feb. 1919.

RADFORD, AUBREY.
Pietermaritzburg College, Natal. First XV. Cadet Corps 1904-7, Sergeant-Major, M.B., Ch.B. 1912. Demonstrator of Anatomy, 1913-14 and 1919. O.T.C. Infantry. June 1909-12, Cadet. R.A.M.C. (T.), Lieut. June 1915; Captain Dec. 1915; Major April 1918. M.C. March 1918.

RADFORD, THOMAS KIRKPATRICK.
George Watson's College. B.Sc. 1910. A.M.I.C.E. O.T.C. Artillery and Engineers, 1908-10, Cadet. R.G.A., 2nd Lieut. March 1915. Wounded June 1916. Invalided out July 1917.

RAE, ALEXANDER MONTGOMERY WILSON.
George Heriot's School. Student of Medicine, 1913-14 and 1918-19. Anatomy Staff, 1919. Scottish Horse (T.), 2nd Lieut. Sept. 1914; Lieut. Nov. 1917. Imperial Camel Corps.

RAE, DAVID ADAMS.
M.A. 1906. Schoolmaster. Glasgow High School O.T.C., Lieut.; Captain Sept. 1918.

Record of War Service

RAE, DOUGLAS.
Kirkcudbright Academy. Student of Arts, 1911-14. 6th Royal Scots (T.), Private Sept. 1914; 2nd Lieut. April 1915; Lieut. July 1917; Captain July 1918; Adjutant, 2nd Royal Scots. France, The Rhine.

RAE, FREDERICK JAMES.
George Watson's College. M.A. 1886. Minister, U.F. Church of Scotland. Chaplain, 4th Class, 1st Highland Brigade (T.); Oct. 1914. 1st Scottish General Hospital, Oct. to Dec. 1914; 16th General Hospital, France, Sept. 1915. 1st Royal Scots Fusiliers, Jan. to Sept. 1916.

RAE, ROBERT.
George Heriot's School. Student of Science, 1912-13. R.A.M.C. (T.) Scottish Horse Field Ambulance, Private Sept. 1914; Lieut. July 1917. 1st Royal Sussex Regiment and 21st Lancers.

RAEBURN, JAMES ALEXANDER.
St George's School, Edinburgh. M.B., Ch.B. 1898; M.D. 1912; D.P.H. (Edin.) 1908. R.A.M.C., Lieut. Aug. 1914. Military Hospital, Pirbright, Surrey.

RAI, DEWAN HAKMUAT.
M.A. 1906; M.B., Ch.B. 1907. No. 4 Coy. Q.R.V.B., Royal Scots, Private. Indian Medical Service, Captain July 1910; Major Jan. 1919. M.C. and Dispatches.

RAINIE, WILLIAM.
Edinburgh Academy. M.A. 1877. Minister, Church of Scotland. Chaplain, Lowland Division (T.), Nov. 1892; Colonel 1912. Coast Defences (Tay), and 9th Cyclist Brigade (T.). T.D. 1912. Mention March 1918.

RAINNIE, WILLIAM ROLAND.
Edinburgh Academy. Student of Law, 1911-15. O.T.C. Engineers, 1912-15, Cadet L/Corporal. R.E. (T.), Scottish Signal Coy., 2nd Lieut. Feb. 1915; Lieut. Sept. 1915. Attached G.H.Q. Signalling Coy. France Jan. 1918 to July 1919.

RAINY, HARRY.
M.A. 1885; M.B., C.M. 1891; M.D. 1899; F.R.C.P. (Edin.) 1896. Lecturer on Physical Methods in Treatment of Disease. R.A.M.C. (T.), Captain July 1908. 2nd Scottish General Hospital.

RALSTON, CLAUDE LYON.
Edinburgh Academy; First XV. Student of Law 1889. Writer to the Signet, 1896. 5th Royal Highlanders (Black Watch) (T.), Captain. Rejoined Sept. 1914.

RAMSAY, GRAHAM COLVILLE.
George Heriot's School. M.B., Ch.B. 1912. R.A.M.C., Lieut. Nov. 1914; Captain Nov. 1915. Liaison Officer, Hedjaz Campaign. Arab Medical Administration, Damascus. Dispatches. O.B.E. Order of El Nahda (Hedjaz).

RAMSAY, MAXWELL.
Otago School, New Zealand. Cadet Corps. M.B., Ch.B. 1911. O.T.C. Infantry, 1908-10, Cadet. R.A.M.C., Lieut. N.Z. Medical Corps, Captain Feb. 1918.

Record of War Service

RANKEN, HENRY.
M.A. 1879; B.D. 1887. Minister, Church of Scotland. Chaplain 1892. 4th Royal Scots Fusiliers, Lieut.-Col. 1907; Colonel 1912. Officiating Chaplain to Troops, Irvine District, from Sept. 1914. Mention June 1918.

RANKEN, THOMAS.
Eton. Athletics. Eton College R.V., 1891-4, Sergeant. Oxford University R.V., 1894-8, Lieut. Student of Law, 1899-1902. Writer to the Signet, 1902. 8th Royal Scots (T.) 1891, Captain 1906; Major Aug. 1916; Brigade Major 2/1st Lothian Infantry Brigade, April 1915. Attached General Staff, 1915-19. T.D.

RANKIN, ADAM LAWSON KELLY.
Galashiels Academy. Student of Medicine, 1916-17 and 1918-20. O.T.C. Artillery, Dec. 1916 to July 1917, Cadet; Officer Cadet July 1917. Forth R.G.A. (T.), 2nd Lieut. Jan. 1918; Lieut.

RANKIN, DONALD.
Fort William School. Student of Medicine, 1913-16 and 1917-19. R.N.V.R., Surgeon-Probationer, Dec. 1915. H.M. Ships *Hind*, *Narbrough*, and *Ulster*.

RANKIN, GEORGE CLAUS.
George Watson's College. M.A. (Hons. Phil.) 1897; B.A. (Camb.). Barrister-at-Law, Lincoln's Inn. R.G.A., Anti-Aircraft Section, June 1916; 2nd Lieut. Aug. 1916; Lieut. Feb. 1918.

RANKIN, VICTOR ALBERT.
George Watson's College. Student of Medicine, 1908-14; L.R.C.P. & S. (Edin.) 1919. 1st Lothians and Border Horse (T.), Private 1910. Mobilised Aug. 1914.

RANKIN, OLIVER SHAW.
George Watson's College. M.A. 1906; B.D. 1909. Minister, Church of Scotland. Chaplain, 4th Class, Dec. 1918. Minister to German Prisoners of War. 712th Labour Coy., Péronne, France.

RANKIN, WILLIAM BLACK.
Student of Law, 1883-8. Writer to the Signet, 1889. 1st and 4th Highland Light Infantry (S.R.) 1900. Mobilised Aug. 1914; Major. 1st Royal Scots Fusiliers, Nov. 1915. India Jan. 1916 to May 1918.

RANKINE, GEORGE.
Dunfermline High School. M.B., Ch.B. 1913. O.T.C. Artillery, 1909-13, Cadet Bombardier. R.A.M.C., Lieut. Oct. 1914; Captain Oct. 1915. D.A.D.M.S. Aug. 1916; Acting Major Feb. 1918. Dispatches Jan. 1916 and May 1918. M.C. 1915; Two Bars to M.C. 1918. Chevalier de la Legion d'Honneur June 1917.

RANKINE, MARY DOUGHTY.
M.B., Ch.B. 1912; D.P.H. (Edin.) 1916. R.A.M.C. Dec. 1916. 2nd Scottish General Hospital, Craigleith.

Record of War Service

RANKINE, WILLIAM HENRY.
Auchterderran School. M.A. 1883; B.D. Minister, Church of Scotland. Chaplain, 4th Class, 1901; 3rd Class, 1911; 2nd Class, June 1916. Lowland Division (T.). Gallipoli 1915; Egypt 1915-16.

RAO, RAJAH MANOOR VENKATA SESHACHELAPATI.
High School, Guntur, Madras. M.A. 1913. Barrister-at-law. Indian Defence Force, Havildar, Jan. 1918.

RAO, STEPHEN RAMCHANDRA.
Student of Medicine, 1913-14. Indian Field Ambulance.

RATTRAY, ALEXANDER MAIR.
M.B., C.M. 1897; M.D. 1903. R.A.M.C., Lieut.

RATTRAY, MALCOLM MacGREGOR.
Edinburgh Collegiate School. M.B., C.M. 1893. R.A.M.C. 1897; Lieut.-Col. March 1915. Crete 1898. South African Campaign, 1899-1902. Dispatches Feb. 1915, Jan. 1916, May and Dec. 1917. D.S.O. June 1917.

RATTRAY, PETER.
Dundee High School. M.B., C.M. 1897; L.R.C.P. & S. (Edin.) and (Glasg.) 1895. No. 4 Coy. Q.R.V.B., Royal Scots, Private. R.A.M.C. (V.), Captain. No. 1 West Riding Field Ambulance. Huddersfield War Hospital A.S.C. (M.T.V.).

RAUCH, JOSEPH.
South African College, Capetown. O.T.C. 1907-12, Sergeant. Student of Medicine, 1914-16 and 1917-18; M.B., Ch.B. 1918. O.T.C. Artillery, 1914-16, Cadet. South African Ambulance, Dresser, 1915. 2nd Scottish General Hospital, 1916. South African Medical Corps, Captain 1918. No. 1 Military Hospital, Wynberg, Capetown.

RAWLENCE, HAROLD ERNEST.
Dean Close, Cheltenham. M.B., Ch.B. 1905; M.R.C.S. (Eng.) and L.R.C.P. (Lond.) 1905; F.R.C.S. (Edin.) 1909. R.A.M.C., Lieut. June 1915; Captain June 1916; Major March 1918. Special Surgical Military Hospital; Alexandra Military Hospital, Cookham. Mention Dec. 1919.

RAWSON, ROBERT EDGAR.
Dumfries Academy. Student of Arts, 1913-15. O.T.C. Artillery, 1914-15, Cadet. R.F.A. (S.R.), 2nd Lieut. June 1915; Lieut. June 1917. Divisional Bombing Officer, 1916 Brigade; Signalling Officer, 1917-19. Dispatches Feb. 1916.

RAY, MATTHEW BURROW.
Lancaster School. M.B., C.M. 1893; M.D. 1903; L.R.C.P. & S. (Edin.) and L.F.P.S. (Glasg.) 1893. No. 4 Coy. Q.R.V.B., Royal Scots, 1888-92, Private. 1st (V.B.), 5th and 7th West Yorkshire Regiment, 2nd Lieut. 1899; Captain 1905. R.A.M.C., Captain May 1914; Major Dec. 1914; Acting Lieut.-Col. Nov. 1915 to May 1919. France. No. 3 Casualty Clearing Station, Nov. 1915. 41st Stationary Hospital, April 1919. D.S.O. and Dispatches Jan. 1917.

Record of War Service

RAYMOND, JOHN KIMBER.
    M.B., C.M. 1895. Royal Navy, Surgeon 1898; Fleet Surgeon. Pacific Station, 1914-16. Grand Fleet, 1916-19.

READMAN, WILLIAM.
    M.B., Ch.B. 1903. R.A.M.C., Temp. Lieut. Dec. 1914. France.

REDDEN, JAMES CHARLES NELSON.
    Student of Arts, 1913-16 and 1919; M.A. 1919. Schoolmaster. Cameron Highlanders, Private July 1916.

REDPATH, JOHN.
    Ednam School, Roxburghshire. M.A. 1903. Schoolmaster. R.G.A., 10th Siege Battery, Gunner Nov. 1915; 2nd Lieut. Nov. 1917. France.

REDPATH, WILLIAM.
    Student of Arts, 1912-15. 16th Royal Scots, Private Dec. 1914. R.E. (Special Brigade), Corporal July 1915. R.G.A., 2nd Lieut. June to Dec. 1918. France Aug. 1915 and Oct. 1916. Gassed June 1916.

REEKIE, CHARLES BARCLAY.
    George Watson's College. Student of Medicine, 1912-15 and 1918-20; M.B., Ch.B. 1920. O.T.C. Artillery, 1914-15, Cadet. R.N.V.R., Surgeon-Probationer, Nov. 1915. Northern Patrol.

REEKIE, JOHN.
    Cliftonbank, St Andrews. Student of Medicine, 1916. O.T.C. Artillery, 1916-17, Cadet Bombardier; Officer Cadet Nov. 1917. R.F.A., 2nd Lieut. July 1918.

REEKIE, JOHN.
    Student of Law, 1913-14. 1/3rd Scottish Horse, Private Sept. 1914; Sergeant. Queen Victoria's Own Corps of Guides, Indian Army, Lieut.; Captain and Adjutant. Egypt, Gallipoli, 1915, and India.

REENEN, JACOB WILLIAM VAN.
    M.B., Ch.B. 1913. Indian Medical Service, Lieut.

REES, AURFRYN MUDIE.
    School for Sons of Missionaries, Blackheath; First XV. and XI. Student of Arts, 1913-15 and 1919; M.A. 1919. O.T.C. Infantry, Dec. 1914 to June 1915, Cadet. 12th and 9th Royal Welsh Fusiliers, 2nd Lieut. June 1915; Lieut. July 1917. France. Wounded at Somme 1916.

REES, D. C.
    Student of Arts. R.A.M.C. (Field Ambulance), Private.

REIACH, JAMES.
    M.B., C.M. 1893. Australian Army Medical Corps, Major. 4th Australian Field Ambulance.

Record of War Service

REID, ALEXANDER.
Lochgelly School. Student of Arts and Science, 1901-6. Royal Highlanders (Black Watch), Private June 1916; 2nd Lieut. March 1917; Lieut. Sept. 1918. France.

REID, ALFRED ROBERT R.
Broughton School, Edinburgh. Student of Arts, 1915-16. Royal Scots to 1915. Highland Light Infantry, Lieut. Rejoined 1917.

REID, ARTHUR GORDON.
M.B., C.M. 1888; B.Sc. (Lond.). 2nd V.B. York and Lancaster Regiment, Captain March 1917. R.A.M.C. (V.), Major Jan. 1918. No. 2 West Riding Field Ambulance.

REID, CHARLES BERRINGTON BALFOUR.
Avenue Academy, Berwick. Student of Medicine, 1911-14 and 1916-17; M.B., Ch.B. 1917. O.T.C. Medical, 1911 and 1916-17; Infantry, 1912-14, Cadet. Scottish Horse (T.), Private Sept. 1914. R.E. (Special Brigade), Corporal 1915. R.A.M.C., Lieut. Aug. 1917; Captain Aug. 1918. France 1915. Gassed at Loos.

REID, ERIC McKAY.
Liverpool College. M.B., Ch.B. 1909. R.A.M.C., Lieut. April 1917; Captain April 1918.

REID, FRANCIS WARRACK.
M.A. (Hons. Classics) 1907. 16th Highland Light Infantry (2nd Glasgow Battn.), 1912; Captain Dec. 1914. M.C. June 1919.

REID, GEORGE ALEXANDER.
Morgan Academy, Dundee. University O.T.C. Artillery, April to Sept. 1916, Cadet. R.F.A., Officer Cadet Sept. 1916. A.S.C. Oct. 1916; 2nd Lieut. Dec. 1916; Lieut. June 1918; Acting Captain July 1918-19. Dispatches March 1919.

REID, HUGH SMITH.
Edinburgh Academy; First XV. and XI. M.B., Ch.B. 1904; M.D. 1907; F.R.C.S. (Edin.) 1910. R.N.V.R., Clyde Division, Surgeon Feb. 1913.

REID, ISIDORE EUGENE ROSENSTEIN.
Royal Italian College. M.B., C.M. 1897. Vol. Medical Service, U.S.A., 1917-19.

REID, JAMES.
Stirling High School. Student of Law, 1903-5. Solicitor. Football "Blue" 1905-11. O.T.C. Infantry, March to Aug. 1916, Cadet. Royal Highlanders (Black Watch), 2nd Lieut. Nov. 1916; Lieut. Jan. 1917 to June 1919.

REID, JAMES.
Edinburgh Academy. O.T.C. 1914-16. University O.T.C. Artillery, May 1917 to Jan. 1918, Cadet Bombardier; Officer Cadet Jan. 1918. R.F.A., 2nd Lieut. July 1918. 94th Brigade, 21st Division.

Record of War Service

REID, JAMES KENELN.
  Sedbergh. M.B., Ch.B. 1913. R.A.M.C., Lieut. June 1917; Captain June 1918. Mesopotamia.

REID, JAMES MARTIN.
  Edinburgh Academy; First XV. and XI. M.B., Ch.B. 1899; M.D. 1903; F.R.C.S. (Edin.) 1903. Rugby International. R.A.M.C., Lieut. Jan. 1918.

REID, JAMES MORE.
  M.B., C.M. 1878; M.D. 1880. R.A.M.C., Lieut.-Col. (retired).

REID, JAMES SCOTT CUMBERLAND.
  Edinburgh Academy. Student of Law, 1911-14. 8th Royal Scots (T.), 2nd Lieut. 1914; Lieut. June 1916. Machine-Gun Corps, Captain July 1915; Temp. Major. France.

REID, JAMES STUART WELLESLEY.
  George Watson's College. O.T.C. 1912-17, Cadet C.S.M. Student of Arts. 1918-19. 4th Argyll and Sutherland Highlanders, 2nd Lieut. Nov. 1917. France 1918. Gassed Aug. 1918.

REID, JOHN.
  Student of Arts and Divinity, 1912-16; M.A. 1916. R.F.A., 2nd Lieut.

REID, JOHN.
  Allan Glen's School, Glasgow. Student of Law, 1912-14. R.F.A., 256th Brigade, Gunner May 1915; Sergeant Sept. 1918. France Oct. 1915 to Jan. 1919.

REID, JOHN.
  Lybster School. M.A. 1906. Schoolmaster. 3rd East Lancashire Regiment, July 1917. Machine-Gun Corps. I.A.R.O., 2nd Lieut. Oct. 1918.

REID, JOHN OWEN.
  Student of Medicine, 1910-15. M.B., Ch.B. 1915. O.T.C. Infantry, Feb. 1910 to June 1912, Cadet. R.A.M.C. (S.R.), Lieut. Nov. 1914; Captain Oct. 1915. France 1914; India, Persian Gulf, and Mesopotamia.

REID, LOUIS ARNAUD.
  Leys School, Cambridge. Student of Arts, 1915-19. M.A. (Hons.) 1919. O.T.C. Engineers, Aug. to Sept. 1914, Cadet. R.E., City of Dundee Fortress (T.), Sapper Sept. 1914. Invalided out 1915.

REID, ROBERT JOHN.
  Buckie School. Student of Medicine, 1918-19. Solicitor. Inns of Court O.T.C., Private, Nov. 1915; Officer Cadet. 9th Royal Scots (T.), 2nd Lieut. March 1917; Lieut. Sept. 1918.

REID, SPENCE DAER.
  M.B., Ch.B. 1911. House Surgeon, R.I.E. R.A.M.C., Captain March 1915. France.

Record of War Service

REID, WALTER RICHARD.
 Malvern College. Student of Medicine, 1897-1900. R.F.A., Staff Captain; Major Oct. 1914; Staff Officer, 2nd Grade, Aug. 1917; Brevet Lieut.-Col. June 1918. Dispatches. D.S.O.

REID, WILLIAM.
 Montrose Academy. M.A. (St Andrews). St Andrews University Battery, Fife R.G.A., Gunner. M.B., Ch.B. 1899. R.A.M.C., Lieut. May 1915; Captain May 1916-19. 2nd Northern General Hospital, Leeds. No. 12 Reserve Cavalry Regiment. No. 12 Stationary Hospital, and 230th Field Ambulance, France.

REID, WILLIAM BREMNER.
 Prince Alfred College, Adelaide, South Australia. First XI. B.D.Sc. (Melb.) L.D.S. (Vict.). Student of Medicine, 1913-14 and 1918-20. Anatomy Staff, 1919. O.T.C. Artillery, Oct. 1913 to Aug. 1914, Cadet. R.F.A., 2nd Lieut. Aug. 1914; Lieut. Feb. 1916; Captain April 1916. France Sept. to Dec. 1915; Salonika Dec. 1915 to Sept. 1917; Palestine Sept. 1917 to June 1918.

REID, WILLIAM WALKER.
 M.A. (Aberdeen); B.D. 1898. Minister, Church of Scotland. Chaplain, 4th Class, April 1917 to Oct. 1918. 1/5th Gordon Highlanders, France, 1917-18.

REILLY, BERNARD JOSEPH.
 Clonmel Grammar School, Co. Tipperary. Student of Science, 1919. 9th Royal Scots, Private April 1915. Royal Air Force, Cadet.

REIS, CYRIL HERBERT STAFFORD.
 Royal High School. Student of Science, 1906-9. C.D.A. President, Agricultural Society, 1908-9. Lothians and Border Horse, 2nd Lieut. Nov. 1916; Lieut. May 1918. Attached G.H.Q., Ireland, Advisory Committee (Educational), Dec. 1918.

REIS, GORDON STANLEY.
 Royal High School. B.Sc. 1909. 28th London Regiment (2nd Artists' Rifles O.T.C.), Cadet Sept. 1918; 2nd Lieut. Timber Supply Department, Dec. 1917 to Sept. 1918.

REIS, HAROLD.
 Royal High School. Lincoln's Inn O.T.C., 2nd Lieut. Student of Science, 1919. R.E., Tunnelling Branch, 2nd Lieut. Dec. 1915; Lieut. July 1917. France.

REMACLE, RENÉ.
 Student of Science, 1914-15. Candidat Ingénieur (Belgian Degree). 54th Coy. T.A.G. (Belgian Army), Private April 1917; Corporal Sept. 1917.

RENDALL, ROBERT.
 Daniel Stewart's College. M.B., C.M. 1893. Volunteer Medical Staff Corps, 1888-93, Corporal. Ex-Admiralty, Surgeon. 1st V.B. Suffolk Regiment, Private May 1915; Sergeant and Musketry Instructor, July 1917. Suffolk R.A.S.C., M.T. (V.), Lieut. April 1918. Suffolk R.A.M.C. (V.), Temp. Lieut. June 1918.

Record of War Service

RENNIE, JOHN.
Trinity Academy. Student of Science, 1919. Scottish Rifles, Private Nov. 1916.

RENTON, ARCHIBALD.
George Heriot's School. O.T.C. 1913-15. Student of Science, 1917. O.T.C. Artillery, Jan. to July 1917, Cadet Sergeant. R.F.A. (S.R.), Officer Cadet Aug 1917; 2nd Lieut. Jan. 1918. 178th Brigade, France.

RENTON, AUGUSTUS CECIL.
Epsom College; First XV. M.B., Ch.B. 1912. Hockey "Blue." R.A.M.C., Lieut. June 1917; Captain June 1918; Major Aug. 1918. No. 1 British General Hospital, Amara, Mesopotamia, and Hamadan, Persia.

RENTON, HORATIO BORROWMAN.
Epsom College; First XV. and XI. Student of Medicine, 1912-17; M.B., Ch.B. 1917. Hockey "Blue." O.T.C. Medical, May 1915 to July 1917, Cadet. R.A.M.C., Lieut. Aug. 1917; Captain Aug. 1918. East Africa.

RENTON, JAMES.
Bathgate Academy. Student of Law, 1918-20. 5th Cameron Highlanders, Private Jan. 1915; 2nd Lieut. March 1917; Lieut. Sept. 1918 to June 1919. Gas Instructor (two months). France Aug. 1915. Invalided home May 1916. France June 1917. Wounded Oct. 1917.

RENTOUL, JOHN LAWRENCE.
M.B., Ch.B. 1900. R.A.M.C., Captain Nov. 1915. 10th General Hospital, St Omer. H.M. Hospital Ship *Britannic*, Dec. 1915; torpedoed Nov. 1917. Med. Exp. Force and France. Dispatches Sept. 1918.

RENWICK, ALEXANDER CAMERON.
M.B., Ch.B. 1898. R.A.M.C., Lieut. April 1915; Captain Oct. 1915. France.

RENWICK, ALEXANDER MACDONALD.
M.A. 1911; B.D. 1913. Minister, U.F. Church of Scotland. Chaplain.

RENWICK, DANIEL.
Fireman, New Buildings. Scottish Horse (T.), Private March 1915. Suvla Bay Sept. 1915; Egypt Dec. 1915. 13th Royal Highlanders (Black Watch), Salonika, Oct. 1916; France June 1918 to March 1919.

REOCH, DOUGLAS JOHNSTON.
Merchiston Castle. O.T.C. 1913-15. University O.T.C. Artillery, May 1917 to Jan. 1918, Cadet. Tank Corps, Private Jan. 1918; Officer Cadet April 1918; 2nd Lieut. Oct. 1918 to Jan. 1919.

REYNARD, ——
M.B., Ch.B. Royal Navy, Fleet-Surgeon.

REYNOLDS, ARTHUR OWEN PLAYFORD.
M.B. Ch.B. 1905. R.A.M.C., Captain Oct. 1915. 1st South Staffordshire Regiment, France. M.C. Aug. 1916.

Record of War Service

REYNOLDS, FRANCIS ESMOND
King Edward VI. High School, Birmingham. M.B., Ch.B. 1908. Assistant to Professor of Pathology, 1911-12. Inns of Court O.T.C., Feb. 1915. Yorkshire Hussars, 2nd Lieut. May; Lieut. July; Captain Dec. 1915. R.A.M.C., Captain Aug. 1917. Salonika, Caucasus, and Asia Minor.

RHYS, OWEN LLEWELLIN.
M.B., Ch.B. 1900; M.D. 1909. R.A.M.C. (T.), Captain March 1913; Lieut.-Col., 2/2nd Welsh Field Ambulance.

RIACH, WILLIAM.
Daniel Stewart's College; First XV. M.B., C.M. 1894; M.D. 1899; D.P.H. 1898. R.A.M.C. 1900. South African Campaign, 1901-2; Major 1912; Lieut.-Col. Sept. 1918; Acting Colonel May 1918 to March 1919; Brevet Colonel June 1919. No. 9 and 74th General Hospitals, and No. 4 Stationary Hospital. France Aug. 1914 to March 1919. Dispatches Dec. 1915 and March 1919. C.M.G. Jan. 1916.

RICE, JOHN PATRICK.
Robert Gordon's College, Aberdeen. Student of Science, 1913-17; B.Sc. 1917; M.R.C.V.S. Royal Army Vet. Corps, Lieut. Nov. 1917; Captain Nov. 1918. Deputy Camel Specialist, Aug. to Dec. 1918. India May 1919.

RICHARDS, EVAN WILLIAMS.
St John's School, Ystradmeurig, and Aberystwith University College. M.B., Ch.B. 1910. R.A.M.C. (T.), Lieut. June 1915; Captain Jan. 1919.

RICHARDS, JOHN KILDAHL.
Ballarat College. M.B., C.M. 1894; M.D. 1897; M.D. (Melb.) 1898. Australian Army Medical Corps, Major Oct. 1915. 2nd and 14th Australian General Hospitals, Cairo, and No. 2 Australian Stationary Hospital, Moascar. S.M.O., Desert Mounted Corps Rest Camp, Port Said.

RICHARDS, SOLOMON HAROLD.
Felsted School. M.B., C.M. 1899; L.R.C.P. & S. (Edin.) and L.F.P.S. (Glasg.) 1896. R.A.M.C., Lieut. Jan. 1916; Captain Jan. 1917 to April 1919. Queen Alexandra Hospital, Millbank, Jan. 1916; Fulham Military Hospital.

RICHARDS, THOMAS EDWARD.
M.B., Ch.B. 1899. R.A.M.C., Quartermaster and Lieut. Aug. 1914; Quartermaster and Captain Aug. 1917.

RICHARDS, WILLIAM GWERNWY.
Aberdare School. Student of Medicine, 1911-16; M.B., Ch.B. 1916. O.T.C. Medical, Nov. 1914-16, Cadet. B.R.C.S. (Dresser), Boulogne, 1914. R.A.M.C. (S.R.), Lieut. Oct. 1916; Captain April 1917.

RICHARDSON, ADAM.
M.B., C.M. 1894; F.R.C.S. (Edin.). R.A.M.C., Captain Jan. 1915. 2nd Northern General Hospital.

Record of War Service

RICHARDSON, ALEXANDER.
Daniel Stewart's College. B.Sc. 1904. Northumberland Fusiliers, 2nd Lieut.

RICHARDSON, DAVID TURNBULL.
M.B., Ch.B. 1910. R.A.M.C., Captain March 1915.

RICHARDSON, GEORGE.
M.B., Ch.B. 1911; M.D. 1913; D.P.H. (Edin.) 1913. R.A.M.C., Lieut.; Captain Dec. 1915; Acting Major Jan. 1918.

RICHARDSON, GEORGE YOUNGER.
M.B., Ch.B. 1906; M.D. 1913; D.P.H. (Edin.) 1910. R.A.M.C., Lieut.; Captain June 1916.

RICHARDSON, HUGH.
Edinburgh Academy; First XV. and XI. M.B., C.M. 1895; M.D. 1903; D.P.H. (St Andrews) 1907. South African Campaign, 1900-2. R.A.M.C. (T.) Major Sept. 1914; Acting Lieut.-Col. Oct. 1915; Acting Colonel May 1917, Scottish Horse Field Ambulance, Gallipoli and Egypt. A.D.M.S., Yeomanry Mounted Division, Palestine, and 4th Cavalry Division, Syria. Dispatches. 1916-17 and 1919. D.S.O. 1918.

RICHARDSON, JOHN.
Student of Law, 1903-5. Solicitor, 1907. 8th Royal Scots (T.), Lieut. Aug. 1914; Captain July 1916. France Nov. 1914 to Aug. 1916, and May 1917 to April 1918. Wounded Aug. 1916 and April 1918.

RICHARDSON, J. FINDLAY.
Student of Medicine, 1886. R.A.M.C., No. 1 Field Ambulance (Sanitary Squadron), Jan. 1916. 53rd Saskatchewan Battn., Corporal March 1916.

RICHARDSON, TOM JENKINSON.
Daniel Stewart's College. Student of Science, 1916. O.T.C. Artillery, Aug. 1917 to May 1918, Cadet. R.F.A., Officer Cadet May 1918 to Jan. 1919.

RICHARDSON, WILLIAM.
M.A. 1882. Schoolmaster. 15th Royal Scots, Private.

RICHMOND, ARCHIBALD HAMILTON DOUGLAS.
Alloa Academy. Student of Medicine, 1918-19. 7th Argyll and Sutherland Highlanders (T.), Private May 1914; Corporal Aug. 1916; 2nd Lieut. Jan. 1917; Lieut. July 1918. 3/1st Highland Field Ambulance. Prisoner of War for eighteen months.

RICHMOND, RALPH LAVERTON.
Durham School; First XI. O.T.C. 1914-16. Student of Law. O.T.C. Artillery, March to Sept. 1916, Cadet Bombardier; Officer Cadet Sept. 1916. R.F.A. (S.R.), 2nd Lieut. Dec. 1916; Lieut. June 1918.

Record of War Service

RICHMOND, THOMAS GUTHRIG.
George Watson's College. Student of Science, 1911-14; B.Sc. 1914. R.E. (T.), City of Dundee (Fortress), Sapper 1914; 2nd Lieut. April 1915; Captain Oct. 1916. 103rd Field Coy., R.E., France. Cambrai and Selle River.

RICKETTS, WILLIAM SYMONDS PERCIVAL.
M.B., C.M. 1886. Indian Medical Service, 1890. Mobilised Nov. 1914; Lieut.-Col. H.M. Hospital Ship *Goorkha*, France, England; Indian General Hospital, Brighton.

RIDDEL, JAMES WILFRID GEORGE HEWAT.
Bath College. O.T.C. 1907-9. Student of Medicine, 1910-15; M.B., Ch.B. 1915. O.T.C. Artillery, Oct. 1911-14, Cadet Acting B.S.M. R.F.A. (T.), 2nd Lieut. Aug. 1914. R.A.M.C. (Regulars), Lieut. July 1915; Temp. Captain Jan. 1916; Captain Jan. 1919; Acting Major 1918-19. France. 1st London Rifle Brigade, 1916-18. D.A.D.M.S., 55th Division, Sept. 1918 to March 1919. The Rhine 1919. M.C. Aug. 1917.

RIDDEL, JOHN ORMOND.
B.Sc. 1908. 17th Northumberland Fusiliers, 2nd Lieut.

RIDDELL, JOHN GERVASE.
Edinburgh Academy. Student of Arts, 1914-15 and 1919-20. O.T.C. Infantry, Oct. 1914 to Aug. 1915, Cadet Sergeant. 11th Gordon Highlanders, 2nd Lieut. Aug. 1915. R.E. (Signal Service), Lieut. May 1916.

RIDDELL, WILLIAM HUNTER.
M.B., Ch.B. 1906. Indian Medical Service, Lieut. 1907; Captain July 1910. Attached 56th Punjab Rifles. Mesopotamia. M.C.

RIDDLE, JAMES SCOTT.
Hawick High School. Student of Medicine, 1918-19. King's Own Scottish Borderers, Private Aug. 1917; L/Corporal Dec. 1917.

RIDDLE, WILLIAM.
Hawick High School; First XV. Student of Arts and Science, 1915-16 and 1918-19. O.T.C. Infantry, Oct. 1915 to June 1916, Cadet. R.F.C., 2nd Air Mechanic, Aug. 1916. Dispatch Rider. France Sept. 1916 to Jan. 1919.

RIDDOCH, JOHN WILLIAM.
George Watson's College. Student of Medicine, 1910-15; M.B., Ch.B. 1915. O.T.C. Medical, Oct. 1914 to July 1915, Cadet. R.A.M.C., Lieut. July 1915; Captain July 1916. Egypt and Salonika; France 1918. M.C. June 1918.

RIPPON, CHARLES SYDNEY URWIN.
Lancing College; First XI. M.B., Ch.B. 1906. R.A.M.C., Lieut. Aug. 1916; Captain Aug. 1917. 2/1st East Anglian Field Ambulance. Egypt and Palestine.

RISSIK, FREDERICK ALTMANN.
M.A. 1913; LL.B. 1914. Royal Fusiliers, 2nd Lieut. Sept. 1914. Northumberland Fusiliers.

Record of War Service

RITCHIE, ANDREW GRAHAM.
   Edinburgh Academy. B.Sc. 1908; M.B., Ch.B. 1910; M.R.C.P. (Edin.) R.A.M.C., Lieut. April 1915; Captain April 1916. 7th Suffolk Regiment. 8th Mobile Laboratory, and A.D.M.S., 12th Division.

RITCHIE, CHARLES DONALDSON.
   Edinburgh Academy; First XV. and XI. O.T.C. 1908-11, Cadet Officer. Student of Medicine, 1911-14. O.T.C. Infantry, 1911-12, Cadet. A.S.C. (T.), Lowland Mounted Brigade, T. and S. Column, 2nd Lieut. 1912; Lieut. Jan. 1915. A.S.C. (Reg.), May 1915; Captain Sept. 1916. Dardanelles 1915-16; Egypt, Salonika, Malta 1916-17; France and The Rhine 1918-19.

RITCHIE, CHARLES RONALD.
   Royal High School. Student of Law, 1906-9. Writer to the Signet, 1911. A.S.C. (T.), 2/1st Lowland Mounted Brigade, T. and S. Column, 2nd Lieut. Sept. 1914; Lieut.; Captain June 1915. Salonika May 1917-19. Greek Order of the Redeemer (Croix de Chevalier) Aug. 1918; Greek Medal of Military Merit, Dec. 1918. Dispatches Nov. 1918 and 1919.

RITCHIE, FREDERICK BARCLAY.
   George Watson's College. Student of Science, 1913-15. O.T.C. Engineers, Oct. 1914 to July 1915, Cadet. R.E. (T.), Highland Division, 2nd Lieut. July 1915; Lieut. June 1916. Transferred to Hants (Fortress) R.E. (T.) Feb. 1917. Staff Lieut., War Office, June 1918. France (two years). Dispatches Dec. 1917.

RITCHIE, JAMES OLIVER.
   George Watson's College. M.A. 1910. Minister, U.F. Church of Scotland. 18th and 11th Royal Scots, Private Jan. 1916; 2nd Lieut. Jan. 1917; Lieut. July 1918. France 1917. Attached 2nd Guides Infantry and 1st Seaforth Highlanders, Egyptian Exp. Force, 1918-19. Wounded in France Dec. 1917.

RITCHIE, JOHN.
   Brechin High School. M.B., Ch.B. 1906; D.P.H. (Edin.) 1907. No. 4 Coy. Q.R.V.B., Royal Scots, 1903-5, Private. R.A.M.C., Lieut. 1917; Captain June 1918. Salonika.

RITCHIE, PATRICK. (See p. 752.)

RITCHIE, ROBERT JEFFREY.
   George Heriot's School. M.A. 1902; B.Sc. 1904. Schoolmaster. George Heriot's School O.T.C. 1909-14, Captain and O.C. 6th and 9th Scottish Rifles (T.), 2nd Lieut. Oct. 1916; Acting Captain March 1917 to Feb. 1918; Lieut. April 1918. Gas Officer Jan. 1917 to Sept. 1918. France April 1918.

RITCHIE, ROBERT LINTON.
   Fettes College. Student of Medicine, 1908-14; M.B., Ch.B. 1914. R.A.M.C. (Reg.), Lieut. April 1915; Captain April 1916; Acting Major and D.A.D.M.S. Sept. 1918 to April 1919. Gallipoli, Egypt, France, and Italy, Oct. 1915 to April 1919. Dispatches March 1919. O.B.E. (Military), June 1919.

Record of War Service

RITCHIE, THOMAS.
Annan Academy; First XV. Student of Medicine, 1916-17. R.E., Sapper Feb. 1917. Royal Air Force, Cadet May 1918; Lieut. Nov. 1918 to March 1919.

RITCHIE, THOMAS CLARK.
Edinburgh Academy. B.Sc. 1909; M.B., Ch.B. 1911; M.D. 1914. R.A.M.C., Lieut. July 1915; Captain July 1916; Acting Major Jan. 1918; Major March 1919. France, 30th Casualty Clearing Station. Médaille d'Honneur des Épidémies en Argent 1916; en Vermeil 1919; Palmes Académiques 1919. Dispatches and O.B.E. (Military) Jan. 1919.

RITCHIE, WILLIAM THOMAS.
George Watson's College. University O.T.C. Artillery, Nov. 1915, Cadet. R.F.A., 1st City of Edinburgh Lowland Brigade, 2nd Lieut. Nov. 1915; Lieut. July 1917; Acting Captain Dec. 1918; Captain Aug. 1919. France 1917-19.

RITCHIE, WILLIAM THOMAS.
M.B., C.M. 1896; M.D. 1899. R.A.M.C. (T.), Captain 1908; Acting Major Jan. 1918. 1/3rd Scottish Horse. Gallipoli and Egypt. Dispatches March 1919. O.B.E. (Military) June 1919.

ROBATHAN, PERCIVAL E.
Student of Law. 17th Welsh Regiment, Captain; Major Jan. 1916. Attached Royal Welsh Fusiliers.

ROBB, DOUGLAS GEORGE.
Blackheath School. Cadet Corps 1900, Sergeant. M.A. (Aberdeen); B.Sc. 1909. A.M.I.C.E. R.E. (Field Coy.), 2nd Lieut. Oct. 1914; Lieut. May 1915; Captain April 1916; Acting Major June 1917; Major May 1918. France Aug. 1915. Dispatches Jan. 1917. M.C. June 1918.

ROBB, HECTOR GEORGE.
Kirkcaldy High School; First XV. O.T.C. 1914-17, Cadet Corporal. University O.T.C. Artillery, Nov. 1917 to Sept. 1918, Cadet Corporal; Officer Cadet Sept. 1918. R.F.A., 2nd Lieut. April 1919.

ROBB, HENRY DRUMMOND.
Dumfries Academy. M.B., Ch.B. 1906; M.D. 1918; D.P.H. (Edin.) 1910. R.A.M.C., Lieut. Aug. 1914; Captain Aug. 1915; Acting Major Sept. 1918. 16th Field Ambulance, France, Aug. 1914. Salonika. M.C. May 1918.

ROBB, IAN ALEXANDER.
Edinburgh Academy. O.T.C. 1914-16, Cadet L/Corporal. University O.T.C. Infantry, Sept. 1916 to Jan. 1917, Cadet; Officer Cadet Jan. 1917. 3rd and 12th Argyll and Sutherland Highlanders, 2nd Lieut. April 1917; Lieut. Oct. 1918. Salonika Nov. 1917 to Jan. 1919.

Record of War Service

ROBB, JOHN JAMES.
: Kemnay School. Student of Medicine, 1915-16 and 1918-19. O.T.C. Artillery, 1915-16, Cadet Corporal. R.F.A., Officer Cadet Dec. 1916; 2nd Lieut. April 1917; Lieut. Oct. 1918. 14th Brigade, R.H.A. France. M.C. Sept. 1918.

ROBB, ROBERT McNAUGHT.
: M.B., Ch.B. 1906. South African Medical Corps, Captain 1916. 1st Battn. Cape Corps.

ROBB, WILLIAM MACKENZIE.
: Blairgowrie High School. Student of Medicine, 1916-17 and 1918-19. O.T.C. Infantry, 1917; Medical, 1918, Cadet; Officer Cadet Oct. 1917.

ROBERTS, ERNEST THEOPHILUS.
: M.B., C.M. 1886; M.D. 1889; D.P.H. (Camb.) 1911; F.R.F.P.S. (Glasg.) 1918. R.A.M.C., Lieut. May 1915; Captain May 1916. President, Travelling Medical Board, Scottish Command, 1918.

ROBERTS, HUGH NORMAN McLAREN.
: Edinburgh Academy. O.T.C. 1912-14. University O.T.C. Artillery, Jan. to May 1917, Cadet. R.F.C., Officer Cadet May 1917; 2nd Lieut. Aug. 1917 to April 1919. Egypt Sept. 1917 to March 1919.

ROBERTS, THOMAS ERNEST.
: Edinburgh Institution. M.B., Ch.B. 1906; M.D. 1909. Resident Physician, R.I.E. No. 4 Coy. Q.R.V.B., Royal Scots. R.A.M.C. (T.), Lieut. Feb. 1915; Captain. Highland Mounted Brigade Field Ambulance and 1/1st Lovat Scouts. Gallipoli and Egypt. Wounded at Suvla Bay Sept. 1915.

ROBERTSON, ALEXANDER.
: Bathgate Academy. B.A. (Hons. Lond.); M.A. 1900. 3rd Cameron Highlanders, Private April 1917. A.S.C., 2nd Lieut. Sept. 1917. 51st Divisional Train, France.

ROBERTSON, ALEXANDER FORD.
: Edinburgh Academy. O.T.C. 1915-16. Student of Science, 1916 and 1919. O.T.C. Artillery, May 1917 to April 1918, Cadet; Officer Cadet April 1918. R.F.A. (S.R.), 2nd Lieut. Feb. 1919.

ROBERTSON, ANDREW.
: George Watson's College. O.T.C. 1909-12, Cadet L/Corporal. Student of Medicine, 1912-17; M.B., Ch.B. 1917. O.T.C. Infantry, Nov. 1912 to April 1918, Cadet C.S.M. R.A.M.C. (S.R.), Lieut. April 1918; Captain April 1919.

ROBERTSON, ANDREW.
: Academy, Newcastle-on-Tyne. M.A. 1882; M.B., C.M. 1888; Rugby and Cricket "Blue." R.A.M.C., Major May 1918. St Luke's War Hospital, Halifax.

ROBERTSON, ANDREW DEAS.
: M.A. 1909. Schoolmaster. 95th Coy., Special Service, V.B. Lowland Brigade, Private June 1918 to Aug. 1919. Recruiting Office, Edinburgh.

Record of War Service

ROBERTSON, ARCHIBALD HECTOR MACCOLL.
Oban High School. M.B., Ch.B. 1907. No. 4 Coy. Q.R.V.B., Royal Scots, 1905-7, Private. R.A.M.C., Lieut. Dec. 1914; Captain Dec. 1915; Major March 1918. Med. Exp. Force, May to Aug. 1915. France May to Sept. 1916.

ROBERTSON, ATHOLL.
Daniel Stewart's College. Student of Medicine, 1911-17; M.B., Ch.B. 1917; M.D. 1920. O.T.C. Infantry, 1912-14, and Medical, 1916, 2nd Lieut. London Scottish (T.), Private Aug. 1914. R.N.V.R., Surgeon-Probationer, Sept. 1915. R.A.M.C. (S.R.), Lieut. May 1917; Captain May 1918. France Jan. 1915; East Africa May 1917; German and Portuguese East Africa. Dispatches Feb. 1919. M.C.

ROBERTSON, CHARLES.
James Gillespie's School. M.A. 1910. Schoolmaster. R.E., Corporal Aug. 1915; Officer Cadet.

ROBERTSON, CHARLES.
Doveton College, Madras. B.A. (Madras). Student of Medicine, 1904-7 and 1916-18; M.B., Ch.B. 1907; M.D. 1917. No. 4 Coy. Q.R.V.B., Royal Scots, 1904-7, L/Corporal. R.A.M.C., Lieut. Sept. 1915. 3rd North Midland Field Ambulance, France.

ROBERTSON, CHARLES JOHN.
Harris Academy, Dundee. Student of Science, 1918-19. Royal Air Force, 3rd Air Mechanic, July 1918.

ROBERTSON, DAVID.
Daniel Stewart's College. M.B., Ch.B. (Hons.) 1907. R.A.M.C., Lieut. Jan. 1918-19.

ROBERTSON, DAVID GORDON.
George Watson's College. Student of Medicine, 1913-16 and 1918-19. R.N.V.R., Surgeon Sub-Lieut. May 1917.

ROBERTSON, DOUGLAS SWAN.
Trinity Academy, Leith. M.A. 1909; M.B., Ch.B. 1913. R.A.M.C., Lieut. Jan. 1916; Captain Jan. 1917. 1st Essex Regiment and 62nd Field Ambulance, France. Wounded Aug. 1917. M.C. Sept. 1917.

ROBERTSON, DOUGLAS WILLIAM.
George Watson's College. O.T.C. 1911-16, Cadet Sergeant. University O.T.C. Infantry, 1916-17, Cadet Corporal; Officer Cadet June 1917. 1st King's Royal Rifles, 2nd Lieut. Sept. 1917. France 1918. Wounded Aug. 1918. Dispatches. D.S.O.; M.C.

ROBERTSON, DUNCAN GLENEROCHIE.
Brighton Grammar School, Australia. M.B., Ch.B. 1909; M.D. 1912; D.P.H. 1911. Freeland Barbour Fellow, 1910. O.T.C. Medical, 1906-12, Cadet Sergeant. South African Campaign, 1902. Australian Army Medical Corps, Captain July 1915.

Record of War Service

ROBERTSON, ERIC A.
Broughton School, Edinburgh. Student of Medicine, 1919. Lothians and Border Horse, Private, Nov. 1914. 9th Royal Scots, Corporal April 1917. France. Prisoner of War April 1917 to December 1918.

ROBERTSON, ERNEST.
Auckland Grammar School, New Zealand. M.B., C.M. 1885; M.D. 1887. N.Z. Medical Corps, Captain Dec. 1915. N.Z. Exp. Force in Europe, Feb. 1916 to Aug. 1919.

ROBERTSON, GEORGE HENRY WHITESIDE.
George Watson's College. M.A. 1893; M.B., C.M. 1898; M.D. 1913. South African Medical Corps, Captain; Major. German West and German East Africa. The Castle, Cape Town. Dispatches. O.B.E.

ROBERTSON, HARRY FERGUSON.
Bathgate Academy. Student of Science, 1914-15. O.T.C. Engineers, Nov. 1914 to May 1915, Cadet. R.E. (T.), 1st Field Coy., Highland Division, 2nd Lieut. May 1915; Lieut. June 1916; Acting Captain Jan. 1919. France.

ROBERTSON, HECTOR ERIC.
Royal High School; First XV. Student of Science, 1917 and 1919. O.T.C. Infantry, May to Nov. 1917, Cadet; Officer Cadet Nov. 1917. 7th Gordon Highlanders, 2nd Lieut. May 1918. M.C. March 1919.

ROBERTSON, IAN MONRO.
Edinburgh Institution; First XV. Cadet Corps 1911-14, Sergeant. Student of Medicine, 1918-19. 9th and 2nd Royal Scots (T.), 2nd Lieut. Oct. 1914; Temp. Lieut. July 1915; Temp. Captain June 1916; Lieut. July 1917. Attached R.E. (Signals), Jan. 1918-19. France.

ROBERTSON, JAMES.
Student of Arts. 11th Royal Scots, Lieut.; Captain.

ROBERTSON, JAMES ANDREW.
Tain Royal Academy. Student of Medicine, 1917-19. R.H.A. and R.F.A., Gunner June 1916; 2nd Lieut. Feb. 1917; Lieut. Aug. 1918.

ROBERTSON, JAMES PHILIP LOGIE.
George Watson's College. Student of Law, 1905-7. Chartered Accountant, 1908. R.F.A., 33rd Battery, Gunner Aug. 1917. 89th Battery, Khyber Pass. Indian Garrison Duty and N.-W. Frontier Operations, 1917-19.

ROBERTSON, JAMES WILLIAM.
Kirkcudbright Academy. M.A. 1890. Minister, U.F. Church of Scotland. Officiating Clergyman, Reigate, Surrey, Dec. 1916 to March 1917. Y.M.C.A. Work, Ypres, May to Oct. 1917. Chaplain, 4th Class, Dec. 1917. Salonika Dec. 1917; Macedonia, Constantinople, and Baku.

Record of War Service

ROBERTSON, JOHN.
    George Heriot's School. M.A., B.Sc. 1906. Baxter and Tait Research Scholar. 16th Royal Scots, Private Nov. 1914; Corporal. R.E. (Special Brigade), Corporal June 1915. Research Department, Royal Arsenal, Woolwich, April 1917.

ROBERTSON, JOHN.
    M.B., C.M. 1884; B.Sc. (P.H.) 1889; M.D. 1887. Professor of Public Health, Birmingham University. R.A.M.C., 1887; Lieut.-Col.; Temp. Hon. Lieut.-Col., Oct. 1914. Sanitary Officer, South Midland Division (T.). 2nd V.B. South Lancashire Regiment. Army Sanitary Committee. Dispatches (four times). C.M.G.; O.B.E.

ROBERTSON, JOHN HENRY MENZIES.
    Berkhampstead and Glenalmond. Student of Law, 1898-1900. Chartered Accountant, 1902. 15th Royal Scots, Sept. 1914; C.Q.M.S. to Feb. 1919. France Jan. 1916 to Nov. 1918.

ROBERTSON, JOHN KEITH GRANT.
    Student of Medicine, 1912-14. R.A.M.C., Driver. A.S.C., Lieut. Royal Air Force. France.

ROBERTSON, JOHN SHERWOOD.
    George Watson's College. Student of Arts and Science, 1913-14. O.T.C. Infantry, 1913-14, Cadet. 12th Argyll and Sutherland Highlanders, 2nd Lieut. Sept. 1914; Lieut. May 1915. Instructor, Scottish Command School of Musketry, 1917-18. France 1916-17 and 1918.

ROBERTSON, MICHAEL WILLIAM.
    M.B., Ch.B. 1901; D.P.H. R.A.M.C., Lieut.; Major. M.C. Dispatches.

ROBERTSON, MILES KENNETH.
    Cheltenham. Student of Medicine, 1909-10; M.R.C.S. (Eng.); L.R.C.P. (Lond.) 1916. R.A.M.C. (T.), 3rd London Field Ambulance, Private Aug. 1914; Hon. Lieut. April 1916; Lieut. July 1916; Captain July 1917. Mesopotamian Field Force, 1916. Station Hospital, Roorkee, India, 1917-19.

ROBERTSON, RICHARD NELSON.
    Annan Academy. Student of Arts and Law, 1912-14 and 1919; M.A. 1919; LL.B. 1920. 9th Royal Scots (T.), Private May 1913; Corporal 1915. 8th King's Own Scottish Borderers, 2nd Lieut. March 1916. Transferred R.E. May 1916; Lieut. 1917. France Feb. 1915-19.

ROBERTSON, ROBERT.
    George Heriot's School. Student of Arts; M.A. 1910. 9th Highland Light Infantry (T.), 2nd Lieut. Royal Air Force, Lieut.

ROBERTSON, ROBERT.
    Dunfermline High School. Student of Arts, 1910-15; M.A. (Hons. Classics) 1914. Bruce of Grangehill and Falkland Classical Scholar. O.T.C. Artillery, 1914-15, Cadet. 1st Lowland Brigade, R.F.A. (T.), Jan. 1915, Bombardier. North Russia.

Record of War Service

ROBERTSON, ROBERT BRUCE.
George Watson's College. O.T.C. 1907-10. Student of Arts and Science, 1910-15; B.Sc. 1913; M.A. 1915. A.M.I.C.E. 1918. O.T.C. Engineers, 1910-13, Cadet. R.E. (T.), Edinburgh Fortress, Sapper Jan. 1916; 2nd Lieut. June 1917; Temp. Lieut. Dec. 1918. France Dec. 1918.

ROBERTSON, ROBERT WILLIAM.
Perth Academy. Student of Arts, 1914-15. O.T.C. Artillery, March to July 1915, Cadet. R.F.A. (T.), 2/1st Lowland Brigade, 2nd Lieut. July 1915; Lieut. June 1916. France Aug. 1917 to June 1919. 15th Divisional Artillery.

ROBERTSON, RONALD MACDONALD.
Edinburgh Academy. O.T.C. 1914-16. Student of Law, 1919. O.T.C. Artillery, Jan. to Aug. 1917, Cadet; Officer Cadet Aug. 1917. R.G.A. (T.), 20th (Forth) Fire Command, 2nd Lieut. March 1918.

ROBERTSON, STUART.
Daniel Stewart's College. M.A. 1893. Minister, U.F. Church of Scotland. Shell Worker. Y.M.C.A., France. Chaplain Dec. 1917.

ROBERTSON, THOMAS ROBERT.
M.B., Ch.B. 1900. R.A.M.C., Lieut.; Captain Dec. 1917. France.

ROBERTSON, WALTER BELL.
M.A. 1911; (Hons. Engl. 1920). Schoolmaster. O.T.C. Artillery, Feb. 1910 to Jan. 1913, Cadet. Ayrshire R.H.A. (T.), 2nd Lieut.; Lieut. June 1916.

ROBERTSON, WILLIAM.
Dollar Academy; First XV. and XI. M.B., C.M. 1893; M.D. 1905. R.A.M.C., Lieut. Jan. 1918; Captain Jan. 1919.

ROBERTSON, WILLIAM ALBERT.
High School and University College, Dundee. M.B., Ch.B. 1907. R.A.M.C. (T.), Lieut. Sept. 1914; Captain April 1915; Acting Major Jan. 1918. Durham R.G.A. (Hartlepool). France Sept. 1915 to Dec. 1918, 50th Divisional Artillery; 2/2nd Northumbrian Field Ambulance. Dispatches Jan. 1917. M.C. April 1919.

ROBERTSON, WILLIAM GEORGE AITCHISON.
Edinburgh Institution. M.B., C.M. 1887; B.Sc. (P.H.) 1889; M.D. 1890; D.Sc. (P.H.) 1892; F.R.C.P. (Edin.) 1891. Examiner, Edinburgh University. R.A.M.C. (V.), 2nd Lieut. Jan. 1915; Major June 1918.

ROBERTSON, WILLIAM JAMES DUNLOP.
Glasgow High School. M.B., Ch.B. 1904. R.A.M.C., Lieut. Aug. 1915; Captain Aug. 1916. 135th Field Ambulance.

ROBERTSON, WILLIAM JOHN.
Robert Gordon's College, Aberdeen. M.B., Ch.B. 1913. R.A.M.C., Lieut. July 1915; Acting Captain June 1918; Captain Jan. 1919. France.

Record of War Service

ROBERTSON, WILLIAM KERR.
Trinity Academy, Leith. B.Sc. 1913. R.E., 2nd Lieut. Sept. 1917; Lieut. March 1919. Inland Waterways and Docks, Mesopotamia. Dispatches Feb. 1919.

ROBERTSON, WILLIAM LATTO.
M.A. (St Andrews); M.B., Ch.B. 1905; F.R.C.S. (Edin.) 1907. R.A.M.C. (T.), Lieut. 1910; Captain April 1914; Acting Major Jan. 1918; Acting Lieut.-Col. June 1918. 3rd Highland Field Ambulance. Dispatches Jan. 1917. M.C. Jan. 1918.

ROBERTSON, WILLIAM MARSDEN FORD.
Edinburgh Academy. O.T.C. 1915-16. Student of Medicine, 1918-19. O.T.C. Artillery, 1917-18, Cadet. R.F.A., Officer Cadet May 1918; 2nd Lieut. Feb. 1919.

ROBERTSON, WILLIAM STEWART IRVINE.
M.B., Ch.B. 1907. R.A.M.C., Lieut.; Captain June 1917.

ROBERTSON-DURHAM, JAMES ALEXANDER.
Edinburgh Academy; First XV. and XI. B.A. (Oxford). Student of Law, 1909-12. Chartered Accountant, 1913. 9th Gordon Highlanders, Captain Sept. 1914. British War Mission in U.S.A., 1917-18. O.B.E. (Military) June 1918.

ROBINSON, GEORGE ALLEN.
Teviot Grove Academy, Hawick. Student of Science, 1911-15; B.Sc. 1915. R.F.A., 2nd Lieut. June 1915; Lieut. Nov. 1915; Adjutant Jan. 1916; Captain June 1917. 3/1st Lowland Field Artillery Depôt and No. 5 Artillery Training School. Transferred R.E. (T.), Lowland Division, Nov. 1918. France.

ROBINSON, EDWARD.
Student of Medicine, 1913-14. R.F.A., 14th Brigade, 2nd Lieut.; Lieut. July 1917.

ROBINSON, JOHN.
Grosvenor College, Carlisle. Student of Medicine, 1912-15 and 1917-19. O.T.C. Infantry, 1914-15, Cadet. R.N.V.R., Surgeon Sub-Lieut. Sept. 1915 to Jan. 1918. H.M. Ships *Nemesis*, *Magic*, and *Defender*. Jutland Battle, May 1916.

ROBINSON, LEONARD NICHOLAS.
Malvern College. M.B., C.M. 1893; M.D. 1898; M.D. (Paris) 1899. Volunteer Medical Staff Corps, 1888-93, Private. R.A.M.C., Hon. Lieut.-Col. June 1915. President, Paris Branch B.R.C.S., Sept. 1914. Dispatches May 1917. C.B.E. March 1920. Chevalier de la Légion d'Honneur, Oct. 1920.

ROBINSON, WILLIAM HUGH.
Student of Medicine, 1903-9. O.T.C. Artillery, Oct. 1908 to May 1910. R.F.A., 87th Battery, 2nd Lieut. 1910; Lieut.; Captain Aug. 1916. France 1914; Russia.

ROBISON, HARRY JACKSON.
Student of Law, 1904-6. Chartered Accountant, 1910. 15th Royal Scots, Private Oct. 1914; 2nd Lieut. July 1915; Lieut. Oct. 1916. Wounded and taken Prisoner Aug. 1918.

Record of War Service

ROBSON, GEORGE.
Royal High School. Student of Medicine, 1918-19. 2/1st Scottish Horse (T.), Private Oct. 1916; L/Corporal.

ROBSON, WILLIAM GORDON.
Daniel Stewart's College; First XV. Student of Arts and Medicine, 1911-15 and 1917-19; M.A. 1915; M.B., Ch.B. 1919. O.T.C. Infantry, Oct. 1911 to Dec. 1914. Cadet L/Corporal. R.N.V.R., H.M.S. *Himalaya*, Surgeon-Probationer, April 1916. Zanzibar Government Hospital, Aug. to Nov. 1916.

RODGER, ALEXANDER.
Edinburgh Academy. M.B., C.M. 1894. Lothians and Border Horse, 1897. Mobilised Aug. 1914. Squadron Sergeant-Major. R.A.M.C. (T.), Lieut. Feb. 1915; Captain Aug. 1915; Acting Major Oct. 1918. 334th Field Ambulance.

RODGER, JOHN.
Ayr Academy; First XV. Student of Medicine, 1910-15; M.B., Ch.B. 1915. O.T.C. Artillery, 1912-15, Cadet. R.A.M.C., Lieut. July 1915; Captain July 1916; Major Jan. 1918. Transferred to Indian Medical Service, 1920. 1/3rd Northumbrian Field Ambulance. Egypt Sept. 1915. 19th Casualty Clearing Station, France, March 1917 to Dec. 1919. M.C. March 1918; Bar to M.C. Nov. 1918.

RODGER, JOHN MURRAY.
East London Technical College. Student of Arts, 1896-9 and 1906-10. Chaplain, 4th Class (Temp.), Aug. 1914; 3rd Class Jan. 1917; 4th Class Sept. 1917. Aldershot, 11th (Northern Division), Guards Depôt. France and The Rhine. 23rd, 32nd, and 64th Casualty Clearing Stations. 8th Labour Corps and No. 5 Convalescent Depôt. Dispatches Jan. 1916.

RODGER, ROBERT JAMES.
Ayr Academy. O.T.C. 1911-16, Cadet Sergeant. Student of Medicine, 1918-19. 12th Argyll and Sutherland Highlanders, Private Feb. 1916. Macedonia 1916-18; Russia Nov. 1918 to March 1919. Wounded in Macedonia May 1917.

RODGER, ROBERT STUART.
M.B., C.M. 1895; D.P.H. Barrister-at-Law, Gray's Inn. R.A.M.C., South African Campaign, 1899-1901; Captain 1902; Major 1915.

ROE, ROBERT LLOYD.
Ranelagh School, Athlone; First XV. M.B., C.M. 1895. Cert. Trop. Med. and Hygiene. South African Campaign, 1900-2; West African Medical Staff, 1904; West African Campaign, 1906. R.A.M.C., Lieut. Aug. 1914; Captain Aug. 1915. Royal Air Force Medical Service, Captain Oct. 1918; Major May 1919. France 1914; Greece; South Russia (Caspian) 1919; Constantinople.

ROGER, GEORGE ALEXANDER.
Student of Arts and Law, 1910-14; M.A. 1914. Royal Naval Air Service and Royal Air Force, Mechanic, Oct. 1915.

Record of War Service

ROGERS, CECIL DERMOT.
  M.B., Ch.B. 1913. R.A.M.C., Lieut. March 1915; Captain Oct. 1915.

ROGERS, CHARLES DAVID.
  Perth Academy. Cadet Corps 1914-17. Student of Arts and Science, 1918-19. 2/2nd Scottish Horse (T.), Private March 1917. Signalling Corporal May 1918.

ROGERS, CHRISTOPHER.
  Sandringham School, Southport. M.B., Ch.B. 1911. R.A.M.C., Lieut. May 1915; Captain Dec. 1915. M.C.

ROGERS, EDMUND THOMAS.
  Royal High School. Student of Medicine, 1914. Northumberland Fusiliers, Private March 1916; Officer Cadet Jan. 1917; 2nd Lieut. June 1917; Lieut. Dec. 1918 to May 1919.

ROGERS, JAMES SAMUEL YEAMAN.
  Dundee Institution and Stanley House, Bridge of Allan. M.B., C.M. 1890. Lecturer, Diseases of Children, St Andrews University. R.A.M.C. (V.) and (T.), 1895; Major 1907; Lieut.-Col. June 1916. 4th Royal Highlanders (Black Watch) (T.). France. T.D. 1915; D.S.O. Jan 1916 and Bar July 1917. Croix de Guerre with Palm July 1918. Associate, St John of Jerusalem.

ROGERS, PHILIP G.
  Dunfermline High School. Student of Arts, 1919. O.T.C. Artillery, Aug. 1917 to April 1918, Cadet. Royal Air Force, Cadet April 1918; Flight Cadet Sept. 1918; Pilot March 1919.

ROGERS, RICHARD SANDERS.
  M.A. (Adelaide) 1897; M.B., C.M. 1887; M.D. 1893. Lecturer, Forensic Medicine, Adelaide University. South African Campaign, 1901. Australian Army Medical Service (Reserve), Major 1909; Lieut.-Col. July 1915. 7th Australian General Hospital, Adelaide, 1915.

ROGERS, WILLIAM.
  St Olave's Grammar School, London. M.B., Ch.B. 1900; M.D. 1911. South African Campaign, 1900-1. R.A.M.C. (T.), Western Command, 1913, Lieut.; Captain Feb. 1915. 5th Cheshire Regiment, France, 1915. East Lancashire Field Ambulance, Gallipoli, 1915-16. 42nd Ammunition Column, Egypt, 1916. 4th Lancashire Fusiliers. R.E. (I.W.T.), 1917. Wounded at Ypres May 1915.

ROLLAND, RALPH ARNOLD.
  Glasgow Academy; First XV. and XI. O.T.C. 1915-17. University O.T.C. Artillery, 1917, Cadet; Officer Cadet Jan. 1918. R.G.A., 2nd Lieut. Aug. 1918.

ROMANES, ARCHIBALD.
  M.A. 1907; M.B., Ch.B. 1912; M.D. 1919. No. 4 Coy. Q.R.V.B., Royal Scots, 1906-8. O.T.C. Infantry, Oct. 1908-11, Cadet Colour-Sergeant. R.A.M.C. (T.), Lieut. June 1915; Captain Dec. 1915. 1st London Sanitary Coy. 58th Sanitary Section, France, Jan. 1917 to March 1919.

Record of War Service

ROMANES, GEORGE.
: Edinburgh Academy. B.Sc. 1905. A.M.I.C.E. Assistant, Engineering Department, 1906-8. No. 4 Coy. Q.R.V.B., Royal Scots, 1902-5, Private. Chief Engineer, H.M. Factory, Craigleith. R.E., Captain July 1917.

ROMANES, JOHN HYSLOP.
: George Watson's College. B.L. 1893. Writer to the Signet, 1894. Royal Defence Corps, 211th Protection Coy., Lieut. July 1915. Prisoners of War Camp, Oldcastle, Co. Meath, 1915-17. 2/1st V.B. Royal Scots, Lieut. May 1917.

RONN, HENRY ALBERT.
: Malvern College. M.B., Ch.B. 1913. R.A.M.C., Lieut. Sept. 1914; Captain Sept. 1915. Dispatches 1915 and 1918. M.C. 1918.

RORIE, DAVID.
: Aberdeen Collegiate School. M.B., C.M. 1890; M.D. 1908; D.P.H. (Hons. Aberdeen) 1911. R.A.M.C. (T.), Lieut. 1903; Captain; Major Aug. 1914; Temp. Lieut.-Col. Jan. 1916; Temp. Col. Dec. 1917; Brevet Lieut.-Col. Dec. 1918. France. 1/2nd Highland Field Ambulance. A.D.M.S., 51st (Highland) Division. Dispatches May 1917 and Dec. 1918. D.S.O. June 1917. Chevalier de la Légion d'Honneur, March 1919. Associate, St John of Jerusalem. T.D.

RORIE, GEORGE ARTHUR.
: Dundee High School. M.B., Ch.B. 1898; M.D. 1906; D.P.H. Surgeon, Red Cross Hospital. R.A.M.C., Captain 1917-19. Egypt.

RORKE, OLIVER.
: Sabsian College. Student of Science, 1918. R.E., Aug. 1914; Corporal 1914; Sergeant 1915; Lieut. 1917. France 1914-18.

ROSA, LEWIS GEORGE.
: Daniel Stewart's College. Student of Medicine, 1916-17. O.T.C. Infantry, 1916-17, Cadet. 1/10th (Cyclists) Royal Scots, Private Feb. 1917 to Sept. 1918.

ROSE, ÆNEAS.
: Royal High School. M.A. (Hons. Mental Phil.) 1898; M.B., Ch.B. 1906. No. 4 Coy. Q.R.V.B., Royal Scots, 1902-6, Private. Royal Navy, Surgeon-Lieut., Nov. 1914. Haslar Hospital, 1914; Dartmouth, 1915. H.M.S. *Cumberland*, N. American and W. Indies Cruiser Squadron, 1917-18; H.M.S. *Almanzara*.

ROSE, FRASER MACINTOSH.
: Nicolson Institute, Stornoway. Student of Medicine, 1918. R.G.A., Ross Mountain Battery, Gunner Aug. 1914.

ROSE, HUGH.
: Leys School, Cambridge; First XV. Student of Law, 1898-1900. Chartered Accountant, 1902. 5th V.B., 7th and 2/7th Royal Scots (T.), 2nd Lieut. 1897; Captain 1912. France. Wounded March 1918. Mention Oct. 1916.

Record of War Service

ROSEBERY, SYDNEY SOLOMON.
Sydney Grammar School and University, New South Wales. Student of Medicine, 1912-17; M.B., Ch.B. 1917. O.T.C. Medical, 1915-17, Cadet. R.A.M.C., Lieut. Jan. 1918; Captain Jan. 1919. Egypt. Dispatches June 1919.

ROSS, ALEXANDER.
North Berwick High School. Cadet Corps 1908-13, Sergeant. Student of Arts, 1913-14 and 1919. 8th Royal Scots (T.) 1913. L/Corporal; Acting Interpreter. France Nov. 1914 to Feb. 1919.

ROSS, ALEXANDER.
Nicolson Institute, Stornoway. O.T.C. 1914-15, 2nd Lieut. Student of Arts and Divinity, 1912-14 and 1919; M.A. 1919. R.F.A., 9th Division, 2nd Lieut. Oct. 1914; Lieut. Jan. 1916; Acting Captain Aug. 1917.

ROSS, ANDREW CLAIR.
Selkirk High School; First XV. and XI. Student of Medicine, 1917-19. Royal Air Force, Cadet Pilot, July 1918; 2nd Lieut. Dec. 1918.

ROSS, ANDREW McKENZIE.
Larchfield and Glasgow High School. Student of Medicine, 1919. R.N.V.R., April 1918, Ord. Telegraphist July 1918; Telegraphist Sept. 1918.

ROSS, ANDREW OLIVER.
Perth Academy and George Watson's College; First XI. Student of Medicine, 1912-17; M.B., Ch.B. 1917. O.T.C. Infantry, Sept. 1914 to March 1915, Cadet. R.N.V.R., Surgeon-Probationer, March 1915 to April 1916. Royal Navy, Surgeon, July 1917. Royal Naval Hospital, Portland. North Sea; Atlantic.

ROSS, ANDREW RUSSELL.
George Watson's College and Loretto. First XV. M.B., Ch.B. 1914. First XV. O.T.C. Medical, 1914, Cadet. R.A.M.C., Lieut. Nov. 1914; Captain May 1918. Gallipoli, Egypt, and East Africa. Dispatches (East Africa).

ROSS, ARTHUR ALEXANDER.
Student of Law, 1903-5. S.S.C., 1908. 9th Royal Scots (T.), Private Sept. 1914; L/Corporal May 1915; Sergeant May 1918. M.S.M. Jan. 1918.

ROSS, CHARLES WILLIAM GRAY.
Student of Law, 1908-10. R.G.A. (Cornwall), Gunner Dec. 1915; Bombardier April 1918.

ROSS, DAVID.
Student of Law. 4th Cameron Highlanders, Major June 1916; Brigade Major.

ROSS, DAVID.
Thurso Academy. M.A. 1914. Schoolmaster. 4th Royal Scots (T.), Private Aug. 1914; L/Corporal. 4th, 10th, and 7th Seaforth Highlanders, 2nd Lieut. Feb. 1915; Lieut. Feb. 1916; Captain Sept. 1918 to March 1919. France, Sept. 1915 to March 1919.

Record of War Service

ROSS, DERMID MAXWELL.
Dumfries Academy. M.B., Ch.B. 1909. No. 4 Coy. Q.R.V.B., Royal Scots, 1905-7, L/Corporal. Red Cross and V.A.D., 1915-17. R.A.M.C., Lieut. May 1917; Captain May 1918; Acting Major Oct. 1919.

ROSS, DONALD.
Dollar Academy. M.B., Ch.B. 1908. University Battery, E.C.A.V., 1902-8, Sergeant. O.T.C. Artillery, 1908-14, Cadet. R.A.M.C., Lieut. April 1916; Captain April 1917. France. No. 12 General Hospital, Rouen. No. 11 Stationary Hospital. 5th Cavalry Division, 13th Brigade, R.H.A. Secunderabad Indian Cavalry Field Ambulance and Lord Derby War Hospital.

ROSS, DONALD MARS MORPHETT.
M.B., C.M. 1888. R.A.M.C., Lieut. Aug. 1916. Military Hospital, Winchester.

ROSS, FRANK.
M.B., Ch.B. 1906. West African Medical Staff, Captain. Cameroons Exp. Force, Southern Nigeria.

ROSS, GEORGE ARCHIBALD PARK.
M.B., Ch.B. 1901; D.P.H. (Edin.) 1902; M.D. 1908. South African Medical Corps, Captain Nov. 1914; Major Dec. 1916. Sanitation Officer and Officer in charge of Sleeping Sickness Quarantine.

ROSS, GEORGE HUGH.
Tarbat School, Ross-shire. M.A. 1913. Schoolmaster. R.G.A., 239th Siege Battery, Private June 1916; Corporal.

ROSS, GEORGE ROBERT THOMSON.
Arbroath High School. M.A. 1897; D. Phil. Rangoon Vol. Rifles, Private Dec. 1914. Indian Defence Force (I.A.R.O.), 2nd Lieut. April 1918.

ROSS, GILBERT MATHESON.
Tain Royal Academy. Student of Medicine, 1917 and 1919. O.T.C. Artillery, Sept. 1917-18, Cadet. R.G.A., Officer Cadet Sept. 1918.

ROSS, JAMES ALEXANDER.
Perth Academy; First XI. M.A. (St Andrews); M.B., Ch.B. 1903. R.A.M.C., Lieut. May 1917; Captain May 1918. Macedonia and Italy.

ROSS, JAMES GILLON.
University College School. M.B., C.M. 1898. Volunteer Medical Staff Corps, 1893-8, Sergeant. Surgeon, West African Frontier Force, Northern Nigeria, 1899-1900. R.A.M.C., Lieut. April 1916. 31st Northumberland Fusiliers, Malta.

ROSS, JAMES NESS MacBEAN.
Fettes College. M.B., Ch.B. 1912; M.D. 1914; F.R.C.S. 1918. O.T.C. Artillery, Oct. 1908 to July 1910, Cadet. Royal Navy, Surgeon, Aug. 1914. H.M.S. *Mars* and 2nd Battn. Royal Marine Light Infantry. Twice Wounded. Twice Mentioned in Dispatches 1917. M.C. July 1917; Bar to M.C. Jan. 1918.

Record of War Service

ROSS, JAMES PAULL.
  M.A. 1902. Writer to Signet, 1909. 5th Royal Scots (T.), Captain Feb. 1914. Gold Coast, April 1913.

ROSS, JOHN.
  M.B., C.M. 1886; M.D. 1895. R.A.M.C., Captain Dec. 1915.

ROSS, JOHN DONALD.
  George Heriot's School. M.A. 1911. Schoolmaster. R.E., Aug. 1915, Sergeant.

ROSS, JOHN HERBERT.
  George Watson's College; First XI. Cadet Corps 1904-6. M.A. 1913. Probationer, U.F. Church. O.T.C. Infantry, Oct. 1914 to May 1915, Cadet. R.A.M.C., Private March 1918. 2nd London General Hospital, and 40th British Field Ambulance, Baku. South Russia.

ROSS, JOHN MACDONALD.
  Warrender Park School, Edinburgh. M.B., Ch.B. 1906; D.P.H. (Edin.) 1909. R.A.M.C., Lieut. Feb. 1916; Captain Feb. 1917. Mesopotamia, India, and France.

ROSS, JOHN ROSS HOME.
  M.B., C.M. 1886; F.R.C.P. (Edin.) 1890. R.A.M.C., Lieut. April 1915; Captain April 1916. Royal Herbert Hospital, Woolwich, 1915. Dispatches Sept. 1917.

ROSS, NORMAN HAMILTON.
  George Watson's College. M.B., C.M. 1896. R.A.M.C., 1898. South African Campaign, 1899-1900; Lieut.-Col. March 1915. India 1913-19.

ROSS, RICHARD.
  Kingswood College, Grahamstown, South Africa. First XV. O.T.C. 1908-13. Cadet Corporal. Student of Medicine, 1918-19. 2/1st Lothians and Border Horse, Private; L/Corporal. Machine-Gun Corps.

ROSS, RICHARD ADOLPHUS.
  Foyle and Magee Colleges, Londonderry. M.B., C.M. 1894; M.D. 1906. Volunteer Medical Staff Corps, 1891-4, Private. Royal Navy, Surgeon 1895; Surgeon-Commander, H.M.S. *Diana*, Cruiser Force, Aug. 1914 to Dec. 1915; H.M.S. *Conqueror*, 1916-17. Battle of Jutland. R.N.A.S. and Royal Air Force, 1917-18, and Admiralty Recruiting Department, 1918-19. Surgeon-Captain July 1920.

ROSS, ROBERT.
  Perth Academy. M.A. (Hons. Mental Phil.) 1909. Minister, U.F. Church of Scotland. R.G.A., 529th Siege Battery, Private May 1917; Signaller.

ROSS, ROBERT B.
  Dingwall Academy. Student of Arts, 1911-14. M.A. 1914. O.T.C. Infantry, Jan. 1912 to Sept. 1914, Cadet L/Corporal. 7th Gordon Highlanders (T.), 2nd Lieut. Sept. 1914; Lieut.; Captain Oct. 1916. France April 1915. Wounded June 1915 and Nov. 1916. Attached War Office, July 1917 to Jan. 1919.

Record of War Service

ROSS, ROBERT DUNCAN.
Dundee High School. Student of Arts and Divinity, 1911-15; M.A. 1915. 5th Royal Scots (T.), Private Aug. 1914; 2nd Lieut. Oct. 1915; Lieut. July 1917. Egypt, Gallipoli, France, and The Rhine.

ROSS, ROBERT MILLER.
George Heriot's School. Student of Science, 1912-14 and 1918-20; B.Sc. 1920. O.T.C. Engineers, Nov. 1913 to Oct. 1914, Cadet. R.E. (T.), City of Dundee Fortress, Sapper Oct. 1914; 2nd Lieut. Sept. 1917. 103rd Field Coy., R.E.

ROSS, THOMAS HUGGIN RIDDELL.
Perth Academy. Student of Arts, 1917. O.T.C. Infantry, Jan. 1917 to July 1918, Cadet Sergeant; Officer Cadet July 1918.

ROSS, THOMAS WILLIAM EDMONDSTON.
M.B., Ch.B. 1902; M.D. 1905; F.R.C.S. (Edin.) 1905. R.A.M.C., Lieut. July 1916; Captain July 1917. Salonika. Order of St Sava (4th Class).

ROSS, WILFRID CHARLES.
Epworth College, Rhyl. Student of Medicine, 1914-15. O.T.C. Infantry, Oct. 1914 to July 1915, Cadet. Royal Air Force, Cadet July 1915; 2nd Lieut.; Lieut. July 1917; Pilot.

ROSS, WILLIAM BEATTIE.
Perth Academy. Student of Medicine, 1913-14 and 1915-20. O.T.C. Medical, Nov. 1915 to May 1919, Cadet. R.E., Corporal July to Oct. 1915.

ROSS, WILLIAM CHARLES.
George Watson's College. M.B., Ch.B. 1900; D.P.H. (Edin.) 1901. Indian Medical Service, 1902; Major Jan. 1914.

ROSS, WILLIAM CHARLES.
Merchiston Castle. O.T.C. 1915-16. Student of Medicine, 1916-17 and 1918-19. O.T.C. Artillery, Oct. 1916 to May 1917, Cadet; Officer Cadet May 1917. R.G.A. (S.R.), 2nd Lieut. Oct. 1917.

ROSS, WILLIAM CHARLES ANGUS.
Royal High School and Fettes College. M.A. 1897. Schoolmaster. Examiner in History, 1914-18. Volunteers, 1915-18. 4th Seaforth Highlanders, Private July 1918; L/Corporal Aug. 1918.

ROSS, WILLIAM DAVID.
Royal High School. M.A. 1895; M.A. (Oxford). Fellow of Oriel College. General List, 2nd Lieut.; Staff Captain April 1915; Captain May 1916; Major Oct. 1918. Ministry of Munitions, 1915-19. Mention Jan. 1917. O.B.E. June 1918.

ROSS, WILLIAM MACKENZIE.
Buckie School. Student of Medicine, 1914-15 and 1918-19. O.T.C. Artillery, Oct. 1914 to May 1915, Cadet. 14th Argyll and Sutherland Highlanders, Private; L/Corporal. Tank Corps, 2nd Lieut. Jan. 1918.

Record of War Service

ROSS, ZACHARY MACAULAY HAMILTON.
Royal High School. M.B., Ch.B. 1906. Military Medical Work. R.A.M.C., Lieut. July 1918.

ROSSER, RICHARD PICTON.
Lancing College, Shoreham. Cadet Corps 1900-2. M.B., Ch.B. 1909. R.A.M.C., Lieut. Nov. 1914; Captain Nov. 1915. Wounded 1917.

ROUT, CHARLES MALCOLM.
M.B., Ch.B. 1912. Lahore British General Hospital, Indian Contingent. N.Z. Rifle Brigade, Captain July 1918.

ROWAN, HENRY DAVIS.
King William's College, Isle of Man. M.B., Ch.B. 1883. R.A.M.C. 1885, Lieut.-Col.; Colonel March 1915. Gallipoli and Serbia 1915; Salonika 1916; France 1917. Croix d'Officier Legion d'Honneur May 1917.

ROWAN-ROBINSON, FREDERICK ENGLAND.
George Watson's College. M.B., Ch.B. 1900. Volunteer Medical Staff Corps, 1894-1901, Staff-Sergeant. R.A.M.C., Lieut. 1901; Captain 1904; Major 1912. South African Campaign, 1901-2; Aden Hinterland 1905; France 1916-19; the Somme, Bourlon Wood. Dispatches March 1919.

ROWAN-ROBINSON, JOHN ROWAN.
King's School, Canterbury. Student of Medicine, 1891-5. Volunteer Medical Staff Corps, 1891-5, Corporal. Indian Army 1900; Captain 1908; Major Sept. 1915; Brevet Lieut.-Col. June 1918. South African Campaign, 1899-1902. France Aug. 1914; Mesopotamia Dec. 1915 to May 1919; Afghanistan and Waziristan 1919. Three times Mentioned in Dispatches. D.S.O.

ROWAN-ROBINSON, LESLIE CHARLES.
George Watson's College. M.B., Ch.B. 1903. University Battery, E.C.A.V., 1899-1902, Gunner. Royal Navy, Surgeon 1904; Staff-Surgeon 1912; Surgeon-Commander July 1919. H.M. Ships *Ark Royal, Prince Eugene*, and *Canterbury*; H.M. Hospital Ship *Somali*, and R.N. Hospital, Shotley. The Dardanelles; Belgian Coast.

ROWLAND, STEPHEN.
M.B., C.M. 1907; D.P.H. (Camb.), 1909. R.A.M.C., Lieut.; Captain Dec. 1916.

ROXBURGH, JOHN ROBERT.
Edinburgh Collegiate School. M.A. 1884; Barrister-at-Law. 1st V.B. Cambridgeshire Regiment, Oct. 1916; 2nd Lieut. June 1917. No. 15 Special Service Volunteer Coy., attached 2/7th Welsh Regiment.

Record of War Service

ROY, JAMES ALEXANDER.
Webster's Seminary, Kirriemuir. M.A. (Hons. Hist.) 1906. Lecturer, St Andrews University. University Battery, E.C.A.V., 1903-6, Gunner. St Andrews University O.T.C. 1914. North Scottish R.G.A. (T.), 2nd Lieut. Jan. 1915; Lieut. July 1916; Captain Oct. 1918. Intelligence Corps Aug. 1915. France. Wireless School, May 1916 to Jan. 1919. Mission, Teschen, Siberia, Feb. to June 1919.

ROYDS, GEORGE DAWSON.
Boroughmuir School; First XV. Student of Science, 1917. O.T.C. Infantry, 1917, Cadet; Officer Cadet Jan. 1918. R.E. (Signals), 2nd Lieut. June 1918 to Aug. 1919. France and The Rhine. Gassed at Reunmont Sept. 1918.

RUBIDGE, JOHN LIESCHING.
Diocesan College, Rondebosch, Cape Colony. First XV. M.B., C.M. 1891; D.P.H. (Edin.) 1895. R.A.M.C., Lieut. Oct. 1916; Captain Oct. 1917. 3rd Highland Light Infantry, Sept. 1917, and 4th Royal Scots, 1917-18.

RUDOLF, HARRY PRIEST.
Hoodstock and Rickering Colleges, Canada. M.B., Ch.B. 1914. O.T.C. Medical, 1914, Cadet. R.A.M.C., Lieut. Oct. 1914; Captain May 1918. R.F.A. Mesopotamia. Dispatches Nov. 1918. M.C. Dec. 1918.

RUDOLF, ROBERT DAWSON.
M.B., C.M. 1889; M.D. 1896; M.R.C.P. (Lond.) 1899. Canadian Army Medical Corps, Lieut.-Col. 1914; Colonel Dec. 1916. Canadian Exp. Force, No. 2 Canadian General Hospital; No. 11 General Hospital, Boulogne. C.B.E.

RUNDALL, LAURENCE.
M.B., Ch.B. 1901. Indian Medical Service, Captain.

RUSK, ARTHUR JOHN.
Merchiston Castle. Student of Arts and Science, 1916-17 and 1918-20. O.T.C. Infantry, May 1917 to March 1918, Cadet Sergeant; Officer Cadet March 1918. Labour Corps, 2nd Lieut. Sept. 1918.

RUSK, GEORGE ARCHER.
George Watson's College. O.T.C. 1904-11, Cadet Pipe Major. Student of Law, 1912-14. O.T.C. Infantry, 1914, Cadet. 9th, 1st, 3rd, and 10th Royal Highlanders (Black Watch), 2nd Lieut. Sept. 1914; Lieut.; Captain June 1915; (Reg.) 1919. France July 1915 and June 1918; Loos, Messigny, and Mons; Salonika March 1917; The Rhine. Wounded and gassed April and July 1916. M.C. June 1919.

RUSSEL, ROBERT GUTHRIE.
Merchiston Castle. B.Sc. 1901. A.M.I.C.E. R.N.V.R., Sub-Lieut. July 1916; Lieut. Mediterranean and Egypt.

RUSSELL, ALEXANDER.
Bathgate Academy. M.A. 1906. Minister, Church of Scotland. Senior Chaplain (Major), Dec. 1914.

Record of War Service

RUSSELL, ALEXANDER.
Broughton School, Edinburgh. Student of Arts, 1917-20; M.A. 1920. 9th Royal Scots, Private Aug. 1915. France, 51st (Highland) Division. Wounded. Invalided out Oct. 1917.

RUSSELL, ALEXANDER FRASER.
M.A. 1877; M.B. C.M. 1881. Army Medical Service (Retired), 1913. Colonel and A.D.M.S., 1914. C..M.G.

RUSSELL, ALEXANDER SCOTT.
George Heriot's School. O.T.C. 1909-12, Cadet L/Corporal. Student of Medicine, 1912-13. O.T.C. Artillery, Aug. to Sept. 1914, Cadet. R.G.A., 2nd Lieut. Sept. 1914; Lieut. Dec. 1915; Captain Aug. 1917. France. Wounded Nov. 1916. Dispatches (Italy) Nov. 1917.

RUSSELL, ARTHUR CLOUSTON.
George Watson's College. M.B., Ch.B. 1910. R.A.M.C., Lieut. June 1917; Captain June 1918. 24th Indian General Hospital, Mesopotamia. Invalided home Dec. 1918.

RUSSELL, ARTHUR WALKER.
Blairlodge. M.A. 1894. Writer to the Signet, 1899. 7th Argyll and Sutherland Highlanders, Captain Feb. 1915.

RUSSELL, CEDRIC.
M.B., Ch.B. 1915. O.T.C. Medical, Nov. 1914, Cadet. R.A.M.C., Lieut. July 1915; Acting Major March 1918; Captain June 1918. M.C.

RUSSELL, DAVID HENRY.
Stanley House, Bridge of Allan. M.B., Ch.B. 1908; F.R.C.S. (Edin.). R.A.M.C., Lieut. Aug. 1914; Captain Aug. 1915; Major March 1918. 2nd Border Regiment. France. Wounded Oct. 1917 and Oct. 1918. Dispatches. M.C.; Bar to M.C.

RUSSELL, EUSTACE.
M.B., Ch.B. 1906. Australian Army Medical Corps, Captain. 31st Battn., 8th Brigade. Egypt. Wounded July 1916.

RUSSELL, GEORGE RAYMOND.
Perth Academy. University O.T.C. Engineers, Oct. 1914 to July 1915, Cadet. R.E. (T.), City of Edinburgh Fortress, 2nd Lieut. June 1916; Lieut. April 1917. France April 1917. Invalided home Oct. 1918.

RUSSELL, JAMES.
M.B., C.M. 1888; M.D. 1892. R.A.M.C., Lieut. June 1915; Captain June 1916; Major Sept. 1917; Acting Lieut.-Col. March 1918. War Hospital, Dewsbury.

RUSSELL, JAMES DEWAR.
Fettes College. O.T.C. 1911-13. Student of Medicine, 1913-14. O.T.C. Infantry, Dec. 1913 to Sept. 1914, Cadet. 11th, 17th, 2nd, and 51st Highland Light Infantry, 2nd Lieut. Sept. 1914; Captain April 1916. France and The Rhine. Twice Wounded. M.C. 1917.

Record of War Service

RUSSELL, JAMES LAWSON.
George Watson's College. M.B., C.M. 1892. Demonstrator, Practical Pathology. Auxiliary Hospital (Military), Todmorden, 1914-15. R.A.M.C., Lieut. Aug. 1915; Captain Aug. 1916. Prees Heath Military and Chester War Hospitals.

RUSSELL, JAMES ROBERTSON.
George Heriot's School. O.T.C. 1910-12. Student of Science, 1912-14; B.Sc. 1920. O.T.C. Engineers, Oct. 1913-14, Cadet. 12th Royal Scots, 2nd Lieut. Oct. 1914; Lieut. June 1915; Captain Nov. 1917; Acting Major Nov. 1919. 21st Squadron, Machine-Gun Corps (Cavalry).

RUSSELL, JOHN.
Morgan Academy, Dundee. M.A. 1907. Schoolmaster. A.S.C. (T.) (51st Highland Division), 2nd Lieut. 1913; Lieut. Oct. 1914; Captain March 1915. France. Dispatches Jan. 1918.

RUSSELL, JOHN.
M.A. 1907. Schoolmaster. 10th Argyll and Sutherland Highlanders, Private May 1917.

RUSSELL, JOHN BLAKE.
Forres School. Student of Arts and Divinity, 1913-16 and 1918-19; M.A. 1919. R.F.A., Gunner; Bombardier.

RUSSELL, OLIVER.
George Watson's College. M.A. 1904. Minister, U.F. Church of Scotland. University Battery, E.C.A.V., 1900-8, B.S.M. R.G.A. (T.), 1st Lowland Heavy Battery, 2nd Lieut. Nov. 1914. Chaplain, 8th Royal Scots (Captain) Dec. 1914. France, Neuve Chapelle.

RUSSELL, STEWART INNES.
Robert Gordon's College, Aberdeen. University O.T.C. Infantry, Feb. to Aug. 1917, Cadet; Officer Cadet Aug. 1917. 9th King's Own Yorkshire Light Infantry, 2nd Lieut. Nov. 1917; Lieut. May 1919. France and The Rhine.

RUSSELL, WILLIAM.
George Watson's College. M.B., Ch.B. 1910; M.D. 1915. Diploma in Psychiatry, 1913. University Battery, E.C.A.V., and O.T.C. Artillery, 1905-11, Cadet Sergeant. R.A.M.C., Lieut. July 1915; Captain July 1916. Dorset Regiment. Malta, Egypt, France (the Somme), German East Africa. M.C. Nov. 1916.

RUSSELL, WILLIAM LYLE.
George Heriot's School. O.T.C. 1914-15. Student of Science and Medicine 1915-16. O.T.C. Artillery, 1915-16, Cadet. Seaforth Highlanders, Private Aug. 1916; Corporal Jan. 1918; Officer Cadet July 1918; 2nd Lieut. March 1919. France.

RUSSELL-JONES, ROY WARREN.
Church of England Grammar School, North Sydney. M.B., Ch.B. 1913. O.T.C. Infantry, July 1909 to July 1912, Cadet. R.A.M.C., Lieut.; Captain July 1917.

Record of War Service

RUTHERFORD, ALLAN FREER.
Glasgow and Dumfries Academies. M.B., C.M. 1890. R.A.M.C. (V.) and (T.), 1899; Major Feb. 1914. Mobilised Aug. 1914. 1/4th King's Own Royal Lancaster Regiment. France May to Nov. 1915 and Jan. 1916 to June 1918. Italy. Ambulance Train. T.D. July 1919.

RUTHERFORD, ANDREW.
M.B., Ch.B. 1912; B.Sc. (P.H.) 1915. Assistant to Professor of Pathology. R.A.M.C., Lieut. Nov. 1915; Captain Nov. 1916.

RUTHERFORD, ANDREW ADAMS.
M.B., Ch.B. 1912; M.D. 1915; B.A., LL.B. (Ireland). Barrister-at-Law (Dublin and Middle Temple). R.A.M.C., Lieut. April 1915; Captain April 1916. Dispatches May 1917.

RUTHERFORD, DAVID SINCLAIR.
Fettes College. O.T.C. 1910-14. Student of Arts, 1914-15. O.T.C. Infantry, March to April 1915, Cadet. 3rd Welsh Regiment (S.R.), 2nd Lieut. April 1915; Lieut. Nov. 1916. Attached 2nd Monmouth Regiment.

RUTHERFORD, JAMES.
Dumfries Academy; First XI. Student of Arts, 1912-14; M.A. 1920. 4th Royal Scots (T.), Private 1912. 12th Scottish Rifles, 2nd Lieut. Feb. 1915. Transferred to Machine-Gun Corps, Jan. 1916; Lieut. Sept. 1916.

RUTHERFORD, JOHN DOUGLAS.
Dollar Academy and George Watson's College. Student of Law, 1904-8. Writer to the Signet, 1910. O.T.C. Artillery, 1907-8 and 1914, Cadet. A.S.C., 2nd Lieut. Sept. 1914; Captain May 1915; Acting Major Aug. to Dec. 1918. France.

RUTHERFORD, JOHN VICTOR WALTON.
Royal High School; First XV. M.B., C.M. 1890; M.R.C.S. (Eng.) 1887. Army Medical Service, 1887; Colonel and A.D.M.S., 1912-17. 50th Northumbrian Division; 1st Northern General Hospital; 1st Northumberland Royal Artillery Volunteers. Dispatches 1915 and 1916.

RUTHERFORD, NORMAN CECIL.
M.B., Ch.B. 1903; L.R.C.P. & S. (Edin.) and L.F.P.S. (Glasg.) 1903. R.A.M.C. (T.), Captain 1912; Major; Acting Lieut.-Col. Aug. 1918. 6th London Field Ambulance and 1/3rd West Riding Field Ambulance, France. D.S.O.

RUTHERFORD, PERCIVAL THOMAS.
Salt Schools, Shipley. First XV. and XI. Student of Medicine, 1902-6; L.R.C.P. & S. (Edin.) and L.F.P.S. (Glasg.) 1907. No. 4 Coy. Q.R.V.B., Royal Scots, 1902-6, L/Corporal. R.A.M.C. (T.), Lieut. 1910. 1/4th London Howitzer Brigade, R.F.A., 2nd Lieut. 1912. R.A.M.C., Captain Oct. 1914; Major Jan. 1918; Lieut.-Col. March 1918. 2/3rd London, Wessex and West Riding Field Ambulances to April 1919. O.B.E. June 1919.

Record of War Service

RUTHERFORD, RICHARD.
Edinburgh Academy. M.B., Ch.B. 1901. R.A.M.C., Captain; Major March 1914. Rangoon.

RUTHERFORD, ROBERT BRYSON.
Berwick-on-Tweed Academy. M.A. 1908; M.B., Ch.B. 1912. O.T.C. Medical, April 1908 to Nov. 1912, Cadet. R.A.M.C., Lieut. Aug. 1914; Captain Aug. 1915; Major March 1918. 91st Field Ambulance, France. M.C. Dec. 1918.

RUTHERFORD, WILLIAM STEWART.
Student of Law, 1901-6 and 1908-10. Law Agent, 1906. Lothians and Border Horse, 1903-10. A.S.C., 25th Divisional Train, Lieut. Nov. 1914; Captain Nov. 1917.

RUTHVEN, MORTON WOOD.
Dollar Academy. M.B., Ch.B. 1910; D.T.M. (Liverpool). Volunteer Medical Staff Corps and O.T.C. Medical, 1905 to Aug. 1909, Cadet Staff Sergeant. R.A.M.C. (S.R.), Lieut. 1909; Captain 1913. Mobilised Aug. 1914; Acting Major March to Aug. 1918. Mention Dec. 1916.

RYAN, SIR CHARLES SNODGRASS.
Church of England Grammar School, Melbourne. M.B., C.M. 1875. Turco-Serbian and Turco-Russian War, 1876-8. Australian Army Medical Corps, 1878; Surgeon-General. A.D.M.S., 1st Australian Division, and Consulting Surgeon to A.I.F. Dispatches (four times). C.B.; C.M.G.; V.D.; K.B.E. June 1919.

RYRIE, ANDREW.
Montrose Academy. Student of Arts, 1914-15 and 1918-19. O.T.C. Artillery, 1914-15, Cadet. R.G.A. (S.R.), 2nd Lieut. April 1915; Lieut. March 1917.

RYRIE, BENJAMIN JAMES.
Montrose Academy. Student of Medicine, 1911-16. M.B., Ch.B. 1916. Anatomy Staff, 1915-16. O.T.C. Medical, Oct. 1915 to July 1916, Cadet. R.A.M.C., Lieut. Jan. 1916; Captain Jan. 1917.

RYRIE, FRANK.
Montrose Academy. M.A. 1912. Missionary, U.F. Church of Scotland. Y.M.C.A. Work, 1914-15. Machine-Gun Corps, Private Sept. 1915; 2nd Lieut. Sept. 1918. M.M. Dec. 1916.

RYRIE, GORDON ALEXANDER.
Montrose Academy. Student of Arts, 1917-20; M.A. (Hons. Maths.) 1920. Scottish Rifles, Private.

SAFFLEY, JOHN.
Dumfries Academy. M.B., Ch.B. 1904. R.A.M.C. (T.), Lieut. Jan. 1914; Captain April 1915. 5th King's Own Scottish Borderers. 48th Division, Italy, Aug. to Nov. 1918. Medical Referee, Ministry of Pensions.

Record of War Service

SAHGAL, GOKAL CHAND.
Sialkot School, India. M.B., Ch.B. 1916; D.P.H. (Edin.). Indian Field Ambulance, Dresser, 1914-15.

SAIDLER, JAMES ROY.
George Watson's College. O.T.C. 1907-11, Cadet Sergeant. Student of Science, 1911-14; B.Sc. (Distinction) 1920. Forth R.G.A. (T.), 2nd Lieut. 1911; Lieut. May 1914; Captain Sept. 1915; Acting Major Nov. 1916. France (Somme, Ancre, Vimy) and The Rhine, Feb. 1916 to Aug. 1919. Siege Battery. Royal Air Force, 12th Squadron. Dispatches Jan. 1918. Croix de Guerre May 1918. M.C. Jan. 1919.

ST LEGER, ROBERT ARTHUR.
Tonbridge School, Kent. M.B., C.M. 1888. No. 4 Coy. Q.E.R., Private. South African Medical Corps, Captain 1913; Temp. Major 1914; Major 1915. R.A.M.C., Major Oct. 1915. German South-West Africa, 1914-15; Senussi, Egypt, 1916; France 1916-18. Dispatches (German South-West Africa and France).

SALE, GILBERT NOEL.
King Alfred's School, Wantage. First XV. and XI. O.T.C. 1911-16, Cadet Sergeant. Student of Science, 1918-19. R.G.A., Officer Cadet Aug. 1916; 2nd Lieut. Feb. 1917; Lieut. Aug. 1918.

SAMPSON, WILLIAM BROOK.
George Watson's College. Student of Science, 1916-17. Officer Cadet April 1917. 4th King's Own Scottish Borderers, 2nd Lieut. Jan. 1918; Lieut. France 1918.

SAMUELSON, GERALD SEPTIMUS.
Sherborne School. M.B., C.M. 1888; M.D. 1893. N. S. Wales Army Medical Corps. South African Campaign, 1899-1902. R.A.M.C., Lieut. May 1915; Captain July 1915; Major April 1917. Dispatches June and Sept. 1918.

SAMUT, ROBERT.
M.B., C.M. 1895. Acting Professor of Pathology, Malta University. Malta Militia, 1897; Surgeon-Major 1912. Military Hospital, Cyprus, Jan. to Aug. 1915; Military Hospital, Forrest, Malta, 1915 to June 1919. Dispatches Feb. 1917.

SAMWELL, CECIL VALE.
Sandringham School, Southport. L.R.C.P. & S. (Edin.) and L.R.F.P.S. (Glasg.) 1917. O.T.C. Medical, Feb. 1916 to Oct. 1917, Cadet L/Corporal. Royal Navy, Surgeon-Lieut., Nov. 1917 to April 1919. Mediterranean.

SAND, CHARLES.
Student of Medicine, 1908-14; M.B., Ch.B. 1914. R.A.M.C., Lieut.

SANDEMAN, CHARLES STEWART.
Sedbergh. M.B., Ch.B. 1909. R.A.M.C. (S.R.), Lieut. 1909; Captain June 1913. France Aug. 1914. Invalided home June 1915. India to Dec. 1919.

Record of War Service

SANDEMAN, DAVID GRANT.
    Morrison's Academy, Crieff. O.T.C. 1914-16. Student of Science, 1916 and 1919. O.T.C. Engineers, March to Aug. 1917, Cadet; Officer Cadet Aug. 1917. R.E., 401st Highland Field Coy., 2nd Lieut. Nov. 1917.

SANDEMAN, GEORGE DAVID STEWART.
    M.A. 1892. Royal Fusiliers (2nd Sportsman's Battn.), Private 1914.

SANDEMAN, IAN.
    Student of Arts, 1913-14. O.T.C. Artillery, Oct. 1913-14, Cadet. R.F.A., 2nd Lieut. Aug. 1914; Lieut. June 1916.

SANDEMAN, LAURA STEWART.
    M.B., Ch.B. 1900; M.D. 1903. Scottish Women's Hospital, Troyes, France, May to Oct. 1915; Leith War Hospital, 1916-17. Q.M.A.A.C. attached R.A.M.C. Controller of Medical Services (Overseas), March 1917 to May 1919. Dispatches Dec. 1918.

SANDEMAN, THOMAS ROBERT.
    Daniel Stewart's College. M.B., Ch.B. 1910; F.R.C.S. (Edin.) 1914. Certificate, Tropical Medicine (Lond.), 1912. West African Medical Service, Lieut. 1912; Captain 1914. Nigerian Regiment, Cameroons, and East Africa. M.C. June 1918.

SANDEMAN, WILLIAM YOUNG.
    Daniel Stewart's College. B.Sc. 1912. A.M.I.C.E. 1915. R.E., 69th Field Coy., 2nd Lieut. Dec. 1915; Lieut. July 1917; Acting Captain and Adjutant March to July 1919. France March 1916. M.C. Jan. 1918.

SANDERS, ERNEST LEONARD.
    Student of Medicine, 1916-19. O.T.C. Infantry, May to Oct. 1915, Cadet. Army, 2nd Lieut.

SANDERS, GERALD GAIRDNER.
    Repton. Student of Medicine, 1916-20. R.N.A.S., Able Seaman Jan. 1915; Chief Petty Officer March 1915. Admiralty, Whitehall, Dec. 1915 to June 1916.

SANDERSON, FRANCIS ROBERT.
    B.A., LL.B. 1901. Advocate, 1901. Judge, Egypt. R.F.A., 2nd Lieut. March 1915; Staff Captain Dec. 1915; Temp. Lieut.-Col. and Legal Adviser, March 1919. East Lancashire Brigade. Gallipoli and Egypt. Dispatches (twice). O.B.E. June 1919; Chevalier de l'Ordre Royal de Georges (Greece) 1919.

SANDERSON, JAMES DURIE.
    Edinburgh Academy. O.T.C. 1908-10, Cadet Corporal. B.Sc. 1914. A.M.I.C.E. O.T.C. Engineers, 1910-13, Cadet. R.E., 100th Field Coy., 2nd Lieut. March 1915; Lieut. July 1917; Captain Sept. 1918.

SANDERSON, NEIL DEWAR.
    Dunfermline High School. Student of Medicine, 1916-19. R.F.A., 94th Brigade, Gunner Dec. 1916; Officer Cadet April 1917; 2nd Lieut. Oct. 1917. France Dec. 1916 to April 1917, and March 1918 to Jan. 1919.

Record of War Service

SANDFORD, GEORGE CALROW.
Shrewsbury. M.B., C.M. 1893; M.D. 1896. No. 4 Coy. Q.R.V.B., Royal Scots, 1888-91, Private. South African Campaign, 1899-1903. R.A.M.C. (T.), Captain 1908. Mobilised 1914; Temp. Major July 1915-19. 4th Southern General Hospital, Plymouth.

SANDILANDS, RICHARD.
Student of Science and Medicine, 1911-15 and 1917-19; B.Sc. 1913; M.B., Ch.B. 1919. R.N.V.R., Surgeon-Probationer.

SANDISON, ALEXANDER ARNOT MITCHELL.
Student of Arts and Medicine, 1913-15 and 1917-20; M.A., B.Sc. 1920. O.T.C. Artillery, 1914-15, Cadet. R.F.A., 2nd Lieut. July 1915; Lieut. Sept. 1917.

SANDISON, CHARLES GILBERT DUNCAN.
George Watson's College. Student of Science, 1911-14; B.Sc. 1914. Royal Aircraft Establishment, Farnborough (Observer), Aug. 1915. R.F.C., 2nd Air Mechanic, Jan. 1916.

SANDISON, JOSEPH HAMILTON MUNDELL.
George Watson's College. Student of Medicine, 1910-14 and 1915-17; M.B., Ch.B. 1917. 18th Royal Scots, Captain 1914-15. Royal Navy, Surgeon 1917-18. Royal Air Force, Captain 1918-19.

SANDISON, ROBERT ELIOT WESTWOOD.
Broughton School, Edinburgh. Student of Arts, 1914-15, and Medicine, 1918-19. 9th Royal Scots, Private June 1915. 1st Royal Scots Fusiliers, 2nd Lieut. Oct. 1917 to March 1919. Machine-Gun Corps. France.

SANDSTON, ALFRED CHARLES.
Boys' High School, New Zealand. M.B., Ch.B. (Hons.) 1898; M.D. 1901 (Gold Medal); F.R.C.S. (Edin.) 1916. R.A.M.C., Lieut. Aug. 1915.

SANSOM, WALTER.
M.B., C.M. 1890; M.D. 1891. R.A.M.C., Captain 1915; Major 1917. Surgeon, German War Hospital, Dartford, and War Hospital, Herne Bay, Kent. President, Pensions Board, 1919. Dispatches Sept. 1917.

SAROLEA, CHARLES HENRY.
Royal High School. Student of Arts and Law, 1916-17 and 1918-19. O.T.C. Artillery, 1917-18, Cadet; Officer Cadet May 1918. R.F.A., 2nd Lieut. Feb. 1919.

SAROLEA, JOHN ROBERT.
Merchiston Castle and Royal High School. Student of Science, 1914-15 and 1920; B.Sc. (Distinction) 1920. O.T.C. Engineers, Oct. 1914 to July 1915, Cadet. R.E., 410th Field Coy., 2nd Lieut. Aug. 1915; Lieut. June 1916. Egypt and Palestine Dec. 1915 to April 1918; France April to Dec. 1918. Wounded at Jerusalem Nov. 1917. Dispatches April 1918.

Record of War Service

SAUNDBY, ROBERT.
M.B., C.M. 1874; M.D.; L.R.C.P. (Edin.) and M.R.C.S. (Eng.) 1874. R.A.M.C. (T.), Lieut.-Col. 1st Southern Military Hospital, Birmingham.

SAUNDERS, FREDERICK ANASTASIUS.
King Edward VI. School, Great Berkhampstead. Student of Medicine, 1879-82; L.R.C.P. & S. (Edin.) 1882; F.R.C.S. (Edin.) 1884. Fife Light Horse, 1885; Bechuanaland Campaign, 1896-7; South African Campaign, 1898-1902. 3rd West Yorkshire Regiment (S.R.), Hon. Captain and Hon. Major. Grahamstown Commands, South Africa, Senior Commandant; Lieut.-Col. Alexandria.

SCALES, CUTHBERT.
Bradford Grammar School. M.B., Ch.B. 1913. O.T.C. Medical, 1909-13, Cadet L/Corporal. R.A.M.C., Lieut. Oct. 1914; Captain Oct. 1915; Acting Major April 1918 to March 1919. 4th Shropshire Light Infantry, 1914-17. Royal Naval Division, 1918-19. India April 1919. Dispatches and M.C. May 1918; Bar to M.C. Oct. 1918.

SCARFF, GORDON RUSSELL.
City of London School. Student of Medicine, 1911-14 and 1918-19. O.T.C. Infantry, Jan. to Feb. 1915, Cadet. B.R.C.S., Boulogne (Dresser). 26th Northumberland Fusiliers, 2nd Lieut. April 1915; Lieut. Aug. 1916; Captain Oct. 1917.

SCARLETT, JAMES THOMAS.
Royal High School. M.A.; B.Sc. 1913. O.T.C. Engineers, Oct. 1911-14, Cadet. R.G.A., 2nd Lieut. Oct. 1914; Lieut. Sept. 1915; Captain Sept. 1917; Acting Major Feb. 1917. France (four years). Dispatches Jan. 1917 and July 1919.

SCARTH, HENRY WILLIAM.
St Paul's School. O.T.C. 1914-16. University O.T.C. Infantry, 1917, Cadet; Officer Cadet Sept. 1917. 1st Scots Guards (S.R.), 2nd Lieut. Jan. 1918; Acting Captain July to Sept. 1919. Orders of St Anne (2nd Class), and St Stanislaus (3rd Class).

SCHULTZ, HENRY JOHN EDWARD.
Student of Medicine, 1917-20; M.B., Ch.B. 1920. South African Medical Corps, Private March 1916. East African Campaign.

SCORESBY-JACKSON, THOMAS.
Blairlodge. M.B., Ch.B. 1905. D.P.H. (Edin.) 1906. No. 4 Coy. Q.R.V.B., Royal Scots, Private. 1/17th B.B. and C.I. Rifles, Indian Defence Force, Surgeon-Lieut. 1912; Surgeon-Captain July 1915.

SCOT-SKIRVING, ARCHIBALD ADAM.
Edinburgh Academy and Cheltenham College; First XV. M.B., C.M. 1893; M.R.C.S. (Eng.) and L.R.C.P. (Lond.) 1895; F.R.C.S. (Edin.) 1897. President, S.R.C. Senior Lecturer, Clinical Surgery. R.A.M.C. (V.) and (T.), 1897. Mobilised Aug. 1914; Captain; Major Sept. 1918. South African Campaign, 1900. 2nd Scottish General Hospital; 58th Scottish General Hospital, France, 1917-18. C.M.G. 1900.

Record of War Service

SCOT-SKIRVING, OWEN.
Edinburgh Collegiate School. Student of Arts, 1872-3. Coorg and Mysore Volunteer Rifles, 1885-1914. 26th Indian Cavalry, Sept. 1914. Kirkcudbrightshire Volunteer Regiment, Jan. 1915. Royal Defence Corps, 2nd Lieut. Oct. 1916; Lieut. April 1918.

SCOT-SKIRVING, ROBERT.
M.B., C.M. 1881; M.B., Ch.M. (Sydney). Australian Army Medical Corps, Hon. Major; New South Wales Forces. South African Campaign, 1899-1902. Census and Queen Alexandra Hospitals, Millbank.

SCOTLAND, ALASTAIR GRAEME.
Viewpark; First XI. University O.T.C. Artillery, Oct. 1914 to Sept. 1915, Cadet Bombardier. Training College, Quetta, India, Dec. 1915 to June 1916. 36th attached 35th and 51st Sikhs, 2nd Lieut. June 1916; Lieut. June 1917. Mesopotamia March 1917; 18th Meerut Division, Palestine, Jan. 1918; Megiddo Sept. 1918. Wounded at Tekrit. M.C. (Palestine) Jan. 1919.

SCOTLAND, GEORGE.
George Heriot's School. Student of Science, 1918-19. 9th Royal Scots (T.), Private Aug. 1914. 12th Highland Light Infantry. France. Wounded at the Somme Sept. 1916.

SCOTT, ALEXANDER.
Dunfermline High School. Student of Medicine, 1918-19. Royal Highlanders (Black Watch), Private May 1916; Officer Cadet Feb. 1917; 2nd Lieut. June 1917; Lieut. Nov. 1918; Captain Feb. 1919. M.C. Aug. 1918.

SCOTT, ALEXANDER BALFOUR.
Arbroath High School; First XI. M.A. 1913; LL.B. 1915. R.F.A., Gunner Nov. 1915; 2nd Lieut. July 1916; Lieut. Jan. 1918; Staff Lieut. April 1917 to Aug. 1918. France July 1916 to Aug. 1918. Wounded Aug. 1918. M.C. Jan. 1919.

SCOTT, ALEXANDER WALTER.
B.L. 1911. Law Agent, 1913. 2/5th King's Own Scottish Borderers (T.), 2nd Lieut. Nov. 1914; Lieut. June 1916; Captain. Wounded Aug. 1918.

SCOTT, ALLAN.
George Heriot's School. Student of Science, 1918-19. R.E., Special Brigade, Corporal July 1915.

SCOTT, ANDREW HENDERSON.
Student of Law, 1902-5. R.G.A., attached Anti-Aircraft, Gunner Dec. 1916 to May 1919.

SCOTT, CHARLES ALEXANDER.
Fettes College. O.T.C. 1911-12. Student of Arts, 1911-14; M.A. 1916. 11th Highland Light Infantry, 2nd Lieut. Sept. 1914; Lieut. Nov. 1914; Captain Sept. 1915; Major Aug. 1919. France. Dispatches Aug. 1919.

Record of War Service

SCOTT, CHARLES ERNEST.
 Milne's Institution, Fochabers. Student of Medicine, 1913-16. O.T.C. Medical, Jan. 1914 to Oct. 1916, Cadet. R.N.V.R., Surgeon Sub-Lieut. Oct. 1916.

SCOTT, DAVID JOBSON,
 M.B., Ch.B. 1903; M.D. 1906. R.A.M.C. (T.), Captain April 1915; Acting Lieut.-Col. June 1918. O.C. Administrative Centre, 1st London Division. M.C.

SCOTT, DOUGLAS D.
 Dunfermline High School. Student of Arts, 1918. 11th Royal Highlanders (Black Watch), Private May 1916. Labour Corps, 40th Division, France.

SCOTT, DUNCAN.
 Perth Academy. M.A. 1912. Schoolmaster. 6th and 1/4th Royal Scots (T.), Private Aug. 1914. Gallipoli May to Aug. 1915. Wounded June 1915. Invalided out March 1916. Forth R.G.A., Gunner May 1916; 2nd Lieut. Dec. 1916; Captain April 1918. France, 181st Siege Battery, July 1916. M.C. June 1919.

SCOTT, FRANCIS LIDDERDALE.
 Otago High School, New Zealand. First XV. and XI. M.B., Ch.B. 1907; M.D. 1909; L.R.C.P. & S. (Edin.) and L.F.P.S. (Glasg.) 1907. N.Z. Medical Corps, Captain May 1915.

SCOTT, GEORGE.
 Edinburgh Academy. O.T.C. 1916-17. University O.T.C. Artillery, June 1917 to Feb. 1918, Cadet; Officer Cadet Feb. 1918. R.G.A., 2nd Lieut. Oct. 1918.

SCOTT, GEORGE ALEXANDER.
 Teviot Grove Academy, Hawick. M.A. 1910; B.Sc. 1913. Schoolmaster. O.T.C. Artillery, Dec. 1914 to March 1915, Cadet. Forth R.G.A. (T.), 2nd Lieut. March 1915; Lieut. June 1916; Acting Captain July 1917; Acting Major Oct. 1918. 70th and 242nd Siege Batteries. France March 1916 to Dec. 1918. Education Officer, 12th Brigade, R.G.A. Dispatches Jan. 1918.

SCOTT, GEORGE MACDONALD.
 Dumfries Academy. Student of Arts, Science, and Medicine, 1908-15; M.A. 1911; B.Sc.; M.B., Ch.B. 1914. O.T.C. Infantry, 1910-14, Medical, 1914-15; Cadet. R.A.M.C., Lieut. Jan. 1915; Captain March 1915. M.C. July 1916.

SCOTT, GORDON SHAW.
 Whitgift Grammar School, Croydon, Surrey. Student of Medicine, 1915-16 and 1918. 8th and 3rd Cameron Highlanders, Private July 1916; Officer Cadet Jan. 1917. 1st King's Liverpool Regiment, 2nd Lieut. April 1917; Lieut. Oct. to Dec. 1918. M.C. Feb. 1918.

SCOTT, HENRY GARNOCK.
 Galashiels Academy. M.A. 1906. Schoolmaster. Inns of Court O.T.C., Private June 1916. King's Own Scottish Borderers, 2nd Lieut. Feb. 1919.

Record of War Service

SCOTT, HERBERT BREBNER.
George Watson's College. O.T.C. 1915-16. University O.T.C. Artillery, Sept. 1916 to April 1917, Cadet Bombardier; Officer Cadet April 1917. R.F.A., 2nd Lieut. Sept. 1917; Lieut. March to May 1919. France 1917-19. M.C. Sept. 1918.

SCOTT, HUGH GALLIE.
Inverness Royal Academy; First XV. M.A. 1907; LL.B. (Distinction) 1909. Solicitor. 2nd Canadian Mounted Rifles, Lieut. June 1915 to 1919. France 1916. British Intelligence Service, Greece, 1918. Wounded at Ypres June 1916.

SCOTT, JAMES.
Dundee University College. M.B., C.M. 1894; M.D. 1898; B.Sc. (P.H.) 1903; D.P.H. Certificate of Tropical Medicine. R.A.M.C. (T.), 1901; Major Jan. 1913; Lieut.-Col. Oct. 1918. Attached 5th Royal Scots (T.). Gallipoli, Egypt, and Greece. Hospitals in Alexandria, Cairo, and Belbeis. T.D.

SCOTT, JAMES.
Daniel Stewart's College; First XV. M.B., Ch.B. 1907. R.A.M.C., Lieut. June 1917; Captain June 1918. M.C. Dec. 1918.

SCOTT, JAMES.
Lanark Grammar School. M.A. 1910. 9th Argyll and Sutherland Highlanders, Private 1907. 1/8th Highland Light Infantry, 2nd Lieut. May 1914; Lieut. Aug. 1914; Captain July 1916. Attached 1/7th Royal Scots. D.A.D.O.S. to Division. France and Palestine. Dispatches April 1918.

SCOTT, JAMES AARON.
Boroughmuir School. Student of Arts, 1912-14 and 1918-19; M.A. 1919. R.F.A. (T.), 1st Lowland Brigade, Gunner; Bombardier Aug. 1914; Corporal Nov. 1914; Sergeant April 1916. 4th Gordon Highlanders, Corporal Oct. 1916. M.M. Nov. 1918.

SCOTT, JAMES MATTHEWS DUNCAN.
Dollar Academy. M.A. (St Andrews) 1908; M.B., Ch.B. 1912. O.T.C. Artillery, Oct. 1908 to Feb. 1911, Cadet. South African Medical Corps, Captain Oct. 1914. Attached 1st Rhodesian Regiment. R.A.M.C., Captain Aug. 1915.

SCOTT, JESSIE ANNE.
M.B., Ch.B. 1909; M.D. 1912; D.P.H. (Lond.). Scottish Women's Hospital, Serbia and Macedonia, July 1915-17. Attached R.A.M.C. Serbian Army, 1917-18. Salonika and France 1918-19. Order of St Sava (4th Class). Serbian Dispatches March 1917.

SCOTT, JOHN.
M.B., Ch.B. 1911. R.A.M.C., Lieut.

SCOTT, JOHN.
Dumfries Academy. M.B., Ch.B. 1908; D.P.H.; D.T.M. and H. Assistant to Professor in Pathology, 1909-10. Indian Medical Service, Lieut. 1911; Captain Jan. 1914; Acting Major July 1918; Brevet Major Jan. 1919. Egyptian Exp. Force. Dispatches Jan. 1916, Jan. 1918, and Jan. 1919. D.S.O. Jan. 1918.

Record of War Service

SCOTT, JOHN ARTHUR NOËL.
  Sedbergh; First XV. and XI. Cadet Corps 1905-8, Corporal. M.B., Ch.B. 1913. R.A.M.C., Lieut. Dec. 1914; Captain Dec. 1915. Wounded April 1918. Invalided out April 1919.

SCOTT, JOHN BARRON.
  M.B., C.M. 1891. R.A.M.C., Captain May 1915. Malta 1915-16. Recruiting Medical Board, Warwick.

SCOTT, JOHN CUNNISON.
  Penrith Grammar School. University O.T.C. Infantry, 1917-18, Cadet L/Corporal; Officer Cadet, June 1918. Royal Fusiliers, 2nd Lieut. Feb. 1919.

SCOTT, JOHN EASTON.
  George Watson's College. M.A. 1899; M.B., Ch.B. 1903. Morden Grange Auxiliary Hospital, 1915-17. R.A.M.C., Lieut. May 1917; Captain May 1918.

SCOTT, JOHN MENZIES BAILLIE.
  Edinburgh Academy and Sedbergh; First XV. Cadet Corps 1902-5, Colour-Sergeant. Student of Law, 1906-10. Writer to the Signet, 1911. R.F.A. (T.), 1st Lowland Brigade, 2nd Lieut. 1908; Lieut. 1909; Captain June 1916; Major May 1918. France Oct. 1915. Wounded. Dispatches Dec. 1917.

SCOTT, PATRICK JOHN HEPBURN.
  Merchiston Castle. O.T.C. 1913-16, Cadet L/Corporal. Student of Arts, 1916-17. O.T.C. Infantry, Oct. 1916 to Nov. 1917, Cadet Corporal; Officer Cadet Nov. 1917. 8th Royal Scots, 2nd Lieut. March 1918. France Sept. to Dec. 1918.

SCOTT, RALPH LESTER.
  M.B., Ch.B. 1907; F.R.C.S. (Edin.). R.A.M.C., Lieut. Aug. 1914; Captain Aug. 1915; Major Jan. 1918. Dispatches Jan. 1917.

SCOTT, ROBERT FREDERICK McNAIR.
  B.A. (Camb.); M.B., Ch.B. 1898. R.A.M.C., Lieut. Aug. 1918 to Feb. 1919. Valenciennes, Jan. 1919.

SCOTT, ROBERT THOMAS HUNTER.
  George Watson's College. University O.T.C. Artillery, Sept. 1915 to Jan. 1918, Cadet B.S.M.; Officer Cadet Jan. 1918. R.F.A., 52nd Army Brigade, 2nd Lieut. July 1918-19. France; Cambrai and Mons.

SCOTT, THOMAS.
  Daniel Stewart's College. Student of Medicine, 1912-15 and 1917-20; M.B., Ch.B. 1920. O.T.C. Artillery, Nov. 1914 to June 1915, Cadet. R.N.V.R., Surgeon Sub-Lieut. July 1915.

SCOTT, THOMAS.
  Moray House. M.A. 1910; B.Sc. 1914. 11th Scottish Rifles, Private Nov. 1914; 2nd Lieut. April 1915; Lieut. July 1916. Transferred to R.E., July 1917; Captain Nov. 1917 to Feb. 1919; Acting Major July to Oct. 1918. France.

Record of War Service

SCOTT, THOMAS.
Dunnottar School, Stonehaven. Student of Arts and Divinity, 1884-90; M.A. 1886. Minister, Church of Scotland. Chaplain, 4th Class, 1894; 3rd Class, 1904; 2nd Class, 1909; 1st Class, 1914. 51st Division (Bedford), Dec. 1914. 4th Gordon Highlanders, France, May 1915. Etaples Area, Oct. 1915, and 2nd Scottish General Hospital, Dec. 1916 to July 1919. T.D. 1914. Dispatches 1918.

SCOTT, THOMAS DUNCAN FALCONER.
Boroughmuir School. Student of Arts and Science, 1911-16; M.A. (Hons. Maths. and Nat. Phil.); B.Sc. 1916. Schoolmaster. R.N.V.R. attached R.N.A.S., Sub-Lieut. Dec. 1917. Royal Air Force, Lieut. Aug. 1918 to March 1919.

SCOTT, THOMAS FRASER.
M.A. 1899. Schoolmaster. 16th Royal Scots, Private.

SCOTT, THOMAS HENRY.
Selkirk High School. M.B., Ch.B. 1906. Certificate Tropical of Medicine. Cricket "Blue," 1901-6. R.A.M.C. (V.), 1900-6, L/Corporal. R.A.M.C., Lieut. 1907; Captain 1910; Major Jan. 1919; Acting Lieut.-Col. Jan. 1917. 1st West Yorkshire Regiment, Aug. 1914; 17th Field Ambulance, Oct. 1915; D.A.D.M.S., 24th Division, Dec. 1915; 14th Field and 1st Cavalry Field Ambulances, 1917-19. France and The Rhine. Dispatches Jan. 1915, Jan. 1917, June 1918, and Jan. 1919. M.C. Jan. 1915; D.S.O. Oct. 1918.

SCOTT, THOMAS ROBERTSON.
Falkirk High School. Student of Arts and Science, 1914-15 and 1918-19. O.T.C. Artillery, Nov. 1914-15, Cadet. 9th and 10th East Yorkshire Regiment, 2nd Lieut. Nov. 1915. R.F.C., Lieut. Oct. 1917. Twice Wounded. D.F.C. Sept. 1918.

SCOTT, WILLIAM EDWARD SAWERS.
Fettes College. M.B., C.M. 1885; M.D. 1889. R.A.M.C., Lieut. Oct. 1915; Captain Oct. 1916. France.

SCOTT, WILLIAM FOREMAN.
Lasswade School. Student of Medicine, 1918-19. 10th Royal Scots Fusiliers, Private Jan. 1917; Corporal Aug. 1918. France Jan. 1918-19.

SCOTT, WILLIAM MACKENZIE.
George Watson's College. Student of Arts, 1916-17 and 1918-19. 2nd Royal Scots Fusiliers, Private April 1917; L/Corporal June 1917; Corporal June 1918; Officer Cadet Sept. 1918; 2nd Lieut. Dec. 1918. France 1918; Somme and Bailleul. Wounded at Voormezeele April 1918.

SCOTT, WILLIAM SIBBALD.
Lasswade School. M.B., Ch.B. 1900. University Battery, 1st E.C.A.V., 1895-8, Gunner. R.A.M.C. (T.), Lieut. 1912; Captain April 1915; Acting Major April 1918. Dispatches May 1919.

Record of War Service

SCOTT-ELLIOTT, GEORGE FRANCIS. (See p. 752.)

SCOTT-MONCRIEFF, CHARLES KENNETH.
Winchester College. Cadet Corps 1907-8. Student of Arts, 1908-14; M.A. (Hons. Engl.) 1914. O.T.C. Artillery, Oct. 1908 to Nov. 1911, Cadet. 3rd King's Own Scottish Borderers, 2nd Lieut. 1913; Captain Feb. 1915. France 1914-17 and 1918-19. Attached General Staff, 1918. Imperial War Museum, 1919. Wounded April 1917. M.C. June 1917.

SCRIMGEOUR, DAVID MUIR.
Bootham School, York; First XI. School Ambulance Corps, 1915-16, Corporal. Student of Medicine, 1916 and 1918-19. Royal Air Force, 2nd Lieut. Sept. 1917; Pilot Nov. 1917; Lieut. May 1918.

SCRIMGEOUR, FREDERICK JOHN.
Dundee High School. Student of Medicine, 1897-1902; L.R.C.P. & S. (Edin.); L.R.F.P.S. (Glasg.) 1902. Army Medical Service, Captain March 1916; Major Nov. 1917. Cairo; Jerusalem; D.A.D.M.S., Northern Palestine. Dispatches 1917, 1918, and 1919. Order of St John of Jerusalem, 1919. O.B.E. (Military) 1919.

SCRIMGEOUR, JAMES.
B.L. 1899. Law Agent, 1900. Recruiting Officer, T.F. Reserve, Lieut. March 1916; Captain Sept. 1917. National Services, Inverness. M.B.E. Jan. 1919.

SCRIMGEOUR, JOHN MURRAY.
M.A. (St Andrews); LL.B. 1907. Barrister and Solicitor. R.G.A., 2nd Lieut. Dec. 1917. 1/1st North Midland Heavy Battery, France.

SEAGAR, EDWARD AITKEN.
M.B., Ch.B. 1913. R.A.M.C., Lieut. Aug. 1914.

SEAL, SATYENDRA NATH.
Student of Medicine, 1910-17; M.B., Ch.B. 1916. Indian Field Ambulance.

SEATON, ALEXANDER WHITE.
Daniel Stewart's College; First XI. University O.T.C. Infantry, Feb. to Oct. 1917, Cadet Corporal; Officer Cadet Oct. 1917. 3rd attached 6th Royal Highlanders (Black Watch), 2nd Lieut. March 1918.

SEATON, JOHN JERDINE.
Daniel Stewart's College; First XV. and XI. Cadet Corps 1915-17. University O.T.C. Infantry, June to Oct. 1918, Cadet. Royal Air Force, Cadet Oct. 1918.

SEELLY, EDWARD St JOHN.
Bradford Grammar School. M.B., Ch.B. 1912. R.A.M.C., Lieut. 1914; Captain 1916. No. 4 Stationary Hospital, France, 1914. Dispatches 1916 and 1917.

SELBY, ROBERT.
George Watson's College. Student of Medicine, 1916-17 and 1918. O.T.C. Artillery, Jan. to Dec. 1917, Cadet Sergeant. R.F.A., Officer Cadet Dec. 1917; 2nd Lieut. June 1918.

Record of War Service

SELKIRK, WILLIAM JOSEPH BURNS.
George Watson's College; First XV. and XI. M.A. 1901; M.B., Ch.B. 1905; M.D. 1908. President, Philomathic Society. R.A.M.C., Lieut. Feb. 1915; Captain Feb. 1916 to April 1919. 6th M.A.C. 10th Royal Fusiliers, and 29th Casualty Clearing Station, France.

SELLAR, THOMAS.
Physiology Department. Forth R.G.A. (T.), Private.

SELLAR, THOMAS ALEXANDER.
Royal High School. Student of Medicine, 1918-19. 4th and 6th Gordon Highlanders, Private 1909; 2nd Lieut. Sept. 1914; Lieut. June 1916. France Dec. 1914 to July 1915; May 1916 to Jan. 1917. Wounded at Givenchy 1915.

SELLAR, THOMAS McCALL.
Royal High School; First XV. M.B., Ch.B. 1910. R.A.M.C., Lieut. Oct. 1915; Captain Jan. 1917. M.C. Nov. 1918.

SELLAR, WILLIAM B.
George Watson's College. O.T.C. 1914-15. University O.T.C. Artillery, Feb. to Sept. 1918, Cadet. R.F.A., Officer Cadet Sept. 1918.

SELLAR, WILLIAM HARPER.
George Watson's College. M.A. 1895; LL.B. 1900. Barrister. 196th (Western Universities) Battn. Canadians, Private May 1916. 4th Royal Scots, 2nd Lieut. July 1918 to March 1919. France and The Rhine 1916-18. Wounded.

SELLERS, ARTHUR.
Manchester Grammar School. M.B., C.M. 1887; M.D. 1893; D.P.H., D.Sc. (Vict.) 1894. R.A.M.C. (T.), Captain 1908; Brevet Major June 1916. Bacteriologist, 2nd Western General Hospital.

SELLS, HUGH LANCELOT.
M.B., Ch.B. 1906. R.A.M.C., Lieut.; Captain Aug. 1915. No. 8 General Hospital.

SEN, JIMUT BAHAN.
St Xavier's College; First XI. Student of Arts and Medicine, 1912-20; M.A. 1920. Indian Volunteer Ambulance Corps.

SETH-SMITH, HOWARD KNOX.
Student of Medicine. 15th Royal Scots, Private. 3rd King's Liverpool Regiment, attached 3/10th Middlesex Regiment, 2nd Lieut.; Lieut. Dec. 1916. France. Twice Wounded.

SHAFTO, WILLIAM ALEXANDER.
M.B., Ch.B. 1910; M.D. 1913; D.P.H. (Edin.) 1913. R.A.M.C., Lieut. March 1916; Captain March 1917. Mesopotamia. Dispatches March 1919.

SHAH, IKBAL ALI.
Student of Medicine, 1915-18. Indian Field Ambulance.

Record of War Service

SHAIKH, ABDUL HAMID.
　　Student of Medicine, 1910-15; M.B., Ch.B. 1914. Indian Medical Service, Lieut. Nov. 1914; Captain 1915. Indian General Hospitals, 1914-16. France, Mhow Field Ambulance, March 1916; India May 1916; 5th (K.E.O.) Cavalry, France, Sept. 1916; Egypt March 1918; Palestine, Syria, and Asia Minor.

SHAKESHAFT, GEOFFREY WHITLOW.
　　Lymm Grammar School, Chester. Student of Science, 1914-15. O.T.C. Artillery, March to June 1915, Cadet. R.F.A. (S.R.), 2nd Lieut. June 1915; Lieut. July 1917 to May 1919. France.

SHAND, JOHN GLENDINNING BRYDEN.
　　George Watson's College. M.B., Ch.B. 1904. Indian Medical Service (40th Pathans), Lieut. 1909; Captain 1912; Acting Major Jan. 1918. Field Hospital, France. Dispatches.

SHANKS, FREDERICK.
　　Arbroath High School. Student of Science, 1916-17 and 1918-19. O.T.C. Infantry, Nov. 1916 to April 1918, Cadet. R.E., Officer Cadet May 1918.

SHANKS, WILLIAM.
　　Airdrie Academy. Student of Medicine, 1910-15. M.B., Ch.B. 1915. O.T.C. Medical, 1914-15, Cadet. R.A.M.C., Lieut. Sept. 1915; Captain Sept. 1916. Dispatches.

SHANNON, FREDERICK.
　　Royal Academy, Belfast; First XV. and XI. M.B., Ch.B. 1907. M.O. in charge of Troops, North London, Aug. 1914. R.A.M.C., Lieut. April 1916; Captain April 1917. France 1916-18. Invalided out April 1918.

SHANNON, JOHN.
　　Daniel Stewart's College University O.T.C. Infantry, Oct. 1917 to Jan. 1918, Cadet. R.F.C., transferred to London Scottish, Private Feb. 1918.

SHANNON, JOHN ALASTAIR.
　　George Watson's College. Student of Arts, 1912-14. 9th Royal Scots, Private Sept. 1914. 1st Highland Light Infantry, 2nd Lieut. Nov. 1915; Lieut. Jan. 1917. Prisoner of War in Turkey for two and a half years.

SHAPIRO, JAPIE HAROLD LEOPOLD.
　　Student of Medicine, 1913-18; M.B., Ch.B. 1918. O.T.C. Infantry, Jan. to Oct. 1915, Cadet. R.N.V.R., Surgeon-Probationer.

SHARP, A. D.
　　Student of Medicine. R.A.M.C. (T.), Lieut.-Col.

SHARP, JAMES.
　　Student of Law. 6th Gordon Highlanders, Captain.

SHARP, JAMES.
　　Merchiston Castle. O.T.C. 1907-12, Cadet Corporal. Student of Medicine, 1912-14 and 1918-19. O.T.C. Infantry, Feb. 1913 to Oct. 1914, Cadet. 5th Royal Scots (T.), Lieut. Oct. 1914. A.S.C. (M.T.), July 1916.

Record of War Service

SHARP, JOHN STUART CADENHEAD.
Glenalmond. O.T.C. 1913-17. University O.T.C. Artillery, May 1917 to March 1918, Cadet Sergeant; Officer Cadet March 1918. R.F.A., 44th Reserve Battery, 2nd Lieut. Sept. 1918 to March 1919.

SHARPE, EDWARD STEVENSON.
Coleraine Academical Institution; First XV. and XI. M.B., Ch.B. 1902. University Battery, 1st E.C.A.V., 1897-1902, Gunner. Royal Air Force Medical Service, Lieut. June 1918.

SHARPE, WILLIAM CECIL.
M.B., C.M. 1890; M.D. 1899. R.A.M.C., Lieut. Sept. 1916; Captain Sept. 1917; Major May 1919. Registrar, Ripon Military Hospital.

SHAW, ALEXANDER MACKINTOSH.
Raining's School, Inverness. M.A. 1902. Schoolmaster. R.A.M.C., Private Jan. 1915; Sergeant July 1915. 24th General Hospital, France.

SHAW, ARCHIBALD CAMPBELL.
Student of Medicine, 1909-14. M.B., Ch.B. 1914. O.T.C. Artillery, 1908-12, Cadet Bombardier. Royal Navy, H.M.S. *Mersey*, Temp. Surgeon, Aug. 1914.

SHAW, HUGH KIRKLAND.
Lanark Grammar School. Student of Medicine, 1908-14. M.B., Ch.B. 1914. Royal Navy, Temp.-Surgeon Captain Nov. 1914. Royal Naval Division, Gallipoli. H.M.S. *Royal Oak*, and Roehampton Hospital.

SHAW, JOHN ALEXANDER.
Bathgate Academy. Student of Medicine, 1918-19. 18th Royal Scots, Private Oct. 1916; Corporal July 1918. Machine-Gun Corps.

SHAW, JOHN JAMES McINTOSH.
M.A. 1906; M.B., Ch.B. 1909; M.D. 1913. President, Students' Union. University Battery, E.C.A.V., 1902-8, Private. O.T.C. Artillery, 2nd Lieut. 1908; Lieut. 1910. R.A.M.C. (S.R.), Captain Oct. 1914; Acting Major Jan. 1918; Major, 2nd and 44th Casualty Clearing Stations, France, 1914-19. Dispatches June 1915 and Dec. 1917. M.C. and Croix de Guerre with Star, June 1918.

SHAW, REGINALD KENWORTHY.
M.B., Ch.B. 1912. Royal Navy, Temp. Surgeon Aug. 1914.

SHAW, ROBERT GLEN.
Daniel Stewart's College; First XV. M.B., Ch.B. 1911. O.T.C. Infantry, Nov. 1908 to Dec. 1911, Cadet Colour-Sergeant. R.A.M.C., Lieut. 1913; Captain Feb. 1915; Acting Major April 1918; Acting Lieut.-Col. May 1919. Gallipoli June 1915; Salonika, Serbia, Macedonia, and 81st Field Ambulance, Black Sea Force. M.C. 1918. Mention 1917 and 1918.

SHAW, ROBERT RUSSELL.
George Watson's College. Student of Law, 1909-11. Chartered Accountant, 1914. Royal Naval Reserve, Assistant Paymaster, May 1915. Royal Air Force. Captain July 1918 to Feb. 1919. H.M.S. *Furious*.

Record of War Service

SHAW, THOMAS BROWN.
    Campbell College, Belfast; First XV. M.B., Ch.B. 1901. Royal Navy, Surgeon Aug. 1901; Staff Surgeon Aug. 1909; Surgeon-Commander Aug. 1915. Battle of Heligoland Bight, Aug. 1914. M.O. Falmouth. H.M.S. *Birmingham*.

SHAW, WILLIAM D.
    Daniel Stewart's College; First XV. University O.T.C. Infantry, March 1909 to June 1912, Cadet. Highland Light Infantry, 2nd Lieut. Aug. 1914; Captain Feb. 1915; Major March 1916. France and East Africa. Wounded at Loos Sept. 1916 and Somme Oct. 1916. Invalided out Dec. 1919. M.C. Oct. 1916.

SHAW, WILLIAM JOHN.
    Stratherrick School. Student of Arts, 1900-3. 4th Cameron Highlanders, May 1914; Captain Sept. 1915; Staff Captain Nov. 1918. France. Instructor of Topography, Italy. Wounded at Neuve Chapelle. Dispatches Aug. and Nov. 1918 and June 1919. Croce di Guerra.

SHEARER, ALFRED LEONARD.
    Royal High School; First XV. and XI. Student of Arts, 1915-16. O.T.C. Infantry, Oct. 1915 to July 1916, Cadet. Cameron Highlanders, Private July 1916; L/Corporal June 1917. Machine-Gun Corps.

SHEARER, DONALD.
    Miller Institution, Thurso. Student of Medicine, 1918-19. 1/8th Argyll and Sutherland Highlanders, 15th Division, Private April 1917.

SHEARER, DONALD ANGUS MacMILLAN.
    George Heriot's School; First XV. O.T.C. 1914-17, Cadet Sergeant. Student of Medicine, 1918-19. 4th Argyll and Sutherland Highlanders (S.R.), May 1917; Officer Cadet June 1917; 2nd Lieut. Jan. to Feb. 1918.

SHEARER, GEORGE.
    George Watson's College. M.A. 1912; B.Sc. Assistant to Professor of Natural Philosophy. Royal Navy, Temp. Instructor-Lieut. Sept. 1915.

SHEARER, JOHN.
    Kirkwall Burgh School. Student of Arts, 1915-17. 2/10th Royal Scots, Private July 1917.

SHEARSBY, JAMES.
    Midwifery Department. A.S.C., Driver.

SHEDDEN, ARCHIBALD JOHN.
    Bathgate Academy. Student of Medicine, 1914-15 and 1918-19. O.T.C. Infantry, Feb. to June 1915, Cadet. 16th Royal Scots, Private; Corporal June 1915; Sergeant March 1916; Officer Cadet; 2nd Lieut. March 1917. France. Wounded at the Somme July 1916. Invalided out Jan. 1918.

Record of War Service

SHENNAN, ARNOLD HOSEASON.
    Edinburgh Academy. O.T.C. 1908-10. Student of Medicine, 1910-13 and 1919; M.B., Ch.B. 1919. O.T.C. Artillery, Oct. 1910 to Aug. 1914, Cadet. R.F.A., 275th Brigade, 2nd Lieut. Aug. 1914; Lieut. June 1916; Acting Captain Nov. 1917. France. Twice Wounded. M.C. Sept. 1918.

SHENNAN, JOHN ROGNVALD.
    Fettes College. O.T.C. 1908-9. B.Sc. 1913. A.M.I.C.E. O.T.C. Engineers, 1910-13, Cadet. R.E., 2nd Lieut. Oct. 1914; Lieut. July 1915; Captain Feb. 1916; Major May 1918. Dispatches June 1918 and June 1919. M.C. Dec. 1916; Officer of Crown of Roumania, March 1919.

SHEPHEARD-WALWYN, RODERICK AYLWARD.
    Bromsgrove School. Student of Medicine, 1914-15. 3rd West Yorkshire Regiment, 2nd Lieut. Oct. 1914; Lieut. June 1915; Captain Nov. 1917. Royal Air Force, Oct. 1918. The Rhine.

SHEPHERD, DAVID.
    Dundee High School. B.Sc. 1906. Canadian Army Service Corps (M.T.), Lieut. Oct. 1914; Captain Jan. 1916. France.

SHEPHERD, JAMES OGILVY.
    Edinburgh Academy. O.T.C. 1908-9. Student of Law, 1913-14. R.F.A. (T.), 2nd Lieut. 1908; Lieut. 1910; Captain June 1916; Acting Major Sept. 1916 to March 1919. France 1915-18. Wounded at Ypres Aug. 1917. M.C. Jan. 1918.

SHEPHERD, JOHN INGRAM.
    Morgan Academy, Dundee. M.A. (St Andrews) 1903; M.B., Ch.B. 1904; M.D. 1913. R.A.M.C., Lieut. Nov. 1914; Captain Nov. 1915. 9th and 7th Leicestershire Regiment. M.C. June 1917.

SHEPHERD, PHILIP G.
    University Library Assistant. 4th Royal Scots (T.), Private Aug. 1914; Corporal July 1918. Gallipoli, Egypt, and Palestine, June 1915 to March 1918. France April 1918 to Sept. 1919.

SHEPHERD, ROBERT FRANCIS.
    Morgan Academy, Dundee. M.A. (St Andrews) 1902; Student of Law, 1902-5. Writer to the Signet, 1905. R.G.A., 2nd Lieut. Dec. 1915; Lieut. June 1916; Acting Captain Aug. 1918.

SHEPHERD, WILLIAM MOIR WEBSTER.
    Wick Academy. M.B., Ch.B. 1912; M.D. 1916; F.R.C.S. 1917. Colonial Office and Navy, East Africa, Sept. 1914 to May 1915. R.A.M.C., Lieut. Nov. 1915; Captain Nov. 1916. France.

SHERIFFS, WILLIAM PERCY DAHERS.
    George Watson's College. University O.T.C. Artillery, Dec. 1917 to Sept. 1918, Cadet Sergeant. R.F.A., Officer Cadet Sept. 1918.

Record of War Service

SHERRIFF, THOMAS CHALMERS.
Dunfermline High School. Student of Arts, 1913-16; M.A. 1919. Forth R.G.A. (T.), Gunner Dec. 1915; 2nd Lieut. Feb. 1918.

SHEWARD, CHARLES RAILTON
Clifton College. M.B., C.M. 1894. First XI. Royal Navy 1897; Surgeon-Commander. Senior M.O. R.N. Hospital Ship *St Margaret of Scotland*, 1916-19. Médaille d'Honneur des Épidémies 1918.

SHIEL, DAVID HASTINGS.
North Berwick High School. Cadet Corps 1903-7, Sergeant. M.A. 1911; B.Sc. 1914. O.T.C. Artillery, Oct. 1909 to Jan. 1913, Cadet. 16th Royal Scots, Sergeant Nov. 1914. R.G.A., 2nd Lieut. Jan. 1915. Invalided out Dec. 1915. Technical Staff, Ardeer Munition Factory, Ayrshire, from Dec. 1915.

SHIELL, ALEXANDER GUTHRIE.
Rugby. B.A. (Oxford) 1906; LL.B. 1908. O.T.C. Infantry, 1914-15, Cadet L/Corporal. 2/1st Highland Cyclist Battn., 2nd Lieut. Oct. 1915; Lieut. July 1917. Attached 4th King's African Rifles. Cantonment Magistrate, Uganda.

SHIELS, PETER McLAREN.
M.B., Ch.B. 1913. R.A.M.C., Lieut.; Captain Nov. 1917.

SHIRCORE, JOHN OWEN.
M.B., Ch.B. 1907; L.R.C.P. & S. (Edin.) and L.F.P.S. (Glasg.) 1906; M.R.C.P. 1911. East African Medical Service, 1908; Captain Oct. 1914 to April 1918. O.C. Native Base Hospital, Mombasa. Dispatches Oct. 1917.

SHIRES, BERTRAM.
M.B., Ch.B. 1914. R.A.M.C. (S.R.), Lieut. Sept. 1914; Captain April 1915; Major June 1918; Brevet Major. Med. Exp. Force and France. Dispatches 1918.

SHIRLAW, HERBERT.
Student of Arts and Divinity, 1908-15; M.A. 1911. O.T.C. Artillery, 1914-15, Cadet. R.F.A., 2nd Lieut. March 1915; Lieut. June 1916. 4th Howitzer Brigade.

SHIRLAW, HUGH.
Lasswade School. M.A. 1907; B.D. 1910. Minister, Church of Scotland. 14th Argyll and Sutherland Highlanders, Private June 1915; Sergeant Dec. 1915. 9th Royal Scots (T.), 2nd Lieut. Jan. 1916; Lieut. July 1917. France.

SHIRLAW, MATTHEW.
Lasswade School. Mus.Bac. 1898; Mus.D. 1913. F.R.C.O. Lecturer in Music. Royal Air Force, Oct. 1918.

SHOOLBREAD, THOMAS BULLIONS.
M.B., C.M. 1897. R.A.M.C., Lieut. May 1916. 8th General Hospital, Rouen, Oct. to Dec. 1916. 2nd West Yorkshire Regiment, Pioneer Battn.

Record of War Service

SIBBALD, ALEXANDER.
Knox Institute, Haddington. M.A. 1910. Schoolmaster. Cameron Highlanders, Private Dec. 1915; L/Corporal. 8th Tank Corps, Sergeant Jan. 1917; Officer Cadet Nov. 1918; 2nd Lieut. March 1919.

SIBBALD, WILLIAM WHYTE.
Harris Academy, Dundee. Student of Science, 1917-18. O.T.C. Artillery 1917-18, Cadet; Officer Cadet June 1918. R.F.A., 2nd Lieut. April 1919.

SILBERBAUER, STANLEY FREDERICK.
South African College School. Cadet Corps 1902-5. M.B., Ch.B. 1911; M.D. 1914; M.R.C.P. (Edin.). O.T.C. Infantry, 1909-11, Cadet. South African Medical Corps, Captain Jan. 1916. East African Exp. Force; Union Defence Force.

SILVER, JOHN PAYZANT.
B.A. (Windsor, N.S.); M.B., C.M. 1893. R.A.M.C. 1894; Lieut.-Col. March 1915; Colonel Feb. 1916 to March 1919. 17th Field Ambulance, Aug. 1914. A.D.M.S., 12th Division, Feb. 1916. France Sept. 1914 to March 1919. Four times Mentioned in Dispatches. D.S.O.; C.B.E. June 1919.

SIM, ALEXANDER.
Student of Medicine, 1907-14. O.T.C. Medical, 1908-10, Cadet. Lovat Scouts (T.), Private Aug. 1914; 10th Northumberland Fusiliers, 2nd Lieut.; Lieut. June 1917; Captain Dec. 1917; Acting Major 1918. France 1915-17; Italy 1917-19. Dispatches Sept. 1917. M.C. June 1918.

SIM, ANDREW.
Gordon Schools, Huntly. Student of Science, 1918-19. 4th Gordon Highlanders, Private May 1916.

SIME, WILLIAM.
George Watson's College. Student of Law, 1896-8. Chartered Accountant, 1899. R.F.A. (T.), 1st Lowland Brigade, 1903; Captain 1908; Major June 1916; Staff Captain, War Office, July 1918. France 1915. Dispatches.

SIMON, BERNARD HILLIARD.
Royal High School. Student of Medicine, 1911-16; M.B., Ch.B. 1916. O.T.C Medical, Oct. 1914-16, Cadet. R.A.M.C. (S.R.), Lieut. Nov. 1916; Captain Nov. 1917

SIMPSON, ALEXANDER.
M.B., Ch.B. 1911. Royal Navy, Surgeon April 1913.

SIMPSON, ALEXANDER BOWDEN.
Linlithgow Academy. B.A. (Hons.); M.A. 1910. 3rd Royal Scots, Private March 1917; L/Corporal June 1917; 2nd Lieut. Oct. 1918.

SIMPSON, ALEXANDER MURRAY.
Daniel Stewart's College. Student of Arts, 1910-15; M.A. (Hons. Mod. Lang.) 1914. O.T.C. Infantry, 1914-15, Cadet. 12th Scottish Rifles, 2nd Lieut. Jan. 1915; Lieut. March 1916; Staff Lieut., 3rd Class, Feb. 1917; 2nd Class, July 1917. Intelligence Corps, 1917-19.

Record of War Service

SIMPSON, ALEXANDER P.
Merchiston Castle. Student of Law, 1888-94. Writer to the Signet, 1894. 10th Royal Scots (T.), 1897; Major 1912; Lieut.-Col. Nov. 1914; Colonel Nov. 1918. General Staff, France, May 1917. Mention 1917. Dispatches Nov. 1918. T.D. Nov. 1917; O.B.E. Jan. 1919.

SIMPSON, ALEXANDER RUSSELL.
Edinburgh Academy. B.A. (Oxford). Student of Law, 1901-3. Writer to the Signet, 1905. North Scottish R.G.A., 2nd Lieut. Oct. 1915; Captain Oct. 1917.

SIMPSON, ANDREW.
Leven School. University O.T.C. Infantry, June to Sept. 1917, Cadet. R.F.C., Officer Cadet Oct. 1917. London Scottish, Private Dec. 1917 to Sept. 1919.

SIMPSON, ANDREW.
Kirkcaldy High School; First XV. and XI. O.T.C. 1914-15, Cadet Corporal. Student of Medicine, 1918-19. 12th Royal Scots, 2nd Lieut. Dec. 1915; Lieut. July 1917.

SIMPSON, ARCHIBALD.
M.B., Ch.B. 1905. R.A.M.C., Lieut.; Captain Aug. 1918.

SIMPSON, CHARLES.
Inverness Royal Academy. Student of Medicine, 1913-18; M.B., Ch.B. 1918. O.T.C. Medical, 1916-18, Cadet L/Corporal. R.A.M.C., Lieut. Aug. 1918; Captain Aug. 1919. 6th King's Own Scottish Borderers. Edinburgh War Hospital, Bangour.

SIMPSON, EDWARD SWAN.
George Watson's College. M.B., Ch.B. 1905; M.D. 1910. University Battery, E.C.A.V., 1901-4, Gunner. R.A.M.C. (T.), Lieut. Sept. 1916; Captain April 1917. 2/2nd Northumbrian Field Ambulance; 4th Yorkshire and 4th East Yorkshire Regiments. France 1916-18; Somme and Lys. Wounded Dec. 1917. M.C. 1918.

SIMPSON, FREDERICK DAVID.
M.B., Ch.B. 1900; M.D. 1903; F.R.C.S. (Edin.) 1903. R.A.M.C., Captain March 1918.

SIMPSON, GEORGE FREELAND BARBOUR.
George Watson's College. M.B., Ch.B. 1898; M.D. 1905; F.R.C.S. (Edin.) 1903; F.R.C.P. (Edin.) 1905. Senior Assistant and Examiner in Midwifery. R.A.M.C., Temp. Lieut. Feb. 1917; Captain April 1917; Major Feb. 1918. President, Medical Board. Military Hospital, Eaton Hall, Chester.

SIMPSON, GEORGE WRIGHT.
George Heriot's School; First XV. Student of Arts, Science, and Medicine, 1912-15 and 1918-19; M.A. 1919. O.T.C. Artillery, 1914-15, Cadet. R.F.A. (T.), 1st Lowland Brigade, 2nd Lieut. Aug. 1915; Lieut. June 1916; Acting Adjutant 1917-19; Acting Captain Oct. 1918. Gallipoli, Egypt, and Palestine.

Record of War Service

SIMPSON, HAROLD CHRISTOPHER.
  Trent College, Derbyshire. M.B., Ch.B. 1908. L.M.S.S.A. (Lond.) 1908. No. 4 Coy. Q.R.V.B., Royal Scots, and 9th Royal Scots (T.), 1902-8. R.A.M.C. (T.), Captain Oct. 1914; Temp. Major Jan. 1919. Military Hospital, Newcastle, Dec. 1916. D.A.D.M.S., Lucknow Division, India, 1919. Dispatches 1919.

SIMPSON, HUBERT LOUIS.
  George Watson's College. M.A. 1901. Minister, U.F. Church of Scotland. No. 4 Coy. Q.R.V.B., Royal Scots, Private. Army Chaplain, 4th Class, 1913. Attached 5th Scottish Rifles (Cameronians).

SIMPSON, IAN GRINDLAY.
  Stramongate School, Kendal. Student of Medicine, 1917. O.T.C. Infantry, 1917, Cadet. R.N.A.S., Probationer Flight Officer May 1917; Flight Sub-Lieut. Oct. 1917. Royal Air Force, Lieut.-Pilot April 1918 to Nov. 1919. France.

SIMPSON, JAMES.
  Dollar Academy; First XV. Student of Science, 1885-6. Fife Light Horse Volunteers, Private 1889; 2nd Lieut. 1897; Lieut. May 1899. Fife and Forfar Yeomanry (T.), Captain June 1902. Mobilised Nov. 1914; Major Feb. 1915. South African Campaign, 1900-1. Invalided out Sept. 1916.

SIMPSON, JAMES BERTIE.
  Inverness Academy. M.A. 1883; M.B., C.M. 1887; M.D. 1892. R.A.M.C. (T.), Major 1914. Attached 5th Seaforth Highlanders. Royal Navy, Temp. Surgeon Dec. 1915 to July 1918. East Indian and Adriatic Squadrons. T.D. 1915. O.B.E. 1920.

SIMPSON, J. C.
  M.B., Ch.B. N.Z. Medical Corps, Captain.

SIMPSON, JOHN FINDLATER.
  M.A. 1905; B.Sc. 1909. O.T.C. Artillery, July to Sept. 1915, Cadet. R.G.A. (S.R.), 2nd Lieut. Sept. 1915; Lieut. July 1917. France.

SIMPSON, JOHN GORDON.
  M.A. (St Andrews); LL.B. 1906. Law Agent, 1907. 4th Royal Highlanders (Black Watch) (T.), 2nd Lieut.; Lieut. June 1916; Acting Captain Oct. 1917. Brigade Musketry Officer.

SIMPSON, JOHN WATSON.
  Merchiston Castle; First XV. and XI. Cadet Corps 1903-8, Sergeant. Student of Medicine, 1910-15; M.B., Ch.B. 1915. Rugby "Blue." O.T.C. Medical, 1914-15, Cadet. R.A.M.C. (T.), Lieut. July 1915; Captain Jan. 1916. 2nd Scottish General Hospital, 1915. 1/3rd Lowland Field Ambulance, Egypt, Palestine, 1916-18.

SIMPSON, JOHN WILLIAM.
  Dollar Academy. M.B., C.M. 1896; M.D. 1906; F.R.C.P. (Edin.) 1903. Scottish Rugby International (13 "Caps"). R.A.M.C. (T.), Captain 1911. 2nd Scottish General Hospital.

Record of War Service

SIMPSON, JOSEPH.
> Harris Institute, Preston. Student of Science, 1900-6. District Volunteers, East Africa, 1914. Belgian Military Transport, Uganda, 1915-16. Military Labour Corps, Private (rejoined) June 1917; Sergeant Dec. 1917; 2nd Lieut. July 1918.

SIMPSON, KERR ALEXANDER.
> Edinburgh Academy. B.L. 1904. 8th Highland Light Infantry (T.), 1906; Captain; Major June 1915. General Staff H.Q., Scottish Command.

SIMPSON, ROBERT FRANCIS.
> Broughton School, Edinburgh. Student of Arts and Science, 1911-15; M.A. 1919. O.T.C. Infantry, Oct. 1911 to Jan. 1915, Cadet Corporal. 9th Gordon Highlanders, 2nd Lieut. Jan. 1915; Lieut. Aug. 1917. France.

SIMPSON, ROBERT JOHN SHAW.
> Edinburgh Collegiate School. M.A. 1878; M.B., C.M. 1882. Army Medical Service, Feb. 1883, Colonel. A.D.M.S., Woolwich District, Aug. 1914 to Jan. 1919. C.M.G. 1900; C.B. 1917.

SIMPSON, ROBERT KENNEDY MUIR.
> Perth Academy; First XV. M.A. (Hons. Engl.) 1914. O.T.C. Artillery, 1910-14, Cadet Corporal. R.F.A. (S.R.), 2nd Lieut. Aug. 1914; Lieut.; Captain Nov. 1917; Acting Major Aug. 1918. Adjutant, 19th Brigade, Nov. 1916. 98th and 131st Batteries, March 1917 to Feb. 1919. France Dec. 1914. Wounded April 1915. Dispatches 1917. M.C. Jan. 1918.

SIMPSON, SAMUEL RALEIGH.
> M.A. 1902. Writer to the Signet, 1906. Labour Corps, 2nd Lieut. Dec. 1917.

SIMPSON, WILFRID JAMES.
> Edinburgh Academy. M.B., Ch.B. 1907. Indian Medical Service, Lieut. 1909; Captain 1911; Major Aug. 1919. France Oct. 1914-16; East Africa Nov. 1917 to Feb. 1918. Dispatches (East Africa) Jan. 1919.

SIMPSON, WILLIAM HAMILTON.
> M.B., Ch.B. 1903; M.D. 1906; D.P.H. (Edin.) 1906. N.Z. Medical Corps, Captain April 1915. N.Z. Hospital Ship *Maheno*, Gallipoli.

SIMSON, ALAN G.
> Edinburgh Academy. Student of Law, 1908-9. Chartered Accountant, 1911. R.F.A. (T.), 1st Lowland Brigade, Lieut. 1910; Captain June 1916; Acting Major Nov. 1917. France Oct. 1915 to Dec. 1916; Mesopotamia June 1917 to Dec. 1918; India Dec. 1918 to Oct. 1919.

SIMSON, ALEXANDER MACDONALD.
> Student of Medicine, 1912-14 and 1917-19. O.T.C. Artillery, 1913-14, Cadet. R.F.A. (T.), 1st Highland Brigade, 2nd Lieut. Aug. 1914; Lieut. June 1916. France (two years).

Record of War Service

SIMSON, HARRY MACDONALD.
    M.A. 1900; LL.B. 1908. Writer to the Signet, 1905. A.S.C. (T.), T. and S. Column, Lowland Division, Lieut. June 1916; Captain May 1918. Palestine.

SIMSON, HENRY JOHN.
    Ashfield College, Sydney, New South Wales. Student of Medicine, 1909-14; M.B., Ch.B. 1914. R.A.M.C., Lieut. Oct. 1916; Captain Oct. 1917. Invalided out Sept. 1918.

SIMSON, JAMES TUDHOPE.
    Merchiston Castle; First XV. and XI. Cadet Corps 1898-1902, 2nd Lieut. M.B., Ch.B. 1908. R.A.M.C. (T.), Captain Oct. 1914.

SIMSON, JOHN THOMAS.
    M.B., Ch.B. 1908. R.A.M.C., Lieut. Aug. 1912; Captain July 1913. 2nd Battn. Egyptian Army. Palestine. Dispatches Jan. 1919.

SIMSON, ROBERT.
    Student of Law, 1890-2. Writer to the Signet, 1894. Mounted Infantry, Q.R.V.B., Royal Scots, 1900-6. 4th Royal Scots (T.), Captain Sept. 1914; Temp. Major Aug. 1915; Temp. Lieut.-Col. Jan. 1916; Lieut.-Col. Dec. 1917 to May 1919. Egypt and Palestine 1916-19. Officers' Base Depôt. Dispatches April 1918. O.B.E. June 1919.

SINCLAIR, ANDREW STEWART.
    Kimberley High School, South Africa. Cadet Corps 1903-4, Corporal. Student of Science, 1913-15. R.F.C., April 1917; 2nd Lieut. Aug. 1917. Royal Air Force, Lieut. May 1918. Prisoner of War (four months); escaped from Le Cateau.

SINCLAIR, ARCHIBALD STEVENSON.
    George Heriot's School; First XV. Student of Law, 1913-14 and 1916-17. Chartered Accountant, 1918. 5th Royal Scots (T.), Private Sept. 1914; L/Corporal 1915; Acting Sergeant 1916. Gallipoli.

SINCLAIR, DAVID.
    Royal High School. University O.T.C. Artillery, Nov. 1915 to March 1916, Cadet Bombardier; Officer Cadet March 1916. R.F.A., 121st Brigade, 2nd Lieut. Sept. 1916; Lieut. March 1918 to April 1919. France, 38th Division.

SINCLAIR, DONALD BOASE.
    Fettes College. B.A. (Oxford) 1908; LL.B. and Writer to the Signet, 1911. 9th Royal Scots (T.), 2nd Lieut. Oct. 1914; Lieut. June 1916; Captain Aug. 1917. Staff Captain, War Office. Intelligence Officer, South-East Coast of Kent. O.B.E. (Military) 1919.

SINCLAIR, FRASER McEWEN.
    George Watson's College. M.B., Ch.B. 1910. R.A.M.C., Lieut. July 1915; Captain.

Record of War Service

SINCLAIR, GEORGE ALEXANDER.
George Watson's College. Student of Arts and Medicine, 1911-15 and 1917-20; M.A. 1919; M.B., Ch.B. 1920. O.T.C. Infantry, Oct. 1912-16, Cadet L/Corporal. R.N.V.R., Surgeon-Probationer, 1916. Haslar Hospital. Invalided out March 1917.

SINCLAIR, JAMES.
George Heriot's School; First XV. and XI. Student of Medicine, 1918-19. 5th Royal Scots, Private Sept. 1914; 2nd Lieut. March 1915; Lieut. June 1917; Temp. Captain Dec. 1916 to Aug. 1917. Royal Air Force. Gallipoli. Wounded Aug. 1915.

SINCLAIR, JAMES RONALD SHERRIFF.
Glasgow Academy. O.T.C. 1912-15, Cadet L/Corporal. University O.T.C. Artillery, March to Dec. 1917, Cadet Bombardier. R.N.V.R., Sub-Lieut. Dec. 1917. Mine-sweeping Operations.

SINCLAIR, JOHN CADZOW.
Campbell College, Belfast. Student of Medicine, 1910-15; M.B., Ch.B. 1915. O.T.C. Medical, 1909-14, Cadet L/Corporal. R.N.V.R., Surgeon Sub-Lieut. Jan. 1915. Royal Navy, Surgeon April 1915. H.M.S. *Bluebell*, Hong-Kong.

SINCLAIR, JOHN GEORGE.
Broughton School, Edinburgh. Student of Arts, 1914-16 and 1918-19; M.A. 1919. Royal Navy, H.M.S. *Valiant*, Able Seaman, Dec. 1916 to Feb. 1919.

SINCLAIR, JOHN UMBRIA.
George Watson's College. O.T.C. 1913-15. Student of Science, 1918-20. O.T.C. Artillery, May to Dec. 1916, Cadet; Officer Cadet Dec. 1916. R.G.A. (S.R.), 2nd Lieut. March 1917; Lieut. Sept. 1918. France.

SINCLAIR, MEURICE.
Clifton College, Bristol. M.B., Ch.B. 1903. R.A.M.C., Lieut. 1904; Captain; Major July 1915. Prisoner of War. Four times Mentioned in Dispatches. C.M.G.

SINCLAIR, PATRICK.
Royal High School. M.A. 1890. Minister, Church of Scotland. Chaplain (T.F.), 4th Class, 1901; 3rd Class, 1911; 2nd Class, March 1916. Senior Chaplain, 51st (Highland) Division, April 1915-19. Wounded Aug. 1917. Prisoner of War March to Nov. 1918. Dispatches Dec. 1917. D.S.O. Jan. 1918.

SINCLAIR, ROBERT ALEXANDER.
George Heriot's School. M.A. 1909; B.Sc. 1909. Schoolmaster. R.E., Sapper June 1917.

SINCLAIR, THOMAS.
George Watson's College. B.Sc. 1912. R.N.V.R., H.M. Motor Launch 140, Sub-Lieut. June 1915; Lieut. June 1916 to April 1919. Special Service, Nov. 1914.

Record of War Service

SINCLAIR, WILLIAM ARNOLD.
Kirkwall Burgh School. Student of Medicine, 1911-14 and 1917-20; M.B., Ch.B. 1920. O.T.C. Infantry, 1911-14, Cadet. 8th Seaforth Highlanders, 2nd Lieut. Sept. 1914; Lieut. June 1916. Attached Trench Mortar Battery.

SINCLAIR, WILLIAM JAMES PENMAN.
George Heriot's School. Student of Science, 1910-14. R.E. (Special Brigade), Corporal July 1915. R.G.A. (S.R.), 2nd Lieut. March 1918. France July 1915-17.

SINCLAIR-LOUTIT, WILLIAM HENRY AUSTIN.
B.A. (Camb.); M.B., Ch.B. 1912. R.N.V.R., H.M.S. *Irresistible*, Surgeon.

SINDERSON, HARRY CHAPMAN.
Clee Grammar School, Lincoln; First XI. Student of Medicine, 1909-14; M.B., Ch.B. 1914. O.T.C. Medical, Nov. 1910-13. R.A.M.C. (S.R.), Lieut. 1913; Captain April 1915; Temp. Major Nov. 1916 to June 1917. H.M. Hospital Ships *Carisbrook Castle*, 1914; *Mandella*, and *Stad Antwerpen*. 65th British General Hospital. Salonika and Mesopotamia.

SINGER, ERNEST OSCAR ADOLPHUS.
Student of Medicine, 1911-16. M.B., Ch.B. 1916. O.T.C. Medical, Oct. 1914 to June 1916, Cadet. R.A.M.C. (S.R.), Lieut. Nov. 1916; Captain Nov. 1917. M.O., 22nd Cavalry, Mesopotamia.

SINGH, NARENDRA PAL.
Student of Arts, 1913-14. Indian Field Ambulance.

SINTON, FREDERICK RITCHIE.
M.B., Ch.B. 1904. R.A.M.C., Lieut. April 1917 to May 1918. Balkans and Italy.

SIRCAR, JYOTIPROKAS.
Hare School, Calcutta. B.Sc. (Calcutta). M.B., Ch.B. 1913. Indian Medical Service, Lieut. Jan. 1916; Captain 1917. Mesopotamia.

SISSON, CHARLES JASPER.
Rutherford College, Newcastle-on-Tyne. M.A. 1907. Professor of English Literature, Bombay University. Bombay Battn., Indian Defence Force, Aug. 1914; Lieut. Oct. 1917. Bombay University Infantry, 1917.

SKAE, ERNEST TRAILL.
St Drostan's College, New Zealand, and Kilmarnock Academy. Student of Law, 1895-7. Solicitor before the Supreme Courts. President, Scots Law Society. 4th Royal Scots (T.), 1906; Captain 1914; Major June 1915. France 1916-17. Twice Wounded in 1917. Invalided home.

SKAE, FREDERICK MACPHERSON TRAILL.
M.B., C.M. 1890; M.D. 1895. R.G.A. (T.) (Orkney), 2nd Lieut. Aug. 1914; Lieut. June 1916.

SKELTON, ARCHIBALD NOEL.
Student of Law, 1904-7. 4th Scottish Horse (T.), Lieut. June 1916.

Record of War Service

SKENE, ALEXANDER.
Pumpherston School. Student of Arts, 1911-14; M.A. 1914. Schoolmaster. O.T.C. Infantry, Oct. 1914 to July 1915, Cadet. 16th Highland Light Infantry, 2nd Lieut. July 1915; Lieut. June 1916 to June 1919. France. Wounded and taken Prisoner at Beaumont Hamel.

SKENE, LESLIE HENDERSON.
George Watson's College. M.B., Ch.B. 1911. Association "Blue." Diploma in Psychiatry. R.A.M.C., Lieut. Sept. 1914; Captain Sept. 1915. Gallipoli. Wounded Sept. 1915 and June 1917. M.C.

SKENE, THOMAS.
M.A. 1907. Student of Medicine, 1913-15. O.T.C. Infantry, Oct. 1914 to March 1915, Cadet. 4th Scottish Rifles (S.R.), 2nd Lieut. March 1915; Lieut. July 1917. 5th Connaught Rangers. Gallipoli and Salonika.

SKINNER, ALEXANDER.
Galashiels Academy. Student of Arts, 1897. King's Own Scottish Borderers, Private May 1916.

SKINNER, CHARLES GUNN.
George Heriot's School. M.B., Ch.B. 1914. R.A.M.C., Lieut.; Captain April 1917.

SKINNER, ERNEST WILLIAM.
Dulwich College. M.B., C.M. 1885; M.D. 1893. R.A.M.C., Captain March 1916; Major Aug. 1916; Acting Lieut.-Col. July 1917. 65th British General Hospital. Macedonia, and Mesopotamia, July 1917 to Jan. 1919. Dispatches. O.B.E.

SLACK, WILLIAM AUGUSTUS.
St Kitts Grammar School; First XI. O.T.C. 1909-11. Student of Medicine, 1911-14 and 1916-19; M.B., Ch.B. 1919. Scottish Horse (T.), Private Aug. 1914. R.E. (Special Brigade), Corporal Aug. 1915, to Dec. 1918. France. Gassed at Loos Sept. 1915.

SLANE, HERBERT FRITHIOF NILSSON.
Ermysted's Grammar School, Skipton-in-Craven. Student of Medicine, 1918-19. Royal Navy Auxiliary Sick Berth Reserve, March 1917 to March 1919. H.M.S. *Royal Arthur*, and R.N. Barracks, Chatham.

SLATER, ALAN BUTLER.
Giggleswick; First XV. and XI; M.B., Ch.B. 1899; M.D. 1905; M.R.C.S. (Eng.) and L.R.C.P. (Lond.) 1899. Royal Navy, Surgeon Oct. 1914 to March 1918. R.A.M.C., Lieut. April 1918-19.

SLATER, ALEXANDER.
Student of Science, 1905-7. A.M.I.C.E. I.A.R.O. 106th Hazara Pioneers, 2nd Lieut. Dec. 1914; Lieut. Dec. 1915; Temp. Captain June 1917; Captain Dec. 1918; Staff Captain June to Sept. 1919. 107th Pioneers, I.E.F.D. France 1915; Baluchistan 1915; Mesopotamia 1916 and 1918-19; N. W. Frontier, India, 1917; Afghan Campaign 1919.

Record of War Service

SLATER, JOHN McDONALD SCOTT.
  Daniel Stewart's College. Student of Medicine, 1916-17. Anatomy Staff, 1919-20. O.T.C. Medical, Oct. 1917-18, Cadet. R.N.V.R., H.M.S. *Verdun*, Surgeon Sub-Lieut. Oct. 1918.

SLAUGHTER, CLEMENT REID.
  Royal High School. 4th Royal Scots (aged 16). University O.T.C. Artillery, Jan. to March 1917, Cadet. R.F.A., Gunner March 1917; Bombardier. Egyptian Exp. Force.

SLAUGHTER, JAMES CRAWFORD.
  Leith Academy. Student of Arts, 1913-15 and 1919-20. 3rd Royal Scots, Private Dec. 1915. 737th Area Employment Coy.

SLAYTER, EDWARD WHEELER.
  Dalhousie University, Halifax, Nova Scotia. M.B., C.M. 1891. Army Medical Service, July 1892; Colonel and A.D.M.S., Dec. 1917; D.D.M.S., 7th Corps, France. Dispatches Feb. and June 1915, June and Dec. 1916, Dec. 1917 and Dec. 1918. C.M.G. June 1916; D.S.O. Jan. 1918.

SLAYTER, JOHN HOWARD.
  Dalhousie University, Halifax, Nova Scotia. M.B., C.M. 1888. Canadian Army Medical Corps, Captain June 1916; Major Nov. 1918. Commandant, Surrey V.A.D. 48. M.B.E. June 1919.

SLEATH, FREDERIC JAMES.
  Anderson Academy, Bo'ness. Student of Arts and Divinity, 1909-15; M.A. 1913. 14th attached 3rd and 2nd Royal Scots, Private Nov. 1914; 2nd Lieut. March 1915; Lieut. July 1917. Attached 4/5th Royal Highlanders (Black Watch), June 1915. Staff Military Intelligence, War Office, Oct. 1916, and G.H.Q., Aug. 1918.

SLEATH, WILLIAM DOUGLAS.
  Bo'ness Academy. M.A. 1909. 15th Royal Scots, Private Sept. 1914. 6/7th Royal Scots Fusiliers, 2nd Lieut. May 1917; Lieut. Nov. 1918. France. Wounded at Fleurbaix March 1916, and at Bois Grenier Aug. 1916.

SLEIGH, ROBERT SKILLEN.
  M.A. 1911. Minister, U.F. Church of Scotland. 14th Royal Scots, 2nd Lieut.

SLEIGH, THOMAS MILLAR.
  Glenalmond. O.T.C. 1913-16. University O.T.C. Artillery, May 1917 to March 1918, Cadet Bombardier. 24th Tank Corps, Officer Cadet April 1918; 2nd Lieut.

SLIGHT, DAVID.
  Falkirk High School. Student of Medicine, 1916-17. R.N.V.R., Surgeon Sub-Lieut. Aug. 1917.

SLIGHT, JAMES DUNCAN.
  Edinburgh Institution. M.A. 1892; M.B., C.M. 1897; M.D. 1900. R.A.M.C. (T.), Major 1908. 5th Northern General Hospital, 1914-19.

Record of War Service

SLOAN, ALLEN THOMSON.
Edinburgh Academy; First XV. O.T.C. 1909-11. Student of Medicine, 1911-14 and 1918-19. Scottish Rugby International, 1914 and 1919. O.T.C. Artillery, Oct. 1912 to Aug. 1914, Cadet. R.F.A., 17th Battery, 2nd Lieut. Sept. 1914; Lieut. Sept. 1915; Captain March 1916; Acting Major Aug. 1916. Prisoner of War in Germany Feb. 1917. Escaped May 1918. Dispatches (twice) 1917. D.S.O. June 1917.

SLOSS, WILLIAM.
South Melbourne College. M.B., Ch.B. 1900; F.R.C.S. (Edin.) 1902. Australian Imperial Forces, Hon. Major 1913. Transport Duty, Melbourne to Cairo. No. 1 Australian General Hospital, Heliopolis, and Seymour Training Camp.

SLUYS, MAURICE.
Student of Science, 1910-11. Ingénieur civil des Mines (Université de Liége). 1er Régiment du Génie, 1st Battn., Private April 1915; Sergeant 1915; 2nd Lieut. 1916; Lieut. 1918. Dispatches Oct. 1916, Nov. 1917, and March 1918. Croix de Guerre avec Palme March 1918.

SMALE, ERNEST HERCULES.
Boroughmuir School. Student of Arts, 1911-14. 4th Royal Scots (T.), Private 1910; Sergeant Dec. 1914; C.Q.M.S. Sept. 1916; R.Q.M.S. April 1917. Egyptian Exp. Force. Dispatches March 1917. Meritorious Service Medal June 1919.

SMALE, PHILIP BRADLEY.
Repton. O.T.C. 1909-13. Student of Medicine, 1914-15 and 1917-20; M.B., Ch.B. 1920. A.S.C. (M.T.), Private (Motor Ambulance Driver) Aug. 1915.

SMALL, HERBERT McDONALD.
Lasswade School. Student of Arts, 1918-19. O.T.C. Infantry, Feb. to March 1916, Cadet. R.E. (Special Brigade), Sapper May 1916. Rifle Brigade, 2nd Lieut. Oct. 1917. Royal Air Force, 2nd Lieut. Aug. 1918 to Jan. 1919. Wounded and Gassed Sept. 1916, and Wounded March 1918.

SMALL, WILLIAM DOUGLAS DENTON.
Merchiston Castle. Cadet Corps 1901-6. M.B., Ch.B. 1911; M.D. 1914; F.R.C.P. (Edin.) 1916. Tutor in Clinical Medicine. No. 4 Coy. Q.R.V.B., Royal Scots, 1906-8, Private. R.A.M.C., Lieut. Jan. 1916; Captain Jan. 1917. France 1916-19. Bacteriologist, 25th General Hospital, 1917-19.

SMART, ARCHIBALD GUELPH HOLDSWORTH.
M.B., Ch.B. 1906; D.T.M. & H. No. 4 Coy. Q.R.V.B., Royal Scots, 1902-5. R.A.M.C., Lieut. April 1915; Captain April 1916. Royal Air Force Medical Service. Croix de Guerre (French) March 1917. M.B.E. June 1919.

SMART, CHARLES MORTON.
Student of Law, 1899-1902. Chartered Accountant, 1903. Lothians and Border Horse, Private Sept. 1914. 7th Royal Scots, 2nd Lieut. Aug. 1915; Lieut. July 1917.

Record of War Service

SMART, DAVID.
Dundee High School. M.B., C.M. 1882; B.Sc. (P.H.) 1886. Junior Assistant Professor of Midwifery, 1882-4. R.A.M.C. (V.), and (T.), Lieut. 1896; Lieut.-Col. 1913; Temp. Colonel 1914; Lieut.-Col. 1914-18; Colonel and A.D.M.S., 57th and 73rd Divisions, Jan. 1916-18. V.D.

SMART, MORTON WARRACK.
George Watson's College. M.B., Ch.B. 1902; M.D. 1912. Volunteer Medical Staff Corps, Private. R.N.V.R., Commander Aug. 1914 to Nov. 1919. Gunboat Flotilla, Belgian Canals, 1914. France 1915; Dardanelles 1915-16; in charge of Motor Launches, Ægean Sea, 1916-17. Admiralty 1917. S.N.O., Trinidad, West Indies. Wounded at Gulf of Smyrna May 1916. Dispatches (Dardanelles). D.S.O. June 1917.

SMEALL, JOHN TELFER.
Nest Academy, Jedburgh. M.B., Ch.B. 1912. R.A.M.C., Lieut. Feb. 1915; Captain Feb. 1916. France. M.C. (Somme) 1916.

SMELLIE, JAMES McILDOWIE.
Lanark Grammar School. Student of Medicine, 1915 and 1919. O.T.C. Infantry, 1916, Cadet; Officer Cadet Aug. 1916. 2nd Seaforth Highlanders, 2nd Lieut. Nov. 1916; Lieut. May 1918; Acting Captain Nov. 1918. France. M.C. May 1917.

SMELLIE, JAMES MACLURE.
Dumfries Academy. Student of Medicine, 1911-16; M.B., Ch.B. 1916. O.T.C. Medical, Nov. 1914 to July 1916, Cadet. R.A.M.C. (S.R.), Lieut. July 1916; Captain Jan. 1917. 43rd General Hospital, Salonika. The Black Sea.

SMELLIE, JOHN McILDOWIE HOPE.
Lanark Grammar School. Student of Medicine, 1912-17; M.B., Ch.B. 1917. O.T.C. Medical, Nov. 1915 to July 1917, Cadet. R.A.M.C., Lieut. Aug. 1917; Captain Aug. 1918. Mesopotamia Sept. 1917 to July 1920.

SMELLIE, KENNEDY.
Student of Law, 1908-10. Chartered Accountant, 1911. 4th and 5th Royal Scots Fusiliers, 2nd Lieut.; Lieut. July 1917.

SMELT, CHARLES ALLEN CASTERTON.
Weymouth and Cheltenham College. M.B., C.M. 1888. R.A.M.C. (T.), Lieut. March 1903; Captain Nov. 1906; Major May 1915.

SMERDON, EDGAR WILMOT.
M.B., Ch.B. 1908; M.D. 1913; F.R.C.S. (Eng.) 1914. R.A.M.C., Lieut.; Captain.

SMILLIE, CHARLES WITHER WILSON.
Student of Law, 1912-14. Chartered Accountant, 1915. R.E., 4/1st Lowland Field Coy., Sapper Aug. 1915; Sergeant Nov. 1915. R.G.A., 2nd Lieut. Feb. 1918. France.

Record of War Service

SMITH, ALAN GEORGE STEWART.
: Edinburgh Academy. Student of Science, 1914-15. O.T.C. Engineers, Oct. 1914 to May 1915, Cadet. R.E. (T.) Signal Coy., Lowland Division, 2nd Lieut. May 1915; Lieut. Dec. 1915.

SMITH, ALEXANDER HUGH DICKSON.
: Llandovery College. First XV. and XI. M.B., Ch.B. (Hons.) 1914. O.T.C. Medical, 1910-12, Cadet. Surgeon, B.R.C.S., No. 14 General Hospital, Boulogne, Oct. 1914 to April 1915. R.A.M.C., Lieut. April 1915; Captain April 1916. 44th General Hospital, Deolali, India, Aug. 1918. M.C. Aug. 1917.

SMITH, ALEXANDER MARTIN.
: George Heriot's School. Student of Science, 1916-17 and 1919. 1/7th Royal Highlanders (Black Watch), Private May 1917; L/Corporal Nov. 1917. France. Wounded at the Marne July 1918. Invalided out Feb. 1919.

SMITH, ARCHIBALD HUGHES.
: Leith Academy. University O.T.C. Artillery, Feb. to May 1915, Cadet. Forth R.G.A., Gunner May 1915. 11th Royal Highlanders (Black Watch), 2nd Lieut. Dec. 1915; Lieut. July 1917. Mesopotamia Aug. 1917. Poona, India, Dec. 1918 to Oct. 1919.

SMITH, ARCHIBALD THORN.
: Dalkeith Burgh School. Student of Arts and Medicine, 1914-16 and 1918-20. R.G.A., Siege Battery, Gunner Oct. 1915 to Jan. 1919.

SMITH, ARTHUR.
: George Watson's College. Student of Medicine, 1918-19. 2nd Royal Scots Fusiliers, Private Jan. 1918. 9th Division, France.

SMITH, AUSTIN NIMMO.
: M.B., Ch.B. 1910. R.A.M.C. (S.R.), Lieut.; Captain. 6th Field Ambulance, France, 1915. Wounded at Festubert March 1915.

SMITH, BRYCE McCALL.
: M.B., Ch.B. 1911. R.A.M.C., Lieut.; Captain Oct. 1915.

SMITH, CLIFFORD HALLIDAY KERR.
: Edinburgh Academy; First XV. M.B., Ch.B. 1914. O.T.C. Artillery, 1909-11, Cadet. R.A.M.C. (T.), Lieut.; Captain May 1915. 3rd Lowland Field Ambulance. France, Dardanelles, Palestine, Mesopotamia. Wounded Aug. 1915. M.C. 1918.

SMITH, DAVID.
: Anderson Institute, Lerwick. M.A. 1911. Schoolmaster. R.A.M.C. (T.), Private Nov. 1915; Sergeant Aug. 1916; Lieut. Oct. 1917; Captain Oct. 1918. Attached R.E. Officer in charge of Anti-Gas Factory, London, Oct. 1917. Education Officer (Forth Garrison), Jan. 1919.

SMITH, DONALD PRINCE.
: Student of Science, 1913-14. O.T.C. Engineers, Oct. 1913-14, Cadet. 7th Royal Dublin Fusiliers, 2nd Lieut.

Record of War Service

SMITH, EVELYN KATE.
Bishop Auckland School. Student of Arts, 1914-18; M.A. 1918. Q.M.A.A.C., Deputy Administrator, Aug. 1918.

SMITH, FLEET FLOYD STROTHER.
Campbell College, Belfast; First XV. and XI. M.B., Ch.B. 1907; M.D. 1912. Indian Medical Service, Captain Aug. 1911; Major Feb. 1920. 137th Combined Field Ambulance. Egypt, Gallipoli, Salonika, South Persia. Dispatches 1916. Order of St Sava (Serbia) April 1918.

SMITH, FRANCIS CLEMENT NIMMO.
M.A. 1908; LL.B. 1910. Writer to the Signet, 1911. 14th and 3rd attached 1st Royal Scots, 2nd Lieut.; Lieut. Jan. 1915. Temp. Captain and Adjutant, Sept. 1917. France.

SMITH, FREDERICK H.
George Heriot's School; First XI. O.T.C. 1912-14. Student of Science, 1915-16 and 1918-20. O.T.C. Artillery, 1915-16, Cadet; Officer Cadet Sept. 1916. R.F.A., attached Trench Mortar Battery, 2nd Lieut. Feb. 1917; Lieut. Aug. 1918. France, 20th Division, 1917-19. Fifth Army, Jan. to March 1919. Gassed Nov. 1917.

SMITH, FREDERICK THOMSON.
George Watson's College. Student of Arts, 1912-14 and 1918-19; M.A. 1919. 15th Royal Scots, Private Oct. 1914. R.E. (Special Brigade), Corporal Aug. 1915; Sergeant Jan. 1917. France Sept. 1915 to May 1917. Wounded at Lens May 1917. Invalided out May 1918.

SMITH, Sir GEORGE ADAM.
Royal High School. M.A. 1877; D.D. 1893. Principal, Aberdeen University. Aberdeen University O.T.C. Chaplain (T.F.), 1st Class, Sept. 1916. Scottish Troops in France Oct. 1916, and U.S.A. April to Aug. 1918.

SMITH, GEORGE ALEXANDER.
Golspie School. Student of Arts, 1918-19. 9th Gordon Highlanders, Private Nov. 1917.

SMITH, GEORGE MEIKLE SHAW.
Student of Medicine, 1913-18; M.B., Ch.B. 1918. O.T.C. Medical, Feb. 1916 to April 1918, Cadet Corporal. R.A.M.C., Lieut. May 1918; Captain May 1919. Greece, Caucasia and Crimea.

SMITH, GEORGE WILLIAM.
George Watson's College. M.B., Ch.B. 1901. Volunteer Medical Staff Corps, 1892-1901, Staff Sergeant. South African Campaign, 1900-1. R.A.M.C., Lieut. Aug. 1914; Captain Aug. 1915; Major Feb. 1918. D.A.D.M.S., Rouen Base. Dispatches Jan. 1917, Jan. 1918, and Jan. 1919. O.B.E. Jan. 1919.

Record of War Service

SMITH, HARRY.
George Watson's College. Student of Law, 1910-11. 1st Royal Dragoons (S.R.), 2nd Lieut. Sept. 1914; Lieut. Sept. 1916. France June 1915 to Dec. 1918. Dispatches 1918.

SMITH, HENRY FAITHFUL.
B.A. (Oxford); M.B., Ch.B. 1909; M.D. 1913. R.A.M.C., Lieut. July 1915; Captain June 1918. 3rd Cheshire Regiment, July 1915 to Jan. 1916. River Sick Convoy Unit, Mesopotamia, July 1917 to April 1919.

SMITH, HERBERT WARD.
George Watson's College. M.B., Ch.B. 1912. O.T.C. Medical, April 1908 to Jan. 1913, Cadet Sergeant-Major. R.A.M.C., Lieut. Aug. 1914; Captain Aug. 1915 to April 1919.

SMITH, HUNTER.
Royal High School. M.A. 1886. Minister, U.F. Church of Scotland. Chaplain, 4th Class, Dec. 1909. Mobilised Sept. 1914. 157th Brigade (T.), 52nd Lowland Division. Med. Exp. Force.

SMITH, IVAN EDWARD.
Dalkeith Burgh School. M.A. 1908; B.Sc. 1911. Lecturer in Agriculture. A.S.C., Private; Sergeant-Major. General Staff.

SMITH, JAMES.
Student of Law, 1904-5. 15th Royal Scots, Private.

SMITH, JAMES GALBRAITH.
M.A. 1895. Minister, U.F. Church of Scotland. 2/7th and 3/7th Gordon Highlanders (T.), Private March 1915; 2nd Lieut. Jan. 1916. France. Wounded. Invalided out. Chaplain, 4th Class, Sept. 1917.

SMITH, JAMES LAUCHLAND.
Morgan Academy, Dundee. Student of Law, 1899-1901. R.G.A., 124th Heavy Battery, April 1917; 2nd Lieut. Dec. 1917.

SMITH, JAMES LINDSAY SALMOND.
Arbroath High School. M.A. 1908; B.Sc. (Distinction) 1914. Lecturer in Botany. O.T.C. Artillery, 1916. Cadet Bombardier; Officer Cadet July 1916. R.G.A., 2nd Lieut. Oct. 1916. Lieut. Aug. 1917; Staff Captain Oct. 1917. France and Italy Nov. 1916 to Feb. 1919. M.C. Dec. 1917; Croce di Guerra Oct. 1918.

SMITH, JAMES MARTIN.
Dundee High School. M.B., Ch.B. 1902. R.A.M.C. (T.), 1908; Captain 1911; Acting Major Jan. 1918. France. 3rd Highland Field Ambulance. Dispatches June 1918. M.C. Oct. 1918. Chevalier de la Légion d'Honneur March 1919.

Record of War Service

SMITH, JAMES MELVILLE.
Campbell College, Belfast. Student of Medicine, 1913-14. O.T.C. Artillery, Oct. 1914 to April 1915, Cadet. R.F.A., 39th Brigade, 2nd Lieut. April 1915; Lieut. July 1917. France. 62nd Brigade, and 5th Brigade, R.F.A., Lahore Division Artillery. Wounded at Ypres Sept. 1917.

SMITH, JAMES ORD PENDER.
Dingwall Academy. Student of Medicine, 1912-17; M.B., Ch.B. 1917. O.T.C. Medical, Feb. 1915-17, Cadet Sergeant. R.A.M.C. (S.R.), Lieut. July 1917; Captain Aug. 1918. Mesopotamia.

SMITH, JOHN.
Student of Law, 1913-14. 5th Reserve Regiment of Cavalry, 2nd Lieut. Sept. 1914. Transferred to 2nd Life Guards, May 1915, Lieut. Jan. 1916. France. Dispatches 1917.

SMITH, JOHN ARTHUR CREASEY.
Albert Memorial College, Framlingham, Suffolk. M.B., Ch.B. 1898. Balkan Convoy Ambulance of French Red Cross, British Section, Oct. 1916 to Sept. 1917. R.A.M.C., Lieut. Oct. 1917; Captain Oct. 1918. France.

SMITH, JOHN CAMPBELL.
George Watson's College. M.A. (St Andrews); M.B., Ch.B. 1912. R.A.M.C., Lieut. Oct. 1915; Captain Oct. 1916.

SMITH, JOHN EDMUND TORRANCE.
Leys School, Cambridge. O.T.C. 1912-14. University O.T.C. Artillery, 1916, Cadet Bombardier; Officer Cadet Sept 1916. R.F.A. (T.), 2nd Lieut. Jan. 1917; Lieut. July 1918. 1st Northumbrian and 296th Brigades, France, March 1917 to April 1919.

SMITH, JOHN GRANT.
George Watson's College; First XV. Student of Science, 1895-6. 6th Seaforth Highlanders (T.), 1898; Lieut.-Col. Oct. 1918; Staff Officer. France 1915-17 and 1918. Dispatches April 1916 and Feb. 1917. D.S.O. June 1916; T.D. July 1916.

SMITH, JOHN HENDERSON.
M.B., Ch.B. 1903. Indian Medical Service, Lieut.; Captain Aug. 1917.

SMITH, JOHN HOPE ROBERTSON.
George Watson's College. Student of Medicine, 1909-17; M.B., Ch.B. 1917. R.A.M.C. (T.), Scottish Horse Brigade Field Ambulance, Private Sept. 1914. R.A.M.C., Lieut. Aug. 1917; Captain Aug. 1918. German East Africa, Nov. 1917 to April 1919.

SMITH, JOHN MACMILLAN.
Greenock Academy. B.Sc. 1914. O.T.C. Engineers, 1911-13, Cadet. R.E. (Special Brigade), Corporal Aug. 1915; 2nd Lieut. June 1916; Lieut. Feb. 1917. France. R.E., Workshops Special Companies, Third Army, 1916-19. Dispatches May and Nov. 1918.

Record of War Service

SMITH, JOHN MITCHELL.
George Watson's College; First XV. O.T.C. 1906-11, Cadet Corporal. Student of Science, 1911-13 and 1918-19; B.Sc. 1919. Lothians and Border Horse, Private Sept. 1914. 17th Royal Scots and 465th Agricultural Labour Coy., France 1915-17; Somme, Ancre.

SMITH, JOHN WILLIAM.
Lancaster School. M.B., C.M. (Hons.) 1886; F.R.C.S. (Eng.). Professor of Systematic Surgery, Manchester University. R.A.M.C., 1898, Lieut.; Colonel 1908; Brevet Colonel Aug. 1917. South African Campaign, 1900. 2nd Western General Hospital, July 1912 to Oct. 1915. T.D. 1919.

SMITH, JULIAN CARTER CARRINGTON.
M.B., C.M. 1878. Indian Medical Service, 1879, Lieut.-Col. (Retired). Afghanistan 1879-80; Burmah 1886-8. R.A.M.C., President, Recruiting Medical Board, and Deputy Commissioner, Medical Services, Glasgow, Feb. 1916 to Jan. 1919. Dispatches Feb. 1917. O.B.E. (Military) June 1919.

SMITH, NOEL JAMES GILLIES.
George Watson's College; First XI. O.T.C. 1914-17. Student of Arts and Science, 1918. O.T.C. Artillery, Sept. 1917 to June 1918, Cadet. R.F.A., Officer Cadet June 1918 to Feb. 1919; 2nd Lieut. March 1919.

SMITH, NORMAN HUBERT.
Victoria College, Jersey. O.T.C. 1907-9. Student of Medicine, 1911-16; M.B., Ch.B. 1916. O.T.C. Medical, 1912-16, Cadet Sergeant. R.A.M.C., attached Indian Army, Lieut. May 1916; Captain May 1917 to Dec. 1919. Egyptian Exp. Force, 1917-18, and 74th Division, R.E., France, 1918-19.

SMITH, PERCY HEBER.
George Heriot's School; First XI. Student of Arts, 1912-15; M.A. 1915. O.T.C. Artillery, July 1915 to March 1916, Cadet; Officer Cadet March 1916. Scottish Horse (T.), 2nd Lieut. Sept. 1916; Temp. Lieut. March 1917; Lieut. March 1918. Palestine June 1917-18; France April 1918 to Feb. 1919.

SMITH, RALPH COLLEY.
Fettes College. O.T.C. 1908-9. B.A. (Oxford) 1912. Student of Law, 1912-14 and 1918-20; LL.B. 1920. Writer to the Signet, 1919. O.T.C. Artillery, Aug. to Nov. 1914, Cadet. R.F.A., 4th Northumbrian (Howitzer) Brigade, 2nd Lieut. Dec. 1914; Lieut. Dec. 1915; Acting Captain Oct. 1916; Acting Major March to April 1917. France April 1915 to May 1917. Wounded Jan. 1916 and April 1917. M.C. April 1917.

SMITH, RALPH JEAN RENAUD.
Daniel Stewart's College. Student of Science, 1914-15. University O.T.C. Infantry, Oct. 1914 to Feb. 1915, Cadet. 9th King's Own Scottish Borderers, 2nd Lieut. Feb. 1915. Army Cyclist's Corps, Oct. 1915. (Lieut., Indian Army, Oct. 1916). Lieut. July 1917. 22nd Punjabis, 1919. France Feb. to July 1916; Mesopotamia and India Dec. 1916 to Oct. 1918. Wounded July 1916.

Record of War Service

SMITH, RICHARD WAYLAND.
: King's School, Worcester. M.B., Ch.B. 1913. O.T.C. Artillery, 1908-13, Cadet Bombardier. R.A.M.C., Lieut. Aug. 1914; Captain Aug. 1915. France Nov. 1914 to June 1917 and Sept. 1918 to July 1919. Wounded June 1917.

SMITH, ROBERT.
: Boroughmuir School. Student of Arts, 1912-14. 4th and 6th Royal Scots (T.), Private Nov. 1912; 2nd Lieut. April 1917; Lieut. Oct. 1918.

SMITH, ROBERT BEVERIDGE.
: Edinburgh Academy. Student of Law, 1906-9. Writer to the Signet, 1910. 10th Seaforth Highlanders, Private; Lieut. Nov. 1914; Captain Dec. 1914. France June 1916. Wounded Oct. 1916. Dispatches.

SMITH, R. C. S.
: M.B., Ch.B. R.A.M.C., Lieut. 1st East Anglian Casualty Clearing Station.

SMITH, ROGER LYNN.
: Dalbeattie School. M.A. 1907. Schoolmaster. Labour Corps March 1917, Sergeant.

SMITH, RONALD EDWARD.
: Edinburgh Academy; First XI. Student of Law, 1903-5. Chartered Accountant, 1907. Scottish Horse, June 1915; 2nd Lieut.; Lieut. July 1917. Gallipoli, Egypt, Salonika, and France. M.C. Oct. 1918.

SMITH, STANLEY ALWYN.
: Repton. Cricket International. M.B., Ch.B. 1905; M.D. 1908; Ch.M. 1911; F.R.C.S. (Edin. and America). No. 4 Coy. Q.R.V.B., Royal Scots, 1900-4, L/Sergeant. Canadian Army Medical Corps, 1912; Captain 1913; Major 1916. R.A.M.C., Major 1917. France 1914-16, 3rd Canadian Field Ambulance. Granville Canadian Special Hospital, Ramsgate, 1916; Welsh Metropolitan War Hospital, Cardiff, 1917-19. Three times Mentioned in Dispatches. D.S.O. (Festubert) May 1915.

SMITH, STEPHEN.
: Edinburgh Institution. B.Sc. 1888. R.E. (V.), 1889. City of Edinburgh R.E. (T.), Major and Hon. Lieut.-Col.; Retired 1912. R.E., Major Oct. 1914; Lieut.-Col. Oct. 1917 to July 1919. France, 39th Division, C.R.E., March 1916. Invalided home Sept. 1916. C.R.E., Mersey Garrison, Dec. 1916 to May 1919.

SMITH, STUART LAURIE.
: Dumfries Academy. Student of Medicine, 1912-17; M.B., Ch.B. 1917. O.T.C. Artillery, Oct. 1914, and Medical, Nov. 1915 to July 1917, Cadet. R.A.M.C. (S.R.), Lieut. Aug. 1917; Captain Aug. 1918. North Russian Exp. Force.

SMITH, SYDNEY ALFRED.
: Victoria College, Wellington, New Zealand. M.B., Ch.B. 1912; M.D. 1914; D.P.H. (Edin.) 1913. O.T.C. Infantry, 1908-11, Cadet L/Corporal. N.Z. Medical Corps (T.), Captain April 1915; Major Sept. 1915. Sanitary Officer, Egypt.

Record of War Service

SMITH, SYDNEY SHEDDEN.
Royal High School. University O.T.C. Infantry, 1917. York and Lancaster Regiment, 2nd Lieut. Jan. 1918; Lieut. July 1919. France 1918-19.

SMITH, SYDNEY WATSON.
High School, and University College, Dundee. M.B., Ch.B. 1903. 3rd V.B. Royal Highlanders (Black Watch), 2nd Lieut. 1900; Captain. R.A.M.C. (T.), 3rd Highland Field Ambulance, Lieut. 1908-9. Lochee Red Cross Auxiliary Hospital, Dundee, 1915-18. R.A.M.C. (T.), Lieut. April 1918. France. Invalided out Sept. 1918.

SMITH, THOMAS.
Ayr Academy. M.A. 1898. Schoolmaster. 24th, 30th, and 6th Royal Fusiliers, Private Dec. 1914; Corporal March 1917.

SMITH, THOMAS ALLAN BERTRAM.
Daniel Stewart's College. M.A. 1904. Minister, U.F. Church of Scotland, Y.M.C.A. Work, France, 1916. Chaplain, 4th Class, June 1917. No. 20 Ordnance Depôt, France.

SMITH, THOMAS STODART WHYTE.
Merchiston Castle. Cadet Corps 1896-8. Student of Law, 1902-5. Writer to the Signet, 1906. O.T.C. Infantry, 1915, Cadet. 14th Royal Scots, 2nd Lieut. March 1915; Lieut. July 1916; Captain Feb. 1918. 1st King's African Rifles. East Africa 1917-19.

SMITH, VIVIAN RAMSAY.
Collegiate School of St Peter, Adelaide. Cadet Corps 1907-8. Student of Medicine, 1909-14; M.B., Ch.B. 1913. O.T.C. Artillery, Feb. 1909-11, and Medical, April to July 1911, Cadet. Royal Australian Navy, H.M.A.S. *Australia*, Surgeon-Lieut. April 1914; Acting Surgeon-Lieut.-Commander 1919.

SMITH, WALTER GIBSON.
M.A. 1900. Minister, Presbyterian Church of England. 4th V.B. Northumberland Fusiliers, Jan. 1917; Captain Aug. 1917.

SMITH, WILLIAM FRANCIS.
St Andrew's College, Grahamstown, South Africa. O.T.C. 1913-15. University O.T.C. Artillery, April to Sept. 1916, Cadet Corporal; Officer Cadet Sept. 1916. R.F.A., 3/1st Highland Brigade, 2nd Lieut. Feb. 1917; Lieut. Aug. 1918. France.

SMITH, WILLIAM RAMSAY.
B.Sc. 1888; D.Sc. (Adelaide) 1904; M.B., C.M. 1892; M.D. 1913. Australian Army Medical Corps, Lieut.-Col. and O.C. 1st Australian General Hospital.

SMITH, Sir WILLIAM ROBERT.
B.Sc. 1883; D.Sc. 1886; M.D. (Aberdeen) 1879. Professor of Forensic Medicine, King's College, London University. R.A.M.C. (V.), and (T.), 1874; Lieut.-Col. and Sanitary Officer, 67th Division, Dec. 1914. Dispatches Sept. 1917. V.D.

Record of War Service

SMITH, WILLIAM THOMAS.
George Watson's College. University O.T.C. Artillery, Feb. to Aug. 1916, Cadet Acting Bombardier; Officer Cadet Aug. 1916. R.G.A., Forth, 2nd Lieut. Nov. 1916; Lieut. May 1918. 34th Siege Battery, France.

SMITH, WILLIAM TORRANCE.
George Watson's College. M.B., Ch.B. 1906. R.A.M.C., Lieut. March 1915; Captain March 1916. France 1915-16. Wounded at the Somme 1916. India.

SMITH-SHAND, ALEXANDER KENNETH.
Glenalmond; First XV. Cadet Corps 1889-94, Sergeant. M.B., Ch.B. 1900. Royal Navy 1902; Staff-Surgeon 1910; Surgeon-Commander Feb. 1918. R.N. Hospital, Chatham, 1914-17. H.M.S. *Glorious*, Grand Fleet, 1918.

SMYTH, THOMAS AUBREY.
M.B., Ch.B. 1901. South African Campaign, 1901. Royal Navy 1902; Staff-Surgeon 1910; Fleet Surgeon May 1918. Wounded through torpedoing of H.M.S. *Pathfinder*, Sept. 1914.

SMYTH, WILLIAM JOHNSON.
M.B., C.M. 1887; M.D. 1890. Army Medical Service, 1891-7. R.A.M.C. (V.), Major. 1st Hants Field Ambulance, Oct. 1917.

SNEDDEN, RICHARD.
George Watson's College. O.T.C. 1914-18. Student of Arts and Law, 1918-19. 4th Royal Scots (T.), April 1918; Officer Cadet Sept. 1918; 2nd Lieut. May 1919.

SNELL, FRANK.
M.A. 1909. A.S.C. (M.T.), Private. France, 25th Divisional Supply Column.

SOKHEY, SAHIB SINGH.
M.A., B.Sc. 1912; M.B., Ch.B. 1911; D.T.M. (Eng.) 1915. Indian Medical Service, Lieut. 1913; Captain July 1915; Temp. Major Feb. 1918.

SOMER, FRANCIS EDWARD.
Royal Grammar School, Worcester; First XV. and XI. O.T.C. 1913-16, Cadet Sergeant. Student of Science, 1918. Royal Air Force, 2nd Air Mechanic, July 1918.

SOMEREN, ALEXANDER GRANT VERMONT VAN.
George Watson's College. M.B., Ch.B. 1905; F.R.C.S. (Edin.) 1908. R.A.M.C. (V.), 1900-7, Sergeant. R.A.M.C. (T.), Lieut. Jan. 1914; Captain April 1915. 9th and 16th Indian Divisions.

SOMEREN, ROBERT ABRAHAM LOGAN VAN.
M.B., Ch.B. 1904; M.D. 1907; D.P.H. (Edin.). Uganda Medical Service, 1905; S.M.O. 1914; Captain June 1915.

Record of War Service

SOMERVILLE, ALEXANDER WELSH.
George Watson's College; First XV. O.T.C. 1905-10, Cadet Lieut. Student of Arts and Divinity, 1910-15; M.A. 1915. O.T.C. Infantry, Oct. 1910 to Aug. 1914, Cadet Sergeant. 1st, 2nd, and 3rd Seaforth Highlanders (S.R.), 2nd Lieut. Aug. 1914; Captain. France 1914-16.

SOMERVILLE, CHARLES WILLIAM.
Royal High School. M.B., Ch.B. 1901; D.P.H. (Edin.) 1902. Whitehill Red Cross Hospital, 1915-18. R.A.M.C., Lieut. April 1918; Captain April 1919.

SOMERVILLE, DAVID.
George Watson's College. M.A. 1904. Minister, U.F. Church of Scotland. Chaplain, 4th Class, March 1916; 3rd Class, Nov. 1917. France Oct. 1916-18.

SOMERVILLE, GEORGE.
Bathgate Academy. University O.T.C. Artillery, April 1917 to Jan. 1918, Cadet; Officer Cadet Jan. 1918. R.F.A., 2nd Lieut. Aug. 1918.

SOMERVILLE, HUGH.
Boroughmuir School. Student of Arts, 1911-15; M.A. (Hons. Engl.) 1919. Schoolmaster. O.T.C. Infantry, 1911-14, Cadet Corporal. 16th Royal Scots, Sergeant Nov. 1914. 23rd and 2nd Manchester Regiment, 2nd Lieut. April 1915; Lieut. Nov. 1915; Captain July 1916. France 1915-18. Ministry of Pensions, 1919. Dispatches May 1917. M.C. June 1917; Bar to M.C. Sept. 1918.

SOMERVILLE, JAMES ALEXANDER.
Dollar Academy. M.A. 1890. Minister, U.F. Church of Scotland. Chaplain, 4th Class, Sept. 1915; 3rd Class, June 1918 to March 1919. Lowland Mounted Brigade (T.). Senior Chaplain, 74th Division. Gallipoli, Egypt, Palestine, and France.

SOMERVILLE, JAMES WALKER.
M.A. 1900; LL.B. and Writer to the Signet, 1903. 8th Royal Scots, Private Dec. 1915; Sergeant to Feb. 1919. 469th Employment Coy., Labour Corps, April 1916.

SOMERVILLE, JOHN LIVINGSTON.
George Watson's College; First XV. Student of Law, 1905-6. Chartered Accountant, 1909. R.G.A. (T.), City of Edinburgh Lowland Heavy Battery, 1909; Captain June 1914; Major June 1916; Staff Captain July 1917 to Feb. 1918. France 1916-18. Twice Wounded.

SOMERVILLE, JOHN R.
George Heriot's School. O.T.C. 1911-13. Student of Medicine, 1918. Border Regiment, 2nd Lieut. June 1915.

SOMERVILLE, WILLIAM.
Hamilton Academy. M.B., C.M. 1892; M.D. 1898. R.A.M.C., Lieut. Sept. 1915. H.M. Hospital Ship *Mauritania*, and No. 7 General Hospital. France.

Record of War Service

SONI, MUL RAJ.
    B.A. Student of Medicine, 1913-18; M.B., Ch.B. 1918. Indian Field Ambulance

SONNTAG, CHARLES FREDERICK.
    Royal High School, and Denstone College, Staffordshire. Cadet Corps 1903. M.B., Ch.B. 1910; M.D. 1912. R.A.M.C., Lieut. April 1915; Captain April 1916. France and Salonika.

SOOTE, DAVID WEBSTER.
    M.A. 1903. R.G.A., 2nd Lieut. Sept. 1917.

SORAPURE, VICTOR EDGAR.
    M.B., Ch.B. 1899; F.R.C.S. (Edin.). R.A.M.C., Captain Feb. 1918.

SOUPER, JAMES LORIMER.
    Aberdeen Grammar School. Student of Science, 1914-15 and 1918-19. A.M.I.C.E. O.T.C. Engineers, Oct. 1914 to March 1915, Cadet. R.E. (T.), 2nd Lieut. March 1915; Lieut. June 1916; Temp. Captain Oct. 1918 to Feb. 1919. 76th Field Coy., France. Wounded at Boesinghe (Ypres Canal), Aug. 1917.

SOUTAR, ALEXANDER.
    Brechin High School. M.A. 1881. Minister, U.F. Church of Scotland. Chaplain, 4th Class, Feb. 1910. Cameron Highlanders and King's Own Scottish Borderers. Scottish Churches Hut, Rouen.

SOUTAR, DAVID HENDERSON.
    George Watson's College. Student of Arts, 1913-14 and 1918-20; M.A. 1920. 2nd Lovat Scouts, Private Aug. 1914. 4th and 5th Cameron Highlanders, 2nd Lieut. July 1915; Temp. Lieut. Nov. 1915; Lieut. July 1917. France. Wounded, Gassed, and Prisoner of War.

SOUTAR, WILLIAM.
    Perth Academy. Student of Medicine, 1918-19. Royal Navy, Able Seaman.

SOUTHALL, STEPHEN.
    Friend's School, York. M.B., Ch.B. 1899; M.D. 1902. R.A.M.C., Lieut. Aug. 1917; Captain Aug. 1918. 14th Casualty Clearing Station, East Africa.

SOUTHAM, HERBERT.
    Leamington College. Student of Medicine, 1877. 1st Shropshires. 4th and 8th Lancashire Volunteer Artillery, 1877; Major 1888; Hon. Colonel 1905-9. Recruiting Officer, Temp. Major, June 1915 to March 1919. Mention 1917. V.D.

SOUTHON, CHARLES EDWARD.
    M.B., Ch.B. 1900; D.T.M. & H. 1911. Indian Medical Service, 1901; Major 1912. East African Exp. Force, 1914-18. Kaisar-i-Hind Medal 1912. O.B.E. Nov. 1918.

SOWDEN, GEORGE SMITH.
    Elgin Academy. M.A. 1905; M.B., Ch.B. 1909. Royal Navy, H.M.S. *Colossus*, Surgeon Dec. 1916.

Record of War Service

SPARKE, WILLIAM MACKAY.
Student of Law, 1905-7. Chartered Accountant. University O.T.C. Infantry, Oct. to Nov. 1915, Cadet. 4th Royal Scots, 2nd Lieut. Nov. 1915; Lieut. 1/4th King's African Rifles, Captain March 1918. British East, German East, and Portuguese East Africa, Nyasaland, Rhodesia, and Uganda, Jan. 1917 to April 1919. M.C. Aug. 1917; Bar to M.C. Nov. 1918.

SPEED, HARRY EXTON.
Leith Academy; First XI. University O.T.C. Infantry, June 1917 to March 1918, Cadet; Officer Cadet March 1918. 24th Tank Corps, 2nd Lieut.

SPEIRS, HAROLD THOMAS.
Galashiels Academy. Student of Arts, 1913-14. R.F.A., 261st Brigade, Gunner Nov. 1916.

SPEIRS, HENRY.
George Watson's College. M.B., Ch.B. 1903; M.D. 1908; F.R.C.S. (Edin.) 1909. R.A.M.C., Lieut. 1916; Captain Jan. 1917.

SPENCE, ARTHUR DUNBAR.
Montrose Academy. M.B., Ch.B. 1900. Volunteer Medical Staff Corps, 1896-1900. Rangoon Mounted Rifles, Surgeon-Lieut. Dec. 1912; Captain. 18th (Rangoon) Battn., Indian Defence Corps.

SPENCE, BASIL HAMILTON HEBDEN.
Edinburgh Academy; First XV. M.B., Ch.B. 1911. O.T.C. Artillery, Oct. 1908 to Nov. 1911, Cadet B.Q.M.S. R.A.M.C., attached Egyptian Army, Lieut. 1911; Captain Jan. 1914. Dispatches (Darfur) 1916, and Egyptian Exp. Force 1918. Order of the Nile (4th Class).

SPENCE, JOSEPH EDWARD.
King William's College, Isle of Man. M.B., Ch.B. (Hons.) 1908; D.P.H. (Edin.) 1910. R.A.M.C., Lieut. Sept. 1916; Captain Sept. 1917. Specialist Sanitary Officer, L. of C. Area, Salonika, 1916-19.

SPENCE, SYDNEY GEORGE.
Kirkwall Burgh School. Student of Law, 1914-15. O.T.C. Artillery, Oct. to Nov. 1914, Cadet. R.F.A., 2nd Lieut. Nov. 1914; Lieut. Feb. 1916; Captain Sept. 1916; Major Feb. 1918. 26th Division. Dispatches Jan. 1918.

SPENCE, THOMAS REGINALD CARWARDINE.
Edinburgh Academy. O.T.C. 1911-13. Student of Medicine, 1913-14 and 1918-19. R.A.M.C. (T.). Scottish Horse Field Ambulance, Private Sept. 1914. 8th Royal Scots (T.), Lieut. Aug. 1915. France. M.C. March 1918.

SPENCER, CHARLES NICHOLAS.
Queen Elizabeth's Grammar School, Wakefield; First XV. Student of Science, 1918-19. Royal Irish Rifles, Cadet Dec. 1915; Cadet L/Corporal Jan. 1916. R.N.V.R., Lieut. March 1917. France Dec. 1915 to July 1916 and 1917. Twice Wounded.

Record of War Service

SPIERS, ANDREW McLAREN.
Dunfermline High School. Student of Arts, 1912-15; M.A. 1915. O.T.C. Artillery, Oct. 1914 to Feb. 1915, Cadet. R.F.A., 2nd Lieut. Feb. 1915; Lieut. Jan. 1917 to March 1919. France. Wounded April 1918.

SPRAGUE, HENRY DOUGLAS.
Edinburgh Collegiate School. M.A. 1895. Chartered Accountant, 1900. R.F.A., Major (Retired) July 1914. Rejoined Sept. 1914; Acting Lieut.-Col. Sept. 1916 and Oct. 1917; Lieut.-Col. (Reserve) July 1919. France, Salonika, Egypt, and Palestine. 301st and 300th Brigades. Dispatches (Palestine) 1918. T.D.

SPRENT, JAMES.
Friend's High School, Hobart. First XV. and XI. B.Sc. (Tasmania) 1903; M.B., Ch.B. 1909. Royal Navy, Acting District Naval Medical Officer, Aug. 1914. Australian Army Medical Corps, Captain March 1915; Major Jan. 1917. Wounded at Noreuil April 1917. M.C.

SPROAT, HARRY BIRD.
Royal High School. M.B., Ch.B. 1899; M.D. 1901. R.A.M.C., 1909; Captain 1912; Acting Major Oct. 1915. 1st West Riding Field Ambulance. France. 48th Division, 1915. Dispatches Jan. 1916 and April 1918.

SPROTT, ALAN FAWCETT.
Student of Medicine, 1912-14. O.T.C. Infantry, May 1913 to Sept. 1914, Cadet. 8th and 10th Gordon Highlanders, 2nd Lieut.; Lieut. July 1917.

SPROTT, WILLIAM ARCHIBALD.
Leith Academy. Student of Arts, 1914-15. 9th Royal Scots (T.), Private June 1915; L/Corporal Dec. 1917. France. Wounded March 1918.

SPROTT, WILLIAM ARTHUR PATRICK.
St Bees, Cumberland; First XV. O.T.C. 1912-15, Cadet Corporal. Student of Medicine, 1919. Royal Air Force, 2nd Lieut. 1915; Lieut. May 1917 to May 1919; Acting Captain 1917.

SPROULE, WILLIAM.
M.B., C.M. 1892; M.D. 1895. Australian Army Medical Corps (Reserve), Hon. Captain 1914.

SPRUNT, WILLIAM RODGER.
Perth Academy. Student of Medicine, 1918. R.E., Sapper Jan. 1915. Wounded May 1917.

STABLES, ALEXANDER.
M.B., C.M. 1883; M.R.C.S. (Eng.) 1884. R.A.M.C. 1885; Major 1897. Re-employed Aug. 1914 to 1919, Aberdeen and Cromarty. Dispatches March 1919.

STALKARTT, CHARLES EDWARD GREY.
M.B., C.M. 1886; M.D. 1890; L.R.C.P. (Lond.) and M.R.C.S. (Eng.) 1889. R.A.M.C. 1891; Major 1903. South African Campaign, 1900. France June 1915-16.

Record of War Service

STALKARTT, WALTER HENRY SKINNER.
M.B., C.M. 1887; M.D. 1895; F.R.C.S. (Edin.) 1900. Royal Navy, 1890, Fleet Surgeon; Acting Surgeon-Captain Sept. 1919. H.M.S. *Minotaur*, 1914-15. S.M.O., R.N. Barracks, Devonport, June 1915; R.N. Auxiliary Hospitals, Greenwich College and Peebles, July 1917 to Aug. 1919.

STALKER, ALEXANDER MITCHELL.
M.A. (Hons.) 1877; M.B., C.M. 1881; M.D. 1890. Professor of Medicine, St Andrews University. R.A.M.C., Captain 1912. 1st Scottish General Hospital.

STALKER, JAMES MILLER.
Dundee High School. Student of Medicine, 1910-12; M.B., Ch.B. (St Andrews) 1916. O.T.C. Artillery, Oct. 1910 to July 1911, Cadet. B.R.C., Surgical Dresser, 1914. R.A.M.C., Lieut. Feb. 1916; Captain Feb. 1917. Wounded May 1917.

STANFIELD, THOMAS ALPHAEUS.
Liscard High School, Wallasey. Student of Medicine, 1918. R.A.M.C., Private March 1915. 2/1st West Lancashire Field Ambulance. M.M.

STANLEY, GILBERT LLEWELLYN.
Student of Medicine, 1907-9. O.T.C. Artillery, Oct. 1912 to Nov. 1913, Cadet, R.F.A., Lieut.

STANLEY, JOHN DOUGLAS.
M.B., C.M. 1889; M.D. 1894; M.R.C.P. (Lond.) 1896. R.A.M.C., Major 1908. 1st Southern General Hospital.

STANSFIELD, THOMAS EDWARD KNOWLES.
Owens College, Manchester. M.B., C.M. 1889. Civil Consultant Neurologist. Eastern Command, 1915 to Aug. 1917. R.A.M.C., Major 1917; Hon. Temp. Lieut.-Col. May 1918. C.B.E. 1919.

STARK, ALLAN ROSS.
George Watson's College. O.T.C. 1912-16, Cadet Sergeant. Student of Science, 1919. O.T.C. Infantry, Aug. 1916-17, Cadet C.S.M.; Officer Cadet Aug. 1917. 2nd Seaforth Highlanders, 2nd Lieut. Dec. 1917; Lieut. June 1918. France and Italy 1918-19. Wounded in France March 1918.

STARK, HUGH GOODWILLIE.
Falkirk High School. Student of Arts and Divinity, 1911-14; M.A. 1914. 3rd Gordon Highlanders, Private April 1915. 8th Royal Lancaster Regiment, 2nd Lieut. April 1915; Lieut. July 1917. Twice Wounded. Invalided out May 1919.

STARK, ROBERT ALEXANDER.
George Watson's College. Cadet Corps 1906-8. M.B., Ch.B. 1913. O.T.C. Infantry, Oct. 1909-12, Cadet. R.A.M.C. (T.), Lieut. Aug. 1914; Captain April 1915; Acting Major Nov. 1918; Acting Lieut.-Col. Feb. 1919. 3rd West Riding Field Ambulance. France 1915-19. M.C. July 1917; Bar to M.C. Oct. 1918.

Record of War Service

STARKIE, ERNEST GEORGE BEST.
 Merchant Taylor's School, Liverpool. M.B., C.M. 1889. R.A.M.C., Lieut. July 1915; Captain July 1916; Local Major March 1917. Malta. Dispatches.

STEDMAN, WILLIAM BLAIR.
 Glenalmond; First XV. O.T.C. 1914-16. University O.T.C. Artillery, 1917, Cadet; Officer Cadet Nov. 1917. Forth R.G.A., 2nd Lieut. May 1918 to Nov. 1919.

STEEL, EBENEZER BROWN.
 Allan Glen's School, Glasgow; Athletics. Student of Medicine, 1918-19. O.T.C. Infantry, Feb. to Sept. 1917, Cadet; Officer Cadet Sept. 1917. Labour Corps, 2nd Lieut. Feb. 1918. France. Wounded Aug. 1918.

STEEL, JAMES WILLIAM.
 M.B., Ch.B. 1913. R.A.M.C., Captain Aug. 1917. 27th Casualty Clearing Station, South Russia. Russian Order of St Stanislaus.

STEELE, JAMES TORRANCE.
 Drumour School, Perthshire. B.Sc. 1910; M.A. 1919. Lothians and Border Horse (T.), Private July 1914; L/Corporal Oct. 1914; Acting Sergeant Jan. 1915. Scottish Horse, 2nd Lieut. April 1915; Temp. Lieut. Dec. 1915; Lieut. July 1917. O.C. 52nd Mule Transport Corps, India.

STEELE, JOHN.
 Dollar Academy. M.B., C.M. 1883; L.R.C.P. & S. 1882. R.N.R. Soudan Campaign, 1885. Commonwealth Military Forces, Lieut.-Col. 1914. O.C. 3rd Light Horse and 15th Field Ambulances; Field Hospital, Port Philip Fortress; No. 5 Australian General Hospital, Melbourne.

STEELE, JOHN PARIS.
 George Watson's College. B.L. 1904; 5th V.B. Royal Scots, 1916; C.Q.M.S., Feb. 1917.

STEELE, LAWSON LAMB.
 St Bees School, Cumberland; First XV. Student of Medicine, 1917-18; L.R.C.P. & S.; M.R.C.V.S. Royal Army Veterinary Corps, 8th Reserve Brigade, Lieut. Feb. 1915; Captain March 1916. 41st Infantry Brigade. Invalided out April 1917.

STEELE, PATRICK.
 Inverness College. M.B., Ch.B. 1904; M.D. 1908; M.R.C.P. (Edin.) 1912. R.A.M.C., Lieut. Jan. 1915; Captain 1917; Lieut.-Col. 1918. 58th Field Ambulance. France.

STEELE, WILLIAM HUGH.
 Kelly College, Tavistock; First XV. M.B., C.M. 1895. Volunteer Medical Staff Corps, 1891-4. R.A.M.C., Lieut. Dec. 1914; Captain Dec. 1915 to March 1919. Radiographer.

Record of War Service

STEEN, HORATIO WALTER JAMES.
Student of Medicine, 1917-19. Glasgow University O.T.C. Engineers, April to Aug. 1915, Cadet. 11th Gordon Highlanders, 2nd Lieut. Aug. 1915.

STEPHEN, ALEXANDER.
M.B., Ch.B. 1906. R.A.M.C., Lieut.

STEPHEN, WILLIAM DOUGLAS M.
Edinburgh Academy. O.T.C. 1916-17. University O.T.C. Artillery, Feb. 1917 to Jan. 1918, Cadet. Tank Corps, Officer Cadet Jan. 1918; 2nd Lieut. Oct. 1918.

STEPHEN, WILLIAM LAING.
M.A. 1893. Minister, U.F. Church of Scotland. Y.M.C.A. Work. Chaplain, 4th Class, 14th Argyll and Sutherland Highlanders, Nov. 1915.

STEPHENS, HAROLD FREDERICK DALE.
Sherborne, Dorset. M.B., C.M. 1884. Royal Navy, Fleet Surgeon (Retired). Royal Naval Canadian Volunteer Reserve, Surgeon-Lieut. Nov. 1917 to Aug. 1919.

STEPHENS, RICCARDO.
M.B., C.M. 1893. R.A.M.C., Lieut.; Captain April 1916.

STEUART, MURRAY BABINGTON.
Edinburgh Academy. M.B., C.M. 1894. R.A.M.C., Lieut. July 1915-16.

STEUART, ROGER St CLAIR.
Wanganui College, New Zealand. First XV. and XI. Cadet Corps 1898-1900, Captain. M.B., Ch.B. 1906; M.D. 1908; F.R.C.S. (Edin.) 1908. Australian Army Medical Corps, Captain May 1915; Major Feb. 1917. Attached R.A.M.C., Australian Casualty Clearing Station, 1918. Dispatches Nov. 1918.

STEVEN, GEORGE DUNLOP.
George Watson's College. Student of Medicine, 1914-15 and 1918. O.T.C. Infantry, Oct. 1914 to July 1915, Cadet. 2/5th Gordon Highlanders (T.), 2nd Lieut. July 1915; Temp. Lieut. May 1916; Lieut. July 1917.

STEVEN, GEORGE HENRY.
George Watson's College; First XI. M.B., Ch.B. 1901. Volunteer Medical Staff Corps, 1896-1901, Private. R.A.M.C., South African Campaign, 1900-1; Lieut. Jan. 1915; Captain Jan. 1916.

STEVEN, THOMAS MORTON.
Student of Arts and Science, 1908-14; M.A. 1914; B.Sc. (Distinction) 1914. O.T.C. Infantry, 1909-12 and June 1915, Cadet Sergeant. Calcutta Light Horse, Private. 25th Cavalry, Frontier Force, 2nd Lieut.; Lieut. and Adjutant. India.

STEVEN, WILLIAM CHARLES.
Student of Law, 1893-5. Chartered Accountant, 1897. Staff Captain, No. 1 District, Perth, 1915. 192nd Infantry Brigade, 1917. Mention April 1917. T.D. July 1917.

Record of War Service

STEVENS, HAROLD SAMUEL EATON.
George Heriot's School. O.T.C. Cadet Lieut. Student of Arts, 1910-14. 12th Royal Scots, 2nd Lieut.; Lieut.; Major April 1918. France. Twice Wounded. M.C.; Chevalier Légion d'Honneur; Croix de Guerre avec Palme.

STEVENS, JOHN.
Waid Academy, Anstruther. M.A. 1909. Schoolmaster. Forth R.G.A. (T.), Sergeant.

STEVENSON, ARTHUR CRICHTON.
Royal High School. Student of Law, 1911-13. R.F.C., 2nd Air Mechanic, Nov. 1915; Sergeant. Invalided out Feb. 1918. R.A.S.C. (T.), 245th (M.T.) Coy., 2nd Lieut. Feb. 1918 to April 1919.

STEVENSON, DAVID ALAN.
Edinburgh Academy. B.Sc. 1912. A.M.I.C.E. Royal Marines, attached Northern Lighthouse Board, Captain 1914 to Aug. 1918. Admiralty, Sept. 1918 to May 1919.

STEVENSON, ERIC JOHN POTT.
Edinburgh Academy. Student of Law, 1912-14. O.T.C. Artillery, Aug. to Sept. 1914. R.F.A., 2nd Lieut. Oct. 1914; Lieut. March 1916; Captain July 1918. France and Italy July 1915 to April 1919. Dispatches May 1918.

STEVENSON, GEORGE HENDERSON.
Royal High School. M.B., Ch.B. 1910; D.P.H. (Eng.) 1913; M.R.C.P. (Eng.) 1914. O.T.C. Medical, April 1908 to Jan. 1910, Cadet Staff Sergeant. R.A.M.C. (S.R.), Lieut. 1910; Captain 1913; Acting Major 1918. Dispatches Jan. 1916. M.C. June 1918; O.B.E. June 1919.

STEVENSON, HENRY JAMES.
Edinburgh Academy; First XV. and XI. M.A. 1890. Writer to the Signet, 1893. Rugby (15 "Caps") and Cricket (10 "Caps") International. Queen's Edinburgh Mounted Rifles, 1893. Lothians and Border Horse, Captain 1908; Brevet Major. A.D.C. to G.O.C. Lowland Mounted Brigade, Aug. 1914; Brigade Major Jan. 1915. Border Regiment, Major 1918. Mention Feb. 1917 and Jan. 1918. Order of St John of Jerusalem. T.D.

STEVENSON, JAMES.
Edinburgh Institution. Student of Law, 1908-10. Chartered Accountant, 1912. Hon. Artillery Coy., Private Nov. 1914. Army Pay Department, Jan. 1915; Lieut. Dec. 1915; Captain July 1918. Palestine. Dispatches June 1919.

STEVENSON, JOHN.
M.B., C.M. 1896; F.R.C.S. (Edin.) 1899. Hon. Captain and Ophthalmic Surgeon to N.Z. Exp. Force.

Record of War Service

STEVENSON, JOHN.
George Watson's College. M.B., Ch.B. 1910; D.P.H. R.A.M.C., Lieut. Nov. 1914; Captain Nov. 1915. France, Mesopotamia, Salonika. Wounded April 1918. M.C. May 1918.

STEVENSON, JOHN AFFLECK.
Hulme, Berwick, and Doncaster Grammar Schools. M.A., B.Sc. 1912. O.T.C. Artillery, Oct. 1909 to Nov. 1913, Cadet. R.F.A., Gunner Dec. 1914; 2nd Lieut. Jan. 1915; Lieut. Feb. 1916. R.F.C., 8th Balloon Coy. Royal Air Force, Captain and Flight Commander Feb. 1918. France March 1916. M.C. Aug. 1917.

STEVENSON, JOHN HORNE.
Edinburgh Collegiate School. Student of Arts and Law; M.A. 1881. Munition Worker. 1st V.B. Royal Scots (Lothian Regiment), Private June 1916. M.B.E. 1918.

STEVENSON, MARGARET SCOTT.
M.A. 1913. Hockey "Blue." W.R.A.F., Assistant Administrator, Aug. 1918.

STEVENSON, ROBERT ELLIOT.
St Andrew's College, Grahamstown, South Africa. O.T.C. 1909-12, Cadet Corporal. Student of Medicine, 1915-16. O.T.C. Infantry, April to June 1916, Cadet. 7th Reserve Battn., The London Regiment, 2nd Lieut. June 1916; Lieut. Dec. 1917. France Oct. 1917. Gassed at Villers Brettoneux April 1918.

STEVENSON, ROBERT SCOTT.
Royal High School; First XV. M.B., Ch.B. 1912; M.D. 1919. President, S.R.C., 1911. O.T.C. Medical, 1908-12, Cadet. R.A.M.C., Captain April 1917. Attached H.Q., Western Command, 1917, and 14th General Hospital. France 1918.

STEVENSON, THOMAS.
George Watson's College. M.B., C.M. 1886; M.D. 1912. R.A.M.C. (T.), 1892; Lieut.-Col. 1912. 2nd West Lancashire Field Ambulance. T.D.

STEVENSON, WILLIAM BLACK.
Edinburgh Academy; First XI. M.A. 1884. Minister, Church of Scotland. Chaplain, 4th Class, 1903; 3rd Class, 1915. 9th and 3rd Royal Scots (T.).

STEVENSON, WILLIAM SCOTT.
George Watson's College. O.T.C. 1906-9, Cadet Corporal. M.A. (Hons. Engl.) 1914. O.T.C. Infantry, 1910-14, Cadet Sergeant. 10th Argyll and Sutherland Highlanders, 2nd Lieut. Sept. 1914; Lieut. May 1915; Captain March 1916; Major and D.A.Q.M.G., March 1918. D.A.A.G., Lowland Division. The Rhine April 1919. Twice Wounded. Four times Mentioned in Dispatches. M.C. Nov. 1916; Croix de Guerre (French) with Gold Star Nov. 1918; D.S.O. March 1919.

STEWART, ABRAM ARCHIBALD.
University O.T.C. Infantry, March to Nov. 1914, Cadet. R.E., 1/1st City of Edinburgh Coy., Sapper Nov. 1914; L/Corporal April 1915; Corporal Sept. 1915; Sergeant Sept. 1918 to Jan. 1919. Egypt 1915; France 1916. Wounded at the Somme June 1916.

Record of War Service

STEWART, ALEXANDER DRON.
: Dundee High School. M.B., Ch.B. 1906; D.T.M. and H.; F.R.C.S. (Edin.) Indian Medical Service, Lieut. 1906; Captain 1909; Major 1918. Egypt 1914; Gallipoli 1915; Egypt and Mesopotamia 1916; Hospital Ship 1917-18.

STEWART, ALISTER JOHN.
: Royal Academy, Inverness. M.A. 1907, (Hons. Engl.) 1908. Minister, U.F. Church of Scotland. Y.M.C.A. Work, France, Jan. to June 1915. Chaplain, 4th Class, Dec. 1915. 155th Brigade, Egyptian Exp. Force and Med. Exp. Force. Dispatches Oct. 1916. M.C. Sept. 1916.

STEWART, ANDREW.
: Broughton School, Edinburgh. Student of Law, 1915-16. Chartered Accountant, 1918. A.S.C., Private Feb. 1915. Invalided out Aug. 1915.

STEWART, ANDREW SINCLAIR.
: Alloa Academy. Student of Law, 1912-13. 7th Argyll and Sutherland Highlanders, 2nd Lieut. Feb. 1915; Lieut. Nov. 1915; Acting Captain Sept. 1916. France and The Rhine 1915-19. Dispatches May 1918.

STEWART, ARCHIBALD MATHISON.
: M.B., Ch.B. 1913. O.T.C. Artillery, Oct. 1908 to Nov. 1911. R.A.M.C. (T.), Lowland Field Ambulance, Lieut.; Captain April 1915.

STEWART, AUGUSTUS SHAW.
: George Watson's College. O.T.C. 1907-11. Student of Law, 1913-14. 9th Royal Scots (T.), Private Sept. 1914. 6th West Riding Regiment, 2nd Lieut. June 1915; Lieut. July 1917; Acting Captain 1918. France. Dispatches.

STEWART, CHARLES.
: Inverness Royal Academy; First XI. Student of Arts, 1916-17 and 1918-19. 4th King's Own Scottish Borderers, Private Aug. 1917; Corporal Sept. 1917. R.E., 2nd Lieut. May 1918.

STEWART, DANIEL.
: Dunfermline High School. Student of Science, 1917-18. O.T.C. Engineers, March to Sept. 1918, Cadet. Royal Air Force, Cadet Sept. 1918.

STEWART, DANIEL.
: George Heriot's School. Student of Arts, 1917. O.T.C. Artillery, Dec. 1917 to June 1918, Cadet Bombardier. R.G.A., Officer Cadet, June 1918.

STEWART, DAVID GEORGE AIMERS.
: Broughton School. Student of Arts and Medicine, 1913-16 and 1919-20; M.A. 1916. Non-Combatant Corps, Private April 1916.

STEWART, DAVID MILNE.
: M.A. 1906; B.Sc. 1908. Schoolmaster. 16th Royal Scots, Private.

Record of War Service

STEWART, DONALD.
Dingwall Academy. Student of Science, 1918; M.A. (Aberdeen) 1916. 4th Cameron Highlanders, 2nd Lieut. Sept. 1915; Lieut July 1917. Croix de Guerre with Palms Nov. 1918.

STEWART, DUNCAN.
Glasgow Academy; First XV. O.T.C., Sergeant. University O.T.C. Artillery, Dec. 1916 to June 1917, Cadet Bombardier; Officer Cadet June 1917. R.F.A. (S.R.), 2nd Lieut. Nov. 1917. France, 17th Corps, Guards Division, Artillery.

STEWART, FRANCIS HUGH.
Oratory School, Birmingham. M.A.; D.Sc. (St Andrews); M.B., Ch.B. 1904; Indian Medical Service 1904, Captain 1907; Major Sept. 1915; Acting Lieut.-Col. Jan. 1919. 74th Punjabis. O.C. Frontier War Hospital (Tank), South Waziristan Field Force, 1917; 39th Indian General Hospital, Mesopotamian Exp. Force, 1917-18; 45th Indian General Hospital and 13th Cavalry Brigade. Combined Field Ambulance, Egyptian Exp. Force.

STEWART, FRANCIS MELVILLE.
Student of Medicine, 1909-14. O.T.C. Medical, Oct. 1912 to Sept. 1914, Cadet Corporal. R.A.M.C., (T.) Scottish Horse Field Ambulance, Private Sept. 1914. 13th and 12th Argyll and Sutherland Highlanders, 2nd Lieut. Aug. 1915; Lieut. July 1917; Acting Captain July 1918 to March 1919.

STEWART, FRANK WHITE.
M.A. 1888. Chaplain, 4th Class, 1902; 3rd Class, 1913; 2nd Class and 1st Class, 1918. Argyll and Sutherland Highlanders, France. Assistant Principal Chaplain, The Rhine. Dispatches May 1915; Dec. 1916 and Dec. 1918. C.B.E. June 1919.

STEWART, FREDERICK NAYLOR.
Royal High School. M.B., C.M. 1889; M.D. 1898; L.R.C.P. & S. (Edin.) and L.F.P.S. (Glasg.) and L.M. 1888. R.A.M.C., Lieut. July 1915; Captain July 1916. Twice Mentioned in Dispatches. M.C. Nov. 1917; D.S.O. March 1918.

STEWART, GEORGE.
Edinburgh Academy. M.B., Ch.B. 1907; B.Sc. (P.H.) 1913. R.A.M.C., Lieut. May 1917; Captain June 1918.

STEWART, GEORGE EDWARD.
Victoria College, Jersey. M.B., C.M. 1895; F.R.C.S. (Edin.) and D.T.M. (Liverpool) 1908. Volunteer Medical Staff Corps, 1892-5, Private. Indian Medical Service, 1898; Major 1910; Lieut.-Col. Jan. 1918. China 1900-1. Somaliland 1909-10. France, Egypt, and India. Dispatches (Waziristan) May 1918.

STEWART, GILBERT MEIKLE.
George Watson's College. Student of Arts, 1912-14 and 1919-20; M.A. 1920. 8th Argyll and Sutherland Highlanders, Private Oct. 1914; 2nd Lieut. March 1915; Lieut. July 1917-19. France 1915-19. G.H.Q. March 1918-19.

Record of War Service

STEWART, HENRY HAY.
M.B., Ch.B. 1911. O.T.C. Artillery, Oct. 1908 to Feb. 1912, Cadet Sergeant. West African Medical Service (Cameroons).

STEWART, HUGH.
Fettes College. Student of Arts, 1903-4. Canterbury (N.Z.) Regiment, 1909. N.Z. Exp. Force, Lieut. Aug. 1914; Captain Sept. 1915; Major Dec. 1915; Lieut.-Col. March 1916; Colonel Nov. 1919. Wounded June 1915. Five times Mentioned in Dispatches. M.C. and Croix de Guerre avec Palme 1915; D.S.O. with Bar 1917; C.M.G. 1919.

STEWART, JAMES.
Perth Academy; Athletics. Student of Arts, 1916. Machine-Gun Corps, May 1917.

STEWART, JAMES.
Pietermaritzburg College. First XV. and XI. O.T.C. 1909-13, Cadet Sergeant. Student of Medicine, 1913-15. O.T.C. Artillery, 1914-15, Cadet. R.F.A., 460th Battery, 2nd Lieut. July 1915; Lieut. (Regulars) and Acting Captain July 1917. R.H.A., 15th Brigade. France, 29th Division. Palestine, 3rd Lahore Division Artillery. Dispatches Jan. 1918. M.C. Dec. 1917.

STEWART, JAMES BELL.
John Watson's Institution. M.A. 1900. Schoolmaster. No. 4 Coy. Q.R.V.B., Royal Scots, 1897-1902, Sergeant, and O.T.C. Artillery, 1916, Cadet; Officer Cadet Aug. 1916. 17th Royal Scots, 2nd Lieut. Nov. 1916; Lieut. May 1918; Captain and Staff Captain Jan. 1919. France Jan. to May 1917. War Office, Nov. 1917-19. Mention Aug. 1919.

STEWART, JAMES CAMERON.
Royal High School. M.A. (Hons. Classics) 1905. Rhind Classical Scholar, 1907. Assistant to Professor of Humanity, 1909-11. 6th Royal Scots (T.), 2nd Lieut. Nov. 1914; Lieut Aug. 1915.

STEWART, JAMES DAVID GRAHAME.
Edinburgh Institution; First XV. and XI. M.B., Ch.B. 1910. R.A.M.C., Lieut. Sept. 1914; Captain Sept. 1915; Egypt. Dispatches June 1919.

STEWART, JAMES DUFF.
Ballymena Academy. Student of Medicine, 1915-16 and 1917-19. O.T.C. Medical, 1916-18, Cadet L/Corporal. R.N.V.R., Surgeon Sub.-Lieut. April 1918.

STEWART, J. H.
M.D. Indian Medical Service, Major.

STEWART, JAMES INNES.
Wick High School. Student of Arts, 1914-17 and 1919-20; M.A. 1920. R.A.M.C., Private April 1917. 33rd Stationary Hospital. Attached Royal Serbian Army.

Record of War Service

STEWART, SIR JAMES PURVES.
Royal High School. M.A. 1889; M.B., C.M. 1894; M.D. 1897; M.R.C.S. (Eng.) 1894; F.R.C.P. (Lond.) 1906. Assistant to Professor of Physiology, 1895. R.A.M.C., Aug. 1914; Colonel June 1915. C.B. (Military) May 1916; K.C.M.G. Jan. 1918; Knight of Grace of St John of Jerusalem; Serbian Order of St Sava.

STEWART, JOHN.
Dalhousie University, Nova Scotia. M.B., C.M. 1877; LL.D. 1913; Professor of Surgery, Dalhousie University, 1919. Canadian Army Medical Corps, Lieut.-Col. Oct. 1915; Colonel March 1918. No. 7 Stationary Hospital, France. War Office, 1918-19. Dispatches May 1918. C.B.E. (Military) Jan. 1919.

STEWART, JOHN.
Daniel Stewart's College. O.T.C. 1914-16. Student of Medicine, 1917 and 1919. O.T.C. Artillery, Dec. 1917 to Aug. 1918, Cadet. R.F.A., Officer Cadet Aug. 1918; 2nd Lieut. April 1919.

STEWART, KENNETH TREVOR.
Haileybury. M.B., C.M. 1889; M.D. 1894. 10th and 12th Essex Regiment, Captain 1900; Retired 1907; Rejoined Oct. 1914. South African Campaign, 1900-2. France. Invalided out Nov. 1916.

STEWART, MALCOLM.
Portree School. M.B., Ch.B. 1910. R.A.M.C., Lieut. May 1917; Captain 1918.

STEWART, MURDO.
Student of Medicine, 1910-16; M.B., Ch.B. 1916. O.T.C. Artillery to Oct. 1914, Cadet. R.F.A. (S.R.), 2nd Lieut. R.A.M.C., Lieut.; Captain Feb. 1917.

STEWART, ROBERT.
Daniel Stewart's College. Student of Law, 1902-5. Solicitor. 9th Highland Light Infantry (T.), Private Jan. 1916; Sergeant Oct. 1916. France.

STEWART, R. A.
Student of Science. Scottish Horse (T.), Private.

STEWART, ROBERT BELL.
George Watson's College. Student of Medicine, 1910-16; M.B., Ch.B. 1916. 9th and 12th Royal Scots (T.), Private Aug. 1914; 2nd Lieut. Sept. 1914; Lieut. Nov. 1914; Captain Sept. 1915. R.A.M.C., Lieut. Aug. 1916; Captain Feb. 1917. France. Wounded Sept. 1915 and Sept. 1916. Dispatches Dec. 1915. M.C. 1915; Bar to M.C. April 1917; second Bar to M.C. Sept. 1918.

STEWART, ROBERT LESLIE.
Student of Medicine, 1912-15 and 1916-17; M.B., Ch.B. 1917. O.T.C. Infantry, 1914-15, Cadet. Royal Navy, Surgeon-Probationer; Surgeon Jan. 1918.

STEWART, ROBERT LOGAN.
M.A. 1908. 2/1st Ayrshire Yeomanry, Private Oct. 1916; L/Corporal Aug. 1917 to Feb. 1919.

Record of War Service

STEWART, ROBERT SCOTT.
  Morgan Academy, Dundee. Student of Medicine, 1918. M.A. (St Andrews) 1916. R.F.A., Gunner April 1916.

STEWART, ROY MACKENZIE.
  Lord Williams' Grammar School, Oxford. M.B., Ch.B. 1911. R.A.M.C., Lieut. May 1915; Captain May 1916. France; Salonika 1917.

STEWART, THOMAS BROWN.
  Dundee High School. University O.T.C. Artillery, Feb. to Aug. 1918, Cadet; Officer Cadet Aug. 1918. R.G.A., 2nd Lieut. April 1919.

STEWART, THOMAS GRAINGER.
  M.B., Ch.B. 1900; M.D. 1912. Royal Navy, Surgeon.

STEWART, THOMAS MORTON JOHNSTON.
  George Watson's College. Student of Medicine, 1910-15; M.B., Ch.B. 1915. O.T.C. Medical, Nov. 1914, Cadet. R.A.M.C., Lieut. July 1915; Captain July 1916. Malta, Egypt, India, France, and North Russia.

STEWART, WILLIAM.
  M.B., Ch.B. 1909. R.A.M.C., Lieut. 1911; Captain Feb. 1915. France and India.

STEWART, WILLIAM.
  Otago High School, New Zealand. Cadet Corps 1897-8; M.B., Ch.B. 1911. O.T.C. Infantry, Jan. 1909-10. R.A.M.C., Lieut. 1915. Netley Hospital.

STEWART, W. BURTON.
  B.A. 1897. Student of Arts. Army, Hon. Lieut. Oct. 1900. Lothians and Border Horse (T.), Major Jan. 1904. T.D.

STEWART, WILLIAM ROSS.
  M.B., Ch.B. 1912. O.T.C. Artillery, Jan. 1910 to April 1913, Cadet. Indian Medical Service, Lieut.; Captain Jan. 1917.

STEWART-MacNEIL, JOHN.
  Edinburgh Institution. Student of Science, 1914 and 1919. O.T.C. Engineers, Oct. 1914 to April 1915, Cadet. R.E. (T.), 2nd Lieut. April 1915; Lieut. July 1916. Attached R.F.C. and Royal Air Force.

STIELL, GAVIN.
  M.B., C.M. 1881; M.D. 1897. R.A.M.C., Captain Sept. 1915; Acting Major May 1918.

STILES, SIR HAROLD JALLAND.
  M.B., C.M. 1885; F.R.C.S. (Edin.) 1889. Professor of Clinical Surgery. R.A.M.C. (T.), Captain 1908; Major; Brevet Lieut.-Col. June 1918; Temp. Colonel Sept. 1918. Edinburgh War Hospital, Bangour, and 2nd Scottish General Hospital.

Record of War Service

STIRLING, JAMES.
Arbroath High School. Student of Law, 1903-5; Law Agent, 1906. O.T.C. Artillery, March to Sept. 1916, Cadet; Officer Cadet Sept. 1916. R.G.A. (North Scottish), 2nd Lieut. Dec. 1916; Lieut. June 1918. 337th Siege Battery, France.

STIRLING, JAMES ALEXANDER.
Robert Gordon's College, Aberdeen. Student of Medicine, 1912-18; M.B., Ch.B. 1917. Senior President, S.R.C. and Union, 1917; O.T.C. Medical, Oct. 1913 to Dec. 1914, Cadet. R.N.V.R., H.M.S. *Meteor*, Surgeon-Probationer, Dec. 1914. Royal Navy, Surgeon-Lieut. Dec. 1917. Invalided out Jan. 1919. D.S.C. and Dispatches (Dogger Bank) Jan. 1915.

STOBIE, WILLIAM.
George Watson's College. M.B., Ch.B. 1908. R.A.M.C. (T.), Lieut. May 1915; Captain Nov. 1915; Acting Major Feb. 1918 to April 1919. 3rd Southern General Hospital, Oxford. 2/1st S.M. Field Ambulance, 2/4th Oxford and Bucks Light Infantry, and 41st Casualty Clearing Station, France (three years). Wounded. Twice Mentioned in Dispatches. O.B.E. (Military).

STOCKLEY, CLEMENT INGS.
Croydon High School. Student of Medicine, 1910-15; M.B., Ch.B. 1915. O.T.C. Medical, 1914-15, Cadet. R.A.M.C., Lieut. Aug. 1916; Captain Aug. 1917.

STOCKLEY, HANDLEY GEORGE.
Croydon Burgh School. Student of Medicine, 1915-16 and 1918-20. O.T.C. Medical, 1915-16, Cadet; Officer Cadet July 1916. West Surrey Regiment, 2nd Lieut. March 1917 to Oct. 1918. India and Mesopotamia.

STOCKMAN, RALPH.
Royal High School. M.B., C.M. 1882; M.D. 1886; F.R.C.P. (Edin.) 1889. R.A.M.C., Lieut.-Col. 1908. 3rd Scottish General Hospital. Mention 1919.

STODART, DAVID EDMUND.
M.B., Ch.B. 1910. R.F.C. 1912. Royal Air Force, Flight Commander.

STODART, M. M.
M.B., Ch.B. Royal Air Force.

STODART, THOMAS.
M.B., C.M. 1891. Indian Medical Service, Lieut.-Col. Jan. 1913.

STODDART, ALEXANDER REID.
Royal High School; First XV. M.B., C.M. 1887. 5th West Yorkshire Regiment, Surgeon-Lieut., 1896; Surgeon-Major 1908. 24th General Hospital, France, April 1915 to Dec. 1918. Dispatches Jan. 1916.

STODDART, JOHN.
George Watson's College. M.B., C.M. 1896; D.P.H. (Camb.) 1901. Barrister-at-Law. Royal Navy 1898, Staff-Surgeon; Surgeon-Commander. Senior M.O. H.M.S. *New Zealand*. Battle of Jutland. Order of St Stanislaus (2nd Class), Sept. 1916.

Record of War Service

STONE, HUGH WILLIAM.
Student of Science, 1893-5. 2nd Artists' Rifles O.T.C., 28th London Regiment, Private; L/Corporal.

STONE, THOMAS WILLIAM.
Holy Cross Academy. Student of Arts, 1913-15. O.T.C. Infantry, Jan. to July 1915, Cadet. 3rd Highland Light Infantry, 2nd Lieut. Jan. 1917. Transferred to 107th Pioneers, India; Lieut.

STOOKES, VALENTINE ALEXANDER.
Merchant Taylors' School. O.T.C. 1907-10, Cadet Staff Sergeant. B.Sc. (St Andrews). St Andrews University O.T.C. 1911-13, Cadet. Student of Medicine, 1914 and 1918-19; M.B., Ch.B. 1919. Scots Greys, Aug. 1914; Captain Jan. 1917. Attached Royal Air Force. Dispatches 1916. M.C. May 1916.

STORIE, WILLIAM STEVENSON.
Jedburgh Grammar School; Dux. Student of Law, 1896-8. Solicitor. No. 12 Coy. A.S.C. (M.T.), Private Dec. 1915; 2nd Lieut. Oct. 1918 to July 1919. New Zealand Division (M.T.), Workshops, Dec. 1918. France and The Rhine.

STORRAR, JOHN.
Student of Law, 1912-14. R.F.A. (T.). 1st Lowland Brigade, Gunner.

STORREY, JAMES RUDOLPH.
George Watson's College. Student of Arts. Scottish Rifles, Meerut, India, 1916.

STORY, COLIN.
George Watson's College. Student of Science, 1897-9. Kaffrarian Rifles, Private Oct. 1914; L/Corporal April 1915. South African Rebellion 1914, and German South West Africa 1914-15.

STOTT, JAMES ROBERT.
M.B., Ch.B. 1910; B.Sc. 1912; M.D. 1918. R.A.M.C., Lieut. April 1917; Captain April 1918. 2nd East Surrey Regiment. Balkans, Turkey, and South Russia. Dispatches. O.B.E. (Military) June 1919.

STOTT, RICHARD CORSAR GORDON.
Daniel Stewart's College; First XI. Student of Science, 1917-19. Royal Air Force, Flight Cadet.

STOUTE, DOUGLAS GARNETT.
Elizabeth College, Guernsey; First XI. O.T.C. 1906-10, Cadet Sergeant. Student of Medicine, 1910-15; M.B., Ch.B. 1916. O.T.C. Medical, Sept. 1914 to July 1916, Cadet L/Corporal. R.A.M.C., Lieut. July 1916; Acting Major Jan. 1917 to Nov. 1919. Dispatches Sept. 1919.

STRACEY, BERNARD.
M.B., Ch.B. 1899. Volunteer Medical Staff Corps, 1896-9, Private. R.A.M.C. (T.), Captain Aug. 1914. 2/1st North Midland Casualty Clearing Station, Jan. 1915. Invalided out March 1918.

Record of War Service

STRACHAN, ARTHUR ROBERT.
George Heriot's School. B.L. 1916. 5th Battn. Machine-Gun Corps, Private.

STRACHAN, DONALD BALFOUR.
George Watson's College. O.T.C. 1914-16. Student of Medicine, 1916-17. O.T.C. Artillery, 1917, Cadet. R.G.A. (Mountain), 2nd Lieut. March 1918.

STRACHAN, EDWARD ALEXANDER.
M.B., Ch.B. 1908. R.A.M.C., Captain March 1915; India.

STRACHAN, GEORGE SMITH GOODALL.
Dollar Academy. Student of Law, 1901-9. Writer to the Signet, 1919. 9th Royal Scots (T.), Lieut; Captain. Mobilised Aug. 1914. France July 1916 and Jan. to May 1917. Wounded at Roeux April 1917.

STRACHAN, HARCUS, *V.C.* (See page 756.)

STRACHAN, JOHN COCKBURN.
Dunbar School. M.A. 1907. Schoolmaster. R.G.A., Gunner July 1917; 2nd Lieut. Aug. 1918.

STRAIN, ARTHUR CHARLES.
Dundee High School. M.B., Ch.B. 1904; M.D. 1907. R.A.M.C., Lieut. Aug. 1917; Captain Aug. 1918.

STRAIN, LAURENCE HUGH.
Uppingham; First XV. School Rifle Corps, 1889-93, Sergeant. B.A. (Camb.); LL.B. Advocate, 1900. King's Counsel. R.N.V.R. attached R.N.A.S., Lieut. Aug. 1914; Lieut.-Commander Oct. 1916; Acting Commander June 1917; Commander Jan. 1918. Transferred to Royal Air Force, Lieut.-Col. April 1918. Dispatches April 1915, April 1916, May 1918, and Jan. 1919. D.S.C. March 1916; Officer of Order of Redeemer (Greek) May 1918. O.B.E. (Military) June 1919.

STRANAGHAN, CYRIL PATRICK ANDREW.
M.B., Ch.B. 1909. R.A.M.C., Captain March 1918.

STRANG, DUNCAN WILLIAM PARK.
M.A. 1910. Minister, U.F. Church of Scotland. O.T.C. Infantry, Sept. 1914, Cadet. 8th Seaforth Highlanders, Private Sept. 1914; 2nd Lieut.; Major April 1916. France. Legion of Honour, Nov. 1916. M.C. and Dispatches Dec. 1916.

STRANG, GEORGE McLAREN.
Stirling High School. Student of Science, 1914-15. R.E., 2nd Lieut. May 1917; Lieut. M.C. Dec. 1918.

STRANG, JAMES LOGAN.
Merchiston Castle. O.T.C. 1908-11. Student of Law, 1914-15. O.T.C. Infantry, Oct. to Nov. 1914, Cadet. 4th Border Regiment, 2nd Lieut. Nov. 1914; Temp. Lieut. Jan. 1915; Lieut. June 1916; Acting Captain May 1918; Acting Major Jan. 1919. 258th Machine-Gun Corps. Mesopotamia.

Record of War Service

STRANG, ROBERT SCOTLAND.
  Stirling High School. Student of Arts, 1918-19. 52nd Gordon Highlanders, Private.

STRANGER, FRANCIS HENRY.
  Taunton School. Student of Science, 1918-19. 19th Canadian Infantry, Private Sept. 1914. 1st Duke of Cornwall's Light Infantry, Lieut. June 1918. France. Wounded at Ypres Oct. 1917.

STRATHAIRN, GEORGE CECIL.
  George Watson's College. M.B., Ch.B. 1901; D.P.H. (Edin.) 1912. University Battery, E.C.A.V., 1897-1901, Sergeant. Uganda Medical Service, Captain Sept. 1914; Major Aug. 1916 to June 1918. Dispatches June 1919.

STRICKLAND, JOHN FLETCHER.
  Carlisle Grammar School. M.B., C.M. 1896. R.A.M.C., Lieut. Oct. 1915; Captain 1916. 30th General Hospital, Palermo, Sicily. France; 3rd (Guards Division) and 102nd (34th Division) and Northumberland (T.) (51st Division) Field Ambulances. The Somme July 1916. Invalided out Feb. 1918.

STRONG, ARTHUR NESBITT.
  Daniel Stewart's College. M.A. 1911. O.T.C. Artillery, 1908-11, Cadet. R.F.A. (S.R.), 2nd Lieut. Dec. 1917. Gassed March and Wounded Aug. 1918.

STRONG, THOMAS ARTHUR.
  Daniel Stewart's College. Cadet Corps 1915-17, Corporal. Student of Science, 1917. O.T.C. Artillery, 1917-18, Cadet Sergeant. R.F.A., Officer Cadet Aug. 1918.

STRONG, WILLIAM BAILLIE.
  B.D. 1874. Minister, Church of Scotland. Chaplain.

STRUTHERS, JOHN WILLIAM.
  Loretto; First XV. and XI. M.B., Ch.B. 1897; F.R.C.S. (Edin.) 1899. Lecturer on Surgery. Scottish R.C. Hospital, Rouen, Sept. 1914 to Oct. 1915. R.A.M.C., Captain May 1916; Major July 1916. 42nd General Hospital, Salonika. Dispatches May 1915 and May 1917. Order of St Sava (Serbia), 4th Class.

STRUTHERS, ROBERT.
  Student of Law, 1906-7 and 1910-11. R.N.V.R., Gunner Nov. 1915 to Oct. 1917. H.M.S. *Constance*, Grand Fleet. R.G.A., Officer Cadet March 1918.

STUART, ALEXANDER.
  George Watson's College. Student of Medicine, 1914-15 and 1918-20. O.T.C. Infantry, 1914-15, Medical, 1918-19, Cadet. R.E., Corporal July 1915 to May 1918.

STUART, CHARLES.
  Perth Academy; First XV. and XI. M.B., C.M. 1891; M.D. 1909. R.A.M.C., Lieut. March 1915; Captain March 1916.

Record of War Service

STUART, DOUGLAS.
Musselburgh Grammar School. Student of Science, 1913-14. O.T.C. Artillery Aug. to Sept. 1914, Cadet. Scottish Horse (T.), Private Sept. 1914; Corporal Aug. 1915. R.F.A., 2nd Lieut. Dec. 1917.

STUART, DONALD NORRIS.
Musselburgh Grammar School. Student of Law, 1913-14. O.T.C. Artillery, Oct. 1913-14, Cadet. R.F.A., 2nd Lieut. Aug. 1914; Lieut. Dec. 1915.

STUART, HENRY CAMPBELL.
Haileybury. Student of Science, 1892-3. 24th Battn. Royal Fusiliers, Private Dec. 1914. Royal Highlanders (Black Watch), 2nd Lieut. Sept. 1915; Lieut. Sept. 1916; Temp. Captain April 1917-19. France, 74th Division. Wounded Sept. 1918.

STUART, SIDNEY WILLIAM HERBERT.
Student of Medicine, 1910-15; M.B., Ch.B. 1914. R.A.M.C., Lieut.; Captain Dec. 1917. Mesopotamia.

STUART, THOMAS.
Darlington Grammar School; First XI. M.B., C.M. 1895; M.D. 1899. N.Z. Medical Corps, Captain Nov. 1917.

STUART, WILLIAM JAMES.
Edinburgh Academy; First XV. and XI. M.A. 1894; M.B., Ch.B. 1899; F.R.C.S. (Edin). Lecturer, Clinical Surgery. R.A.M.C. (T.), Captain 1908; Acting Major, Sept. 1917 to Jan. 1919. 2nd Scottish General Hospital, Aug. 1914 to June 1916. Salonika July 1916 to Dec. 1918.

STUART, WILLIAM LEITCH.
Edinburgh Academy. M.A. (St Andrews). Student of Law, 1911-14 and 1918-19. Writer to the Signet, 1919. 9th Royal Scots (T.), Private Aug. 1914. 1/7th Royal Highlanders (Black Watch) (T.), 2nd Lieut. Oct. 1914; Lieut. June 1916. France May 1915. Invalided home Nov. 1917.

STUMP, CLAUDE WITHERINGTON.
Student of Medicine, 1910-17. M.B., Ch.B. 1917. O.T.C. Medical, Nov. to Dec. 1914, Cadet Sergeant. 8th King's Own Scottish Borderers, Lieut. Australian Army Medical Corps, Captain Oct. 1917.

STUNGO, SYMON.
Royal High School. Student of Arts, 1904-6 and 1914-15; M.A. 1915. A.S.C., Private May 1916; Corporal Jan. 1919. France.

STURROCK, ALEXANDER CORSAR.
George Watson's College. M.A. 1892; M.B., C.M. 1896; M.D. 1898; M.R.C.P. (Lond.) 1906. Assistant to Professor of Physiology, 1896-8. B.R.C., No. 4 Hospital, Wimereux, France, 1915. Salonika 1915-17. R.A.M.C., May 1917; Major Dec. 1917. Dispatches 1920.

Record of War Service

STURROCK, DOUGLAS LLOYD.
Daniel Stewart's College; First XV. and XI. Student of Arts and Medicine, 1912-15. O.T.C. Infantry, Oct. 1914 to May 1915, Cadet. R.N.V.R., Chief Petty Officer, May 1915; Sub-Lieut. Feb. 1917; Lieut. Feb. 1918 to March 1919. H.M. Drifter *Buck*, Sept. 1917 to March 1919.

SULLIVAN, JOHN.
Daniel Stewart's College. M.B., Ch.B. 1901. R.A.M.C., Lieut. March 1915; Captain March 1916. France. Prisoner of War April to Nov. 1918.

SUMNER, SYDNEY SCOTT.
George Heriot's School. O.T.C. 1914-15. Student of Medicine, 1915-18. O.T.C. Artillery, Sept. 1916 to April 1917, Cadet. R.G.A., Officer Cadet April 1917. Invalided out July 1917.

SUMNER, THEODOTUS JOHN.
Student of Medicine, 1911-14. R.N.V.R., Surgeon-Probationer.

SUTHERLAND, ANDREW.
Inverness Royal Academy. Student of Science, 1905-8. 4th Cameron Highlanders, 2nd Lieut. Aug. 1914; Lieut. June 1915; Captain July 1915. R.E., Captain March 1916; Acting Major June and July 1917. France, Neuve Chapelle, Festubert, and Loos; Palestine and Egypt, first and second Gaza, and Jerusalem. Wounded at Givenchy June 1915. M.C. and Dispatches June 1915.

SUTHERLAND, DAVID.
Royal High School; First XV. M.B., Ch.B. 1902. Royal Navy, Surgeon Jan. 1915.

SUTHERLAND, DAVID.
M.A. 1896. Schoolmaster. 5th Seaforth Highlanders, Jan. 1902. Mobilised Aug. 1914; Captain Feb. 1916. France, 51st (Highland) Division. M.C. and Dispatches Jan. 1916; Bar to M.C. July 1918.

SUTHERLAND, DAVID WATERS.
South Melbourne College, Australia. M.B., C.M. (Hons.) 1893; M.D. 1902; M.R.C.P. (Lond.) 1902. Fellow of Punjab University, 1904. Indian Medical Service, Surgeon-Lieut. 1894; Lieut.-Col. Jan. 1914. Chitral 1895; Afghanistan 1919. Mention (India) June 1918. C.I.E. June 1917.

SUTHERLAND, GEORGE.
George Watson's College. M.B., Ch.B. 1910. R.A.M.C., Lieut. Jan. 1916; Captain 1917. Station Hospital, Quetta, Baluchistan; Royal Herbert Hospital, Woolwich; 118th Field Ambulance. Seistan Field Force, Persia, and 1st Cameronians, France.

SUTHERLAND, GEORGE WILLIAM GORDON.
Kirkwall Burgh School. Student of Medicine, 1911-14. O.T.C. Infantry, Sept. to Oct. 1914, Cadet. 4th and 10th Gordon Highlanders, 2nd Lieut.; Lieut. Jan. 1917; Acting Captain April 1918.

Record of War Service

SUTHERLAND, HALLIDAY GIBSON.
Merchiston Castle. M.B., Ch.B. 1906; M.D. 1908. Royal Navy, H.M.S. *Empress of Britain*, Surgeon Aug. 1914. R.N.A.S. and Royal Air Force, Captain.

SUTHERLAND, HECTOR WILLIAM.
Galashiels Academy. Student of Medicine, 1906-8 and 1918-19. University Battery, E.C.A.V., 1907-8, Gunner. 7th King's Own Scottish Borderers, Private Sept. 1914; 2nd Lieut. Dec. 1914; Captain Sept. 1915; Major July 1918; Lieut.-Col. Aug. 1918. Four times Wounded. Dispatches 1916 and 1918. D.S.O. Jan. 1919.

SUTHERLAND, HENRY ERIC GIBBS.
Edinburgh Institution; Dux; First XV. Student of Arts and Law, 1912-14 and 1919-20; M.A. 1920. O.T.C. Infantry, April 1913 to Aug. 1914, Cadet. 9th Royal Scots (T.), Private Aug. 1914. 4th Royal Scots Fusiliers (T.), 2nd Lieut. Sept. 1914; Lieut. June 1915; Captain June 1916. Transferred to 1st Gordon Highlanders (Regulars), Lieut. Sept. 1917 to July 1919. Gallipoli, Palestine. Dispatches Oct. 1916. M.C. May 1917; Bar to M.C. Dec. 1917.

SUTHERLAND, JOHN.
Wick High School. Student of Arts, 1915-16 and 1918-19. R.G.A., Gunner Jan. 1916; Acting Sergeant Nov. 1917. Northern Command, Jan. 1917 to Sept. 1918.

SUTHERLAND, JOHN DONALD.
Inverness Academy. Student of Law, 1886-91. Law Agent and Notary Public. Home Timber Supplies, 1915-17. R.E., Lieut.-Col. May 1917; Colonel Sept. 1917. Assistant Director of Forestry in France, 1917-19. Dispatches May 1918 and March 1919. Chevalier of the Legion of Honour, Feb. 1919. C.B.E. (Military) June 1919.

SUTHERLAND, JOHN WILLIAM ROSS.
George Watson's College. Student of Medicine and Science, 1912-14 and 1920. O.T.C. Infantry, May 1913 to Oct. 1914, Cadet. 2nd Scottish Horse (T.), Private Aug. 1914; Corporal Oct. 1915; Sergeant Nov. 1915. Dorset Yeomanry, attached 3rd Hussars, 2nd Lieut. Dec. 1917. Gallipoli, Egypt, Salonika, and France.

SUTHERLAND, ROBERT KERR SOUTAR.
George Watson's College. M.B., Ch.B. 1912. R.A.M.C., Captain Aug. 1914. France, 55th Field Ambulance, 15th Division. Staff Captain; The Rhine. Wounded.

SUTHERLAND, THOMAS HARVEY.
Boroughmuir School. Student of Science, 1914-16 and 1918-19. Royal Air Force, 2nd Lieut. (Meteorological Officer) Sept. 1918.

SUTHERLAND, WILLIAM DUNBAR.
M.B., C.M. 1888; M.D. 1907. Indian Medical Service, Lieut.-Col. March 1910.

Record of War Service

SUTHERLAND, WILLIAM NEIL.
M.A. 1910. Minister, Church of Scotland. O.T.C. Infantry, Nov. 1908 to May 1910, Cadet Corporal. R.F.A., 4th Lowland Brigade, Captain June 1916; Major June 1917. Wounded Nov. 1917. Dispatches Nov. 1917. M.C. Jan. 1918.

SWAFFIELD, WALTER HENRY.
M.B., Ch.B. 1901; M.D. 1903; F.R.C.S. (Edin.) 1903. R.A.M.C., Lieut. Sept. 1914; Captain Sept. 1915.

SWAN, ALLISON.
Student of Arts, 1916-18. Women's Legion, attached 606th Coy. (M.T.), R.A.S.C., Mechanic Driver July 1918.

SWAN, ANDREW EDWARD.
Student of Science, 1913-14. Mobilised with Yeomanry, Aug. 1914. R.F.A. (S.R.), 112th Brigade, 2nd Lieut. Sept. 1917. France and Salonika.

SWAN, JAMES.
M.B., Ch.B. 1909. R.A.M.C. (S.R.), Lieut. Nov. 1914; Captain May 1915; Acting Major Jan. 1918. M.C.

SWAN, MATTHEW ARNOLD.
Paisley Grammar School. M.B., Ch.B. 1901. R.A.M.C., Lieut. Feb. 1915; Captain Feb. 1916. 13th General Hospital. 41st Brigade, R.F.A.; 2nd Highland Light Infantry and 1st Cavalry Field Ambulance. France March 1915 to Nov. 1918. Wounded 1916. M.C. June 1916; Bar to M.C. March 1918.

SWAN, THOMAS MILNE.
Kirkcaldy High School; First XV. and XI. Cadet Corps 1903-8, Corporal. Student of Science, 1912-14. 15th Royal Scots, Private Aug. 1914; Sergeant. 7th Border Regiment, 2nd Lieut. Feb. 1915; Captain April 1917; Adjutant June 1917.

SWEETEN, BENJAMIN.
Queen Elizabeth's Grammar School, Penrith. M.B., C.M. 1889; D.P.H., R.C.S. 1907. R.A.M.C., Lieut. April 1915; Captain April 1916; Acting Major. Sanitary Officer and General Military Hospital, Colchester, Nov. 1918. Mention Sept. 1917.

SWIFT, BRIAN HERBERT.
St Peter's College, Adelaide. First XI. O.T.C. 1909-10, Lieut. B.A., M.B., B.C. (Camb.) 1916. Student of Medicine, 1910-16. R.A.M.C., Lieut. Aug. 1916; Captain Aug. 1917. 61st Field Ambulance. Royal Air Force Medical Service, 1918-19. M.C. Feb. 1918.

SWINBURNE, THORDUR JOHN WILHELM.
George Watson's College. O.T.C. 1907-8. M.B., Ch.B. 1914. O.T.C. Medical, 1910-14, Cadet L/Corporal. R.A.M.C., Lieut. Aug. 1915; Captain Aug. 1916. France.

Record of War Service

SYDENHAM, FREDERICK WILLIAM.
Appleby Grammar School. M.B., C.M. 1893; M.D. 1899; F.R.C.S. (Edin.) 1906; D.P.H. (Vict.) 1895. R.A.M.C., Lieut. 1909; Captain Aug. 1913.

SYED, RAHMAT KADUI.
St George's School, Hyderabad. First XI. Student of Arts, 1914-15 and 1918-19. Tennis "Blue." Indian Field Ambulance, Cadet Dec. 1914.

SYM, JAMES PITCAIRN.
Craigmount, Edinburgh; First XV. M.A. 1877. Rugby "Blue." Writer to the Signet, 1878. 1st V.B. Royal Scots, Private Dec. 1914.

SYME, GEORGE.
Dunfermline High School. M.A. 1912. Schoolmaster. 6th and 8th Royal Scots (T.), Private Sept. 1914; L/Sergeant Oct. 1916; 2nd Lieut. May 1917; Lieut. Nov. 1918. France Nov. 1914.

SYMON, JACK.
George Heriot's School. O.T.C. 1912-14. Student of Medicine, 1918-19. 8th Scottish Rifles, Private Nov. 1916. Egypt and Palestine, Feb. 1917 to March 1918. France April 1918 to Feb. 1919. Wounded July 1918.

TAIT, ADAM.
Biggar High School. M.B., Ch.B. 1908. R.A.M.C., Lieut. June 1917; Captain June 1918.

TAIT, ARTHUR EDWIN.
Blyth National School. M.B., Ch.B. 1908. R.A.M.C. (T.), Lieut. Dec. 1914; Captain June 1915. 2nd Northern Field Ambulance, London Field Ambulance, and 63rd General Hospital, Salonika, Dec. 1916 to Feb. 1919.

TAIT, CHARLES KINGSLEY.
Edinburgh Institution. Student of Music, 1911-15. 3rd and 6th Royal West Surrey Regiment, Private Nov. 1915; L/Corporal. Inns of Court O.T.C., Cadet. Royal Air Force, 2nd Lieut. Aug. 1916; Lieut. Feb. 1918; Acting Captain June 1918 to March 1919. Machine-Gun Corps. Croix de Guerre with Palm 1917.

TAIT, GEORGE CRIGHTON.
Daniel Stewart's College; First XI. Cadet Corps 1914-16. University O.T.C. Artillery, 1917-18, Cadet; Officer Cadet Feb. 1918. R.F.A., 2nd Lieut. Sept. 1918.

TAIT, JAMES.
George Heriot's School. Student of Arts, 1909-14. Lothians and Border Horse (T.), Private Aug. 1914; Sergeant. Machine-Gun Corps, 2nd Lieut. Dec. 1917. M.M. Nov. 1916.

TAIT, JOHN.
B.Sc. 1901; M.B., Ch.B. (Hons.) 1903; M.D. 1906; D.Sc. 1907. Lecturer in Experimental Physiology. R.A.M.C., Lieut. May 1917; Captain May 1918. 66th and 62nd General Hospitals, and 9th Casualty Clearing Station.

Record of War Service

TAIT, RALPH JOHNSTON.
　　Crieff Academy. M.B., Ch.B. 1913; D.P.H. 1920. R.A.M.C., Lieut. Aug. 1914; Captain Aug. 1915. 2/2nd Northumbrian Field Ambulance. 34th Brigade R.F.A.

TALBOT, MATHEW WRIGHT.
　　M.B., C.M. 1892. R.A.M.C., Lieut. Dec. 1915; Captain Dec. 1916.

TARLETON, JOHN A.
　　Student of Science, 1914-15. O.T.C. Artillery, Nov. 1914 to May 1915, Cadet. R.F.A., 2nd Lieut. May 1915; Lieut. June 1916.

TARR, WILLIAM.
　　West Buckland School, N. Devon. First XI. M.B., Ch.B. 1898; M.D. 1909; F.R.C.S. (Edin.) 1909. Indian Medical Service, 1904; Captain 1907; Major July 1915. No. 1 Ambulance Train, India, 1914-15, and Officers' Convalescent Depôt, Baghdad, 1917. Dispatches (Mesopotamia) March 1918.

TASSELL, ARCHIBALD RONALD.
　　Carlisle Grammar School. 1st Cumberland Volunteers, Private April 1916. University O.T.C. Infantry, Dec. 1917 to June 1918, Cadet; Officer Cadet June 1918. Royal Fusiliers (City of London Regiment), 2nd Lieut. March 1919.

TAUNTON, RICHARD EUSTACE MAXWELL.
　　St John's College, Winnipeg. Student of Medicine, 1918-19. 11th Reserve and 27th Canadian Infantry, Aug. 1914; L/Corporal Nov. 1914. Invalided out 1915. Rejoined Oct. 1916. R.F.C., 63rd Squadron, Lieut. Jan. 1917; Flying Officer (Observer) June 1917 to March 1919. Royal Air Force. Mesopotamia.

TAYLOR, ALEXANDER.
　　M.A. (Aberdeen). Student of Medicine, 1903-4. M.R.C.V.S. N.Z. Veterinary Corps. Second Army Brigade, N.Z. Field Ambulance, Captain Aug. 1914. Egypt. France April 1916.

TAYLOR, ALEXANDER.
　　M.A.; LL.B. 1896. 9th Royal Scots (T.), March 1908; Captain Aug. 1914.

TAYLOR, ALEXANDER JEFFERSON.
　　Durban High School, S. Africa. Student of Science, 1918; B.A. (Cape) 1914. 102nd Brigade, S. African Field Ambulance, Private Aug. 1915; Corporal Feb. 1916; Sergeant Sept. 1917. R.F.A., 2nd Lieut. June 1917; Lieut. Dec. 1918.

TAYLOR, ARTHUR CAMPBELL.
　　Edinburgh Academy. Student of Arts, 1896-9. 2nd Scottish Rifles, Captain; Major Sept. 1915.

Record of War Service

TAYLOR, ARTHUR LOUDOUN.
Edinburgh Academy. B.Sc. 1907; M.B., Ch.B. 1909; F.R.C.P. (Edin.) 1917. R.A.M.C., Lieut. Feb. 1915; Captain Feb. 1916; Acting Major Feb. 1919. Neurologist, Dieppe Area, June 1916 to Feb. 1919.

TAYLOR, CHARLES CAMERON.
Fettes College; First XV. O.T.C. 1914-18, Cadet Sergeant. Student of Arts, 1918-19. R.G.A., Gunner Sept. 1919.

TAYLOR, CHARLES MELDRUM.
Kirkwall Burgh School. Student of Arts, 1915-16 and 1918-19. O.T.C. Artillery, Nov. 1915 to April 1916, Cadet. 2nd Royal Scots Fusiliers, Private April 1916. France. Wounded at Arras April 1917, and invalided out Nov. 1917.

TAYLOR, CHARLES WILLIAM GRAY.
Daniel Stewart's College. Student of Arts and Divinity, 1896-1904; M.A. 1900. Minister, Church of Scotland. Chaplain, 4th Class, March 1916.

TAYLOR, DAVID LIVINGSTONE KIDD.
Kirkcaldy High School. M.A. 1913. Schoolmaster. 11th Royal Highlanders (Black Watch), Private Nov. 1915.

TAYLOR, ERIC.
George Heriot's School, Dux. M.A. (Hons. Maths.) and B.Sc. 1910. R.E., L/Corporal; Captain. M.C.

TAYLOR, EUSTACE TREVOR NEAVE.
Student of Medicine, 1911-14 and 1915-18; M.B., Ch.B. 1917. O.T.C. Medical, 1912-14 and 1917, Cadet Sergeant. Scottish Horse (T.), Private Sept. 1914. R.E., July 1915 to June 1916. Indian Medical Service, Captain Feb. 1918. France 1915-16.

TAYLOR, FRANCIS OUTRAM.
Edinburgh Academy. O.T.C 1908-10. Student of Medicine, 1909-14 and 1916-17; M.B., Ch.B. 1916. O.T.C. Artillery, 1910-14, Cadet. R.F.A., 2nd Lieut. Aug. 1914. R.A.M.C., Lieut. May 1917; Captain May 1918. France 1915.

TAYLOR, GEORGE PETER.
Ushaw College, Co. Durham. M.B., C.M. 1883. R.A.M.C., Lieut. May 1915; Captain May 1916-19; Acting Major. Queen Mary's Military Hospital, Whalley. Hospital Ships *Aberdonian, Glencairn Castle, Dunluce Castle, Aquitania*.

TAYLOR, GEORGE PRITCHARD.
Trent College. M.B., Ch.B. 1908. Volunteer Medical Staff Corps and O.T.C. Medical, Nov. 1903 to Jan. 1909, Cadet Acting Sergeant-Major. R.A.M.C., Lieut. 1909; Captain July 1912; Acting Lieut.-Col. April 1917. France. North Russia 1919. Four times Mentioned in Dispatches. D.S.O. and Bar; M.C.; Croix de Guerre with Silver Star (French).

Record of War Service

TAYLOR, HENRY AUGUSTUS.
: Royal High School; First XV. University O.T.C. Infantry, Sept. to Oct. 1914, Cadet. 23rd Royal Fusiliers, 2nd Lieut. Nov. 1914; Lieut. April 1915; Captain June 1915. Wounded July 1916 and March 1918. M.C. Dec. 1917.

TAYLOR, HENRY VERNON.
: Oakham School. M.B., Ch.B. 1905. R.A.M.C., Lieut. Aug. 1916; Captain Aug. 1917.

TAYLOR, HERBERT OWEN.
: Christ Church, Oxford. M.B., C.M. 1872; M.D. 1879; L.R.C.P. & S. (Edin.) 1873. 10th and 11th Battn., N.V.R., Sherwood Foresters, Captain (M.O.) 1915. Military Hospital, Nottingham.

TAYLOR, HUGH WILLIAM YOUNG.
: Elgin Academy. Student of Arts, Science, and Medicine, 1910-15 and 1917-19; M.A. 1913; B.Sc. 1915. O.T.C. Infantry, Oct. 1914 to Dec. 1915, Cadet. R.N.V.R., Surgeon-Probationer, Dec. 1915 to May 1918. Mine-sweeping, April 1916 to March 1917. Mediterranean, North and Arctic Seas.

TAYLOR, JAMES.
: Uppingham. Student of Law, 1912-14 and 1918-19. R.F.A., Captain. M.C. Sept. 1916.

TAYLOR, JAMES.
: Lochgelly School. Student of Science, 1911-14; B.Sc. 1914. R.G.A., 278th Siege Battery, Gunner June 1917.

TAYLOR, JAMES.
: Kirkcudbright Academy. M.A. 1913. Schoolmaster. 6th attached 4th Royal Scots, 1910, Corporal. Mobilised Aug. 1914. 1st Argyll and Sutherland Highlanders, 2nd Lieut. July 1916; Lieut. Jan. 1918. Wounded at Gallipoli June 1915.

TAYLOR, JAMES BRAID.
: Edinburgh Academy, Dux. O.T.C. 1908-9. M.A. 1912. Vans Dunlop Scholar. O.T.C. Infantry, Oct. 1909 to April 1914, Cadet Corporal. 1/4th East Kent Regiment (T.), 2nd Lieut. March 1915; Lieut. July 1917 to April 1919. Arabia.

TAYLOR, JAMES McBAIN.
: Merchiston Castle. Cadet Corps 1891-4. M.B., Ch.B. 1904. No. 4 Coy. Q.R.V.B., Royal Scots, 1894-1902, Colour-Sergeant. R.A.M.C. (T.), Lieut. Oct. 1914; Captain April 1915 to Jan. 1919. Eastern Mounted Brigade Field Ambulance. Motor Ambulance Convoy, Dec. 1914, Gallipoli. Attached 1/1st Suffolk Yeomanry, Sept. 1915 to Feb. 1918. 71st and 27th General Hospitals, Egypt; 47th Ambulance Train, 1918; Palestine.

TAYLOR, JOHN ARCHIBALD.
: M.B., Ch.B. 1906. Uganda Medical Service, Captain Oct. 1914 to Nov. 1917.

Record of War Service

TAYLOR, JOHN BINNIE.
Falkirk High School. Student of Medicine, 1915-19. O.T.C. Artillery, Sept. to Dec. 1916, Cadet. R.N.V.R., Surgeon-Probationer, April 1917.

TAYLOR, JOHN ORR.
Glasgow Academy; First XV. and XI. M.A. 1908 and LL.B. 1911 (Glasg.). Advocate, 1914. University O.T.C. Infantry, Aug. to Oct. 1914, Cadet. 1/4th Royal Scots (T.), Captain Sept. 1914; Acting Major May 1916 to Sept. 1917. Gallipoli. Twice Wounded.

TAYLOR, JOHN SUTHERLAND.
Edinburgh Academy. O.T.C. 1908-9. M.B., Ch.B. 1914. O.T.C. Infantry, Oct. 1909-14, Cadet Corporal. R.A.M.C., Lieut. Feb. 1915; Captain Feb. 1916. France; Loos, Ypres, the Somme.

TAYLOR, LEONARD WHITAKER OWEN.
Oundle. Cadet Corps 1903-4. M.B., Ch.B. 1910; F.R.C.S. (Edin.) 1912. R.A.M.C. (S.R.), Lieut. 1911; Captain Sept. 1914; Acting Major and Brevet Major Jan. 1918. Dispatches Jan. 1917 and Jan. 1918.

TAYLOR, MOWBRAY.
M.B., C.M. 1889. R.A.M.C. (T.), Lieut.-Col. 4th London Field Ambulance.

TAYLOR, RICHARD JAMES OGILVIE.
George Watson's College. Student of Medicine, 1913-15 and 1918. O.T.C. Infantry, Oct. 1914 to March 1915, Cadet. 14th attached 3rd Royal Scots, 2nd Lieut. March 1915; Lieut. April 1916; Acting Captain June 1916-17. France 1915-16. Wounded June 1916. Invalided out Dec. 1917.

TAYLOR, SARAH.
Clerical Staff. W.R.N.S., Typist, May 1918 to July 1919.

TAYLOR, STUART HOPCRAFT STANLEY.
Malvern College. B.A. (Camb.); M.B., Ch.B. 1904. R.A.M.C., Lieut. March 1917; Captain March 1918 to Jan. 1919.

TAYLOR, WALTER DUFF.
Broughton School, Edinburgh. M.A. 1911. Schoolmaster. 1/8th Scottish Rifles (Cameronians), Private June 1917.

TAYLOR, WILLIAM ATKINSON.
George Watson's College. M.B., C.M. 1893. No 4 Coy. Q.R.V.B., Royal Scots, 1888-93, Sergeant. R.A.M.C. (T.), Major 1912. Mobilised Aug. 1914 to April 1919. France 1915. T.D.

TAYLOR, WILLIAM EDMUND.
Royal High School. Student of Science, 1917. O.T.C. Artillery, 1917-18, Cadet; Officer Cadet May 1918. R.G.A., Coast Defence, 2nd Lieut. Nov. 1918.

Record of War Service

TAYLOR, WILLIAM MACRAE.
Edinburgh Academy. M.B., C.M. 1895; F.R.C.S. (Edin.). No. 4 Coy. Q.R.V.B., Royal Scots, 1890-4, Private, and Volunteer Medical Staff Corps, 1894-5, Corporal. Midlothian Artillery Volunteers, Surgeon-Lieut. 1899. R.A.M.C. (T.), Lieut. South African Campaign, 1900-1. Major Sept. 1913. Mobilised Aug. 1914. 1st Lowland R.F.A. (T.), France.

TAYLOR, WILLIAM STUART.
Edinburgh Academy. Student of Law, 1910-12. Chartered Accountant, 1913. O.T.C. Infantry, Jan. to Aug. 1914, Cadet. 9th Royal Scots (T.), Private Aug. 1914. 7th Royal Highlanders (Black Watch) (T.), 2nd Lieut. Aug. 1916; Lieut. Feb. 1918. France. Wounded May 1915 and June 1917.

TAYLOR-SMITH, MORAY.
Germiston Central School, South Africa. Student of Medicine, 1916-18. Royal Navy, Surgeon Sub-Lieut. Oct. 1918.

TEAGUE, DANIEL GILBERT MILLER.
Melbourne Church of England Grammar School. First XV. M.B., Ch.B. 1896. Australian Army Medical Corps, Australian Imperial Force.

TEAGUE, HENRY WILLIAM.
M.B., Ch.B. 1909. R.A.M.C., Lieut.

TEDCASTLE, ROBERT.
Hastings Grammar School. Student of Law, 1913-15. 2nd Scots Guards, Private Aug. 1915. 1/7th Cheshire Regiment, 2nd Lieut. Jan. 1918; Captain Sept. 1918. France Aug. 1916 and June 1918. Wounded at Somme Sept. 1916, and at Marne Aug. 1918. M.C. July 1918.

TELFORD, ALEXANDER McMENAGAL.
George Watson's College. O.T.C. 1909-11. Student of Science, 1912-15; B.Sc. 1915. O.T.C. Engineers, Oct. 1913 to July 1914, Cadet. R.E., 2nd Lieut. July 1915; Lieut. June 1916. France. Wounded March 1918. Dispatches June 1918.

TEMPLETON, JAMES.
Broughton School, Edinburgh. Student of Science, 1911-15; B.Sc. 1914. Assistant Lecturer in Botany. 9th Royal Scots, Private April 1915. R.E. (Special Brigade), July 1915; Sergeant June 1917 to Jan. 1919. France.

TENNANT, WILLIAM.
Daniel Stewart's College. Student of Law, 1906-9. Law Agent, 1909. 8th and 1/7th Highland Light Infantry, Lieut. 1912. Mobilised Aug. 1914; Captain Sept. 1914. Attached 8th Royal Scots Fusiliers.

TERRELL, CHARLES GIRDLESTONE.
Kendal School; First XV. and XI. Student of Medicine, 1912-17; M.B., Ch.B. 1917. O.T.C. Medical, Dec. 1914 to Jan. 1916, Cadet. R.N.V.R., Surgeon-Sub-Lieut. Jan. 1916. Royal Navy, Surgeon-Lieut. April 1917.

Record of War Service

TERRY, WILLIAM ROBERT.
Sussex Grammar School. Student of Medicine, 1919. R.A.M.C., Private Feb. 1916; L/Corporal May 1916; Sergeant May 1917. 2nd Scottish General Hospital.

TEWSLEY, CYRIL HOCKEN.
Otago High School, Dunedin, New Zealand. M.B., Ch.B. 1906; M.D. 1909; F.R.C.S. 1909 and M.R.C.P. (Edin.) 1919. Examiner in Materia Medica, New Zealand University. N.Z. Medical Corps (T.), 1910, Captain; Major 1915; Lieut.-Col. Sept. 1917. C.M.G. 1918.

THATCHER, CHARLES MALCOLM RUSSEL.
Edinburgh Academy. M.B., Ch.B. 1911. O.T.C. Infantry, Oct. 1908-11, Cadet Sergeant. Royal Navy, Surgeon 1911; Surgeon-Lieut.-Commander Nov. 1917. H.M. Ships *Dreadnought* and *Revenge*.

THATCHER, LEWIS HAY FREDERICK.
Edinburgh Academy; First XV. M.B., Ch.B. 1907; M.D. 1910; F.R.C.P. (Edin.). R.A.M.C., Lieut. Sept. 1914; Captain Sept. 1915.

THERON, CHARLES PETRUS.
South African College, Cape Town. B.A. (South Africa). M.B., Ch.B. 1907. South African Medical Corps, Captain 1914. South African Rebellion and German West Campaign. 5th Mounted Brigade, 1914-15. Dispatches 1915.

THIN, JAMES AINSLIE.
George Watson's College. Student of Arts, 1906-7 and 1909-11. Lothians and Border Horse, Private Aug. 1914; 2nd Lieut.; Lieut. Oct. 1917. France 1915-17. Prisoner of War April 1917. Dispatches April 1917.

THIN, RUSSELL GIBSON.
George Watson's College. O.T.C. 1909-10. Student of Science, 1910-14; B.Sc. 1914. A.I.C. 9th Royal Scots (T.), Private Aug. 1914. 4th King's Own Scottish Borderers (T.), 2nd Lieut. July 1915; Acting Captain June 1917. France 1915; Egypt and Palestine 1916-18.

THOM, FRANK CHISHOLM HARTLEY.
Linlithgow Academy. Student of Law, 1911; B.L. 1917. 10th Royal Scots (T.), 2nd Lieut. Sept. 1914; Lieut. Feb. 1915; Captain March 1916; Staff Captain Feb. 1919; Bombing Officer 1915-19. Wounded Oct. 1916.

THOM, GEORGE St CLAIR.
Dollar Academy; First XV. M.B., C.M. 1893. Rugby "Blue." R.A.M.C. 1894; Lieut.-Col. March 1915; Colonel Dec. 1917. South African Campaign, 1900-2; Gallipoli 1915; France 1916-18; North Russia 1919. C.M.G. 1916; C.B. June 1918; C.B.E. Jan. 1920.

THOM, GEORGE VICTOR.
Dunfermline High School. Student of Science, 1915-16 and 1918-19. O.T.C. Artillery, Sept. 1915 to Aug. 1916, Cadet Acting Sergeant; Officer Cadet Aug. 1916. Forth R.G.A. (T.), 279th Siege Battery, Lieut. May 1918. Attached Royal Air Force. France.

Record of War Service

THOM, HERBERT JAMES.
 Daniel Stewart's College; First XV. Student of Arts, 1912-14; M.A. 1920. 5th Dragoon Guards, Private Aug. 1914; Corporal; Officer Cadet Sept. 1916. 12th Royal Scots, 2nd Lieut. Nov. 1916; Acting Captain July 1917; Captain March 1918 to Aug. 1919. France May 1915-19. M.C. June 1918.

THOM, JAMES ALEXANDER.
 Merchiston Castle. O.T.C. 1908-10. Student of Science, 1913-14. Highland Cyclist Battn. (T.), 1912; Captain Aug. 1914; Major Oct. 1918. 51st Highland Division, Army Cyclist Corps, attached 4th Border Regiment.

THOM, JOHN GIBB.
 Linlithgow Academy. M.A. 1911; LL.B. 1917. 10th and 6th Gordon Highlanders, Sept. 1914; Lieut.-Col. Jan. 1917; Brevet Lieut.-Col. Jan. 1919. France. Wounded at Ypres July 1917, Bapaume March 1918, and Cambrai Oct. 1918. Four times Mentioned in Dispatches. M.C. Jan. 1917; D.S.O. July 1917.

THOMARSON, JOHN.
 M.B., C.M. 1897; M.D. 1907; L.R.C.P. & S. (Edin.) 1897. R.A.M.C., Lieut. June 1915; Captain 1916 to March 1919. Portsmouth and Weymouth Military Hospitals, 1915-16. Troopship and Hong Kong Military Hospital, 1917. 1st and 2nd Birmingham Hospitals, 1917-18, and 7th General Hospital, St Omer, France, 1918.

THOMAS, ARTHUR HENRY.
 M.B., Ch.B. 1898. Volunteer Medical Staff Corps, 1893-8, Sergeant. R.A.M.C., Lieut. May 1915; Captain May 1916; Acting Major Jan. 1919. France. Wounded April 1917. M.B.E. (Military) June 1919.

THOMAS, CYRIL MARSINGALL.
 Blundell's, Tiverton. O.T.C. 1908-10. Student of Medicine, 1912-14. 4th Duke of Cornwall's Light Infantry, 2nd Lieut. Sept. 1914; Lieut. June 1916. India Dec. 1914 to Jan. 1917, and Palestine Jan. 1917 to Feb. 1919.

THOMAS, DAVID GWILYN.
 Queen's College, Taunton. Student of Science, 1909-13; B.Sc. 1920. O.T.C. Infantry, 1909-10, Artillery, 1910-13, Cadet. R.F.A., 2nd Lieut. Sept. 1914; Lieut. April 1916; Acting Captain June 1916. France. Dispatches April 1917.

THOMAS, JOHN MONTAGUE RIDLEY.
 Oswestry Grammar School; First XV. and XI. Student of Medicine, 1917 and 1919. O.T.C. Infantry, June to Dec. 1917, Cadet; Officer Cadet Jan. 1918. 24th Battn., Royal Welsh Fusiliers, 2nd Lieut. June 1918.

THOMAS, LESLIE GWYN.
 Neath County School. Student of Medicine, 1910-12 and 1918-19. R.A.M.C. (T.), Scottish Horse Brigade Field Ambulance, Private.

Record of War Service

THOMPSON, ALBERT GEORGE.
: Edinburgh Institution. M.B., C.M. 1891; D.P.H. (Edin.) 1905. Army Medical Service 1892, Lieut.-Col. March 1915; Colonel Sept. 1918. Special Service at Battle of La Catrine, 1914. 19th Casualty Clearing Station. Prisoner of War Sept. 1914 to June 1915. Dispatches Jan. 1916, June and Dec. 1917, May and Dec. 1918. D.S.O. Jan. 1917; C.M.G. June 1918.

THOMPSON, BRIAN GEORGE.
: King's College, Auckland, New Zealand. First XV. O.T.C. 1911-15, Cadet Sergeant. Student of Medicine, 1919. N.Z. Medical Corps, Private March 1917; Corporal July 1917 to April 1919. No. 2 Field Ambulance, N.Z. Exp. Force.

THOMPSON, CUTHBERT.
: Academical Institution, Londonderry. M.B., C.M. 1892. United States Army Medical Reserve Corps, Captain June 1918.

THOMPSON, EDWARD RONALD.
: Hymers College, Hull. M.B., Ch.B. 1906. R.A.M.C., Lieut. Oct. 1916; Captain Oct. 1917 to May 1919. 42nd General Hospital and 143rd Field Ambulance, Salonika. Dispatches June 1919.

THOMPSON, FRANK STEWART CORBETT.
: Eastbourne School. M.B., C.M. 1895. No. 4 Coy. Q.R.V.B., Royal Scots, Private. Indian Medical Service, 1898; Major Jan. 1910; Lieut.-Col. Jan. 1918. China 1900, Aden, Hinterland and Somaliland. Kitchener Hospital, Brighton, 1915. O.B.E. Jan. 1919.

THOMPSON, FREDERICK TROUGHTON.
: M.B., Ch.B. 1900. Indian Medical Service, Major June 1913.

THOMPSON, HERBERT MARSHALL.
: Barnard Castle. M.B., Ch.B. 1904. R.A.M.C., Lieut. April 1917 to June 1918.

THOMPSON, HERBERT PANK.
: Queen's College, Taunton; First XV. M.B., Ch.B. 1902; M.D. 1906; F.R.C.S. (Edin.) 1907. University Battery, E.C.A.V., Gunner. Assistant in Anatomy and Clinical Medicine. Beaulieu Auxiliary Military Hospital, Harrogate, 1914-15. War Hospital, Dunkirk, March 1915. R.A.M.C., Lieut. Nov. 1915; Captain Jan. 1918. 31st General Hospital, Egypt; Etaples, France.

THOMPSON, IAN MACLAREN.
: Musselburgh Grammar School. Student of Science and Medicine, 1914-18; B.Sc. 1919; M.B., Ch.B. 1920. O.T.C. Medical, Oct. 1915 to April 1917, Cadet. Anatomy Staff, 1919. R.N.V.R., H.M.S. *Strongbow*, Surgeon-Probationer, April 1917. Wounded Oct. 1917. Dispatches March 1918.

THOMPSON, JAMES.
: Queen Elizabeth's Grammar School, Penrith. Student of Medicine, 1912-17; M.B., Ch.B. 1917. O.T.C. Medical, 1914-17, Cadet. R.A.M.C. (S.R.), Lieut. Nov. 1917; Captain Nov. 1918. France Dec. 1917 to Feb. 1920. 92nd Field Ambulance, attached 2nd Bedfordshire Regiment, 1918-19. M.C. Oct. 1918.

Record of War Service

THOMPSON, JAMES ALEXANDER RICHARD.
George Watson's College. M.B., Ch.B. 1905; M.D. 1920; D.P.H. (Camb.) 1911. Certif. Trop. Med., Edinburgh. R.A.M.C., Lieut. Nov. 1915; Captain Nov. 1916. O.C. 71st and 45th Sanitary Section. France 1917-18.

THOMPSON, JEAN GLASS.
B.Sc. 1907. Q.M.A.A.C., Deputy Assistant Chief Controller, Aug. 1917-19. O.B.E. (Military) Jan. 1919.

THOMPSON, JOHN ALEXANDER.
The College, Lurgan, Ireland; First XV. M.B., Ch.B. 1909. Royal Navy, Surgeon, Dec. 1914 to March 1919. H.M. Ships *Sirius, Hamadryad*. R.N. Air Station, Chingford.

THOMPSON, ROBERT JAMES.
Old Aberdeen Grammar School. M.A. 1887. Minister, Church of Scotland. Y.M.C.A. Work, Arras. King's Own Scottish Borderers, Volunteer Defence Corps, Private March 1917.

THOMPSON, WILLIAM EGBERT.
St John's High School, N.B. B.A. (Mount Allison, Canada); Student of Medicine, 1911-15; M.B., Ch.B. 1915. O.T.C. Medical, Oct. 1914 to June 1915, Cadet L/Corporal. B.R.C.S. Villa Trento Hospital, Italy, 1915-18. R.A.M.C., Lieut. Jan. 1918 to June 1919; Bose, Italy.

THOMPSON, WILLIAM GEORGE.
Royal School, Cavan. M.B., Ch.B. 1899; M.D. 1902; F.R.C.S. (Edin.) 1914. R.A.M.C., Lieut. Dec. 1914; Captain Dec. 1915. 15th General Hospital. Egypt 1915, France 1916, Salonika and Palestine 1917.

THOMSON, ALEXANDER BUTCHART MacARTHUR.
Dundee High School. M.B., Ch.B. 1902; M.D. 1914; D.P.H. (Eng.) 1910. R.A.M.C., Lieut. May 1915-16.

THOMSON, ALEXANDER GRAY.
Perth Academy. Student of Arts and Medicine, 1916-17 and 1918-20. O.T.C. Infantry, Sept. 1916 to May 1917, Cadet L/Corporal; Officer Cadet April 1917. 7th Gordon Highlanders, 2nd Lieut. Aug. 1917.

THOMSON, ALEXANDER RAVEN.
Merchiston Castle, O.T.C. 1913-18, Cadet Sergeant. Student of Science, 1919. Officer Cadet June 1918. R.E., 2nd Lieut. Nov. 1918 to Jan. 1919.

THOMSON, ANDREW RUTHERFORD.
B.A. (Manitoba). M.B., Ch.B. 1914. Canadian Army Medical Corps, Lieut. March 1915. R.A.M.C., Lieut. June 1915; Captain June 1916.

THOMSON, ARCHIBALD ANGUS McDONALD.
Tynemouth School. Student of Arts, 1914-15. Officer Cadet April 1916. R.F.A. (S.R.), 2nd Lieut. May 1917; Lieut. Nov. 1918. India and Mesopotamia.

Record of War Service

THOMSON, ARTHUR.
M.B., C.M. 1888; D.P.H. (Camb.) 1891. R.A.M.C., Lieut. April 1915; Captain April 1916. Mudros, Sinai Peninsula, and Egypt, 1915-18.

THOMSON, CHARLES.
M.B., C.M. 1892. Indian Medical Service, 1894; Major 1906; Retired 1910. Rejoined Dec. 1914 to Jan. 1919. Chitral and Mohmand Campaigns.

THOMSON, DANIEL STEWART.
Daniel Stewart's College; First XV. Cadet Corps 1915-17. Student of Science, 1918-19. O.T.C. Infantry, May to Sept. 1917, Cadet. Royal Air Force, Cadet Sept. 1917; 2nd Lieut. Feb. 1918-19.

THOMSON, DAVID.
George Heriot's School. M.B., Ch.B. 1907; D.P.H. (Camb.) 1909. No. 4 Coy. Q.R.V.B., Royal Scots, 1903-6, Private. R.A.M.C., Lieut. Oct. 1914; Captain Oct. 1915 to April 1919. 69th Field Ambulance, 1914-15. Pathologist, Egypt, 1915; and London, 1916-19. O.B.E. June 1919.

THOMSON, DAVID GEORGE.
M.B., C.M. 1878; M.D. 1881. R.A.M.C., Lieut.-Col. May 1915-19. Norfolk War Hospital, Norwich. Mention May 1916. C.B.E. June 1919.

THOMSON, EDMUND JOHN.
Brechin High School. Student of Medicine, 1913-14. Forth R.G.A. (T.), 1913; Captain June 1916; Acting Major March 1917 to May 1919. Royal Air Force. France. M.C. Jan 1918.

THOMSON, EDWARD CHRISTIE.
Merchiston Castle. O.T.C. 1910-15. Student of Arts, 1915-16. O.T.C. Artillery, Feb. to Aug. 1916, Cadet Sergeant; Officer Cadet Aug. 1916. R.G.A., 12th Siege Battery, 2nd Lieut. Nov. 1916; Lieut. May 1918. France.

THOMSON, EDWARD G.
Edinburgh Academy. Student of Law, 1908-10. Chartered Accountant, 1912. R.G.A. (T.), Lowland, 2nd Lieut. Jan. 1914; Captain June 1916. France. Wounded. Dispatches April 1917. M.C. April 1918.

THOMSON, ERIC ROGNVALD.
George Watson's College; First XV. Cadet Corps 1904-8, Colour-Sergeant. M.A. 1911. O.T.C. Infantry, Nov. 1908-11, Cadet L/Corporal. 2nd Canadian Auxiliary Horse Coy., Driver, April 1916. France 1917-18.

THOMSON, FRANK BLACKLOCK.
George Watson's College. Student of Medicine, 1913-15 and 1918-19. O.T.C. Artillery, 1914. R.G.A., 102nd Siege Battery, 2nd Lieut. Nov. 1914; Lieut. Oct. 1916; Acting Captain Dec. 1916. France 1916-18. Wounded June 1916 and May 1918. Invalided out Feb. 1919.

Record of War Service

THOMSON, FREDERICK CHARLES.
Edinburgh Academy; First XV. B.A. (Oxford); LL.B. 1901. Advocate, 1901. M.P. (South Aberdeen). 3rd Scottish Horse (T.), 2nd Lieut. Sept. 1914; Lieut. Sept. 1915. 10th (Lovat Scouts) Cameron Highlanders, Oct. 1916 to Jan. 1918. Egypt and Salonika Jan. 1916-18. Wounded at Salonika Oct. 1917. War Office, June 1918 to Jan. 1919. M.B.E.

THOMSON, GEORGE CLARK.
McLaren High School, Callander. Student of Law, 1906-8. 6th Royal Highlanders (Black Watch) (V.). 15th Royal Scots, Private Nov. 1914. 14th Highland Light Infantry, Lieut. Feb. 1915. 18th Royal Scots, Captain May 1916. 1st Garrison Battn., Bedfordshire Regiment, and Highland Light Infantry. Wounded at Gallipoli June 1915.

THOMSON, GEORGE GILCHRIST.
Boroughmuir School. University O.T.C. Artillery, Sept. 1917 to April 1918, Cadet; Officer Cadet April 1918. R.F.A., 2nd Lieut. April 1919.

THOMSON, GEORGE RITCHIE.
Glasgow High School. M.B., C.M. 1887. South African Campaign, 1899-1902. South African Medical Corps, Major March 1915; Lieut.-Col. Aug. 1915 Dispatches June 1918. C.M.G. July 1919.

THOMSON, GEORGE THOMAS.
Daniel Stewart's College. B.A. (Oxford); M.A. 1909; B.D. 1915. Assistant to Professor of Greek. Licentiate, Church of Scotland. O.T.C. Infantry, Oct. 1914 to Jan. 1915, Cadet Sergeant. Lothians and Border Imperial Yeomanry, 1905. 8th Royal Scots (T.), 2nd Lieut. Jan. 1915; Lieut. June 1916; Acting Captain Nov. 1917. France 1914. Brigade Gas Officer, 94th Infantry Brigade. Intelligence Staff (Arabic) G.H.Q. Egyptian Exp. Force, Nov. 1918.

THOMSON, GERALD MACALISTER.
Merchiston Castle and Edinburgh Institution; First XV. O.T.C., Corporal. University O.T.C. Artillery, Dec. 1917 to July 1918, Cadet; Officer Cadet Aug. 1918. R.H. and R.F.A., 2nd Lieut. April 1919.

THOMSON, HENRY.
Robert Gordon's College, Aberdeen. Student of Medicine, 1913-14 and 1918-20; M.B., Ch.B. 1920. O.T.C. Medical, May 1915-16, Cadet. R.N.V.R., Surgeon-Probationer, May 1916. H.M. Ships *Maenad* and *P.Q.* 44.

THOMSON, HENRY ALEXIS.
Royal High School. M.B., C.M. (Hons.) 1885; M.D. (Gold Medal) 1889; B.Sc. (P.H.) 1888; M.R.C.S. (Eng.) 1885. Professor of Surgery. R.A.M.C., Captain Aug. 1914; Major; Colonel Aug. 1915. 2nd Scottish General Hospital, Craigleith. Surgical Consultant, Third Army, France, May 1915. Dispatches Nov. 1915. C.M.G. Aug. 1916.

Record of War Service

THOMSON, HENRY TORRANCE.
Leys School, Cambridge; First XV. and XI. M.B., C.M. 1892; M.D. 1898. B.R.C.S., No. 11 Stationary Hospital, Rouen, June 1915-17, Hon. Lieut. 1916; Hon. Captain 1917. R.A.M.C., Captain Sept. 1918.

THOMSON, HUGH BARBOUR.
Edinburgh Academy. O.T.C. 1909-11. Student of Medicine, 1912-14 and 1918-20. O.T.C. Medical, 1913-14 and 1918-19, Cadet Corporal. R.A.M.C. (T.), Scottish Horse Field Ambulance, Corporal Sept. 1914. B.R.C.S., No. 11 Stationary Hospital, Rouen (Dresser), 1915-17. 1st Artists' Rifles, Private June 1917; L/Corporal to March 1918. France.

THOMSON, JAMES ALEXANDER MONTEATH.
George Watson's College; First XI. O.T.C. 1911-14, Cadet Corporal. Student of Law, 1914 and 1919. O.T.C. Artillery, Dec. 1914 to Nov. 1915, Cadet. Argyll and Sutherland Highlanders, Private Nov. 1915. R.F.A., 124th Brigade, 2nd Lieut. Aug. 1917. France 1916-19. M.C. March 1919.

THOMSON, JAMES FREDERICK GORDON.
Clayesmore, Pangbourne. O.T.C. 1912-14, Cadet Sergeant. Student of Arts, 1918. 5th Royal Scots, 2nd Lieut. March 1915; Lieut. Sept. 1917. Discharged on account of Wounds Feb. 1919.

THOMSON, J. K.
Student. 16th Royal Scots, Private.

THOMSON, JAMES WILLIAM.
George Watson's College. M.A. (Hons. Engl.) 1915. 14th and 7th Argyll and Sutherland Highlanders, Private Nov. 1915; L/Corporal May 1917. 10th King's Liverpool Regiment, 2nd Lieut. Sept. 1917. 154th T.M. Battery, Machine-Gun Corps.

THOMSON, JOHN ALEXANDER.
George Watson's College. Student of Medicine, 1914-15 and 1917-19. O.T.C. Infantry, Sept. 1914 to May 1915, and Medical, April 1918-19, Cadet. 14th Argyll and Sutherland Highlanders, Private May 1915. France 1916-17.

THOMSON, JOHN GORDON.
Bathgate Academy. M.A. 1903; M.B., Ch.B. 1908. Lecturer, London University School of Tropical Medicine. No. 4 Coy. Q.R.V.B., Royal Scots, L/Corporal. R.A.M.C., Lieut. Jan. 1915; Captain Jan. 1916. Protozoologist and Pathologist, Alexandria, Egypt.

THOMSON, JOHN JAMES.
Lanark Grammar School. M.B., Ch.B. 1908. Assistant to Professor of Clinical Medicine. R.A.M.C. and Canadian Army Medical Corps, Captain 1914; Reverted to Lieut. 1915; Captain June 1916; Acting Major June 1918-19. Dardanelles 1915; Egypt 1915; France 1916. Dispatches 1919. O.B.E. (Military) June 1919.

Record of War Service

THOMSON, JOHN JAMES SCOTT.
Teviot Grove Academy, Hawick. Student of Arts and Divinity, 1912-15; M.A. 1915. 9th Royal Scots (T.), March 1915, Sergeant. 9th and 1/4th King's Own Scottish Borderers, 2nd Lieut. Aug. 1916; Lieut. Feb. 1918; Captain April 1919. Egypt, Palestine, France, and The Rhine. M.C. Sept. 1918.

THOMSON, JOHN PIRIE.
George Watson's College; First XV. and XI. O.T.C. 1914-19, Cadet Lieut. Student of Medicine, 1918-19. Royal Air Force, Cadet July 1918.

THOMSON, LAWRENCE RAMSAY.
M.B., Ch.B. 1911. R.A.M.C., Captain Sept. 1916. Camp Hospital, Ghain, Tuffieha, Malta.

THOMSON, LESLIE GRAHAME.
Merchiston Castle. O.T.C. 1910-14. Student of Arts, 1914-15. 2nd Scottish General Hospital, Craigleith, Voluntary Worker, Sept. 1915. 3rd Highland Light Infantry, Private Nov. 1916. Army Pay Corps, Corporal Dec. 1917. Egypt Oct. 1917-19.

THOMSON, MARY.
George Watson's Ladies' College. Student of Arts, 1912-16; M.A. 1916. W.R.N.S., attached H.M.S. *Pactolus*, Assistant Principal, March 1918. Invalided out Oct. 1918.

THOMSON, RICHARD BURDON HALDANE.
George Heriot's School. Student of Arts, 1918-19. R.N.R. Jan. 1916; Leading Deck Hand April 1917; 2nd Hand July 1918.

THOMSON, ROBERT.
George Heriot's School. M.B., Ch.B. 1912. O.T.C. Artillery, Oct. 1908 to Feb. 1911, Cadet. R.A.M.C., Lieut. Nov. 1914; Captain Nov. 1915; Major and D.A.D.M.S., June 1919. 10th Division, R.E., France and The Rhine. Médaille de l'Assistance Publique " en Argent," June 1918.

THOMSON, ROBERT BARCLAY.
M.A. 1903. Royal Welsh Fusiliers, 2nd Lieut.

THOMSON, ROBERT BLACK.
Wallace Hall Academy, Dumfries. M.B., Ch.B. 1905; M.D. Assistant to Professor of Anatomy, 1906-11. Professor of Anatomy, Cape Town. South African Medical Corps, Captain 1914; Major and Adjutant 1916. German South-West Africa; Wynberg Camp and Alexandra Hospital, Cape Town, and Potchefstroom Hospital. Dispatches (South Africa).

THOMSON, ROBERT CUNNINGHAM.
Daniel Stewart's College. Student of Science, 1918-19. O.T.C. Infantry, March to Nov. 1916, Cadet Corporal. 9th and 15th Royal Scots, 2nd Lieut. April 1917; Lieut. Sept. 1918. France.

Record of War Service

THOMSON, ROBERT DOUGLAS.
Student of Medicine, 1913-15. O.T.C. Infantry, Oct. 1912 to March 1915, Cadet. 8th Royal Scots Fusiliers, 2nd Lieut.; Lieut. July 1917.

THOMSON, ROBERT MACNIE.
Falkirk High School. Student of Medicine, 1918-19. Royal Highlanders (Black Watch), Private Nov. 1916. Invalided out April 1918.

THOMSON, ROBERT ORR COLQUHOUN.
Student of Medicine, 1909-14; M.B., Ch.B. 1914. O.T.C. Artillery, 1910-13, Cadet. R.A.M.C., Lieut. May 1915; Captain Nov. 1915. 9th Cheshire Regiment.

THOMSON, THOMAS.
Student of Medicine. O.T.C. Infantry, April to Aug. 1915, Cadet. 2nd Lieut. in the Army.

THOMSON, THOMAS JAMES.
St George's School, Edinburgh. M.B., C.M. 1893; M.D. 1899. R.A.M.C. (T.), Lieut. Dec. 1914; Captain June 1915. 4th Royal Scots (T.). France.

THOMSON, WILBERT TURNER.
George Watson's College. O.T.C. 1909-11. Student of Science, 1912-14. O.T.C. Infantry, Sept. 1914, Cadet. 12th Argyll and Sutherland Highlanders, 2nd Lieut. Sept. 1914; Lieut. July 1915; Captain Oct. 1916. France 1915; Macedonia 1915-16. M.C. Nov. 1916.

THOMSON, WILLIAM.
Student of Law, 1912-14. 16th Royal Scots, Private.

THOMSON, WILLIAM ANDREW.
George Watson's College. M.A. 1913. Schoolmaster. O.T.C. Infantry, March 1910-13, Cadet. 3rd Cameron Highlanders, 2nd Lieut. Nov. 1915; Lieut. July 1917 to April 1919. France 1916-18; The Rhine 1918-19.

THOMSON, WILLIAM WILSON.
Ayr Academy; First XV. and XI. M.B., Ch.B. 1907. R.A.M.C., Lieut. March 1915; Captain March 1916. Fargo Military Hospital, Salisbury Plain, 1915-16. 66th Field Ambulance, Salonika, 1916-18.

THORBURN, DAVID HAY.
Edinburgh Academy. Student of Arts, 1897-9. No. 4 Coy. Q.R.V.B., Royal Scots, 1898-1900, Private. 4th (Militia Battn.) Cameronians, 1900. 2nd Cameronians (Scottish Rifles), May 1901; Major Sept. 1915. South African Campaign. Egyptian Army, 10th Sudanese Battn. Twice Mentioned in Dispatches. Order of the Nile (4th Class).

THORBURN, HAROLD HAY.
M.B., Ch.B. 1906. Indian Medical Service, Captain Sept. 1909. C.I.E. June 1917.

Record of War Service

THORBURN, JOHN.
Portobello School. Student of Arts and Science, 1911-15 and 1918-19; M.A. 1914. 1st Scots Guards, Private Jan. 1915. 11th Royal Scots, 2nd Lieut. April 1916. France. Wounded. Invalided out Feb. 1918.

THORBURN, JOHN BURNETT.
George Watson's College. M.B., Ch.B. 1901; L.R.C.P. & S. (Edin.) and L.F.P.S. (Glasg.) 1900. R.A.M.C., Lieut. Oct. 1915; Captain Oct. 1916. Cambuslang War Hospital. Salonika. National Service Recruiting Board, Edinburgh, 1917-18.

THORBURN, JOHN MACCAIG.
Stranraer High School. M.A., B.Sc. 1904. Artists' Rifles, Private Dec. 1915; Officer Cadet Aug. 1916. R.G.A., 2nd Lieut. 1916.

THORBURN, WILLIAM.
Sessional School, Jedburgh. Student of Arts, 1888-9. 5th King's Own Scottish Borderers (T.), Lieut.-Col.

THORNE, THEOPHILUS HERBERT.
Student of Science, 1910-12. R.F.A., 20th Anti-Aircraft Battery, 2nd Lieut.; Lieut. June 1916. France. M.C. Dec. 1918.

THORNHILL, JOHN.
M.B., Ch.B. 1900; L.M. (Dublin). University Battery, E.C.A.V., 1895-7, Gunner. Royal Navy, Surgeon, 1901; Surgeon-Lieut.-Commander 1909; Surgeon-Commander Feb. 1917. H.M. Ships *Endymion*, *Caribbean*, and *Victorian*, Aug. 1914-17. R.N. Barracks, Chatham, Aug. 1917. H.M.S. *Hannibal*, Egypt, Nov. 1917-19.

THORNLEY, JOHN HARDWICK.
Cheltenham College. M.B., Ch.B. 1900. R.A.M.C., Lieut. May 1915; Captain Nov. 1916; Acting Major Jan. 1918; Surgeon Specialist 1918. France (two and a half years). M.C. June 1918.

THORNLEY, NORMAN GARFIELD.
Epworth College, Rhyl; First XI. M.B., Ch.B. 1908. R.A.M.C., Lieut. Dec. 1914; Captain Dec. 1915.

THORNTON, CECIL TAYLOR.
Merchiston Castle; First XI. Cadet Corps 1899-1904, Sergeant. B.D. 1910. Minister, Church of Scotland. O.T.C. Infantry, May to Aug. 1916, Cadet L/Corporal; Officer Cadet Aug. 1916. Royal Scots, 2nd Lieut. Nov. 1916; Lieut. Jan. 1918. France.

THORNTON, CONRAD D.
Arbroath High School. Student of Science, 1918-19. 40th Training Reserve Brigade, April 1917. Royal Air Force, 2nd Lieut. Feb. 1918.

THORNTON, CONYNGHAM VERNON.
M.B., Ch.B. 1912. R.A.M.C., Captain March 1915. M.C.

Record of War Service

THORNTON, PETER.
M.B., Ch.B. 1890. R.A.M.C. (S.R.), Lieut. Sept. 1914; Captain April 1915. M.C.

THORNTON, ROBERT.
M.B., C.M. 1897; D.P.H. (St Andrews) 1902. R.A.M.C. (T.), Major Oct. 1914. 4th Royal Highlanders (Black Watch).

THORP, ROLAND.
Bradford Grammar School. Student of Medicine, 1909-14; M.B., Ch.B. 1914. Athletics. O.T.C. Artillery, Oct. 1908-14, 2nd Lieut. R.F.A. (S.R.), 2nd Lieut. Aug. 1914; Lieut. Oct. 1915; Acting Captain Aug. 1916. R.A.M.C., Captain Dec. 1917. France 1914-17. Wounded at Arras April 1917. M.C. Jan. 1917.

THWAITES, HAROLD VERDON.
St Peter's College, Adelaide. Student of Medicine, 1914-15 and 1918-20. R.A.M.C. (T.), Transport Section, Highland Field Ambulance (Driver), April 1915. R.E., Corporal Sept. 1915. Tank Corps, 2nd Lieut. July 1917 to Jan. 1919. France Sept. 1915 to March 1917, and June to Aug. 1918. Wounded at Monchy-le-Preux Aug. 1918.

THWAITES, WILLIAM St CLAIR.
Queen's Royal College, Trinidad, B.W.I. M.B., Ch.B. 1913. Indian Medical Service, Sept. 1914; Lieut. Dec. 1914; Captain Dec. 1915.

TIBBITS, WALTER.
M.B., C.M. 1892. R.A.M.C., Major Oct. 1905.

TIFFEN, CHARLES JOHN.
M.B., C.M. 1882; M.D. 1885. 5th Border Regiment (T.), Captain and Hon. Major Oct. 1914. Eastbourne Division, National Reserve. Regimental Surgeon, 15th King's Royal Rifle Corps. Resigned Oct. 1918. V.D.

TILLYARD, FREDERICK EDWARD.
Student of Medicine, 1909-14. M.B., Ch.B. 1914. R.A.M.C., Lieut.; Captain Sept. 1915.

TIMS, HENRY WILLIAM MARETT.
Reading School. M.A. (Camb.), M.B., C.M. 1887; M.D. 1890. Reader in Zoology, London University. R.A.M.C., Captain Aug. 1915; Major May 1916; Acting Lieut.-Col. March 1918. Bermondsey Military Hospital, 1916-19. Mention Sept. 1916. O.B.E. June 1919.

TINMAN, JAMES TELFER.
Stobhill School. Student of Law, 1914-15. 2/10th Royal Scots, Sept. 1916. 1/6th Royal Sussex Regiment.

TISDALE, CHARLES JEROME.
M.B., Ch.B. 1912. R.A.M.C., Lieut. June 1915. 16th Red Cross Train, France. Invalided out 1916. B.R.C.S. and Ministry of Pensions.

Record of War Service

TITTERTON, JOHN TARRATT.
Edinburgh Academy. M.B., C.M. 1898. R.A.M.C., Lieut. Feb. 1917; Captain March 1918. Tuberculosis Specialist, Aldershot Command, Aug. 1917-19.

TOCHER, FORBES S.
Fordyce Academy. B.D. 1909. Minister, Church of Scotland. R.F.A., 2nd Lieut. Aug. 1917; Lieut. Feb. 1919. M.C. March 1919.

TOD, DAVID LIVINGSTONE MACRAE.
Huddersfield College; First XI. Student of Arts, Science, and Medicine; M.A., B.Sc. 1915; M.B., Ch.B. 1920. Secretary, S.R.C.; President and Secretary, The Union, 1918. O.T.C. Medical, Feb. 1915 to May 1916, Cadet L/Corporal. R.N.V.R., Surgeon-Probationer. French Interpreter, 1917. Grand Fleet and Mediterranean.

TOD, FREDERICK LEWIS MAITLAND.
Edinburgh Academy. Student of Law, 1902-6. Writer to the Signet, 1907. 9th Royal Scots (T.), Private Aug. 1914. A.S.C. (T.), Lowland Division, 2nd Lieut. Nov. 1914; Lieut. Jan. 1916. Egypt June to Sept. 1915; Serbia, Macedonia, and Palestine, Oct. 1915; France April to Sept. 1918. Accidentally wounded Sept. 1918. Dispatches. O.B.E.

TODD, ARTHUR THEODORE.
M.B., Ch.B. (Hons.) 1912. R.A.M.C., Lieut Aug. 1914; Captain Aug. 1915. East Yorkshire Regiment.

TODD, EDWIN ERNEST ENEVER.
Daniel Stewart's College. M.A. (Hons. Hist.) 1907. Army Pay Corps, Paymaster-Captain Nov. 1916; Major May 1917; Lieut.-Col. Sept. 1918. Regimental Paymaster, Warley, Sept. 1918. O.B.E. (Military) Jan. 1918.

TODD, HARRY CAMPBELL.
Fettes College. M.B., Ch.B. 1910. O.T.C. Artillery, 1905 to Nov. 1910, Cadet B.S.M. R.A.M.C., Lieut. 1911; Captain Jan. 1915; Brevet Major June 1919. D.A.D.M.S. France, Mesopotamia. Dispatches June 1919.

TODD, HERBERT WILLIAM.
The Western College, Harrogate; First XI. University O.T.C. Artillery, Dec. 1915 to June 1916, Cadet Bombardier; Officer Cadet June 1916. R.F.A. (T.), 3/1st Lowland Brigade, 2nd Lieut. Sept. 1916; Lieut. March 1918; Acting Captain April 1918. France Jan. 1917-19. M.C. Sept. 1918.

TODD, JAMES.
Edinburgh Academy. O.T.C. 1913-15. Student of Medicine, 1914-16. 2nd Royal Scots, 2nd Lieut. 1916. Prisoner of War April 1918.

Record of War Service

TODD, JAMES.
 The Western College, Harrogate; First XI. M.A. (Camb.). University O.T.C. Artillery, Dec. 1915 to April 1916, Cadet; Officer Cadet April 1916. R.F.A. (S.R.), 2nd Lieut. Aug. 1916; Lieut. Feb. 1918. France Aug. to Dec. 1916; Salonika June 1917 to Nov. 1918.

TODD, JAMES ALEXANDER.
 M.A. 1902; B.Sc. 1911. Schoolmaster. 8th Royal Scots (T.), 1900; Lieut.; Captain; Major Sept. 1914; Acting Lieut.-Col. Twice Wounded. Prisoner of War April 1918. Dispatches Jan. 1917. T.D. June 1919.

TODD, JAMES EADIE.
 George Watson's College. M.A. (Hons. Hist.) 1907; M.A. (Oxford). Professor of History, Dalhousie University. O.T.C. Infantry, May to Sept. 1916, Cadet Corporal; Officer Cadet Sept. 1916. 3rd Scottish Rifles, 2nd Lieut. Jan. 1917; Lieut. July 1918. Attached 1st Royal Sussex Regiment and 8th Cheshire Regiment. India and Mesopotamia.

TODD, JOHN.
 Student of Science, 1918-20; B.Sc. 1920. 3rd Royal Highlanders (Black Watch), Lieut. March 1916; Acting Captain May 1917.

TODD, JOHN.
 Student of Medicine, 1916-17 and 1919. O.T.C. Infantry, Feb. to April 1917, Cadet; Officer Cadet April 1917. Royal Air Force, 2nd Lieut. Aug. 1917; Lieut. April 1918; Captain May 1918. M.C. May 1918; D.F.C. July 1918.

TODD, JOHN BARBER.
 George Heriot's School. B.Sc. 1909. A.M.I.M.E. Lecturer in Engineering. O.T.C. Artillery, Oct. 1908 to Jan. 1916, Cadet B.S.M. 1911-12; 2nd Lieut. 1912; Temp. Captain April 1915. Transferred North Midland Brigade, R.F.A. (T.), Captain March 1916; Major April 1918. C/197th Brigade, R.F.A., March to June 1916. 2nd Reserve Brigade, R.F.A., 1916-17, and 294th Siege Battery, R.G.A., Aug. 1918 to Jan. 1919. France 1917-18. Croix de Guerre Sept. 1918.

TODD, PERCY EVERARD.
 M.B., C.M. 1882. R.A.M.C. (V.), Lieut. Aug. 1916; Captain Sept. 1917.

TODD, ROBERT WILLIAM LANG.
 B.Sc. 1906; M.B., Ch.B. 1908. R.A.M.C., Lieut.; Captain Oct. 1915. France 1914.

TODD, THOMAS ROBERT RUSHTON.
 Edinburgh Institution. 1st (Highland) Cadet Battn., 1912-13, L/Sergeant. Student of Medicine, 1912-14 and 1917-19. O.T.C. Medical, Oct. 1913 to Sept. 1914, Cadet Corporal. R.A.M.C. (T.), Scottish Horse Field Ambulance, Corporal Sept. 1914 to July 1915. 8th and 10th Seaforth Highlanders, 2nd Lieut. July 1915; Lieut. April to Dec. 1917.

Record of War Service

TODD, WILLIAM ALEXANDER.
George Watson's College. M.B., Ch.B. 1910. O.T.C. Medical, April 1908 to Dec. 1910, Cadet Staff Sergeant. R.A.M.C., Lieut. Oct. 1914; Captain Oct. 1915; Acting Major June to Nov. 1919. France and The Rhine.

TODRICK, ARCHIBALD.
M.B., Ch.B. 1906. Royal Navy, Surgeon.

TOFFT, WALTER HENRY. (See p. 752.)

TOLMIE, JAMES.
M.A. 1893. Minister, U.F. Church of Scotland. Army Chaplain, 4th Class, March 1917. Egypt and Palestine.

TOLMIE, JOHN ALEXANDER.
Inverness School. L.R.C.P. & S. (Edin.) and L.R.F.P.S. (Glasg.) 1917. University O.T.C. Medical, March 1916 to Jan. 1917, Cadet. R.A.M.C., Lieut. Jan. 1917; Captain Jan. 1918; Acting Lieut.-Col. June to Oct. 1919. India, N.-W. Frontier Provinces. Afghan War.

TOLMIE, PETER MORRISON.
Inverness High School. Student of Medicine, 1919. L.R.C.P. and S. (Edin.) 1908. R.A.M.C., Lieut. Feb. 1917; Captain Feb. 1918.

TOMB, JAMES ALEXANDER.
Coleraine Academical Institution. M.B., Ch.B. 1911; D.P.H. (Manchester) 1913. R.A.M.C., Lieut. Dec. 1914; Captain June 1915. 3rd East Lancashire Field Ambulance, Egypt. Wounded April 1918.

TOMB, JOHN SLOAN.
Foyle College, Londonderry. M.B., Ch.B. 1913. R.A.M.C., Lieut. Feb. 1915; Captain Aug. 1915. 1st Welsh Field Ambulance.

TOMORY, KENNETH ALEXANDER MACDONALD.
Aberdeen Grammar School. Student of Medicine, 1909-14; M.B., Ch.B. 1914. O.T.C. Infantry, May 1909-13, Cadet Sergeant. R.A.M.C. (S.R.), Lieut. 1913. Mobilised Nov. 1914; Lieut. (Regulars) Jan. 1917; Captain May 1918. France.

TONNOCHY, ALEXANDER BAIN.
Fettes College. M.A. 1911. 13th London Regiment, Feb. 1916; 2nd Lieut. Dec. 1916; Lieut. June 1918. Attached 13th and 53rd Rifle Brigades. France and The Rhine.

TORRANCE, GUY MELCHOIR.
Glasgow High School. Cadet Corps 1904-6. Student of Medicine, 1910-15; M.B., Ch.B. 1915. R.A.M.C. (T.), Lieut. Dec. 1915; Captain July 1916. 2/1st Highland Field Ambulance, France. Prisoner of War March 1918. M.C. July 1916.

TORRANCE, MAURICE CALMAN.
George Watson's College. M.B., Ch.B. 1913. R.A.M.C., Lieut. Nov. 1914-15. France.

Record of War Service

TORRANCE, THOMAS STIRLING.
Penicuik School. Student of Medicine, 1918-19. R.A.M.C., Private Sept. 1914; Sergeant Dec. 1915; Staff Sergeant Dec. 1916; Q.M.S. Dec. 1917. Wounded Aug. 1918.

TOUGH, DAVID WESTON CHANT.
George Watson's College. Student of Medicine, 1915-18. O.T.C. Medical, Dec. 1915 to Oct. 1918, Cadet. R.N.V.R., Surgeon Sub-Lieut. Oct. 1918.

TOWERS, ARTHUR HENRY.
M.B., Ch.B. 1912. R.A.M.C., Lieut.; Captain Feb. 1916.

TOWERS, FRANK.
Sir J. Deane's Grammar School, Norwich. B.A. (Durham) 1914. Student of Medicine, 1918-19. Durham University O.T.C., 1912-14. 19th and 1st Manchester Regiment, Acting Corporal Aug. 1914; 2nd Lieut. Sept. 1914; Lieut. Jan. 1915; Captain Dec. 1918 to March 1919. Wounded in France May 1916, and in Mesopotamia Nov. 1917.

TOWNLEY, EDMUND JAMES.
Bradfield College, Berkshire. Student of Science, 1918-19. 4th and 1st Lancashire Fusiliers, 2nd Lieut. July 1915; Lieut. July 1917. France. Prisoner of War May 1917 to Jan. 1918.

TOWSE, HAROLD BECKWITH.
Charterhouse. Cadet Corps 1880-4, Sergeant. B.A. (Camb.) 1889. Student of Law, 1890. Writer to the Signet, 1893. Lothians and Border Yeomanry, Captain. South African Campaign, 1900-2. Royal Scots Greys, Captain (Regulars), June 1902. Retired Dec. 1913. Staff Captain Aug. 1914. 25th Royal Fusiliers, Major March 1915; Lieut.-Col. East Africa, March 1915 to Jan. 1918. D.A.Q.M.G., G.H.Q., France, March 1918 to July 1919. Three times Mentioned in Dispatches.

TRAFFORD, WILLIAM LEIGH.
M.B., Ch.B. 1901; F.R.C.S. Indian Medical Service, Major Jan. 1914. Dispatches.

TRAIL, RICHARDSON ROBERTSON.
Robert Gordon's College, Aberdeen. M.A. (Hons.) Aberdeen 1918. University O.T.C. Artillery, Dec. 1915 to May 1916, Cadet. R.G.A., Officer Cadet May 1916; 2nd Lieut. Jan. 1917; Temp. Captain April 1918. France. M.C. Aug. 1917.

TRANN, DAVID.
Buckhaven School, Wemyss. Student of Science, 1915-16 and 1918-20. R.N.V.R., Signalman, July 1916. H.M.S. *Isis*.

TREN, RUDOLPH MONTAGUE.
Student of Medicine. O.T.C. Artillery, 1909-10, Medical, 1913-14, Cadet. A.S.C., Captain Dec. 1914. 16th Divisional Train. 145th Coy., France. M.C.

Record of War Service

TROTTER, JOHN.
Boroughmuir School. Student of Science and Medicine, 1914-15 and 1918-19. O.T.C. Infantry, Oct. 1914 to April 1915, Cadet. 4th Highland Light Infantry (S.R.), 2nd Lieut. April 1915; Lieut. April 1916; Captain Aug. 1917. Dispatches Nov. 1917.

TRUTER, ROBERT MEESER.
M.B., C.M. 1892; L.M.R.C.P. (Ireland) 1892. South African Medical Corps, Captain 1915; Major 1916. German West and East Africa. Dispatches.

TUKE, ALAN LEONARD SMITH.
Cargilfield. M.B., C.M. 1887. Fife and Forfar Light Horse and Yeomanry for thirteen years. R.A.M.C. (T.), Lieut. 1907; Captain Dec. 1910; Major Jan. 1918. R.M.O., Fife and Forfar Yeomanry. Citadel and 27th General Hospitals, Cairo. D.A.D.M.S., 53rd Division, Gallipoli, Egypt, and Palestine. Dispatches July 1916. M.C. Jan. 1918; T.D. 1919.

TULLIS, GEORGE DONALDSON EDIE.
Sherborne School, Dorset. Cadet Corps 1904-7, L/Corporal. M.B., Ch.B. 1912. Hampton Grange Auxiliary Hospital. R.A.M.C., Lieut. Dec. 1915; Captain Dec. 1916. 50th Casualty Clearing Station, France, July 1916 to Dec. 1918.

TULLOCH, FREDERICK LIVINGSTONE.
Lossiemouth School. M.B., Ch.B. 1911. O.T.C. Medical, April 1908 to Oct. 1911, Cadet Sergeant. R.A.M.C. (S.R.), Lieut. 1913; Captain April 1915. France Aug. 1914 to March 1919.

TULLOCH, ROBERT.
Broughton School, Edinburgh; First XI. Student of Arts and Science, 1918-20. Highland Light Infantry, Private June 1918.

TULLOCH, WILLIAM.
M.A. 1913. Schoolmaster. 10th East Kent Regiment, 2nd Lieut.

TULLY, THOMAS.
George Heriot's School. O.T.C. 1916-17. Student of Medicine, 1919. O.T.C. Infantry, Oct. 1917 to June 1918, Cadet. 4th Highland Light Infantry, Officer Cadet June 1918; 2nd Lieut. Feb. 1919.

TURCAN, CHARLES SOMERVILLE.
Edinburgh Academy; First XV. Student of Law, 1904-5. Chartered Accountant, 1906. 7th Royal Scots (T.), 2nd Lieut. March 1915; Temp. Captain Sept. 1915; Lieut. June 1916. France.

TURFERY, JOSEPH COSSAR OLDMEADOW.
Student of Medicine, 1914-15. O.T.C. Infantry, May to Sept. 1915, Cadet. 11th Argyll and Sutherland Highlanders, 2nd Lieut.; Lieut. July 1917.

Record of War Service

TURNBULL, ARCHIBALD.
> Boroughmuir School. M.A. (Hons. Engl.) 1913. 9th Royal Scots Fusiliers, 2nd Lieut. May 1915; Lieut. Feb. 1917; Captain Oct. 1918. Army Signal Service. France (Guards Division) Sept. 1916 to Feb. 1919. Dispatches Dec. 1917. M.C. June 1918.

TURNBULL, ARCHIBALD GORDON.
> George Watson's College. M.A. 1911. Schoolmaster. No. 4 Coy. Q.R.V.B., Royal Scots, 1905-8, Private. 8th Royal Scots (T.), April 1916; 2nd Lieut. Nov. 1916; Lieut. May 1918. France 1917.

TURNBULL, ERIC LESLIE LOWE.
> George Heriot's School; First XV. and XI. Student of Science, 1913-15 and 1918-20; B.Sc. 1920. O.T.C. Engineers, Oct. 1913 to Dec. 1914, Cadet. R.E., 2nd Lieut. Dec. 1914; Lieut. May 1917. Royal Air Force, Captain (Flight Commander) Dec. 1917. Dardanelles and Egypt 1914-17; France 1917-18.

TURNBULL, JAMES NISBET.
> Royal High School. M.B., Ch.B. 1906; L.M. (Dublin) 1906; F.R.C.S. (Edin.) 1910. Volunteer Medical Staff Corps, 1902-6, Corporal. R.A.M.C., Lieut. Sept. 1918. India.

TURNBULL, JOHN.
> Teviot Grove Academy, Hawick. B.Sc. 1909. Royal Scots Fusiliers, Private Jan. 1915. Dispatches Jan. 1919.

TURNBULL, ROBERT.
> Edinburgh Academy. O.T.C. 1913-14. University O.T.C. Artillery, Aug. 1916 to Feb. 1917, Cadet Acting Bombardier; Officer Cadet. R.G.A., 2nd Lieut. May 1917; Lieut. Nov. 1918.

TURNBULL, ROBERT WILSON.
> Hawick High School. Student of Arts and Divinity, 1910-16; M.A. 1913; B.D. 1919. Minister, Church of Scotland. O.T.C. Infantry, Nov. 1915 to Jan. 1916, Cadet. 3rd Royal Highlanders (Black Watch), Private Jan. 1916; L/Corporal. 1st and 2nd Royal Scots Fusiliers, 2nd Lieut. March 1917. Gordon Highlanders.

TURNBULL, WILLIAM F.
> Blairgowrie High School. Student of Law, 1914-15. 14th Argyll and Sutherland Highlanders, Private May 1915; Corporal. France. Wounded March 1918. Invalided out Feb. 1919.

TURNBULL, WILLIAM GOVER.
> George Watson's College. B.Sc. 1910. O.T.C. Engineers, Oct. to Dec. 1915, Cadet. R.E., 2nd Lieut. Dec. 1915; Lieut. July 1917; Captain Oct. 1918. India.

TURNBULL, WILLIAM JACKSON.
> B.Sc. 1913. A.M.I.C.E. O.T.C. Engineers, 1910-13, Cadet L/Corporal. Canadian Engineers, 2nd Lieut. Aug. 1914. R.E., Nov. 1916; Lieut. May 1918 to July 1919. France Feb. 1915 to Aug. 1916; India May 1917; Mesopotamia Aug. 1917 to March 1919.

Record of War Service

TURNER, ARTHUR LOGAN.
    Fettes College. M.B., C.M. 1889; M.D. 1894; F.R.C.S. (Edin.) 1891. Lecturer on Larynx, Ear and Nose. R.A.M.C. (T.), Captain Aug. 1914. 2nd Scottish General Hospital.

TURNER, HUGH PHILLIPS.
    Kingskettle School. Student of Arts, 1906-8 and 1910-11. 6th Royal Irish Fusiliers, Private Sept. 1914; 2nd Lieut. Oct. 1915; Lieut. Jan. 1917. Attached R.E., Signals. Wounded Sept. 1916.

TURNER, JAMES FRANCIS GEORGE.
    University O.T.C. Engineers, Aug. to Oct. 1914, Cadet. Lothians and Border Horse, Private Oct. 1914. 13th, 11th, 3rd, and 14th Royal Scots, 2nd Lieut. Nov. 1914; Captain May 1917. France Oct. 1915 and April 1917. Wounded Sept. 1916 and July 1917. M.C. Nov. 1916; Bar to M.C. Sept. 1917.

TURNER, JOHN.
    Milne's Institution, Fochabers; First XI. Student of Arts, 1918-19. 6th Royal Scots (T.), Private. France 1914.

TURNER, RALPH HINELICLIFFE.
    Student of Arts, 1915-16. R.A.M.C. (T.), Private. 1st Welsh Field Ambulance.

TURNER, WILLIAM.
    Castle Douglas School. M.A. 1909. Royal Scots Fusiliers, Private. 11th Scottish Rifles, 2nd Lieut.; Lieut. July 1917; Captain; Major. Base Commandant, Afghan Frontier, India.

TURNER, WILLIAM ALDREN.
    Fettes College. M.B., C.M. 1887; M.D. 1892; F.R.C.P. (Lond.) 1896. R.A.M.C., Lieut.-Col. (Special Duty) Aug. 1914; Colonel 1917. C.B. 1917.

TURNER-SMITH, NOWELL ASHTON.
    Bishop's Stortford College. Student of Arts, 1911-15; M.A. 1915. O.T.C. Infantry, March 1912 to April 1915, Cadet Corporal. 4th Highland Light Infantry (S.R.), 2nd Lieut. April 1915; Lieut. July 1917; Captain Oct. 1917. R.E., Signal Service, March 1916.

TURTON, PHILIP HENRY JOB.
    Palmer's School, Grays, Essex. O.T.C. 1910-12. Student of Medicine, 1912-14 and 1917-19. O.T.C. Medical Nov. 1917 to Feb. 1919, Cadet. R.A.M.C. (T.), Private Sept. 1914; 2/1st Highland Field Ambulance. France; Festubert, May 1915; Somme 1916.

TWEEDIE, GILBERT.
    Student of Law, 1899-1900 and 1901-3. Writer to the Signet, 1903. 7th King's Own Scottish Borderers, 2nd Lieut. 7th (Reserve) Cavalry Regiment.

Record of War Service

TWEEDIE, HARLEY ALEC.
Charterhouse and Trinity College, Cambridge; First XI. Student of Medicine, 1908-10. Inns of Court O.T.C., Private Aug. 1914. 10th Hussars, 2nd Lieut. Sept. 1914. R.F.C., Sept. 1915; Major 1918. France 1915; Loos. Staff Officer, S.E. Area, London, 1918; India 1919. Staff College, Quetta, 1920. A.F.C.

TWEEDIE, JOHN ALEXANDER.
Royal High School. Student of Arts and Law, 1884-92. R.A.S.C., Private.

TYERMAN, GEORGE VERNON.
Durham School; First XV. O.T.C. 1914-15, Cadet L/Corporal. University O.T.C. Artillery, Dec. 1916 to June 1917, Cadet Bombardier; Officer Cadet June 1917. R.F.A., 2nd Lieut. Dec. 1917. France.

TYLER, OWEN WILLIAM BLATHWAYTE.
Edinburgh Academy. Student of Arts, 1912-13. 9th Royal Scots (T.), Captain. France. M.C. and Bar to M.C. Oct. 1918.

TYRIE, GEORGE AITKEN.
Harris Academy, Dundee. University O.T.C. Artillery, Sept. 1917 to June 1918, Cadet. R.F.A., Officer Cadet, July 1918 to Jan. 1919.

TYRRELL, EDWARD JAMES.
Dundee High School. M.B., Ch.B. 1901; M.D. 1903. R.A.M.C., Lieut. Oct. 1915; Captain Oct. 1916 to March 1919. Salonika 1915-16; Mesopotamia 1917-18; France July to Nov. 1918; The Rhine.

TYRRELL, JAMES MUNRO.
Galashiels Academy. Student of Medicine, 1912-17; M.B., Ch.B. 1917; D.P.H. 1920. O.T.C. Medical, Feb. 1916 to July 1917, Cadet. Royal Navy, Surgeon-Lieut. July 1917. H.M.S. *Victorious II*.

ULLO, JOSEPH RICHARD.
Student of Medicine, 1912-13. O.T.C. Infantry, Nov. 1914 to March 1915, Cadet Sergeant. 8th South Lancashire Regiment, 2nd Lieut. March 1915; Lieut.; Captain May 1917.

UNDERHILL, JAMES WALTER OCTAVIUS.
Aldenham. M.B., C.M. 1884. Royal Navy, 1886; Fleet Surgeon; Retired 1907. Mobilised Aug. 1914. H.M.S. *Excellent*. Invalided out April 1916.

UNWIN, THOMAS BARTON.
Rugby. M.B., C.M. 1899. R.A.M.C., 1900; Captain 1903; Major Nov. 1912; Acting Lieut.-Col. April 1917. South African Campaign, 1899-1901. A.D.M.S., Aug. 1916 to May 1917, Cameroons. 39th Stationary Hospital, France. Dispatches Jan. 1915, June 1918, and Jan. 1919. O.B.E. Jan. 1919.

URQUHART, ALEXANDER COLIN.
Gordon's College, Aberdeen. Student of Science, 1916-17 and 1918. R.F.A., Driver Nov. 1916.

Record of War Service

URQUHART, ALEXANDER LEWIS.
Edinburgh Academy; First XV. and XI. M.B., Ch.B. 1911; D.P.H. (Lond.). R.A.M.C., Lieut. 1912; Captain March 1915; Acting Major Dec. 1917 to June 1919. France and Salonika. Dispatches (Salonika) June 1917 and June 1918. O.B.E. June 1918.

URQUHART, ALEXANDER ROBERT.
Royal High School; First XV. Student of Science, 1916-17. R.F.A., Gunner April 1917; 2nd Lieut. June 1918. Dispatches March 1919.

URQUHART, COLIN LINDSAY WALTON.
Christ's Hospital; First XI. O.T.C. 1912-15. University O.T.C. Infantry, May 1917 to Jan. 1918, Cadet; Officer Cadet Jan. 1918. 3rd Royal Highlanders (Black Watch), 2nd Lieut. May 1918.

URQUHART, WILLIAM MACDUFF.
Edinburgh Institution; First XV. M.A. 1909; LL.B. 1912. Solicitor before the Supreme Courts, 1913. 9th Royal Scots (T.), 1911; Lieut. Sept. 1914; Captain June 1916; Major March 1918. Royal Air Force. France. Wounded Sept. 1917. M.C. Sept. 1917.

URQUHART, WILLIAM SINCLAIR.
Dingwall Academy. Student of Medicine, 1918-19. 2/1st Highland Cyclist Battn., Private April 1918. Attached Royal Highlanders (Black Watch).

VALENTINE, WILLIAM STAINER.
Ashton Grammar School. Student of Medicine, 1913-15. O.T.C. Infantry, Feb. to Dec. 1914, Cadet Sergeant. 4th Cameron Highlanders, 2nd Lieut. Dec. 1914; Lieut. Oct. 1915. Machine-Gun Corps, March 1916. 9th Gurkha Rifles, Indian Army, Feb. 1918. France July 1915 to Aug. 1916, and Aug. to Nov. 1917. Wounded at the Somme Aug. 1916. India Feb. 1918. Invalided home Jan. 1919.

VARMA, BATUKDEVA PRASAD.
Muzaffarpur Government School. Student of Medicine, 1910-15; M.B., Ch.B. 1915; F.R.C.S. (Edin.) Indian Field Ambulance, Dec. 1914.

VARTAN, CHARLES SAMUEL.
Royal High School. M.B., Ch.B. 1899. R.A.M.C., Lieut. Dec. 1915; Captain Dec. 1916.

VAUDIN, MATHEW LIVINGSTONE MITCHELL.
Victoria College, Jersey. M.B., C.M. 1894. Royal Navy 1896, Surgeon Commander. South African Campaign, 1899-1902.

VAUGHAN, EDMUND WAYNE.
Bandon Grammar School. M.B., Ch.B. 1906. University Battery, E.C.A.V., 1900-5, Corporal. R.A.M.C., Lieut. 1908; Captain 1912; Acting Lieut.-Col. Dec. 1917. France Aug. 1914-19; 3rd Division, 2nd Cavalry Division, and 7th Division; 4th Cavalry and 23rd Field Ambulance. Dispatches June 1918 and June 1919. M.C. Jan. 1918; D.S.O. June 1919.

Record of War Service

VAUGHAN, JOSEPH CHARLES STÖLKE.
    M.B., C.M. 1885. Indian Medical Service, Lieut.-Col. 1909 and April 1917.

VAUGHAN-WILLIAMS, HERBERT WYNNE.
    M.B., C.M. 1893. South African Medical Corps, Lieut. 1894; Captain 1897; Lieut.-Col. Nov. 1915. France Dec. 1914 to April 1915; No. 2 South African Field Ambulance. German East Africa, Nov. 1915, and A.D.M.S., 3rd South African Division, April to Dec. 1916. General Hospitals, South Africa. Invalided out April 1919. D.S.O. and four times Mentioned in Dispatches.

VAWDREY, DANIEL LLEWELYN.
    Rugby. B.A. (Hons. Oxford) 1914. Student of Arts, 1918-19. 5th attached 2nd Worcestershire Regiment, 2nd Lieut. Sept. 1914; Lieut. July 1915; Acting Captain Oct. 1916. Cadet Instructor, Oxford, 1917-18.

VEEL, GEORGE REGINALD.
    Student of Arts, 1911-14; M.A. 1914. Priest, Church of England. King's Royal Rifle Corps, 1914-15. Hon. Chaplain, Military Hospitals, 1915-18. Hon. Artillery Coy., 309th Siege Battery, Gunner 1918. France.

VEITCH, JAMES.
    Student. Canadian Contingent.

VEITCH, ROBERT McLEOD.
    M.B., Ch.B. 1903; M.D. 1907. Volunteer Medical Staff Corps, 1899-1902, Private. R.A.M.C., Lieut. Dec. 1914; Captain Dec. 1915. Bacteriologist, Cambridge Hospital, Aldershot; 22nd General and Isolation Hospitals, Etaples, France. Invalided home Aug. 1916. Ministry of National Service and Ministry of Pensions, Dec. 1917-20. Bradford and London. O.B.E. 1920.

VEITCH, WILLIAM.
    George Watson's College. M.A. 1880. Minister, Church of Scotland. Chaplain, 2nd Class, 1899. Lothians and Border Horse, attached Lowland Mounted Brigade (T.), April 1914.

VELLNOT, GEORGE ALBERT.
    Student of Medicine, 1911-14. French Army Hospital Service, Aug. 1914. Médecin Auxiliaire, Jan. 1916; Médecin Aide Major, Jan. 1918. 97th Territorial Infantry Regiment, Feb. 1916; 355th Infantry Regiment, March 1917, and 237th Field Ambulance, Oct. 1917. Dispatches Jan. 1917 and March 1918. Croix de Guerre (French).

VEREL, RAYMOND.
    Glenalmond. M.B., Ch.B. 1908; F.R.C.S. (Edin.) 1911. R.A.M.C. (T.), Captain Sept. 1914. Scottish Horse Brigade Field Ambulance. Gallipoli and Egypt. Dispatches and O.B.E. June 1919.

Record of War Service

VERLEY, REGINALD CHARLES.
   Blairlodge; First XV. and XI. Black Watch Cadet Corps, Private. M.B., Ch.B. 1898; B.Sc. (P.H.) 1900; M.R.C.S. (Eng.) and L.R.C.P. (Lond.) 1898. South African Campaign, 1900-1. R.A.M.C., Lieut. Sept. 1914; Captain Sept. 1915. 57th Infantry Brigade; S.M.O. 28th and 29th General Hospitals, Salonika; 11th Stationary Hospital, France; 10th Worcestershire Regiment, and 58th Field Ambulance.

VERNON, EDWARD THOMSON.
   Arbroath High School. M.A. 1911. Minister, U.F. Church of Scotland. O.T.C. Artillery, Oct. 1909 to Feb. 1912, Cadet. R.F.A., 2nd Lieut. Nov. 1914; Lieut. July 1917; Acting Captain. Signalling Officer, Aldershot, May 1917 to Nov. 1918. France and Salonika.

VERNON, HAROLD RUSSELL.
   George Watson's College. Student of Medicine, 1916-17 and 1918-20. O.T.C. Artillery, Jan. to Nov. 1917, Cadet; Officer Cadet Nov. 1917. R.F.A., 2nd Lieut. April 1918. Prisoner of War Oct. 1918.

VERSTER, JOHN MICHAEL.
   South African College, Cape Town. First XV. and XI. Student of Medicine, 1909-14 and 1919; M.B., Ch.B. 1919. O.T.C. Artillery, 1910-13, Cadet. R.A.M.C., Lieut. July 1915. South African Medical Corps, Captain Aug. 1916. No. 13 Casualty Clearing Station. Anzac Beach, Dardanelles; Malta and South Africa.

VICKERS, HENRY CHAMBERS.
   George Watson's College. Student of Arts, 1914-16 and 1918-20; M.A. 1920. R.G.A., 199th Siege Battery, Gunner Aug. 1916. France 1917. Wounded.

VIDEON, JAMES MORTON.
   Daniel Stewart's College; First XV. and XI. Cadet Corps 1914-17. University O.T.C. Infantry, Feb. to June 1918, Cadet. Royal Air Force, Cadet June 1918. No. 3 Cadet Wing, Egypt.

VIEYRA, PETER.
   M.B., Ch.B. 1911. Indian Medical Service, Captain Aug. 1917; Mesopotamia. N.-W. Frontier, India, and Eastern Waters.

VIJVER, GIFFORD TRAILL VAN DER.
   Gill College, Somerset East, South Africa. First XV. and XI. Cadet Corps 1905-7, Sergeant-Major. M.B., Ch.B. 1914. O.T.C. Artillery, Oct. 1908-14, Cadet Sergeant; Medical, 1914, Cadet L/Corporal. R.A.M.C. (S.R.), Lieut. Dec. 1914; Captain May 1915; Acting Major Jan. 1918; Acting Lieut.-Col. April 1918 to March 1919. France. Dispatches (Somme) Sept. 1916. M.C. April 1918.

VIZARD, ARTHUR HENRY HINGSTON.
   St John's College, Hurstpierpoint, Sussex. M.B., C.M. 1893; M.D. 1901. Royal Navy, 1894, Surgeon-Commander, 1910. H.M.S. *Fisgard*.

Record of War Service

VOGE, CECIL INNES BOTHWELL.
Merchiston Castle. O.T.C. 1911-12. Student of Medicine, 1915-17. O.T.C. Infantry, Oct. 1916 to April 1917, Cadet. R.F.C., 3rd Air Mechanic, April 1917; 2nd Lieut. July 1917; Lieut. July 1919. Royal Air Force. France.

VOS, GERRIT HENDRIK WILLEM DE.
M.B., Ch.B. 1911. South African Medical Corps.

WADDY, EDMOND WILLIAM.
Merchiston Castle. O.T.C. 1908-12, Cadet L/Corporal. Student of Arts, 1912-15. O.T.C. Infantry, Oct. 1913-14, Cadet. 12th, 9th, and 10th Scottish Rifles, 2nd Lieut. Oct. 1914; Lieut. Nov. 1915; Acting Captain July 1917. 56th T.R.B. Dec. 1916. France, Aug. to Oct. 1916, and April to Dec. 1917. Wounded.

WADE, HENRY.
Royal High School. M.B., Ch.B. (Hons.) 1898; M.D. (Gold Medal) 1907; F.R.C.S. (Edin.) 1903. Lecturer on Surgery. R.A.M.C. (V.) and (T.), 1908-13, Captain. R.A.M.C. (T.), Captain Sept. 1914; Lieut.-Col. Aug. 1916. Army Medical Service, Colonel Sept. 1918. Scottish Horse. Consulting Surgeon, Egyptian Exp. Force, 1916-19. Order of the White Eagle, July 1916; D.S.O. 1918; C.M.G. 1919.

WADE, NOEL NATHANIEL.
King's School, Warwick; First XV. M.B., ChB. 1901; M.D. 1904. No 4 Coy. Q.R.V.B., Royal Scots, 1895-1901, Sergeant. Royal Navy, Surgeon Dec. 1914.

WADE, WILFRED FRANCIS EUGENE.
University O.T.C. Infantry, Oct. 1917 to Jan. 1918, Cadet. Royal Navy, Ordinary Seaman, Jan. 1918. H.M. Ships *Actaeon* and *Champion*. Injured Nov. 1918. Invalided out Feb. 1919.

WAKEFIELD, FRANCES MARGARET.
St Leonard's School, St Andrews and St Helens, Clifton. M.B. Ch.B., and D.T.M. 1905. Scottish Women's Hospital, Serbia, 1914-15. Kragujevác. Hall Memorial Hospital, Omdurman, 1917-18. Royal Air Force, Mechanic, 1918-19, Abukir. Serbian Red Cross Medal, June 1915.

WAKEFIELD, THOMAS CLEAVE.
Taunton School. Student of Medicine, 1912-15 and 1917-19. M.B., Ch.B. 1920. R.N.V.R., Surgeon-Probationer, Dec. 1914 to Aug. 1917.

WAKELIN, JAMES GLENCORSE.
Edinburgh Academy. M.A. 1913; LL.B. 1918. Advocate, 1919. O.T.C. Artillery, Jan. 1909 to Dec. 1911. 5th Royal Scots Fusiliers, 2nd Lieut. Sept. 1914; Captain April 1916. Egypt. Wounded at Gallipoli July 1915. Recruiting and National Service, Ayrshire and Wigtownshire, 1916-19. O.B.E. (Military) 1918.

Record of War Service

WALCOT, THOMAS.
Edinburgh Institution. M.B., C.M. 1887; M.D. 1892; M.R.C.S. (Eng.) 1887. R.A.M.C., Captain Nov. 1915; Major June 1917. Hospital Ships *Britannic, Llandovery Castle, Guildford Castle*, and *Assaye*.

WALDEN, ALFRED E.
Caterham, Surrey. B.Sc. (Lond.) 1913. Assistant in Chemistry. R.G.A., 2nd Lieut. Dec. 1914; Lieut. July 1917. France. Indian Mountain Artillery, Aug. 1916 to Feb. 1919.

WALDON, FREDERICK JAMES.
M.B., C.M. 1897. Australian Army Medical Corps Reserve, Captain Aug. 1915; Major; Temp. Lieut.-Colonel; Lieut.-Colonel; Acting P.M.O., 5th Military District, West Australia. President, Pensions Board.

WALINCK, CHARLES DODS.
Broughton School, Edinburgh. Student of Arts and Science, 1912-15 and 1919; M.A. (Hons. Maths. and Nat. Phil.) 1919; B.Sc. 1920. O.T.C. Infantry, Jan. to Aug. 1915, Cadet. 13th Reserve, attached 6th Highland Light Infantry, 2nd Lieut. Aug. 1915; Lieut. July 1917. Royal Air Force, Lieut. April 1918 to Feb. 1919. Egypt, Salonika, and Palestine, Jan. 1916 to Dec. 1918.

WALKER, ALEXANDER IZAT.
Dollar Academy. O.T.C. 1905-10. Student of Science, 1912-15. O.T.C. Engineers, 1912-14, Cadet Corporal. 9th Royal Scots (T.), Private Oct. 1914. R.E., 2nd Lieut. Jan. 1915; Lieut. Nov. 1915; Acting Captain March 1917. France. Dispatches July 1916. M.C. Dec. 1917.

WALKER, ALLAN LINDSAY.
Berwickshire High School. M.A. 1913. 9th Royal Scots (T.), Private Sept. 1914. 8th and 1st Cameron Highlanders, 2nd Lieut. Oct. 1915; Lieut. July 1917. France.

WALKER, ALLAN ROBERTSON.
Elgin Academy. Student of Medicine, 1913-14. R.A.M.C. (T.), Scottish Horse Brigade Field Ambulance, Private Sept. 1914. 6th Seaforth Highlanders, 2nd Lieut July 1915. Attached R.F.C., Sept. 1916. 15th Ludhiana Sikhs, Lieut. April 1917; Captain May 1918. India. Wounded April and Sept. 1916.

WALKER, ARCHIBALD STODART.
M.B., C.M. 1891; F.R.C.P. (Edin.) 1897. R.A.M.C., Major. Registrar, Lancashire Convalescent Hospital, Blackpool, 1914. Dispatches.

WALKER, ARTHUR SAMUEL.
Uppingham. M.B., Ch.B. 1906; M.D. 1914; D.P.H. 1910. R.A.M.C. (T.), Lieut. Nov. 1914; Captain May 1915. 2/7th Royal Scots, Nov. 1914. 2/7th Durham Light Infantry, Dec. 1917. Italy, Sanitary Officer, May 1918.

Record of War Service

WALKER, CHARLES DERWENT.
Falmouth Grammar School. M.B., Ch.B. 1911. R.A.M.C., Lieut. Nov. 1915. Captain Nov. 1916. Dispatches Jan. 1918.

WALKER, CLARENCE.
North Berwick High School. Student of Law, 1910-12. 16th Royal Scots, Private; 2nd Lieut. June 1916; Lieut. Dec. 1916. France.

WALKER, DAVID MERRICK.
Lorne Street School, Leith. Student of Arts, 1889-90. Royal Navy, 1915. Acting Chaplain to Nonconformists, Grand Fleet in Scottish Waters, April 1915-19.

WALKER, DAVID SAMUEL HILL.
George Heriot's School; First XV. O.T.C. 1909-11, Cadet Corporal. Student of Medicine, 1911-14. O.T.C. Artillery, 1911-14, Cadet Bombardier. R.F.A. (S.R.), 2nd Lieut. Aug. 1914; Regulars, Feb. 1915; Lieut. Dec. 1916. 93rd Battery. Gallipoli July 1915; Egypt Jan. 1916; France March 1916 to April 1917; Mesopotamia Oct. 1917, and India, June 1918-20. Wounded April 1917.

WALKER, DOUGLAS GRAHAME.
Leighton Park School, Reading. Student of Science, 1918-19. Cambridge University O.T.C. and Sandhurst Military College. 2nd Highland Light Infantry, Lieut.; Acting Captain July to Oct. 1917.

WALKER, DOUGLAS STEWART.
Aberdeen Grammar School; First XI. University O.T.C. Artillery, June 1916 to Jan. 1917, Cadet; Officer Cadet Jan. 1917. R.F.A. (T.), 1st Highland Brigade, 2nd Lieut. May 1917; Lieut. Nov. 1918. France July 1917 to Oct. 1918. Wounded March 1918. Invalided out June 1919.

WALKER, EDWARD ARCHIBALD.
Cheltenham College. M.B., Ch.B. 1908; M.D. 1912; D.P.H. (Camb.) 1914. R.A.M.C., Lieut. Oct. 1914; Captain Oct. 1915 to March 1919. France 1915 and 1917; Mesopotamia 1916. Prisoner of War March to Nov. 1918. M.C. Aug. 1917.

WALKER, EDWARD ROBERT CHARLES.
Edinburgh Academy. O.T.C. 1912-16, Cadet Officer. University O.T.C. Infantry, June to Oct. 1917, Cadet L/Corporal; Officer Cadet Oct. 1917. 9th Royal Highlanders (Black Watch), 2nd Lieut. Feb. 1918. France.

WALKER, ERNEST ALEXANDER.
Forfar Academy. M.B., Ch.B. 1901; F.R.C.S. (Edin.) 1912. Indian Medical Service, No. 1 Field Ambulance, Major Jan. 1914. Kut-el-Amara, Mesopotamia, Dec. 1915. 6th Division, Indian Exp. Force. Dispatches Oct. 1919.

WALKER, FRANK WARRACK.
Edinburgh Academy. O.T.C. 1913-17, Cadet Sergeant. University O.T.C. Artillery, Jan. to Sept. 1917, Cadet Sergeant; Officer Cadet Sept. 1917. R.F.A. (S.R.), 255th Highland Brigade, 2nd Lieut. Feb. 1918. France. M.C. April 1919.

Record of War Service

WALKER, FREDERICK.
　Edinburgh Academy. O.T.C. 1914-15. Student of Science, 1915-17. O.T.C. Artillery, Oct. 1915 to July 1917, Cadet; Officer Cadet July 1917. Forth R.G.A. (T.), 2nd Lieut. Dec. 1917 to Nov. 1918.

WALKER, GEORGE.
　M.A. 1883; B.D. 1886. Minister, Church of Scotland. Chaplain, April 1901; 2nd Class, 1916. Highland Division, R.E. 2/6th and 2/8th Argyll and Sutherland Highlanders, and 2nd Scottish General Hospital.

WALKER, GEORGE DAVID.
　George Heriot's School. M.A. 1904; B.Sc. 1905. Assam Valley Light Horse, Corporal. 2/8th Gurkha Rifles (I.A.R.O.), 2nd Lieut.; Lieut. M.B.E. (Military) July 1920.

WALKER, HUGH.
　Glasgow High School. M.A. (Glasg.) 1887; M.B., C.M. (Hons.) 1903. R.A.M.C., Captain 1908; Major July 1915. Ophthalmic Surgeon, Victoria Infirmary, Glasgow. Order of St Sava (4th Class).

WALKER, HUGH.
　M.A. 1910. Schoolmaster. Army Ordnance Corps, Private May 1916; L/Corporal July 1916; Local Sergeant Aug. 1916; Local Staff Sergeant Dec. 1916. Transferred to Reserve April 1917.

WALKER, HUGH STEWART.
　St Mary's School, Melrose. M.A. (Hons. Engl.) 1910. Schoolmaster. Kelvinside Academy O.T.C., Captain and O.C. Hockey International. 6th Cameron Highlanders, Captain March 1915. Taken Prisoner, Feb. 1916. O.C. Russian Prisoners Camp, Hamelin, Nov. 1918. British Military Mission, Siberia.

WALKER, JAMES.
　Daniel Stewart's College. M.A. 1908. Schoolmaster. R.G.A., Gunner Feb. 1917. R.E. (Topographical Section), Sapper.

WALKER, JAMES.
　Dollar Academy. O.T.C. 1912-15, Cadet Corporal. Student of Arts, 1915-16. O.T.C. Infantry, Oct. 1915 to May 1916, Cadet. 3rd and 7th Argyll and Sutherland Highlanders, Private May 1916; Corporal Nov. 1916; 2nd Lieut. June 1917; Lieut. Nov. 1918. France.

WALKER, JAMES.
　Ewart High School, Newton-Stewart. M.A. (Glasg.) 1913. Student of Law, 1913-15. Advocate, 1914. O.T.C. Artillery, Nov. 1914 to Oct. 1915, Cadet. 4th Royal Scots, Private Feb. 1916. Machine-Gun Corps, Oct. 1917; Officer Cadet Nov. 1917. Machine-Gun Corps, 2nd Lieut. Feb. 1918 to May 1919. France.

WALKER, JAMES CAMPBELL.
　Grove Academy, Broughty Ferry. Student of Law, 1914-16. R.F.A., Gunner Dec. 1915. France. M.M. Aug. 1918.

Record of War Service

WALKER, JAMES ROBERT HALL.
    Edinburgh Academy. M.B., C.M. 1897; M.D. 1902. Indian Medical Service, Temp. Lieut. Dec. 1914; Temp. Captain June 1915. R.A.M.C., Temp. Captain Dec. 1915; Hon. Captain Sept. 1918. Mont Dore Military Hospital for Indians at Bournemouth. Radiographer.

WALKER, JOHN.
    Student of Medicine, 1914-16 and 1917-19. O.T.C. Infantry, April 1915 to June 1916, Cadet. R.N.V.R., Surgeon-Probationer.

WALKER, JOHN.
    Falkirk School. Chartered Accountant, 1919. University O.T.C. Infantry, Sept. 1914-15, Cadet Sergeant. 7th Royal Scots, Sergeant Sept. 1915. Army Gymnastic Staff, Jan. 1916; C.S.M. April 1917 to Jan. 1919.

WALKER, JOHN FORBES.
    Grove Academy, Broughty Ferry. M.A. (Hons. Maths.) and B.Sc. 1913. O.T.C. Artillery, Oct. 1909 to Feb. 1914, Cadet Corporal. Calcutta Volunteer Battery, Gunner Oct. 1915. British and German East Africa, Oct. 1915 to Jan. 1917. Invalided out Jan. 1917.

WALKER, JOSEPH.
    M.B., Ch.B. 1913. O.T.C. Medical, 1909-12, Cadet. R.A.M.C. (S.R.), Lieut. Aug. 1914; Captain April 1915; Acting Major Feb. 1918. D.A.D.M.S., 17th Division. France Aug. 1914 to March 1919. Dispatches Jan. 1918 and July 1919. M.C. Jan. 1918.

WALKER, LINDSAY.
    Greenock Academy; First XV. M.A. 1911; M.B., Ch.B. 1917. O.T.C. Medical, Nov. 1915 to July 1917, Cadet. R.A.M.C., Lieut. Aug. 1917; Captain Sept. 1918. Mesopotamia.

WALKER, MARY BROADFORT.
    M.B., Ch.B. 1913. Attached R.A.M.C., Sept. 1916 to June 1919. Malta and Salonika.

WALKER, NORMAN DUNBAR.
    Merchiston Castle. M.B., Ch.B. 1899; D.P.H. 1909. R.A.M.C. 1902; Major June 1914. Mesopotamia 1916-19. D.A.D.M.S. (Sanitary), Peshawar, India. Dispatches Aug. 1917, Aug. 1918, and June 1919. O.B.E. June 1919.

WALKER, OSWALD.
    George Heriot's School. Student of Arts and Divinity, 1909-14 and 1918-19; M.A. 1912. O.T.C. Infantry, 1911-14, Cadet. 2/9th Royal Scots (T.), Private April 1915. 4th Highland Light Infantry, 2nd Lieut. Sept. 1915; Lieut. July 1917.

WALKER, PETER KEIR.
    Dunfermline High School; First XV. Student of Medicine, 1916-20. O.T.C. Infantry, May to Sept. 1917, and Medical, April 1918 to Feb. 1919, Cadet. 4th Highland Light Infantry, Private Nov. 1917. Royal Air Force, Cadet Jan. 1918.

Record of War Service

WALKER, ROBERT BURGESS.
Student of Law, 1911-13. Chartered Accountant, 1918. 15th Royal Scots, Private. 3rd East Lancashire Regiment, 2nd Lieut. Wounded.

WALKER, ROBERT CLIVE.
George Watson's College. M.B., Ch.B. 1905; M.D. 1913. R.A.M.C., Lieut. May 1917; Captain May 1918. 245th R.A.S.C. (M.T.), Salonika.

WALKER, RUSSELL ERNEST.
Haileybury. Rifle Volunteer Corps, 1904-6. M.B., Ch.B. 1912; F.R.C.S. (Edin.) 1914. R.A.M.C., Lieut. Aug. 1914; Captain Aug. 1915. 17th Field Ambulance and 2nd Durham Light Infantry. France. Wounded.

WALKER, THOMAS GAMBIER PRESLAND.
Royal High and George Heriot's Schools. M.A. 1913. Schoolmaster. 9th Royal Scots, Private Sept. 1914; Corporal; Sergeant. 1/7th Gordon Highlanders, 2nd Lieut. July 1916; Lieut. Jan. 1918. France 1915. Wounded Nov. 1916.

WALKER, THOMAS JULIEN MONTGOMERY.
Umtata School, South Africa. Student of Medicine, 1912-14 and 1918. O.T.C. Medical, June 1918-19, Cadet 2nd Lieut. Lothians and Border Horse (T.), Private 1912; L/Corporal Aug. 1915; Acting Corporal June 1916; Corporal Sept. 1916; Sergeant Oct. 1916. Macedonia.

WALKER, VANE.
M.A. 1914. Clergyman, Church of England. R.A.M.C., Sergeant.

WALKER, WALTER OLIPHANT.
George Heriot's School; First XV. M.B., Ch.B. 1908. Indian Medical Service, Lieut. 1910; Captain 1913. 1st and 8th Gurkha Rifles. N.-W. Frontier, India, 1914-15. Mesopotamia March 1916 to Jan. 1920. Dispatches 1917.

WALKER, WILLIAM DICKINSON.
Student of Medicine, 1913-14. 8th Durham Light Infantry, 2nd Lieut.; Lieut.; Captain.

WALKER, WILLIAM ROBERT.
Merchiston Castle. Student of Arts and Law, 1905-12; M.A. 1909; LL.B. 1912; Advocate 1914. 2/4th Border Regiment (T.), 2nd Lieut. Jan. 1915; Lieut. June 1917; Staff Captain May 1918. India 1915. Adjutant, H.Q., Delhi.

WALL, ARTHUR PERCY.
M.B., Ch.B. 1906. Australian Army Medical Corps, Major. 6th Australian Field Ambulance.

WALL, CHARLES PERCIVALE BLIGH.
Bradfield College. Cadet Corps 1886-90, Sergeant. M.A., M.B., C.M. 1897; M.D. 1905. Tembuland Field Force, Surgeon-Captain 1899. South African Campaign. Retired July 1908. 19th Mounted Rifles, Captain July 1914. South African Medical Corps, Captain Aug. 1916. D.A.D.M.S., Nov. 1917; A.D.M.S. G.H.Q., East African Exp. Force, April 1918; Lieut.-Col. Aug. 1918. Dispatches 1918 and 1919. O.B.E. (Military) 1919.

Record of War Service

WALL, DOUGLAS LARMER.
Cheltenham. M.B., Ch.B. 1901. R.A.M.C., Lieut. Feb. 1912; Captain April 1915. R.G.A. (Kent); 2/1st West Riding Field Ambulance. Attached 8th West Yorkshire Regiment. Dispatches Oct. 1917. M.C. Nov. 1917.

WALLACE, CHARLES MAWER.
George Heriot's School. Student of Law, 1913-15. 3rd and 17th Royal Scots, Private Nov. 1915. 3rd King's Royal Rifles, 2nd Lieut. Aug. 1917; Lieut. March 1919. France, Salonika. Educational Officer, 8th Oxford and Bucks Light Infantry, the Black Sea.

WALLACE, CHARLES STUART.
George Watson's College. M.A. 1899. Minister, Church of Scotland. Chaplain 4th Class, Jan. 1917. France Jan. 1917-18; Salonika March 1918 to May 1919.

WALLACE, SIR DAVID.
M.B., C.M. 1884; F.R.C.S. Senior Lecturer, Clinical Surgery. South African Campaign, 1900-2. R.A.M.C. (T.), Major 1908; Brevet Lieut.-Col. June 1917. Inspector of Auxiliary Hospitals and Red Cross Commissioner, Eastern District, Scotland. Mention 1917. C.M.G. 1900; C.B.E. 1917; K.B.E. 1920.

WALLACE, DAVID MITCHELL.
M.A. 1905. Schoolmaster. O.T.C. Artillery, 1915, Cadet Bombardier. R.F.A., 2nd Lieut. Sept. 1915; Lieut. June 1916; Acting Captain Oct. 1918.

WALLACE, EDWIN DANIEL MACKAY.
Royal High School; First XV. and XI. Student of Medicine, 1918-20. 14th Argyll and Sutherland Highlanders, Private June 1915; L/Corporal Feb. 1917. Wounded April 1917. Invalided out Dec. 1917.

WALLACE, GEORGE BRUNTON.
George Heriot's School. O.T.C. 1916. Student of Science, 1919-20. O.T.C. Artillery, Jan. to Dec. 1917, Cadet; Officer Cadet Dec. 1917. R.G.A., 2nd Lieut. June 1918 to Aug. 1919.

WALLACE, GEORGE WILLOUGHBY.
Edinburgh Academy; First XI. M.A. 1912; Student of Law, 1912-14. Writer to the Signet, 1919. Forth R.G.A. (T.), 2nd Lieut. Nov. 1914; Lieut. June 1916; Acting Captain March 1916 to Sept. 1918; Acting Major Sept. 1918 to Jan. 1919.

WALLACE, HERBERT SMITH.
M.B., Ch.B. 1908. R.A.M.C., Lieut.; Captain April 1915. Notts and Derby Mounted Brigade Field Ambulance. France.

WALLACE, JOHN ANDREW LESLIE.
M.B., Ch.B. 1903; M.D. 1909. South African Campaign, 1900-1. Australian Army Medical Corps (Reserve), Hon. Captain Feb. 1917. No. 13 and No. 28 Australian Auxiliary Military Hospitals, Sydney.

Record of War Service

WALLACE, ROBERT JOHNSTON.
Edinburgh Academy. M.A. (Oxford); LL.B. 1912. Advocate 1913. 9th Royal Scots (V.) 1905; (T.) 1908; Captain 1912. Forth Defences, Staff Captain March 1915 to May 1916. Royal Air Force, Feb. 1918; Acting Captain (Wing Gunnery Officer) Dec. 1918.

WALLACE, ROBERT WILLIAM LESSEL.
George Watson's College. M.B., Ch.B. 1904; M.D. 1914. R.A.M.C., Lieut. June 1915; Captain June 1916. M.C. Sept. 1918.

WALLACE, SAMUEL THOMAS DICKSON, *V.C.* (See p. 757.)

WALLACE, THOMAS WILLIAM.
George Heriot's School. M.A. 1909; B.L. 1920. 16th and 6th Royal Scots, Private Dec. 1914; 2nd Lieut. April 1915; Lieut. July 1917. France.

WALLACE, VICTOR GEORGE HENRY.
Fettes College. O.T.C. 1912-16, Cadet Corporal. Student of Medicine, 1917-20. 10th Liverpool Regiment (The Liverpool Scottish), Private May 1916; Officer Cadet; 2nd Lieut. Oct. 1916. France. Wounded July 1917. Invalided out March 1918.

WALLER, GEORGE RONALD.
Selborne College, East London, South Africa. Cadet Corps 1906-10, Sergeant. Student of Medicine, 1911-14 and 1918-19; M.B., Ch.B. 1919. O.T.C. Medical, June 1911 to Sept. 1914, Cadet L/Corporal. R.A.M.C. (S.R.), Lieut. (on Probation) Aug. 1914 to Jan. 1915. 9th East Lancashire Regiment (Combatant), 2nd Lieut. Jan. 1915; Lieut. July 1916 to March 1918.

WALLS, CHARLES.
Student of Arts and Divinity, 1913-16; M.A. 1916. Guards' Machine-Gun Corps, Private.

WALLS, WILLIAM.
Kilmarnock Academy. Student of Arts, 1919. O.T.C. Infantry, 1915-16, Cadet. 8th Cameron Highlanders, Private Feb. 1916. 6th Royal Highlanders (Black Watch), L/Corporal; Officer Cadet. 12th King's Own Yorkshire Light Infantry, 2nd Lieut. Jan. 1918 to Feb. 1919.

WALSH, JOHN ALOYSIOUS.
St Bonaventure's College, St John's, Newfoundland. Student of Medicine, 1918. 1st Royal Newfoundland Regiment, Private Dec. 1914. France 1915.

WALSH, ROY WILLIAM WHISTON.
M.B., Ch.B. 1912. Australian Army Medical Corps, Major Nov. 1916. D.S.O.

WALSHE, SARSFIELD JAMES AMBROSE HALL.
M.B., Ch.B. 1912. O.T.C. Medical, April 1908 to Aug. 1910, Cadet Acting Sergeant. R.A.M.C. (S.R.), Lieut. 1910; Captain Feb. 1914; Temp. Major May 1918; Captain (Regulars) 1919. No. 6 Field Ambulance, Aug. 1914 to Sept. 1916. France Aug. 1914 to Sept. 1916. D.A.D.M.S., 7th Division. Italy Nov. 1917. Dispatches Jan. 1915, Jan. 1916, and Jan. 1919. D.S.O. (Ypres) Oct. 1914.

Record of War Service

WALTON, ROBERT HENRY.
Auckland Grammar School, New Zealand. First XV. and XI. M.B., Ch.B. 1906; M.D. 1909. N.Z. Medical Corps, Captain Aug. 1914; Major Nov. 1915; Lieut.-Col. Dec. 1917. Dispatches Jan. 1918.

WARD, FRANCIS.
Sedbergh. M.B., C.M. 1894; M.D. 1897. R.A.M.C. (V.), 1898; (T.) Major Oct. 1914. Gallipoli, Palestine, and France. Dispatches June 1917. Croix de Guerre April 1917.

WARD, JOSEPH HUGH.
St Mary's College, Dundalk. M.B., Ch.B. 1913. O.T.C. Medical, Jan. 1909 to June 1912, Cadet L/Corporal. R.A.M.C. (S.R.), Lieut. 1912; Captain April 1915; Captain (Regulars) Feb. 1918; Acting Lieut.-Col., Cavalry Field Ambulance, Dec. 1917 to April 1919. France Aug. 1914. Dispatches Jan. 1916 and Dec. 1918. M.C. Jan. 1918; D.S.O. July 1918; Médaille de l'Assistance Publique June 1918.

WARD, KENNETH LANGHAME STANLEY.
Student of Medicine, 1912-17; M.B., Ch.B. 1917. Royal Navy, Surgeon-Probationer; Surgeon Oct. 1917.

WARD, THOMAS HAMILTON.
Epsom College. M.B., C.M. 1887; M.D. 1892. R.A.M.C. (T.), Lieut. 1914; Captain Jan. 1915; Brevet Major June 1917.

WARD-SMITH, WARD.
Newcastle-under-Lyne High School. M.B., Ch.B. 1898; M.D. 1905; F.R.C.S. (Eng.) 1902; L.R.C.P. (Lond.) 1900. Volunteer Medical Staff Corps, 1894-8, L/Corporal. R.A.M.C., Lieut. April 1916; Captain April 1917; Acting Major 1918-19; Major.

WARDEN, HERBERT LAWTON.
George Heriot's School. Student of Law, 1893-6. Solicitor before the Supreme Courts, 1905. No. 4 Coy. Q.R.V.B., Royal Scots, 1901; (T.) Captain 1908-12. 16th Royal Scots, Major 1915. 13th East Surrey Regiment, Lieut.-Col. and O.C. Feb. 1917. France 1915-18. Director of Pensions, Scotland. Dispatches May 1917, May and Dec. 1918. D.S.O. Feb. 1918; Bar to D.S.O. Sept. 1918.

WARR, ALFRED ERNEST.
Glasgow Academy. M.A. (Hons. Classics) 1911; B.D. 1914. Spence Bursar, 1908; First Bursar (Divinity), 1911. Senior President, S.R.C. Minister, Church of Scotland. O.T.C. Infantry, Oct. 1908 to April 1910, Cadet. 16th Royal Scots, Private Nov. 1914; 2nd Lieut. Dec. 1914; Lieut.; Captain March 1915; Major Feb. 1917. France 1915-18. Prisoner of War April to Nov. 1918.

WARR, CHARLES LAING.
Glasgow Academy. Student of Arts, 1910-14; M.A. 1914. Simson Bursar, 1910. Minister, Church of Scotland. O.T.C. Infantry, April to Aug. 1914, Cadet. 9th Argyll and Sutherland Highlanders (T.), 2nd Lieut. Aug. 1914. France Feb. 1915. Wounded at second Ypres March 1915, and invalided out April 1916.

Record of War Service

WARREN, DONALD WILLIAM.
    Daniel Stewart's College. Student of Medicine, 1911-17; M.B., Ch.B. 1917. Royal Navy, Surgeon-Probationer, March 1915; Surgeon-Lieut. April 1917 to May 1919.

WARREN, WILLIAM DOUGLAS MARDEN.
    Nairn Academy. Student of Science, 1918. 4th Gordon Highlanders. Mobilised 1914. R.F.A., 2nd Lieut. Feb. 1918 to March 1919. France Feb. 1915. Invalided home Sept. 1916. France June 1918 to March 1919.

WARWICK, ARTHUR MACGREGOR.
    George Watson's College. M.B., Ch.B. 1910. O.T.C. Infantry, Oct. 1908 to May 1911, Cadet. R.A.M.C., Lieut. April 1915; Captain April 1916. 1st Indian Field Squadron, R.E. France. M.C. (Hindenburg Line) Sept. 1918.

WASH, WILLIAM ARTHUR.
    Colchester and Wallasey Schools. M.A. 1913. Minister, Congregational Church. R.G.A., No. 2 Reserve Brigade, Siege Artillery, 2nd Lieut. Sept. 1914; Lieut. July 1917; Acting Captain May 1919. Assistant Education Officer, 1919.

WATER, FRANS KAREL TE.
    Gràaff Reinet College, Cape Colony. M.B., Ch.B. 1908; M.R.C.S. (Eng.); L.R.C.P. (Lond.). No. 4 Coy. Q.R.V.B., Royal Scots, 1906-8, Private. South African Medical Corps, Captain Aug. 1914 to Feb. 1919. M.C. 1915.

WATERHOUSE, SIR HERBERT FURNIVALL.
    Brighton College. M.B., C.M. 1887; M.D. 1889; F.R.C.S. (Eng.) 1890; L.R.C.P. (Lond.) 1887. Demonstrator in Anatomy. R.A.M.C. (V.) and (T.), 1904; Captain; Major Feb. 1916; Brevet Lieut.-Col. Surgeon-in-Chief, Anglo-Russian Hospitals, Russia, Nov. 1915-16. Knighted June 1917.

WATERS, ERNEST EDWIN.
    Wesley College, Sheffield. M.B., Ch.B. 1893; M.D. 1903; M.R.C.P. (Lond.) 1911. University Battery, E.C.A.V., 1890-3, B.S.M. Indian Medical Service, 1895; Lieut.-Col. Jan. 1915. Nalakand 1897; Tirah 1898. H.M. Ships *Karmala* and *Manora*, 1914-15.

WATERSTON, JAMES.
    M.A. 1901; B.Sc. (Distinction) 1906; B.D. 1905. R.A.M.C., Lieut.; Captain May 1918. 1st City of London Sanitation Coy.

WATKINS, WILLIAM RICHARD SPENCER.
    Llandovery College; First XV. M.B., Ch.B. 1903; F.R.C.S. (Edin.) 1908. R.A.M.C., Lieut. Dec. 1914; Captain Dec. 1915. Surgical Specialist, 19th General Hospital.

WATLING, FRANCIS HAMMOND.
    Mussoorie School. M.B., C.M. 1893. No. 4 Coy. Q.R.V.B., Royal Scots, 1887-92, Private. Indian Medical Service, 1895; Lieut.-Col. Jan. 1915. Chitral 1895; Tochi Valley 1897; China 1900-1; Mohmand and Swat 1915; Mesopotamia 1915-18. Dispatches (Mesopotamia) Aug. 1917.

Record of War Service

WATSON, ADAM FYFE.
   Student of Law, 1902-4. Chartered Accountant, 1905. National Reserve, Private.

WATSON, THE HON. ADAM GEORGE.
   Student of Law, 1899-1900. Writer to the Signet, 1901. 8th Royal Scots (T.), 2nd Lieut.; Lieut. June 1916.

WATSON, ALEXANDER EDWARD.
   M.B., C.M. 1892. R.A.M.C., Captain Sept. 1917.

WATSON, ALEXANDER PIRIE.
   Trinity Academy, Leith. M.A. 1908; M.B., Ch.B. 1908; Ch.M. 1911; F.R.C.S. (Edin.) 1911. Assistant in Surgery. R.A.M.C. (V.) and (T.), 1900; Captain Nov. 1914; Acting Major Jan. 1918. Attached 4th Royal Scots. Gallipoli and Egypt. Dispatches Feb. 1917 and Jan. 1919. O.B.E. (Military) Jan. 1919.

WATSON, ALEXANDRA MARY CAMPBELL, *née* GEDDES.
   St Leonard's School, St Andrews. First XI. M.B., Ch.B. 1896; M.D. 1898, W.A.A.C., Organiser and Chief Controller, 1916; Hon. Organising Secretary, Women's Emergency Corps, Edinburgh. C.B.E. (Military).

WATSON, ALLAN.
   M.B., Ch.B. 1909; M.D. 1914. D.T.M. & H. 1910; D.P.H. (Edin.) 1912. No. 4 Coy. Q.R.V.B., Royal Scots, 1904-8, Corporal. O.T.C. Infantry, April 1909 to July 1910, Cadet L/Corporal. R.A.M.C. (Regulars), Lieut. Jan. 1914; Captain March 1915. 1/4th Hampshire Regiment, Northern Persia Force. Wounded 1914 and 1916. Dispatches Aug. 1917 and Aug. 1918. D.S.O. Feb. 1917.

WATSON, ANDREW GORDON.
   Stanley House, Bridge of Allan. M.B., Ch.B. 1900; M.D. 1908. University Battery, E.C.A.V., 1895-9, Acting Bombardier. South African Campaign, 1901-2. 11th East Lancashire Regiment, Captain Sept. 1914 to June 1916. Transferred to R.A.M.C., June 1916. France 1914-16. Invalided home Sept. 1916, and out Sept. 1917.

WATSON, ANTHONY ALFRED.
   Western College, Harrogate. Student of Medicine, 1909-15; M.B., Ch.B. 1915. O.T.C. Medical, Jan. 1910-15, Cadet L/Corporal. R.A.M.C., Lieut. Nov. 1915; Captain Nov. 1916. 26th and 72nd General Hospitals, 35th and 58th Divisions.

WATSON, ARTHUR CLARK.
   Royal High School. Student of Arts, 1917-18. O.T.C. Infantry, Feb. to Dec. 1917, Cadet; Officer Cadet Dec. 1917. Royal Scots, 2nd Lieut. July 1918. Attached 52nd Highland Light Infantry.

WATSON, BENJAMIN PHILP.
   M.B., Ch.B. 1902; M.D. 1905; F.R.C.S. (Edin.) 1905. Canadian Army Medical Corps, Captain April 1915. No. 4 Canadian General Hospital.

Record of War Service

WATSON, DONALD.
High School, Mames, New Zealand. M.B., Ch.B. 1911. Anatomy Staff, 1912-14 and 1919. O.T.C. Infantry, Jan. 1909 to Aug. 1911, Cadet L/Corporal. R.A.M.C., Lieut. Jan. 1915; Captain Jan. 1916. India and Dardanelles.

WATSON, FRANK HERBERT CHENEY.
Royal School, Dungannon; First XV. and XI. M.B., Ch.B. 1912. O.T.C. Artillery, Oct. 1906 to July 1912, Cadet Sergeant. R.A.M.C., Lieut. Oct. 1914; Captain April 1915; Major Jan. 1918. Dispatches Jan. 1918. French Médaille des Épidémies (en Vermeille).

WATSON, GEORGE OLIVER DODDS.
Berwickshire High School, Duns. M.A. 1909; LL.B. 1912. O.T.C. Infantry, Oct. to Dec. 1915, Cadet. 4th King's Own Scottish Borderers, 2nd Lieut. Dec. 1915; Lieut. June 1917; Acting Captain Aug. 1917. Ministry of National Service, Jan. to Nov. 1918. Three times Wounded.

WATSON, HARRY M. D.
Merchiston Castle. Student of Law, 1896-8. Chartered Accountant, 1899. 8th and 5th Cameron Highlanders, Dec. 1915; 2nd Lieut.; Lieut. July 1917. France. Chevalier Ordre de Leopold and Croix de Guerre (Belgian).

WATSON, HUGH.
Royal High School. Student of Arts, 1915-16. O.T.C. Infantry, May 1915-16, Cadet Sergeant. Cameron Highlanders, Sept. 1916; 2nd Lieut.; Lieut. March 1918. Attached 12th Argyll and Sutherland Highlanders.

WATSON, HUGH BALLINGALL.
M.A. 1902; M.B. Ch.B. (Hons.) 1908; M.D. (Hons.) 1913. R.A.M.C., Captain. Edinburgh and Border Hospital, Dunkirk.

WATSON, HUGH KELSO.
Broughton School, Edinburgh. Student of Medicine 1918-20. 7th Cameron Highlanders, Private Feb. 1916; Corporal April 1917; Officer Cadet Sept 1918. France.

WATSON, JAMES ANDERSON SCOTT.
Harris Academy, Dundee. B.Sc. 1908. Lecturer in Agriculture. Lothians and Border Horse, Private Aug. 1914. R.F.A., 2nd Lieut. July 1915; Lieut. June 1916. France. M.C.

WATSON, JAMES KENNETH.
Fettes College. M.B., C.M. 1892; M.D. 1896. R.A.M.C., Lieut. Dec. 1916; Captain Dec. 1917 to March 1918.

WATSON, JAMES PITT.
George Heriot's School. M.A. 1916. Labour Corps. 290th Prisoner of War Coy., France, 2nd Lieut. Dec. 1917.

Record of War Service

WATSON, JOHN.
Foyle College, Londonderry. M.B., Ch.B. 1911. R.A.M.C., Lieut. Sept. 1915; Captain Sept. 1916; Major Jan. 1918. No. 4 Field Ambulance, Guards Division. France. M.C. June 1916.

WATSON, JOHN.
Student of Arts, 1911-14 and 1919. M.A. 1919; B.Sc. 1920. R.A.M.C. (T.), Private Feb. 1911; Corporal; Sergeant 1918. 3rd Lowland Field Ambulance, attached 3rd Royal Scots and R.E.

WATSON, JOHN BALLINGALL FORBES.
Dollar Academy. M.A. 1900; LL.B. 1908. Advocate, 1919. Senior President, S.R.C., and Union. General List, Staff Lieut. Nov. 1915. Royal Air Force, Staff Major April 1918. France (Special Duty) 1915-16. Ministry of Munitions; Treasury; Foreign Office; War Office, and Air Ministry. Mention Jan. 1919.

WATSON, JOHN CHARLES.
John Neilson Institution. M.A. (Hons.) and LL.B. (Glasg.). Advocate, 1906. Student of Law, 1908-9. O.T.C. Infantry, Oct. 1908, Cadet. 15th Royal Fusiliers, 2nd Lieut. March 1915. R.F.C., Lieut. (Observer) 1916. Royal Air Force, Captain (Staff Captain) May 1918. Secret R.F.C. Exp. to Hedjaz, Nov. 1915 to Feb. 1916. Egypt, Sinai, Arabia, Palestine, and Syria, Nov. 1915 to May 1919. M.B.E. (Military) Jan. 1919.

WATSON, JOSEPH CUNNINGHAM.
M.B., Ch.B. 1910. 1st Monmouthshire Regiment, Lieut. July 1915; Captain July 1916. France. Invalided out Oct. 1916.

WATSON, PETER.
Morrison's Academy, Crieff. M.A. 1914. 16th Royal Scots, Private Dec. 1914; L/Corporal; Sergeant. Machine-Gun Corps, 2nd Lieut. Dec. 1917. France.

WATSON, REGINALD WALTER ROBERTS.
Clitheroe Grammar School; Athletics. Student of Medicine, 1916 and 1919. Royal Navy (Sick Berth), Reservist, Aug. 1917; Surgeon Sub.-Lieut. Jan. 1918 to March 1919.

WATSON, ROBERT FRENCH MONCUR.
George Watson's College. Student of Arts, 1912-16; M.A. 1916. Schoolmaster. 9th Royal Scots (T.), Private 1910; L/Corporal. Mobilised Aug. 1914. Invalided out April 1915.

WATSON, THE HON. RONALD BANNATYNE.
Marlborough. B.A. 1909. Student of Law, 1905-7. Advocate, 1909. 8th Royal Scots (T.), 2nd Lieut. Oct. 1914; Lieut. Aug. 1915.

Record of War Service

WATSON, STANLEY.
Fettes College; First XV. O.T.C. 1908-9. Student of Science, 1909-14; B.Sc. 1919. Rugby "Blue." O.T.C. Infantry, Oct. 1909-13, Cadet Corporal. 12th Cheshire Regiment, 2nd Lieut. Sept. 1914; Lieut. Nov. 1914; Temp. Captain May 1915; Temp. Major Sept. 1917; Captain (Regulars) Jan. 1917; Acting Lieut.-Col. Oct. 1918. France and Macedonia 1915-18; The Black Sea. Dispatches Nov. 1917 and June 1919. M.C. Jan. 1918; D.S.O. June 1919. French Legion of Honour.

WATSON, THOMAS ALFRED.
M.B., C.M. 1884. R.A.M.C., Lieut.

WATSON, WILLIAM.
Dundee High School. Student of Science, 1917-19; B.Sc. 1920. R.E., Signal Service, Sapper.

WATSON, WILLIAM BROWNLEE.
Daniel Stewart's College. Student of Medicine, 1914-18; L.D.S. 1917; L.R.C.P. & S. 1919. O.T.C. Medical, March 1916 to Feb. 1919, Cadet L/Corporal. R.A.M.C. (S.R.), Lieut. Feb. 1919.

WATSON, WILLIAM HERIOT.
Broughton School. Student of Arts, 1917-20. O.T.C. Artillery, Sept. 1917 to July 1918, Cadet Bombardier. R.G.A., Officer Cadet July 1918; 2nd Lieut. April 1919.

WATSON-WEMYSS, HERBERT LINDESAY.
Marlborough. M.B., Ch.B., 1908; M.D. 1910; F.R.C.P. (Edin.) 1914. Dalmeny House, Auxiliary Military Hospital, Oct. 1914 to Jan. 1917. R.A.M.C., Lieut. Jan. 1917; Local Captain (Malta) April 1917; Temp. Captain Jan. 1918.

WATT, DAVID TWEEDIE.
Student of Medicine, 1911-19. O.T.C. Artillery, Oct. 1914 to Dec. 1915, Cadet. R.N.V.R., H.M.S. *Zinnia*, Surgeon-Probationer, Dec. 1915.

WATT, FRANCIS CLIFFORD.
Berwickshire High School, Duns. Student of Arts and Law, 1913-15 and 1918-19. O.T.C. Infantry, Oct. 1914 to June 1915, Cadet. 14th Argyll and Sutherland Highlanders, Private June 1915. 4th and 2nd King's Own Scottish Borderers, 2nd Lieut. Jan. 1916; Lieut. July 1917 to March 1919. 1/5th Royal Warwickshire Regiment, Sept. 1916 to March 1917. France and Italy Sept. 1916 to Aug. 1918. Wounded Aug. 1918.

WATT, GEORGE LORIMER.
Broughton School, Edinburgh. M.A. 1909. Schoolmaster. R.E. (Special Brigade), Corporal Sept. 1915.

WATT, IAN GEORGE.
Dundee High School. B.Sc. 1909. 28th R.E., American Exp. Force, Lieut.

Record of War Service

WATT, JAMES PETER.
M.B., C.M. 1887. R.A.M.C. (T.), Captain and Sanitary Officer, 1909.

WATT, JOHN MITCHELL.
Student of Medicine, 1910-16; M.B., Ch.B. 1916. O.T.C. Medical, 1911-14, Cadet Corporal. R.A.M.C. (S.R.), Lieut. March 1916; Captain Sept. 1916.

WATT, LAUCHLAN MacLEAN.
Dalkeith High School. M.A. 1893; B.D. 1897; D.D. 1920. Minister, Church of Scotland. Chaplain, 3rd Class, 1913. Attached Y.M.C.A., France, Dec. 1914. France, 1916-17, in 7th Division with 2nd Gordon Highlanders (Somme and Ancre), and in 39th Division with 4/5th Royal Highlanders (Black Watch) (Ypres). British Mission to America, 1918.

WATT, NORVAL JAMES.
George Watson's College. M.B., Ch.B. 1909. University Battery, E.C.A.V., Nov. 1906 to May 1908, Gunner. South African Medical Corps and R.A.M.C., Captain July 1914. German South-West Africa. France 1915-16; Egypt and India 1916 and 1917.

WATT, ROBERT CAMERON.
Fettes College; First XV. O.T.C. 1913-16, Cadet Corporal. University O.T.C. Artillery, Sept. 1916 to March 1917, Cadet Bombardier; Officer Cadet April 1917. Forth R.G.A., 2nd Lieut. June 1917; Lieut. Dec. 1918.

WATT, ROBERT RITCHIE.
Morrison's Academy, Crieff. Student of Arts, 1912-14 and 1918-19; M.A. 1919. 3rd Scottish Horse (T.), Sergeant Aug. 1914; Acting Sergeant-Major March 1917. R.F.A., 2nd Lieut. June 1918.

WATTEVILLE, IAN DE.
Merchiston Castle. O.T.C. 1907-10, Cadet Corporal. Student of Arts, 1910-15; M.A. 1913; (Hons. Classics) 1915. 4th Cameron Highlanders, 2nd Lieut. Oct. 1915; Lieut. July 1917. Royal Air Force. France. Wounded April 1918. Croix de Guerre avec Palme, July 1918.

WATTHEWS, JOHN WILFRED.
Silcoates School, Wakefield. Student of Medicine, 1910-15; M.B., Ch.B. 1915. Red Cross Edinburgh and Border Hospitals, Dunkirk (Dresser), Nov. 1914 to Jan. 1915. R.A.M.C., Lieut. June 1916; Captain June 1917. M.C. Nov. 1917; Bar to M.C. July 1918.

WATTHEWS, OSWALD ALEXANDER.
Silcoates School, Wakefield. Student of Medicine, 1914-16. O.T.C. Artillery, Oct. 1914 to April 1916, Cadet; Officer Cadet March 1916. 4th Gordon Highlanders, 2nd Lieut. May 1917; Lieut. Nov. 1918.

Record of War Service

WAUGH, ARTHUR ALLEN.
George Watson's College; First XV. O.T.C. 1907-9. M.A. 1912. United Provinces Light Horse, Trooper, 1914-19. Indian Civil Service, District Recruiting Officer, 1916.

WAUGH, WILLIAM GRANT.
M.A. 1905; M.B., Ch.B. 1910; M.D. 1913. O.T.C. Medical, April 1908-10, Cadet. R.A.M.C., Lieut.; Captain Aug. 1915; Major.

WEARING, WILLIAM THOMAS.
M.B., C.M. 1893. R.A.M.C., Lieut. Aug. 1915; Captain 1916-17. H.M. Hospital Ships *Oxfordshire*, *Aquitania*, *Panama*, and H.M. Troopship *Osterley*.

WEATHERBE, LEWIS JOHNSTONE.
M.B., C.M. 1890. South African Campaign, 1900-1, Captain (Retired). R.A.M.C., Captain Aug. 1916 to Dec. 1918.

WEATHERBE, PHILIP.
M.B., Ch.B. 1901. South African Campaign, 1901-2. Canadian Army Medical Corps, 1902, Major. Military and Convalescent Hospitals, Halifax, N.S.

WEATHERHEAD, KENNETH KILPATRICK.
Dundee High School; First XV. and XI. Student of Arts, 1916-17. Scots Guards, April 1917; L/Corporal Nov. 1917. France Feb. 1918 to Feb. 1919.

WEATHERHEAD, WILLIAM ANDREW.
George Heriot's School. Student of Medicine, 1912-17; M.B., Ch.B. 1917. O.T.C. Medical, Oct. 1915 to July 1917, Cadet. R.A.M.C., Lieut. Aug. 1917; Captain Aug. 1918. India Aug. 1917; Macedonia; South Russia Dec. 1918, 81st Field Ambulance; The Black Sea (Tiflis).

WEATHERSON, RICHARD ROBERT STEVENSON.
George Watson's College; First XV. Student of Medicine, 1911-16; M.B., Ch.B. 1916. O.T.C. Medical, Nov. 1914 to July 1916, Cadet L/Corporal. R.A.M.C. (S.R.), Lieut. Aug. 1916. France 1914-19. Invalided out. Order of St George (Russia).

WEBB, FREDERICK HENRY.
George Watson's College. O.T.C. 1913-16. Student of Medicine, 1916-17. O.T.C. Artillery, April to Dec. 1917, Cadet; Officer Cadet Dec. 1917. R.G.A., 36th and 86th Siege Batteries, 2nd Lieut. June 1918.

WEBB, HERMANN WATSON.
Campbell College, Belfast; First XV. M.B., Ch.B. 1911; F.R.C.S. (Edin.) 1913. O.T.C. Infantry, Jan. 1909 to June 1910, Cadet L/Corporal. R.A.M.C., Lieut. Sept. 1914; Captain Sept. 1915.

WEBSTER, ADAM BLYTH.
Christchurch High School, New Zealand. M.A. (Hons. Engl.) 1905. Lecturer in English. R.G.A., Gunner June 1916; Sergeant; 2nd Lieut. April 1918. General Staff, Intelligence, G.H.Q., France, April 1918 to March 1919.

Record of War Service

WEBSTER, ARTHUR DOUGLAS.
Dalhousie College, Nova Scotia. B.Sc. (P.H.) 1888; D.Sc. 1890; M.D. (McGill College) 1878; F.R.C.P. 1884. King's Cavalry, Nova Scotia, 1876-7. Surgeon, Q.R.V.B., Royal Scots, 1884. Lothian Volunteer Brigade, Surgeon; Lieut.-Col. 1902. M.O., 15th Royal Scots. School of Instruction for N.C.O's. V.D. 1905; O.B.E. 1919.

WEBSTER, DAVID MACKAY.
Falkirk High School. Student of Science, 1918-20. R.E., July 1915, 2nd Corporal; Officer Cadet June 1917. R.G.A., 2nd Lieut. Nov. 1917 to Dec. 1918. France March 1916 to April 1917.

WEBSTER, IRVIN.
Student of Arts, 1905-6. West Riding Regiment, Captain Dec. 1914. France.

WEBSTER, JAMES SCOTT.
George Watson's College. Student of Medicine, 1909-14. O.T.C. Infantry, Dec. 1909 to May 1913, Cadet. Scots Guards, Private Aug. 1914. R.E. (Special Brigade), Corporal Aug. 1915; Sergeant April 1916; 2nd Lieut. March 1917; Lieut. Sept. 1918. France.

WEBSTER, THOMAS.
George Heriot's School. Student of Law, 1914-15. Chartered Accountant, 1918. O.T.C. Artillery, Jan. to April 1916, Cadet. R.G.A. (T.), East Anglian, Gunner April 1916; Bombardier June 1916.

WEBSTER, WILLIAM LECKIE.
Edinburgh Academy. M.B., Ch.B. 1910. University Battery, E.C.A.V., 1906-8, Sergeant. R.A.M.C., Lieut. 1911; Captain Jan. 1915; Brevet Major Jan. 1919; Major. O.C. 16th Field Ambulance, Egypt, to Oct. 1914; Malta Sept. 1915 to March 1917. France March 1917. Dispatches April and Nov. 1918. Croix de Guerre May 1918.

WEBSTER, WILLIAM MAURICE.
Lord Weymouth's Grammar School; First XI. Student of Medicine, 1916-17. Royal Army Veterinary Corps (Lowland Division), Dispenser, June 1916. 56th Battn., Machine-Gun Corps, France, L/Corporal Sept. 1918 to Feb. 1919.

WEDDERBURN, ALEXANDER ARCHIBALD INNES.
Edinburgh Academy. O.T.C. 1913-15. Student of Arts, 1916-19; M.A. 1920. 18th Royal Scots, Private June to Aug. 1916. Ministry of National Service. Munitions.

WEDDERBURN, ERNEST MACLAGAN.
George Watson's College. M.A. 1904; LL.B. 1906; D.Sc. 1913. Writer to the Signet, 1907. R.E., Meteorological Section, Captain Sept. 1915. G.H.Q., Gallipoli; G.H.Q., Salonika, 1916, and Assistant Superintendent of Experiments, Shoeburyness, 1918. Dispatches (Salonika) 1917 and 1919. O.B.E. 1919.

Record of War Service

WEDDERBURN, JOSEPH HENRY MACLAGAN.
George Watson's College. M.A. 1903; D.Sc. 1908. O.T.C. Infantry, 1908-10, 2nd Lieut. Assistant Professor of Mathematics, Princeton University, New Jersey. 10th Seaforth Highlanders, Lieut. Dec. 1914; Captain Jan. 1915. Transferred R.E. (Field Survey Battn.), Feb. 1918. France. Dispatches July 1919.

WEDDERBURN, LAURENCE CRAIGIE MACLAGAN.
Forfar High School. M.B., Ch.B. 1899; M.D. 1906. South African Campaign, 1901. R.A.M.C., Captain Feb. 1915-16. Royal Navy, Surgeon June 1917. Royal Air Force Medical Service, Captain April 1918; Major Oct. 1918.

WEDDERSPOON, GEORGE.
Royal Academy, Inverness. M.A. 1899. 4th and 7th Cameron Highlanders, 2nd Lieut. April 1915; Captain July 1915. France. Wounded June 1917.

WEDDERSPOON, WILLIAM FARQUHARSON GIBSON.
Student of Arts, 1911-14 and 1916; M.A. 1915. O.T.C. Infantry, March 1913 to June 1914, Cadet. 2nd Devonshire Regiment (S.R.), Lieut. Jan. 1915; Captain and Adjutant to 1917.

WEDECLEFSKY, HARRY EZEKIEL.
Boroughmuir School. Student of Arts, 1912-16; M.A. 1916. 2/5th Gordon Highlanders, Private Sept. 1916; L/Corporal May 1918. Attached 1st Battn. Gordon Highlanders, India.

WEIR, ALEXANDER THOM.
Miller Institution, Thurso. Student of Arts, 1910-14; M.A. 1914. Schoolmaster. 3/2nd Lovat Scouts, Private Nov. 1915; Sergeant Dec. 1916.

WEIR, ANDREW HERON WILSON.
Viewpark School, Edinburgh. Student of Science, 1910-14 and 1918; B.Sc. 1920. O.T.C. Artillery, Oct. 1914 to July 1915, Cadet Bombardier. R.F.A. (T.), 1st Lowland Brigade, 2nd Lieut. July 1915; Lieut. June 1916; Acting Captain July 1917; Acting Major Nov. 1918. India and Mesopotamia. Dispatches (Mesopotamia) Feb. 1919.

WEIR, JOHN HENRY.
George Watson's College. O.T.C. Student of Law, 1911-13. Chartered Accountant, 1914. 9th Royal Scots (T.), Private Aug. 1914. Argyll and Sutherland Highlanders, 2nd Lieut. Dec. 1914; Captain Sept. 1915. Salonika. Invalided out April 1918.

WEIR, JOHN WILLIAM.
Daniel Stewart's College. Cadet Corps 1911-15. University O.T.C. Artillery, March 1917 to Jan. 1918, Cadet; Officer Cadet Feb. 1918. R.G.A., 121st Siege Battery, 2nd Lieut. Aug. 1918.

Record of War Service

WEIR, ROBERT YAXLEY.
Edinburgh Academy; First XI. Student of Law, 1906-8. Chartered Accountant, 1909. 9th Royal Scots, Private Aug. 1914. 1st Lovat Scouts (T.), Captain Dec. 1914; Acting Major March 1917 to Jan. 1919. Dispatches Aug. 1917, Nov. 1918, and March 1919. O.B.E. March 1919.

WELCH, ADAM CLEGHORN.
M.A. 1883; B.D. 1886; D.D. 1913; D.Th. Lecturer in Post Graduate Divinity School. Professor in New College. Chaplain, 4th Class, 1909.

WELLS, H. J.
Student. British East African Mounted Rifles, Trooper.

WELLS, HENRY JAMES GORDON.
St Paul's, London. Cadet Corps 1902-4. M.B., Ch.B. 1910. O.T.C. Artillery, Oct. 1908 to Nov. 1910, Cadet Sergeant. R.A.M.C., Lieut. 1911; Captain Jan. 1915. N.-W. Frontier, India, 1914 and 1917-19; Mesopotamia 1915-16.

WELLS, JOSEPH DOUGLAS.
George Watson's College. M.B., Ch.B. 1905. Volunteer Medical Staff Corps, 1900-6, L/Corporal. R.A.M.C. (T.), Lieut. 1909; Captain 1913; Acting Major June 1918. 4th Suffolk Regiment, France, Nov. 1914-17; Italy 1917-19. O.B.E. and Dispatches Jan. 1918.

WELSH, DAVID CHARLES.
M.B., Ch.B. 1903. No. 4 Coy. Q.R.V.B., Royal Scots, 1898-1903, Sergeant. R.A.M.C., Lieut. May 1915; Captain May 1916.

WELSH, THOMAS SCOTT.
Edinburgh Academy and Fettes College. Student of Arts and Law, 1892-9. Writer to the Signet, 1899. Royal Army Ordnance Corps, Private Sept. 1917.

WELSH, WILLIAM HALLIDAY.
Merchiston Castle; First XV. and XI. Cadet Corps 1894-9, Captain. M.B., Ch.B. 1906; M.D. (Gold Medal) 1910. Scottish Rugby International. R.A.M.C., Lieut. Oct. 1915; Captain 1916; Major Jan. 1918. 21st Stationary Hospital, Salonika. Greek M.M. for Merit.

WEST, LEONARD.
M.B., Ch.B. 1903. R.A.M.C. (T.), Lieut.; Captain April 1915; Acting Major Jan. 1918. Herts Yeomanry.

WESTHUIJZEN, JOHAN FREDERICK VAN DER.
Student of Medicine, 1910-15; M.B., Ch.B. 1914. O.T.C. Medical, Nov. 1914, Cadet. R.A.M.C. (S.R.), Lieut.

WESTON, WILLIAM GORDON.
Student of Medicine, 1907-15; M.B., Ch.B. 1915. R.A.M.C., Lieut.; Captain.

Record of War Service

WESTWATER, JOHN SINCLAIR.
George Watson's College, Edinburgh, and Eltham College, Kent; First XV. and XI. Student of Medicine, 1910-19; M.B., Ch.B. 1919. O.T.C. Medical, Oct. 1915 to Feb. 1916, Cadet. R.N.V.R., Surgeon Sub-Lieut. March 1916. Invalided out Oct. 1917. D.S.C. May 1917.

WESTWOOD, JOHN SHARPE.
Royal High School. Student of Science, 1914 and 1919. O.T.C. Engineers, Oct. 1914 to Sept. 1915, Cadet. 9th Gordon Highlanders, 2nd Lieut. Sept. 1915; Lieut. July 1917.

WHAIT, JOHN ROBERT.
University College, London. M.B., C.M. 1892; B.Sc. (P.H.) 1893; M.R.C.S. (Eng.) and L.R.C.P. (Lond.) 1893. R.A.M.C. (V.) and (T.), 1894; Lieut.-Col. 1912. France. 85th (3rd London) Field Ambulance, 28th Division, 1914-19. Dispatches 1915 (twice); 1916 (twice); 1917 and 1918. Order of White Eagle, 4th Class (with Swords), Serbia, 1917. D.S.O. 1918; T.D.

WHEATLEY, LEONARD ABERCROMBY.
Royal High School. M.A. 1913. O.T.C. Infantry, Dec. 1914 to April 1915, Cadet. 9th Royal Scots Fusiliers, 2nd Lieut. April 1915. 61st Battn. Machine-Gun Corps, Lieut. July 1917. Gallipoli and France.

WHETTER, JOHN PEARCE.
M.B., Ch.B. 1909. R.A.M.C., Lieut. 1915-16. N.Z. Medical Corps, Captain Nov. 1917. Regimental M.O., 1/5th Argyll and Sutherland Highlanders, Gallipoli and Egypt, 1915-16.

WHIGHAM, WALTER KENNEDY.
Student of Law, 1898-1900. Chartered Accountant, 1901. 6th North Staffordshire Regiment (T.), Lieut. Aug. 1914; Captain June 1915. France March 1915 to Jan. 1919. Three times Mentioned in Dispatches. O.B.E.

WHITAKER, HARRY.
M.B., Ch.B. 1911. R.A.M.C., Captain April 1915. M.C.

WHITAKER, J. RYLAND.
Viewpark School, Edinburgh. University O.T.C. Artillery, May 1915 to July 1916, Cadet Sergeant; Officer Cadet July 1916. R.F.A., 2nd Lieut. Sept. 1916; Lieut. March 1918-19. France 1916-19. M.C. April 1917.

WHITE, ADAM.
Edinburgh Institution. M.B., Ch.B. 1908. D.T.M. & H. 1910; D.P.H. (Camb.) 1912. R.A.M.C., Lieut. April 1915; Captain Dec. 1915. Dispatches Nov. 1918.

WHITE, CHARLES.
George Heriot's School; First XV. O.T.C. 1909-13, Cadet L/Corporal. Student of Science, 1918. R.E. (Signal Service), 2nd Lieut. July 1915; Lieut. June 1917.

Record of War Service

WHITE, CHARLES RICHARDSON.
Daniel Stewart's College; First XV. M.B., ChB. 1909; L.R.C.P. & S. (Edin.) and L.F.P.S. (Glasg.) 1898. South African Campaign, 1900-2. R.A.M.C. (V.) and (T.), Surgeon-Lieut. 1903; Surgeon-Captain 1907; Major Aug. 1914 to March 1919; Temp. Lieut.-Col. 2nd Welsh Field Ambulance; Welsh Casualty Clearing Station. Suvla Bay, Egypt, Palestine, and 47th General Hospital, France, 1915-19. Dispatches Sept. 1917 and Jan. 1918. D.S.O. Jan. 1918.

WHITE, GEORGE THOMAS FROOD.
B.Sc. 1913. O.T.C. Engineers, Jan. 1910 to Sept. 1914, Cadet Acting Sergeant. R.E. (S.R.), 2nd Lieut. Oct. 1914; Captain Nov. 1917. Twice Wounded.

WHITE, HENRY ELLIS YEO.
Bradford Grammar School; First XV. M.B., Ch.B. 1911. Royal Navy, Surgeon 1913; Surgeon-Lieut.-Commander April 1919. H.M. Ships *Commonwealth* and *Renown*.

WHITE, HORACE POWELL WINSBURY.
Marlborough College, New Zealand. Cadet Corps 1904-8, Colour-Sergeant. M.B., Ch.B. 1914; F.R.C.S. (Edin.) 1917. O.T.C. Infantry, 1909-12, Cadet Corporal. R.A.M.C., Lieut. Nov. 1914. N.Z. Medical Corps, Captain April 1917. France and The Rhine. Wounded at second Ypres May 1915.

WHITE, JOHN LETHAM.
George Watson's College. B.Sc. 1906. A.M.I.C.E. Lothians and Border Horse, 1909. R.E., 2nd Lieut. Aug. 1915; Lieut. May 1916; Captain May 1918. Staff Officer to Chief Engineer, 8th Corps, Nov. 1918. Dispatches (Egypt) April 1918, (France) Jan. and July 1919. Cavalier of Order of Crown of Italy, Nov. 1918.

WHITE, JOHN MAIR.
Glasgow Academy. O.T.C. 1914-16. University O.T.C. Artillery, Feb. to Aug. 1917, Cadet Sergeant; Officer Cadet Aug. 1917. R.F.A., 72nd Battery, 2nd Lieut. Feb. 1918. 38th Brigade, France, June 1918. Wounded Oct. 1918.

WHITE, JOHN WALTON.
Edinburgh Academy; First XV. O.T.C. 1908-11. B.Sc. 1913. O.T.C. Engineers, Nov. 1910 to Feb. 1914, Cadet. Loyal North Lancashire Regiment, 2nd Lieut. 1914. Machine-Gun Corps, 1916. Tank Corps, Lieut. July 1916; Captain Dec. 1917. France. Wounded.

WHITE, JOSHUA CHAYTOR.
M.B., C.M. 1887; M.D. 1893. Indian Medical Service, Lieut.-Col. Chitral 1895. O.C. Indian Convalescent Depôt, Barton, Hants, Nov. 1914 to April 1919. C.M.G. Mention March and Aug. 1916.

WHITE, RICHARD.
Edinburgh Academy. Student of Law, 1901-4. Writer to the Signet, 1906. O.T.C. Artillery, May to Nov. 1916, Cadet Acting Bombardier; Officer Cadet Nov. 1916. R.G.A., 2nd Lieut. Feb. 1917. Invalided out Feb. 1918.

Record of War Service

WHITE, ROBERT LEISHMAN.
Daniel Stewart's College; First XV. and XI. Cadet Corps 1914-17. University O.T.C. Infantry, Dec. 1917 to Aug. 1918, Cadet. Cameron Highlanders, Officer Cadet Sept. 1918; 2nd Lieut. March 1919.

WHITE, ROBERT SIDNEY.
Allan Glen's, Glasgow. University O.T.C. Artillery, Feb. to Aug. 1916, Cadet; Officer Cadet Sept. 1916. R.F.A., 2nd Lieut. Jan. 1917; Lieut. July 1918. France. Gassed April 1918.

WHITE, WALTER CROKER POOLE.
M.B., Ch.B. 1904. Royal Navy, Surgeon Oct. 1914. R.N. Hospital, Haslar.

WHITEFORD, JAMES HARRIS GARCIA.
Merchiston Castle; First XV. and XI. M.B., C.M. 1891; D.P.H. 1900 and B.A. (Camb.) 1886. R.A.M.C. (V.) and (T.), 1892; Major 1904; Lieut.-Col. June 1916. Sanitary Officer, Clyde Defences, 1914-19. Mention March 1919.

WHITEFORD, ROBERT PATRICK.
Kelso High School. M.A. 1915. R.A.M.C., 3rd Lowland Field Ambulance, Private Oct. 1915. 3rd King's Own Scottish Borderers, 1917. 12th Royal Scots, 1918-19.

WHITEHEAD, WILLIAM.
Falkirk High School; First XI. Student of Arts, 1913-15; M.A. 1919. O.T.C. Infantry, Oct. 1914 to March 1915, Cadet. Gordon Highlanders, Private April 1915; L/Corporal June 1915. R.E., Corporal Sept. 1915; 2nd Lieut. June 1917; Lieut. Dec. 1918 to Feb. 1919. France 1915-19. M.M. June 1917.

WHITELAW, WILLIAM MENZIES.
Collegiate School, Toronto. B.A. (Toronto) 1910; B.D. (New York) 1914. Student of Divinity, 1914. Y.M.C.A., Egypt, 1915; Mesopotamia 1916, and German East Africa 1917. Canadian Army, Hon. Lieut. Sept. 1917.

WHITELEY, REGINALD FREDERICK.
Daniel Stewart's College. Student of Arts and Divinity; M.A. 1915. O.T.C. Infantry, Feb. 1912 to March 1915, Cadet. Duke of Cornwall's Light Infantry, 2nd Lieut. March 1915; Lieut. Feb. 1917. Prisoner of War, Karlsruhe, Nov. 1917.

WHITELOCKE, RICHARD HENRY ANGLIN.
M.B., C.M. (Hons.) 1884; M.D. 1903; F.R.C.S. (Eng.) 1893; M.A. (Hons. Oxford) 1910. R.A.M.C. (T.), Major 1908. Mobilised Aug. 1914; Lieut.-Col. 1916. 3rd Southern General and Somerville Hospitals, Oxford, 1915-19.

WHITTOME, ARTHUR.
M.B., Ch.B. 1899; F.R.C.S. (Edin.) 1903. R.A.M.C., Lieut. Jan. 1916. H.M. Hospital Ship *Aquitania*.

Record of War Service

WHITTON, ALFRED BELL.
 M.B., C.M. 1885. 6th Gordon Highlanders (T.), Lieut.-Col. (Retired). R.A.M.C. (T.), Major on rejoining June 1915. 4/1st Highland Field Ambulance.

WHYTE, ALEXANDER FREDERICK.
 M.A. 1905. M.P. R.N.V.R., Hon. Lieut. Nov. 1914.

WHYTE, ARCHIBALD CAWDOR CAMPBELL.
 Inverness Royal Academy. M.A. 1909; LL.B. 1912. 4th, 3rd, and 2nd Cameron Highlanders, Private Nov. 1915; L/Corporal. 6th and 11th Royal Scots, 2nd Lieut. May 1918. Salonika, France, and The Rhine.

WHYTE, GEORGE FRANCIS.
 M.B., C.M. 1896. R.A.M.C. (V.) and (T.), 1900; Major 1912; Acting Lieut.-Col. April 1918. Attached 5th Royal Highlanders (Black Watch) (T.). Dundee War Hospital and O.C. 30th Casualty Clearing Station. 2/1st Highland Field Ambulance. France 1914. Dispatches Jan. 1919. T.D. Croix de Guerre 1918.

WHYTE, GUSTAVUS AIRD.
 Merchiston Castle. Cadet Corps 1902-4. Student of Science, 1908-14; B.Sc. 1914. Scottish Horse (T.), 2nd Lieut. Aug. 1914; Lieut. April 1915; Captain Aug. 1915; Major March 1917. M.C.

WHYTE, JAMES.
 Broughton School, Edinburgh; First XI. Student of Arts and Science, 1918-19. 2nd Scottish Rifles, Private July 1916; L/Corporal. Wounded.

WHYTE, JOHN MACKIE.
 Royal High School. M.A. 1878; M.B., C.M. 1882; M.D. 1897. Examiner in Systematic Medicine, 1916-19. R.A.M.C. (T.), Captain Dec. 1912. 1st Scottish General Hospital, Aug. to Dec. 1914; Dundee War Hospital, Sept. 1915 to Jan. 1918; 58th General Hospital, France, March to July 1918.

WHYTE, JOHN PATTULLO MACKIE.
 Edinburgh Academy; First XV. O.T.C. 1914-17. Student of Science, 1919. O.T.C. Artillery, May to Dec. 1917, Cadet Bombardier; Officer Cadet Dec. 1917. R.F.A., 2nd Lieut. June 1918. France. Gassed Sept. 1918.

WHYTT, ALEXANDER.
 Birkenhead School. M.B., C.M. 1894; M.D. 1897. R.A.M.C., Lieut. Nov. 1915; Captain Nov. 1916. Hospital Ship *St David*. France.

WICKHAM, HARRY TOWNSHEND.
 Harrow. M.B., Ch.B. 1888; M.D. 1894. Volunteer Medical Corps, Lieut. April 1918. M.O. in charge of Twickford Abbey Auxiliary Hospital.

WICKS, MARGARET CAMPBELL WALKER.
 M.A. (Hons. Mod. Lang.) 1914. Q.M.A.A.C., Assistant Administrator, Aug. 1917; Deputy Administrator, Dec. 1918; Acting Unit Administrator, April 1919. France.

Record of War Service

WEIR, HENRY WOOD.
Campbell College, Belfast. M.B., Ch.B. 1914. O.T.C. Medical, 1908-11, Cadet. R.A.M.C., 83rd Field Ambulance Lieut. Dec. 1914; Captain June 1915. France Dec. 1914; Salonika 1915-19. Dispatches June 1918.

WIGHT, ANDREW.
Royal High School. M.B., Ch.B. 1905. M.O. Lady Bagot Hospital, Adinkerke, Feb. to May 1915. R.A.M.C., Lieut. Sept. 1915. 41st Field Ambulance, Gallipoli, and 8th Cheshire Regiment, Oct. 1915-16; 41st Field Ambulance, Mesopotamia, March to Aug. 1916. Dalmeny House Hospital, 1917.

WIGHT, JOHN DONALD.
Trinity Academy, Leith. University O.T.C. Engineers, March to Oct. 1918, Cadet; Officer Cadet Oct. 1918. Tank Corps, 2nd Lieut.

WIGHTMAN, ARTHUR ROBERTSON.
Merchiston Castle. Cadet Corps 1902-7. M.B., Ch.B. 1912. R.A.M.C., Lieut. Feb. 1915; Captain Feb. 1916.

WIGHTMAN, GEORGE LINDORES.
Merchiston Castle. Cadet Corps 1903-7. Student of Law, 1908-13. Chartered Accountant, 1913. O.T.C. Infantry, Sept. to Oct. 1914, Cadet. 3rd Gordon Highlanders, 2nd Lieut. Nov. 1914; Lieut. 1915; Captain 1916; Major 1917. Royal Air Force. Dispatches Jan. 1917 and April 1918.

WIGHTMAN, ROBERT BROWN.
Royal High School. University O.T.C. Medical, 1917, Cadet. Royal Air Force, Officer Cadet Sept. 1917; 2nd Lieut. Feb. 1918. Flying Officer May 1918.

WILKIE, DAVID PERCIVAL DALBRECK.
Edinburgh Academy; First XV. M.B., Ch.B. 1904; M.D. 1908; Ch.M. (Gold Medal) 1909; F.R.C.S. (Edin.) 1907 and (Eng.) 1918. Assistant Surgeon, R.I.E. R.N.V.R., H.M. Hospital Ship *Margaret of Scotland*, Staff Surgeon. R.N. Barracks, Portsmouth. Lent to Army, Casualty Clearing Station, France, 1918. O.B.E. (Military) Sept. 1919.

WILKIN, BERTRAM OSBORNE.
Student of Medicine, 1911-14. O.T.C. Medical, May 1912 to Aug. 1914, Cadet. 6th Duke of Cornwall's Light Infantry, 2nd Lieut. Aug. 1914. Wiltshire Regiment. Prisoner of War.

WILKINS, RICHARD.
Rydal Mount, Colwyn Bay. M.B., Ch.B. 1905; F.R.C.S. (Edin.) 1910. V.A.D. Hospital, Moor Park, Preston. Royal Navy, Temp. Surgeon April 1917. Dispatches 1919. Médaille d'Honneur des Épidémies, 1918.

Record of War Service

WILKS, ARTHUR STRINGER.
    Brighton College. Student of Arts, 1891-2. A.S.C., Lieut. Dec. 1914; Captain July 1915.

WILL, WILLIAM JOHNSTONE.
    East Taieri School, New Zealand. M.B., C.M. 1884. Q.E.R. 1880-4, Private. N.Z. Medical Corps, 1885; Colonel and A.D.M.S. Mobilised Aug. 1914. V.D. 1906. Knight of Grace of Order of St John of Jerusalem, 1915.

WILLCOCK, MAURICE EXELL.
    Fettes College. O.T.C. 1908-10. Student of Medicine, 1910-15; M.B., Ch.B. 1915. O.T.C. Medical, Nov. 1914-15, Cadet. R.A.M.C., Lieut. July 1915; Captain July 1916. Salonika, Egypt, and Mesopotamia.

WILLIAMS, ALFRED ERNEST.
    M.B., C.M. 1896; M.D. 1904; D.P.H. (Liverpool) 1907. R.A.M.C., Lieut.; Captain Feb. 1915. Sanitary Officer.

WILLIAMS, CHARLES LOUIS.
    Liverpool College; First XI. M.B., C.M. 1886; M.D. 1889. Indian Medical Service, 1889; Major 1901. Retired 1907. Rejoined Nov. 1914. Surgeon.

WILLIAMS, FREDERICK JAMES HORSLEY.
    M.A. 1911. Schoolmaster. Royal Scots Fusiliers, 2nd Lieut.; Lieut. July 1917.

WILLIAMS, GEORGE BRUCE.
    Wick High School. Student of Science, 1916-17 and 1918. O.T.C. Artillery, Dec. 1916 to April 1917, Cadet. R.F.C., Officer Cadet April 1917; 2nd Lieut. Aug. 1917; Royal Air Force, Lieut. April 1918.

WILLIAMS, GOMER.
    M.B., Ch.B. 1913; M.D. 1914. O.T.C. Infantry, 1910, Cadet. Assistant in Materia Medica. Royal Navy, Surgeon Oct. 1914. R.N. Hospital, Plymouth.

WILLIAMS, ILLTYD GWYN.
    Llandovery College. Student of Medicine, 1914-15 and 1918-20. O.T.C. Infantry, Oct. 1914 to Aug. 1915, Cadet. R.E. (Special Brigade), Corporal; Sergeant.

WILLIAMS, JAMES LAWSON.
    Edinburgh Collegiate School. M.B., C.M. 1890; M.D. 1896. R.A.M.C., Lieut. May 1915; Captain May 1916. France.

WILLIAMS, JOHN ROBERT.
    M.B., C.M. 1890. R.A.M.C. (V.) and (T.), 1900, Major Sept. 1914. S.M.O., North Wales Infantry Brigade. Attached B.R.C.S., France, Assistant Medical Assessor, 1917-19.

Record of War Service

WILLIAMS, JOHN WILLIAM.
Christ's College, Christchurch, New Zealand. M.B., C.M. 1891; M.D. 1898. N.Z. Medical Corps, Captain. 2nd N.Z. General Hospital, Walton-on-Thames.

WILLIAMS, OWEN HERBERT.
Liverpool Institute. M.B., Ch.B. 1906; F.R.C.S. (Edin.) 1909; D.P.H. (Oxford) 1911. R.A.M.C. (T.) (West Lancs. Division), Major Jan. 1915. 51st (Highland) Casualty Clearing Station, France.

WILLIAMS, SEYMOUR.
M.B., Ch.B. 1910. R.A.M.C., Lieut.; Captain March 1916.

WILLIAMS, THOMAS SAMUEL BEAUCHAMP.
Magdalen College School, Oxford, and H.M.S. *Conway* Training Ship. M.B., Ch.B. 1901. Indian Medical Service, 1902; Major 1913; Brevet Lieut.-Col. June 1917. Attached 87th Punjabis, N. W. Frontier, India, 1915. Mesopotamia 1916-18. Dispatches (Mesopotamia).

WILLIAMS, WILLIAM EDWARD REES.
Wellingborough School. M.B., Ch.B. 1906. Indian Medical Service, 1907; Captain 1910; Temp. Major Aug. 1918; Major Feb. 1919. France Oct. 1914 to Dec. 1915; Mesopotamia Jan. 1916-18. Dispatches Nov. 1917 and June 1919. O.B.E. June 1919.

WILLIAMS, WILLIAM REGINALD EYTON.
Oswestry Grammar School. M.B., Ch.B. 1899; M.R.C.S. (Eng.) and L.R.C.P. (Lond.) 1900. South African Campaign, 1899-1901. R.A.M.C., 1904; Major March 1916. Invalided out Jan. 1919.

WILLIAMS, WYNDHAM.
Student of Medicine, 1911-16. M.B., Ch.B. 1915. O.T.C. Medical, May 1911 to Sept. 1914, Cadet. R.A.M.C. (S.R.), Lieut. Sept. 1914; Captain July 1916.

WILLIAMSON, ALEXANDER BOYD.
Ayr Academy. Student of Arts, Science and Medicine, 1913-15; M.A. 1920. O.T.C. Artillery, 1914-15, Cadet. R.F.A. (T.), 2nd Lowland Brigade, 2nd Lieut. June 1915; Lieut. June 1916; Acting Adjutant Sept. to Nov. 1918; Acting Captain Jan. to Aug. 1919. 52nd Lowland and 7th (Indian) Meerut Divisions. Egypt, Palestine, and Syria, Aug. 1917-19.

WILLIAMSON, ALEXANDER JEANS.
Knox Institute, Haddington. M.B., Ch.B. 1900. R.A.M.C., 1901; Major 1913; Acting Lieut.-Col. Dec. 1915. 138th Field Ambulance; 12th Casualty Clearing Station, and 2nd Scottish General Hospital, Singapore, Aug. 1914 to Oct. 1915. France, May to Oct. 1916, and April 1918 to July 1919. Dispatches July 1919.

WILLIAMSON, ANDREW WALLACE.
M.A. 1878; D.D. Minister, Church of Scotland. Chaplain, 1st Class, Aug. 1913. 1st Lowland Brigade, R.F.A. (T.).

Record of War Service

WILLIAMSON, ARCHIBALD MOIR.
Aberdeen Grammar School. University O.T.C. Infantry, 1917-18, Cadet; Officer Cadet. 1st Garrison Reserve Battn., Highland Light Infantry, 2nd Lieut. Sept. 1918.

WILLIAMSON, DAVID HARDIE.
Perth Academy. Student of Medicine, 1912-14 and 1918. R.N.V.R., H.M.S. *Peyton*, Surgeon-Sub.-Lieut. Oct. 1915. Battle of Jutland, May 1916.

WILLIAMSON, DAVID JAMES.
M.B., Ch.B. 1907; M.D. 1908. R.N.V.R. (Drake Battn.), 1st Brigade. R.N. Division, Surgeon. Antwerp Expedition.

WILLIAMSON, GEORGE ROBERTSON.
Daniel Stewart's College. Cadet Corps 1912-17, Sergeant. Student of Arts and Commerce, 1919. O.T.C. Artillery, Jan. to Aug. 1917, Cadet Corporal. Forth R.G.A. (T.), Officer Cadet Aug. 1917; 2nd Lieut. Dec. 1917; Lieut. July 1920.

WILLIAMSON, GEORGE SCOTT.
Barnard Castle. M.B., Ch.B. 1914; L.R.C.P. & S. (Edin.) and L.F.P.S. (Glasg.) 1907. Volunteer Medical Staff Corps, 1903-7. R.A.M.C. (T.), 1909; Lieut.-Col. April 1917. France. Prisoner of War. Dispatches July 1915. M.C. 1918.

WILLIAMSON, JAMES HENRY.
George Watson's College. Student of Law, 1912-15. Chartered Accountant, 1916. Royal Scots, 2nd Lieut. Dec. 1915; Lieut. May 1918. Twice Wounded.

WILLIAMSON, JAMES WALKER-MORISON.
George Watson's College and Repton. M.A. 1904. Secretary and President, S.R.C. Minister, Church of Scotland. Chaplain, 4th Class, July 1916. 2/9th Argyll and Sutherland Highlanders, July 1916; 14th Scottish Rifles, Dec. 1916; 6th King's Own Scottish Borderers, Aug. 1917; 20th Casualty Clearing Station, Sept. to Dec. 1918; Hon. Chaplain 1919.

WILLIAMSON, JOHN.
Wick Academy. M.A. 1905. Schoolmaster. R.G.A., Gunner Feb. 1918.

WILLIAMSON, JOHN RUTTER.
M.B., Ch.B. 1898; M.D. 1902. Indian Medical Service, Captain (Retired). Lady Hardinge's Hospital, Brockenhurst. R.A.M.C., Captain Jan. 1916. Military Hospital, Edmonton. Mention Feb. 1917.

WILLIAMSON, KENNETH BAMFORD.
Mill Hill School. O.T.C. 1911-13, Cadet Sergeant. Student of Medicine, 1913-14 and 1918. O.T.C. Artillery, Oct. 1913 to Nov. 1914, Cadet. R.G.A., 2nd Lieut. Nov. 1914; Lieut. Sept. 1915; Captain Sept. 1917; Acting Major Jan. 1917. Dispatches Jan. 1917. M.C. Oct. 1917.

WILLIAMSON, RICHARD ERNEST. (See p. 752.)

Record of War Service

WILLOX, LEONARD STEPHEN.
: M.B., Ch.B. 1911; M.D. (Gold Medal) 1914; D.P.H. (Camb.) 1913. R.A.M.C. (T.), Lieut. Aug. 1915; Captain March 1916. Sanitary Specialist, Macedonia and Caucasus, Bulgaria and France. Attached R.E. on H.Q. Staff.

WILLS, CHARLES RICHARD.
: Repton. M.B., Ch.B. 1906. Yeomanry, Private 1900. R.A.M.C., Lieut. June 1915; Captain June 1916; Major May 1918. Wounded. Prisoner of War.

WILLS, EDWARD FERRIS.
: School for Sons of Missionaries, Blackheath. M.B., C.M. 1896. R.A.M.C., Lieut. May 1917; Captain May 1918. No. 3 Native Labour General Hospital, France.

WILSON, ANDREW.
: Royal High School; First XV. Student of Science, 1901-2. M.I.C.E. Officer Cadet Aug. 1916. R.E., 2nd Lieut. Nov. 1916; Lieut. Feb. 1917; Captain March 1918; Major June 1918. Assistant Controller of Labour, Independent Air Force, France. Dispatches Dec. 1918. O.B.E. Jan. 1919.

WILSON, ANDREW JOHN.
: Madras College, St Andrews. Student of Science, 1908-10. C.D.A. 1910. Northern Rhodesian Rifles, Private 1914. 1st King's African Rifles, 2nd Lieut. May 1916; Lieut. Dec. 1916. German East African Frontier, Nyasaland. Wounded 1917. M.C. June 1918.

WILSON, ANDREW ROBERTSON.
: Edinburgh Collegiate School. M.A. 1890; M.B., C.M. 1895; M.D. 1901. No. 4 Coy. Q.R.V.B., Royal Scots, 1888-96, Colour-Sergeant. Assistant to Professor of Materia Medica, 1896-7. R.A.M.C. (V.) and (T.), 1888. Mobilised Aug. 1914; Lieut.-Col. Nov. 1914. 3rd Welsh Field Ambulance. Mention Sept. 1917.

WILSON, ARTHUR JAMES.
: St Joseph's College, Dumfries. O.T.C. 1914-16, Cadet Sergeant. Student of Medicine, 1916-17 and 1918. O.T.C. Infantry, March to Sept. 1917, and Medical, April 1918 to Jan. 1919. R.F.C., Sept. 1917. R.A.M.C., Corporal.

WILSON, DAVID.
: Daniel Stewart's College; First XV. Cadet Battn. 1912-17. Student of Arts, 1918. O.T.C. Infantry, 1918, Cadet; Officer Cadet Sept. 1918. Royal Scots, 2nd Lieut. Dec. 1918.

WILSON, DAVID.
: Boroughmuir School. Student of Medicine, 1916-17 and 1919. Seaforth Highlanders, L/Corporal Jan. 1917.

WILSON, DAVID.
: Bathgate Academy. M.A. 1913. Dundas Bursar. Schoolmaster. A.S.C. (M.T.), 13th Coy., attached R.G.A., Private Aug. 1916. Caterpillar Section, attached 62nd Siege Battery, France.

Record of War Service

WILSON, DAVID COOK.
Edinburgh Academy. O.T.C. 1912-14. Student of Medicine, 1913-14 and 1918. O.T.C. Infantry, Oct. 1914 to May 1915, Cadet. 4th Royal Highlanders (Black Watch) (T.), 2nd Lieut. May 1915; Lieut. July 1918. France 1916-17.

WILSON, DONALD McDONALD.
M.B., Ch.B. 1911. R.A.M.C., Lieut.; Captain. M.C.

WILSON, DUNCAN KIPPEN.
Perth Academy. M.A., B.Sc. 1910. Royal Scots. Transferred R.E., Aug. 1915. R.G.A., 2nd Lieut. July 1916. France. Wounded at Ypres Aug. 1917.

WILSON, EDWARD.
Burntisland School. M.A. 1892. Schoolmaster. 2nd Royal Scots (V.), Private April 1917.

WILSON, EDWARD ALEXANDER.
Dollar Academy; First XV. O.T.C. 1913-16, Cadet L/Corporal. Student of Medicine, 1915-17 and 1918. Anatomy Staff, 1919. O.T.C. Infantry, May 1916-17, Cadet. R.N.V.R., H.M.S. *Jonquil*, Surgeon-Sub-Lieut. April 1918 to Feb. 1919.

WILSON, EDWARD JOHN.
Berwickshire High School. M.A. 1914. O.T.C. Artillery, 1914-15, Cadet. Forth R.G.A. (T.), 2nd Lieut. April 1915; Lieut. June 1916; Acting Captain April 1917. France. Wounded at Ypres Nov. 1917 and at Nesle Aug. 1918.

WILSON, FERGUS SMITH ROSSLYN.
Student of Law, 1909-10. Chartered Accountant, 1913. Cameron Highlanders, Private.

WILSON, FORSYTH JAMES.
B.Sc. 1901; D.Sc. 1910; Ph.D. 12th Highland Light Infantry, Sept. 1914; Captain Jan. 1915. Chemical Adviser, XI. Corps, France.

WILSON, FREDERIC ERNEST.
M.B., Ch.B. 1901. R.A.M.C., Lieut.; Captain May 1918. India.

WILSON, FREDERICK.
M.B., C.M. 1896. R.A.M.C., Lieut. Aug. 1914; Captain Aug. 1917.

WILSON, GEORGE.
Dumfries Academy. M.B., C.M. 1881; M.R.C.S. (Lond.). R.A.M.C., Surgeon 1884; Major 1896; Lieut.-Col. 1904. Ashanti Expedition, 1895; Sierra Leone, 1898; South African Campaign, 1899-1902. Reading War Hospital, March 1915; O.C. Cambridge Hospital, Aldershot.

WILSON, GEORGE.
George Watson's College. Student of Medicine, 1918. 4th Royal Scots, Private Aug. 1916; L/Corporal March 1917; Corporal Sept. 1917. Labour Corps. National Service, 1918.

Record of War Service

WILSON, GEORGE.
  M.B., Ch.B. R.A.M.C., Captain. 9th North Staffordshire Regiment. France.

WILSON, GEORGE.
  George Watson's College. Student of Medicine, 1912-13 and 1918. O.T.C. Artillery, Nov. 1912 to April 1916, Cadet. R.F.A., 17th Battery, Gunner March 1916; Bombardier June 1916; Corporal Jan. 1917; Officer Cadet 1918.

WILSON, GEORGE D.
  Student of Law, 1910-13. Chartered Accountant, 1914. F.F.A. 8th Royal Scots (T.), 2nd Lieut.; Lieut. June 1916. France.

WILSON, GEORGE RICHARD.
  Collége de Beaucamps, Lille, France. M.B., C.M. 1892. University Battery, E.C.A.V., 1890-1, Gunner. 4th East Lancashire Regiment, 2nd Lieut. 1899; Lieut. 1900; Captain 1901. R.A.M.C. (T.), Major 1915. Attached 2/8th Manchester Regiment, 11th Battn. Norfolk Regiment, and Bedfordshire Regiment, Oct. 1915 to March 1919.

WILSON, GORDON.
  Waresly Lodge, Cheltenham. M.B., Ch.B. 1908. Army Medical Service, Lieut. 1911; Captain July 1914; Acting Major 1918 to April 1920. Mesopotamia 1914-16; Waziristan Field Force, 1917; India 1918-20. Twice Mentioned in Dispatches (Mesopotamia). M.C. (Ctesiphon).

WILSON, GREGG.
  Royal High School. M.A. 1885; B.Sc. 1891; D.Sc. 1897. Demonstrator in Zoology, Edinburgh University, and Professor of Zoology, Queen's University, Belfast. Belfast University O.T.C. (T.), Major and O.C. 1910. School of Instruction, 1915-16.

WILSON, HAROLD WILLIAM.
  Wanganui Collegiate School, New Zealand. Athletics. Cadet Corps 1902-7, Lieut. M.B., Ch.B. 1913. R.A.M.C., Lieut. Feb. 1915; Captain Feb. 1916. 51st and 34th Field Ambulances, and 9th and 8th Northumberland Fusiliers, France. N.Z. Medical Corps, Feb. 1918.

WILSON, HUGH CAMERON.
  George Watson's College. M.B., Ch.B. 1905; M.D. 1908; F.R.C.S. (Eng.) 1911. Volunteer Medical Staff Corps, 1900-4, Private. R.A.M.C., Lieut. July 1916; Captain July 1917; Major Jan. 1918.

WILSON, JAMES.
  George Watson's College; First XV. M.B., C.M. 1887. Q.E.R., 1880-6. R.A.M.C. (V.) and (T.), 1898; Major 1910; Brevet Lieut.-Col. 1917; Acting Lieut.-Col. 1917-19. Military Hospital, Edinburgh Castle, Aug. 1914; 69th General Hospital, Egypt and Palestine, July 1917 to May 1919. T.D. 1915.

WILSON, JAMES ALEXANDER SUTHERLAND.
  George Watson's College. M.A. 1903; B.A. (Oxford) 1908; L.C.P. Minister, Church of Scotland. Chaplain, 4th Class, Jan. 1917. Egypt and Palestine.

Record of War Service

WILSON, JAMES HOURSTON.
Stromness School. R.G.A. (Orkney). Student of Arts and Science; M.A. 1913; B.Sc. 1920. O.T.C. Engineers, Oct. 1912-14, Cadet. R.E. (T.), City of Dundee (Fortress), Sapper Oct. 1914; Sergeant March 1915; 2nd Lieut. Aug. 1917; Lieut. Feb. 1919; Acting Captain Jan. 1919. France May 1915-19. M.C. 1919.

WILSON, JAMES LESLIE.
George Watson's College. O.T.C. 1909-13, Cadet Sergeant. Student of Medicine, 1913-15 and 1918; M.B., Ch.B. 1919. O.T.C. Artillery, 1914-16, Cadet. R.N.V.R., Surgeon-Sub-Lieut. April 1916. H.M. Ships *Crusader*, *Express*, and *Osiris*.

WILSON, JAMES MILLAR.
Student of Medicine, 1909-14. R.G.A., 2nd Lieut.

WILSON, JAMES RANKINE HALL.
Stonyhurst College. O.T.C. 1909-16, Cadet Sergeant. University O.T.C. Artillery, Feb. to Aug. 1917, Cadet; Officer Cadet Aug. 1917. R.F.A., 382nd Battery, 2nd Lieut. Jan. 1918; Lieut. July 1919. France.

WILSON, JAMES ROBERT.
Dumfries Academy. Student of Law, 1915-16 and 1919. O.T.C. Artillery, Cadet. Motor Machine-Gun Corps, Private Sept. 1916; Corporal Jan 1917; Sergeant Feb. 1917; Officer Cadet; 2nd Lieut. March 1918. Tank Corps.

WILSON, JOHN.
Student of Law, 1879-81. Chartered Accountant, 1884. Q.R.V.B., Royal Scots, 1887-1907; Major Jan. 1905. 2/5th Royal Scots, Oct. 1914. T.F. Reserve, 1916.

WILSON, JOHN.
Leith Academy. M.A. 1912. Schoolmaster. 10th Royal Fusiliers, Private. Dec. 1916; Sergeant Nov. 1917. Attached Intelligence Corps.

WILSON, JOHN GORDON.
M.A. 1883; M.B., C.M. 1889. Canadian Army Medical Corps, Captain Aug. 1916. Westcliff Hospital, Folkestone. France. Medical Referee Board, Chicago, United States Army.

WILSON, JOHN HECTOR ALEXANDER.
Student of Medicine, 1916-17. O.T.C. Artillery, May 1916-17, Cadet. 17th Lancers, 2nd Lieut. April 1918.

WILSON, JOHN LYON.
Student of Medicine; L.R.C.P. (Edin.) 1879. R.A.M.C., Lieut.; Captain Sept. 1917. 46th Field Ambulance.

WILSON, JOHN McLAREN.
Rose's Academical Institution, Nairn. Highland R.G.A., Volunteers. M.A. (Aberdeen) 1910. University O.T.C. Artillery, Aug. to Nov. 1914, Cadet. R.G.A., Heavy Artillery, 2nd Lieut. Nov. 1914.

Record of War Service

WILSON, JOHN THOMAS.
Lockerbie Academy. Student of Medicine, 1913-14 and 1918. 2/1st and 1/1st Lanarkshire Yeomanry (T.), Private Sept. 1914; L/Corporal April 1915; Corporal Sept. 1915. 7/8th King's Own Scottish Borderers, 2nd Lieut. June 1917 to May 1918. Gallipoli and Egypt Sept. 1915 to Jan. 1917. France Dec. 1917 to April 1918.

WILSON, MALCOLM.
Wreight's School, Faversham, Kent. D.Sc. (Lond.). A.R.C.Sc. Lecturer in Mycology. Pathologist, London County War Hospital, Aug. 1915 to Sept. 1916. R.A.M.C., 1st London Sanitary Coy., Lieut. Oct. 1916; Captain May 1917 to Feb. 1919. Salonika Jan. 1917 to Feb. 1919.

WILSON, NORMAN GRAHAME.
Daniel Stewart's College. Student of Science, 1916-17 and 1918. O.T.C. Artillery, Oct. 1916 to June 1917, Cadet; Officer Cadet June 1917. R.F.A. (S.R.), 2nd Lieut. Nov. 1917.

WILSON, RICHARD ARDERNE.
Diocesan College, Rondebosch, South Africa. First XV. M.B., C.M. 1893. R.A.M.C., Lieut. 1915. Principal Surgeon, Serbian Relief Fund Hospitals, Salonika and Serbia. No. 17 General Hospital, Alexandria. Order of St Sava (4th Class).

WILSON, ROBERT.
Royal High School. Student of Arts, 1917. O.T.C. Infantry, Oct. 1917 to March 1918, Cadet. R.A.M.C., Private May 1918; Acting Corporal June 1919. Military Hospital, Hemel Hempstead, Herts.

WILSON, ROBERT BALLANTYNE.
Berwickshire High School. Student of Science, 1912-15. R.A.M.C. (T.). 3rd Lowland Field Ambulance, Private Dec. 1914. R.F.A. (T.), 2nd Lieut. May 1915; Lieut. June 1916; Acting Captain Aug. 1917 to March 1918.

WILSON, RODERICK JAMES.
Student of Arts, 1915-16. O.T.C. Artillery and Infantry, Feb. to Aug. 1916, Cadet; Officer Cadet. 4th Loyal North Lancashire Regiment, Lieut. May 1918.

WILSON, ROWLAND PATERSON.
Wellington College, New Zealand. First XI. Student of Medicine, 1918; B.Sc. 1920. N.Z. Medical Corps, Private 1912-15. No. 3 New Zealand Hospital.

WILSON, THOMAS WARRINGTON.
Student of Science, 1907-9. 9th King's Own Scottish Borderers, 2nd Lieut.

WILSON, WALTER MELVILLE.
George Watson's College. O.T.C. 1915-17. Student of Science, 1918. O.T.C. Artillery, 1918, Cadet Bombardier. R.G.A., Officer Cadet Oct. 1918 to Jan. 1919.

Record of War Service

WILSON, WILLIAM.
George Watson's College. M.A. 1906; LL.B. 1909; Advocate, 1910. Secretary to the University. General List, Lieut. 1916. Appeal Military Representative.

WILSON, WILLIAM.
Boroughmuir School. Student of Arts, 1911-14. 9th Royal Scots (T.), Private 1911. R.E. (Special Brigade), Corporal 1915. R.F.A., 2nd Lieut. 1918-19.

WILSON, WILLIAM CHEYNE.
M.B., C.M. 1886; M.D. 1896. R.A.M.C. (T.), Major Jan. 1912. 4th Southern General Hospital, Plymouth.

WILSON, WILLIAM MUIRHEAD.
George Watson's College; First XV. O.T.C. 1914-15. Student of Arts and Medicine, 1915 and 1917. Anatomy Staff, 1919. O.T.C. Infantry, Oct. to Dec. 1915, Cadet L/Corporal. 9th Royal Scots, Private Dec. 1915; L/Corporal April 1917. 1/5th Scottish Rifles. France 1916-17; Somme, Arras. Wounded. Invalided out March 1918.

WILSON-SMITH, WILLIAM ARTHUR.
M.B., Ch.B. 1904; M.D. 1907; D.P.H. R.A.M.C., Lieut. Aug. 1914-15 and July 1917; Captain Jan. to Dec. 1918.

WIMBERLEY, CHARLES NEIL CAMPBELL.
Inverness College. M.B., C.M. (Hons.) 1889. Indian Medical Service, 1890, Lieut.-Col. 1910; Colonel July 1916. Chitral 1895; Tirah 1898; Tibet 1904; France 1915. A.D.M.S., 14th and 17th Divisions, Mesopotamia, 1916-19. Dispatches Aug. 1917 and Aug. 1918. C.M.G. Aug. 1917.

WINCH, GEORGE HAMILTON.
Durham School; First XV. and XI. M.B., Ch.B. 1904. R.A.M.C., Lieut. July 1918; Captain July 1919. Litchfield Military Hospital.

WINCHESTER, CHARLES CAMPBELL.
Edinburgh Academy; First XV. and XI. O.T.C. 1910-13, Cadet Corporal. Student of Medicine, 1913-14. 11th, 1st, and 15th Royal Scots, 2nd Lieut. Sept. 1914, Captain July 1916; Officer Cadet Instructor 1917. France 1915-16 and 1918, Staff Captain. Germany Jan. to April 1919. Wounded in France July 1915. M.C. July 1916. Croix de Guerre (Belgian) Dec. 1918.

WINCHESTER, HUGH SINCLAIR.
M.A. 1899; B.D. 1912. Minister, Church of Scotland. Chaplain, 4th Class, May 1917. 5th King's Own Scottish Borderers.

WINCHESTER, WILLIAM DOUGLAS.
George Watson's College; First XV. M.A. 1906; LL.B. 1908. 4th and 14th Royal Scots, Private March 1909; L/Corporal; 2nd Lieut. April 1915; Lieut. July 1916. Twice Wounded.

Record of War Service

WINDER, ARTHUR BENJAMIN.
Huddersfield College. M.B., C.M. 1884; M.D. 1892. R.A.M.C., Lieut. June 1915; Captain Dec. 1915.

WINNING, THOMAS GIRDWOOD.
Student of Law, 1908-10. Solicitor. Lothians and Border Horse (T.), Private.

WISEMAN, JOHN FREDERICK STEWART.
Dollar Academy; First XV. and XI. Student of Medicine, 1913-14 and 1918. Royal Highlanders (Black Watch), Private Sept. 1914. 12th Argyll and Sutherland Highlanders, Sept. 1914. Transferred R.E. (Special Brigade), to Jan. 1919. France June 1915 to Jan. 1919.

WISHART, AYLMER JAMES REIDFORD.
Edinburgh Academy. Student of Science, 1912-14. O.T.C. Engineers, Jan. 1913 to Oct. 1914, Cadet L/Corporal. Royal Military College, Oct. 1914. R.E., 2nd Lieut. April 1915; Lieut. Sept. 1917; Captain and Adjutant Dec. 1917. France Nov. 1915. M.C. June 1917.

WISHART, DAVID GARRICK.
Royal High School. Student of Medicine, 1910-14. M.B., Ch.B. (Hons.) 1914. O.T.C. Medical, Nov. 1914 to July 1915, Cadet. R.A.M.C., Lieut. June 1915; Captain June 1916; Major Dec. 1918. 27th Casualty Clearing Station, Salonika.

WISHART, DAVID GEORGE.
Kilmarnock Academy. O.T.C. 1911-13, Cadet Sergeant. Student of Science, 1915-18. M.R.C.V.S. (Edin.) 1917. Royal Army Veterinary Corps, Lieut. Feb. 1918; Captain Feb. 1919. 3rd Afghan War, India.

WISHART, JAMES MATTHEW.
Kirkcaldy High School. O.T.C. 1904-10, Cadet Colour-Sergeant. Student of Medicine, 1910-15. M.B., Ch.B. (Hons.) 1915. O.T.C. Infantry, 1911-14, Medical, 1914-15, Cadet L/Corporal. R.A.M.C., Lieut. Aug. 1915; Captain Aug. 1916. France Nov. 1915 to Sept. 1917; Mesopotamia Jan. 1918 to April 1919.

WISHART, JOHN.
Student of Arts and Science, 1916-17. 7th attached 9th Royal Highlanders (Black Watch), 2nd Lieut. Aug. 1918.

WISHART, JOHN.
George Heriot's School. M.A. 1901 Schoolmaster. 9th Royal Scots, Private Dec. 1915, 2nd Lieut. April 1917; Captain Oct. 1918. Education Officer, 15th Division. France. Dispatches March 1919.

WISHART, JOHN REIDFORD.
Edinburgh Academy. O.T.C. 1907-10, Cadet L/Corporal. Student of Arts and Law, 1911-14 and 1917-19; M.A. 1914. O.T.C. Artillery, Oct. 1911 to Aug. 1914, Cadet. R.F.A., 1st Lowland and 86th Brigades, 2nd Lieut. Aug. 1914; Lieut. Oct. 1915; Acting Captain Aug. 1917. France, 51st Division. Wounded at Passchendaele Nov. 1917, and invalided out Dec. 1917.

Record of War Service

WISHART, ROBERT McLAREN.
George Watson's College. Student of Medicine, 1911-16; M.B., Ch.B. 1916; L.R.C.P. & S. (Edin.) and L.F.P.S. (Glasg.) 1908; D.P.H. 1912. Edinburgh and Border Hospital, Dunkirk, Nov. 1914 to March 1915. R.A.M.C., Lieut. May 1915; Captain Aug. 1916. 7th Argyll and Sutherland Highlanders, France. 27th Division, Salonika, and South Russia.

WISHART, ROBERT SCOTT.
Kirkcaldy High School; Athletics. Cadet Corps 1902-7, Sergeant. M.A. (Hons. Maths.), and B.Sc. (Distinction, Maths. and Nat. Phil.), 1912. O.T.C. Artillery, Feb. 1910 to Nov. 1912, Cadet. R.F.A. (T.), 177th Brigade, 2nd Lieut. Oct. 1914, Lieut. Feb. 1915; Captain Sept. 1915. France, 2nd Highland Brigade.

WISHART, WILLIAM.
M.A. 1890; B.Sc. 1892. Schoolmaster. First Morayshire Volunteer Regiment, Nov. 1916; 2nd Lieut. April 1917; Captain June 1917.

WISHART, WILLIAM GARRICK.
Kirkcaldy High School; First XV. Cadet Corps 1900-3, Bombardier. B.Sc. (Distinction) 1910. O.T.C. Engineers, 1909-10, Cadet. R.G.A., 2nd Lieut. March 1915; Lieut. July 1917; Captain Feb. 1918. Attached 46th Division, Signal Coy., Poona, and Indian Signal Service, Oct. 1918.

WISHART, WILLIAM MUIR.
George Heriot's School. University O.T.C. Infantry, June to Oct. 1916, Cadet. 8th Seaforth Highlanders, 2nd Lieut. Jan. 1917; Lieut. France. Wounded.

WOLFE, JAMES FRANCIS.
M.B., C.M. 1896. R.A.M.C., Lieut. May 1915; Captain May 1916.

WOLFENDEN, ALFRED ERNEST.
Brooksbank Grammar School, Elland. Student of Arts, 1914-16. R.A.M.C. (T.), Welsh Field Ambulance, Private Nov. 1915; L/Corporal Dec. 1915; Corporal Oct. 1916. West Yorkshire Regiment, 2nd Lieut. Dec. 1917.

WOOD, ALBERT EDWARD BATHURST.
Plymouth College. M.B., Ch.B. 1900; L.R.C.P. & S. (Edin.), and L.F.P.S. (Glasg.) 1898. University Battery, E.C.A.V., 1893-8, Senior Sergeant. R.A.M.C., 1903; Major Jan. 1915; Temp. Lieut.-Col. 46th Field Ambulance, 15th Division, France, July 1915 to March 1917. Liaison Officer, with U.S.A. Base Hospitals. No. 13 General Hospital, France, May 1917 to Aug. 1918.

WOOD, ALEXANDER LINDSAY.
Mackie Academy, Stonehaven. University O.T.C. Artillery, Feb. to Aug. 1918, Cadet; Officer Cadet Aug. 1918. R.F.A., 2nd Lieut. April 1919.

WOOD, ARTHUR MURRAY.
Edinburgh Institution. M.B., Ch.B. 1900; M.D. 1904; D.P.H. (Edin.) 1904; F.R.C.P. (Edin.). R.A.M.C., Captain Aug. 1914; Acting Major April 1918. France and Italy. Prisoner of War in Germany.

Record of War Service

WOOD, CHARLES.
: Student of Medicine, 1913-15 and 1916-17. O.T.C. Medical, Oct. 1913 to Sept. 1914, Cadet. 12th Royal Scots, 2nd Lieut.

WOOD, DAVID JAMES.
: Royal High School. M.B., C.M. 1888. South African Medical Corps, Major 1914. Ophthalmic Surgeon to Military Hospitals, Cape Town, and to Warships at Simonstown.

WOOD, HARRY STATESBURY.
: M.B., C.M. 1888. Indian Medical Service, Lieut.-Col. July 1911.

WOOD, JAMES.
: Kelso High School; First XV. Cadet Corps 1900-4, Sergeant. Student of Law, 1907-9. Chartered Accountant, 1911. Royal Canadian Dragoons, Private Sept. 1914. A.S.C., 2nd Lieut. Dec. 1915; Lieut. Oct. 1916; Captain July 1918. France May 1915 to Feb. 1919. Dispatches May 1918.

WOOD, JAMES ALEXANDER.
: Broughton School, Edinburgh. M.A. 1914. Schoolmaster. O.T.C. Infantry, 1912. 16th Royal Scots, Private. R.E., Corporal Aug. 1915. France. Wounded near Armentières Oct. 1916.

WOOD, JOHN BURN.
: M.B., C.M. 1895. R.A.M.C.

WOOD, JOHN B.
: Student. 10th Gordon Highlanders, 2nd Lieut. M.C.

WOOD, JOHN FAIRLEY.
: Mackie Academy, Stonehaven. University O.T.C. Artillery, Feb. to Aug. 1918, Cadet; Officer Cadet. R.F.A., 2nd Lieut. April 1919.

WOOD, MARGUERITE.
: St George's School for Girls. M.A. 1913. Q.M.A.A.C., Deputy Administrator, July 1917; Unit Administrator, March to July 1919. Morfa Camp, Conway.

WOOD, MURDO MACKENZIE.
: Fordyce Academy. M.A. 1903. Secretary, S.R.C. Barrister-at-Law (Gray's Inn). 6th Gordon Highlanders (T.), 2nd Lieut. Aug. 1914; Lieut. March 1915; Captain June 1916. Royal Air Force, Acting Major April 1918. France Nov. 1914. Wounded at Neuve Chapelle March 1915. O.B.E. Jan. 1919.

WOOD, ORBY RUSSELL MORGAN.
: Woodbridge Grammar School. M.B., C.M. 1890; L.R.C.P. & S. (Edin.) and L.F.P.S. (Glasg.) 1889. Finborough Hall Red Cross Hospital. 2nd (Vol.) Suffolk Regiment, Lieut.

Record of War Service

WOOD, ROBERT.
Royal High School. Student of Science, 1903-4. O.T.C. Artillery 1915, Cadet. R.F.A., 2nd Lieut. Sept. 1915; Lieut. July 1917; Captain June to Oct. 1918.

WOOD, ROBERT SCOTT TAIT.
Glasgow High School and Royal Technical College. University O.T.C. Infantry, May to June 1916, Cadet; Officer Cadet. 10th Seaforth Highlanders, 2nd Lieut. Jan. 1917; Lieut. Aug. 1918. A.S.C. (M.T.). Royal Air Force. France.

WOOD, ROBERT TURNBULL.
Royal High School. Student of Science, 1911-12. O.T.C. Infantry, Sept. to Oct. 1914, Cadet. R.F.A., 2nd Lieut. Oct. 1914; Lieut. March 1916; Acting Captain June 1918; Acting Major Dec. 1918. France July 1915 to June 1916, and Feb. 1917-19. Dispatches July 1919.

WOOD, WILLIAM WILSON.
Edinburgh Institution. M.B., C.M. 1896. R.A.M.C., Lieut. May 1915.

WOODBURN, JAMES LAURITZ.
Merchiston Castle. O.T.C. 1914-16. Student of Science, 1918. 4th Highland Light Infantry, Private; L/Corporal. Royal Air Force.

WOODBURN, WILLIAM YOUNG.
Hamilton School, Victoria, Australia. First XI. M.B., Ch.B. 1903; M.D. 1906. Mackenzie Bursar. Prosector in Anatomy. R.A.M.C., Captain June 1915 to March 1919.

WOODCOCK, JOHN NORMANDALE.
Bridlington Grammar School. Student of Science, 1918. Leeds University O.T.C., Cadet. King's Own Yorkshire Light Infantry, 2nd Lieut. July 1916; Lieut. Dec. 1917.

WOODE, CHARLES.
Brundels and Sydney Grammar School. Student of Medicine, 1913-15. O.T.C. Medical, 1913-14, Cadet. 12th Royal Scots, 2nd Lieut. Aug. to Dec. 1914; Surgeon-Probationer, 1915.

WOODHEAD, Sir GERMAN SIMS.
Huddersfield College; First XV. and XI. M.B., C.M. 1878; M.D. 1881; F.R.C.P. (Edin.) 1882. Assistant to Professor of Pathology. Professor of Pathology, Cambridge. Volunteer Medical Staff Corps, 1885-90, Unit Captain. R.A.M.C. and Army Medical Service, Captain 1886; Lieut.-Col. Jan. 1909; Brevet Colonel June 1917. Eastern Command, San Sao, Sept. 1914. Irish Command, Tipperary, Oct. 1915. Adviser in Pathology and Inspector of Military Hospital Laboratories, Sept. 1917 to Aug. 1919. V.D. 1910. Mention Jan. 1917. O.B.E. Jan. 1918; K.B.E. June 1919.

WOODWARD, ALEXANDER TAYLOR.
Student of Medicine, 1912-17; M.B., Ch.B. 1917. Anatomy Staff, 1916. O.T.C. Medical, Oct. 1913-17, Cadet L/Corporal. R.N.V.R., Surgeon-Probationer, Feb. 1915; Royal Navy, Surgeon-Lieut. July 1917. China.

Record of War Service

WOODWARD, ALFRED CHAD TURNER.
Radley College; First XI. M.B., Ch.B. 1904; F.R.C.S. (Edin.) 1904 and (Eng.) 1911. Demonstrator in Anatomy, 1904-5. French Red Cross, Sept. 1914 to Jan. 1915. R.A.M.C., Lieut. Sept. 1915; Captain Sept. 1916; Major Jan. 1918.

WOOLER, ERNEST WILLIAM NOWELL.
Sedbergh; First XI. Student of Medicine, 1909-14; M.B., Ch.B. 1914. R.A.M.C., Lieut. Nov. 1915; Captain Nov. 1916. Dispatches 1919.

WRAY, GERALD GAGE.
Academical Institution, Coleraine. First XV. and XI. M.B., Ch.B. 1908; D.P.H. (Manchester). Volunteer Medical Staff Corps, 1905-8, Private. R.A.M.C. (T.), Lieut. Nov. 1914; Captain May 1915. 2/3rd East Lancashire Field Ambulance.

WRIGHT, ARCHIBALD FRANCIS.
Edinburgh Academy. M.B., Ch.B. 1906. R.A.M.C., Lieut. 1914; Captain May 1916; Acting Major to Aug. 1919. 3rd Field Ambulance, 1st Division and Guards Division, France. Bacteriologist, Central Hospital, Lichfield. Dispatches. M.C.

WRIGHT, ARTHUR.
M.B., Ch.B. 1912. R.A.M.C., Lieut. June 1916; Captain June 1917. France 1916.

WRIGHT, BERTRAM ERNEST.
Student of Medicine, 1912-14; M.B., Ch.B. 1914. R.A.M.C., Lieut.

WRIGHT, DAVID.
Edinburgh Institution; First XV. and XI. Cadet Corps 1913-16. University O.T.C. Infantry, Nov. 1916 to April 1917, Cadet. Royal Defence Corps, 2nd Lieut. April 1917. Royal Air Force, Dec. 1917; Lieut. May 1918.

WRIGHT, GARNETT.
St Bees School, Cumberland; First XV. M.B., Ch.B. 1900; F.R.C.S. (Eng.). Lecturer in Operative Surgery, Manchester University. R.A.M.C., Captain 1908. 2nd Western and 57th General Hospitals.

WRIGHT, GEORGE GIBSON NEILL.
M.A. (Hons. Engl.) 1914. Bachelor of Education, 1920. O.T.C. Infantry, Aug. to Oct. 1915, Cadet. 1st and 5th Cameron Highlanders, 2nd Lieut. Nov. 1915; Lieut. July 1917. France, Sept. 1916 to Aug. 1918. Wounded at Meteren Aug. 1918.

WRIGHT, HEDLEY DUNCAN.
Queen's College, Hobart, Tasmania. First XI. B.A. (Tasmania). Student of Medicine, 1909-16; M.B., Ch.B. 1916. O.T.C. Medical, Aug. 1914 to March 1916, Cadet L/Corporal. R.A.M.C. (S.R.), Lieut. March 1916; Captain Oct. 1916.

WRIGHT, JOHN HOWARD.
King Edward's High School, Birmingham. First XV. Student of Medicine, 1914-16 and 1917-19. O.T.C. Medical, Oct. 1915 to March 1916, and April 1918 to June 1919, Cadet. Non-Combatant Corps, Private April 1916-18.

Record of War Service

WRIGHT, LEWIS JAMES.
Dumfries Academy. M.A. 1912. Schoolmaster. 6th Royal Scots (T.), 1910, Corporal; Sergeant. Palestine.

WRIGHT, ROBERT YOUNG MURRAY.
Hull Grammar School. M.A. 1889. 1st Cadet Battn., Royal Dublin Fusiliers (Dublin Schools Cadet Corps), Cadet-Lieut. April 1915; Captain Sept. 1915; Major May 1919. Acting Sub-Director of Recruiting, Nov. 1915 to May 1916.

WRIGHT, THOMAS.
M.B., Ch.B. 1904; M.D. 1912. R.A.M.C., Lieut. April 1915-16.

WRIGHT, VERNON OSWALD.
York High School. Student of Music, 1918. A.R.C.M. (Lond.). 7th Argyll and Sutherland Highlanders, Lieut. Dec. 1912.

WRIGHT, WILLIAM DUNDAS.
M.B., Ch.B. 1903. Indian Medical Service, attached 110th Mahratta Light Infantry, Captain; Major March 1917. Mesopotamia.

WRIGHTSON, JOHN HAROLD.
Royal Lancaster Grammar School. M.B., Ch.B. 1900. R.A.M.C., Lieut. Feb. 1915; Captain Feb. 1916. Attached 8th York and Lancaster Regiment, and 32nd General Hospital, Wimereux, France.

WYATT, WALTER.
Broughton School, Edinburgh. 1st Highland Cadet Battn., Royal Scots, 1916-18. Student of Medicine, 1918. O.T.C. Artillery, April to Oct. 1918, Cadet. R.F.A., Officer Cadet Nov. 1918.

WYLIE, ANDREW ROBERTSON.
Kelvingrove and McLaren High School. Cadet Corps 1913-15, Sergeant. Student of Science, 1919. O.T.C. Artillery, Aug. 1916 to April 1917, Cadet Bombardier; Officer Cadet April 1917. R.F.A., 106th Brigade, 2nd Lieut. Oct. 1917; Lieut. April 1917. France, 24th Division. Dispatches June 1919.

WYLIE, JOHN KERR.
George Watson's College. M.A. 1906; LL.B. and Advocate, 1909. 14th and 13th Royal Scots, Private Aug. 1914; 2nd Lieut. March 1915; Lieut. Aug. 1917; Captain and Courts Martial Officer, Dec. 1918. 188th Prisoner of War Coy. France May 1916.

WYLIE, THOMAS.
Boroughmuir School. Student of Arts, 1911-14 and 1918; M.A. (Hons. Maths.) 1920. 8th Royal Scots (T.), Private Aug. 1914. France 1914.

WYLIE, THOMAS MURRAY.
M.A. 1911. Schoolmaster. R.A.M.C., 3rd Lowland Field Ambulance, Private.

Record of War Service

WYLIE SMITH, ANDREW.
 M.A. 1887. Minister, Church of Scotland. 5th Black Watch, Volunteers, 2nd Lieut. Nov. 1916; Lieut. July 1917. 2nd Special Service Battn., 1918.

WYLLIE, WILLIAM GIFFORD.
 Edinburgh Academy. M.B., Ch.B. 1914; M.D. 1920. O.T.C. Infantry, 1909-11, Cadet. Royal Navy, Surgeon March 1915. H.M.S. *Invincible;* R.N. Auxiliary Hospital, Dungavel, Strathaven; H.M. Monitor 33, Archangel, 1919.

WYNNE-DAVIES, LLEWELYN.
 Oswestry School. M.B., Ch.B. 1897; M.D. R.A.M.C., Lieut. Aug. 1914; Captain. Amara and 57th Casualty Station Hospital, Quirnah. Ibi Column, West African Forces, Cameroons. Twice Mentioned in Dispatches. O.B.E. (Military) Spring 1919.

WYON, GUY ALFRED.
 Highgate School. B.Sc. (Lond.) 1904; M.B., Ch.B. 1910; M.D. 1915. R.A.M.C., Lieut. May 1915; Captain March 1918. 13th Casualty Clearing Station and 19th Mobile Laboratory, France.

YATES, ARTHUR GURNEY.
 Spalding Grammar School, Lincolnshire. M.A. 1904; M.B., Ch.B. 1908; M.D. 1910. R.A.M.C., Captain Nov. 1914; Major May 1915. 3rd Northern General Hospital. Mention Oct. 1917.

YATES, GEORGE DOUGAL.
 Fettes College; First XV. M.B., Ch.B. 1914. O.T.C. Artillery, 1909-12, Cadet. R.A.M.C., Lieut. Nov. 1914; Captain Nov. 1915. Dispatches Dec. 1916.

YATES, ROBERT BURTON MEIKLE.
 Sedbergh. Cadet Corps 1901-2. M.B., Ch.B. 1911. R.A.M.C., Lieut. Sept. 1914; Captain April 1915. 2nd North Midland Field Ambulance.

YEATTS, WILLIAM WALTER MURRAY.
 Royal High School. Student of Arts, 1913-16; M.A. 1916, (Hons. Maths.) 1919. O.T.C. Infantry, Oct. 1914 to Sept. 1916, Cadet. R.F.A., Gunner Sept. 1916; Bombardier Jan. 1917; Officer Cadet Jan. 1917, 2nd Lieut. April 1917; Lieut. Oct. 1918. Three times Wounded.

YELF, ROBERT EDWARD BURNET.
 Campden Grammar School. M.B., C.M. 1888. No. 4 Coy. Q.R.V.B., Royal Scots, Private. R.A.M.C., Lieut. Sept. 1915-16.

YEOMAN, ALEXANDER ROSS.
 George Watson's College. M.A. 1895. Jeffrey Scholar. Chaplain 1903; 3rd Class; 2nd Class July 1917. Interpreter in High and Cape Dutch. France. Wounded at second Ypres, April 1915. Three times Mentioned in Dispatches. C.M.G.

Record of War Service

YEOMAN, JAMES TELFORD.
George Heriot's School. O.T.C. 1911-13. Student of Arts, 1913-14. O.T.C. Infantry, Aug. to Sept. 1914, Cadet. 14th Royal Scots (T.), Private Sept. 1914; 2nd Lieut. Sept. 1915; Lieut. July 1917; Captain Aug. 1918. Transferred to 17th and 3rd Battns. Tank Corps. France.

YEOMAN, JOHN BROWN.
M.B., C.M. 1893; M.D. 1898; F.R.C.S. (Edin.) 1900; D.P.H. (Liverpool) 1905. Demonstrator in Anatomy. R.A.M.C., Major and D.A.D.M.S., Oct. 1914. Acting Lieut.-Col. July 1917 in charge of 43rd Stationary Hospital, El Arish, Egypt.

YIN, MOUNG BA.
M.B., Ch.B. 1912. Indian Medical Service, Lieut. Dec. 1914.

YORSTON, ROBERT MacDONALD.
Montrose Academy; First XV. Student of Science, 1912-14 and 1918. O.T.C. Infantry, Oct. 1912 to Sept. 1914, Cadet. 4th North Staffordshire Regiment, 2nd Lieut. Aug. 1914; Lieut. May 1917; Captain March 1917. France. Wounded at the Somme July 1916. Military Posting Officer, Dublin, Aug. 1918 to Jan. 1919.

YOUNG, ALEXANDER MILLER.
Dunfermline High School. M.A. 1907. Schoolmaster. 3/7th, 4th, and 12th Royal Scots, Private June 1916; L/Corporal Jan. 1917; Officer Cadet May 1917; 2nd Lieut. Sept. 1917. France. Prisoner of War April to Nov. 1918.

YOUNG, ALEXANDER WAUGH.
M.B., Ch.B. 1906; M.D. 1911; F.R.C.S. (Edin.) 1908. Anatomy Staff, 1910. R.A.M.C., Lieut. Nov. 1914; Captain Nov. 1915. Lemnos, Egypt, and France. M.C. Médaille des Épidémies (French).

YOUNG, ANDREW.
Kilmarnock Academy. M.A. 1907. Schoolmaster. R.F.C., 2nd Lieut. July 1916, Lieut. Feb. 1917; Captain Nov. 1917. Royal Air Force, Major June 1918. O.B.E. (Military) May 1919.

YOUNG, ANDREW HAMILTON.
George Watson's College. Student of Science, 1918-19. O.T.C. Artillery, Sept. 1917 to May 1918, Cadet; Officer Cadet June 1918. R.G.A., 2nd Lieut. Feb. 1919.

YOUNG, ARCHIBALD DUNCAN MacCONNELL.
Dunfermline High School. Student of Medicine, 1914-15 and 1918-20. O.T.C. Infantry, 1915, Cadet. R.G.A., Private Nov. 1915; Lieut. Royal Air Force.

YOUNG, CHARLES JAMES.
Student of Medicine, 1910-15; M.B., Ch.B. 1915. O.T.C. Infantry, Oct. 1911 to March 1915, Cadet. R.A.M.C., Lieut. July 1915; Captain July 1916. Gallipoli, France, and Mesopotamia.

Record of War Service

YOUNG, DAVID MURRAY.
Kilmarnock Academy. Student of Medicine, 1912-17; M.B., Ch.B. 1917. O.T.C. Medical, Oct. 1915 to May 1918, Cadet. R.A.M.C., Lieut. May 1918 to April 1919.

YOUNG, DAVID ROBERT.
George Watson's College. O.T.C. 1914-16. Student of Law, 1917-19. Y.M.C.A. France 1917. O.T.C. Artillery, 1917-18, Cadet; Officer Cadet April 1918. R.F.A., 1st Lowland Brigade, 2nd Lieut. Feb. 1919.

YOUNG, GEORGE.
George Watson's College. M.A. 1905. Schoolmaster. 4th Royal Scots, Private Aug. 1916; 2nd Lieut. June 1917; Lieut. Dec. 1918. Egypt and France. Wounded.

YOUNG, GEORGE ERNEST ROBERTSON.
Glasgow Academy; First XI. M.A. 1904; LL.B. 1907. 28th London Regiment (Artists' Rifles), Private Dec. 1915. Royal Highlanders (Black Watch), 2nd Lieut. Nov. 1916. France. Wounded at Ypres Aug. 1917. Invalided out Jan. 1918.

YOUNG, GEORGE GRAFTON JOSEPH.
M.B., Ch.B. 1898. Indian Medical Service, Major June 1912.

YOUNG, HUBERT TURNER PENN.
Oundle School. Cadet Corps 1903-7. M.B., Ch.B. 1912. O.T.C. Artillery, 1907-8, Cadet. R.A.M.C., Lieut. June 1917; Captain June 1918.

YOUNG, JAMES.
M.A. 1904. Schoolmaster. 8th Royal Scots (T.), 2nd Lieut.; Lieut. July 1917.

YOUNG, JAMES.
George Heriot's School. Student of Law, 1908-10. Solicitor. 8th Royal Scots, (T.), Sergeant Nov. 1914; 2nd Lieut. Oct. 1915; Lieut. July 1917; Acting Captain Oct. 1918. France.

YOUNG, JAMES.
George Heriot's School. M.B., Ch.B. (Hons.) 1905; M.D. (Gold Medal) 1910, No. 4 Coy. Q.R.V.B., Royal Scots, 1901-5. R.A.M.C. (T.), Lieut. 1910; Captain 1913; Major May 1915; Lieut.-Col. Aug. 1916. 3rd Lowland Field Ambulance France. Dispatches June 1918 and Jan. 1919. D.S.O. Jan. 1919.

YOUNG, JAMES ANDERSON.
Alloa Academy. St Andrews University Battery, R.G.A., 1906-8. M.B., Ch.B. 1914. R.A.M.C., Lieut. Nov. 1915; Captain May 1916; Acting Major April 1918 to March 1919. 2/2nd North Midland Field Ambulance, France 1917-19. M.C. Feb. 1918.

YOUNG, JAMES ROY STEPHENS.
Edinburgh Institution. M.A. (Hons. Hist.) 1912. Schoolmaster. 9th Royal Scots, Private April 1917. R.N.A.S., Temp. Sub.-Lieut. (Observer) Aug. 1917, Royal Air Force, Temp. Lieut. (Observer) April 1918. D.F.C. Dec. 1918.

Record of War Service

YOUNG, JOHN BENSON.
    Rossall. Cadet Corps 1902-6, Corporal. Student of Medicine, 1909-14; M.B., Ch.B. 1914; F.R.C.S. (Edin.) 1919. R.A.M.C., Lieut. Aug. 1914; Captain Aug. 1915. France Sept. 1914-15. Invalided out 1916.

YOUNG, JOHN EDWARD.
    Student of Science, 1913-15. A.S.C. 2nd Lieut.; Lieut. March 1916; Acting Captain July 1918.

YOUNG, JOHN PERCY.
    Edinburgh Academy. University O.T.C. Infantry, Nov. 1916 to Aug. 1918. Cadet C.Q.M.S. Seaforth Highlanders, Officer Cadet Aug. 1918.

YOUNG, MEREDITH.
    Bradford Grammar School. M.B., Ch.B. 1892; M.D. 1897; D.P.H. 1902. Barrister-at-Law. V.A.D. Hospital, Chester, Oct. 1914. R.A.M.C. (V.), Lieut. 1917; Captain 1918. 3rd Volunteer Battn., Cheshire Regiment.

YOUNG, ROBERT STEELE.
    Academical Institution, Coleraine; First XV. and XI. M.B., Ch.B. 1896. Rugby and Cricket "Blue." R.A.M.C. (T.), Lieut. Sept. 1914; Captain May 1915. 1st East Lancashire Field Ambulance.

YOUNG, THOMAS ADAIR.
    George Watson's College. B.Sc. 1905. A.M.I.C.E. Nigeria Regiment, Lieut. Aug. 1917. East and West Africa.

YOUNG, THOMAS PETTIGREW.
    Daniel Stewart's College. M.A. 1900; D.Litt. (Dijon). Officier d'Académie. Lecturer in French, St Andrews University. St Andrews University O.T.C., 2nd Lieut. Dec. 1915. Munitions, 1915. Attached Second Army H.Q., Jan. 1919.

YOUNG, WILLIAM.
    Wellington College, New Zealand. M.B., C.M. 1892; M.D. 1894; F.R.C.S. (Edin.) 1901. R.A.M.C., Lieut. July 1915; Captain Dec. 1915.

YOUNG, WILLIAM.
    George Watson's College. M.A. (Hons. Classics) 1914. 1/6th Royal Scots, Private Nov. 1914; L/Corporal May 1915. 9th East Lancashire Regiment, 2nd Lieut. April 1916; Lieut. Oct. 1917. Egypt 1915-16; Macedonia 1916-17. Wounded. Invalided out Sept. 1918. Dispatches (Struma Front) Sept. 1916.

YOUNG, WILLIAM ALLAN.
    Daniel Stewart's College. M.B., Ch.B. 1908; M.D. 1918; D.P.H. (Camb.) and (Eng.) 1911. No. 4 Coy. Q.R.V.B., Royal Scots, 1904-8, Private. R.A.M.C., Lieut. Aug. 1915; Captain Aug. 1916. Dardanelles (Anzac), Egypt, and France. D.S.O. Jan. 1917.

Record of War Service

YOUNG, WILLIAM PAULIN.
: Glasgow Academy; First XI. M.A. 1906. Minister, U.F. Church of Scotland. 9th Royal Scots (T.), Private Sept. 1914; Wounded and Discharged Jan. 1916. Chaplain, 4th Class, Feb. 1916, 5th Seaforth Highlanders. Royal Air Force A.P.C., April to May 1919. Prisoner of War March to Nov. 1918. France 1915. Dispatches May 1918. D.C.M. Jan. 1916; M.C. June 1919.

YOUNGER, ROBERT.
: Daniel Stewart's College. M.A. 1902. Schoolmaster. 2/7th Royal Highlanders (Black Watch), Private Oct. 1916 to Feb. 1919. Transferred R.A.M.C., attached Royal Serbian Army, Salonika.

YOUNIE, WILLIAM SIMPSON.
: Student of Arts, 1910-13. O.T.C. Infantry, Oct. 1910 to Nov. 1914, Cadet. 1st Dorsetshire Regiment, 2nd Lieut. M.C.

YUILLE, DUNCAN FERGUSON.
: George Heriot's School. Student of Medicine, 1913-16 and 1918-20. O.T.C. Infantry, Sept. 1914 to April 1916, Cadet. R.N.V.R., Surgeon-Probationer.

YULE, ARTHUR DAVID.
: Arbroath High School. M.B., C.M. 1896; B.Sc. (P.H.) 1898. R.A.M.C., Lieut. July 1917; Captain July 1918.

ANDERSON, WILLIAM LOWE.
: Falkirk High School. Student of Medicine, 1919. 2nd Seaforth Highlanders, Private April 1915; 2nd Lieut. March 1918. Wounded April 1917 and Sept. 1918.

BAKER, ARCHIBALD DONALD.
: Royal High School. Student of Science, 1919. 8th Argyll and Sutherland Highlanders, Private Sept. 1914; Sergeant May 1915; 2nd Lieut. May 1918 to April 1919.

BELL, ARCHIBALD.
: Kingussie School. Student of Divinity, 1919. 4th Cameron Highlanders, Private 1911; L/Corporal Feb. 1916; 2nd Lieut. Feb. 1917; Lieut. Aug. 1918. 51st Division, Cyclist Coy. 17th Lancashire Fusiliers.

BELL, VERNON.
: Rossall School. O.T.C. 1915-17. Student of Medicine, 1919. General List, attached Macedonian Labour Battn., 2nd Lieut. Nov. 1917.

BROWN, CYRIL WILLIAM GILLINGHAM.
: Dulwich College. Student of Arts, 1919. Royal Navy, Cadet and Midshipman, 1914; Sub-Lieut. 1918-19.

Record of War Service

BURNS, FRANCIS PETER.
Bathgate Academy. Student of Arts, 1919. 4th Royal Scots (Res.), Private March 1916. Discharged. Royal Air Force, Gunnery Instructor.

CAIE, JOHN MYLES.
Forfar Academy. Student of Medicine, 1919. Seaforth Highlanders, Private Feb. 1916. Loyal North Lancashire Regiment, 2nd Lieut. Jan. 1918. M.C. Sept. 1918.

CAMPBELL, GEORGE MacDONALD.
Boroughmuir School. Student of Medicine, 1919. 3rd Gordon Highlanders, May 1916. Northamptonshire Regiment, 2nd Lieut. Jan. 1918 to April 1919.

CAMPBELL, JAMES IAN.
Perth Academy. Student of Medicine, 1919. R.F.C., 1st Air Mechanic, Nov. 1915. Northumberland Fusiliers, 2nd Lieut. June 1918.

CARROTHERS, WILLIAM ALEXANDER.
B.A. Manitoba University O.T.C., 1914-16. Student of Arts, 1919. Manitoba Regiment, Lieut. Feb. 1916; Captain Nov. 1917. Royal Air Force, 1918-19 France and The Rhine. D.F.C. and Croix de Guerre (Belgian).

COATS, JOHN DUNDAS ORR.
Edinburgh Academy; First XV. O.T.C. 1908-12. B.A. (Oxford); Student of Law, 1919. 5th Royal Highlanders (Black Watch), 2nd Lieut. Sept. 1914; Lieut. June 1916; Temp. Captain April 1915. Attached Machine-Gun Corps. Aug. 1916; Acting Captain Sept. 1918. France and Mesopotamia.

CONDIE, ROBERT M.
Buckhaven School. Student of Medicine, 1919. 2nd Shropshire Light Infantry, Private June 1915.

CROLE, GERARD BRUCE.
Edinburgh Academy; First XV. and XI. O.T.C. 1910-11. B.A. (Oxford); Student of Law, 1919. 2nd Dragoon Guards, 2nd Lieut. Aug. 1914; Lieut. May 1916; Captain Sept. 1917. R.F.A. and Royal Air Force. France 1915-17, Wounded and Prisoner of War Nov. 1917 to Dec. 1918. M.C. Sept. 1917.

DAVIE, PETER COUSIN.
Timaru High School. B.Sc. (N.Z.). M.B., Ch.B. 1915; M.R.C.P.(Edin.) 1919. R.A.M.C., Lieut. Aug. 1915; Captain Aug. 1916 to May 1920. Dispatches Nov. 1917 and July 1918.

DAVIES-JONES, CYRIL.
St David's College, Lampeter; First XV. Student of Medicine, 1919. R.F.A., Driver Oct. 1916. France.

FAIRLEY, JAMES HENRY BARRIE.
St Paul's, Darjeeling, India. Cossipore Artillery Volunteers, 1904-13. Student of Science, 1919. 9th Royal Scots, Private Aug. 1914. R.F.A. (S.R.), 2nd Lieut. May 1915; Lieut. July 1917. 29th Division. Gallipoli, Egypt, and France.

Record of War Service

FERGUSON, DUNCAN LAMONT.
Gill College, South Africa. First XV. and XI. Student of Medicine, 1919. 7th South African Infantry, Private. German East Africa.

FINDLAY, JOHN MERRIEVALE.
Southland High School; First XV. Student of Arts, 1919. N.Z. Exp. Force, L/Corporal. M.M. Oct. 1918.

GALL, DAVID MENMUIR.
Broughton School, Edinburgh. Student of Science, 1919. 4th Royal Scots, Private Aug. 1914; 2nd Lieut. Jan. 1917; Lieut. July 1918. 6th attached 2nd Scottish Rifles. M.C. Nov. 1917.

GAVIN, FREDERICK WILLIAM.
George Watson's College. Student of Medicine, 1918. 9th Highland Light Infantry, 2nd Lieut. Sept. 1915. France. Wounded at Menin Road Sept. 1917.

GLAISTER, THOMAS DERRICK.
Lanark Grammar School. Student of Medicine, 1919. N.Z. Field Artillery, Gunner March 1917. Wounded March 1918.

GOODWIN, ERNEST WILLIAM.
Wyggeston Grammar School. O.T.C. 1915-16, Cadet-Sergeant. Student of Medicine, 1919. 31st Royal Fusiliers, Private Oct. 1916; L/Corporal; Corporal; Sergeant to Jan. 1919.

HARRISON, JAMES LEES.
George Watson's College. Student of Science, 1919. 9th Royal Scots, Private Aug. 1914. R.E., 2nd Lieut. Oct. 1915; Lieut. Jan. 1917-19.

HENDRY, RIDLEY.
Madras College, St Andrews. Student of Science, 1919. 89th Field Coy., R.E., Private Sept. 1914; Corporal June 1915; Sergeant April 1916. 9th Seaforth Highlanders, 2nd Lieut. Sept. 1916; Lieut. March 1918. Wounded April 1917 and Feb. 1919.

HORNE, JOHN L.
Falkirk High School. Student of Medicine, 1919. Royal Air Force, May 1917; 2nd Lieut. Aug. 1917; Lieut. April 1918; Acting Captain Oct. 1918 to Feb. 1919. Air Force Cross, Jan. 1919.

HUGO-BRUNT, HUGO.
South African College School. Cadet Corps 1910-14. Student of Science, 1919. South African Heavy Artillery, 552nd Siege Battery, Gunner Aug. 1915; Bombardier Nov. 1917; 2nd Lieut. Aug. 1918. France. Wounded Feb. 1917. M.M. Feb. 1917.

Record of War Service

HUNTER, JAMES KERR.
Royal Grammar School, Newcastle. Student of Medicine, 1919. 7th, 21st and 24th Royal Fusiliers, Private June 1915. France Nov. 1916 to Dec. 1917. Wounded at Vimy Ridge June 1916. Wounded and taken Prisoner of War at Cambrai Dec. 1917.

JACK, DONALD GEORGE.
Broughton School, Edinburgh. Student of Law, 1919. Lothians and Border Horse, Private Nov. 1914. 15th Royal Scots, Corporal May 1917. France. Taken Prisoner of War at Ypres Oct. 1917.

JAMES, BENJAMIN.
Carmarthen County School. Student of Medicine, 1919. R.E. (Signal Service), Sapper June 1917 to Jan. 1919.

JOHNSON, ERNEST HUGH.
Gresham's School, Holt; First XV. and XI. O.T.C. 1906-11, Cadet Colour-Sergeant. B.A. (Cambridge); Student of Arts, 1919. R.F.A., Northumbrian Brigade, 2nd Lieut. Aug. 1914; Lieut. June 1916; Captain Oct. 1918. Wounded May and Sept. 1917. Dispatches and M.C. June 1918.

KEIGHLEY, JAMES PHILIP.
Mount St Mary's College, Chesterfield; First XI. O.T.C. 1915-16. Student of Medicine, 1919. 9th South Lancashire Regiment, Private Dec. 1915; 2nd Lieut. March 1917; Lieut. Sept. 1918 to Feb. 1919.

LANG, FERDINAND WILSON.
Auckland Grammar School; First XV. O.T.C. 1908-11, Cadet Sergeant-Major. M.A. (N.Z.) 1916; Student of Medicine, 1919. Auckland Regiment, N.Z. Exp. Force, Corporal; Sergeant; 2nd Lieut. M.C. Oct. 1918.

LEADBETTER, JAMES GREENSHIELDS GREENSHIELDS.
Rugby. O.T.C. 1906-10, Cadet Corporal. B.A. (Oxford) 1914; Student of Law, 1919. Lanarkshire Yeomanry, 2nd Lieut. Jan. 1914; Lieut. Oct. 1915; Captain June 1917. Machine-Gun Squadron, Imperial Camel Corps. Cape Helles, Egypt, Palestine, and Syria. M.C. March 1918.

LOVELOCK, CHARLES WILLIAM.
The Grocers' Company School, London. O.T.C. 1910-12. Student of Science, 1919. 12th Rifle Brigade, Rifleman Sept. 1914; Lewis Gun Sergeant June 1915; 2nd Lieut. May 1917; Lieut. Nov. 1918 to April 1919. Four times Wounded.

MACCABE, JOSEPH.
Holy Cross Academy, Leith. Student of Medicine, 1919. 5/6th Royal Scots, Private June 1917. Invalided out April 1918.

McCULLOCH, JOHN LEITCH.
Student of Medicine, 1919. 5/6th Royal Scots.

Record of War Service

MACDONALD, DONALD ROBERTSON.
Royal Academy, Inverness. Student of Medicine, 1919. 5th Cameron Highlanders, Private April 1916; 2nd Lieut. Aug. 1917; Lieut. Feb. 1919. Wounded April 1918.

McDOWALL, WILLIAM ANDSON.
Dumfries Academy. Student of Medicine, 1919. 4th Royal Scots Fusiliers, Private Sept. 1917. 4th Argyll and Sutherland Highlanders. 7th Royal Highlanders (Black Watch) to Feb. 1919. France, 51st Division.

MacGREGOR, IAN GREGOR.
Broughton School, Edinburgh. Student of Medicine, 1919. R.G.A., Gunner Aug. 1914. R.F.A. attached R.G.A., 136th Heavy Battery.

McGUIRE, THOMAS.
Bathgate Academy. Student of Medicine, 1919. Royal Air Force, 3rd Air Mechanic April 1918 to Feb. 1919.

MACKINTOSH, HUGH CAMERON.
Merchiston Castle. O.T.C. 1910-13. Student of Law, 1919. 7th Royal Highlanders (Black Watch), Feb. 1914; Lieut. Nov. 1914; Captain Nov. 1915. M.C. July 1917.

MacLENNAN, ALISTAIR.
Inverness High School. Student of Science, 1919. 4th Cameron Highlanders. 1911; Sergeant. Mobilised Aug. 1914.

MARSHALL, ROBERT WADDELL.
Edinburgh Academy. Student of Law, 1919. 16th Rifle Brigade, Private May 1916; 2nd Lieut. Aug. 1917 to Jan. 1919; Acting Captain April to July 1918. France.

MILLAR, WILLIAM GILBERT.
Reading School. O.T.C. 1910-13. Student of Medicine, 1919. R.A.M.C., Private June 1915. R.G.A., 2nd Lieut. Feb. 1917; Lieut. Aug. 1918. Mention.

MOWAT, JAMES COBBAN ROSS.
Aberdeen Grammar School. Student of Medicine, 1919. R.A.M.C., Private Nov. 1916.

NEWCOMBE, HAROLD BERNARD.
Ebbw Vale School. University College, Aberystwyth. O.T.C. 1915-16. Student of Medicine, 1919. R.G.A., 15th Siege Battery, Aug. 1916; 2nd Lieut. Nov. 1916; Lieut. May 1918. 1st Field Survey Coy. R.E.

ORD, ARTHUR FREDERIC TROTTER.
George Watson's College and Nottingham High School. O.T.C. 1914-15. Student of Medicine, 1919. West Yorkshire Regiment, Lieut. Attached Royal Air Force.

Record of War Service

PHILIP, NORMAN McLEOD.
Linlithgow Academy. Student of Science, 1919. 2nd Dragoons, Royal Scots Greys, Sept. 1914; Assistant Sergeant-Accountant Jan. to June 1915; L/Corporal Aug. 1917; Corporal June 1918; Acting Sergeant Jan. 1919. Gordon Highlanders.

PRESTON, CLASSON O'DRISCOLL.
Royal Military Academy, Woolwich. Student of Arts, 1919. R.F.A., 2nd Lieut. 1906; Lieut. 1909; Captain Oct. 1914; Major April 1917. France and Salonika. Dispatches Aug. 1914, June 1915, and Oct. 1917. D.S.O.

PRICE, FREDERICK NOEL RITCHIE.
George Watson's College. O.T.C. 1914-17. Student of Medicine, 1919. Royal Air Force, Lieut. 1917-19. Kite Balloon Section, Med. Exp. Force.

RITCHIE, PATRICK.
George Heriot's School. Student of Engineering, 1916-17. O.T.C. Artillery, 1916-17. Royal Flying Corps and R.A.F., 2nd Lieut. April 1917; Acting Flight Lieut. Nov. 1919. Palestine and Russia. A.F.C. Orders of St Anne and St Stanislaus (Russia).

SCOTT-ELLIOTT, GEORGE FRANCIS.
B.Sc. 1887. 1/5th King's Own Scottish Borderers, Lieut.; Captain June 1916. Egypt and Palestine, Romani and Gaza. Dispatches. Order of the Nile (4th Class).

TOFFT, WALTER HENRY.
Hobart High School. M.B., C.M. 1887. A.M.C. (Australian), Captain Aug. 1915; Major Oct. 1917. M.B.E. 1918.

WILLIAMSON, RICHARD ERNEST.
Giggleswick School. M.B., C.M. 1880. 2/6th Duke of Wellington's Regiment, Lieut.-Col. Transferred to R.A.M.C. (T.), Major Jan. 1916. Attached 62nd Division Artillery. France, Somme. Ministry of National Service, Nov. 1917. Ministry of Pensions, April 1919. V.D.

PLATE XCV.

ALLAN EBENEZER KER.

ORDERS, DECORATIONS AND DISPATCHES

VICTORIA CROSS

KER, ALLAN EBENEZER (*b.* 1883).   Pl. xcv.
Edinburgh Academy. Student of Law, 1903-8. Writer to the Signet, 1908. Queen's Edinburgh Mounted Infantry. 3rd Gordon Highlanders, 2nd Lieut. June 1915; Lieut. Jan. 1917. Attached 61st Battn. Machine-Gun Corps, March 1916. France Oct. 1915; Salonika July 1916; Battle of Muchkovo, near Vardar River. Invalided home Dec. 1916. Returned to France May 1917, and present at the Battles of the Somme, Passchendaele, Arras, Ypres, Cambrai, and St Quentin. Taken Prisoner at St Quentin March 1918. Secretary and Food Controller for British Officers at Karlsruhe and Beeskow, March to Dec. 1918. V.C. March 1918.

Extract from the " London Gazette," 4th Sept. 1919:—

VICTORIA CROSS

For most conspicuous bravery and devotion to duty. On the 21st March 1918, near St Quentin, after a very heavy bombardment, the enemy penetrated our line, and the flank of the 61st Division became exposed. Lieut. Ker, with one Vickers gun, succeeded in engaging the enemy's infantry, approaching under cover of dead ground, and held up the attack, inflicting many casualties. He then sent back word to his Battalion Headquarters that he had determined to stop with his sergeant and several men who had been badly wounded, and fight until a counter-attack could be launched to relieve him. Just as ammunition failed his party were attacked from behind by the enemy with bombs, machine-guns, and with the bayonet. Several bayonet attacks were delivered, but each time they were repulsed by Lieut. Ker and his companions with their revolvers, the Vickers gun having by this time been destroyed. The wounded were collected into a small shelter, and it was decided to defend them to the last and to hold up the enemy as long as possible. In one of the many hand-to-hand encounters a German rifle and bayonet and a small supply of ammunition were secured, and subsequently used with good effect against the enemy. Although Lieut. Ker was very exhausted from want of food and gas poisoning, and from the supreme exertions he had made during ten hours of the most severe bombardment, fighting, and attending to the wounded, he refused to surrender until all his ammunition was exhausted and his position was rushed by large numbers of the enemy. His behaviour throughout the day was absolutely cool and fearless, and by his determination he was materially instrumental in engaging and holding up for three hours more than 500 of the enemy.

Orders, Decorations and Dispatches

VICTORIA CROSS

LASCELLES, ARTHUR MOORE (*b.* 1880). Pl. XCVI.
Uppingham. House XV. and XI. Student of Medicine, 1899-1902. 1st South African Mounted Rifles, Rifleman 1914; Quartermaster-Sergeant 1915. 3rd, 14th, and 15th Durham Light Infantry, 2nd Lieut. 1915; Acting Captain 1916; Lieut. July 1917; Captain Aug. 1917. German West Africa and South Africa under General Botha, 1914-15. France 1916-18. Wounded at the Somme in 1916; and again at Masnière, near Cambrai, on 3rd Dec. 1917. M.C. and V.C., Jan. 1918. Killed in action at Limont Fontaine near Maubeuge on 7th November 1918.

Extract from the "London Gazette," 1st Jan. 1918:—

MILITARY CROSS

In the 15 Bis Sector, near Loos, on 15th June 1917, showed great courage endurance and initiative in a very successful daylight raid. He commanded a party of forty other ranks. He led them with great gallantry, capturing all his objectives, taking five prisoners and killing twenty Germans. He conducted operation throughout with great coolness and it was largely due to his fine work that the withdrawal of the whole raid was carried out without a casualty. He was the last to leave the trench. The success of the raid was largely due to the valuable reconnaissance carried out by this officer before the raid. This officer has many times been brought to notice for his gallantry in action and has commanded his company very well.

Extract from the "London Gazette," 11th Jan. 1918:—

VICTORIA CROSS

Theatre of War in which V.C. was gained, and Date of Services. } Masnière, France, 3rd *Dec.* 1917.

For most conspicuous bravery, initiative and devotion to duty when in command of his company in a very exposed position. After a very heavy bombardment, during which Captain Lascelles was wounded, the enemy attacked in strong force but was driven off, success being due in a great degree to the fine example set by this officer, who, refusing to allow his wound to be dressed, continued to encourage his men and organise the defence.

Shortly afterwards the enemy again attacked and captured the trench, taking several of his men prisoners. Captain Lascelles at once jumped on to the parapet, and, followed by the remainder of his company—twelve men only—rushed across under very heavy machine-gun fire, and drove over sixty of the enemy back, thereby saving a most critical situation.

He was untiring in reorganising the position, but shortly afterwards the enemy again attacked and captured the trench and Captain Lascelles, who escaped after.

The remarkable determination and gallantry of this officer in the course of operations, during which he received two further wounds, afforded an inspiring example to all.

ARTHUR MOORE LASCELLES.

DAVID LOWE MACINTYRE.

Orders, Decorations and Dispatches

VICTORIA CROSS

MACINTYRE, DAVID LOWE (*b.* 1895). Pl. xcvii.
Portnahaven School, Islay, and George Watson's College. Student of Arts, 1914-15 and 1918. O.T.C. Infantry, Feb. to May 1915, Cadet. 13th and 4th Argyll and Sutherland Highlanders, 2nd Lieut. May 1915; Lieut. July 1917; Acting Captain and Adjutant June to Sept. 1918. 6th Highland Light Infantry, Jan. 1916-19. Egypt and Palestine; France, Spring 1918. Wounded Sept. 1918. V.C. Oct. 1918.

Extract from the " London Gazette," 26th Oct. 1918 :—

VICTORIA CROSS

For most conspicuous bravery in attack when, acting as Adjutant of his battalion, he was constantly in evidence in the firing line, and by his coolness under most heavy shell and machine-gun fire inspired the confidence of all ranks.

Three days later he was in command of the firing line during an attack, and showed throughout most courageous and skilful leading in face of heavy machine-gun fire. When barbed wire was encountered he personally reconnoitred it before leading his men forward. On one occasion, when extra strong entanglements were reached, he organised and took forward a party of men, and under heavy machine-gun fire supervised the making of gaps. Later when the latter part of our line was definitely held up, Lieut. Macintyre rallied a small party, pushed forward through the enemy barrage in pursuit of an enemy machine-gun detachment, and ran them to earth in a "pill-box" a short distance ahead, killing three and capturing an officer, ten other ranks and five machine-guns. In this redoubt he and his party raided three "pill-boxes" and disposed of the occupants, thus enabling the battalion to capture the redoubt.

When the battalion was ordered to take up a defensive position, Lieut. Macintyre, after he had been relieved of command of the firing line, reconnoitred the right flank which was exposed. When doing this an enemy machine-gun opened fire close to him. Without any hesitation he rushed it single-handed, put the team to flight and brought in the gun. On returning to the redoubt he continued to show splendid spirit while supervising consolidation.

The success of the advance was largely due to Lieut. Macintyre's fine leadership and initiative, and his gallantry and leading was an inspiring example to all.

Orders, Decorations and Dispatches

VICTORIA CROSS

STRACHAN, HARCUS (*b.* 1884). Pl. xcviii.
Royal High School; First XV. and XI. Student of Medicine, 1903-5 and 1913. Fort Garry Horse, Canadian Expeditionary Force, Private June 1915; L/Corporal Dec. 1915; Corporal Feb. 1916; Sergeant June 1916; Lieut. Sept. 1916; Captain Dec. 1917; Major June 1918. France and Belgium. Wounded July 1917. M.C. Aug. 1917; V.C. Dec. 1917.

Extract from the " London Gazette," 16th Aug. 1917 :—

MILITARY CROSS

For conspicuous gallantry and devotion to duty. He commanded a party which attacked the enemy's outposts. He handled his men with great ability and dash, capturing eight prisoners and killing many more. The operation was carried out without a single casualty to the party.

Extract from the " London Gazette," 18th Dec. 1917 :—

VICTORIA CROSS

For most conspicuous bravery and leadership during operations.
He took command of the squadron of his regiment when the squadron leader, approaching the enemy front line at a gallop, was killed. Lieut. Strachan led the squadron through the enemy line of machine-gun posts, and then, with the surviving men, led the charge on the enemy battery, killing seven of the gunners with his sword. All the gunners having been killed and the battery silenced, he rallied his men and fought his way back at night through the enemy's line, bringing all unwounded men safely in, together with fifteen prisoners.

The operation—which resulted in the silencing of an enemy battery, the killing of the whole battery personnel and many infantry, and the cutting of three main lines of telephone communication two miles in rear of the enemy's front line—was only rendered possible by the outstanding gallantry and fearless leading of this officer.

PLATE XCVIII.

HARCUS STRACHAN.

PLATE XCIX.

SAMUEL THOMAS DICKSON WALLACE.

Orders, Decorations and Dispatches

VICTORIA CROSS

WALLACE, SAMUEL THOMAS DICKSON (*b.* 1892). Pl. xcix. Dumfries Academy. Student of Science, 1911-14; B.Sc. 1914. O.T.C. Infantry, April 1912 to Oct. 1914. R.F.A., 2nd Lieut. Oct. 1914; Lieut. July 1917; Captain Aug. 1918. France, 63rd Brigade, R.F.A. V.C. Feb. 1918, for service at the Battle of Cambrai on 30th Nov. 1917.

Extract from the " London Gazette," 13th Feb. 1918:—

VICTORIA CROSS

For most conspicuous bravery and devoted services in action in command of a section.

When the personnel of the battery was reduced to five by the fire of the artillery, machine-guns, infantry, and aeroplanes; had lost its commander and five of the sergeants, and was surrounded by enemy infantry on the front right flank, and finally in rear, he maintained the fire of the guns by swinging the trails round close together, the men running and loading from gun to gun. He thereby not only covered other battery positions, but also materially assisted some small infantry detachments to maintain a position against great odds.

He was in action for eight hours, firing the whole time, and inflicting serious casualties on the enemy. Then, owing to the exhausted state of his personnel, he withdrew when infantry support arrived, taking with him the essential gun-parts and all wounded men.

His guns were eventually recovered.

Orders, Decorations and Dispatches

ORDER OF THE BATH

KNIGHT GRAND CROSS (G.C.B.)

BEATTY, DAVID (EARL) KEOGH, ALFRED.
KITCHENER, THE RIGHT HON. EARL KITCHENER OF KHARTOUM

KNIGHT COMMANDER (K.C.B.)

BEATSON, GEORGE THOMAS GEDDES, AUCKLAND CAMPBELL
BRUCE, DAVID PORTER, JAMES
DONALDSON, HAY FREDERICK

COMPANION (C.B.)
(*Total* 35)

ALDRIDGE, ARTHUR RUSSELL
BALFOUR, ANDREW
BEGG, CHAS. MACKIE
BEVERIDGE, WILFRED WM. OGILVY
BIRCH, DE BURGH
BIRRELL, EDWIN THOMAS FAIRWEATHER
BOYD, FRANCIS DARLEY
BRUCE, DAVID
CHEYNE, WM. WATSON
CLARK, JAMES
CRANSTON, ROBERT
DEWAR, THOMAS FINLAYSON
DONALDSON, HAY FREDERICK
FORREST, JOHN VINCENT
GEDDES, AUCKLAND CAMPBELL
GORDON-HALL, FREDERICK WILLIAM GEORGE
GRAYFOOT, BLENMAN BUHÔT
HAIG, PATRICK BALFOUR
HANDYSIDE, PATRICK BRODIE
HENDERSON, ROBERT SAMUEL FINDLAY
HUNTER, WILLIAM
HUTCHISON, ROBERT
JOHNSTON, CHARLES ARTHUR
JOHNSTON, HENRY HALCRO
KIRKPATRICK, ROGER
LYNDEN-BELL, EDWARD HORACE LYNDEN
MACPHERSON, JOHN
MACPHERSON, WILLIAM GRANT
MANIFOLD, COURTENAY CLARKE
PRIMROSE, ALEXANDER
RYAN, CHARLES SNODGRASS
SIMPSON, ROBERT JOHN SHAW
STEWART, JAMES PURVES
THOM, GEORGE ST CLAIR
TURNER, WILLIAM ALDREN

ORDER OF MERIT (O.M.)

BALFOUR, ARTHUR J. (RT. HON.) KITCHENER, EARL KITCHENER OF KHARTOUM
BEATTY, DAVID (EARL)

ORDER OF THE STAR OF INDIA

KNIGHT GRAND COMMANDER (G.C.S.I.)

KITCHENER, EARL KITCHENER OF KHARTOUM

KNIGHT COMMANDER (K.C.S.I.)

DUNLOP-SMITH, JAMES ROBERT

COMPANION (C.S.I.)

ALDRIDGE, ARTHUR RUSSELL BANNERMAN, WILLIAM BURNEY

Orders, Decorations and Dispatches

ORDER OF SAINT MICHAEL AND SAINT GEORGE

KNIGHT GRAND CROSS (G.C.M.G.)

KITCHENER, EARL KITCHENER OF KHARTOUM

KNIGHT COMMANDER (K.C.M.G.)

CHEYNE, WM. WATSON
HENDERSON, ROBERT S. F.
HUTCHISON, ROBERT
MACPHERSON, WILLIAM GRANT
PORTER, JAMES
STEWART, JAMES PURVES

COMPANION (C.M.G.)

(*Total* 72)

ALDRIDGE, ARTHUR RUSSELL
BADGEROW, GEORGE WASHINGTON
BALFOUR, ANDREW
BARNETT, LOUIS EDWARD
BEGG, CHAS. MACKIE
BILTON, LEWIS LEONARD
BIRD, JOHN TURNBULL
BIRRELL, EDWIN THOMAS FAIRWEATHER
BLAIR, ALEXANDER STEVENSON
BOYD, FRANCIS DARLEY
BUIST, HERBERT JOHN MARTIN
CHOYCE, CHARLES COLEY
COTTERILL, JOSEPH MONTAGU
DICK, JAMES ADAM
FORREST, JOHN VINCENT
GRANGER, THOMAS ARTHUR
GRAY, WILLIAM LEWIS
GRIFFITHS, JOSEPH
GULLAND, GEORGE LOVELL
HAMILTON, JOHN ARCHIBALD
HEPBURN, DAVID
HUXTABLE, ROBERT BEVERIDGE
JAFFRAY, W. STEVENSON
KENWOOD, HENRY RICHARD
KIRKPATRICK, ROGER
LESLIE, ARCHIBALD STEWART
LINDSAY, CREIGHTON HUTCHINSON
LYELL, DAVID
McDONALD, SAMUEL
MACDOUGALL, ALEX. JAMES
McINTOSH, ALEXANDER MORRISON
MACKAY, WILLIAM BERTIE
MACKELVIE, THOMAS
MACKENZIE, RONALD PIERSON
MACLAREN, MURRAY
MACLEAN, ALEXANDER MILLER
MACPHERSON, WILLIAM GRANT
MANIFOLD, COURTENAY CLARKE
MARTIN, CLAUDE BUIST
MARTIN, JAMES FITZGERALD
MASON-MACFARLANE, DAVID JAMES
MELVILLE, CHARLES HENDERSON
MILL, THOMAS
MOFFAT, ROBERT UNWIN
MURRAY, CHARLES DAVID
MURRAY, DONALD NORMAN WATSON
MYERS, BERNARD
NICHOL, CHARLES EDWARD P. S.
OGILVIE, WALTER HOLLAND
PARKES, WILLIAM HENRY
POTTS, EDMUND THURLOW
PROUT, WILLIAM THOMAS
RIACH, WILLIAM
ROBERTSON, JOHN
RUSSELL, ALEXANDER FRASER
RYAN, CHARLES SNODGRASS
SCOT-SKIRVING, ARCHIBALD ADAM
SIMPSON, ROBERT JOHN SHAW
SINCLAIR, MEURICE
SLAYTER, EDWARD WHEELER
STEWART, HUGH
SYMONS, FRANK ALBERT
TEWSLEY, CYRIL HOCKEN
THOM, GEORGE ST CLAIR
THOMPSON, ALBERT GEORGE
THOMSON, GEORGE RITCHIE
THOMSON, HENRY ALEXIS
WADE, HENRY
WALLACE, DAVID
WHITE, JOSHUA CHAYTOR
WIMBERLEY, CHARLES NEIL CAMPBELL
YEOMAN, ALEXANDER ROSS

Orders, Decorations and Dispatches

ORDER OF THE INDIAN EMPIRE

KNIGHT GRAND COMMANDER (G.C.I.E.)
KITCHENER, EARL KITCHENER OF KHARTOUM

COMPANION (C.I.E.)

ANDERSON, JOHN
BARNARDO, FREDERICK ADOLPHUS FLEMING
BELL, GEORGE JAMES HAMILTON
BELL, ROBERT DUNCAN
BREBNER, ALICK
DUNLOP-SMITH, JAMES ROBERT
GREIG, EDWARD DAVID WILSON
HERON, DAVIS
JOLLY, GORDON GRAY
LAMONT, JOHN CHARLES
MACWATT, ROBERT CHARLES
MADDOX, RALPH HENRY
MELL, FELIX OSWALD NEWTON
MELVILLE, HARRY GEORGE
MILNE, JAMES WILLIAM
MUNRO, DAVID
SUTHERLAND, DAVID WATERS
THORBURN, HAROLD HAY

ROYAL VICTORIAN ORDER

KNIGHT GRAND CROSS (G.C.V.O.)
BEATTY, DAVID (EARL)
KEOGH, ALFRED

KNIGHT COMMANDER (K.C.V.O.)
CRANSTON, ROBERT
DUNLOP-SMITH, JAMES ROBERT

COMMANDER (C.V.O.)
BANKART, ARTHUR REGINALD

MEMBER (M.V.O.)
BARDSWELL, NOEL DEAN
CAMERON, EWEN
CARRUTHERS, JAMES
GORDON, A. A.

KNIGHT (KT.)

BRUCE, DAVID
COTTERILL, JOSEPH MONTAGU
HEWAT, JOHN
WATERHOUSE, HERBERT FURNIVALL

ORDER OF THE BRITISH EMPIRE

KNIGHT COMMANDER (K.B.E.)

BEATSON, GEORGE THOMAS
HANDYSIDE, PATRICK BRODIE
HODSDON, JAMES WILLIAM BEEMAN
MITCHELL-THOMSON, WILLIAM
RYAN, CHARLES SNODGRASS
WALLACE, DAVID
WOODHEAD, GERMAN SIMS

Orders, Decorations and Dispatches

ORDER OF THE BRITISH EMPIRE—*continued.*

COMMANDER (C.B.E.)
(*Total* 40)

BARNARDO, FREDERICK ADOLPHUS FLEMING
BEVERIDGE, WILFRED WILLIAM OGILVY
BRANDER, WILLIAM BROWNE
BRIDGES, JAMES WHITESIDE
BROATCH, GEORGE THOMAS

CATHCART, CHARLES WALKER
CHOYCE, CHARLES COLEY
CRANSTON, ROBERT

FAYRER, JOSEPH

GABITES, GEORGE EDWARD
GORDON, ARCH. ALEXANDER

HOME, GEORGE

JAFFRAY, W. STEVENSON
JOHNSTON, HENRY HALCRO
JOHNSTONE, ROBERT WILLIAM

LORD, JOHN ROBERT
LYELL, DAVID
LYLE, SAMUEL

MACCORMAC, HENRY

MACDONALD, WILLIAM MARSHALL
MACKAY, PATRICK ROBSON
MCLEAN, HENRY JOHN
MARTIN, JAMES FITZGERALD
MASON-MACFARLANE, DAVID JAMES
MILL, THOMAS
MONFRIES, CHARLES BABINGTON SMITH
MORTON, HUGH MURRAY
MORTON, WILLIAM COTHBERT

PARKES, WILLIAM HENRY

ROBINSON, LEONARD NICHOLAS
RUDOLF, ROBERT DAWSON

SILVER, JOHN PAYZANT
STANSFIELD, THOMAS EDWARD KNOWLES
STEWART, FRANK WHITE
STEWART, JOHN
SUTHERLAND, JOHN DONALD

THOM, GEORGE ST CLAIR
THOMSON, DAVID GEORGE

WALLACE, DAVID
WATSON, ALEXANDRA M. C. (*née* GEDDES)

OFFICER (O.B.E.)
(*Total* 174)

ADDISON-SMITH, CHILTON LIND
ALLEN, CHARLES HENRY
ANDERSON, ALEXANDER
ANDERSON, DAVID IRVING

BALFOUR, HARRY HYNDMAN
BALFOUR, JAMES MONCREIFF (THE HON.)
BARKLEY, THOMAS YUILLE
BASHFORD, ERNEST FRANCIS
BAXTER, CHAS. BOTTERIL
BELL, THOMAS CARMICHAEL
BENNETT, WILLIAM
BLACK, NORMAN
BOWERBANK, FRED THOMPSON
BROWN, FRANCIS ROBERT
BROWN, WILLIAM
BRUCE, GEORGE ROBERT

BRUCE, JOHN
BRUCE, WILLIAM
BURNS, HENRY

CAIRNS, JOHN
CARMICHAEL, JAS. CHAS. GORDON
CHAMBERS, ROBERT ALEXANDER
CHILD, ARMANDO DUMAS
CHILL, EDWIN ALBERT
COWAN, JOHN
COWARD, NOEL ANTHONY
COX, JOSHUA JOHN
CRABBIE, JOHN E.
CRAIG, JOHN GIBSON
CRAN, PETER MCLELLAN
CRAWFORD, JAMES MUIR
CUNNINGHAM, BARBARA MARTIN

Orders, Decorations and Dispatches

ORDER OF THE BRITISH EMPIRE (OFFICER)—*continued*.

DAVIDSON, HUGH STEVENSON
DAVISON, WM. HENDERSON
DEAS, PERCY
DINWIDDIE, MELVILLE
DUKES, CUTHBERT
DUNBAR, HENRY JOHN
DUNCAN, GEORGE SIMPSON
DUNLOP, WILLIAM
DUNNETT, GEORGE VICTOR

ELLIOTT, ARTHUR CAMPBELL

FERGUSON, JOHN ALEXANDER
FINDLAY, GEORGE WM. MARSHALL

GIBSON, RICHARD EDWARD
GILL, JOHN GALBRAITH
GORDON, PHILIP JAMES
GRAHAM, DAVID JAMES
GRAHAM, WM. THOMSON
GRANT, ANDREW (ACTING MAJOR)
GRAY, ALEXANDER CHARLES EDWARD
GREER, WM. NIVEN
GUTHRIE, ROBERT LYALL

HALL, JAMES THOMAS
HAMILTON, ALEXANDER GEORGE
HANNA, WILLIAM G. C.
HARDIE, ROBERT
HARPER NELSON, JOHN JOSEPH
HARTLEY, JAMES NORMAN JACKSON
HAULTAIN, WM. FRANCIS THEODORE
HASTIE, STUART HENDERSON
HOME, GEORGE
HOME, WILLIAM EDWARD
HOPE, EDWARD WILLIAM
HUNTER, EVAN AUSTIN
HUTCHINSON-LOW, RICHARD M.

INCH, THOMAS DOUGLAS

JACKSON, GEORGE ERSKINE
JARDINE, JOHN
JARVIS, OSWALD DUKE
JENKINS, GEORGE JOHN
JOHNSTON, JOHN
JOHNSTONE, ROBERT WILLIAM

KELMAN, JOHN
KENNEDY, WM. NICOL WATSON
KERR, CHARLES

KIDD, ALEXANDER EDWARD
KING, DAVID BARTY
KNIGHT, JAMES ST PIERRE
KNUTHSEN, LOUIS FRANCIS

LEASK, JAMES B.
LEGGAT, GEORGE LEGGAT
LEIGHTON, GERALD ROWLEY
LENNOX, JOHN
LINDSAY, WALKER STEWART
LINKLATER, GEORGE JAMES IRVINE
LORNIE, PETER
LOW, JAMES LAWSON

MACARTHUR, DONALD HECTOR COLIN
MACAULAY, DONALD
MACDIARMID, PETER
MACDONALD, ANGUS GRAHAM
MACDONALD, RANALD
MACFIE, RONALD BUTE
MCHUTCHON, EDWIN GRAY
MACKENZIE, ALEX. DONALD
MACKENZIE, ERIC FRANCIS WALLACE
MACKENZIE, JOHN WILLIAM
MCNAUGHTON, WILLIAM
MACPHAIL, HECTOR DUNCAN
MACPHERSON, M. M.
MARGETTS, HORACE PALMER
MARSHALL, LEGH RICHMOND HERBERT PETER
MARTIN, WILLIAM LEWIS
MAXWELL, RAYMOND
MENZIES, ROBERT
MILNE, G. WARDLAW
MITCHELL, LACHLAN MARTIN VICTOR
MOLONY, JOHN BARRÉ DE WINTON
MONFRIES, CHARLES BABINGTON SMITH
MORE, PAXTON ST CLAIR
MORRISON, JOHN TERTIUS
MOTHERWELL, GAVIN BLACK LONDON
MUNRO, EDMUND BRODIE
MURSELL, HENRY TEMPLE

NELSON, JOHN JOSEPH HARPER
NEWMAN, R. E. UPTON
NICOL, GEORGE

OGILVIE, ALEXANDER
OLIVER, ARCHIBALD

POLLOCK, JOHN DONALD
PRIMROSE, ALEXANDER FERGUSON

Orders, Decorations and Dispatches

ORDER OF THE BRITISH EMPIRE (OFFICER)—*continued*.

PROUT, WILLIAM THOMAS

RABAGLIATI, DUNCAN SILVESTRO
RADCLIFFE, FRANK
RAMSAY, GRAHAM COLVILLE
RITCHIE, ROBERT LINTON
RITCHIE, THOMAS CLARK
RITCHIE, WILLIAM THOMAS (R.A.M.C.)
ROBERTSON, GEORGE HENRY WHITESIDE
ROBERTSON, JOHN
ROBERTSON-DURHAM, JAMES A.
ROSS, WILLIAM DAVID
RUTHERFORD, PERCIVAL THOMAS

SANDERSON, FRANCIS ROBERT
SCRIMGEOUR, FREDERICK JOHN
SIMPSON, ALEXANDER P.
SIMPSON, JAMES BERTIE
SIMSON, ROBERT
SINCLAIR, DONALD BOASE
SKINNER, ERNEST WILLIAM
SMITH, GEORGE WILLIAM
SMITH, JULIAN CARTER CARRINGTON
SOUTHON, CHARLES EDWARD
STEVENSON, GEORGE HENDERSON
STOBIE, WILLIAM
STOTT, JAMES ROBERT
STRAIN, LAURENCE HUGH

THOMPSON, FRANK STEWART CORBETT

THOMSON, DAVID
THOMSON, JOHN JAMES
TIMS, HENRY WILLIAM MARETT
TOD, FRED. LEWIS MAITLAND
TODD, EDWIN ERNEST ENEVER

UNWIN, THOMAS BARTON
URQUHART, ALEXANDER LEWIS

VEITCH, ROBERT MCLEOD
VEREL, RAYMOND

WAKELIN, JAMES GLENCORSE
WALKER, NORMAN DUNBAR
WALL, CHARLES PERCIVAL BLIGH
WATSON, ALEXANDER PIRIE
WEBSTER, ARTHUR DOUGLAS
WEDDERBURN, ERNEST MACLAGAN
WEIR, ROBERT YAXLEY
WELLS, JOSEPH DOUGLAS
WHIGHAM, WALTER K.
WILKIE, DAVID PERCIVAL DALBRECK
WILLIAMS, WILLIAM EDWARD REES
WILSON, ANDREW
WOOD, MURDO MACKENZIE
WOODHEAD, GERMAN SIMS
WYNNE-DAVIES, LLEWELYN

YOUNG, ANDREW

MEMBER (M.B.E.)

BALFOUR, HARRY HYNDMAN

CAVAYE, RONALD J.

FARQUHAR, HENRY
FORBES, DUNCAN
FRASER, CATHERINE
FRASER, GEORGE ALEXANDER

GRANT, ANDREW
GREEN, JOSEPH

HAMILTON-GRIERSON, PHILIP FRANCIS

KENNEDY, DUNCAN

MARTINE, WILLIAM ROBERT
MACLEAN, CHARLES A.

PATRICK, NEIL JAMES KENNEDY COCHRAN

SCRIMGEOUR, JAMES
SLAYTER, JOHN HOWARD
SMART, ARCHIBALD GUELPH HOLDSWORTH
STEVENSON, JOHN HORNE

THOMAS, ARTHUR HENRY
THOMSON, FREDERICK CHARLES

WALKER, GEORGE DAVID
WATSON, JOHN CHARLES

Orders, Decorations and Dispatches

COMPANION OF HONOUR

Keogh, Alfred

DISTINGUISHED SERVICE ORDER

COMPANION (D.S.O.)

(*Total* 175)

Anderson, Charles
Anderson, Lewis
Angus, A. W.
Archibald, Robert George

Babington, Marcus Hill
Barkley, James
Barrington-Ward, Victor Michael
Beatty, David (Earl)
Bedingfield, Harry
Bell, John Grenville
Bell, Whiteford James Edward
Bennett, William
Beveridge, Wilfred Wm. Ogilvy
Black, Robert Barclay
Blackwood, William
Bomford, Leslie Raymond
Booth, Patrick Dick
Bowie, John Darling
Bradley, Frederick Hoysted
Brash, James
Brebner, Charles Stuart
Bremner, George
Brown, George Herbert James
Buist, Herbert John Martin
Butchart, Henry Jackson

Cameron, James Black
Carruthers, James
Cobb, William Grahame
Cochrane, Charles William
Connell, J. C. W.
Craig, Archibald Hay
Craig, George
Craig, William Bannerman
Craig-Brown, Ernest
Crombie, John Frank
Cunningham, Francis Wm. Murray
Cuthbert, Thomas Wilkinson

Darling, John May

Davidson, James
Davidson, James Eadie
De La Pryme, Percy Christopher
Dickson, Maurice Rhynd
Dinwiddie, Melville
Dobson, John Greenlaw
Dods, Joseph Espie
Donaldson, Herbert
Dunn, James Churchhill

Eames, Charles William

Ferguson, George Douglas
Fergusson, Vivian Moffat
Findlay, James Leslie
Fisher, David Leonard
Fleming, Arch. Nicol
Fleming, Charles Christie
Fletcher, William
Foggie, Wm. Edward
Forsyth, William Henry
Foulis, Douglas Ainslie
Fraser, Alastair Norman
Fraser, Henry

Gardner, William Ross
Gibson, George Herbert Rae
Gill, John Galbraith
Girdwood, Robert Lawrie
Gordon, Alexander Maclennan
Gordon, Reginald Glegg
Green, Thomas Arthur
Gunson, Edward Carwardine
Gunter, Francis Ernest

Haig, William
Hardyman, John Hay Maitland
Heddle, Malcolm
Henderson, Patrick Hagart
Holmden, Frank Alfred Amphlett
Husband, George Staunton

Orders, Decorations and Dispatches

DISTINGUISHED SERVICE ORDER (COMPANION)—*continued.*

HUTCHISON, ROBERT
HUXTABLE, ROBERT BEVERIDGE
HYSLOP, JAMES

JOHNSTON, CHARLES ARTHUR

KAY, DAVID MILLER
KNOX, ROBERT WELLAND

LANG, ERIC CHRISTISON
LEES, DAVID
LINDSAY, CREIGHTON HUTCHINSON
LYELL, DAVID

MCALLUM, STUART GERALD
MCCONAGHY, WILLIAM
MACDONALD, JAMES ALEXANDER
MCDONALD, SAMUEL
MCINTYRE, HUGH ROSS
MACKENZIE, DONALD FRANCIS
MACKENZIE, FRANCIS BURNETT
MACKENZIE, KENNETH WILLIAM
MACKENZIE, LIONEL DE AMARAL
MACKENZIE, WILLIAM
MACKIE, GEORGE
MACLAGAN, DOUGLAS CRAIG
MACLEAN, ALEXANDER
MACLEOD, JAMES STRACHAN
MACMILLAN, CHARLES CLARKE
MACMILLAN, ROBERT JAMES ALAN
MANIFOLD, JOHN ALEXANDER
MAUGHAN, JOHN ST AUBYN
MEADOWS, ROBERT THORNTON
MEEKE, HUGH CRAIG
MENZIES, ARTHUR JOHN ALEXANDER
MENZIES, JACK MCKENZIE
MILLER, GEORGE WATERSTON
MILLER, WILLIAM ARCHIBALD
MITCHELL, JAMES THOMSON RANKIN
MOFFAT, F. J. C.
MORGAN, WM. D.
MORRISON, WILLIAM KENNETH
MORTON, HUGH MURRAY
MULLER, CHARLES HEROLD
MURRAY, DONALD NORMAN WATSON
MURRAY-LYON, DAVID MURRAY

NAISMITH, JOHN OLIVER
NEWTON, CHARLES TREWEEKE HAND
NICHOL, CHARLES EDWARD P. S.

PANTON, HENRY FORBES
PATERSON, DAVID
PATON, MONTGOMERY PATERSON
PAWLETT, FRANCIS
PENFOLD, ERNEST ALFRED
PERCIVAL, EDGAR
PHILIP, GEORGE MORRISON
POOLE, LEOPOLD THOMAS
PORTEOUS, NORMAN
PORTER, WILLIAM GUTHRIE
POTTS, EDMUND THURLOW
PRESTON, CLASSON O'DRISCOLL
PRINGLE, ROBERT NORMAN
PUCKLE, B. HALE
PURVES, ROBERT BLACK

RATTRAY, MALCOLM MCGREGOR
RAY, MATTHEW BURROW
REID, WALTER RICHARD
RICHARDSON, HUGH
ROBERTSON, DOUGLAS WILLIAM
ROGERS, JAMES SAMUEL YEAMAN
RORIE, DAVID
ROWAN-ROBINSON, JOHN ROWAN
RUTHERFORD, NORMAN CECIL

SCOTT, JOHN
SCOTT, THOMAS HENRY
SILVER, JOHN PAYZANT
SINCLAIR, PATRICK
SLAYTER, EDWARD WHEELER
SLOAN, ALLEN THOMSON
SMART, MORTON WARRACK
SMITH, JOHN GRANT
SMITH, STANLEY ALWYN
SOMERVAIL, WILLIAM FULTON
STEVENSON, WILLIAM SCOTT
STEWART, FREDERICK NAYLOR
STEWART, HUGH
SUTHERLAND, HECTOR WILLIAM
SYMONS, FRANK ALBERT

TAYLOR, GEORGE PRITCHARD
THOM, JOHN GIBB
THOMPSON, ALBERT GEORGE

VAUGHAN, EDMUND WAYNE
VAUGHAN-WILLIAMS, HERBERT WYNNE

WADE, HENRY
WALSH, ROY WILLIAM WHISTON

Orders, Decorations and Dispatches

DISTINGUISHED SERVICE ORDER (COMPANION)—*continued.*

WALSHE, SARSFIELD JAMES AMBROSE HALL
WARD, JOSEPH HUGH
WARDEN, HERBERT LAWTON
WATSON, ALLAN
WATSON, STANLEY

WHAIT, JOHN ROBERT
WHITE, CHARLES RICHARDSON

YOUNG, JAMES
YOUNG, WILLIAM ALLAN

DISTINGUISHED SERVICE CROSS (D.S.C.)

GLEGG, WILLIAM LITTLE
JOE, ALEXANDER

STIRLING, JAMES ALEXANDER
STRAIN, LAURENCE HUGH

WESTWATER, JOHN SINCLAIR

MILITARY CROSS (M.C.)

(Total 705)

ADAM, GEORGE MIN
ADAM, JAMES NEILSON
ADDIS, WILLIAM ROBERT
AIKMAN, JAMES HISLOP
AITCHISON, WILLIAM
ALEXANDER, DAVID C.
ALEXANDER, GEORGE JAMES
ALEXANDER, ROBERT H.
ALLAN, ROBERT MARSHALL
ALLAN, WILLIAM NIMMO
ALLISON, THOMAS BISSET
ANDERSON, CHARLES
ANDERSON, FREDERIC A.
ANDERSON, JOHN GEORGE
ANDERSON, LEWIS
ANDERSON, MARK LOUDON
ANDERSON, ROBERT JOHN
ANDERSON, ROBERT PRINGLE
ANDERSON, WILLIAM
ANDREW, ALEXANDER K.
ANDREW, THOMAS F.
ANDREWS, JOHN ALBAN
ANTHONY, JOHN
ARMIT, NAPIER
ASH, ROBERT VACY C.
AVERILL, LESLIE CECIL L.

BAIN, DANIEL
BAIN, JAMES
BAIRD, W. J. STIRLING
BALFOUR, THOMAS HENRY
BALL, GEORGE FALCONER
BALMAIN, ROY FREDERICK

BARCLAY, HUGH B.
BARCLAY, WILLIAM
BARRON, RODERICK
BARTHOLOMEW, GEORGE G.
BARTHOLOMEW, JOHN
BAXTER, DAVID LEISHMAN
BEATON, GEORGE MACKIE
BEATTIE, JOHN MENZIES
BECKERLEG, VIVIAN C.
BEGG, ROBERT CAMPBELL
BELL, DELVINE
BELL, FRANCIS GORDON
BELL, JAMES GORDON
BELL, JOHN DOUGLAS
BELL, WILLIAM IVOR
BENNETT, W. GORDON
BENTLEY, JAMES
BEVERIDGE, GORDON
BEVERIDGE, ROBERT
BEZUIDENHOUT, PETER H. S.
BIDEN, WILLIAM MERVYN
BIGGAM, JAMES
BISSET, WALTER
BLACK, DAVID CHRISTIE
BLACK, NORMAN
BLACKWOOD, ROBERT CECIL
BLACKWOOD, WILLIAM T.
BLAIR, EDWARD JAMES
BLAIR, PATRICK ALEXANDER
BLAIR, WILLIAM ROBERT
BLANDY, GURTH S
BLOOM, ARTHUR
BOAG, JOHN HAMILTON

BOMFORD, LESLIE RAYMOND
BOOTH, PATRICK DICK
BORWICK, GEORGE
BOWEN-REES, RICHARD ERIC
BOYD, JAMES ROBERTS
BRADLEY, FRED. HOYSTED
BRASH, JAMES
BRASH, JAMES COUPER
BREMNER, ALEXANDER
BREMNER, GEORGE
BREWIS, ROBERT R.
BROADWOOD, ROBERT GRANT
BROWN, CHARLES ROLLAND
BROWN, GAVIN STIELL
BROWN, KENNETH ROBERT
BROWN, WILLIAM THOMSON
BROWNE, BERNARD SCORE
BROWNLIE, JAMES R.
BROWNLIE, WILLIAM
BRUCE, LEWIS CAMPBELL
BULLOCK, ARTHUR EDWIN
BURGH, EDWARD HENRY
BURNET, GILBERT
BURNS, J. RATTRAY
BURTON, ALEXANDER B.

CAIE, JOHN MYLES
CALLEN, JAMES ANDERSON
CALWELL, ANDREW FISHER
CAMERON, ANGUS
CAMERON, DUGALD
CAMERON, RODERICK D.
CAMPBELL, ALEXANDER

Orders, Decorations and Dispatches

MILITARY CROSS—*continued.*

CAMPBELL, ARTHUR
CAMPBELL, DAVID
CAMPBELL, LACHLAN G.
CAMPBELL, SAMUEL B. B.
CANT, ANDREW MCGREGOR
CANT, ROBERT BREMNER
CHALMERS, THOMAS E. B.
CHAMBERS, JAMES
CHANDLER, FRED. CHARLES
CHARLES, JOHN JAMES P.
CHEVES, ALEXANDER BRUCE
CHODAK, HENRY ALEXIS
CHRISTIE, GRAHAM WILSON
CLARK, ARTHUR GRUCHY
CLARK, EDWARD JAMES
CLARK, FRANCIS WILLIAM
CLARKE, FREDERICK O.
CLARKE, THOMAS WILLIAM
CLEGHORN, ALFRED M.
CLEMENTS, THOMAS E.
COLLIER, DAVID ERIC
COLLIER, HOWARD E.
CONDER, ARCHIBALD F. R.
CONNELL, ROBERT M.
COOK, ALAN GIBB
COOPER, C. G. T.
CORKILL, THOMAS F.
CORMACK, HARRY SLATER
COURT, ALEXANDER C.
COUSLAND, KENNETH H.
COWAN, ANDREW
CRAIG, ARCH. CAMPBELL
CRAIG, ARCHIBALD HAY
CRAIG, DAVID DUNCAN
CRAIG, NICHOLAS SMITH
CRAWFORD, GILBERT M.
CRAWFORD, WILLIAM
CREASER, FRED. GEORGE
CROLE, GERARD BRUCE
CROSBIE, KENNETH C.
CRUICKSHANK, JAMES A.
CUNNISON, THOMAS JOHN
CUSHNY, ALEXANDER OGILVY
CUTHBERT, DAVID A. R.
CUTHBERT, JOHN

DALZIEL, EWEN G.
DANDIE, JAMES NAUGHTON
DARLING, JAMES WALKER
DARLING, WILLIAM
DAVIDSON, ALAN MUNRO

DAVIDSON, ALEXANDER W.
DAVIDSON, FREDERICK C.
DAVIDSON, HERBERT JOHN
DAVIDSON, JOHN POLSON
DAVIE, JAMES MURRAY
DAVIE, THOS. MACNAUGHTON
DAVIES, PURSER
DAVIN, LAURENCE FRANK
DEANE, CHARLES GORDON
DERRY, DOUGLAS ERITH
DICK, JAMES H.
DICKIE, EDGAR PRIMROSE
DICKSON, IAN DUNBAR
DICKSON, JAMES
DINWIDDIE, MELVILLE
DODS, JOSEPH ESPIE
DONALD, DOUGLAS ALAN
DOUGLAS, GEORGE PURVES
DOUGLAS, GEORGE R. P.
DOUGLAS, IAN VICTOR
DOUGLAS, WILLIAM LOW
DRUMMOND, ROBERT K.
DRUMMOND, WM. MILLER
DRUMMOND SHIELS, THOMAS
DUFF, ALEX. MACGREGOR
DUFF, DONALD GORDON
DUFFES, ARTHUR PATERSON
DUNCAN, GEORGE WILSON
DUNCAN, JOHN ALFRED A.
DUNDEE, CHARLES
DUNLOP, ALFRED JOSEPH
DUNN, JAMES CHURCHILL
DURWARD, ANDREW B.
DURWARD, WALTER S.

EAGLES, VICTOR THOMAS W.
EATON, RICHARD OLIVER
EDMOND, JOHN JAMES B.
ELDER, EDWARD MEDCALF
EWING, JOHN

FAIRGRIEVE, THOMAS D.
FAIRWEATHER, GEORGE M.
FAIRWEATHER, R. M. D.
FALCONER, ARCHIBALD B.
FALCONER, KEITH DOUGLAS
FARIE, GILBERT JOHN
FARMER, WILLIAM SYDNEY
FENWICK, STANLEY
FERGUSON, JOHN JAMES H.
FERGUSON, WILLIAM HAIG

FERGUSON, WILLIAM PIKE
FERGUSSON, DONALD C.
FERRIE, ARCH. MCLAREN
FINDLAY, RONALD STUART
FINLAYSON, DONALD
FITZGERALD, WM. ERNEST
FLEMING, DAVID
FLEMING, DAVID PINKERTON
FLEMING, IAN GRANT
FLETT, HENRY WILLIAM
FORBES, ALASTAIR GORDON
FORBES, ALEX. KEITH
FORMAN, ARTHUR
FORRESTER, WILLIAM R.
FORSYTH, CHARLES C.
FORTUNE, MACKENZIE
FRASER, DOUGLAS JAMES
FRASER, DUNCAN MENZIES
FRASER, JOHN
FRASER, JOHN ALEXANDER
FREW, DAVID BENNY
FREW, JOHN WILLIAMSON

GALL, DAVID MENMUIR
GALLETLY, ALEXANDER
GALLOWAY, ROBERT ANGUS
GANAPATHY, CODANDA M.
GARDINER, PATRICK P. L.
GARDINER, WILLIAM TYLER
GARRETT-FISHER, WM. E.
GAVIN, WILLIAM STRACHAN
GEDDES, ALASTAIR COSMO B.
GEORGESON, HAROLD
GIBLIN, NORRIS
GIBSON, ROBERT GRAY N.
GILCHRIST, KENNETH A.
GILES, AUSTIN CHARLES
GILL, JOHN GALBRAITH
GILLESPIE, HOPE MURRAY
GILLESPIE, JOHN MARCHBANK
GILLIES, JOHN
GILLIESON, WILLIAM PHIN
GILMOUR, JOHN
GOLDIE, WILLIAM
GORDON, ALEXANDER M.
GOURLAY, GEOFFRY B.
GOURLAY, WM. BALFOUR
GOW, JOHN MILLER
GRAHAM, MALCOLM
GRAHAM, THOMAS
GRAINGER-STEWART, THOMAS

Orders, Decorations and Dispatches

MILITARY CROSS—*continued*.

GRANT, GEORGE REGINALD
GRANT, GERALD WALLACE
GRANT, JOHN CHARLES B.
GRANT, JOHN PETER
GRANT, JOHN VICTOR L.
GRANT, THOMAS F.
GRAYSTON, JOHN WILLIAM
GREENWOOD, ROBERT ALFRED
GREER, WILLIAM WELLS
GRIEVE, JOHN CALDWELL
GROENEWALD, ALBERT
GUNN, JOHN
GUY, JAMES CAMPBELL M.

HADDON, DAVID A. R.
HADDOW, ROSS T.
HALL, ROBERT
HALLIWELL, BASIL T.
HAMILTON, E. STUART BURT
HAMILTON, ANDREW S. L.
HANNAH, ROBERT
HANNAY, HARRY
HARDYMAN, JOHN HAY M.
HARLE, RICHARD JOHN P.
HARPER, FREDERICK GEORGE
HARPER-NELSON, JOHN J.
HARRIS, CHESTER
HART, FRED. G.
HASELL, GODFREY SINCLAIR
HASLAM, JOHN FEARLEY C.
HASTIE, STUART HENDERSON
HASTINGS, THOMAS ERNEST
HAULTAIN, WM. FRANCIS T.
HAY, JAMES
HAYCROFT, JOHN BERRY
HEATHCOTE, GEORGE F. P.
HEDDLE, MALCOLM
HENDERSON, FRANCIS
HENDERSON, GEORGE F.
HENDERSON, JAMES ELMSLIE
HENDRIE, JOHN GAIRDNER W.
HENDRY, PATRICK
HEPBURN, WM. ALLAN F.
HEPPLE, ROBERT ALEXANDER
HERD, WALTER
HERRIDGE, DAVID RUSSELL
HILL, JAMES GILL
HIRD, FRED WAISTELL
HODGSON, STEWART
HOWARD, DOUGLAS WALTER
HUNTER, ALAN DAVID

HUNTER, ARTHUR JOSEPH G.
HUNTER, NORMAN C.
HURST, JOHN THOMAS
HUTCHISON, ADAM FRASER
HUTCHISON, WILLIAM M.

IMPEY, ROBERT LANCE
INCH, ROBERT STUART MARK
INCH, THOMAS DOUGLAS
INGLIS, GORDON STEWART
INGLIS, JOSEPH ELLIS
IRELAND, JOHN

JACKSON, GEORGE ERSKINE
JACKSON, THOMAS WILLIAM
JAMIESON, ARTHUR
JEFFREY, JOHN GEORGE A.
JENKINS, GERALD KERR
JENKINS, GEORGE M.
JOHNS, FREDERICK NOEL
JOHNSON, ERNEST HUGH
JOHNSTON, MATTHEW JAMES
JONES, LIONEL BAKER
JOYNT, NORMAN LOCKHART

KEEP, ARTHUR CORRIE
KEITH, DAVID BARROGILL
KELLY, JOHN LAWSON
KENNEDY, ALEXANDER
KENNEDY, ANGUS JOHN A.
KENNEDY, NORMAN DOUGALL
KENT, JOHN ROBERT
KERR, FRANCIS KENNETH
KIRK, JAMES
KIRSOPP, EDGAR CRAIG B.
KITCHEN, HUGH MILLER
KNIGHT-COUTTS, CECIL

LAIDLAW, WILLIAM
LAING, ARTHUR CECIL
LAING, JOHN MACKINTOSH
LAMBIE, CHARLES GEORGE
LANG, FERDINAND WILSON
LARGE, DAVID TORQUIL M.
LASCELLES, ARTHUR M. (V.C.)
LAURIE, ALBERT ERNEST
LAWRIE, MAURICE BERTRAM
LAWSON, JOHN WILSON
LAWSON, JOSEPH I.
LAWSON, ROBERT
LEADBETTER, JAMES G.

LECKIE, JOHN
LEE, ALAISTER FRASER
LETHEM, WILLIAM ASHLEY
LINDSAY, ROBERT STRATHERN
LINDSAY, W. C. S.
LINTON, ALEXANDER
LINZELL, STANLEY JAMES
LITTLE, PAUL MACDONALD
LIVINGSTONE, ARCH. McD.
LLOYD, RAYMOND LIONEL
LOCKHART, ROBERT
LOCKHART, THOMAS T. R.
LOW, HERBERT BRUCE
LOW, JOHN JACKSON
LUMSDEN, GEORGE J. S.
LYELL, THOMAS

McAFEE, DUNCAN JOHN
McAINSH, DUNCAN TAYLOR
MACASKIE, WILFRID VICTOR
McCALLUM, JAMES RUSSELL
McCALLUM, PETER
McCASKIE, ROY WHITE
McCONNELL, ALBERT E. P.
McCONNELL, PRIMROSE
McCRACKEN, ANGUS MURRAY
MACDONALD, ALASTAIR HUGH
MACDONALD, ANGUS HUGH
MACDONALD, ERIC
MACDONALD, IAN F.
McDONALD, JOHN ROUGH
MACDONALD, JOHN V.
MACDONALD, NORMAN JAMES
MACDONALD, RODERICK O. C.
McDONALD, WILLIAM S.
McELNEY, ROBERT GERALD
McEWEN, EWYN ALASTAIR
McEWEN, THOMAS
McFARLANE, WILFRID
MACGIBBON, JAMES
MACGREGOR, ARCH. GORDON
MACGREGOR, DAVID H.
McGREGOR, ERIC
McGREGOR, GEORGE B.
McGREGOR, JAMES ALLISTER
MACGREGOR, ROBERT F. D.
McHARDY, ARCHIBALD
M'INTOSH, HUGH P. F.
M'INTYRE, HUGH ROSS
M'INTYRE, WILLIAM K.
M'IVER, DONALD PATRICK

Orders, Decorations and Dispatches

MILITARY CROSS—*continued.*

MACIVER, S. L.
MACKAY, DONALD
MACKAY, GEORGE
MACKAY, GEORGE R. E. G.
MACKAY, GEORGE STIBBARD
MACKAY, JAMES A. C.
MACKAY, JOHN CHIENE
MCKAY, MAGNUS ROSS
MCKEAND, WILLIAM IAN
MCKELVEY, DANIEL
MACKENZIE, DONALD ROSS
MACKENZIE, ERIC F. W.
MACKENZIE, ERIC LOFTS
MACKENZIE, FRANCIS B.
MACKENZIE, JOHN A.
MACKENZIE, JOHN TOLME
MACKENZIE, KENNETH W.
MACKENZIE, LIONEL DE A.
MACKENZIE, MALCOLM D.
MACKENZIE, R. W. K.
MCKERROW, MUNGO
MCKIE, HENRY ERSKINE
MCKINNA, HENRY D.
MCKINNON, PATRICK
MACKINTOSH, CHARLES
MACKINTOSH, HUGH C.
MACKINTOSH, IAN
MACKINTOSH, WILLIAM D.
MACLACHLAN, ALASTAIR D. B.
MACLACHLAN, CHARLES F.
MACLAGAN, PHILIP W.
MACLEAN, CHARLES A.
MCLEAN, JAMES YOUNGER
M'LEAN, WILLIAM F.
M'MENAMIN, FRANCIS DE S.
MACMILLAN, HUGH A.
MCMURTRIE, ALEX. C. B.
MACNAE, ROBERT
MCNAIR, HERBERT
MCNEIL, ROBERT PATRICK
MCPHEE, ARTHUR DAVID
MACPHERSON, CHARLES J.
MACPHERSON, HUGH B.
MACRAE, KENNETH M.
MCVICKER, DANIEL
MAIN, JOHN ALEXANDER
MAIR, ROBERT CUMMING T.
MALCOLM, JOHN WRIGHT
MALLACE, ALEXANDER C.
MALLOCH, DUNCAN
MALSEED, ALFRED

MANFORD, GILBERT C.
MANIFOLD, JOHN A.
MANION, ROBERT JAMES
MANN, ALAN COWAN
MANNING, EDYR RODESTON
MANUEL, JAMES
MARSHALL, DAVID
MARSHALL, JOHN FORSYTH
MARSHALL, WILLIAM E.
MARTIN, JOHN
MASON, JOHN WHARTON
MASON, VICTOR HAROLD
MASON-MACFARLANE, F. N.
MAXWELL, AYMER D.
MAXWELL, JOHN HUGH
MAYBIN, WILLIAM
MEISTER, CHARLES G. C.
MENZIES, DANIEL
MENZIES, JACK MCKENZIE
MERCER, WILFRID BERNARD
MIDDLETON, ARTHUR G. M.
MILLAR, GEORGE
MILLER, GEORGE MACKENZIE
MILLER, JAMES
MILLER, JAMES MACBRIDE
MILLER, WILLIAM A.
MILLIGAN, OSWALD BELL
MILNE, THOMAS
MITCHELHILL, JAMES
MITCHELL, ARCHIBALD B.
MITCHELL, WILLIAM McG.
MITCHELL, WILLIAM McK.
MITTON, JAMES BERTRAM
MOIR, ALEXANDER H. M.
MOODIE, ANDREW MORRIS
MOORE, HAMILTON STEPHEN
MORGAN, WM. D.
MORISON, DUNCAN M.
MORRIS, GEORGE
MORRIS, JOHN
MORRISON, DAVID LYALL
MORRISON, WM. (R.A.M.C.)
MORRISON, WM. (R.F.A.)
MORRISON, WILLIAM S.
MUKERJI, KALYAN KUMAR
MUNRO, STEWART GRAHAM
MURDOCH, JOHN DUNCAN
MURDOCH, WILLIAM
MURRAY, ALEXANDER F.
MURRAY, ANGUS DONALD
MURRAY, ROBERT McD.

MURRAY-LYON, DAVID M.
MURRAY-LYON, OVINGTON

NELSON, JOHN JOSEPH H.
NEWMAN, R. E. UPTON

O'BRIEN, ARTHUR J. R.
OGILVIE, GEORGE HAMILTON
ORBELL, RONALD GRAEME S.
ORME, JOHN MCCALLUM
OVENS, ROBERT BLACKSTOCK
OWEN-MORRIS, WILL. G. F.

PANTON, HENRY FORBES
PARKER, WYNDHAM
PATERSON, JAMES RALSTON K.
PATERSON, ROBERT W.
PATON, LEONARD CECIL
PATON, MONTGOMERY P.
PATON, WILLIAM CALDER
PATTEN, JOHN ALEXANDER
PATTEN, MURRAY GLADSTONE
PATTULLO, HENRY A.
PEARCE, JOHN LINDESAY
PERCIVAL, EDGAR
PESEL, HOWARD GEORGE
PHILIP, GEORGE MORRISON
POOLE, LEOPOLD THOMAS
POPE, JUSTIN JOHN
PORTEOUS, NORMAN
POSTLETHWAITE, WILLIAM B.
POTTINGER, DAVID
POWER, MICHAEL PATRICK
PRINGLE, GEORGE L. K.
PRINGLE, JOHN MILLIE
PRINGLE, ROBERT NORMAN
PRIOR, NORMAN HENRY
PROSSER, DAVID GRIFFITHS

RADFORD, AUBREY
RAE, JOHN CAIRNS
RAI, DEWAN HAKUMAT
RANKINE, GEORGE
REID, FRANCIS WARRACK
REID, WILLIAM DOUGLAS
RENDELL, HERBERT
REYNOLDS, ARTHUR OWEN P.
RIDDELL, JAMES W. G. H.
RIDDELL, WILLIAM HUNTER
RIDDOCH, JOHN W.
ROBB, DOUGLAS GEORGE

Orders, Decorations and Dispatches

MILITARY CROSS—*continued*.

ROBB, HENRY DRUMMOND
ROBB, JOHN JAMES
ROBERTSON, ATHOLL
ROBERTSON, CHARLES
ROBERTSON, DOUGLAS SWAN
ROBERTSON, DOUGLAS W.
ROBERTSON, HECTOR ERIC
ROBERTSON, MICHAEL WM.
ROBERTSON, WM. ALBERT
ROBERTSON, WILLIAM LATTO
RODGER, JOHN
ROGERS, CHRISTOPHER
RONN, HENRY ALBERT
ROSS, FINDLAY MCFADYEN
ROSS, JAMES NESS MACBEAN
RUDOLF, HARRY PRIEST
RUSK, GEORGE ARCHER
RUSSELL, CEDRIC
RUSSELL, DAVID HENRY
RUSSELL, JAMES D.
RUSSELL, WILLIAM
RUTHERFORD, ROBERT B.

SAIDLER, JAMES ROY
SANDEMAN, THOMAS ROBERT
SANDEMAN, WILLIAM YOUNG
SCALES, CUTHBERT
SCOTLAND, ALASTAIR GRAEME
SCOTT, ALEXANDER
SCOTT, ALEXANDER BALFOUR
SCOTT, DAVID JOBSON
SCOTT, DUNCAN
SCOTT, GEORGE MACDONALD
SCOTT, GORDON SHAW
SCOTT, HERBERT BREBNER
SCOTT, JAMES
SCOTT, THOMAS HENRY
SCOTT-MONCRIEFF, CHAS. K.
SCOUGAL, ALEX. GRAHAM
SELLAR, THOMAS MCCALL
SHAW, JOHN JAMES M'INTOSH
SHAW, ROBERT GLEN
SHAW, WILLIAM D.
SHENNAN, ARNOLD HOSEASON
SHENNAN, JOHN ROGNVALD
SHEPHERD, JAMES OGILVY
SHEPHERD, JOHN INGRAM
SIM, ALEXANDER
SIMPSON, EDWARD SWAN
SIMPSON, ROBERT K. M.
SKENE, LESLIE HENDERSON

SMALL, HUGH ALEXANDER
SMEALL, JOHN TELFER
SMELLIE, JAMES MCILDOWIE
SMITH, ALEXANDER HUGH D.
SMITH, CLIFFORD H. K.
SMITH, JAMES LINDSAY S.
SMITH, JAMES MARTIN
SMITH, RALPH COLLEY
SMITH, RONALD EDWARD
SOMERVAIL, WILLIAM FULTON
SOMERVILLE, HUGH
SPARKE, WILLIAM MACKAY
SPENCE, THOMAS R. C.
SPOOR, HERBERT MATHER
SPRENT, JAMES
STARK, ROBERT ALEXANDER
STEVENS, HAROLD SAMUEL E.
STEVENSON, GEORGE H.
STEVENSON, JOHN
STEVENSON, JOHN AFFLECK
STEVENSON, WILLIAM SCOTT
STEWART, ALISTER JOHN
STEWART, CHARLES EDWARD
STEWART, FREDERICK N.
STEWART, HUGH
STEWART, JAMES
STEWART, JAMES AITCHISON
STEWART, JOHN WALCOT
STEWART, ROBERT BELL
STEWART, THOMAS
STOOKES, VALENTINE A.
STRACHAN, HARCUS
STRANG, DUNCAN WM. PARK
STRANG, GEORGE MCLAREN
STUART, WILLIAM G. S.
SUTHERLAND, ANDERSON
SUTHERLAND, ANDREW
SUTHERLAND, DAVID
SUTHERLAND, HENRY E. G.
SUTHERLAND, WILLIAM NEIL
SWAN, JAMES
SWAN, MATTHEW ARNOLD
SWIFT, BRIAN HERBERT

TAYLOR, ERIC
TAYLOR, GEORGE PRITCHARD
TAYLOR, HENRY AUGUSTUS
TAYLOR, JAMES
TEDCASTLE, ROBERT
TENNENT, BERNARD CHARLES
THATCHER, FRANCIS G.

THOM, HERBERT JAMES
THOM, JOHN GIBB
THOMPSON, JAMES
THOMSON, EDMUND JOHN
THOMSON, EDWARD G.
THOMSON, JAMES ALEX. M.
THOMSON, JOHN JAMES SCOTT
THOMSON, WILBERT TURNER
THORNE, THEOPHILUS H.
THORNLEY, JOHN HARDWICK
THORNTON, CONYNGHAM V.
THORNTON, PETER
THORP, ROLAND
TOCHER, FORBES S.
TODD, HERBERT WILLIAM
TODD, JOHN
TORRANCE, GUY MELCHIOR
TRAIL, RICHARDSON R.
TREN, RUDOLPH MONTAGUE
TUKE, ALAN LEONARD SMITH
TURNBULL, ARCHIBALD
TURNER, JAMES FRANCIS G.
TYLER, OWEN WILLIAM B.

URQUHART, WM. MACDUFF

VAUGHAN, EDMUND WAYNE
VAN DER VIJVER, GIFFORD T.
VENABLES, JOSEPH KENDRICK

WALKER, ALEXANDER IZAT
WALKER, EDWARD ARCH.
WALKER, FRANK WARRACK
WALKER, GIDEON
WALKER, JOSEPH
WALL, DOUGLAS LARMER
WALLACE, ROBERT WM. L.
WARD, JOSEPH HUGH
WARWICK, A. MACGREGOR
WATER, FRANS KAREL TE
WATSON, JAMES ANDERSON S.
WATSON, JOHN
WATSON, STANLEY
WATSON, WILLIAM NORMAN
WATTHEWS, JOHN WILFRED
WELSH, TOM
WHITAKER, HARRY
WHITAKER, J. RYLAND
WHITE, THOMAS JAMES
WHYTE, GUSTAVUS AIRD
WILLIAMSON, GEORGE H.

Orders, Decorations and Dispatches

MILITARY CROSS—*continued*.

WILLIAMSON, GEORGE SCOTT
WILLIAMSON, KENNETH B.
WILSON, ANDREW JOHN
WILSON, DONALD MCDONALD
WILSON, GORDON
WILSON, JAMES HOURSTON
WINCHESTER, CHARLES C.
WISHART, AYLMER JAMES R.
WOOD, JOHN B.
WRIGHT, ARCH. FRANCIS
YOUNG, ALEXANDER WAUGH
YOUNG, JAMES ANDERSON
YOUNG, WM. ALEXANDER
YOUNG, WILLIAM PAULIN
YOUNIE, WILLIAM SIMPSON

DISTINGUISHED FLYING CROSS (D.F.C.)

CARROTHERS, WM. ALEX.
MCLAREN, HAMISH DUNCAN
MACPHERSON, WILLIAM E.
SCOTT, THOMAS ROBERTSON
TODD, JOHN
YOUNG, JAMES ROY STEPHENS

AIR FORCE CROSS (A.F.C.)

HORNE, JOHN L.
KERR, JAMES
MORTIMER, CYRUS MAXWELL
RITCHIE, PATRICK
TWEEDIE, HARLEY ALEC.

ORDER OF ST JOHN OF JERUSALEM

CATHCART, CHARLES WALKER
COATES, JOHN MANDALL
CROMBIE, JOHN FRANK
DONALD, DAVID
DUNLOP-SMITH, JAMES ROBERT
FAYRER, JOSEPH
FOGGIE, WM. EDWARD
FORREST, JOHN VINCENT
JENNINGS, WILLIAM ERNEST
KNUTHSEN, LOUIS FRANCIS
LYNDEN-BELL, EDWARD HORACE LYNDEN
MACKAY, WILLIAM BERTIE
MARTIN, JAMES FITZGERALD
PARKES, WILLIAM HENRY
PATERSON, ALEXANDER GORDON
ROGERS, JAMES SAMUEL YEAMAN
RORIE, DAVID
SCRIMGEOUR, FREDERICK JOHN
STEVENSON, HENRY JAMES
STEWART, JAMES PURVES
WILL, WILLIAM JOHNSTONE

DISTINGUISHED CONDUCT MEDAL (D.C.M.)

COULTER, WILLIAM
GILCHRIST, JOHN J.
MORRISON, JOHN STEWART
MURRAY, GEORGE BOYD
YOUNG, WILLIAM PAULIN

MILITARY MEDAL (M.M.)

(Total 34)

AMES, FRANCIS W.
BARNIE, WILLIAM EDWARD
BLANCHARD, HENRY H.
BURLEIGH, THOMAS H.
BUTTER, ANDREW JAMES M.
CAMPBELL, ALEXANDER S.
CLUNESS, ANDREW THOMAS
CUMMING, HERBERT GRANT
CUTT, JOHN
DOW, NORMAN DAVID
DUNCANSON, FRANCIS
FINDLAY, JOHN MERRIEVALE
GILCHRIST, WILLIAM RITCHIE
HOPE, JAMES
HUGO-BRUNT, HUGO
INNES-SMITH, STUART W.
KNIGHT, JOHN TAYLOR
KOHLER, LEO JOHN
LOW, JOHN JACKSON
MACFIE, ROBERT ANDREW S.
MCINTOSH, ALEXANDER P.
MCLAREN, ALISTAIR JAMES
MACPHERSON, STANLEY N.
MACRAE, DONALD CAMERON
MARWICK, WILLIAM
MAYBIN, WILLIAM
MILLER, WILLIAM ARMOUR
MORRISON, JOHN
RYRIE, FRANK
SCOTT, JAMES AARON
STANFIELD, THOMAS A.
TAIT, JAMES
WALKER, JAMES CAMPBELL
WHITEHEAD, WILLIAM

Orders, Decorations and Dispatches

MERITORIOUS SERVICE MEDAL

Bryce, James
Nairn, Matthew
Ross, Arthur Alexander
Smale, Ernest Hercules

KAISAR-I-HIND MEDAL

Holland, Henry Tristram
Irvine, Thomas Walter
Macwatt, Robert Charles
Maddox, Ralph Henry
Neve, Ernest Frederick
Prasad, Kanta
Southon, Charles Edward

VOLUNTEER OFFICERS' DECORATION (V.D.)

(Total 30)

Birch, De Burgh
Cairns, John (M.A.)
Cairns, John
Campbell, Alex. John
Cranston, Robert
Currie, Duncan William
Douglas, Charles Edward
Elliot, Stuart Douglas
Forsyth, William
Fraser, Alexander
Fraser, Charles Lachlan
Fulton, Robert Valpy
Graham, Robert Balfour
Hepburn, David
Hope, James Arthur
Hugo-Brunt, Hugo
Huxtable, Robert B.
Inglis, James McDonald
Kirk, Robert
McClymont, James Alex.
Mackenzie, Thomas
Main, Robert Maxwell
Millar, Robert Hoyer
Ryan, Charles Snodgrass
Smart, David
Smith, William Robert
Southam, Herbert
Tiffen, Charles John
Webster, Arthur Douglas
Woodhead, German Sims

TERRITORIAL DECORATION (T.D.)

(Total 76)

Adamson, Thomas
Anderson, Alford William

Barrie, William Turnbull
Blair, Alexander S.
Bruce, John
Burns, James Golder

Cadell, Hew Francis
Cameron, John Sproat T.
Capper, Stewart Henbest
Cochrane, Charles Wm.
Colman, Horace C.
Craig, James
Crombie, John Frank
Cunningham, Robert J.

Dewar, Thomas Finlayson
Dodgson, Henry

Edgar, Frank
Elliot, Andrew

Foggie, William Edward
Forsyth, William
Frankish, Thomas

Greenway, Alexander S.
Greig, David Middleton
Griffiths, Joseph

Haig, William
Horne, Robert John Maule
Howard-Jones, John

Inglis, James McDonald

Jackson, Robert
Johnstone, Michael P.

Kerr, Peter Murray

Laing, David
Leslie, Archibald Stewart
Livingstone, John
Lumsden, John Lowson

Macdonald, James Harold
Macdonald, William A.
Macduff, Peter
McIntosh, Alexander M.
Mackay, William Bertie
Maclean, Alexander M.
Macpherson, John L.
Martin, William Lewis
Mason-Macfarlane, D. J.
Millar, John
Miller, Alexander C.
Miller, Alfred Tennant

Orders, Decorations and Dispatches

TERRITORIAL DECORATION—*continued.*

MILLER, GEORGE WATERSTON
MONCRIEFF, RICHARD H. F.
MUNRO, ALEXANDER ROSE

NEWTON, DUNCAN GRAY
NIGHTINGALE, JOHN
NIVEN, JAMES P.
NORMAN, LOUIS S. F. DE R.

OGILVIE, ALEXANDER

RAINIE, WILLIAM

RANKINE, THOMAS
ROGERS, JAMES SAMUEL Y.
RORIE, DAVID
RUTHERFORD, ALLAN FREER

SCOTT, JAMES
SCOTT, THOMAS
SIMPSON, ALEXANDER P.
SIMPSON, JAMES BERTIE
SMITH, JOHN GRANT
SMITH, JOHN WILLIAM
SPRAGUE, HENRY DOUGLAS

STEVEN, WILLIAM CHARLES
STEVENSON, HENRY JAMES
STEVENSON, THOMAS

TAYLOR, WILLIAM ATKINSON
TODD, JAMES ALEXANDER
TUKE, ALAN LEONARD SMITH

WHAIT, JOHN ROBERT
WHYTE, GEORGE FRANCIS
WILSON, JAMES

FRANCE

LEGION OF HONOUR

BEATSON, GEORGE T.
BEATTY, DAVID (EARL)
BEVERIDGE, WILFRED W. O.
BROATCH, GEORGE THOMAS
BUIST, HERBERT JOHN M.
CLARK, STEPHEN FRAZER
CRANSTON, ROBERT
DICKSON, MAURICE RHYND

GEDDES, ALASTAIR C. B.
FISHER, DAVID LEONARD
KEOGH, ALFRED
LYELL, DAVID
MACPHERSON, WM. GRANT
MOFFATT, ALEC. MCRITCHIE
PEFFERS, ANDREW
RANKINE, GEORGE

ROBINSON, LEONARD N.
RORIE, DAVID
ROWAN, HENRY DAVIS
SMITH, JAMES MARTIN
STEVENS, HAROLD S. E.
STRANG, DUNCAN W. P.
SUTHERLAND, JOHN DONALD
WATSON, STANLEY

MÉDAILLE D'HONNEUR EN ARGENT

ANDERSON, JAMES ROBERTSON

ORDRE DU MÉRITE

MACDONALD, JAMES ALEX.

CROIX DE GUERRE

(*Total* 63)

ANDERSON, JOHN NORRIE
ANDERSON, LEWIS

BARKER, ALEXANDER
BARRINGTON-WARD, V. M.
BEGG, CHAS. MACKIE
BENNETT, WILLIAM
BOWIE, JOHN MACAULAY
BROWNLIE, JAS. RUTHERFORD
BUIST, HERBERT JOHN M.

CALLEN, JAMES ANDERSON
CHRISTIE, ARTHUR WM. S.
CLARK, STEPHEN FRAZER
COUSLAND, KENNETH H.

DAVIDSON, JAMES EADIE
DEAS, LEONARD JOSEPH M.
DRUMMOND, WM. MILLER
DUFF, DAVID KERR

EDINGTON, ALEXANDER D.
EDINGTON, JAMES WILLIAM

FLEMING, DAVID
FORMAN, ARTHUR
FRASER, KENNETH GRANT

GARDNER, WILLIAM ROSS
GIBSON, GEORGE HERBERT R.
GORDON, ARCHIBALD A.
GOURLAY, GEOFFRY BALFOUR

Orders, Decorations and Dispatches

FRANCE (CROIX DE GUERRE)—*continued.*

HAY, FREDERICK WILLIAM
HEATHCOTE, GEORGE F. P.
HOPE, JOHN CHARLES DAVID
HUGHSON, A. J.

JAMIE, WILLIAM DALLAS

LAING, ARTHUR CECIL
LINZELL, STANLEY JAMES
LUMSDEN, JOHN

MACDONALD, JAMES A.
MCEWAN, PETER
MCKELVEY, DANIEL
MCLAREN, HAMISH DUNCAN
MACLEAN, CHARLES A.

MANIFOLD, C. C.
MILLER, GEORGE WATERSTON
MITCHELL, JAMES T. R.
MOWAT, JAMES LAWSON
MUIR, JOHN REID
MUNRO, STEWART GRAHAM
MURRAY, JAMES MACKINNON

PORTEOUS, EDWARD JOHN

ROGERS, JAMES SAMUEL Y.

SAIDLER, JAMES ROY
SHAW, JOHN JAMES M'INTOSH
SMART, ARCHIBALD G. H.

STEVENS, HAROLD SAMUEL E.
STEVENSON, WILLIAM SCOTT
STEWART, DONALD
STEWART, HUGH

TAIT, CHARLES KINGSLEY
TAYLOR, GEORGE PRITCHARD
TODD, JOHN BARBER

VELLNOT, GEORGE ALBERT

WARD, FRANCIS
WATTERVILLE, IAN DE
WEBSTER, WILLIAM LECKIE
WHYTE, GEORGE FRANCIS

MÉDAILLE DE RECONNAISSANCE

KNUTHSEN, LOUIS FRANCIS

MACDONALD, WILLIAM ALEXANDER

MÉDAILLE DE L'ASSISTANCE PUBLIQUE

BALDIE, ALEXANDER

MACCORMACK, HENRY
THOMSON, ROBERT

WARD, JOSEPH HUGH

MÉDAILLE DES ÉPIDÉMIES

ALDRIDGE, ARTHUR RUSSELL
CROLIUS, JOHN ROBERT
CROMBIE, JOHN FRANK
GAMBLE, CROMWELL

HILL, WILLIAM HUGH
KNUTHSEN, LOUIS FRANCIS
OLIVER, ARCHIBALD
RITCHIE, THOMAS CLARK
SHEWARD, CHARLES RAILTON

WATSON, FRANK HERBERT C.
WILKINS, RICHARD
WILSON, MARION ELIZABETH
YOUNG, ALEXANDER WAUGH

BELGIUM

CHEVALIER DE L'ORDRE DE LA COURONNE

DAVIDSON, JAMES EADIE

GORDON, A. A.
HUTCHISON, ROBERT

KEOGH, ALFRED

ORDER OF LEOPOLD

CORKILL, THOS. FREDERICK
GORDON, ARCHIBALD A.

HUTCHISON, ROBERT
LYELL, DAVID

PEARSON, JOHN HENRY H.
WATSON, HARRY M. D.

Orders, Decorations and Dispatches

BELGIUM—*continued.*

CROIX DE GUERRE

BELL, WM. IVOR
BILTON, LEWIS LEONARD
CARROTHERS, WM. A.
CLEGHORN, ALFRED M.
CORKILL, THOS. FREDERICK
CUNNISON, THOMAS JOHN
DAVIDSON, JAMES EADIE
DRUMMOND-SHIELS, THOMAS
EWING, JOHN
FLEMING, DAVID P.
GILCHRIST, ALEXANDER
GORDON, A. A.
HENDRIE, JOHN G. W.
HUME, JOHN
HUTCHISON, ROBERT
LAING, FREDERICK ROBERT
LYELL, DAVID
MACGREGOR, ARCH. GORDON
MCGREGOR, DUNCAN
MASON, JOHN BLACK
MORGAN, WM. D.
PEARSON, JOHN HENRY H.
SLUYS, MAURICE
WATSON, HARRY M. D.
WINCHESTER, CHARLES C.

CROIX CIVIQUE

GORDON, A. A.

RUSSIA

ORDER OF ST ANNE

FITZWILLIAMS, DUNCAN C. L.
GORDON, A. A.
RITCHIE, PATRICK
SCARTH, HENRY WILLIAM

ORDER OF ST STANISLAUS

BEVERIDGE, WILFRED WM. O.
FITZWILLIAMS, DUNCAN C. L.
GLEGG, WILLIAM LITTLE
MCALLAN, JAMES
PENFOLD, ERNEST ALFRED
RITCHIE, PATRICK
SCARTH, HENRY WILLIAM
STEEL, JAMES WILLIAM
STODDART, JOHN

ORDER OF ST VLADIMIR

FITZWILLIAMS, DUNCAN CAMPBELL LLOYD

ORDER OF ST GEORGE

CRAWFORD, EDWARD JAMES
INGLIS, ELSIE MAUD
WEATHERSON, R. R. S.

SERBIA

ORDER OF THE WHITE EAGLE

BIRRELL, EDWIN THOMAS F.
CARLYLE, ROBERT CARLYLE
GRAY, FRANCIS HENRY T.
INGLIS, ELSIE MAUD
KEOGH, ALFRED
KNOX, ROBERT WELLAND
PROUDFOOT, ROBERT
WADE, HENRY
WHAIT, JOHN ROBERT

Orders, Decorations and Dispatches

SERBIA—*continued*.

ORDER OF ST SAVA

BARRINGTON-WARD, L. E.
BENNETT, AGNES E. L.
BUIST, HERBERT JOHN M.
CARMICHAEL, NORMAN SCOTT
CARSON, JOSEPH THOMPSON
CLARK, STEPHEN FRAZER
FORBES, ALEX. KEITH
HILL, JOHN MCADAM
HUNTER, WILLIAM

HUTCHISON, ALICE MARION
INGLIS, ELSIE MAUD
JAFFRAY, W. STEVENSON
KIDD, ALEXANDER EDWARD
MARTIN, CLAUDE BUIST
MITCHELL, WILLIAM G.
MONSARRAT, KEITH W.
MACGIBBON, JAMES
MCTURK, JOHN NORMAN

MARTIN, CLAUDE BUIST
ROSS, THOMAS WM. E.
SCOTT, JESSIE ANNE
SMITH, CHARLES EDGAR H.
SMITH, FLEET FLOYD S.
STEWART, JAMES PURVES
STRUTHERS, JOHN WILLIAM
WALKER, HUGH
WILSON, RICHARD ARDERNE

RED CROSS MEDAL

BENNETT, AGNES E. L.

MCDOUGALL, HELEN

RIDLEY, WILLIAM ROBERT

ORDER OF CHARITY

MAXWELL, JAMES

ITALY

CAVALIERE DELLA CORONA D'ITALIA

HUTCHISON, ROBERT
KNOX, ROBERT WELLAND

LOGAN, GEORGE
MACPHERSON, WILLIAM G.

PEEK, JOHN HAROLD
WHITE, JOHN LETHAM

CROCE DI GUERRA

INCH, THOMAS DOUGLAS
COCHRANE, EDWARD A.

FINDLAY, J. L.
GILL, CECIL ERNEST G.

SHAW, WILLIAM JOHN
SMITH, JAMES LINDSAY S.

ENCOMIUM COMMANDO SUPREMO

LOCKHART, THOMAS THOMSON RANKIN

ASIAGO PLATEAU MEDAL

BROWN, HENRY HILTON

DOVE, ROLLAND ATKINSON

MELVILLE, KENMURE D.

BRONZE MEDAL

MACKAY, GEORGE REGINALD EDWARD GRAY

MOWAT, GEORGE THOMSON

Orders, Decorations and Dispatches

ROUMANIA

CHEVALIER OF THE CROWN OF ROUMANIA

ADAM, WILLIAM GEORGE
GLEGG, WILLIAM LITTLE
FITZWILLIAMS, DUNCAN C. L.
SHENNAN, JOHN ROGNVALD

STAR OF ROUMANIA

ARMSTRONG, FERGUS
BUTCHART, HENRY JACKSON

GREECE

ORDER OF THE REDEEMER

ALDRIDGE, ARTHUR RUSSELL
BIRRELL, EDWIN THOMAS F.
KIDD, ALEXANDER EDWARD
LITT, JOHN PERCY
OLIVER, ARCHIBALD
RITCHIE, CHARLES RONALD
STRAIN, LAURENCE HUGH

ORDRE ROYAL DE GEORGES

SANDERSON, FRANCIS ROBERT

MILITARY CROSS

McINTYRE, WILLIAM KEVERALL

MILITARY MERIT MEDAL

BIRRELL, EDWIN THOMAS F.
RITCHIE, CHARLES RONALD
WELSH, WILLIAM HALLIDAY

MONTENEGRO

ORDER OF DANILO

CRAIG-BROWN, ERNEST

PORTUGAL

COMMANDER OF THE ORDER OF AVIS

BOYDEN, PERCY HAMILTON
GORDON, PHILIP JAMES
LYELL, DAVID

NORWAY

KNIGHT OF ST OLAF

CRANSTON, ROBERT

Orders, Decorations and Dispatches

SWEDEN

KNIGHT COMMANDER OF NORTH STAR

Dunlop-Smith, James Robert

EGYPT

ORDER OF THE NILE

Allen, Charles Henry
Buist, David Stirling
Leask, James B.
McConaghy, William
Marshall, William E.
Ogilvie, Walter Holland
Spence, Basil Hamilton H.
Thorburn, David Hay

HEDJAZ

ORDER OF EL NAHDA

Ramsay, Graham Colville

JAPAN

IMPERIAL ORDER OF THE SACRED TREASURE

Handyside, Patrick Brodie
Macpherson, William Grant

DECORATION FOR DISTINGUISHED SERVICES, RED CROSS SOCIETY

Macpherson, William Grant

CHINA

ORDER OF WEN-HU

Addison-Smith, Chilton Lind

UNITED STATES

DISTINGUISHED SERVICE MEDAL

Hutchison, Robert

Orders, Decorations and Dispatches

DISPATCHES, Etc.

MENTIONED IN DISPATCHES AND FOR VALUABLE WAR SERVICE

(*Total* 1068)

ADAM, WILLIAM GEORGE
ADAMS, DAN VERE MAXWELL
ADAMSON, THOMAS
ADDISON-SMITH, CHILTON L.
ADIE, WILLIAM JOHN
AIKMAN, JAMES HISLOP
ALDRIDGE, ARTHUR RUSSELL
ALEXANDER, DAVID C.
ALEXANDER, GEORGE JAMES
ALEXANDER, JOHN
ALEXANDER, RICHARD C.
ALLEN, CHARLES HENRY
ANDERSON, ABNER GALLIE
ANDERSON, CHARLES
ANDERSON, DAVID IRVING
ANDERSON, JOHN ALLAN
ANDERSON, LEWIS
ANDERSON, ROBERT YUILL
ANDREW, ALEXANDER KEITH
ANGUS, A. W.
ANGUS, THOMAS CURR
ARBUCKLE, HENRY ERNEST
ARCHIBALD, ROBERT GEORGE
ASHRUFF, MOHOMED
ATKINSON, ALBERT A.

BADGEROW, GEORGE W
BAEZA, JOSHUA ISADORE
BAIN, DANIEL
BAIN, FRANCIS O.
BAIRD, ARCHIBALD WILLIAM
BAIRD, JOSEPH HAROLD
BALFOUR, HARRY HYNDMAN
BALFOUR, THOMAS HENRY
BALL, GEORGE FALCONER
BALLANTINE, JAMES
BALMAIN, ROY FREDERICK
BANKART, ARTHUR R.
BARCLAY, IVAN CURROR C.
BARCLAY, WILLIAM
BARKER, THOMAS L.
BARKLEY, JAMES

BARKLEY, THOMAS YUILLE
BARNETT, LOUIS EDWARD
BARRINGTON-WARD, V. M.
BARRON, DAVID CUTHBERT
BARTHOLOMEW, JOHN
BASHFORD, ERNEST FRANCIS
BEATSON-BELL, JOHN
BEATTY, MARTIN CECIL
BEDINGFIELD, HARRY
BEGG, ROBERT CAMPBELL
BEILBY, JULIUS HENRY
BELFORD, WALTER CHEYNE
BELL, DELVINE
BELL, WILLIAM IVOR
BENNETT, WILLIAM
BENNETT, W. GORDON
BENTLEY, JAMES
BERRY, JOHN PARTON
BEST, STEPHEN W.
BEVERIDGE, ROBERT
BEVERIDGE, THOMAS L.
BEVERIDGE, WILFRED W. O.
BIDEN, WILLIAM MERVYN
BIGGAM, JAMES
BILTON, LEWIS LEONARD
BIRCH, DE BURGH
BIRD, JOHN TURNBULL
BIRRELL, EDWIN THOMAS F.
BIRRELL, WILLIAM GEORGE
BLACK, DAVID CHRISTIE
BLACK, JOHN
BLACK, ROBERT BARCLAY
BLACKADDER, WILLIAM
BLACKWOOD, ROBERT CECIL
BLACKWOOD, WILLIAM
BLAIR, ALEXANDER S.
BLAIR, PATRICK ALEXANDER
BLAIR, RALPH
BLANCHARD, ROBERT J.
BOAG, JOHN HAMILTON
BOMFORD, L. R.
BONALLO, JAMES

BOOTH, HERBERT
BOOTH, PATRICK DICK
BOSTOCK, JOHN SOUTHEY
BOWEN-REES, RICHARD E.
BOWERBANK, FRED. T.
BOWES, JOHN
BOWIE, JOHN DARLING
BOWIE, JOHN MACAULAY
BOYACK, RUSSELL
BOYD, FRANCIS DARBY
BOYD, JOHN CAMPBELL
BRAMWELL, HERBERT
BRAND, GEORGE BELL
BRASH, JAMES
BRASSEY, LAWRENCE P.
BREBNER, CHARLES STUART
BREMNER, ALEXANDER
BREMNER, GEORGE
BRINK, JOHANNES H.
BROCK, GEORGE SELBY
BROOK, ALEXANDER
BROOK, ALEXANDER B.
BROWN, GEORGE HERBERT J.
BROWN, FRANCIS ROBERT
BROWN, WILLIAM
BROWNE, BERNARD SCORE
BRUCE, ALEXANDER C. A.
BRUCE, GEORGE ROBERT
BRUCE, JAMES
BRUCE, JOHN
BRUCE, LEWIS CAMPBELL
BRUCE, WILLIAM
BRUMMITT, ELLIOTT A.
BRYCE, JAMES
BRYDONE, THOMAS
BUCHAN, WILLIAM TAYLOR
BUCHANAN, JOHN CECIL R.
BUIST, DAVID STIRLING
BUIST, HERBERT JOHN M.
BULLOCK, ARTHUR EDWIN
BULLOCK, WILLIAM EWART
BURGESS, CHARLES HERBERT

Orders, Decorations and Dispatches

DISPATCHES, ETC.—*continued*.

BURNET, WILLIAM
BURNS, JAMES GOLDER
BURNS-BEGG, ROBERT
BURROW, JOSEPH LE F. C.
BUTCHART, HENRY JACKSON
BUTLER, EDWIN
BYRES, GEORGE M.

CAIRD, FRANCIS MITCHELL
CAIRNS, JAMES WILLIAM
CALLEN, JAMES ANDERSON
CAMERON, ALEXANDER T.
CAMERON, DUNCAN A.
CAMERON, JAMES BLACK
CAMERON, JOHN HUNTER
CAMERON, RODERICK D.
CAMPBELL, ALEX. JOHN
CAMPBELL, ERNEST KENNETH
CAMPBELL, JAMES DUNCAN
CAMPBELL, JOHN YOUNG
CAMPBELL, LACHLAN G.
CAMPBELL, SAMUEL B. B.
CAMPBELL, WILLIAM
CANNON, JOHN WILSON
CANT, ANDREW MCGREGOR
CAPPER, STEWART HENBEST
CARMICHAEL, JAMES C. G.
CARRUTHERS, VINCENT T.
CASSILLIS, ARCH. K. (EARL OF)
CAVERHILL, AUSTIN MACK
CHALKER, ERIC
CHAMBERS, ROBERT A.
CHAMBERS, WALTER D.
CHARLES, JOHN JAS. P.
CHARNOCK, JOHN PLETHEAN
CHAUDHURI, MANMATHA N.
CHEVES, ALEXANDER BRUCE
CHEW, WILLIAM ROGER
CHILD, ARMANDO DUMAS
CHILDS, TOM W. J.
CHOYCE, CHARLES COLEY
CHRISTIE, ARTHUR WM. S.
CHRISTIE, WILLIAM FRANCIS
CLARK, CHARLES INGLIS
CLARK, GILBERT
CLARK, JAMES
CLARK, STEPHEN FRAZER
CLARKE, THOS. WILLIAM
CLEEVES, FREDERICK R.
CLEGHORN, ALFRED M.
CLEMENT, HUBERT ARNOLD

CLEMENTS, JOHN BURTON
COCHRANE, CHARLES W.
COCHRANE, EDWARD A.
COCHRANE, WILLIAM T.
CONNELL, J. C. W.
COOK, ADRIAN HENRY
COOPER, WM. RICHARD
COPELAND, ROBERT JAMES
CORKILL, THOMAS F.
CORMACK, ROBERT PAIRMAN
CORMACK, HARRY SLATER
COTTERILL, JOSEPH M.
COULLIE, ALEXANDER G.
COULTER, WILLIAM
COURTNEY, BERTRAM JOSEPH
COUSLAND, KENNETH H.
COUTTS, WILLIAM ALEX.
COWAN, GEORGE DEAS
COWAN, JOHN
COWAN, JOHN MACQUEEN
COWARD, NOEL ANTHONY
COWPER, JOHN J. MCPHAIL
COX, JOSHUA JOHN
CRAIG, ARCHIBALD HAY
CRAIG, DAVID DUNCAN
CRAIG, GEORGE
CRAIG, JAMES
CRAIG-BROWN, ERNEST
CRAN, PETER MCLELLAN.
CREASER, FRED. GEORGE
CROLL, ANDREW
CROMBIE, JOHN FRANK
CUNNINGHAM, BARBARA M.
CUNNINGHAM, FRANCIS W. M.
CUNNISON, THOMAS JOHN
CUTHBERT, JOHN
CUTHBERT, THOMAS W.

DANDIE, JAMES NAUGHTON
DARLING, JOHN MAY
DARLING, WILLIAM
DAUTH, DIEDERIK JOHN
DAVIDSON, FREDERICK C.
DAVIDSON, HUGH S.
DAVIDSON, JAMES
DAVIDSON, JAMES EADIE
DAVIDSON, ROGER STEWART
DAVIE, JAMES MURRAY
DAVIE, PETER COUSIN
DAVISON, WM. HENDERSON
DEAS, LEONARD JOSEPH M.

DE LA PRYME, PERCY C.
DELGADO, ALFRED ERROLL
DEWAR, THOMAS FINLAYSON
DEWAR, WILLIAM SHAW
DICK, ALAN MACDONALD
DICK, JAMES ADAM
DICK, WILLIAM CHARLES
DICKSON, IAN DUNBAR
DICKSON, MAURICE RHYND
DICKSON, WILLIAM F.
DILL, MARCUS GRAHAM
DILLON, FREDERICK
DINWIDDIE, MELVILLE
DOBELL, CLARENCE BRIAN
DODS, JOSEPH ESPIE
DONALD, DAVID
DONALDSON, HERBERT
DOUGLAS, CHARLES
DOUGLAS, GEORGE PURVES
DOUGLAS, GEORGE ROBERT P.
DOWDEN, ARTHUR ERNEST
DRUMMOND, JOHN
DRUMMOND, WM. MILLER
DRUMMOND-SHIELS, THOMAS
DUFF, ALEX. MACGREGOR
DUFF, DONALD GORDON
DUFF, WM. RICHMOND
DUGGAN, CHARLES WILLIAM
DUKES, CUTHBERT
DUN, ROBERT CRAIG
DUNBAR, HENRY JOHN
DUNCAN, GEORGE SIMPSON
DUNCAN, GEORGE WILSON
DUNDAS, JAMES
DUNLOP, WILLIAM
DUNN, BERNARD VENN
DUNN, JAMES CHURCHHILL
DUNNETT, GEORGE VICTOR
DURWARD, WALTER STEWART
DYKES, ANDREW LESLIE
DYKES, JAMES JOHNSTONE

EAGLES, VICTOR THOMAS W.
EAMES, CHARLES WILLIAM
EDINGTON, ALEXANDER D.
EDINGTON, DAVID CAMERON
EDWARDS, PETER WILLIAMS
ELDER, ALEXANDER AUSTIN
ELLIOT, ANDREW
ELLIOT, EDWARD JOHN
EWING, ALEX. JAMES

Orders, Decorations and Dispatches

DISPATCHES, ETC.—*continued*.

EWING, JOHN

FARMER, WILLIAM SYDNEY
FASSON, FRANCIS HAMILTON
FAULKNER, HUGH
FAYRER, JOSEPH
FERGUSON, GEORGE DOUGLAS
FERGUSON, JAMES
FERGUSON, JOHN (S.R.)
FERGUSON, WILLIAM HAIG
FERGUSSON, DONALD C.
FERGUSSON, VIVIAN MOFFATT
FERREIRA, P. D. F.
FETHERSTON, RICHARD H.
FINDLAY, J. L.
FINLAY, GILBERT LAURIE K.
FISHER, DAVID LEONARD
FISHER, JOHN W. D.
FITZWILLIAMS, DUNCAN C. L.
FLEMING, ARCH. NICOL
FLEMING, CHARLES CHRISTIE
FLEMING, DAVID P.
FLEMING, IAN GRANT
FLEMING, SAMUEL
FOGGIE, WM. EDWARD
FORREST, JOHN VINCENT
FORSYTH, CHARLES CALDER
FORSYTH, WILLIAM ALLAN
FORSYTH, WILLIAM HENRY
FORSYTH-GRANT, IVOR
FOSTER, FRANCIS GREGORY
FOSTER, MALCOLM
FOTHERGILL, REG. HANNAY
FOULIS, DOUGLAS AINSLIE
FOWLER, WM. ALEXANDER
FRASER, ALASTAIR NORMAN
FRASER, ALEXANDER
FRASER, HENRY
FRASER, JOHN
FRASER, KENNETH GRANT
FRASER, ROBERT
FRASER, WILLIAM JAMES
FREW, DAVID BENNY
FULLER, THOMAS ARTHUR

GAMBLE, CROMWELL
GARDINER, WILLIAM TYLER
GARDNER, WILLIAM ROSS
GEORGESON, DAN HORACE
GERRARD, ROBERT FINLAY

GIBB, HAMILTON A. R.
GIBSON, HERBERT ROBERT B.
GIFFORD, JOHN
GILCHRIST, KENNETH A.
GILDARD, JAMES GRAHAM A.
GILES, AUSTIN CHARLES
GILL, JOHN GALBRAITH
GILLESPIE, JOHN MARCHBANK
GILLIESON, WILLIAM PHIN
GILLISON, ANDREW
GIRDWOOD, ARTHUR INGLIS
GLANVILL, ERNEST MUIR
GLASSE, JOHN MORLEY
GLEGG, WILLIAM LITTLE
GLYNN, ARTHUR SAMUEL
GOLDIE, WILLIAM
GOODFELLOW, ERIC HECTOR
GORDON, CLEMENTINA MARY
GORDON, REGINALD GLEGG
GORDON-HALL, FRED. W. G.
GORMAN, JOHN PATRICK
GORRIE, ROBERT MACLAGAN
GOURLAY, GEOFFRY BALFOUR
GOW, JOHN MILLER
GOWAN, ALASTAIR A.
GOWANS, THOMAS
GRAHAM, DAVID JAMES
GRAHAM, WILLIAM THOMSON
GRANGER, THOMAS ARTHUR
GRANT, ALEXANDER
GRANT, ANDREW (ACT. MAJOR)
GRANT, JOHN CHARLES B.
GRANT, JOHN PETER
GRANT, PERCY KENMURE
GRAY, JOHN WILLIAM
GRAY, WILLIAM LEWIS
GRAYFOOT, BLENMAN BUHÔT
GREEN, ARTHUR C. V.
GREEN, THOMAS ARTHUR
GREENWOOD, ROBERT ALFRED
GREER, WILLIAM WELLS
GREGORY, JOHN BONAR
GRIEVE, JOHN
GRIFFITHS, ALFRED
GULLAND, GEORGE LOVELL
GUNN, ALBERT ALEXANDER
GUNN, JOHN WM. CORMACK
GUNTER, FRANCIS ERNEST
GUTHRIE, HUGH L. C.
GUTHRIE, W. A.
GUY, JAMES C. MORRISON

HADDON, DAVID A. ROSS
HAIG, PATRICK BALFOUR
HALL, JAMES THOMAS
HALL, PETER TAYLOR
HALL, ROBERT
HALLIWELL, BASIL T.
HAMILTON, ALEXANDER G.
HAMILTON, JOHN ARCHIBALD
HAMILTON-GRIERSON, P. F.
HANMER, HASSAL
HANNA, WILLIAM G. C.
HANNAY, HARRY
HARDIE, ROBERT
HARDING, HOWARD
HARDYMAN, JOHN HAY M.
HARPER-NELSON, JOHN J.
HART, F. J. A.
HARVEY, ALEXANDER W. M.
HARVEY, WILLIAM FREDERICK
HASELL, GODFREY SINCLAIR
HASLAM, JOHN FEARLEY C.
HASTINGS, THOMAS ERNEST
HASWELL, JOHN FRANCIS
HAULTAIN, WILLIAM F. T.
HAY, FREDERICK WILLIAM
HAY, WILLIAM
HAYCROFT, JOHN BERRY
HEDDLE, MALCOLM
HELM, HENRY PAUL DUNDAS
HENDERSON, JAMES ELMSLIE
HENDERSON, PATRICK H.
HEPBURN, DAVID
HEPPLE, ROBERT ALEXANDER
HERD, WALTER
HERDMAN, RONALD TYDD
HERRIDGE, DAVID RUSSELL
HEWAT, ANDREW FERGUS
HEWAT, JOHN
HILL, WILLIAM HUGH
HILLCOAT, ROBERT GUY
HIRD, FREDERICK WAISTELL
HODSDON, JAMES WILLIAM B.
HOLE, RICHARD BRASSEY
HOLLAND, HENRY TRISTRAM
HOLMDEN, FRANK ALFRED A.
HOLMDEN, HARRY FOSTER
HOLMES, MATHEW
HOLMES, NOEL ROWLAND H.
HORNE, ROBERT JOHN MAULE
HOWARD-JONES, JOHN
HUGGAN, JAMES LAIDLAW

Orders, Decorations and Dispatches

DISPATCHES, ETC.—*continued*.

HUME, DAVID LIONEL L.
HUMPHRIS, FRANCIS H.
HUNTER, EVAN AUSTIN
HUNTER, WILLIAM
HUNTER, WILLIAM A.
HURST, JOHN THOMAS
HURWORTH, JAMES ERNEST
HUSBAND, JAMES
HUSBAND, JOSEPH SIM
HUSBAND, THOMAS GIBSON
HUTCHINSON, DONALD H. A.
HUTCHISON, ROBERT
HUTCHISON, WM. MURRAY
HUTTON, JAMES
HUXTABLE, ROBERT B.

IMPEY, ROBERT LANCE
INCH, THOMAS DOUGLAS
INGLIS, GORDON STEWART
INGLIS, JOHN ANDREW
INGLIS, JOSEPH ELLIS
INGLIS, MAURICE PATERSON
INNES, LESLIE W.
IRVINE, ROBERT CHARLES

JACKSON, GEORGE ERSKINE
JACKSON, ROBERT
JACKSON, THOMAS
JACKSON, WALTER DALGLEISH
JAFFRAY, W. STEVENSON
JAMESON, JAMES CONWAY
JAMIESON, ERIC
JARDINE, JOHN
JARVIS, OSWALD DUKE
JENKINS, GEORGE JOHN
JENNINGS, WILLIAM ERNEST
JOHNSON, ERNEST HUGH
JOHNSTON, JAMES HALCRO
JOHNSTON, JOHN
JOHNSTON, J. MACPHERSON
JOHNSTON, THOMAS BAILLIE
JOHNSTONE, FREDERICK J. C.
JOLLY, GORDON GRAY

KAY, ALFRED GOODWYN
KAY, DAVID MILLER
KELLIE, JOHN
KENNEDY, JAMES CRAWFORD
KENNEDY, JAMES TURNER
KENNEDY, THOMAS DYMOCK
KENNEDY-FRASER, DAVID

KENWOOD, HENRY RICHARD
KERR, CHARLES
KERR, PETER MURRAY
KIDD, ALEXANDER EDWARD
KIRK, JAMES
KIRK, JOHN PAUL
KIRKPATRICK, ROGER
KNIGHT, JAMES ST PIERRE
KNOX, ROBERT WELLAND
KNUTHSEN, LOUIS FRANCIS

LAING, DAVID
LAING, GEORGE DAVISON
LAIRD, DAVID ANDERSON
LANDSBOROUGH, WILLIAM
LANG, ERIC CHRISTISON
LAURIE, ALAN RUPERT
LAURIE, ALBERT ERNEST
LAWRENCE, LEONARD ARTHUR
LAWRIE, MAURICE BERTRAM
LAWSON, CHARLES BUNBURY
LAWSON, JAMES
LAWSON, JOSEPH I.
LEARY, GERALD F. V.
LEASK, JAMES BRUCE
LECHLER, ARTHUR NORMAN
LECKIE, JOHN
LECKIE, WILLIAM GORDON
LEES, DAVID
LEES, HARRY RANKINE
LEGGAT, GEORGE LEGGAT
LEIGHTON, GERALD R.
LENNOX, JOHN
LESLIE, ARCHIBALD STEWART
LESLIE, JAMES
LESLIE, LEONARD
LESLIE, ROBERT MILLER
LETHEM, WILLIAM ASHLEY
LINDSAY, CREIGHTON H.
LINDSAY, W. C. S.
LINKLATER, GEORGE J. I.
LINTON, ALEXANDER
LITT, JOHN PERCY
LLOYD, JOHN STANLEY
LOCHRANE, NEALE LEO
LOCKHART, THOMAS T. R.
LOGAN, GEORGE
LOGAN [ALEX. S.] INNES
LORD, JOHN ROBERT
LORIMER, ALEX. PATRICK G.
LOUW, ADRIAN HOFMEYER

LOW, HERBERT BRUCE
LOW, JAMES LAWSON
LUCAS, FREDERICK RICHARD
LUMSDEN, GEORGE JAMES S.
LYELL, DAVID (R.E.)
LYNDEN-BELL, EDWARD H. L.
LYON, DAVID MURRAY

MACALLISTER-HEWLINGS, W.F.
MCALLUM, STUART GERALD
MACARTHUR, DONALD H. C.
MACASKIE, WILFRED VICTOR
MCCALLUM, JAMES RUSSELL
MCCLINTOCK, LAWSON TAIT
MCCLYMONT, JAMES ALEX.
MCCONAGHY, WILLIAM
MCCONNELL, PRIMROSE
MACCORMAC, HENRY
MCCRACKEN, ANGUS MURRAY
MACDONALD, ADAM DAVIDSON
MACDONALD, ANGUS HUGH
MACDONALD, JOHN V.
MACDONALD, RANALD
MACDONALD, RODERICK O. C.
MCDONALD, SAMUEL
MCDOUGAL, JOHN WALTER
MACDOUGALL, ALEX. JAMES
MCEWEN, BRUCE
MACEWEN, WM. GEORGE
MACFIE, ROBERT ANDREW S.
MACFIE, RONALD BUTE
MACGIBBON, JAMES
MACGILLIVRAY, FRANCIS P.
MACGLASHEN, KEITH B.
MACGREGOR, DAVID H.
MCGREGOR, ERIC
MACGREGOR, GEORGE B.
MACGREGOR, ROBERT F. D.
MCHARDY, IAN
MCHUTCHON, EDWIN GRAY
MCINTOSH, ALEXANDER M.
MCINTOSH, GEORGE WISHART
MCINTYRE, HUGH ROSS
MACINTYRE, PAT. B.
MCINTYRE, WILLIAM K.
MACIVER, ISAAC HUNTER
MCIVER, JOHN CHRISTIAN
MACKAY, ALEX. MORRISON
MACKAY, DONALD
MACKAY, GEORGE
MACKAY, IAN

Orders, Decorations and Dispatches

DISPATCHES, ETC.—*continued*.

MACKAY, PATRICK ROBSON
MACKAY, WILLIAM BERTIE
MACKEAN, HUGH
MCKELVEY, DANIEL
MACKELVIE, THOMAS
MACKENZIE, ALISTER T.
MCKENZIE ARCHIBALD D.
MACKENZIE, DONALD F.
MACKENZIE, DONALD ROSS
MACKENZIE, ERIC F. W.
MACKENZIE, ERIC LOFTS
MACKENZIE, FRANCIS B.
MACKENZIE, JOHN EDWIN
MACKENZIE, JOHN WILLIAM
MACKENZIE, KENNETH W.
MACKENZIE, LIONEL DE A.
MACKENZIE, THOMAS
MACKENZIE, WILLIAM
MCKINLAY, ROBERT
MCKINNEY, JAMES WILFRED
MACKINNON, PATRICK
MACKINTOSH, CHARLES
MACKINTOSH, JOHN
MACKINTOSH, WILLIAM D.
MACLACHLAN, C. F. M.
MACLAGAN, DAVID W.
MACLAGAN, PHILIP W.
MCLAREN, JAMES B. P.
MACLAREN, MURRAY
MCLAUGHLIN, JAMES NEIL
MACLEAN, ALEXANDER M.
MACLEAN, CHARLES A.
MACLEAN, D. MACDONALD
MACLEAN, HENRY JOHN
MCLEAN, JAMES YOUNGER
MACLEAN, RICHARD
MCLEAN, WILLIAM F.
MACLEOD, JAMES STRACHAN
MACLEOD, JOHN ANDREW
MACLEOD, NEIL
MACMILLAN, HUGH AGNEW
MACMILLAN, JOHN MCC. A.
MACMILLAN, ROBERT J. A.
MACNAE, ROBERT
MCNAUGHTON, WILLIAM
MCNEIL, CHARLES
MCNEIL, DAVID BELL
MACNEILL, ROBERT ARCH.
MACPHERSON, CHARLES JAS.
MACPHERSON, DONALD J. R.
MACPHERSON, JAMES EWAN

MACPHERSON, JOHN L.
MACPHERSON, M. M.
MACPHERSON, STANLEY N.
MACPHERSON, WILLIAM G.
MACQUEEN, JOHN
MACRAE, KENNETH M.
MACROSTY, HENRY HUGH
MCVICKER, DANIEL
MADDOCK, EDWARD C. G.
MADDOX, RALPH HENRY
MAGRATH, CHARLES WM. S.
MALCOLM-SMITH, GEORGE L.
MALLACE, ALEXANDER CROSS
MALLOCH, DUNCAN
MANIFOLD, COURTENAY C.
MANIFOLD, JOHN ALEXANDER
MANN, ALAN COWAN
MANSFIELD, GERALD S.
MANUEL, JAMES
MARSDEN, JAMES ALFRED
MARSHALL, GEORGE GUTHRIE
MARSHALL, JOHN FORSYTH
MARSHALL, LEGH R. H. P.
MARSHALL, WILLIAM E.
MARTIN, ARTHUR A.
MARTIN, CLAUDE BUIST
MARTIN, GEORGE EWART
MARTIN, JAMES FITZGERALD
MASON, JOHN WHARTON
MASON-MACFARLANE, D. J.
MATHEWSON, GEORGE D.
MATHEWSON, GEORGE G.
MATTHEWS, ALEXANDER
MAUGHAN, JOHN ST AUBYN
MAXWELL, JAMES REID
MAYBIN, WILLIAM
MAYNARD, EDWARD FORSTER
MAYNE, WILLIAM JOHN F.
MEARNS, ALEXANDER
MEEKE, HUGH CRAIG
MEIKLE, ALEXANDER J.
MEISTER, CHARLES G. C.
MELVILLE, CHARLES H.
MELVILLE, HARRY GEORGE
MELVILLE, KENMURE D.
MENZIES, ARTHUR JOHN A.
MENZIES, JACK MCKENZIE
MENZIES, ROBERT
MENZIES, WILLIAM MENZIES
MEYER, WILLIAM C. B.
MILL, THOMAS

MILL, W. A.
MILLAR, GEORGE
MILLAR, WILLIAM GILBERT
MILLER, ALEXANDER G. S.
MILLER, GEORGE WATERSTON
MILLER, HUGH MORISON
MILLER, JAMES
MILLER, WILLIAM A.
MILLIGAN, OSWALD BELL
MILLSON, ALVAN EWEN
MILNE, EWAN THOMAS M.
MILNE, GEORGE WARDLAW
MILNE, JAMES ROBERTSON
MILNE, JAMES WILLIAM
MITCHELL, JAMES T. R.
MITCHELL, LACHLAN M. V.
MITCHELL, WILLIAM MCG.
MITTON, HAROLD
MOFFAT, F. J. C.
MOFFATT, ALEXANDER MCR.
MOIR, ARCHIBALD GIFFORD
MOLONY, JOHN BARRÉ DE W.
MONCRIEFF, RICHARD H. F.
MONRO, DAVID CARMICHAEL
MONSARRAT, KEITH W.
MONTEATH, HARRY H.
MONTGOMERY, ROBERT
MOODY-STUART, KENNETH A.
MOORHEAD, ARTHUR H.
MORGAN, BENJAMIN B.
MORGAN, WM. D.
MORISON, DUNCAN METCALFE
MORRIS, JAMES ARTHUR
MORRISON, JAMES STEWART
MORRISON, JOHN TERTIUS
MORRISON, WILLIAM K.
MORRISON, WILLIAM S.
MORTON, HUGH MURRAY
MOTHERWELL, GAVIN BLACK
MOYES, JOHN MURRAY
MUIR, JOHN REID
MUNRO, ALEXANDER ROSE
MUNRO, DAVID
MUNRO, HUGH LENNOX
MURDOCH, BARCLAY BROWN
MURDOCH, JOHN DUNCAN
MURDOCH, THOMAS FLEMING
MURRAY, DAVID KEITH
MURRAY, DONALD N. W.
MURRAY, JOHN OLIVER
MURRAY, PETER

783

Orders, Decorations and Dispatches

DISPATCHES, ETC.—*continued.*

MURRAY, RONALD RODERICK
MURRAY-LYON, DAVID M.
MURSELL, HENRY TEMPLE
MYERS, BERNARD

NAIDU, B. P. BALAKRISHNA
NAISMITH, JAMES BERTRAM
NAISMITH, JOHN OLIVER
NAPIER, ARCHIBALD D. M.
NEWMAN, R. E. UPTON
NEWTON, CHARLES T. H.
NICHOL, CHARLES E. P. S.
NICOL, ANDREW
NICOL, GEORGE
NIGHTINGALE, JOHN
NIVEN, JAMES PARKER
NOBBS, ERIC ARTHUR
NORFOR, ROBERT C.
NORMAND, CHARLES W. B.

O'BRIEN, ARTHUR JOHN R.
OGILVIE, ALEXANDER
OGILVIE, GEORGE HAMILTON
OGILVIE, PHILIP G.
OGILVIE, WALTER HOLLAND
O'HALLORAN, HENRY
OLIVER, ARCHIBALD
ORBELL, RONALD GRAEME S.
ORCHARD, ALBERT JOHN
ORMROD, GARFIELD
ORR, MATTHEW YOUNG
OSWALD, JOHN

PALMER, HUGH SALISBURY
PARKER, WYNDHAM
PARR, ALFRED ERNEST
PATERSON, ALEXANDER G.
PATERSON, GEORGE WM. S.
PATERSON, JAMES LEE H.
PATERSON, JOHN C.
PATERSON, ROBERT WALKER
PATERSON-BROWN, KEITH
PATON, LEONARD CECIL
PATON, MONTGOMERY P.
PATON, WILLIAM CALDER
PATTEN, JOHN ALEXANDER
PATTERSON, NORMAN J.
PAWLETT, FRANCIS
PEEK, JOHN HAROLD
PEFFERS, ANDREW
PEILL, ERNEST JOHN

PENFOLD, ERNEST ALFRED
PERCIVAL, EDGAR
PHILIP, GEORGE MORRISON
PIRIE, GEORGE STEPHEN
PIERCE, HOWEL BULKLEY
PITCAIRN, ANDREW
POOLE, LEOPOLD THOMAS
PORTEOUS, NORMAN
POTTS, EDMUND THURLOW
PRESTON, CLASSON O'D.
PRICE, EDMUND GEORGE C.
PRIMROSE, ALEXANDER
PROUDFOOT, ROBERT
PROUT, WILLIAM THOMAS
PUCKLE, HALE
PURVES, ROBERT BLACK

RABAGLIATI, DUNCAN S.
RAE, JOHN CAIRNS
RAI, DEWAN HAKUMAT
RAINIE, WILLIAM
RAMSAY, GEORGE BENNETT
RAMSAY, GRAHAM COLVILLE
RANKEN, HENRY
RANKINE, GEORGE
RATTRAY, MALCOLM McG.
RAWLENCE, HAROLD ERNEST
RAWSON, ARTHUR
RAWSON, ROBERT EDGAR
RAY, MATTHEW BURROW
REID, GEORGE ALEXANDER
REID, WALTER RICHARD
RENDELL, HERBERT
RENTOUL, JOHN LAWRENCE
RIACH, WILLIAM
RICHARDS, HUBERT H. L.
RICHARDSON, HUGH
RITCHIE, CHARLES RONALD
RITCHIE, FREDERICK B.
RITCHIE, ROBERT LINTON
RITCHIE, THOMAS CLARK
RITCHIE, W. T. (R.A.M.C.)
ROBB, DOUGLAS GEORGE
ROBERTSON, ATHOLL
ROBERTSON, DOUGLAS W.
ROBERTSON, GEORGE H. W.
ROBERTSON, JOHN
ROBERTSON, MICHAEL W.
ROBERTSON, WILLIAM A.
ROBERTSON, WILLIAM KERR
ROBERTSON, WILLIAM LATTO

ROBINSON, LEONARD N.
RODGER, J. MURRAY
RONN, HENRY ALBERT
RORIE, DAVID
ROSE, HUGH
ROSEBERY, SIDNEY SOLOMON
ROSS, ANDREW RUSSELL
ROSS, JAMES NESS MACBEAN
ROSS, JOHN ROSS HOME
ROSS, WILLIAM DAVID
ROWAN-ROBINSON, FRED. E
ROWAN-ROBINSON, JOHN R.
RUDOLF, HARRY PRIEST
RUSSELL, ALEXANDER SCOTT
RUSSELL, DAVID HENRY
RUSSELL, JOHN (A.S.C.)
RUSSELL, WILLIAM BLACK
RUTHERFORD, ANDREW A.
RUTHERFORD, JOHN V. W.
RUTHVEN, MORTON WOOD
RYAN, CHARLES SNODGRASS

SAIDLER, JAMES ROY
ST LEGER, ROBERT A.
SAMUELSON, GERALD S.
SAMUT, ROBERT
SANDEMAN, LAURA STEWART
SANDERSON, FRANCIS R.
SANSOM, WALTER
SAROLEA, JOHN ROBERT
SCALES, CUTHBERT
SCARLETT, JAMES THOMAS
SCOTT, CHARLES ALEXANDER
SCOTT, GEORGE ALEXANDER
SCOTT, JAMES
SCOTT, JESSIE ANNE
SCOTT, JOHN
SCOTT, JOHN, M.B.
SCOTT, RALPH LESTER
SCOTT, THOMAS
SCOTT, THOMAS HENRY
SCOTT, WILLIAM SIBBALD
SCRIMGEOUR, FREDERICK J.
SEELLY, EDWARD ST JOHN
SHAFTO, WILLIAM A.
SHAND, JOHN G. B.
SHANKS, WILLIAM
SHAW, JOHN J. M'INTOSH
SHAW, ROBERT GLEN
SHAW, WILLIAM JOHN
SHENNAN, JOHN ROGNVALD

Orders, Decorations and Dispatches

DISPATCHES, ETC.—*continued.*

SHIRCORE, JOHN OWEN
SHIRES, BERTRAM
SILVER, JOHN PAYZANT
SIM, ALEXANDER
SIME, WILLIAM
SIMPSON, ALEXANDER P.
SIMPSON, HAROLD C.
SIMPSON, ROBERT K. M.
SIMPSON, WILFRID JAMES
SIMSON, JOHN THOMAS
SIMSON, ROBERT
SINCLAIR, MEURICE
SINCLAIR, PATRICK
SKINNER, ERNEST WILLIAM
SLAYTER, EDWARD WHEELER
SLOAN, ALLEN THOMSON
SLUYS, MAURICE
SMALE, ERNEST HERCULES
SMART, MORTON WARRACK
SMITH, FLEET FLOYD S.
SMITH, GEORGE WILLIAM
SMITH, HARRY
SMITH, JAMES MARTIN
SMITH, JOHN
SMITH, JOHN GRANT
SMITH, JOHN MACMILLAN
SMITH, JULIAN CARTER C.
SMITH, ROBERT BEVERIDGE
SMITH, STANLEY ALWYN
SMITH, WILLIAM ROBERT
SOMERVAIL, WILLIAM FULTON
SOMERVILLE, HUGH
SOUTHAM, HERBERT
SPENCE, BASIL HAMILTON H.
SPENCE, SYDNEY GEORGE
SPRAGUE, HENRY DOUGLAS
SPROAT, HARRY BIRD
STABLES, ALEXANDER
STARKIE, ERNEST GEORGE B.
STEUART, ROGER ST CLAIR
STEVEN, WILLIAM CHARLES
STEVENS, NORMAN WALTER
STEVENSON, ERIC JOHN POTT
STEVENSON, GEORGE H.
STEVENSON, HENRY JAMES
STEVENSON, JAMES
STEVENSON, WILLIAM SCOTT
STEWART, ALISTER JOHN
STEWART, ANDREW SINCLAIR
STEWART, AUGUSTUS SHAW
STEWART, FRANK WHITE

STEWART, FREDERICK N.
STEWART, GEORGE EDWARD
STEWART, HUGH
STEWART, JAMES
STEWART, JAMES BELL
STEWART, JAMES DAVID G.
STEWART, JOHN
STEWART, MUNGO
STEWART, ROBERT BELL
STEWART, THOMAS
STIRLING, JAMES ALEXANDER
STOBIE, WILLIAM
STOCKMAN, RALPH
STODDART, ALEXANDER REID
STOOKES, VALENTINE A.
STOTT, JAMES ROBERT
STOUTE, DOUGLAS GARNETT
STRAIN, LAURENCE HUGH
STRANG, DUNCAN WILLIAM P.
STRATHAIRN, GEORGE CECIL
STRUTHERS, JOHN WILLIAM
STURROCK, ALEXANDER C.
SUTHERLAND, ANDERSON
SUTHERLAND, ANDREW
SUTHERLAND, DAVID
SUTHERLAND, DAVID WATERS
SUTHERLAND, HECTOR WM.
SUTHERLAND, HENRY ERIC G.
SUTHERLAND, JOHN DONALD
SUTHERLAND, WILLIAM NEIL
SWEETEN, BENJAMIN
SYMONS, FRANK ALBERT

TARR, WILLIAM
TAYLOR, GEORGE PRITCHARD
TAYLOR, LEONARD W. O.
TELFORD, ALEX. MCMENAGAL
TENNANT, ALEXANDER SMITH
THERON, CHARLES PETRUS
THIN, JAMES AINSLIE
THOM, JOHN GIBB
THOMAS, DAVID GWILYN
THOMPSON, ALBERT GEORGE
THOMPSON, EDWARD ROLAND
THOMPSON, IAN MACLAREN
THOMSON, DAVID GEORGE
THOMSON, EDWARD G.
THOMSON, GEORGE RITCHIE
THOMSON, HENRY ALEXIS
THOMSON, JOHN JAMES
THOMSON, ROBERT BLACK

THOMSON, SYDNEY JAS. KERR
THORBURN, DAVID HAY
THORNTON, LESLIE IRVINE L.
TIMS, HENRY WM. MARETT
TOD, FRED. LEWIS MAITLAND
TODD, HARRY CAMPBELL
TODD, JAMES ALEXANDER
TODRICK, THOMAS
TOWSE, HAROLD BECKWITH
TRAFFORD, WILLIAM LEIGH
TROTTER, JOHN
TRUTER, ROBERT MEESER
TUKE, ALAN LEONARD SMITH
TURNBULL, ARCHIBALD
TURNBULL, JOHN

UNWIN, THOMAS BARTON
URQUHART, ALEX. LEWIS
URQUHART, ALEX. ROBERT

VAUGHAN, EDMUND WAYNE
VAUGHAN-WILLIAMS, H. W.
VELLNOT, GEORGE ALBERT
VEREL, RAYMOND
VIJVER, GIFFORD T. VAN DER

WALKER, ALEXANDER IZAT
WALKER, ARCHIBALD S.
WALKER, CHARLES DERWENT
WALKER, ERNEST ALEX.
WALKER, JOSEPH
WALKER, NORMAN DUNBAR
WALKER, WALTER OLIPHANT
WALL, CHARLES P. B.
WALL, DOUGLAS LARMER
WALLACE, DAVID
WALSHE, SARSFIELD J. A. H.
WALTON, ROBERT HENRY
WARD, FRANCIS
WARD, JOSEPH HUGH
WARDEN, HERBERT LAWTON
WATLING, FRANCIS HAMMOND
WATSON, ALEXANDER PIRIE
WATSON, ALLAN
WATSON, DAVID GALLOWAY
WATSON, FRANK HERBERT C.
WATSON, JOHN B. FORBES
WATSON, STANLEY
WATSON, WILLIAM NORMAN
WEBSTER, WILLIAM LECKIE
WEDDERBURN, E. MACLAGAN
WEDDERBURN, JOSEPH H. M.

Orders, Decorations and Dispatches

DISPATCHES, ETC.—*continued.*

WEIR, ANDW. HERON WILSON
WEIR, ROBERT
WEIR, ROBERT YAXLEY
WELLS, JOSEPH DOUGLAS
WELSH, TOM
WHAIT, JOHN ROBERT
WHIGHAM, WALKER K.
WHITE, ADAM
WHITE, CHARLES R.
WHITE, JOHN LETHAM
WHITE, JOSHUA CHAYTOR
WHITEFORD, JAMES H. G.
WHITTAKER, CHARLES B.
WHYTE, GEORGE FRANCIS
WIER, HENRY WOOD
WIGHTMAN, GEORGE L.
WILKINS, RICHARD
WILLIAMS, THOMAS S. B.
WILLIAMS, WILLIAM E. R.
WILLIAMSON, ALEXANDER J.
WILLIAMSON, GEORGE H.
WILLIAMSON, GEORGE SCOTT
WILLIAMSON, JOHN RUTTER
WILLIAMSON, KENNETH B.
WILSON, ANDREW
WILSON, ANDREW R.
WILSON, GORDON
WIMBERLEY, CHARLES N. C.
WISHART, JOHN
WOOD, JAMES
WOOD, ROBERT TURNBULL
WOODHEAD, GERMAN SIMS
WOOLER, ERNEST W. N.
WRIGHT, ARCHIBALD F.
WYLIE, ANDREW ROBERTSON
WYNNE-DAVIES, LLEWELYN

YATES, ARTHUR GURNEY
YATES, GEORGE DOUGAL
YEOMAN, ALEXANDER ROSS
YOUNG, JAMES
YOUNG, NORMAN MITCHELL
YOUNG, WILLIAM ALEXANDER
YOUNG, WILLIAM
YOUNG, WILLIAM PAULIN

www.ingramcontent.com/pod-product-compliance
Lightning Source LLC
Chambersburg PA
CBHW080406230426
43662CB00016B/2329